ICISS

PROPERTY OF
THE CARTER CENTER
RESOURCE ROOM
PLEASE DO NOT REMOVE

# THE RESPONSIBILITY TO PROTECT

## RESEARCH, BIBLIOGRAPHY, BACKGROUND

DECEMBER 2001

SUPPLEMENTARY VOLUME TO THE REPORT OF
THE INTERNATIONAL COMMISSION ON INTERVENTION
AND STATE SOVEREIGNTY

Published by the
International Development Research Centre
PO Box 8500, Ottawa, ON, Canada K1G 3H9
http://www.idrc.ca

© International Development Research Centre 2001


**National Library of Canada cataloguing in publication data**

International Commission on Intervention and State Sovereignty

The Responsibility to Protect: Research, Bibliography, Background
Supplementary Volume to the Report of the International Commission on Intervention and
State Sovereignty

Issued by the International Development Research Centre.
ISBN 0-88936-963-1

1.  Intervention (International law).
2.  Sovereignty.
3.  Security, international
4.  United Nations. Security Council.
5.  Humanitarian assistance.
I.  International Development Research Centre (Canada)
II. Title.

JZ6368.I57 2001                         327.1'7                         C2001-980329-X

All rights reserved. No part of this publication may be reproduced, stored in a retrieval
system, or transmitted, in any form or by any means, electronic, mechanical, photocopying,
or otherwise, without the prior permission of the International Development Research
Centre. Mention of a proprietary name does not constitute endorsement of the product and
is given only for information.

IDRC Books endeavours to produce environmentally friendly publications. All paper used
is recycled as well as recyclable. All inks and coatings are vegetable-based products. The full
catalogue of IDRC Books is available at http://www.idrc.ca/booktique.

# TABLE OF CONTENTS

# CO-CHAIRS' FOREWORD

The Report of the Commission on Intervention and State Sovereignty could not have been produced in an intellectual vacuum. There is an enormous literature on the subject, in many languages and going back many years, which the Commission had a responsibility to take into account – and every reason to want to. In order to aid our own work, and as a contribution to future scholarship, we asked our research team to prepare an annotated list – necessarily selective, but as wide-ranging as possible – of the best writing on the subject. The Bibliography thus produced, set out in Part II, is an important component of the present volume.

Notwithstanding the wealth of existing literature, the Commission felt the need to generate a good deal of additional research of its own, to fill gaps in that literature, to bring it up to date and to draw together in a more manageable way information and ideas scattered through many primary and secondary sources in many languages. Thus the Research Essays in Part I, which constitute the bulk of this volume. Between them, the nine essays cover, in depth, the full range of issues with which the Commission had to grapple. We were particularly concerned to ensure that we had before us, as an input into our deliberations, a thoroughly balanced analysis of all those issues, with all the major arguments and counter-arguments fully laid out. To the extent that views or conclusions are expressed from time to time in these essays – almost unavoidable in an exercise of this kind – they are, of course, those of the researchers and not the Commission.

The primary authors of these essays in their final published form were Thomas G. Weiss and Don Hubert, of the Commission's research team, to whom the Commission owes an enormous debt of gratitude. Their writing was based, in turn, on substantial contributions from over fifty other scholars and specialists, whose names are listed in the acknowledgements which follow, who submitted either specially commissioned research papers, or who made specifically requested contributions to the regional and national roundtables further described below.

The Commission's Report – and in particular its central theme of "The Responsibility to Protect" – goes in a number of ways beyond the discussion in the Research Essays collected here. But those essays were very much the quarry from which the Report was mined. They should also be seen as supplementing, and adding a great deal of detail (for example in its descriptions of past interventions, both before and after 1990) to a Report which was deliberately limited in length to increase its chances of being read. The Commission very much hopes that the Research Essays will in turn prove to be, for policy makers and commentators of the future, a mine of detailed and useful information and analysis.

Access to high quality written research was a necessary, but not sufficient, condition for the Commission to produce its report. Dealing with subject matter of this kind, involving such sensitive and volatile policy issues, and with many different views evident in different parts of the world, it was absolutely crucial for the Commission to hear directly from those actually or potentially affected by interventions, or in a position to undertake them, or with strong and well-considered views on the issues in question. So, as an integral part of our work, we conducted a series of lengthy roundtable discussions in Beijing, Cairo, Geneva, London, Maputo, New Delhi, New York, Ottawa, Paris, St Petersburg, Santiago and Washington. The meetings involved representatives from governments and intergovernmental organizations, from nongovernmental organizations and civil society, and from universities, research institutes and think-tanks – in all, over 200 people. These roundtable meetings proved to be a wonderfully rich source of information, ideas and diverse political perspectives, and an excellent real world environment in which the Commission could test its own ideas as they evolved. Summary accounts of each of the roundtable meetings, together with lists of those who participated in them, are also included in Part III of this volume.

As much as we might hope otherwise, nothing is more likely than that the international community will sooner or later again be confronted by events all too reminiscent of the agonies of the last decade in the Great Lakes, the Balkans, Haiti, Somalia, Sierra Leone, East Timor and elsewhere. Reacting to these situations in the ad hoc, and often ineffective or counter-productive, way we have in the past is not good enough for interdependent global neighbours in the twenty-first century. We have to do better.

The material gathered and described in this volume has played an important part in the deliberations of the Commission, and we warmly thank all those involved in writing, collecting or contributing to it. If the Report that has grown out of this material can help bring about a more systematic, balanced and less ideological debate of the main issues by the international community – and even more if it comes to provide an accepted framework for dealing with these matters, as they arise in the future, in concrete and positive ways – then our work will have been ground-breaking indeed.

GARETH EVANS
MOHAMED SAHNOUN
*Co-Chairs*
*15 August 2001*

# ACKNOWLEDGEMENTS

ICISS is indebted to the following scholars and specialists who have contributed to the research essays and bibliography in this supplementary volume. While the two primary authors, Thomas G. Weiss and Don Hubert, wrote and deserve full credit for the essays as they finally appear, they received substantial written input from all those other contributors listed, who between them brought an extraordinary store of knowledge and experience to ICISS's deliberations.

## PRIMARY AUTHORS

**Thomas G. Weiss** is Presidential Professor at The CUNY Graduate Center (The City University of New York) and Director of the Ralph Bunche Institute for International Studies, where he is also co-director of the United Nations Intellectual History Project, and editor of *Global Governance*. Among other positions, he was a Research Professor at Brown University's Watson Institute for International Studies, Executive Director of the International Peace Academy, a member of the United Nations (UN) Secretariat, and a consultant to several public and private agencies. He has written extensively on the UN and on intervention, and his latest books include *Military–Civilian Interactions: Intervening in Humanitarian Crises* (1999); *Humanitarian Challenges and Intervention* (2000); *The United Nations and Changing World Politics* (2000); and *Ahead of the Curve? UN Ideas and Gobal Challenges* (2001).

**Don Hubert** is a Senior Policy Advisor in the Peacebuilding and Human Security division of the Canadian Department of Foreign Affairs and International Trade, currently on leave. He is also a Research Fellow at the Centre for Foreign Policy Studies at Dalhousie University. He has a PhD in social and political science from the University of Cambridge and was a Post-Doctoral Fellow at the Centre for Foreign Policy Studies at Dalhousie University and with the Humanitarianism and War Project at Brown University. He has also worked for the Canadian Immigration and Refugee Board. He is author of *The Landmine Ban: A Case Study in Humanitarian Advocacy* (2000) and co-editor of *Human Security and the New Diplomacy: Protecting People, Promoting Peace* (2001).

## OTHER CONTRIBUTORS

**Howard Adelman**
University of Toronto

**Adonia Ayebare**
Embassy of Uganda in Rwanda, Kigali

**Mohamed Ayoob**
Michigan State University, East Lansing

**Dipankar Banerjee**
Regional Centre for Strategic Studies, Colombo

**Vladimir Baranovsky**
University of St Petersburg

**Mwesiga Baregu**
Southern African Regional Institute for Policy Studies, Harare

**Ken Berry**
Canberra

**Chaloka Beyani**
London School of Economics and Political Science

**Louis Bitencourt**
Woodrow Wilson Center, Washington, DC

**Chen Luzhi**
China Institute of International Studies,
Beijing

**Simon Chesterman**
International Peace Academy, New York

**Jarat Chopra**
Brown University, Providence

**Chester A. Crocker**
Georgetown University, Washington, DC

**Dennis Driscoll**
National University of Ireland, Gallway

**Richard Falk**
Princeton University

**Fan Guoxiang**
China Society for Human Rights Studies,
Beijing

**Christopher Greenwood**
London School of Economics and Political
Science

**Steven Haines**
Oxford University

**Morton Halperin**
US Institute of Peace, Washington, DC

**Tudor Hera**
Department of Foreign Affairs
and International Trade, Ottawa

**Peter Joshua Hoffman**
The CUNY Graduate Center, New York

**Nicholas Howen**
Consultant, London

**Ahmed Tawfic Khalil**
Egyptian Council for Foreign Affairs, Cairo

**Zalmay Khalilzad**
RAND Corporation, Washington, DC

**Konstantin Khudoley**
State University of St Petersburg

**Keith Krause**
Graduate Institute for International Studies,
Geneva

**Igor Leshukov**
University of St Petersburg

**Jeremy Levitt**
DePaul University, Chicago

**Edward Luck**
Columbia University, New York

**S. Neil MacFarlane**
Oxford University

**Mark Malan**
Institute for Strategic Studies, Johannesburg

**William Maley**
Refugee Council of Australia, Sydney

**Kenneth Menkhaus**
Davidson College, Charlotte

**Jennifer Milliken**
Graduate Institute of International Studies,
Geneva

**Kevin Vedat Ozgercin**
The CUNY Graduate Center, New York

**David Petrasek**
International Council on Human Rights
Policy, Geneva

**Veselin Popovski**
University of Exeter

**Gwyn Prins**
London School of Economics and Political
Science

**Adam Roberts**
Oxford University

**Severine Rugumamu**
Organization of African Unity, Addis Ababa

**Eric Schwartz**
Woodrow Wilson Center, Washington, DC

**Omran El Shafei**
Egyptian Council for Foreign Affairs, Cairo

**Michael J. Smith**
University of Virginia, Charlottesville

**Janice Gross Stein**
University of Toronto

**Matthias Stieffel**
War-Torn Societies Project, Geneva

**John Stremlau**
University of Witwatersrand, Johannesburg

**Tran Ngoc Thach**
Institute for International Relations, Hanoi

**Carolin Thielking**
Oxford University

**Chin Kin Wah**
Singapore Institute of International Affairs

**Nicholas J. Wheeler**
University of Aberystwyth

**Yuan Jian**
China Institute of International Studies, Beijing

# RESEARCHERS' PREFACE

Given the divisive views about the topic of intervention and state sovereignty, a first thought was to produce an edited volume containing essays with representative views from all points of the spectrum. This approach was abandoned after an initial meeting of researchers in London in October 2000. It would have been impossible in a volume of manageable length to reflect so many geographical, philosophical, political, and moral positions on so many different dimensions of the debate. Instead, some 15 specialists were asked to spell out the range of contemporary views, with the understanding that their raw material would be transformed by us. During this transformation, we also drew on the background papers and summary reports prepared for the various roundtables and consultations held by ICISS, which are summarized in Part III of this volume. The names of both types of colleagues figure in the acknowledgements to this volume as contributors, but few of them would recognize their building blocks in the present text. We have written and rewritten texts, moved parts of arguments, and inserted a substantial body of new material.

The task given to us by ICISS was to lay out in straightforward and nonargumentative terms the main issues behind the debate about humanitarian intervention that has taken place over the last decade. Working within these parameters, the three main sections of the research part of this volume are designed to provide readers with a common framework to understand its various dimensions.

Section A lays out the elements in the debate. Three essays discuss the range of meanings associated with the potentially politically charged and emotionally laden terms of state sovereignty and intervention, as well as the related notion of prevention. These essays provide a foundation for reviewing the subsequent historical overview and analysis.

Section B consists of two essays that systematically review the evolution of state practice toward humanitarian intervention since the founding of the United Nations Charter regime. This story, and the legitimate and illegitimate uses of "humanitarian" to justify intervention, are as old as the Westphalian system of international relations. The first essay provides an overview of nonconsensual interventions that had humanitarian objectives or resulted in substantial humanitarian benefits between 1945 and 1990. The real emphasis is, however, on interventions after 1990, which are summarized in the second essay of this section. The post-Cold War era has not changed everything, but it certainly has altered the prospects for intrusions into what had formerly been considered the more protected domain of sovereign states – to manage their domestic human rights policy without outside interference.

Section C builds on the essential elements and past history to explore the moral, legal, operational, and political dimensions of humanitarian intervention. Virtually all analyses of intervention and state sovereignty have examined the issues from the point of view of an intervener. When is intervention for humanitarian purposes justified? How is it authorized? What is the most effective way to conduct it? And how can sufficient political will be mobilized to mount and maintain an intervention? A further essential perspective running throughout the four essays is how intervention is viewed by, and what effect it has on, populations at risk.

Part II of the volume is an extensive bibliography on the intervention debate. In a field that has burgeoned in the contemporary era, it is impossible to be comprehensive. However, more than 2,200 entries are listed under 12 basic headings, and they provide an impressive listing of key literature from a variety of perspectives. This part, and in particular the electronic version available on CD-ROM or on the web, provides an important resource for researchers.

We are grateful for having had the challenging assignment of providing this input into the work of this Commission. We are especially indebted to a number of individuals. Throughout the process, Co-Research Director and rapporteur Stanlake Samkange has proved to be an insightful reader and most supportive colleague; this volume bears his fingerprints, even if he would take issue with some of our interpretations. Carolin Thielking played a principal role in preparation of the bibliography, with supervision from Neil MacFarlane at Oxford University. Kevin Ozgercin and Peter Hoffman, doctoral candidates from the Political Science Program at The CUNY Graduate Center, tirelessly furnished us with essential back-up research and criticism of arguments and prose; the volume would not have been possible without them. Ken Berry, executive assistant to the two Co-Chairs, compiled the summaries of the roundtables and national consultations included in Part III on which we drew. Finally, we are extremely grateful for the essential support emanating from the Secretariat of the Canadian Department of Foreign Affairs and International Trade – especially Jill Sinclair, Heidi Hulan, and Susan Finch.

The layout and presentation are our responsibility as primary authors. Such views as are expressed are not to be taken as those of ICISS; nor are they necessarily those of any of the contributors, or of the institutions that sponsored regional roundtables or national consultations.


THOMAS G. WEISS
DON HUBERT
*ICISS Research Directorate*
*15 August 2001*

# LIST OF ACRONYMS

| | |
|---|---|
| AFL | Armed Forces of Liberia |
| AFRC | Armed Forces Revolutionary Council [Sierra Leone] |
| AI | Amnesty International |
| ASEAN | Association of Southeast Asian Nations |
| CIS | Commonwealth of Independent States |
| DD&R | disarmament, demobilization, and reintegration |
| DPKO | Department of Peacekeeping Operations [UN] |
| DRC | Democratic Republic of the Congo |
| EC | European Community |
| ECOMOG | ECOWAS Cease-fire Monitoring Group |
| ECOWAS | Economic Community of West African States |
| EO | Executive Outcomes |
| EU | European Union |
| FEWS | Famine Early Warning System [USAID] |
| FRY | Federal Republic of Yugoslavia [Serbia and Montenegro] |
| FSAU | Food Security Assessment Unit [EU] |
| GIA | Governor's Island Agreement [Haiti] |
| GIEWS | Global Information and Early Warning System on Food and Agriculture [FAO] |
| ICC | International Criminal Court |
| ICISS | International Commission on Intervention and State Sovereignty |
| ICJ | International Court of Justice |
| ICRC | International Committee of the Red Cross |
| IDPs | internally displaced persons |
| IFOR | Implementation Force [Bosnia] |
| IHL | international humanitarian law |
| IMF | International Monetary Fund |
| INTERFET | International Force in East Timor [Australian-led multinational force] |
| IOM | International Organization for Migration |
| KLA | Kosovo Liberation Army |
| MISAB | Inter-African Force to Monitor the Implementation of the Bangui Agreements [Central African Republic] |
| MNF | Multinational Force |
| MOU | Memorandum of Understanding |
| MSF | Médecins sans Frontières [Doctors Without Borders] |
| NAM | Non-Aligned Movement |
| NATO | North Atlantic Treaty Organization |
| NGO | nongovernmental organization |

| | |
|---|---|
| NPFL | National Patriotic Front of Liberia |
| NPRC | National Provisional Revolutionary Council [Sierra Leone] |
| OAS | Organization of American States |
| OAU | Organization of African Unity |
| ODI | Overseas Development Institute |
| OECD | Organisation for Economic Co-operation and Development |
| OECS | Organisation of Eastern Caribbean States |
| ONUC | UN Operation in the Congo |
| OSCE | Organization for Security and Co-operation in Europe |
| P-5 | five permanent members of the UN Security Council |
| PLO | Palistine Liberation Organization |
| ROEs | rules of engagement |
| RPF | Rwanda Patriotic Front |
| RSLMF | Republic of Sierra Leone Military Forces |
| RUF | Revolutionary United Front [Sierra Leone] |
| SADC | Southern African Development Community |
| SIPRI | Stockholm International Peace Research Institute |
| SFOR | Stabilization Force [NATO] [Bosnia] |
| SRSG | Special Representative of the Secretary-General |
| UK | United Kingdom |
| ULIMO | United Liberation Movement of Liberia for Democracy |
| UN | United Nations |
| UNAMET | UN Mission in East Timor |
| UNAMIR | UN Assistance Mission in Rwanda |
| UNAMSIL | UN Mission in Sierra Leone |
| UNHCR | UN High Commissioner for Refugees |
| UNITAF | Unified Task Force [Somalia] |
| UNMIH | UN Mission in Haiti |
| UNMIK | UN Interim Administration Mission in Kosovo |
| UNOMIL | UN Observer Mission in Liberia |
| UNOMSIL | UN Observer Mission in Sierra Leone |
| UNOSOM | UN Operation in Somalia |
| UNPROFOR | UN Protection Force [former Yugoslavia] |
| UNTAET | UN Transitional Administration in East Timor |
| US | United States |
| USAID | US Agency for International Development |

# LIST OF TABLES AND FIGURES

# PART I

# RESEARCH ESSAYS

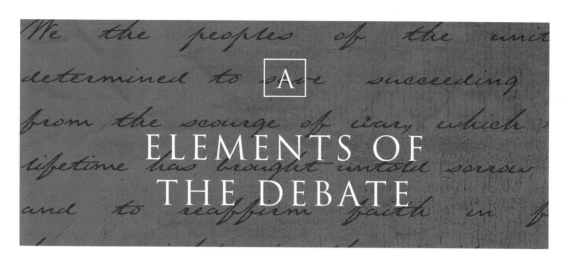

# ELEMENTS OF THE DEBATE

Sovereignty, intervention, and prevention are three essential elements of the contemporary debate on the use of coercive means to secure humanitarian objectives. Each is covered by a separate essay in Section A, and particular attention is devoted to the relationship between them. Two of them, state sovereignty and intervention, are often assumed to be irreconcilable and contradictory. A fundamental question to be addressed in the pages that follow, then, is the extent and manner in which these two concepts are actually in tension.

Essay 1, Sovereignty, approaches the concept of sovereignty from the perspective of law and politics. By setting out the historical origins of the concept in international law and in state practice, it demonstrates that sovereignty remains a cornerstone of contemporary international relations but that the actual exercise of state sovereignty has always been more constrained and porous than the stark legal definition would imply. The analysis illuminates the changing nature of the concept of sovereignty. Four challenges have appeared to the traditional and static conception of sovereignty: the increased salience of self-determination and the willingness to redraw borders, the ever-widening definition of threats to international peace and security, the recurring collapse of state authority, and the heightened importance attached to popular sovereignty.

Essay 2, Intervention, places the concept of intervention in historical context and examines it in light of both legal definitions and state practice. The norm of noninterference in internal affairs has lost ground. Activities that decades ago would have been conceived as interference are now widely acknowledged, if not accepted, as part of day-to-day politics. Nevertheless, the norm of nonintervention, where intervention is understood as the employment of coercive measures without the consent of the respective state, remains remarkably robust. Three specific dimensions of nonconsensual coercion are examined – military enforcement, sanctions and embargoes, and international criminal prosecution – before concluding with an overview of the contemporary debate on humanitarian intervention.

Essay 3, Prevention, deals with prevention as an integral part of this debate. Successful preventive efforts may obviate the need for coercion or at least reduce the need for robust military interventions and the human and financial costs that they entail. In the wake of a series of crises in the late 1990s – particularly Rwanda, East Timor, Kosovo, Liberia, and Sierra Leone – the United Nations and many member states have concluded that greater priority should be given to prevention. Beyond their instrumental benefits, genuine preventive measures also increase the ultimate legitimacy of intervention when prevention fails. The text reviews the growing field of conflict prevention, identifies the various activities and initiatives included under the broad rubric of prevention, assesses the various conceptual distinctions along both thematic and temporal lines, and illuminates the challenges that at present appear to result in many words but little action.

# 1. STATE SOVEREIGNTY

State sovereignty has, for the past several hundred years, been a defining principle of interstate relations and a foundation of world order. The concept lies at the heart of both customary international law and the United Nations (UN) Charter and remains both an essential component of the maintenance of international peace and security and a defence of weak states against the strong. At the same time, the concept has never been as inviolable, either in law or in practice, as a formal legal definition might imply. According to former Secretary-General Boutros Boutros-Ghali, "The time of absolute sovereignty ... has passed; its theory was never matched by reality."[1]

Empirically, sovereignty has routinely been violated by the powerful. In today's globalizing world, it is generally recognized that cultural, environmental, and economic influences neither respect borders nor require an entry visa. The concept of state sovereignty is well entrenched in legal and political discourse. At the same time, territorial boundaries have come under stress and have diminished in significance as a result of contemporary international relations. Not only have technology and communications made borders permeable, but the political dimensions of internal disorder and suffering have also often resulted in greater international disorder.[2] Consequently, perspectives on the range and role of state sovereignty have, particularly over the past decade, evolved quickly and substantially.

The purpose of this essay is to set out the scope and significance of state sovereignty as a foundation on which to explore contemporary debates on intervention. Students and scholars are aware of the enormous and contentious literature on this subject. As one scholar has summarized,

> Few subjects in international law and international relations are as sensitive as the notion of sovereignty. Steinberger refers to it in the *Encyclopedia of Public International Law* as "the most glittering and controversial notion in the history, doctrine and practice of international law." On the other hand, Henkin seeks to banish it from out vocabulary and Lauterpacht calls it a "word which has an emotive quality lacking meaningful specific content," while Verzijl notes that any discussion on this subject risks degenerating into a Tower of Babel. More affirmatively, Brownlie sees sovereignty as "the basic constitutional doctrine of the law of nations" and Alan James sees it as "the one and only organising principle in respect of the dry surface of the globe, all that surface now ... being divided among single entities of a sovereign, or constitutionally independent kind." As noted by Falk, "There is little neutral ground when it comes to sovereignty."[3]

Nevertheless, a quick review of the basics is useful for less specialized readers. The analysis begins with a review of the origins of the concept and its role in the evolution of state practice. This is followed by a discussion of the legal meaning of sovereignty and of its counterpart principle, nonintervention in domestic affairs. Together they comprise the fundamental bedrock of the contemporary international order. The widely acknowledged limits of state sovereignty are then examined, before turning to four contemporary challenges.

## MEANING AND PURPOSE OF SOVEREIGNTY

State sovereignty denotes the competence, independence, and legal equality of states. The concept is normally used to encompass all matters in which each state is permitted by international law to decide and act without intrusions from other sovereign states. These matters include the choice of political, economic, social, and cultural systems and the formulation of foreign policy. The scope of the freedom of choice of states in these matters is not unlimited; it depends on developments in international law (including agreements made voluntarily) and international relations.

The concept of sovereign rule dates back centuries in the context of regulated relationships and legal traditions among such disparate territorial entities as Egypt, China, and the Holy Roman Empire. However, the present foundations of international law with regard to sovereignty were shaped by agreements concluded by European states as part of the Treaties of Westphalia in 1648.[4] After almost 30 years of war, the supremacy of the sovereign authority of the state was established within a system of independent and equal units, as a way of establishing peace and order in Europe.[5] The core elements of state sovereignty were codified in the 1933 Montevideo Convention on the Rights and Duties of States. They include three main requirements: a permanent population, a defined territory, and a functioning government. An important component of sovereignty has always been an adequate display of the authority of states to act over their territory to the exclusion of other states.

The post-1945 system of international order enshrined in the UN Charter inherited this basic model. Following decolonization, what had been a restrictive and eurocentric (that is, Western) order became global. There were no longer "insiders" and "outsiders" because virtually every person on Earth lived within a sovereign state. At the same time, the multiplication of numbers did not diminish the controversial character of sovereignty.

In accordance with Article 2 (1) of the UN Charter, the world organization is based on the principle of the sovereign equality of all member states. While they are equal in relation to one another, their status of legal equality as a mark of sovereignty is also the basis on which intergovernmental organizations are established and endowed with capacity to act between and within states to the extent permitted by the framework of an organization. In 1949 the International Court of Justice (ICJ) observed that "between independent States, respect for territorial sovereignty is an essential foundation of international relations."[6] Thirty years later, the ICJ referred to "the fundamental principle of state sovereignty on which the whole of international law rests."[7]

As a hallmark of statehood, territorial sovereignty underlies the system of international order in relations among states. An act of aggression is unlawful, not only because it undermines international order, but also because states have exercised their sovereignty to outlaw war. In addition, the failure or weakening of state capacity that brings about a political vacuum within states leads to human tragedies and international and regional insecurity. Repressive, aggressive, or collapsed states may result in threats to international peace and security.

The principle of noninterference in affairs that are within the domestic jurisdiction of states is the anchor to state sovereignty within the system of international relations and obligations. Jurisdiction broadly refers to the power, authority, and competence of a state to govern persons and property within its territory. It is labelled "prescriptive" and "enforcement." Prescriptive jurisdiction relates to the power of a state to make or prescribe law within and outside its territory, and enforcement jurisdiction is about the power of the state to implement the law within its territory. Jurisdiction exercised by states is then the corollary of their sovereignty. Jurisdiction is clearly founded on territorial sovereignty but extends beyond it. Jurisdiction is *prima facie* exclusive over a state's territory and population, and the general duty of nonintervention in domestic affairs protects both the territorial sovereignty and the domestic jurisdiction of states on an equal basis.

Within the Charter of the UN, there is an explicit prohibition on the world organization from interfering in the domestic affairs of member states. What may be the Charter's most frequently cited provision, Article 2 (7), provides that "[n]othing contained in the present Charter shall authorise the United Nations to intervene in matters that are essentially within the domestic jurisdiction of any State or shall require the Members to submit such matters to settlement under the present Charter."

In sum, sovereignty is a key constitutional safeguard of international order. Despite the pluralization of international relations through the proliferation of nonstate actors – evidenced by an accelerated rate of economic globalization, democratization, and privatization worldwide – the state remains the fundamental guarantor of human rights locally, as well as the building block for collectively ensuring international order.

The equality in legal status of sovereignty also offers protection for weaker states in the face of pressure from the more powerful. This sentiment was captured by Algerian President Boueteflika, who, as President of the Organization for African Unity (OAU), addressed the UN General Assembly in 1999, immediately after the Secretary-General, and called sovereignty "our final defense against the rules of an unjust world."[8]

## LIMITS OF SOVEREIGNTY

There are important and widely accepted limits to state sovereignty and to domestic jurisdiction in international law. First, the Charter highlights the tension between the sovereignty, independence, and equality of individual states, on the one hand, and collective international obligations for the maintenance of international peace and security, on the other.[9] According to Chapter VII, sovereignty is not a barrier to action taken by the Security Council as part of measures in response to "a threat to the peace, a breach of the peace or an act of aggression." In other words, the sovereignty of states, as recognized in the UN Charter, yields to the demands of international peace and security. And the status of sovereign equality only holds effectively for each state when there is stability, peace, and order among states.

Second, state sovereignty may be limited by customary and treaty obligations in international relations and law. States are legally responsible for the performance of their international obligations, and state sovereignty therefore cannot be an excuse for their nonperformance. Obligations assumed by states by virtue of their membership in the UN and the corresponding powers of the world organization presuppose a restriction of the sovereignty of member states to the extent of their obligations under the Charter.

Specifically, Article 1 (2) stipulates that "[a]ll Members, in order to ensure to all of them the rights and benefits resulting from membership, shall fulfil in good faith the obligations assumed by them in accordance with the present Charter." Furthermore, under "Purposes and Principles," this same article obliges member states to achieve international cooperation in solving problems of an economic, social, cultural, or humanitarian character and in promoting and encouraging respect for human rights and for fundamental freedoms for all, without distinction as to race, sex, language, or religion. This article further recognizes the UN as a centre for harmonizing the actions of states in the attainment of these common ends. Thus, the Charter elevates the solution of economic, social, cultural, and humanitarian problems, as well as human rights, to the international sphere. By definition, these matters cannot be said to be exclusively domestic, and solutions cannot be located exclusively within the sovereignty of states.

Sovereignty therefore carries with it primary responsibilities for states to protect persons and property and to discharge the functions of government adequately within their territories. The quality and range of responsibilities for governance have brought about significant changes in state sovereignty since 1945. In particular, since the signing of the UN Charter, there has been an expanding network of obligations in the field of human rights. These create a dense set of state obligations to protect persons and property, as well as to regulate political and economic affairs. Sovereignty is incapable, then, of completely shielding internal violations of human rights that contradict international obligations.

Similarly, Article 2 (7) of the Charter is also subject to widely accepted limits. In the first place, this article is concerned chiefly with the limits of the UN as an organization. In the second place, the words *"essentially* within the domestic jurisdiction of States" refer to those matters that are not regulated by international law. As the ICJ has concluded, "[T]he question whether a certain matter is or is not solely within the domestic jurisdiction of a State is an essentially relative question; it depends on the development of international relations."[10] The ICJ has further concluded that it hardly seems conceivable that terms like "domestic jurisdiction" were intended to have a fixed content, regardless of the subsequent evolution of international law.[11]

Sovereignty has been eroded by contemporary economic, cultural, and environmental factors. Interference in what would previously have been regarded as internal affairs – by other states, the private sector, and nonstate actors – has become routine. However, the preoccupation here is not these routine matters but the potential tension when the norm of state sovereignty and egregious human suffering coexist. As Kofi Annan suggested, in his opening remarks at the 1999 General Assembly, "States bent on criminal behaviour [should] know that frontiers are not the absolute defence."[12] In this respect, events in the last decade have broken new ground.

## EMERGING CHALLENGES TO SOVEREIGNTY

The limits on sovereignty discussed above are widely accepted. They originate in the Charter itself, in authoritative legal interpretations of that document, and in the broader body of international law that has been agreed on by states. In recent decades, and particularly since the end of the Cold War, four more radical challenges to the notion of state sovereignty have emerged: continuing demands for self-determination, a broadened conception of international peace and security, the collapse of state authority, and the increasing importance of popular sovereignty.

In many ways, a central contemporary difficulty arises from the softening of two norms that had been virtually unchallenged during the Cold War, the sanctity of borders and the illegitimacy of secession. For almost half a century, collective self-determination was limited to the initial process of decolonization. Existing borders were sacrosanct, and it was unthinkable that an area of a state would secede, even with the consent of the original state. The OAU's Charter was clear that colonial borders, although it is generally agreed that they were arbitrarily drawn, still had to be respected, or chaos would ensue. *Uti possidetis, ita possideatis* (as you possess, so may you possess) was accepted as the necessary trade-off for a modicum of international order.

At the end of the Cold War, however, these relatively clear waters became muddied. First, the Soviet Union became a "former superpower." Russia inherited the Soviet Union's legal status, including a permanent seat on the Security Council, but 14 other new states were created. Shortly thereafter, Yugoslavia broke up into 6 independent states. Later in the decade, Eritrea seceded from Ethiopia.

That weakening of the norms relating to borders and secessions is creating new tensions. Contemporary politics in developing countries is deeply conditioned by the legacy of colonialism. As European states ruled so many Asian and African countries without their consent, respect for state sovereignty is the preemptive norm *par excellence* of ex-colonial states. In light of history, it is difficult for representatives of developing countries to take at face value altruistic claims by the West. What may appear as narrow legalism – for instance, that Security Council authorization is a prerequisite for intervention – often appears in the South as a necessary buttress against new forms of imperialism.

The second challenge is the broadening interpretation of threats to international peace and security, the Charter-enshrined licence to override the principle of nonintervention. It arises from the fact that the Charter's collective system of international peace and security was crafted on the experience of the Second World War, some of which is of doubtful contemporary relevance. The focus was principally on the external unlawful use of sovereignty by states in committing acts of aggression. Collective efforts by the UN to deal with internal problems of peace and security, and gross violations of human rights, including genocide, have therefore run against the grain of the claim to sovereign status as set out in the Charter.

State actions approved or authorized after the Cold War's end by the Security Council have routinely broadened the notion of what is considered a threat to international peace and security. This process actually began during the Cold War with the Security Council's coercive decisions in the form of economic sanctions and arms and oil embargoes against apartheid in Southern Rhodesia and South Africa. In both cases, the Security Council described the recourse to Chapter VII action as a response to "threats to international peace and security." However, what clearly motivated state decision making was the human costs resulting from aberrant domestic human rights policies of white-minority regimes. An affront to civilization was packaged as a threat to international peace and security in order to permit action.

The evolution of the definition of a threat to international peace and security accelerated in the 1990s. For instance, while recalling Article 2 (7) of the Charter, the Security Council, in Resolution 688 (1991), nonetheless condemned "the repression of the Iraqi civilian population in many parts of Iraq, including most recently in Kurdish populated areas."[13] The Security Council has repeatedly condemned attacks on civilians, in Bosnia and Herzegovina, in Sierra Leone, and in Kosovo, which constitute grave violations of international law. It has reaffirmed that persons who commit or order the commission of grave breaches of the Geneva Conventions and the Additional Protocols are individually responsible in respect of such breaches.[14] Similarly, the establishment of international tribunals with criminal jurisdiction and the negotiation of the Rome Statute on the International Criminal Court signal that atrocities committed against human beings by their own governments – including war crimes, crimes against humanity, and the perpetration of genocide – may trump claims of sovereignty.[15]

The main interventions of the 1990s were justified, at least in part, on humanitarian grounds, though again the humanitarian dimensions were framed as threats to international peace and security. In most cases, the dire humanitarian situation was explicitly mentioned in the Security Council's authorization – the most extreme case being Somalia, where "humanitarian" appeared 18 times in Resolution 794 (1992). In a session devoted to Africa in January 2000, the AIDS pandemic was also framed as falling within the Security Council's mandate. In short, the range of interpretations of international peace and security – the concept that defines the Security Council's mandate – has been substantially broadened, albeit not without controversy.

The third challenge to traditional interpretations of state sovereignty has arisen because of the incapacity of certain states to effectively exercise authority over their territories and populations. In some cases, sovereignty is a legal fiction not matched by an actual political capacity. They are, in the words of one analyst, "quasi-states."[16] And as mentioned earlier, the display of actual control over territory is a prominent dimension of sovereign status. Some commentators have even argued that failed states violate the substantive UN membership requirement in Charter Article 4 that they "are able to carry out" their obligations.

This perspective is important in light of the growing awareness that state capacity and authority are essential conditions for the protection of fundamental rights. These conditions do not invoke nostalgia for repressive national-security states, but they recognize that a modicum of state authority and capacity is a prerequisite for the maintenance of domestic and international order and justice.

The absence or disappearance of a functioning government can lead to the same kinds of human catastrophe as the presence of a repressive state or the outbreak of a deadly civil war. Resounding features of these so-called failed states are anarchy, chronic disorder, and civil war waged without regard for the laws of armed conflict. These features, individually or collectively, inhibit or prevent a state from acting with authority over its entire territory. The failure of state sovereignty is most obviously evidenced by the lack of control where territorial sovereignty is effectively contested by force internally. In this situation, insurgents may occupy and control large portions of the territory, inhibiting the state from carrying out its responsibility to protect lives and property and maintain public security.

The political vacuum resulting from these circumstances leads to nonstate actors' taking matters into their own hands, the massive flight of refugees, and the forced displacement of populations. These issues also create consequences of concern to other states, international organizations, and civil society. In lending support to the intervention by the Economic Community of West African States in Liberia, Zimbabwe went so far as to take the position that "when there is no government in being and there is just chaos in the country," domestic affairs should be qualified as meaning "affairs within a peaceful environment."[17]

The grave humanitarian consequences of the failure of state capacity has led the Security Council to override state sovereignty by determining that internal disorder may pose a threat to international peace and security. In one case in particular, Somalia, the complete absence of state capacity prompted the Security Council to authorize a Chapter VII intervention.

The fourth challenge to traditional state sovereignty emerges from the changing balance between states and people as the source of legitimacy and authority. The older version of the rule of the law of states is being tempered by the rule of law based on the rights of individuals. And a broader concept of sovereignty, encompassing both the rights and the responsibilities of states, is now being more widely advocated.

One formulation has been proposed by Kofi Annan in his widely cited article in *The Economist* on the "two concepts of sovereignty," which helped launch the intense debate on the legitimacy of intervention on humanitarian grounds. In it he argued that one concept of sovereignty is oriented around states and the other around people:

> State sovereignty, in its most basic sense, is being redefined – not least by the forces of globalization and international co-operation. States are now widely understood to be instruments at the service of their peoples, and not vice versa. At the same time individual sovereignty – by which I mean the fundamental freedom of each individual, enshrined in the Charter of the UN and subsequent international treaties – has been enhanced by a renewed and spreading consciousness of individual rights. When we read the Charter today, we are more than ever conscious that its aim is to protect individual human beings, not to protect those who abuse them.

For Annan and others, sovereignty is not becoming less relevant; it remains the ordering principle of international affairs. However, "it is the peoples' sovereignty rather than the sovereign's sovereignty."[18]

Another way of approaching the increasing importance of popular sovereignty is the notion of "sovereignty as responsibility," most explicitly formulated by Francis M. Deng, the Representative of the Secretary-General on Internally Displaced Persons. This doctrine stipulates that when states are unable to provide life-supporting protection and assistance for their citizens, they are expected to request and accept outside offers of aid.[19] Should they refuse or deliberately obstruct access to their displaced or other affected populations and thereby put large numbers at risk, there is an international responsibility to respond. Sovereignty then means accountability to two separate constituencies: internally, to one's own population; and internationally, to the community of responsible states and in the form of compliance with human rights and humanitarian agreements. Proponents of this view argue that sovereignty is not absolute but contingent. When a government massively abuses the fundamental rights of its citizens, its sovereignty is temporarily suspended.

A third variant on this theme revolves around the concept of human security. Security has traditionally been conceived in terms of the relations between states, but for a growing number of states the security of individuals is becoming a foreign policy priority in its own right. According to a group of states participating in the Human Security Network, "[H]uman security means freedom from pervasive threats to people's rights, their safety or even their lives."[20] Though the state remains the principal provider of security, it is seen in instrumental terms – as a means to an end, rather than an end in itself. In the face of repressive or weak states, advocates of human security argue that international actors have a responsibility to come to the aid of populations at risk. Ultimately, "peace and security – national, regional and international – are possible only if they are derived from peoples' security."[21]

These approaches all see the basis for sovereignty shifting from the absolute rights of state leaders to respect for the popular will and internal forms of governance based on international standards of democracy and human rights.[22] Their advocates suggest that on a scale of values the sovereignty of a state does not stand higher than the human rights of its inhabitants.[23]

Some observers charge that humanitarian intervention is simply the latest phase of Euro-centric domination. Human rights are the contemporary Western values being imposed in place of Christianity and the "standard of civilization"[24] in the 19th and early 20th century.

Nevertheless, from many quarters the view is emerging that sovereignty is no longer sacrosanct.[25] Sovereignty as the supreme power of a state has always been limited, originally by divine law, respect for religious practices, and natural law; and subsequently, limitations have resulted from the consent-based system of the law of nations.[26] "The doctrine of national sovereignty in its absolute and unqualified form, which gave rulers protection against attack from without while engaged within in the most brutal assault on their own citizens," writes Ramesh Thakur, "has gone with the wind."[27]

## NOTES

1   Boutros Boutros-Ghali, *An Agenda for Peace* (New York: United Nations, 1992), para. 17.

2   Mohammed Ayoob, "The New-Old Disorder in the Third World," *Global Governance* 1, no. 1 (Winter 1995), pp. 59–78.

3   Nico Schrijver, "The Changing Nature of State Sovereignty," *The British Year Book of International Law 1999* (Oxford: Clarendon Press, 2000), pp. 69–70.

4   Francis Hinsley, *Sovereignty* (London: Basic Books, 1966), p. 126; Francis Abiew, *The Evolution of the Doctrine and Practice of Humanitarian Intervention* (The Hague: Kluwer, 1999), pp. 26–27; Louis Henkin, *International Law: Politics and Values* (London: Martinus Nijhoff, 1995), pp. 9–10; and W. Michael Reisman, "Sovereignty and Human Rights in Contemporary International Law," *American Journal of International Law* 84 (1990), p. 867.

5   Stephen D. Krasner, "Compromising Westphalia," *International Security* 20 (Winter 1995–1996), p. 115.

6   ICJ Reports, 1949, p. 4.

7   ICJ Reports, 1986, para. 263.

8   Quoted by Shashi Tharoor and Sam Daws, "Humanitarian Intervention: Getting Past the Reefs," *World Policy Journal* XVIII, no. 2 (Summer 2001), p. 25.

9   Christopher M. Ryan, "Sovereignty, Intervention, and the Law: A Tenuous Relationship of Competing Principles," *Millennium: Journal of International Studies* 26 (1997), p. 77; and Samuel M. Makinda, "Sovereignty and International Security: Challenges for the United Nations," *Global Governance* 2, no. 2 (May–August 1996), p. 149.

10   Emphasis added. This is an interpretation similar to that of the Permanent Court of International Justice in its Advisory Opinion concerning the *Tunis and Morocco Nationality Decrees* (1923), Series B, no. 4, p. 4.

11   *Aegean Sea Case*, in ICJ Reports, 1978, p. 32.

12   Kofi A. Annan, "Secretary-General's Speech to the 54th Session of the General Assembly," September 20, 1999.

13   This resolution was adopted in the framework of "consequences which threaten international peace and security in the region." It was criticized by the states that abstained (China and India) and voted against (Cuba, Yemen, and Zimbabwe) for being concerned with a domestic issue.

14   Statement by the President of the Security Council, October 30, 1992, UN Document S/24744.

15   Theodore Meron, "International Criminalization of Internal Atrocities," *American Journal of International Law* 89 (July 1995), p. 554; and Louis Henkin, "Kosovo and the Law of Humanitarian Intervention," *American Journal of International Law* 93 (1999), p. 824.

16   Robert H. Jackson, *Quasi-States: Sovereignty, International Relations, and the Third World* (Cambridge: Cambridge University Press, 1990). See also Christopher Clapham, *Africa and the International System: The Politics of State Survival* (Cambridge: Cambridge University Press, 1996); I. William Zartman, ed., *Collapsed States* (Boulder: Lynne Rienner, 1995); and Kal J. Holsti, *The State, War, and the State of War* (Cambridge: Cambridge University Press, 1996). The debate began in earnest following Gerald B. Helman and Steven Ratner, "Saving Failed States," *Foreign Policy*, no. 89 (Winter 1992–1993), pp. 3–20.

17   Statement by President Robert Mugabe of Zimbabwe, quoted by Lori F. Damrosch, ed., *Reinforcing Restraint: Collective Intervention in Internal Conflicts* (New York: Council on Foreign Relations, 1993), p. 364.

18   Kofi Annan, "Two Concepts of Sovereignty," *The Economist* 352 (September 18, 1999), pp. 49–50.

19   Francis Deng, *Protecting the Dispossessed* (Washington, DC: Brookings Institution, 1993); and Abiew, *The Evolution of the Doctrine and Practice*, pp. 1–2.

20  Knut Vollebaek, "A Perspective on Human Security: Chairman's Summary," presented at 1st Ministerial Meeting of the Human Security Network, Lysøen, Norway, May 20, 1999. At that time, participants of the network included Austria, Canada, Chile, Ireland, Jordan, The Netherlands, Norway, Slovenia, Switzerland, and Thailand.

21  Lloyd Axworthy, "Human Security and Global Governance: Putting People First," *Global Governance* 7, no. 1 (January–March 2001), p. 23.

22  Reisman, "Sovereignty and Human Rights in Contemporary International Law," pp. 867–69.

23  Henkin, "Kosovo and the Law of Humanitarian Intervention," p. 824.

24  See Robert Jackson, *The Global Covenant: Human Conduct in a World of States* (Oxford: Oxford University Press, 2000), especially chapter 10, "Armed Intervention for Humanity," and chapter 11, "Failed States: Interantional Trusteeship." See also Mohammed Ayoob, "Humanitarian Intervention and International Society," *Global Governance* 7, no. 3 (July–September 2001), pp. 225-230.

25  Jarat Chopra and Thomas G. Weiss, "Sovereignty Is No Longer Sacrosanct: Codifying Humanitarian Intervention," *Ethics and International Affairs* 6 (1992), p. 95.

26  Charles E. Merriam, *History of the Theory of Sovereignty since Rousseau* (New York: Columbia University Press, 1958), p. 11.

27  Ramesh Thakur, "Global Norms and International Humanitarian Law: An Asian Perspective," *International Review of the Red Cross* 83, no. 841 (March 2001), p. 35.

# 2. INTERVENTION

Intervention means various forms of nonconsensual action that are often thought to directly challenge the principle of state sovereignty. With the exception of the subsequent examination of prevention, the remainder of this volume focuses on various aspects and instances of intervention. What follows is thus not an exhaustive account of the notion, but rather the conceptual foundation for subsequent analyses.

Many commentators would prefer to eliminate the "h" word, the modifier "humanitarian," before "intervention." Civilian humanitarians dislike the association with the use of military force, viewing "humanitarian intervention" as an oxymoron. Former colonies recall the disingenuous application of the term for purposes that were anything except humanitarian. And many observers do not want the high ground automatically occupied by those who claim a humanitarian justification for going to war without a serious scrutiny of the specific merits of the case or prejudging whether a particular intervention is defensible or not. "Of course military intervention may be undertaken for humanitarian motives," cautions UN Secretary-General Kofi Annan, but "let's get right away from using the term 'humanitarian' to describe military operations."[14]

Such concerns are understandable and may serve some diplomatic or analytical purposes. However, "humanitarian intervention" is used throughout this volume because the term is employed in virtually all academic and policy literature. Semantics aside, truth in packaging requires an accurate short-hand description for military coercion to protect civilians. It made no sense to insert either "so-called" throughout the text or to use scare quotes around the term. Human suffering and the need to provide humanitarian relief to affected populations are prominent in the support of publics and politicians who back the use of military force to support humanitarian objectives – and they almost always employ "humanitarian intervention" in their arguments.

For many audiences, "humanitarian" thus retains great resonance.[15] The definition of "humanitarian," as a justification for intervention, is a high threshold of suffering. It refers to the threat or actual occurrence of large scale loss of life (including, of course, genocide), massive forced migrations, and widespread abuses of human rights. Acts that shock the conscience and elicit a basic humanitarian impulse remain politically powerful.

The specific objectives are to explore the meaning and evolution of the concept, the implications of the United Nations (UN) Charter, and nonmilitary forms of intervention and to summarize the various dimensions of the contemporary intervention debate.

## MEANING OF INTERVENTION

The actual meaning of the term "intervention" can be derived from the contexts in which it occurs, in addition to the purposes for which it is invoked. Actions do not amount to intervention if they are based on a genuine request from, or with the unqualified consent of, the target state. Consent, if it is to be valid in law, should emanate from the legal government of a sovereign state and be freely given. Forms of interference that fall short of coercion in the internal affairs of a state also do not amount to intervention. In fact, a central purpose of foreign policy is to persuade other states, friend and foe alike, to enact changes in behaviour that are consistent with foreign policy objectives.

Of course, wider definitions of intervention have always existed. In a world of asymmetrical power, economic activities and foreign direct investment are considered by some observers as types of "intervention." And with interdependence and globalization rising over the last few decades, anxiety levels among many governmental officials have increased because there are substantial new vulnerabilities about which they can do virtually nothing. Heightened state sensitivities to economic and cultural influences across borders have also meant even greater sensitivities to human rights pressures that occur without the assent of governments. Moreover, there are gray areas regarding "consent" – for economic as well as military measures. Some observers note, for instance, that a request for military intervention may involve so much arm-twisting, including economic pressure from Washington-based financial institutions, as to effectively constitute coercion.

Various terms have been coined in thinking about the problem of what amounts to coerced consent, including "coercive inducement."[1] Intervention may be better framed, in effect, as a matter of factual intrusiveness, rather than merely an absence of consent, to ensure that a so-called request is not actually spurious. As for many definitions, it may be more useful to think of consent as a continuum, rather than as an absolute concept.

Notwithstanding these realities, the actual expression of consent is a critical dividing line in this volume, both legally and conceptually. And given the legacy of colonialism, it is not surprising that it is the benchmark against which developing countries measure international action.

Obviously the use of armed force against another state without its consent constitutes intervention, but so too does the use of such nonmilitary measures as political and economic sanctions, arms embargoes, and international criminal prosecution. Intervention is a concept with a distinct character.[2] This character lies in the use of "forcible" or "nonforcible" measures against a state, without its consent, solely on account of its internal or external behaviour. Although intervention has most frequently been employed for the preservation of the vital interests – legitimately or illegitimately perceived – of intervening states,[3] there is also a long history of intervention justified on the grounds of grave human suffering.

## THE CONCEPT OF HUMANITARIAN INTERVENTION

References to humanitarian intervention first began to appear in the international legal literature after 1840.[4] Two interventions in particular were most directly responsible: the intervention in Greece by England, France, and Russia in 1827 to stop Turkish massacres and suppression of populations associated with insurgents; and the intervention by France in Syria in 1860 to protect Maronite Christians.[5] In fact, there were at least five prominent interventions undertaken by European powers against the Ottoman Empire from 1827 to 1908.[6] By the 1920s, the rationale for intervention had broadened to include the protection of nationals abroad.[7]

Intervention was invoked against a state's abuse of its sovereignty by brutal and cruel treatment of those within its power, both nationals and nonnationals. Such a state was regarded as having made itself liable to action by any state or states that were prepared to intervene. One writer, in 1921, depicted humanitarian intervention as "the reliance upon force for the justifiable purpose of protecting the inhabitants of another state from the treatment which is so arbitrary and persistently abusive as to exceed the limits of that authority within which the sovereign is presumed to act with reason and justice."[8]

Intervention was surrounded by controversy, however, and many looked, and continue to look, askance at the earliest cases of so-called humanitarian intervention.[9] Critics argued that the humanitarian justifications were usually a pretext for intervention motivated by strategic, economic, or political interests. Furthermore, there can be no doubt that even when objectives were less objectionable, the paternalism of intervening powers – which were self-appointed custodians of morality and human conscience, as well as the guarantors of international order and security – undermined the credibility of the enterprise.[10]

One noted legal authority concluded in 1963 that "no genuine case of humanitarian intervention has occurred with the possible exception of the occupation of Syria in 1860 and 1861."[11] The scale of the atrocities in that case may well have warranted intervention – more than 11,000 Maronite Christians were killed and 100,000 were made homeless in a single four-week period. But by the time the 12,000 European troops had been deployed, the violence was largely over, and after undertaking some relief activities the troops withdrew.

At the end of the 19th century, many legal commentators held that a doctrine of humanitarian intervention existed in customary international law, though a considerable number of scholars disagreed. Contemporary legal scholars disagree on the significance of these conclusions. Some argue that the doctrine was clearly established in state practice prior to 1945 and that it is the parameters, not the existence, of the doctrine that are open to debate. Others reject this claim, noting the inconsistency of state practice, particularly in the 20th century, and the substantial number of scholars who had earlier rejected the proposition. What is clear is that this notion of intervention evolved substantially before the appearance of an international system with institutions responsible for maintaining international order and protecting human rights.

The first restrictions on recourse to war were developed in the Kellogg-Briand Pact in 1928. Later, the system crystallized into its current form, under the UN Charter. Since 1945, the threat or use of force against the territorial integrity and political independence of states is prohibited by Article 2 (4), with exceptions granted for the collective use of force under Chapter VII and for individual or collective self-defence in the event of an armed attack in Article 51. Although the prohibition seems clear, questions about the legality of humanitarian intervention remained. In 1946, for example, an eminent legal scholar continued to argue that intervention is legally permissible when a state is guilty of cruelties against its nationals in a way that denied their fundamental human rights and shocked the conscience of humankind.[12]

## MILITARY INTERVENTION AND THE UN CHARTER

The advent of the UN Charter fundamentally affected earlier interpretations of the legality of intervention. Not only did the Charter set out the circumstances under which intervention was permissible, it also changed the terms of debate by employing the term "the threat or use of force" instead of "intervention."

As "intervention" had been used, historically, as a synonym for the threat or use of force, the question was and remains: Did the Charter's prohibition on the unilateral threat or use of force prohibit intervention altogether, or was intervention subsumed by the system of the collective use of force? Even more controversial: Was there an interpretation of the term "intervention" that would place this concept outside the frame of the Charter's prohibition on the use of force against the territorial integrity and political independence of a state? Does the Charter prohibit the use of force without the authorization of the Security Council, even when exceptional circumstances arise?

As the Charter explicitly permits the use of force in self-defence and enables the Security Council to authorize force to confront threats to international peace and security, a recurring aspect of debate has been the use of force to protect human rights. The 1990s were not the beginnings of the dispute. Various interpretations of the legality of humanitarian intervention were fiercely debated, particularly beginning in the late 1960s.[13]

The ideological competition of the Cold War lent a particular character to interventions during that period. With much of the world aligned with one of the two superpowers, there was considerable pressure from both sides to intervene in both internal and international armed conflicts. The deadlock in the Security Council and the existence of the veto also increased the likelihood that interventions would either not occur at all or be undertaken in the absence of a Council mandate. In fact, interventions during the Cold War were far more likely to be undertaken by a single state (for example, the United States [US] in Vietnam, the Soviet Union in Afghanistan, and South Africa and Cuba in Angola), whether directly or by proxy, than they were to be multilateral.

On two occasions during this period, the International Court of Justice (ICJ) ruled on cases that involved assessing the legality of interventions for which humanitarian purposes had been declared: the United Kingdom in the Corfu Channel and the US in Nicaragua. In both cases, the ICJ adhered to the position that the principle of nonintervention involves the right of every sovereign state to conduct its affairs without outside interference and that international law requires territorial integrity to be respected. The ICJ rejected intervention that impedes a state from conducting those matters that each state is permitted, by the principle of sovereignty, to decide freely – namely, its political, economic, social, and cultural system and the formulation of its foreign policy.

More specifically, in the case of *Nicaragua vs. United States*, the ICJ reiterated the attributes of humanitarian aid or assistance, that might also be applicable to military intervention for humanitarian purposes. If the provision of humanitarian assistance is to escape condemnation as an intervention in the internal affairs of a state, the ICJ took the view that it must be "limited to the purposes hallowed in practice, namely to prevent and alleviate human suffering, and to protect life and health and to ensure respect for the human being without discrimination to all in need" and that it be "linked as closely as possible under the circumstances to the UN Charter in order to further gain legitimacy." These criteria should be applicable in extreme situations where the need to "prevent and alleviate human suffering, and to protect life and health and to ensure respect for the human being" constitutes a humanitarian crisis threatening international or regional peace and security. The ICJ rejected the notion of the use of force to ensure the protection of human rights: "[W]here human rights are protected by international conventions, that protection takes the form of such arrangements for monitoring or ensuring the respect for human rights as are provided for in the conventions themselves … . In any event … the use of force could not be the appropriate method to monitor or ensure such respect."[16]

Such a conclusion, however, does not appear to be definitive. The protection of human rights by international conventions presupposes a stable and orderly system of monitoring and ensuring respect for human rights based on those conventions. Cases may arise where the existing arrangements are inappropriate for protecting human rights, owing to the nature and scale of the violations. Furthermore, in extreme situations, where the Security Council is unable to act, political and moral imperatives may leave no choice but "to act outside the law."[17]

Further clarification of the meaning of intervention in the context of the Charter can be drawn from UN negotiations over the past decade. The end of the Cold War was seen by many as the rebirth of the UN, and it bore witness to an urge for intervention to sort out problems of civil strife.[18] Throughout the 1990s there was an unpredictable and diverse pattern of interventions by the UN, stretching from Iraq to Bosnia, Somalia to Haiti, Kosovo to East Timor.

Within the General Assembly, the tensions between intervention and state sovereignty initially focused on the delivery of humanitarian assistance.[19] Already in 1988, Resolution 43/131 was a contentious milestone acknowledging that nongovernmental organizations (NGOs) had a role to play in responding to the effects of deadly conflicts. The resolution maintained that humanitarian aid could and should be provided to affected populations in need of access to "essential" supplies. By implication, states were obliged to grant such access. A number of governments, however, objected on the grounds that NGOs might urge states to interfere in what the dissenters considered to be strictly domestic affairs.

Three years later, in the wake of the intervention in northern Iraq, the General Assembly passed Resolution 46/182. Somewhat surprisingly, in light of the actual intervention that had preceded it, this resolution gives weight, first and foremost, to the consent of the state inhabited by severely affected populations. The most relevant section reads, "The sovereignty, territorial integrity and national unity of states must be fully respected in accordance with the Charter of the UN. In this context, humanitarian assistance should be provided with the consent of the affected country and in principle on the basis of an appeal by the affected country." Though the implications of the resolution were wide-ranging, the debate preceding its adoption in the General Assembly focused largely on the issue of military intervention for humanitarian purposes and the accompanying clash with state sovereignty. Already in these debates, the views of developing and developed countries were polarized, and the ensuing negotiated text represented a delicate balance.

The result of this consensus is open to interpretation. Consent may reflect less the wishes of a government than severe international pressure, as was arguably the case with Indonesia over East Timor in 1999. Moreover, the government of a state requesting assistance may be disputed, as was arguably the case with the government-in-exile of Jean-Bertrand Aristide over Haiti in 1994. Behind the consensus is an assumption that the state concerned has a government with effective territorial control, allowing it to offer or refuse consent. Where no such government exists, the requirement for consent, by definition, cannot be met, as was the case in Somalia in 1992. Furthermore, some observers point out that the phrase "in principle" may, in practice, mean that consent may be subordinate to the necessity to provide assistance in the face of an overwhelming human tragedy, or indeed that consent should come from citizens, rather than governments.

## NONMILITARY INTERVENTIONS

The bulk of the contemporary policy and academic literature about intervention is concerned with the application of military force to pursue humanitarian objectives. But the present analysis would be incomplete without also introducing nonmilitary intervention, both sanctions and criminal prosecution.

### Sanctions

International economic and political sanctions, as well as embargoes of various types, became widespread in the 1990s. They are the main element of "nonmilitary" interventions designed to impose a course of conduct – including a change of policy – on a state, by banning or restricting that state's economic, military, or political relations. Sanctions are a punitive countermeasure against illegal acts, whether they be criminal (for example, alleged acts of aggression) or civil (for example, alleged breaches of international obligations).

Economic sanctions include trade and commercial restrictions and sometimes embargoes on imports and exports, shipping, flights, investment, or assistance and the seizure of a state's assets abroad. Political sanctions include embargoes on arms, denial of military assistance and training, restraint on the means and extent of a state's level of armament, the nonrecognition of illegal acts perpetrated by a state, and the refusal of entry of political leaders into the territories of other states.[20]

An analysis of the use of sanctions under the auspices of the UN Charter in the 1945–1990 and post-Cold War periods indicates three broad trends. First, there was a combination of unilateral and collective sanctions during the Cold War by individual states and by the UN, chiefly in the process of decolonization – specified in Charter Chapters XI–XIII and elsewhere[21] – against Portugal (in relation to Angola and Mozambique before 1975), Rhodesia's Unilateral Declaration of Independence, in 1965, and South Africa's illegal presence in Namibia,[22] as well as its practice of apartheid between 1975 and 1979.[23] Only in the clearest of cases was it possible for the Security Council to reach decisions on the collective use of sanctions. Consequently, many "nonbinding" resolutions on sanctions were passed by the General Assembly during debates on decolonization.

Second, there is increasing use in the 1990s of unilateral and collective sanctions in the context of diplomatic efforts to coerce state behaviour with respect to maintaining international peace and security under Chapter VII. Compliance with sanctions regimes is often voluntary at the outset in order to generate consensus and only later do they sometimes become mandatory under Chapter VII.

The third discernible element is the use of sanctions as a means of intervening in aid of democracy, not only by the UN but more emphatically by the British Commonwealth, the European Union (EU), the Organization of American States (OAS), and other regional organizations. The Haiti case is central because both the General Assembly and the OAS condemned the 1991 military coup that overthrew the elected government. The Security Council subsequently prohibited specified commercial passenger flights destined for Haiti and denied entry of the Haitian military and others to territories of UN member states. The Security Council also imposed embargoes on the supply of arms and petroleum to the Union for the Total Liberation of Angola, a rebel organization fighting the government of Angola in breach of the Lusaka Peace Agreement and UN-supervised elections.[24] The Economic Community of West African States also launched an "economic blockade" against the junta in Sierra Leone in 1997.

The Commonwealth Ministerial Action Group[25] intervened on the authority of the Harare Declaration of 1991, by imposing economic and political sanctions on military governments that had thwarted democracy or overthrown democratically elected governments in Nigeria, Pakistan, and Fiji. Commonwealth membership of these states was also suspended. The Commonwealth is unusual among regional arrangements in its capacity and willingness to suspend or expel member states if they act in serious breach of the standards of human rights. But the sanctions imposed on Nigeria were mirrored by the EU, which restricted member states from granting visas to members of the Nigerian military government and security forces, alongside other measures.[26]

A central difficulty with sanctions is assessing their impact and effectiveness on the objectives for which they are imposed. Research suggests little real impact over what is often a very long time.[27] Moreover, it is methodologically difficult to disaggregate the impact of sanctions from other measures.[28] The Security Council establishes a sanctions committee to review each episode of sanctions, but there is rarely sufficient data to enable sound assessments.

Sanctions tend, more often than not, to harm the economic and social well-being of the general population, rather than that of the political leadership against whom the coercive measures are imposed.[29] "Smart sanctions," which target elites through such measures as freezing foreign assets and preventing travel, have had, to date, more impact on theorizing than Security Council practice.[30] Concern about the plight of civilians has meant, in almost every case endorsed by the Security Council, humanitarian exceptions for food and medical supplies to alleviate the plight and suffering of the population. Yet, these exemptions cannot compensate for the massive economic dislocations, and the UN remains ill-equipped to oversee them.[31]

The dramatic suffering caused by economic sanctions – the plight of innocent civilians deteriorates with little discernable policy change from repressive regimes – suggests that sanctions and embargoes may not be an intervention tool of preference in the future. Former UN Secretary-General Boutros-Ghali captured the troubling tensions between dramatic civilian pain and elusive political gain in his 1995 *Supplement to An Agenda for Peace*. Sanctions are a "blunt instrument" that inflict suffering on vulnerable groups, complicate the work of humanitarian agencies, cause long-term damage to the productive capacity of target nations, and generate severe effects on neighbouring countries. Although he stopped short of rejecting sanctions, he urged reforms in their implementation.[32] Paradoxically, the logic of the Charter to use forcible measures only as a last resort may be inappropriate to foster humanitarian objectives. Rather than gradually ratcheting up to more interventionist measures, it is plausible that an earlier resort to military force may be more "humane" than extended and extensive sanctions.[33]

## International Criminal Prosecution

After almost a half-century since the war crimes tribunals in Nuremberg and Tokyo following the Second World War, the 1990s have witnessed the renewed use of international criminal prosecution as a form of nonmilitary intervention. Basic principles for prosecution under international criminal law were set out in the late 1940s – that violations of the laws of war were subject to penal sanctions, that superiors' orders do not release an individual from responsibility, and that certain acts constitute crimes against humanity. Yet, almost no progress was made over the intervening 45 years. The 1990s have witnessed a series of almost revolutionary changes. Not only are war criminals and human rights abusers occasionally being brought to account, but a series of transformations in international criminal law suggests that this form of intervention may become more routine. The pursuit of indicted criminals is slow and time-consuming, and hence it is hardly an effective intervention instrument on the edge of the abyss of a humanitarian crisis in the same way that military intervention may be. In fact, a case can be made that international criminal prosecution may better be framed as an effective instrument for prevention through deterrence and eventually as a contribution to post-conflict reconciliation. At the same time, the use of this tool effectively requires moving beyond consent, and the consequences are important for humanitarian action.

The establishment of the ad hoc war crimes tribunals for the former Yugoslavia in 1993 and Rwanda in 1994 were major innovations. Despite initial scepticism and considerable criticism about the pace, both tribunals have convicted senior officials and made progress in setting the record straight. They have also contributed to the development of international criminal jurisprudence. They have clearly established that criminal liability exists for war crimes during internal armed conflicts and that crimes against humanity extend beyond periods of armed conflict, and rape is now legally considered an aspect of genocide.

Considerable erosion has also taken place in the rules relating to the immunity of leaders. Until recently it was commonly accepted that leading officials (including those retired) could not be tried in courts in another country for acts committed in their own country while in office.[34] The capture in 1989 and subsequent conviction by the US of former Panamanian General Manuel Noriega was the first major crack in that particular bastion of international law. More recently, the House of Lords – acting as Britain's highest court in the third Pinochet case – established a very strong precedent for no longer treating government officials as having absolute protection under the rules of the sovereign immunity of states.[35]

The arrest and trial in Senegal of the former president of Chad, Hissène Habré, suggests that the reach of this type of thinking is expanding to other continents. This followed the new legal ground broken by the Arusha Tribunal, which convicted Jean Kambanda, the former Prime Minister of Rwanda, the first head of government to be convicted of genocide and crimes against humanity. In March 2001, Biljana Plavsic, the former president of the Republika Srpska, voluntarily surrendered herself to the Tribunal in The Hague after being indicted for genocide and complicity in genocide. The indictment of a sitting head of state for war crimes, the Federal Republic of Yugoslavia's President Slobodan Milosevic, for his direction of efforts in Kosovo is yet another precedent.

Moving from the heads of state, some commentators saw as even more exceptional the conviction in spring of 2001 in Belgium of Rwandan nuns charged with complicity in the 1994 genocide. These developments begin to form a pattern that suggests the emergence of universal jurisdiction for egregious human rights abuses. "The notion that heads of state and senior public officials should have the same standing as outlaws before the bar of justice is quite new," writes former US Secretary of State Henry A. Kissinger, himself accused by some of being a "war criminal" for his role in the Vietnam War. Speaking for many who caution against this general trend, he argues that "[t]he danger lies in pushing the effort to extremes that risk substituting the tyranny of judges for that of governments; historically, the dictatorship of the virtuous has often led to inquisitions and even witch-hunts."[36]

While still waiting to enter into force, the Rome Statute will undoubtedly lead to the creation of a permanent tribunal, the International Criminal Court (ICC). The court will have jurisdiction over three crimes – genocide, crimes against humanity, and war crimes – and has provided definitions for each. As well as having a deterrent effect, indictments, some argue, may also serve as a disincentive to leaders who would be left with no reason to compromise. This was not the problem that some expected, however, when the indictment of Milosevic was made public during the North Atlantic Treaty Organization (NATO) air campaign.

The Rome Statute has also formalized in international law many of the precedents set out by the ad hoc tribunals. One of the more important aspects of the ICC is that it may answer partially the allegation that international justice is always of the victors' sort. The statute allows for criminal proceedings to be initiated, not only by states and the Security Council, but also by the ICC prosecutor independently.

## CONTEMPORARY DEBATE

Intervention has long been one of the most controversial issues for diplomats, lawyers, and academics. In the post-Cold War era, and particularly since the NATO intervention in Kosovo, state practice and scholarly analyses have sharpened the cutting edges of these long-standing controversies.[37] Two senior UN officials have summarized: "To its proponents, it marks the coming of age of the imperative of action in the face of human rights abuses, over the citadels of state sovereignty. To its detractors, it is an oxymoron, a pretext for military intervention often devoid of legal sanction, selectively deployed and achieving only ambiguous ends. As some put it, there can be nothing humanitarian about a bomb."[38]

In broad brush strokes, two overarching positions have emerged about humanitarian intervention. Among the members of the trans-Atlantic community, there appears to be a general consensus on the legitimacy of humanitarian intervention in extreme circumstances, even in the absence of Security Council authorization. Although some of the five permanent members of the Security Council (P-5) share this view, all agree that matters pertaining to the use of force should be in the hands of the great powers and thus they jealously guard their vetoes. Among developing countries, the predominant view is a deep-seated scepticism toward humanitarian intervention because it seems to be yet another rationalization for unwanted interference. The dichotomy in views is exacerbated to the extent that the Third World has been relegated to the role of norm-takers, while developed countries act as norm-enforcers.

The essence of the contemporary debate stems from two basic questions: Does a right of humanitarian intervention exist? And if so, whose right is it?[39] The broader contours of the debate revolve around the following more specific questions:

❏ Are self-defence and Security Council-authorized enforcement under Chapter VII the only legitimate exceptions to the UN Charter's prohibition on the use of force, or is there an independent right of humanitarian intervention based in either natural law or emerging state practice?

❏ Should the Security Council retain the legitimacy to make decisions on intervention, given that its composition, and the veto held by the P-5, is unrepresentative of the distribution of power and population in today's world?

❏ Are there limitations on expanding the meaning of "international peace and security" to include humanitarian crises, or is the Security Council entitled to define the scope of its own mandate?

❏ Is the most pressing challenge to develop barriers to limit the possible abuse of the right to intervene on humanitarian grounds, or is it to ensure that interventions widely believed necessary to stop mass atrocities are actually undertaken?

❏ Is sovereignty best conceived mainly as a barrier to unwarranted external interference and the foundation of a stable world order, or does it also imply a responsibility to both domestic populations and an international constituency?

❑   Are the inconsistency and selectivity of international action to stop mass atrocities evidence of its illegitimacy (as a result of hidden agendas and biases from interests and media coverage), or is it the result of choices that must be made when the capacity does not exist to intervene everywhere it is warranted?

❑   Will developing criteria for humanitarian intervention be more likely to stop illegitimate interventions, or simply provide a further rationale for inaction; and if developed, is it desirable that such criteria remain ad hoc, or should they be formalized through negotiations?

❑   Does military intervention inevitably do more harm than good, or are the consequences generally positive, despite the inevitable failings and shortcomings?

❑   Is the priority during an intervention to provide the greatest protection possible to populations at risk, or is it to minimize casualties among the intervening armies, to ensure that fragile domestic support for interventions is maintained?

❑   Does the long-term legitimacy of an intervention require the early withdrawal of forces to demonstrate a lack of ulterior motives, or does legitimacy in some cases require the establishment of protectorates even where these may facilitate secessionism?

## NOTES

1   Kofi Annan, "Peace Operations and the United Nations: Preparing for the Next Century," unpublished paper, February 1996, pp. 4–5. This is the starting point for Donald C.F. Daniel and Bradd C. Hayes, with Chantal de Jonge Oudraat, *Coercive Inducement and the Containment of International Crises* (Washington, DC: US Institute of Peace, 1999).

2   Robert Jennings and Arthur Watts, eds., *Oppenheim's International Law* (London: Longmans, 1996), pp. 428–434; and Ian Brownlie, *International Law and the Use of Force by States* (Oxford: Clarendon Press, 1963), pp. 44–45. It is worth noting that some analysts include both "solicited" (that is, consensual) and "unsolicited" military force in their definitions of intervention. See, for example, Martin Wright, *Power Politics* (Harmondsworth: Penguin, 1979), chapter 11.

3   For a recent overview, see Stephen D. Krasner, *Sovereignty: Organized Hypocrisy* (Princeton: Princeton University Press, 2000).

4   Augustus Stapleton, *Intervention and Non-Intervention* (London: Murray, 1866); *The Foreign Policy of Great Britain from 1790 to 1865* (London: Murray, 1866); Ellery Stowell, *Intervention in International Law* (Washington, DC: J. Bryne, 1921); and Brownlie, *International Law and the Use of Force by States.*

5   France's intervention was approved subsequently by European countries and Turkey. See Stowell, *Intervention in International Law*, pp. 126, 489.

6   The others were the intervention by Austria, France, Italy, Prussia, and Russia in 1866–1968 to protect the Christian population in Crete; Russian intervention in the Balkans in 1875–1978 in support of insurrectionist Christians; and interference by European powers from 1903 to 1908 in favour of the oppressed Christian Macedonian community. See Danish Institute of International Affairs, *Humanitarian Intervention: Legal and Political Aspects* (Copenhagen: Danish Institute of International Affairs, 1999), p. 79.

7   Brownlie, *International Law and the Use of Force by States*, pp. 338–339.

8   Stowell, *Intervention in International Law*, p. 53.

9   Dino Kritsiotis, "Reappraising Policy Objections to Humanitarian Intervention," *Michigan Journal of International Law* 19 (1998), p. 1005.

10   This legacy continues to colour the intervention debate, for, as Ramesh Thakur points out, developing countries "are neither amused nor mindful at being lectured on universal human values by those who failed to practice the same during European colonialism and now urge them to cooperate in promoting 'global' human rights norms." Ramesh Thakur, "Global Norms and International Humanitarian Law: An Asian Perspective," *International Review of the Red Cross* 83, no. 841 (March 2001), p. 31.

11   Brownlie, *International Law and the Use of Force by States*, p. 340.

12  Hersch Lauterpacht, "The Grotian Tradition in International Law," *British Year Book of International Law* 23 (1946), p. 1.

13  See, for example, Richard Lillich, *Humanitarian Intervention and the United Nations* (Charlottesville: University Press of Virginia, 1973).

14  Kofi Annan, "Opening Remarks," Humanitarian Action: A Symposium," November 20, 2000, *International Peace Academy Conference Report* (New York: International Peace Academy, 2001), p. 11.

15  One searches in vain for a solid definition of "humanitarian" in international law. The International Court of Justice was provided an opportunity in the case of Nicaragua against the United States, but it declined to define the term. It engaged in a tautology of sorts by stating that humanitarian action is what the International Committee of the Red Cross does. The *Oxford English Dictionary* (Oxford: Oxford University Press, 1933) is not of much help, by stating that humanitarian is "having regard to the interests of human-ity or mankind at large; relating to, or advocating, or practising humanity or human action." A second definition notes that the term is "often contemptuous or hostile."

16  International Court of Justice, *Military and Paramilitary Activities in and Against Nicaragua (Nicaragua v United States)*, June 27, 1986, paras. 267–268 and 243.

17  Bruno Simma, *The Charter of the United Nations: A Commentary* (Oxford: Oxford University Press, 1995), p. 7.

18  *Report of the Secretary General on the Work of the Organization, Supplement to An Agenda for Peace: Position Paper of the Secretary General on the Occasion of the Fiftieth Anniversary of the United Nations*, UN Document S/24111 (1992); and *Supplement to An Agenda for Peace*, A/50/60, S/1995/1. See also Stephen J. Stedman, "The New Interventionists," *Foreign Affairs* 72, no. 1 (1993), pp. 1–16; Thomas G. Weiss, "Whither the United Nations," *The Washington Quarterly* 17, no. 1 (1993), pp. 109–128; and *Report of the Advisory Committee on Problems of International Public Law*, Report no. 15, June 18, 1992, The Hague.

19  Thomas G. Weiss, "Military–Civilian Humanitarians: The Age of Innocence is Over," *International Peace Keeping* 2, no. 2 (Summer 1995), pp. 157–174.

20  W. Michael Reisman and Douglas L. Sterick, "The Applicability of International Law Standards to the UN Economic Sanctions Programmes," *European Journal of International Law* 9 (1998), p. 86.

21  In relation to decolonization, the regime of the Charter develops standards for the conduct of colonial states in 1945 by establishing a framework for decolonization, based on the right to self-determination and the rights and duties of the Mandatory powers with regard to the protection of the inhabitants of Trust and Mandated territories. See "Declaration on the Granting of Independence to Colonial Countries and Peoples," General Assembly Resolution 1514 (XV), December 14, 1960.

22  See *Legal Consequences for States of the Continued Presence of South Africa in Namibia (South West Africa) notwithstanding Security Council Resolution 276, ICJ Report* (1970), p. 16.

23  See for example, General Assembly Resolution 204 (XX) of November 11, 1965, and Security Council Resolution 216 (1965) of November 12, 1965. For detail, see *United Nations Action in the Field of Human Rights* (New York: United Nations, 1983), pp. 16–38.

24  Reisman and Sterick, "The Applicability of International Law Standards to the UN Economic Sanctions Programmes," p. 124.

25  Commonwealth Heads of Government Meeting, *The Auckland Communiqué*, November 1995, p. 5.

26  EU Decisions 95/515/CFSP OJL 298/1995; 95/544/CFSP OJL 309/1995; and Toby King, "Human Rights in European Foreign Policy: Success or Failure for Post-modern Diplomacy," *European Journal of International Law* 10, no. 2 (1999), pp. 313–337.

27  Gary C. Hufbauer, Jeffery J. Schott, and Kimberly Ann Elliott, *Economic Sanctions Reconsidered: History and Current Policy*, 2nd ed. (Washington, DC: Institute for International Economics, 1990). Despite appearing as an alternative to the use of force, they are often meant to "punish" a target. See Kim Richard Nossal, "International Sanctions as International Punishment," *International Organization* 43, no. 2 (Spring 1989), pp. 301–323. See also Robert A. Pape, "Why Economic Sanctions Do Not Work," *International Security* 22, no. 2 (Fall 1997), pp. 90–136.

28  For a discussion of these and other circumstances associated with the increased use of sanctions, see David Cortright and George A. Lopez, eds., *Economic Sanctions: Panacea or Peacebuilding in a Post-Cold War World?* (Boulder: Westview Press, 1995); and Margaret P. Doxey, *International Sanctions in Contemporary Perspective*, 2nd ed. (New York: St. Martin's Press, 1996).

29   See, for example, Ramesh Thakur, "Sanctions: A Triumph of Hope Eternal over Experience Unlimited," *Global Dialogue* 2, no. 3 (Summer 2000), pp. 129–141. In fact, the entire issue is devoted to this topic.

30   David Cortright and George A. Lopez, eds., *The Sanctions Decade. Assessing UN Strategies in the 1990s* (Boulder: Lynne Rienner, 2000).

31   See, for example, Paul Conlon, "The UN's Questionable Sanctions Practice," *Aussenpolitik* [German foreign affairs review] 46, no. 4 (1995), pp. 327–338.

32   Boutros Boutros-Ghali, *Supplement to An Agenda for Peace* (New York: United Nations, 1995), paras. 66–76.

33   For the humanitarian issues, see Thomas G. Weiss, David Cortright, George A. Lopez, and Larry Minear, eds., *Political Gain and Civilian Pain: The Humanitarian Impacts of Economic Sanctions* (Lanham: Rowman & Littlefield, 1997); and Larry Minear, David Cortright, Julia Wagler, George A. Lopez, and Thomas G. Weiss, *Towards More Humane and Effective Sanctions Management* (New York: UN Department of Humanitarian Affairs, 1997).

34   The International Law Commission between 1977 and 1986 produced a "Draft Convention on the Jurisdictional Immunities of States and Their Property," which sought to change the then existing rules, including allowing legal actions against officials who committed crimes. However, the draft rules still required a nexus between where the crime was committed and the court in which the action was brought. More generally, moves to negotiate the draft Convention into existence failed.

35   The Pinochet case illustrates the limits on sovereign immunity in regard to crimes committed while in office. However, it does not affect serving heads of state or serving diplomats. It remains an as yet untested possibility that the 1949 Geneva Conventions and Additional Protocols of 1977 on humanitarian law in armed conflict, which are regarded as being *jus cogens*, could provide sufficient authority for an armed intervention to enforce them. Common Article I of the Conventions states that "[t]he High Contracting Parties undertake to respect and to ensure respect for the present Convention in all circumstances." See Geoffrey Robertson, *Crimes against Humanity: The Struggle for Global Justice* (London: Penguin, 1999), p. 398.

36   Henry A. Kissinger, "The Pitfalls of Universal Jurisdiction," *Foreign Affairs* 80, no. 4 (July–August 2001), pp. 86–87.

37   Adam Roberts, "Humanitarian War: Military Intervention and Human Rights," *Journal of International Affairs* 69, no. 4 (1993), pp. 429–449; "The Road to Hell: A Critique of Humanitarian Intervention," *Harvard International Review* 16 (1993), pp. 10–13 and 63–65; Rosalyn Higgins, "The New UN in Former Yugoslavia," *Journal of International Affairs* 69, no. 4 (1993), pp. 465–483; Richard Falk, "The Complexities of Humanitarian Intervention: A New World Order Challenge," *Michigan Journal of International Law* 17, no. 491 (1996), pp. 491–513; Christopher Greenwood, "Is There a Right of Humanitarian Intervention?" *The World Today* 49 (1993), p. 40; Thomas G. Weiss, "Intervention: Whither the United Nations," *The Washington Quarterly* 17, no. 1 (1993), pp. 109–128; and Thomas G. Weiss, "Triage: Humanitarian Interventions in a New Era," *World Policy Journal* 11 (1994), pp. 59–68.

38   Shashi Tharoor and Sam Daws, "Humanitarian Intervention: Getting Past the Reefs," *World Policy Journal* XVIII, no. 2 (Summer 2001), p. 21.

39   Christopher Greenwood, "Is There a Right of Humanitarian Intervention?," *The World Today* 49 (1993), p. 40.

# 3. PREVENTION

The appeal of conflict prevention – as a policy, strategy, and paradigm – is enhanced by the widespread consensus that intervention is problematic and costly. Successful preventive measures could spare at-risk populations from the scourge of war, displacement, and death; save the international system the cost, risk, and political controversy of peace operations and direct humanitarian intervention; and shield the community of states from the "spill-over" and "spill-in" effects of intrastate wars, including refugee flows, arms trafficking, transnational criminality, and the spread of disease. Preventive strategies are appealing both from the point of view of a liberal humanitarian ethos and that of a *Realpolitik*, national-security logic. Hence, it is treated as central to the sovereignty versus intervention debate and not as an afterthought. The focus here is on forestalling the human costs from violence and war, or, in the words of the Carnegie Commission, to "prevent extremely deadly conflicts."

Not surprisingly, conflict prevention as a general principle has been repeatedly endorsed in international fora, national-security documents, and academic analyses. "There is near-universal agreement that prevention is preferable to cure," notes the United Nations (UN) Secretary-General Kofi Annan, "and that strategies of prevention must address the root causes of conflicts, not simply their violent symptoms."[1]

Yet, in practice, conflict prevention has remained underdeveloped, undervalued, ephemeral, and largely elusive. A wealth of theoretical and applied research has been generated since the 1950s, and a promising array of international, regional, and nongovernmental mechanisms for conflict prevention, focused particularly on intrastate conflict, were established or expanded in the 1990s.[2] But many seemingly avoidable intrastate conflicts have inspired only token international efforts at prevention. Moreover, when sustained measures have been undertaken, results have been mixed. There are only a few unambiguous examples of successful preventive diplomacy in the post-Cold War era, while the catalogue of failed preventive action and missed opportunities is lengthy.

Part of the problem has been the gap between rhetorical support and tangible commitments. As the 2000 *Report of the Panel on United Nations Peace Operations* points out, when it comes to improving UN preventive diplomatic and military capacity, there remains a "gap between verbal postures and financial and political support for prevention."[3]

A fundamental resource constraint is the declining levels of foreign assistance for economic development. Virtually all observers of war and conflict concur that underdevelopment, poverty, and resource scarcity are among the root causes of conflict.

For some observers, calls coming mainly from the affluent West for more robust rules of intervention ring somewhat hollow when set against the weakening commitment to economic development in poor countries. As to priorities, the main concern in policy making and scholarly debates in the West has overwhelmingly appeared to be reaction to humanitarian catastrophes, especially by military intervention, rather than on efforts to ensure that such disasters did not occur in the first place. At the same time, the lack of certainty among developmentalists about what works and what does not gives pause as to the precise link between enhanced economic and social development and a reduction in violent conflict.

Prevention is sometimes invoked as a solution to the sovereignty versus intervention dilemma. According to this logic, if proactive measures could be taken to defuse tensions before they reach the point of armed violence, then the most nettlesome questions relating to the debate about international intervention versus state sovereignty could be finessed. Many measures in the "toolbox" depicted in Table 3.1 are, in actuality, relatively nonintrusive. The "structural" preventive measures to address the root causes of poverty and many armed conflicts, for instance, work best with the full consent and participation of host governments. Targeted development assistance, promotion of private investment, training and capacity building programmes for governments and civil society are relatively uncontroversial.

The same could be said for such direct prevention efforts as offers of mediation or good offices. But other direct tools commonly cited in the literature are far more intrusive: sanctions, war crimes tribunals, human rights monitoring, arms embargoes, aid conditionality, preventive deployment of peacekeeping forces, and threat of force. These arrows in the quiver of conflict prevention unquestionably move into the debate over intervention and state sovereignty. It is one of the reasons why many countries have become leery about the "continuum" of prevention.

## TABLE 3.1
## STRUCTURAL AND DIRECT PREVENTION OPTIONS

|  | Consensual | Nonconsensual |
|---|---|---|
| Structural "Root Cause" Prevention | Poverty alleviation<br>Economic growth and investment<br>Democratic development<br>Training and capacity building<br>Security sector reform | |
| Direct Prevention | Good offices and special envoys<br>Economic incentives<br>Mediation and arbitration<br>Preventive deployment | Diplomatic sanctions<br>Economic sanction<br>War crimes tribunals<br>Arms embargoes<br>Threat of military force |

There are numerous criticisms of conflict prevention – that some violent conflicts are simply inevitable, that some actions can produce "compromises that kill,"[4] that the entire concept has been "oversold,"[5] or that in some instances it stands in the way of "just wars," wherein armed resistance against oppression is justified. But even if one subscribes to these arguments, it still stands to reason that improving conflict prevention at every level – conceptually, operationally, and strategically – is urgent and essential. The following pages assess the "state of the art" of conflict prevention in theory and practice, with special attention to its place in the debate over intervention and state sovereignty.

## RECENT DEVELOPMENTS

Conflict prevention is by no means new to international diplomacy; the Concert of Europe, the League of Nations, and the UN were all established with the explicit intent to construct collective measures for the prevention and removal of threats to peace. Indeed, Chapter VI of the UN Charter contains a catalogue of many consensual direct prevention devices that are linked to "the pacific settlement of disputes." But prevention has garnered greater attention in the post-Cold War era. Reasons for the ascendance of conflict prevention to the "front burner" of international diplomacy include the improved capacity for cooperative action in the UN Security Council after the end of the Cold War; alarm at the number of dangerous intrastate wars and collapsed states; sobering international experiences with belated intervention into complex political emergencies; revolutionary advances in information technology, which have made it more difficult for leaders to ignore violent crises in distant lands; and growing, organized public pressure on states and international organizations to intervene to prevent or halt genocide, war crimes, and deadly conflicts.

The shift in emphasis toward prevention prominently manifested itself in 1992, when Secretary-General Boutros Boutros-Ghali released *An Agenda for Peace* in response to the Security Council's request for recommendations to improve the UN's capacity for preventive diplomacy, peacekeeping, peace enforcement, and peace building. This document identified preventive diplomacy as "the most desirable and efficient" option for managing conflicts and identified several essential capacities on the part of the international community – confidence-building measures, early-warning and fact-finding capabilities, and rapid preventive deployment capacity.[6] Frustration and setbacks with UN peace operations in the years following the release of *An Agenda for Peace* reinforced the original emphasis on conflict prevention. The declining enthusiasm for UN peace operations in the *Supplement* published only three years later by the UN made prevention seem even more attractive.[7]

In recent years, the UN has continually underscored the importance of conflict prevention.[8] This increased emphasis has not, however, been matched by an equal commitment by member states to build UN preventive capacities. Between 1992 and 1993, initial measures were undertaken toward internal restructuring to improve its preventive capacities, but UN resources dedicated to preventive diplomacy remain dwarfed by the resources dedicated to efforts after wars and especially to peacekeeping. In 1996, Norway established a Fund for Preventive Action for use by the Secretary-General to support the work of special envoys and special representatives in emerging conflicts. More recently, the UN Executive Committee on Peace and Security created an Inter-agency/Interdepartmental Framework for Coordination in an effort to improve the UN system's ability to predict and prevent conflict, but that effort has "not accumulated knowledge in a structured way and does no strategic planning."[9]

The UN may not always be the most appropriate instrument. While the world organization remains the centerpiece for discussions of improved international capacity for conflict prevention, prospects for strengthening the role of regional organizations are also being explored. The Organization of African Unity, for instance, established in 1993 a Mechanism for Conflict Prevention, Management, and Settlement, with support from external donors. The Economic Community of West African States established a Mechanism for Conflict Prevention, Management, Resolution, Peace and Security in 2000. The Organization for Security and Co-operation in Europe (OSCE) has developed a number of innovative internal mechanisms and practices designed to prevent conflict in Europe.

Two of the most powerful political actors in the post-Cold War period, the European Union (EU) and the United States (US), have also embraced conflict prevention as a priority. In Washington, the first Bush administration affirmed that "the most desirable and efficient security strategy is to address the root causes of instability and to ease tensions before they result in conflict," a view that informed the subsequent decision to insert US troops as part of a preventive UN military presence in Macedonia. The Clinton administration placed crisis prevention at the centre of its national-security strategy. The 1994 *National Security Strategy of Engagement and Enlargement* emphasized preventive diplomacy via support for democracy, development aid, overseas military presence, and diplomatic mediation "in order to help resolve problems, reduce tensions, and defuse conflicts before they become crises."[10] This position informed the decision to assist the African Crisis Response Initiative and the Greater Horn of Africa Initiative and led to the establishment of the Secretary of State's Preventive Action Initiative.

Meanwhile, conflict prevention has come to enjoy a central place in discussions about the future of European foreign policy. Indeed, nowhere else is conflict prevention explored with such seriousness of purpose (with the exceptions of Canada and Australia), and nowhere else has it been institutionalized as deeply. The OSCE was founded to foster conflict prevention on the continent. Several European states have trained and earmarked rapid-response peacekeeping forces, and a number have played leading mediating roles in preventive diplomacy. And the EU itself is under great pressure to restructure to better execute preventive diplomacy.[11] In 2001, Sweden used its EU presidency to promote this capacity. Innumerable workshops and conferences, many sponsored by nongovernmental organizations (NGOs), are helping to drive this agenda and explore the technical reforms needed in the European Commission to harness its funds and power toward conflict prevention.[12] Many European states are major proponents in their own right.

Particularly impressive has been the post-Cold War explosion in the growth, activities, and capacity of international NGOs devoted to various aspects of conflict prevention. Illustrative examples include lobbying, coordinating, and advocacy; public education on conflict prevention; sponsorship of conflict prevention research; analysis of conflict prevention concepts, techniques, tools, and trends; direct engagement in early warning of conflict; local capacity building in conflict prevention; dissemination of information among NGOs; training of development NGO staff in peace building; and direct mediation or provision of good offices in incipient crises. These types of organizations exist in the South (for example, Inter-Africa Group and Nairobi Peace Initiative), as well as in the North (for example, the Carter Center and Communita St. Egidio).

In addition, a growing number of development NGOs, such as Oxfam, are reshaping their aid programmes in order to more explicitly address peace building and conflict prevention as integral themes of relief and development assistance.[13] This greater sensitivity on the part of some relief and development agencies to conflict prevention is welcome and much-needed. In the recent past, relief agencies tended to adopt a narrower, apolitical view of humanitarian action. Widespread indifference to, and ignorance of, the role that aid resources play in local conflicts has led to cases of relief and development resources actually fueling, rather than defusing, armed conflict.[14] In the context of war and scarcity, aid becomes a precious resource. The nature and extent of its distribution is, therefore, loaded with political ramifications. The fact that NGOs are now acknowledging the "do no harm" principle in their emergency efforts is a step toward harnessing their considerable resources as a force for prevention.

Collectively, international NGOs are becoming better organized and funded. They have been emboldened by such recent successes as the anti-land mine campaign and the Jubilee 2000 movement to forgive Third World debt. The "soft power" of NGOs in this and other fields is often exaggerated, but it is clear that they are becoming a driving force in the campaign to improve global capacities to prevent deadly conflicts.

Complementing this expansion of governmental and nongovernmental programmes and projects devoted to conflict prevention is the explosion of academic and policy research on the topic since the end of the Cold War. The quality of this body of research is variable. On the one hand, it has helped to provide a more sophisticated set of conceptual tools. On the other hand, this mushrooming research has also created considerable confusion over terminology.

## SCOPE OF CONFLICT PREVENTION

One of the first obstacles to strengthening preventive strategies is reaching consensus on the scope and definition of the concept. Some definitions are so expansive as to include virtually all development work and post-conflict peace building; others insist on a very narrow definition. The result is conceptual confusion and muddled strategies. Coming to some consensus about how conflict prevention is defined is an unavoidable point of departure, as the definition establishes the parameters of strategies.

Though there is no universal agreement on the precise causes of deadly conflict, observers do agree that it is useful to differentiate between precipitating versus underlying causes of armed conflict. There is a growing and widespread recognition that armed conflicts cannot be understood without reference to such "root" causes as poverty, political repression, and uneven distribution of resources. Ignoring these underlying factors, critics charge, amounts to addressing the symptoms, rather the causes, of deadly conflict, an accusation that has been frequently leveled at UN peacekeeping and peace enforcement operations.[15]

Diplomats, activists, and analysts who take seriously the view that deadly conflicts have structural causes are thus drawn toward preventive strategies that address underlying causes of conflict. "Every step taken towards reducing poverty and achieving broad-based economic growth," argues Kofi Annan, "is a step toward conflict prevention."[16] Preventive strategies must therefore work "to promote human rights, to protect minority rights and to institute political arrangements in which all groups are represented." Advocates applaud the trend of viewing humanitarian and development work through a "conflict prevention lens" as an example of a more integrated, holistic approach to development and peace building.[17] Critics, however, suspect that development agencies are merely pouring old wine into new bottles in order to attract donor funding. They also point out that decades of development assistance and investment have still not shed much light on what kinds of efforts truly lessen the propensity to lethal violence. War is clearly an enemy of development, but the links between development and prevention are still only partially understood.

There is an obvious logic to the argument that root causes should be addressed if deadly conflict is to be prevented and that preventive diplomacy that waits until conflict is imminent stands a much lower chance of success. Yet, it is not universally accepted that broadening the definition of conflict prevention to include development and governance issues is appropriate. An overly elastic definition equates prevention with correction of all social inequities.

Critics argue that this holistic approach effectively amounts to defining prevention out of existence. Taking such a broad approach may divert attention away from the behavioural origins of violent conflict that are ultimately political. Too heavy an emphasis on structural causes of conflict is also empirically inaccurate – social inequities and resource scarcity do not in fact always lead to deadly conflict, and they can in some instances produce healthy nonviolent conflict that catalyzes positive social change. Protests in democratic societies are an obvious example, but even armed struggle for self-determination against a repressive regime may remain within acceptable bounds of violence.

Definitions of conflict prevention can also include post-conflict activities, including assistance and diplomatic efforts. From this perspective, armed conflicts themselves typically feature "windows of opportunity" for effective responses to prevent the conflict from cascading to a new, more destructive, and more intractable level. Conflict prevention would then include efforts to forestall armed hostilities from getting worse, as well as preventing armed violence in the first place. Boutros-Ghali advocated this vision in *An Agenda for Peace* by defining it as "action to prevent disputes from arising between parties, to prevent existing disputes from escalating into conflicts and to limit the spread of the latter when they occur."[18] This view was confirmed by the UN Security Council, which "recognizes that early warning, preventive diplomacy, preventive deployment, preventive disarmament, and post-conflict peace-building are interdependent and complementary components of a comprehensive conflict prevention strategy."[19]

The Carnegie Commission on Preventing Deadly Conflict distinguishes between "structural prevention," which encompasses "strategies to address the root causes of deadly conflict," and "operational prevention," described as "early engagement to help create conditions in which responsible authorities can resolve tensions before they lead to violence."[20] Likewise, the findings of the Krusenberg Seminar on Preventing Violent Conflict distinguish between "upstream" and "downstream" conflict prevention efforts. In this continuum, or "ladder," of measures, upstream prevention refers to "long-term structural measures," while downstream initiatives are "short-term, crisis management actions."[21]

There appears to be a growing consensus on a broad but not unlimited understanding of strategies – what the G-8 Miyazaki Initiative for Conflict Prevention terms "chronological comprehensiveness."[22] Such an approach would include both structural prevention and post-conflict peace building. But care should be taken to distinguish among different types of prevention along a temporal scale:

❑ "structural prevention" (ongoing efforts that target issues of economic development, human rights, arms trafficking, and governance and that help build international regimes or a "culture of prevention");

❑ "early prevention" (initiatives generated as soon as early warnings indicate a serious dispute in the context of uneasy stability);

❑ "late prevention" (crisis diplomacy when serious armed conflicts appear imminent or have begun); and

❑ "post-conflict peace building" (initiatives designed to prevent a recurrence of armed conflict).

To be effective and comprehensive, a strategy must integrate these different types of prevention and differentiate between the measures appropriate for each stage of a conflict. Of these types, early prevention is likely to be the most useful, yet it is also least developed or employed. Six prerequisites for effective prevention are outlined in the following sections:

conflict analysis, early warning, operational capacity, strategy, institutional capacity, and political will. Each of them constitutes a link in the "chain" of prevention, which is only as strong as the weakest of the links.

## CONFLICT ANALYSIS

By definition, preventive action is founded on, and proceeds from, accurate prediction of conflict. To be effective, it is also necessary to address effectively the root causes of an emerging or imminent lethal conflict. If either of these levels of analysis is flawed, then preventive measures will either miss key warning signs (and hence miss opportunities for early action) or will correctly foresee violent conflicts but misread their nature (and hence apply the wrong tools).

One need not be directly involved in the art of political analysis in any of the world's troubled war zones to appreciate that human predictive capacities are modest. Many of the most dramatic political events over the past decade – from the fall of the Berlin Wall, to the Iraqi invasion of Kuwait, to the Ethiopian–Eritrean War (to mention but a few) – were not foreseen by intelligence agencies, international institutions, scholars, or policy analysts.

A number of distinct problems weaken analytic capacities to predict violent conflict. First is the multiplicity of variables associated with structural causes of conflict and the complexities of their interactions. The Carnegie Commission's final report provides a typical list:

> Many factors and conditions make societies prone to warfare: weak, corrupt, or collapsed states; illegitimate or repressive regimes; acute discrimination against ethnic or other social groups; poorly managed religious, cultural, or ethnic differences; politically active religious communities that promote hostile and divisive messages; political and economic legacies of colonialism or the Cold War; sudden economic or political shifts; widespread illiteracy, disease, and disability; lack of resources such as water and arable land; large stores of weapons and ammunition; and threatening regional relationships.[23]

These factors were certainly in play in countries such as Somalia and Liberia, but they are also present in any number of other countries where armed conflict does not appear on the horizon. Predictive models predicated on systemic variables thus tend to see trouble everywhere.[24]

Second, there is the perennial problem of securing accurate information on which to base analysis and action. Even in relatively peaceful and open settings, key indicators of "systemic causes" of conflict, such as declining gross national product per capita or unemployment, are often inaccurate or crude. Moreover, access to reliable information worsens in direct relationship to the deterioration of local politics; rising insecurity and polarized politics hamper independent information-gathering and politicize the views of local informants. This is an especially sensitive problem in "imminent conflicts," where the type of "estimative intelligence" needed tends to shift from early-warning modeling to field analysis by country experts in governments, the UN, NGOs, or academia. Close, field-based assessments, which can at their best anticipate "triggering," or precipitating, causes of conflict, are most difficult to achieve precisely when they are most needed. The existing body of literature thus catalogues underlying factors and permissive conditions, "but it is weak when it comes to identifying the catalytic factors – the triggers or proximate causes – of internal conflicts."[25]

Third, the predictive value of our models of "systemic causes of conflict" progressively diminishes as conflicts move from emerging to imminent. At that point, precipitating causes become paramount, and precipitating causes are much more likely to be driven by capricious decisions and unforeseeable, random events that defy prediction. Moreover, as crises mount, decision makers invariably encounter fiercely competing interpretations of events, both from local actors and from external analysts. The considerable energies being devoted to improving the capacity to predict violent conflict will no doubt yield some fruit. But it is important not to overstate the ability to predict.

That said, genuine advances have been made in understanding some dimensions of contemporary conflict, and analysts are therefore in a better position to diagnose conflicts accurately. Understanding the nature of ethnic conflict and the manner in which ethnic identity can be mobilized by power-seeking elites, for instance, is much more sophisticated and has at least in academic circles laid to rest "primordialist" interpretations of ethnopolitics.[26] The Carnegie Commission summarizes:

> To label a conflict simply as an ethnic war can lead to misguided policy choices by fostering a wrong impression that ethnic, cultural, or religious differences inevitably result in violent conflict and that differences therefore must be suppressed … as violence almost invariably results from the deliberately violent response of determined leaders and their groups to a wide range of social, economic, and political conditions that provide the environment for violent conflict, but usually do not independently spawn violence.[27]

Similar advances have been made in our comprehension of resource-driven conflict, the politics of warlordism, the role of "conflict constituencies" and spoilers, and the role of foreign aid and globalization in internal conflict.[28] This more sophisticated understanding of the economic motives and forces behind many intrastate conflicts in turn helps to improve and expand strategies of prevention. They include expanding preventive policies into the realm of global trade. Commerce is coming under the growing scrutiny of broader efforts to prevent and manage conflict. For instance, prevention-based analysis considers how global trade in oil, timber, or conflict diamonds fuels local conflicts.[29]

This increased capacity to diagnose emerging conflicts, however, seemingly has not yet widely penetrated policy making circles. Decision makers often fall back on more stereo-typical (and fatalistic) explanations for "intractable" conflicts. NGO officials – particularly those working on development – also are not immune from embracing crude and inaccurate theories about disputes and identity politics. The gap between scholarly and popular understanding of intrastate conflict (especially conflicts with ethnic dimensions) should be closed. Strengthening this particular link in the chain of prevention is partly a matter of education and dissemination.

Another important way in which diagnoses of conflicts can be improved is through greater involvement of regional actors and neighbouring states with intimate local knowledge. Although emerging conflicts tend to share a number of characteristics, each is also unique in some ways. Regional actors are usually better placed to understand local dynamics, although they also have shortcomings, not least of which is that they are often not disinterested in the outcomes of deadly conflicts.

# EARLY WARNING

The capacity to predict and diagnose emerging conflicts should be housed in some type of early-warning system. Good analysis is ultimately wasted if it does not get into the hands of decision makers. And in recent years, considerable emphasis has been placed on the need for a conflict early warning system that can better guarantee that political actors will hear the alarms.

The idea of a global early-warning system for conflict is not at all new. Decades ago, Kenneth Boulding called for a global network of "social data stations" to monitor and warn about emerging conflict conditions.[30] The idea gained strength for humanitarian issues in the 1970s in response to the spread and recurrence of famines and overwhelming refugee flows.[31] International agencies and donors trying to cope with these humanitarian emergencies sought to build early-warning systems in order to more effectively respond to crises and when possible act to avert them. The ensuing success of early-warning systems for food security led to the call in the 1990s to establish comparable early-warning systems for conflict prevention.[32]

Monitoring for conflict prevention is not, in fact, as doable as monitoring food security – crop yields, rainfall, and market prices for foodstuffs are much more amenable to precise measurement, both on the ground and from satellites. But the parallel was compelling enough to stimulate discussions of developing early-warning systems for conflict prevention and response.

To date, early warning of deadly conflict has been essentially ad hoc and unstructured. A wide range of players have been involved, including embassies and intelligence agencies, UN peacekeeping forces, relief and development NGOs, human rights groups, the International Committee of the Red Cross (ICRC), faith groups, academics, and the media. Quality is variable, and coordination among groups has been rudimentary or nonexistent. Moreover, UN specialized agencies and development NGOs have the advantage of a grass-roots presence in countries, but they lack both the expertise and human resources to be consistently accurate and engaged.

UN headquarters is often identified as the logical place to centralize early warning. Efforts have been made for more than two decades to improve the world organization's information-gathering and analytical capacities. However, the difficulties involved in the UN's establishment of the Office for Research and the Collection of Information in the 1980s should be kept in mind. Although billed as a clearinghouse for conflict early warning, it was unceremoniously dismantled in 1992.

One of the particular strengths of the Secretary-General is his special mandate under Article 99 of the UN Charter to "bring to the attention of the Security Council any matter that in his opinion may threaten the maintenance of international peace and security." The secretariat possesses, in other words, a formidable capacity as a "bully pulpit" to alert the world of impending conflicts, either loudly or discreetly. But efforts to improve the organization's early-warning capacity have so far fallen short. In addition, the value of the oft-discussed Article 99 may be overstated. Security Council inaction seldom takes such a form that the Secretary-General's forcing debate would result in effective action. Furthermore, one should not overestimate the intelligence-gathering and analytical capacities of major powers, particularly in parts of the world where they no longer perceive strategic interests.

The most organized and comprehensive early-warning capacities are currently housed within intelligence bodies of individual governments. The most powerful states – those with the resources and interests to follow events closely around the world – usually (but not always) possess somewhat better access to key political indicators and intelligence than the UN, NGOs, and other nonstate actors. Efforts to build a better early-warning system by harnessing this preexisting governmental capacity is an idea worth pursuing, but realism is in order about the extent to which states are willing to divulge information that may compromise their own intelligence network. Though one should not overestimate the intelligence capacity of the major powers, even in parts of the world where they no longer perceive major strategic interests.

Dissatisfaction with this situation has prompted the rise of a new type of NGO, one dedicated exclusively to conflict early warning. Organizations such as International Crisis Group and International Alert monitor and report on areas of the world where conflict appears to be emerging, and they are aggressive in alerting governments and the media if they believe preventive action is urgently required. Their work is complemented by the monitoring and reporting capacity of international and national human rights organizations such as Amnesty International and Human Rights Watch. These organizations, which previously devoted most of their energies to reporting on human rights violations against individuals and groups, have made a conscious effort to expand their work to include early warning about conflicts that could result in massive violations of human rights or even genocide. The impressive growth of such human rights centres in the post-Cold War period gives this set of actors an increasingly powerful network for sharing information and lobbying. Still, it is taking time for these organizations to learn how better to coordinate among themselves, mobilize constituents globally, work with the media, and move governments.

All this falls well short of a system of early warning. Some, including Kofi Annan, have concluded that "loose, creative … global policy networks" are adequate foundations on which to build effective international cooperation, and he praises them for being "non-hierarchical." But even this relatively optimistic assessment of these networks is tempered. "Our involvement with global policy networks," he concludes, "has been extensive but largely unplanned. We need a more focused and systematic approach."[33]

In sum, a "network" of early warning is not a "system." Networks are patchy and less than comprehensive in coverage, informal in their information-sharing, and variable in the quality of their participants, and typically they have no central clearinghouse. These are potentially fatal shortcomings. The *Report of the Panel on United Nations Peace Operations* is one of many that reiterates the call for that clearinghouse role to be played by the UN, noting "the need to have more effective collection and assessment at UN headquarters, including an enhanced conflict early-warning system that can detect and recognize the threat or risk of conflict or genocide."[34] This report also makes very detailed proposals for building an early-warning capacity within the UN Secretariat.

A further suggestion is to meld the UN Secretary-General's agenda-setting power with the growing information-gathering and assessment capacity of NGOs. The development of stronger and more routinized coordination of the network of NGOs, UN agencies, and the Secretariat would go some way toward redressing the weakness of the UN's intelligence-gathering and the NGO's difficulty in "making noise" effectively.

Even an improved early-warning system will face a range of bureaucratic and political obstacles. One is the commonly cited problem of "information overload." Policy makers are confronted with so many reports and information that it is difficult for warnings to make themselves adequately "loud" and difficult for decision makers to discern high-quality warnings from flawed analyses. That is, early warning has three components: having the information, transmitting it to policy makers, and making sure that the latter act. The third component is clearly the most formidable. The very crisis-driven nature of decision making in the UN and in government ministries also works against considered attention to warnings about crises that have yet to occur. Reward systems in governmental and international agencies are not designed to recognize "nonevents," such as a prevented conflict; indeed, officials drawn into preventive actions often believe they are "being set up for failure."[35]

In addition, early warning often forces policy makers to make hard choices. Yet, these same people are inclined to delay making choices for as long as possible because of the short-term nature of political rewards. In such a case, additional information or warning may not prompt additional action. Were an effective early-warning system in place inside the UN Secretariat, political sensitivities about emerging conflicts in members states would create precisely these kinds of "unpalatable decisions." And as the UN's own hard-hitting report on the Rwanda debacle demonstrates, this could result in the Secretariat's downplaying reports and ignoring warnings.[36]

Despite all these obstacles, however, the present ad hoc system of early warning has still managed to provide adequate signals of impending trouble to anyone inclined to watch closely. For example, governments, members of the UN system, and numerous NGOs rang alarm bells in late 1993 and early 1994 about the impending bloodbath in Rwanda. While existing capacities can and should be strengthened, early warning is far from the weakest link in the chain. Information about deadly conflicts is a necessary but far from sufficient condition for effective prevention.

## OPERATIONAL CAPACITY

No other aspect of the debate has received as much useful attention as the toolbox of preventive methods. Dozens of studies and reports, informed by decades of diplomatic experience and empirical observation, have generated lengthy lists of tools appropriate for various types of situations, produced careful assessments of the strengths and weaknesses of these tools, and explored the experience of using specific tools in detail.[37] The attention is due to their obvious importance in the execution of preventive diplomacy.

There is no shortage of tools, and various reports list dozens to hundreds. Furthermore, much has been learned about their effective use. Analysts stress that these measures have both strengths and drawbacks, which are in turn affected by the degree to which tools are properly matched to the type and stage of emerging conflicts. When preventive tools are used half-heartedly, they can actually precipitate rather than forestall conflict, by emboldening the warring factions.

The most successful use of these instruments is as part of a multilateral initiative and when preventive measures are taken early – before parties to an emerging conflict mobilize political followings or armed forces. Success is also improved when several different tools are employed to address different dimensions of a conflict and when they are chosen to match different levels in the chronology of a conflict, an approach known as a "ladder of prevention."

One problem is that the successful use of preventive tools requires almost surgical precision in application and timing, yet many of the decision making bodies that approve or mandate action wield them as blunt instruments. The poor contemporary track record of economic sanctions imposed by the US, for instance, is due in part to the fact that Congress mandates them, giving diplomacy very little flexibility. The EU and the Security Council face comparable problems on this score in that resolutions are passed for many reasons, but rarely with the impact on diplomacy in the forefront of concerns. Committee decision-making processes are simply incompatible with skillful and refined diplomatic use of preventive measures.

Although a comprehensive review cannot be included here, several of the more prominent preventive measures – whether especially effective, innovative, or controversial – are highlighted below, under the categories of structural and direct tools.

### Structural or "Root Cause" Prevention Tools

Ample evidence suggests that bad governance – lack of the rule of law, flawed justice systems, corruption, human rights abuses, and poor accountability, transparency, minority rights, and democracy – are important contributing factors to violent conflicts. Consequently, major emphasis over the last decade has been placed on "good governance" as a central goal of development assistance and public investments.[38] Development aid has shifted toward technical assistance for judicial and police reform, municipalities, political decentralization, civil society, and a range of other programmes that fall under the umbrella of good governance. It has gained top billing as a development goal, in part because it is seen as a pillar of conflict prevention. Good governance has become an institutionalized objective in both development assistance and investment programmes and, in that sense, is now less of a tool than an ongoing programme that may bear fruit in the years to come. A related trend has been the growing consensus within development NGOs that relief and development aid cannot be divorced from the political context and that an integral goal of all aid must be to avoid fueling conflict and to enhance local peace building.

Repeated calls have been made in recent years to bring the lending practices of the World Bank and the International Monetary Fund (IMF) more directly in line with conflict prevention goals.[39] These same institutions also play a central role in post-conflict peace building and reconstruction. Their reputations for heavy-handed pressures on recipient countries have led to less than enthusiastic endorsement by some observers of using their conditionality as part of a meaningful preventive strategy. And critics charge that the policies of the Bretton Woods institutions have actually fueled deadly conflicts. Instead, given the resources of these two institutions, their engagement in coordinated conflict prevention efforts would considerably expand the range of inducements offered to cooperative parties.[40]

Studies of preventive measures consistently stress the need to strengthen indigenous capacities. This ethos of "local solutions to local problems" emphasizes the primary responsibility of both governments and local communities to manage their own conflicts and their enormous advantages in understanding and operating in their own political milieu. International NGOs have been on the front line of efforts to build local capacity.

### Direct Prevention Tools

There are a number of methods of direct conflict prevention available to actors who are concerned with conflict before it reaches catastrophic proportions. These include the use of special envoys, "naming and shaming," international criminal prosecution, NGO involvement, the use of the media, and, finally, the deployment of UN or other forces.

The use of special envoys and special representatives by the UN Secretary-General in potential conflict zones is an important part of consensual prevention. Envoys can – by merit of their reputations and role as honest brokers – achieve breakthroughs and catalyze domestic and international support for peace at low cost and in a discrete manner. They do not, however, wield much direct influence in terms of "carrots and sticks" and can succeed only as part of a package of other preventive measures. Many observers applaud the increased use of this type of diplomacy, which can also include "friends'" groups, eminent-persons commissions, and fact-finding missions.[41] The capacity to appoint and send special envoys has been enhanced by Norway's establishment of the Fund for Preventive Action in 1996.

The time-honoured technique of "naming and shaming" is one of the more effective and important tools of conflict prevention. As human rights reporting has become an established, routinized practice, it has become a source of information to be skillfully used to embarrass and pressure governments or political movements to cease violations that endanger the peace. International support for local human rights organizations helps to build up this capacity, which could well be expanded.

International criminal prosecution is in the first instance a form of intervention, but its existence may also have a deterrent effect. One of the most powerful ideas in conflict prevention is the notion that many deadly conflicts are facilitated by a "culture of impunity." If government figures, opposition leaders, merchants, and warlords perceive that they can literally get away with murder, then they are more likely to resort to deadly conflict in pursuit of their political or economic goals. To establish limits to impunity, the UN Secretary-General contends that it is crucial to "reassert the centrality of international humanitarian and human rights law. We must strive to end the culture of impunity – which is why the creation of the International Criminal Court is so important."[42] War crimes tribunals may have an impact far beyond the immediate armed crisis for which they are established. The more that potential perpetrators of crimes against humanity must consider the possibility that they will be held accountable for their actions in a future court of law, so the argument goes, the less likely they will be to commit atrocities against civilians. As discussed earlier, it can also have the opposite effect, by eliminating potentially face-saving ways of withdrawing from a deadly conflict.

NGOs also grew in importance throughout the 1990s, as they injected themselves into conflict prevention, not only as pressure groups and as part of early-warning systems, but also as direct mediators in conflict prevention and management. Track II diplomacy has been studied and explored as an option for building peace.[43] At the civil society and grass-roots levels, they have demonstrated some successes in "citizen-based diplomacy," which has produced considerable interest and enthusiasm for a direct mediating role for NGOs.[44] There is an important distinction, however, between NGOs' working at a civil society level and their playing direct diplomatic roles. NGOs have not, in fact, distinguished themselves in the formal conduct of preventive diplomacy, and it is not clear that they possess the ability and experience for this role. Indeed, there are serious concerns about NGOs, including their lack of experience and accountability.[45] Given the consequences of failure, the current rush by enthusiastic NGOs to assist in conflict prevention may be counterproductive. More recently, interest has been expressed in drawing the for-profit sector into conflict prevention, especially in an early-warning role, on grounds that businesses have strong interests in preventing conflict in their zones of activity.[46]

In the aftermath of the Rwandan genocide, the world is more aware of the potential for local media to incite deadly conflict.[47] Greater use of jamming techniques is under discussion where "hate media" is being used to incite violence. Conversely, mass media also have the capacity to promote communal understanding and peace building. A variety of international engagements with local media – ranging from journalist training, to media monitoring, to the establishment of, or support to, "peace radio" projects – have been attempted with some promise.

Mounting pressure is being placed on governments from NGOs, human rights groups, and peace activists to consider direct coercive measures to monitor, restrict, and in some instances embargo the flow of small arms to zones of emerging or imminent conflict. A coalition of NGOs organized by Saferworld and International Alert, for instance, lobbied the Swedish and Belgian governments to use their turns on the rotating presidencies of the EU in 2001 to pass an EU code of conduct on arms transfers and to push for a comparable measure in the UN.[48] The UN Millennium Report highlighted the need to curtail illicit small-arms trafficking.[49] Because of the success of the International Campaign to Ban Landmines in the 1990s and because most deaths in armed conflicts are caused by small arms, the campaign to place tighter controls on small-arms trafficking may have an impact in the coming decade.[50] Although it cannot stop armed conflict from breaking out, effective embargoes on small-arms trading can serve as a powerful signal to local belligerents.[51]

Where armed conflict or genocide appears imminent and belligerents are unwilling to explore peaceful alternatives to their disputes, preventive deployment of UN forces is an option. The UN Preventive Deployment Force in Macedonia is the clearest example to date, and it garnered credibility for this preventive device.[52] The experience seems to have been strengthened by the precarious situation that developed in Macedonia in 2001, after the UN's departure. While consensual, this preventive measure can also be coercive if the Security Council decides to send buffer or observer forces without the agreement of one or more local authorities. Calls to institutionalize a UN capacity to deploy a "thin blue line" via the establishment of a rapid-reaction force have also been repeated in numerous studies.[53]

## STRATEGY

Tools of prevention, however well developed, are of only limited use without a coherent strategy. The recent flood of studies and commissioned reports on preventive action has helped improve this situation somewhat. Yet, there is a great distance to travel before a strong strategic capacity exists. What emerges from these studies is best described as contributions to a strategic framework. One of the most important observations is that there can be no "one size fits all" strategy – each situation requires tailoring.

For observers concerned with the weak link between early warning and actual responses, a critical aspect of a preventive strategy is ensuring that the decibel levels for early warnings are not only loud enough to be heard but also trigger effective action. For NGOs, human rights organizations, and others, this involves a fairly straightforward but essential strategy of pressuring governments and international organizations. Where discrete action is required, pressure can be mounted through normal political channels; where urgent action is required, "making noise" through the media and through holding elected officials accountable for inaction is essential.

Others argue that almost all preventive actions require "mixed strategies," combining elements of coercion and inducements. Preventive strategies that embrace sticks to the virtual exclusion of carrots, or vice versa, have limited persuasive value. In this regard, constituency politics shape strategic frameworks for prevention by highlighting the political and economic interests at stake in emerging conflicts. Negotiations should allow all sides to show their constituencies real gains.[54] Where conflict constituencies or spoilers have vested interests in triggering deadly conflict, external actors should move quickly to support and empower the local leaders embracing nonviolent positions and work to limit the impact of spoilers. One can add to this strategy a tactic of using economic inducements to buy off spoilers who resist preventive diplomacy because they see little benefit in peace. Well-timed and well-conceived economic aid, such as demobilization or job-skills training for armed unemployed youth, has the potential to change spoilers into stakeholders.

The Carnegie Commission's extensive work on the strategic employment of conflict prevention efforts sets a standard. The report argues for two distinct strategies – for imminent crises and for underlying causes. The operational strategy emphasizes early action, when prevention stands a greater likelihood of success. A "lead player" is required to manage multi-actor prevention, to avoid the prospect of "prevention by committee" and all the strategic incoherence that implies. Initiatives are also desirable that not only prevent violence but also take specific, comprehensive, and balanced actions to reduce pressures that trigger violence. In practice, this approach would integrate "quick-impact projects" into diplomatic initiatives. The availability of a pool of flexible development funds for use at very short notice is necessary. This capacity does not presently exist within the UN, and this has long been a major constraint on the ability of mediators to "sweeten the pot" for parties to a dispute and engage in even rudimentary confidence-building measures.[55]

Another approach to preventive strategies emphasizes the importance of timing. Strategies should be informed by an understanding of whether actors in an emerging conflict are ready to negotiate. Thus, a strategy must first determine if an emerging conflict is "ripe for prevention."[56] This position challenges the common idea that when it comes to prevention, earlier is always better.

Despite some progress, there is still much work to be done. Even with a well-honed strategic framework to provide general direction to specific preventive actions, success is ultimately dependent on an appropriate strategy, one which should be case-specific and be designed by individuals and organizations with close knowledge of the conflict. Success also depends on the ability of those crafting it to avoid committee-driven decisions (which are prone to compromises and hence rarely coherent strategically) and bureaucratically driven approaches (relying on standard operating procedures). Studies of failure have demonstrated that a successful preventive strategy requires an ability to "think outside the box" and tailor new approaches to new types of problems.[57]

## INSTITUTIONAL CAPACITY

Conflict prevention is and will remain a thoroughly multilateral endeavour, with numerous structures and organizations playing different roles at different times. By adopting a broad definition of conflict prevention, there is virtually no limit to the number of organizations and institutions whose activities are relevant to the task at hand. Yet these actors – states, the UN, regional organizations, NGOs, religious groups, the business community, the media, and the scientific and educational communities – are judged collectively as mediocre by the Carnegie Commission.[58]

Effective conflict prevention depends on these disparate organizations' working together strategically. The capacity to conduct preventive diplomacy ultimately relies on the international ability to coordinate multilateral initiatives and identify logical divisions of labour. The mention of "coordination" normally makes eyes glaze over, and this topic remains a perennial concern for numerous UN conferences and reports. The number of coordinating committees and meetings is large, but they do not necessarily improve coordination. It is obvious that states and nonstate organizations often have varying interests and agendas; and in zones of potentially catastrophic conflict where external actors have significant interests (and usually more than a few rivals), coordination of preventive actions can be especially difficult. This provides easy ammunition for indigenous actors to exploit divisions among external players. Combined with the need to coordinate and create divisions of labour across agencies and be flexible in sequencing preventive measures over time, the prospects for strategic coherence are formidable.

In many respects the institutional challenges to effective preventive action parallel those for early warning. Most observers have accepted the reality that the structures of preventive response will be "loose and temporary," to return to Kofi Annan's characterization. But where does responsibility for preventive action ultimately rest? For when everyone is responsible for preventive measures, then no one is compelled to act.

## POLITICAL WILL

The final link in the chain of prevention is political will. The overwhelming majority of studies cite lack of will as the major cause of failed prevention. On this score, the Rwandan genocide casts an especially long shadow. Assessments of this sad display of highly inadequate international backbone all conclude that the world's inaction was due to a failure of the major states and the UN Secretariat. "There was a persistent lack of political will by member states to act, or to act with enough assertiveness," concluded the UN's own independent inquiry into Rwanda.[59]

One suggestion is for advocacy or political organizations to exert sustained pressure on governments to make prevention a priority. Yet, there is no guarantee that forcing governments to act will yield appropriate outcomes. One of the hard lessons about humanitarian intervention in the 1990s is that public pressure can produce window dressing instead of meaningful action: "When humanitarian policy is driven only by media images and public pressure, there is a strong tendency on the part of administrations to measure success by how effectively they *appear* to be addressing the problem, rather than by how effectively they *actually* resolve it. If the stakes are political, not strategic, then the policy choices will also be political, not strategic."[60]

Advocacy and political pressure should, therefore, be coupled with other measures if sustained and successful preventive diplomacy is to become the norm. If leaders are persuaded that preventive action is in the national interests of their states, if the public is sceptical that preventive diplomacy is warranted, or if officials perceive that the political risks of preventive action are too great, then early warnings will either go unheeded or will yield risk-averse, half-hearted measures. Such responses may actually make things worse.

Some observers argue that governments should become persuaded that conflict prevention addresses important security interests. The paradigm of prevention as a cornerstone of national interest, not just special interests, should be thoroughly "soaked" into both the leadership and the foreign policy branches of governments and international organizations. If preventing deadly conflicts is framed and ultimately accepted as a vital strategic goal, then preventive responses are more likely to engage sustained attention from governments. This means that arguments for conflict prevention should be articulated in the language of interest as much as moral or humanitarian appeals.[61] At the same time, skeptics argue that broadening definitions of vital interests is counterproductive and that humanitarian action should be justified in its own terms.

Advocates go still further, arguing that cultivating a regime of prevention is essential.[62] The notion of a "culture of prevention" has taken on a wide range of meanings, but its core presumes that certain norms gradually become so pervasive and globalized that there are real costs – to individual careers, to governments, and to would-be transgressors – for violating or dismissing them. And, importantly, these norms permeate governmental agencies and international organizations, so that acting on them becomes almost second nature. Evidence suggests that neither creating nor maintaining a regime is easy. For example, regimes based on such long-standing concerns as human rights and sustainable development still remain relatively weak.

## TOWARD EFFECTIVE PREVENTION

Conflict prevention has received far more rhetorical than political, financial, and institutional support. Nonetheless, significant improvements in capacity and the growth of organized public pressure have created a more fertile atmosphere for the growth of a culture of prevention.

Prevention is broadly understood to involve strategies addressing both proximate and underlying causes. The vast majority of preventive measures, particularly those that address root causes, are nonintrusive and actively championed by many poor countries that are potential targets for outside intervention when prevention fails. Some direct preventation measures are merely intrusive, however, while others actually are coercive. Dimensions of conflict prevention are therefore part of a "continuum" of intervention that can conjure up visceral negative reactions. In this respect, genuine preventive efforts are both attractive and repellent. This reality, along with the fact that internationalizing a conflict is not necessarily in the interests of governments or belligerents, explains why prevention is not always uncontested.

The effectiveness of prevention depends on six distinct capacities, which together form the links in a chain, with the results being only as strong as the weakest of these links. At this time, some are stronger than others. The analytic capacity to predict and understand conflicts is not as strong as many believe and needs serious attention. The capacity to provide early warning is weak and ad hoc, but it has been sufficient in many instances to provide adequate notice. The operational capacity to prevent conflict is in place – that is, a well-honed and increasingly sophisticated toolbox of prevention is at the disposal of policy makers. However, the strategic capacity to prevent conflict – to know which tools to use when – remains underdeveloped. Although each conflict requires a distinct strategy, a general strategic framework requires more attention. The capacity to respond is, and will likely remain, multiactored and decentralized. This basic reality places a premium on coordination and the establishment of clear divisions of labour among states, the UN, regional organizations, NGOs, and local actors.

Finally, the political will to act has been a chronic weakness. While a growing network of advocacy groups is trying to place political pressure on states to engage, conflict prevention needs to be understood by governments as being in their strategic, as well as in their political, interests before the concept is fully institutionalized.

## NOTES

1  Kofi Annan, the UN Millennium Report, *"We the Peoples": The Role of the United Nations in the 21st Century* (New York: United Nations, 2000), p. 44. For the most recent interview, see Kofi Annan, *Prevention of Armed Conflict: Report of the Secretary-General*, UN Document A/55/985/S/2001/574, June 7, 2001.

2  Hugh Miall, Oliver Ramsbotham, and Tom Woodhouse, *Contemporary Conflict Resolution* (Cambridge: Polity Press, 1999), pp. 39–64.

3  *Report of the Panel on United Nations Peace Operations* (New York: United Nations, 2000), para. 33.

4  Richard Betts, "The Delusion of Impartial Intervention," *Foreign Affairs* 73, no. 6 (November–December 1994), p. 24.

5  Stephen John Stedman, "Alchemy for a New World Order: Overselling 'Preventive Diplomacy'," *Foreign Affairs* 74, no. 3 (May–June 1995), pp. 14–20.

6  Boutros Boutros-Ghali, *An Agenda for Peace* (New York: United Nations, 1992), para. 23.

7  Boutros Boutros-Ghali, *Supplement to An Agenda for Peace* (New York: United Nations, 1995).

8    Annan, "*We the Peoples*," Chapter IV; and *Facing the Humanitarian Challenge – Towards a Culture of Prevention*, The Report of the Secretary-General on the Work of the Organization for 1999 (New York: UN Secretary-General, 1999), paras. 68–100.

9    *Report of the Panel on United Nations Peace Operations*, para. 31.

10   The White House, quoted in Michael Lund, *Preventing Violent Conflict: A Strategy for Preventive Diplomacy* (Washington, DC: US Institute of Peace, 1996), p. 5.

11   Peter Cross, ed., *Contributing to Preventive Action* (Baden-Baden: Nomos, 1998); Peter Cross and Guenola Rasaloelina, eds., *Conflict Prevention Policy of the European Union, CPN Yearbook 1998/1999* (Baden-Baden: Nomos, 1999); and Michael Lund and Guenola Rasamoelina, *The Impact of Conflict Prevention Policy, CPN Yearbook 1999/2000* (Baden-Baden: Nomos, 2000).

12   International Security Information Service, *Restructuring for Conflict Prevention and Management: EU Restructuring Conference Report and Comments* (Brussels: International Security Information Service Europe, 1999); Nicole Ball et al., *The European Commission and the World Bank: Exploring Fields of Cooperation, Joint Workshop of the EU and the World Bank* (Brussels: Stiftung Wissenschaft und Politik and the Conflict Prevention Network, 2000; and Saferworld, *Preventing Violent Conflict: Opportunities for the Swedish and Belgian Presidencies of the European Union in 2001* (Saferworld and International Alert, 2000), http://www.oneworld.org/euconflict/whatsnew/eulobbydoc.html

13   Mary B. Anderson, *Do No Harm: Supporting Local Capacities for Peace through Aid* (Cambridge, MA: Development of Collaborative Action Inc., 1996); Giovanni Rufini, "The Potential of Non-governmental Organization in Peacekeeping Negotiation and Mediation," *Peacekeeping and International Relations* 24, no. 2 (1995); and Haneef Atmaar et al., *From Rhetoric to Reality: The Role of Aid in Local Peacebuilding in Afghanistan* (York: Post-War Reconstruction and Development Unit, University of York, 1998).

14   Larry Minear and Thomas G. Weiss, *Humanitarian Action in Times of War* (Boulder: Lynne Rienner, 1993); Mats Berdal and David Malone, eds., *Greed and Grievance: Economic Agendas in Civil Wars* (Boulder: Lynne Rienner, 2000); Joanne Macrae and Anthony Zwi, eds., *War and Hunger: Rethinking International Responses to Complex Emergencies* (London: Zed Books, 1994); Mary B. Anderson, *Do No Harm*; and Peter Uvin, *Aiding Violence: The Development Enterprise in Rwanda* (West Hartford: Kumarian Press, 1998).

15   Some analyses go further and differentiate between systemic or background causes (such as resource scarcity), enabling or proximate causes (such as political repression or ethnic mobilization), and triggering or immediate factors (specific acts of repression or a sudden economic crisis). See, for example, Creative Associates International, *Preventing and Mitigating Violent Conflicts: A Guide for Practitioners* (Washington, DC: Greater Horn of Africa Initiative and US Agency for International Development, 1996).

16   Annan, "*We the Peoples*," p. 45. For a more sophisticated view of the connection between aid and conflict, see Kofi Annan, "Peace and Development – One Struggle, Two Fronts," Address to World Bank Staff, October 19, 1999.

17   *Report of the Panel on United Nations Peace Operations*, para. 30.

18   Boutros-Ghali, *An Agenda for Peace*, para. 20.

19   UN Security Council, November 30, 1999. Statement by the President of the Security Council, UN Document S/PRST/1999/34, p. 2.

20   Carnegie Commission on Preventing Deadly Conflict, *Preventing Deadly Conflict – Final Report* (Washington, DC: Carnegie Commission on Preventing Deadly Conflict, 1997), pp. 40 and 69.

21   Stockholm International Peace Research Institute, *Preventing Violent Conflict: The Search for Political Will, Strategies and Effective Tools – Report of the Krusenberg Seminar* (Stockholm: Stockholm International Peace Research Institute, 2000), p. 3. Available at http://editors.sipri.se/pubs/Krusenberg.html

22   G-8 Foreign Ministers Meeting, *G-8 Miyazaki Initiative for Conflict Prevention* (Miyazaki, Japan: G-8, July 13, 2000), p. 1.

23   Carnegie Commission on Preventing Deadly Conflict, *Preventing Deadly Conflict*, pp. 4–5.

24   Analytic models designed to predict conflicts are, however, improving. A useful compilation of the findings of these systemic conflict prediction models can be found in John L. Davies and Ted Robert Gurr, *Preventive Measures: Building Risk Assessment and Crisis Early Warning Systems* (Lanham: Rowman & Littlefield, 1998).

25   Michael E. Brown, "Introduction" in Michael E. Brown, ed., *The International Dimensions of Internal Conflict* (Cambridge: MIT Press, 1996), p. 13.

26    David A. Lake and Donald Rothchild, *Ethnic Fears and Global Engagement: The International Spread and Management of Ethnic Conflict* (La Jolla: Institute on Global Conflict and Cooperation, 1996), pp. 5–7; and Bruce Jentleson, "Preventive Diplomacy: Analytical Conclusions and Policy Lessons," in Jentleson, ed., *Opportunities Missed, Opportunities Seized: Preventive Diplomacy in the Post-Cold War World* (Lanham: Rowman & Littlefield, 2000), pp. 322–323.

27    Carnegie Commission on Preventing Deadly Conflict, *Preventing Deadly Conflict*, p. 29

28    Macrae and Zwi, *War and Hunger*; Uvin, *Aiding Violence*; Berdal and Malone, *Greed Grievance*; Jean-Francois Bayart et al., *The Criminalization of the State in Africa* (Oxford: James Currey, 1999); William Reno, *Warlord Politics and African States* (Boulder: Lynne Rienner, 1998); and Jonathan Goodhand and David Hulme, "From Wars to Complex Emergencies: Understanding Conflict and Peace-Building," *Third World Quarterly* 20, no. 1 (1999), pp. 13–26.

29    *Report of the Panel of Experts on Violations of Security Council Sanctions against UNITA*, UN Document S/2000/203, March 10, 2000.

30    Miall et al., *Contemporary Conflict Resolution*, p. 100.

31    See, for example, Leon Gordenker, *Refugees in International Politics* (London: Croom Helm, 1987).

32    Food security early-warning systems include US Agency for International Development's Famine Early Warning System, or FEWS; the Food and Agriculture Organization's Global Information and Early Warning System on Food and Agriculture, or GIEWS; and the European Community's Food Security Assessment Unit, or FSAU.

33    Annan, "*We the Peoples*," pp. 70–71.

34    *Report of the Panel on United Nations Peace Operations*, para. 6, pp. 66–75.

35    J. Brian Atwood, "Conflict Prevention in Today's World," remarks delivered at Georgetown University, October 8, 1998, http:www.usaid.gov/press/sp_test/speeches/1998/sp981014.html

36    *Report of the Independent Inquiry into the Actions of the United Nations during the 1994 Genocide in Rwanda* (New York: United Nations, December 15, 1999).

37    Also, see Lund, *Preventing Violent Conflict*; Carnegie Commission on Preventing Deadly Conflict, *Preventing Deadly Conflict*; Swedish Ministry of Foreign Affairs, *Preventing Violent Conflict – A Swedish Action Plan* (Stockholm: Swedish Ministry of Foreign Affairs, 1999); and Annika Björkdahl, "Developing a Toolbox for Conflict Prevention," *Preventing Violent Conflict – The Search for Political Will Strategies, and Effective Tools*, Appendix I (Stockholm: Stockholm International Peace Research Institute, 2000).

38    United Nations Development Programme, *Governance for Sustainable Growth and Equity* (New York: United Nations, 1997); and World Bank, *World Development Report 1997: The State in a Changing World* (New York: Oxford University Press, 1997).

39    Ball et al., *The European Commission*; Carnegie Commission on Preventing Deadly Conflict, *Preventing Deadly Conflict* – Executive Summary, p. 41; John Stremlau and Francisco Sagasti, *Preventing Deadly Conflict: Does the World Bank Have a Role?* (New York: Carnegie Commission on Preventing Deadly Conflict, 1998); and Saferworld, *Preventing Violent Conflict*, pp. 8–11.

40    See, for example, James Boyce and Manuel Pastor, "Aid for Peace: Can International Financial Institutions Help Prevent Conflict?," *World Policy Journal* 15, no. 2 (Summer 1998), pp. 42–49.

41    Cyrus R. Vance and David A. Hamburg, *Pathfinder for Peace: A Report to the UN Secretary-General on the Role of Special Representatives and Personal Envoys* (Washington, DC: Carnegie Commission on Preventing Deadly Conflict, 1997); Jean Krasno, *The Group of Friends of the Secretary-General: A Useful Diplomatic Tool* (Washington, DC: Carnegie Commission on Preventing Deadly Conflict, 1996); and Jentleson, ed., *Opportunities Missed and Opportunities Seized*, pp. 336–337.

42    Annan, "*We the Peoples*," p. 46.

43    Louise Diamond and John McDonald, *Multi-Track Diplomacy: A Systems Approach to Peace*, 3rd ed. (West Hartford: Kumarian Press, 1996); Pamela Aall, "Nongovernmental Organizations and Peacemaking," in Chester Crocker and Fen Osler Hampson, eds., *Managing Global Chaos* (Washington, DC: US Institute of Peace, 1996), pp. 433–444; and John Paul Lederach, *Building Peace: Sustaining Reconciliation in Divided Societies* (Washington, DC: US Insitute of Peace, 1997).

44    Kumar Rupesinghe, *Strategies for Conflict Prevention, Management, and Resolution* (Washington, DC: Winston Foundation for World Peace, 1999), http://www.wf.org/kumar/html

45    Stedman, "Alchemy for a New World Order," p. 15; and Robert I. Rotberg, *Vigilance and Vengeance: NGOs Preventing Ethnic Conflict in Divided Societies* (Cambridge: World Peace Foundation, 1996).

46    Jordana Friedman and Nick Killick, "The Partnership Model," *Conflict Prevention Newsletter* 2, no. 2 (1999), http://www.oneworld.org/euconflict/publicat/nl2.2/page7.html; Claire Short, "Conflict Prevention, Conflict Resolution and Post-Conflict Peace-building – From Rhetoric to Reality," speech to *International Alert*, November 2, 1999, http://www.international-alert.org/cssspeech.html; and Carnegie Commission on Preventing Deadly Conflict, *Preventing Deadly Conflict* – Executive Summary, pp. 34–36.

47    Nik Gowing, *Media Coverage: Help or Hindrance in Conflict Prevention* (New York: Carnegie Commission on Preventing Deadly Conflict, 1997); and Jamie F. Metzl, "Information Intervention: When Switching Channels Isn't Enough," *Foreign Affairs* 76, no. 6 (November–December 1995), pp. 15–21.

48    Saferworld, *Preventing World Conflict*, sec. 2a.

49    Annan, "*We the Peoples*," p. 53.

50    See Don Hubert, *The Landmine Ban: A Case-Study in Humanitarian Advocacy* (Providence: Watson Institute, 2000), occasional paper #42; and Richard Price, "Reversing the Gun Sights: Transnational Civil Society Targets Land Mines," *International Organization* 52, no. 3 (Summer 1998), pp. 613–644.

51    Jeffrey Boutwell and Michael Klare, *Light Weapons and Civil Conflict: Controlling the Tools of Violence* (Lanham: Rowman & Littlefield, 1999).

52    Annika Björkdahl, "Conflict Prevention from a Nordic Perspective: Putting Prevention into Practice," *Journal of International Peacekeeping* 6, no. 3 (1999), pp. 54–72; and Michael Lund, "Preventive Diplomacy to Macedonia, 1992–1999: From Containment to Nation-Building," in Jentleson, ed., *Opportunities Missed, Opportunities Seized*, pp. 173–208.

53    Carnegie Commission on Preventing Deadly Conflict, *Preventing Deadly Conflict* – Executive Summary, pp. 17–18.

54    Jentleson, ed., *Opportunities Missed, Opportunities Seized*, pp. 13 and 336.

55    Carnegie Commission on Preventing Deadly Conflict, *Preventing Deadly Conflict* – Executive Summary, pp. 7, 15.

56    Creative Associates International, *Preventing and Mitigating Violent Conflicts*, pp. 6–18.

57    Kenneth Menkhaus and Louis Ortmayer, "Somalia: Missed Crises and Missed Opportunities," in Jentleson, ed., *Opportunities Missed, Opportunities Seized*, p. 326.

58    Carnegie Commission on Preventing Deadly Conflict, *Preventing Deadly Conflict* – Executive Summary, p. x.

59    Alison Des Forges, *Leave None to Tell the Story: Genocide in Rwanda* (New York: Human Rights Watch; Paris: International Federation of Human Rights, 1999); Astri Suhrke and Bruce Jones, "Dilemmas of Protection: The Log of the Kigali Battalion," in Howard Adelman and Astri Suhrke, eds., *The Path of a Genocide: The Rwanda Crisis from Uganda to Zaire* (New Brunswick: Transaction Publishers, 1999); Gerard Prunier, *The Rwanda Crisis, 1959–1994: History of a Genocide* (London: Hurst & Co., 1995); Scott Feil, *Preventing Genocide: How the Early Use of Force Might Have Succeeded in Rwanda: A Report to the Carnegie Commission on Preventing Deadly Conflict* (Washington, DC: Carnegie Commission on Preventing Deadly Conflict, 1998); Carnegie Commission on Preventing Deadly Conflict, *Preventing Deadly Conflict* – Final Report; *Report of the Independent Inquiry into the Actions of the United Nations during the 1994 Genocide in Rwanda*, UN Document S/1999/1257, December 15, 1999, p. 1; and Joint Evaluation of Emergency Assistance to Rwanda, *The International Response to Conflict and Genocide: Lessons from the Rwanda Experience* (Copenhagen: Steering Committee of the Joint Evaluation of Emergency Assistance to Rwanda, 1996).

60    Kenneth Menkhaus, "Complex Emergencies, Humanitarianism, and National Security," *National Security Studies Quarterly* 4, no. 4 (1998), p. 56.

61    See, for example, S. Neil MacFarlane and Thomas G. Weiss, "Political Interest and Humanitarian Action," *Security Studies* 10, no. 1 (Autumn 2000), pp. 120–152.

62    Kofi Annan, *Report on the State of the Organization* (New York: United Nations, 1998); and Gareth Evans, *Cooperating for Peace: The Global Agenda for the 1990s and Beyond* (New York: Allan and Unwin, 1993), pp. 40–41.

# B

# PAST HUMANITARIAN INTERVENTIONS

The second group of essays in this part of the volume provides a historical overview of humanitarian intervention – the nonconsensual use of outside military force on humanitarian grounds – since the founding of the United Nations (UN) in 1945. The definition of "humanitarian" refers to the threat or occurrence of large scale loss of life (including, most obviously, genocide), forced migration, and abuses of human rights. The specific cases have been selected where a humanitarian justification was actually employed by the intervening states or where the intervention resulted in clearly beneficial impacts on humanitarian conditions in the target state. Military force applied at the request of a target state is not "intervention"; it is not unwanted interference in state sovereignty, because states have the right to seek outside military assistance. Thus, when genuine consent is present, a request to defend state sovereignty is legitimate and not considered unacceptable interference in domestic politics.

In each case, information is included on the nature of the crisis and the subsequent events on the ground, pertinent developments at the Security Council and in regional bodies, the justifications employed by the intervening forces, and the views of other states. The latter are particularly significant, for the evidence of the legitimacy or illegitimacy in behaviour resides in the claims and counterclaims of states as they debate the propriety of various interventions.

Essay 4, Interventions Before 1990, is an overview of interventions in the post-1945 period, from the birth of the UN Charter regime to the end of the Cold War. Considerable attention is given to the three cases from this period that are widely cited – East Pakistan, Cambodia, and Uganda – but seven others are also examined. Although in retrospect these three cases are often invoked as evidence of the norm of humanitarian intervention, on balance they were carried out by single states that justified them on grounds of self-defence. At the end of this period, most commentators argued that no such norm existed or that it was so contentious that it was necessary to justify intervention on other grounds.

Essay 5, Interventions After the Cold War, focuses on interventions after 1990. The post-Cold War era has not changed everything. There are strong similarities between the challenges posed by the Congo in the early 1960s and in 2001. The armed conflict was internal and civilians constituted the overwhelming majority of casualties. However, the political context of the 1990s certainly has altered the prospects for intrusions into what had formerly been considered the more protected domain of sovereign states – to conduct domestic policy as they pleased. During this period, the balance in the UN Charter between state sovereignty and human rights has been tipped so that the latter occasionally assumes the same or more importance than the claims of states.

In looking toward the future, these cases illuminate emerging trends in the use of coercive measures to address humanitarian needs. The willingness of outside actors (military and civilian, governmental and intergovernmental and nongovernmental), as well as the resources devoted to aiding and protecting severely affected local populations, have increased dramatically. Not only has the use of the ultimate tool of coercion, military force, increased in the last decade, but other nonconsensual interventions as well. Economic sanctions and arms embargoes, along with international criminal prosecutions, have been commonly employed over the past decade.

In contrast to the cases of humanitarian intervention during the Cold War, the cases examined from the 1990s are remarkable for their legitimacy. The Security Council was seized by each case and made decisions about coercion; the conscious-shocking and truly humanitarian dimensions of each case were more central to international actions; and military responses were more multilateral.

The cases are covered relatively briefly. There is much more to be said about all of them. References have been included to assist future research, but for those seeking further information, the cases in the 1990s and the three main ones from the 1970s are covered in the Bibliography.

# 4. INTERVENTIONS BEFORE 1990

The purpose here is to survey the episodes of nonconsensual military interventions that were conducted for claimed humanitarian purposes or that resulted in clear humanitarian benefits during the Cold War period, 1945–1989. There is substantial evidence in these cases about why controversy surrounds what constitutes an actual incidence of "humanitarian" intervention. Sometimes this qualifying adjective provides a smoke screen for other foreign policy objectives; sometimes humanitarian motives are present but not primary; and sometimes the adjective is not used at all, but the humanitarian impact is undeniable.

Ten cases of military intervention are discussed: Belgium in the Congo (1960); Belgium and the United States (US) in Stanleyville (1964); the US in the Dominican Republic (1965); India in East Pakistan (1971); France and Belgium in Shaba province (1978); Vietnam in Cambodia (1978); Tanzania in Uganda (1979); France in Central Africa (1979); the US and certain Caribbean countries in Grenada (1983); and the US in Panama (1989).[1]

## BELGIUM'S INTERVENTION IN THE CONGO, 1960

The Congo declared independence from Belgium on June 30, 1960.[2] However, because of the immediate breakdown of law and order, national celebration was short-lived. On July 4, troops of the Congolese Army mutinied, and chaos spread throughout the country. Congolese and foreign civilians were murdered, others were beaten, and women were raped. "During the night of July 7–8 alone, more than 1,300 women and children, mostly Belgians, fled in panic across the Congo River to Brazzaville."[3] On July 10, Belgian battalions left their barracks in the Belgian bases at Kitona and Kamina and took control of a number of Congolese cities to restore order; and more troops were flown in from Belgium.

On July 11 Moise Kapenda Tshombe, the prime minister of mineral-rich Katanga province, declared Katangese independence. Two days later, Congolese President Joseph Kasavubu and Prime Minister Patrice Lumumba sent a joint telegram to UN Secretary-General Dag Hammarskjöld, appealing for United Nations (UN) assistance and accusing Belgium of aggression, fomenting secession in the province of Katanga, and "colonialist machinations."[4] Invoking Charter Article 99, Hammarskjöld requested an urgent meeting of the Security Council, which met later that day.

The Belgian intervention was harshly condemned by Congolese authorities and throughout Africa. Belgium was accused of having instigated the army mutiny and Tshombe's revolt. Belgium's opposition to Congolese independence and the precipitous manner in which it had withdrawn the colonial administration and infrastructure prior to independence had seriously destabilized the fledgling country. Many saw the events that followed as an effort by Belgium to provoke a crisis and create a pretext to reassert control and authority.

Before the Security Council, Belgium argued that it had intervened because of the complete breakdown of law and order and the compelling need to protect life generally, asserting a broad claim to intervene on humanitarian grounds:

> When the "Force Publique" [the Congolese Army] ceased to be an instrument of order in the hands of the new Congolese State, the latter was no longer in a position to ensure the safety of the inhabitants and it was at this point that the Belgian Government decided to intervene, with the sole purpose of ensuring the safety of European and other members of the population and of protecting human lives in general.[5]

Under such circumstances, Belgium claimed that it was under a "sacred duty to take the measures required by morality and by public international law."[6] Later statements emphasized Belgium's right to protect its own nationals, rather than a more general right to intervene for humanitarian purposes. The next day, the Belgian representative stated: "I should like to make our present position clear. We sent troops; they intervened to the extent necessary to fulfil our sacred duty to protect the lives and honour of our nationals."[7]

In the Cold War environment of the 1960s, Belgium's actions were strongly supported by its North Atlantic Treaty Organization (NATO) allies. The most emphatic defender was France, arguing that "in many instances the Belgian troops have alone been able to protect lives and property" and that "their mission of protecting lives and property" was in accordance "with a recognized principle of international law, namely intervention on humanitarian grounds."[8] Britain observed that the Belgian effort was directed at facilitating "the withdrawal of Belgian nationals [and] of other communities threatened with violence" and that the Belgian troops had performed a "humanitarian task" for which Britain was grateful "and for which … the international community should be grateful."[9] For its part, Italy argued that because the Belgian troops had intervened only to protect human life and to restore law and order, the Belgian action should not even be considered an intervention, but rather "a temporary security action."[10] The US simply observed that Belgium had not committed aggression, that matters were too critical to spend time trying to apportion blame, and that what was required was immediate UN assistance.[11]

A number of countries rejected the Western arguments. The Soviet Union and Poland insisted that Belgium's claim to protect human life was simply a pretext; the real reason was to further its own commercial interests.[12] Nevertheless, even the protection of human life could not justify an intervention by one state in the affairs of another.[13] Tunisia and Ecuador joined in arguing that the Belgian intervention was unjustifiable.[14] African countries were also categorical, arguing that the effort was transparently colonial, rather than humanitarian.

On July 14, the Security Council unanimously passed Resolution 143, sponsored by Tunisia, which called on Belgium "to withdraw its troops," and authorized the Secretary-General to consult with the Congolese government in order to provide it "with such military assistance as may be necessary until … the national security forces may be able … to meet fully their tasks." The resolution, which was the legal basis for the subsequent establishment of the UN Operation in the Congo (ONUC, or Opération des Nations-Unies au Congo), was ambiguously drafted in order to avoid either a Soviet or a Western veto, and it was adopted by a vote of 8–0–3.[15] Although many non-NATO states expressed the view that the Belgian military action was unlawful, the resolution did not accuse Belgium of an unlawful act, but the request was "an implied censure."[16] A further purposeful element of ambiguity was that the resolution did not directly link the establishment of a UN force with the withdrawal of Belgian troops, which would have given an implicit endorsement to the Belgian argument that some non-Congolese force was necessary to preserve law and order.[17]

Following the Security Council mandate for ONUC, the mission deployed rapidly. The first troops were in the country the following day, and by July 17 (only three days later) more than 3,500 troops were on the ground.[18] Despite the controversy over the presence of the Belgian troops, their presence did not create any serious difficulties for UN forces, and the Belgians were withdrawn by early September.

## BELGIUM AND THE US'S INTERVENTION IN STANLEYVILLE, 1964

The immediate post-independence turmoil and Belgium's subsequent intervention resulted in the deployment of ONUC, a peacekeeping force that remained for four years. Although a number of secessionist struggles had ended by the time of the UN force's departure, civil strife certainly had not.[19] Insurgencies had arisen in a number of provinces, and if anything they were inflamed by the establishment, in July 1964, of what was meant to be a government of national reconciliation, led by one former secessionist leader, Moise Tshombe. Congolese President Joseph Kasavubu had appointed Tshombe as prime minister in the hopes that a more broadly based government would help quell the unrest. The opposite proved to be the case. The contempt in which Tshombe was held in much of Africa was shown only a few days after he assumed office, when African foreign ministers, meeting in Cairo to prepare for the Second Assembly of Heads of State and Government, declared that Tshombe would not be welcome.[20]

On August 5, 1964, rebel forces seized control of Stanleyville, the northeastern provincial capital and former stronghold of deceased Prime Minister Patrice Lumumba. By this time, rebel forces controlled approximately half of the Congo. The rebel advance had become so rapid that it was thought that the central government might fall in a matter of weeks.[21] A desperate Tshombe decided to hire white mercenaries from South Africa and Rhodesia. The rapid arrival of the mercenaries, supported by US-supplied aircraft, began to turn the tide of the rebel advance. On September 3, one of the rebel leaders sent a message to UN Secretary-General U Thant to the effect that he was holding as hostages 500 "white men, women and children" and would begin to execute them if the Tshombe government continued its use of mercenaries and its air attacks on rebel positions. The gravity of the message was confirmed by a number of radio interceptions in October, when US intelligence sources overheard rebel radio messages concerning the executions.[22]

Belgium and the US decided to mount a rescue attempt if negotiations to free the hostages were unsuccessful. After meeting a rebel intermediary in Nairobi, the two countries formed the opinion that unacceptable conditions had been placed on the release of the hostages,[23] and there was no real alternative to a rescue attempt.[24] On November 21, Prime Minister Tshombe authorized Belgium and the US to mount a rescue operation. Three days later, Belgian paratroopers were transported by US military aircraft into Stanleyville to commence rescue operations. Hours after the rescue attempt began, Brussels and Washington sent letters to the president of the Security Council emphasizing the request from the Congolese government. The intervention was strictly limited to the humanitarian goal of rescuing the hostages, who now numbered about 1,000 civilians from many different countries.[25]

In five days, approximately 2,000 foreign residents were evacuated. The Organization of African Unity's (OAU's) ad hoc Commission on the Congo protested that the action was likely to have made matters worse for both foreign residents and Congolese. Five or six foreign residents had been executed before the intervention, almost 200 were executed afterward, along with thousands of Congolese. While the Belgian and US governments publicly presented the intervention as a considerable success, the opinion of the OAU's ad hoc Commission may have been more accurate. Many more foreigners and Congolese might have lived if the ongoing OAU negotiations had been given more time.[26] In any event, the intervention benefited the Tshombe government in its fight against the rebels.

The intervention occasioned a firestorm of protest in Africa. Many African governments argued in the Security Council that the real objective was to support a neocolonialist government and Western economic and political interests. At the request of 22 African and Asian member states, the Security Council met on December 9 to consider what the requestors called the Belgian and American aggression against the Congo.[27] What followed was one of the most acrimonious debates in the Security Council's history, taking 17 sessions to complete.[28]

Many African states believed that the Tshombe government had no legitimacy[29] and that claims from Belgium and the US were disingenuous. Egypt argued that the Belgian–American intervention represented nothing less than "naked aggression."[30] To invite the former colonial master, even under the trappings of governmental consent and authority, was simply to reintroduce colonialism by the back door.[31] Algeria made the allegation pointedly, claiming that "it is only natural that the main motive of those who helped the prime mover of Katanga's secession or who handed over the leadership of the Leopoldville Government to him should have been to retain a monopoly over the exploitation of enormous wealth."[32] Moreover, the Belgian–US intervention was an affront to the recently established OAU, whose ad hoc Commission on the Congo had been set up to deal with the civil strife and was, they claimed, making serious progress in the negotiations.[33] The affront to the dignity of the OAU was compounded by the seeming spectacle of whites killing blacks to save whites.[34] The Soviet Union and Czechoslovakia essentially reiterated African and Asian claims.

The Belgian and US representatives confessed to having been stunned by what they regarded as the ugly tone of the debate. Paul-Henri Spaak, the Belgian foreign minister, called it "violent" and "insulting."[35] US Permanent Representative Ambassador Adlai Stevenson referred to it as "irrational, irresponsible, insulting and repugnant language."[36] Both countries repeated orally the claims that they each had made in writing on November 24 in letters to the president of the Security Council: the reason for the intervention was the humanitarian one of saving civilians, with the authorization of the lawful government of the Congo. On Belgium's behalf, Spaak argued that "the Stanleyville operation was not a military operation. It was not a matter of helping the Congolese National Army … . It was a question of saving between

1,500 and 2,000 persons whose lives were in danger. It was to save people who were regarded as hostages by the rebel authorities."[37] Stevenson argued that the intervention "was exactly what we said it was when we notified this Council at the very beginning – nothing more and nothing less than a mission to save the lives of innocent people of diverse nationalities." Stevenson stated that beyond the primary objective of the US to rescue its own nationals, "we are proud that the mission rescued so many innocent people of eighteen other nationalities."[38] Britain, France, Norway, Nationalist China, Bolivia, and Brazil accepted the legitimacy of the claims. Côte d'Ivoire, supported by Morocco, remarked that the "question at issue" was in fact the relatively straightforward one of a state's right to protect its own nationals, a concept that is "recognized in international law."[39]

The Security Council eventually passed Resolution 199 (1964) unanimously. It appealed for a cease-fire and requested all states to refrain from intervening in the domestic politics of the Congo. Because it requested all states to refrain from intervening in Congolese affairs, the US and Belgium were able to argue that this request implicitly referred, not simply to their military action, but also to alleged Soviet support for the rebel forces.

The legacy of actions in the early 1960s in Central Africa continues to colour the debate about intervention and state sovereignty. Colonial powers misused humanitarian justifications to mask self-interested motives. The end of colonialism did not mean that former colonial powers were readily given the benefit of the doubt by post-colonial countries when "humanitarianism" was invoked.

## THE US'S INTERVENTION IN THE DOMINICAN REPUBLIC, 1965

On April 24, 1965, a group of army officers revolted against the Dominican Government.[40] Some members of the military expressed a preference for inviting back the exiled leader Juan Bosch, who had been ousted in a coup d'état in September 1963. Others preferred the formation of a junta that would rule until elections could be held. Fighting began between the "loyalists," who favoured the formation of a junta, and the "constitutionalists," who preferred the return of the constitutionally elected but deposed president.

The US intervened on April 28, citing the need to protect American and other foreign civilians living in the Dominican Republic. Announcing that he had sent 400 Marines, President Lyndon B. Johnson declared that, "I have ordered the Secretary of Defense to put the necessary American troops ashore in order to give protection to hundreds of Americans who are still in the Dominican Republic and to escort them to safety … .This same assistance will be available to nationals of other countries"[41] Within the next few days, thousands of additional troops were deployed. While the US was concerned about the safety of its nationals, it is widely accepted that the real reason for intervening was to affect the authority structure in the Dominican Republic. Washington had decided to intervene when it was felt that the constitutionalists might win the struggle and usher in a left-wing regime.[42] One analyst comments: "The military outcome was a foregone conclusion once the Marines landed, for it was clear from the start which side they were supporting … . Despite their official neutrality, the Marines invaded the rebel strongholds and permitted [loyalist] forces safe conduct through the US Security Zone."[43]

At the request of the Soviet Union,[44] the Security Council held a series of meetings beginning on May 3. Defending its military action, the US argued that its intervention served two goals: "to save the lives of our people and … of all people." And, the US representative openly confessed, "to help prevent another communist State in this hemisphere."[45] Nationalist China enthusiastically supported both goals.[46] Britain and The Netherlands expressed approval of the US evacuation of their nationals[47] but avoided addressing the legitimacy of Washington's political objective. They supported the US call for the Dominican intervention to be left in the hands of the Organization of American States (OAS).

In the context of the Cold War rivalry, especially given its seeming manifestation in the streets of Santo Domingo itself, bitter opposition by the Soviet Union and Cuba was unsurprising.[48] Soviet Ambassador Nikolai Fedorenko accused the US of "sanctimonious hypocrisy" because the claim to protect nationals was a pretext to aiding conservative elements in the civil struggle. The claim that Ambassador Stevenson made later in the debate that the "lives of thousands of people from nearly 40 countries hung in the balance" seems exaggerated.[49] Unlike the case in Stanleyville, foreigners were not singled out and victimized, but rather suffered the same fate as the residents of Santo Domingo in coping with civil war. By the time the Security Council began to meet on May 3, President Johnson had appeared on national television to declare that the US would not allow the civil struggle to be won by the constitutionalist side, which he claimed had been "taken over and really seized and placed into the hands of a band of Communist conspirators ... . The American nations cannot, must not, and will not permit the establishment of another Communist Government in the Western Hemisphere."[50]

More revealing than the Soviet and Cuban opposition to the US military action was the opposition to the intervention by France, Uruguay, Jordan, Malaysia, and Côte d'Ivoire. While accepting the possible legitimate rescue of endangered nationals by states under certain circumstances, France argued that the essential purpose of the US intervention "appears to be directed against those who claim to have constitutional legality."[51] In a careful and detailed legal analysis by Security Council standards, Uruguay trenchantly criticized the intervention as violating both UN Charter and OAS norms.[52]

The first phase of the Security Council debate on the Dominican crisis lasted until May 14, when Resolution 203 was passed unanimously, inviting the Secretary-General to send a fact-finding mission to the Dominican Republic.[53] Meanwhile, various OAS organs had been meeting in Washington since the day after the initial landing – on April 30 – to call on all factions in the Dominican Republic to accept a cease-fire; on May 1, to establish a five-member commission to work for a negotiated solution; and finally, on May 6, to request OAS member states to create an Inter-American Force to take over from US troops. The debate at the OAS demonstrated a sharp division between the five states (Chile, Ecuador, Mexico, Peru, and Uruguay) that opposed the intervention as unjustifiable and contrary to both universal (that is, UN) and regional (that is, OAS) norms of nonintervention and the other 14 states (including the US). Of these 14, some argued that the intervention was necessary and legitimate, while others urged an urgent, peaceful resolution to the crisis. The resolution of May 6 enabled the deployment of an Inter-American Force under the command of a Brazilian general, but half of the US forces remained to constitute the core of the 12,000-strong Inter-American Force.

The intervention further fueled Latin American scepticism about disinterested motives, including humanitarian ones, invoked by the US or other major powers. Earlier experiences with gunboat diplomacy and the Monroe Doctrine asserting US hegemony in the Americas were substantially confirmed by this so-called humanitarian intervention in the Dominican Republic.

## INDIA'S INTERVENTION IN EAST PAKISTAN, 1971

The Indian intervention in East Pakistan arose out of a self-determination struggle in East Pakistan that eventually resulted in civil war in March 1971.[54] After the Awami League, a party advocating autonomy for East Pakistan, won the majority of seats in the National

Assembly in the December 1970 elections, Pakistani President Yahya Khan responded by refusing to convene the parliament. His decision provoked widespread demonstrations in East Pakistan, to which the government responded by invoking martial law. This, in turn, prompted Sheikh Mujibur Rahman, the leader of the Awami League, to issue a declaration, on March 23, that the struggle for emancipation would continue. Anticipating trouble, the Khan government had been sending additional troops into East Pakistan, and on March 26 civil war erupted.

The West Pakistani troops displayed a brutality that the Indian parliament then, and many commentators since, labeled "genocide."[55] The army was certainly guilty of widespread pillage, rape, torture, and murder. In all likelihood, hundreds of thousands were slaughtered. The Hindus of East Pakistan, in particular, were especially marked for extermination.[56] In a study of the events published some months later, the International Commission of Jurists summarized the Pakistani Army's behaviour in this way:

> The principal features of this ruthless oppression were the indiscriminate killing of civilians, including women and children … ; the attempt to exterminate or drive out of the country a large part of the Hindu population; the arrest, torture, and killing of Awami League activists, students, professional and business men and other potential leaders among the Bengalis; the raping of women, the destruction of villages and towns; and the looting of property. All this was done on a scale which was difficult to comprehend.[57]

By late autumn, 10 million refugees had fled into India. In addition to the tremendous social, economic, and administrative burden on India, the refugees fled to a politically volatile area of India.[58] New Delhi feared the creation of social and political upheaval that could undermine India's own stability.

Relations between India and Pakistan deteriorated rapidly. India began to support the Mukti Bahini, the Bengali liberation movement, by allowing India to be used as a safe haven in the autumn and by providing air cover for guerrilla forces. Border incidents multiplied, with each side accusing the other of repeated violations.[59] On December 3, in a surprising move, Pakistan bombed 10 Indian military airfields, hoping, it seems, to disable the Indian Air Force.[60] India responded with an all-out offensive into East Pakistan the next day, completely cutting off East from West Pakistan. Two days later, India recognized former East Pakistan as the independent state of Bangladesh. Within a few days, Indian forces occupied most parts of the former province, and on December 16 the Pakistani Army surrendered.

Within hours of the Indian entry into East Pakistan, representatives from a number of countries requested an immediate session of the Security Council, which met later that day. India's principal justification was that it was acting in self-defence, having been attacked by Pakistan on December 3.[61] Further, India also claimed that the influx of 10 million refugees amounted to "refugee aggression" and represented such an intolerable burden that it constituted a kind of "constructive" attack.[62] The Soviet Union later pointed out that this number was larger than the populations of 88 out of the then 131 member states of the UN.[63]

In addition to the principal justification of self-defence, India also made reference to the need to provide support to the Bengali victims of the Pakistani Army's onslaught. At the end of his initial statement to the Security Council, the Indian representative said that "we have on this particular occasion absolutely nothing but the purest of motives and the purest of intentions: to rescue the people of East Bengal from what they are suffering."[64] During the debates in both the Security Council and the General Assembly between

December 5 and 21, this statement came closest to justifying India's intention to intervene as being to protect the people of East Pakistan. At no time did India claim a right of human-itarian intervention, but rather insisted that it had used military force in self-defence.[65] However, in statement after statement, India repeatedly referred to the massive abuses committed by the Pakistani Army and linked the atrocities to the disenchantment of the people of East Pakistan with the central government and to the need for a genuine political settlement in East Pakistan.[66]

International reaction at the UN to the Indian claims was striking. In a debate that involved more than half of the member states, few countries accepted that the circumstances actually justified India's claimed use of force in self-defence,[67] and not a single country argued that India had a right to intervene militarily in order to rescue the beleaguered people of East Pakistan. Although India had not expressly invoked a right to intervene for humanitarian reasons, the countries participating in the debate were well aware of claims of mass murder, and even of genocide, in East Pakistan.[68] Except for the Soviet-bloc countries, states that participated in either the Security Council or General Assembly debates chose to ignore the well-founded claims concerning egregious human rights violations. Many coun-tries emphasized the importance of the principle of nonintervention,[69] and few even addressed the delicate issue of intervention to improve a desperate humanitarian situation. No country did so in the Security Council. And when the matter was transferred to the General Assembly under the Uniting for Peace resolution, the statements of Iran,[70] Jordan,[71] Sweden,[72] and Mauritania[73] can be read as having condemned the idea that an intervention could be legitimate under such circumstances.

New Delhi endeavoured, to some extent, to portray itself as a hapless bystander to the events in East Pakistan that had used military force only reluctantly and in self-defence.[74] Most states were not prepared to accept the argument. That a weakened Pakistan was in India's strategic interest was lost on no one, nor was the fact that India's assistance to the Mukti Bahini over many months had considerably strengthened its fighting capacity against the Pakistani Army. Moreover, the heavy fighting actually made the refugee situation signif-icantly worse. It is also likely that a number of states may have taken the view that India had attacked Pakistan first, which the latter had argued in the Security Council.[75]

Whatever the reasons, no state raised them as grounds for legitimizing the intervention. Moreover, diplomatic support for India's military action was conspicuously absent. The Security Council was blocked by Soviet vetoes, and consideration of the intervention moved to the General Assembly under the Uniting for Peace procedure. Resolution 2793 (XXVI) was passed on December 7 by a vote of 104–11–10. It called for a cease-fire between India and Pakistan and also for the withdrawal of their armed forces from each other's territory. Since there were virtually no Pakistani forces in India, the resolution was, effectively, a call for Indian troops to leave East Pakistan. The resolution, and the call for military forces to return to their own territory, was considered a diplomatic defeat for New Delhi. Nonetheless, Indian troops continued their military campaign in East Pakistan until the Pakistani Army surrendered.

## FRANCE AND BELGIUM'S INTERVENTION IN SHABA PROVINCE, 1978

After infiltrating into Shaba province, a southern province of Zaire, bordering on Angola and Zambia, a rebel force of a few thousand men attempted to seize the town of Kolwezi on May 11, 1978, as part of an ongoing guerrilla campaign to overthrow the government of President Mobutu Sese Soko.[76] Kolwezi was the heart of Zaire's copper-mining industry, which was central to Zaire's foreign exchange earnings, and more than 2,000 Westerners, mostly Belgian and French, lived there. On May 14, the Zairean Government requested assistance in suppressing the rebellion from Belgium, France, the US, China, and Morocco.[77] Two days later, reports that the rebels had murdered some members of the European population began to circulate. Belgium and France decided to mount a rescue operation, and the US agreed to provide the necessary transport.

France had declared that it would mount the rescue operation in close cooperation with Belgium, but French troops actually landed in Kolwezi first, in the early morning of May 19. The French claimed that they had intercepted a radio message from a rebel commander to the effect that Europeans would be killed in the event of a rescue attempt. On learning of the imminent intervention, the rebels murdered about 60 Europeans.

Differences of viewpoints between the French and the Belgians concerning the objective of their intervention soon surfaced. Whereas France declared an intention both to rescue its nationals and to help the Zairean Government restore order, Belgium said its goal was the purely humanitarian one of rescuing its nationals and whomever else among the foreign population who wished to leave.[78]

In a telegram to UN Secretary-General Kurt Waldheim, on May 19, President Mobutu complained about the invasion, which he claimed was supported by Angola. But he would not request a Security Council meeting because he considered the rebellion to be an African affair. As a result, the Security Council did not meet, nor did the OAU. As it happened, the Fifth Franco-African Conference of Heads of State and Government, attended by 20 African countries, was taking place in Paris from May 22 to 23, during the last, more pronouncedly French, phase of the operation. President Eyadema of Togo, speaking for the African states, endorsed the Shaba intervention.[79] Few formal state protests seem to have been made,[80] in contrast to the heated African protests regarding the Stanleyville intervention.[81]

The subsequent debate at a meeting of the OAU in Khartoum demonstrated that African states were divided about the propriety of accepting military help from non-African powers. A number took the view that the essential issue concerning the French–Belgian intervention was not the protection of nationals abroad, but rather a legitimate request from a lawful government.[82]

## VIETNAM'S INTERVENTION IN CAMBODIA, 1978

After a lengthy civil war, the Khmer Rouge came to power in Cambodia in April 1975, with the intention of "purifying" Cambodian politics.[83] Commentators estimate that 1 to 2 million people were murdered by the government or died from malnutrition or disease.[84] Amnesty International (AI) estimated that the figure of those calculatedly murdered, as opposed to those who died in other ways, amounted to hundreds of thousands.[85] Minorities were especially subject to victimization, and "more than half of the total 1975 Cham population of 400,000 was killed."[86] Under the weight of such devastating figures, it seems unnecessary to detail the broad and systematic violations of other rights, such as the right to liberty, freedom from slavery and slave-like practices, the right to a fair trial, the right to privacy and family life, and the right to freedom of expression.[87]

Immediately after their assumption of power, the Khmer Rouge began a series of cross-border attacks on Vietnam. During the summer and autumn of 1978, heavy fighting occurred along the border, with both the Cambodian and the Vietnamese governments blaming the other for acts of aggression. Vietnam ultimately invaded Cambodia with more than 100,000 troops, supported by 20,000 soldiers of the newly formed National United

Front for an Independent, Neutral, Peaceful, and Cooperative Cambodia. The Vietnamese troops quickly overran most of Cambodia, and by January 7, 1979, Phnom Penh fell. On January 8, the United Front formed a People's Revolutionary Council.

Because mass murder in Cambodia had been well documented, by the autumn of 1978, it could be argued that rescuing people from one of the most extraordinary examples of mass murder in the 20th century would be an outstanding example of humanitarian intervention. However, when Vietnam justified its conduct before the Security Council, it did not claim such a right. Rather, Vietnam invoked the right of self-defence because of Khmer Rouge aggression against Vietnam since 1975.[88] What Vietnam termed a "border war" justified its use of force in self-defence. Vietnam argued further that the "inhumane policies" of the Khmer Rouge regime, which had made Cambodia a "living hell," had caused the people of Cambodia to rebel against the regime and that it was this people's uprising which "overthrew the Pol Pot–Ieng Sary clique." There had been, in other words, two wars in Cambodia: "one, the border war started by the Pol Pot–Ieng Sary clique against Viet Nam," with regard to which Vietnam used force in self-defence; and "the other, the revolutionary war of the Kampuchean people."[89] With regard to the second, it was the Cambodian people themselves, Vietnam claimed, who had overthrown the Khmer Rouge regime.

Vietnam therefore did not describe its presence in Cambodia as a use of military force to pursue humanitarian objectives. In fact, Vietnam did not mention its presence in Cambodia at all. In none of the Vietnamese statements to the Security Council did the government acknowledge that Vietnamese forces were actually in Cambodia, let alone a presence of some 100,000 troops. Indeed, the Vietnamese representative referred to the "alleged invasion of the Vietnamese Army."[90] The disingenuousness of the Vietnamese argument undoubtedly stunned most members of the Security Council. However, neither the Soviet Union nor the other Eastern-bloc countries acknowledged the invasion.[91] Each argued that the Cambodian people themselves had overthrown the Khmer Rouge regime.[92] The presence of Vietnamese troops in Cambodia was never formally acknowledged.[93]

The Western countries participating in the debate rejected Vietnam's claim to self-defence, and then went on to address the issue of whether a humanitarian claim could have been legitimate. None of the five NATO countries that spoke – France, Norway, Portugal, the United Kingdom, and the US – thought that Vietnam's intervention could have been justified. Four of them expressly raised the issue of human rights and said emphatically that even massive violations would not have justified military intervention. Given what was known about abuses by the Khmer Rouge, Western responses are worth examining more closely. For instance, Norway said,

> The Norwegian Government and public opinion in Norway have expressed strong objections to the serious violations of human rights committed by the Pol Pot Government. However, the domestic policies of that Government cannot – we repeat, cannot – justify the actions of Vietnam over the last days and weeks. The Norwegian Government firmly rejects the threat or use of force against the territorial integrity or political independence of any State.[94]

France agreed:

> The notion that because a regime is detestable foreign intervention is justified and forcible overthrow is legitimate is extremely dangerous. That could ultimately jeopardize the very maintenance of international law and order

and make the continued existence of various regimes dependent on the judgement of their neighbours. It is important for the Council to affirm, without any ambiguity, that it cannot condone the occupation of a sovereign country by a foreign Power.[95]

Portugal also agreed:

> Neither do we have any doubt about the appalling record of violation of the most basic and elementary human rights in Kampuchea … [Nonetheless], there are no nor can there by any socio-political considerations that would justify the invasion of the territory of a sovereign State by the forces of another State …[96]

The United Kingdom (UK) also put the matter emphatically: "Whatever is said about human rights in Kampuchea, it cannot excuse Vietnam … for violating the territorial integrity of Democratic Kampuchea."[97] Of the other Western states in the debate, Australia also raised the human rights issue and put the matter every bit as categorically as NATO members: "We cannot accept that the internal policies of any Government, no matter how reprehensible, can justify a military attack upon it by another Government."[98]

All five of the Association of Southeast Asian Nations (ASEAN) participating in the Security Council debate argued that Vietnam's intervention was unjustifiable. Given suspicions about Vietnam's long-standing expansionary behaviour in the region, reactions from these neighbouring countries were united in their rejection of the intervention. Only Singapore directly raised the issue of massive human rights violations:

> It has been said by others that the Government of Democratic Kampuchea has treated its people in a barbarous fashion. Whether that accusation is true or false is not the issue before the Council … . No other country has a right to topple the Government of Democratic Kampuchea, however badly that Government may have treated its people.[99]

Without mentioning the human rights situation in Cambodia explicitly, Indonesia argued that, "[W]e may not like, we may even abhor, the political and social system in a country, but that fact cannot justify an armed intervention with the aim of changing that system."[100] Malaysia and the Philippines, not even mentioning the issue of human rights violations directly, argued that intervention was unacceptable for any reason.[101]

Among other countries participating in the debate, Bolivia and Jamaica referred to the issue of massive human rights violations by the Khmer Rouge but argued that they could not justify Vietnam's intervention.[102] Without referring directly to the human rights situation in Cambodia, Nigeria and Yugoslavia both argued that a domestic situation could not be used as a justification for foreign intervention in any form.[103] Bangladesh, Kuwait, Sudan, Gabon, and Zambia emphasized the importance of the nonintervention principle.[104]

The only countries that supported Vietnam's intervention were the Soviet Union and its political allies. Of the remaining 22 states, half directly addressed the issue of whether substantial human rights violations could justify a military intervention and argued emphatically that such violations could not. The debate ended on January 15, when a draft resolution calling for the withdrawal of all foreign (that is, Vietnamese) forces from Cambodia, although supported by 13 members of the Council, was vetoed by the Soviet Union.

Some time later, ASEAN countries requested the inclusion of an agenda item about Cambodia at the next autumn session of the General Assembly. Fifty-two countries presented their views during three full days of debate. Aside from the Socialist bloc and Soviet allies, Vietnam found no support but somewhat shifted the justification for its use of military force. Vietnam continued to claim to the General Assembly that it had acted in self-defence and that the Khmer Rouge regime had been overthrown by the Cambodian people themselves, but now it also admitted that its forces had in fact assisted the Cambodian people in their overthrow of the regime – without, however, at any time acknowledging the massive nature of Vietnamese assistance.[105] Vietnam was, once again, supported by the Soviet Union, other Eastern-bloc countries, a number of Soviet political allies, and Grenada – a total of 17 countries, essentially on the ground that the Khmer Rouge regime had committed aggression against Vietnam.

Particular note should be taken of arguments used by three of Vietnam's supporters, the German Democratic Republic, Laos, and Afghanistan. After detailing Khmer Rouge human rights violations and arguing that such violations had reached genocidal proportions, each state claimed that intervention under such extraordinary circumstances had a legitimate character. For instance, the German Democratic Republic claimed that "the assistance of Vietnam in the struggle for a new Kampuchea was primarily a humanitarian matter. It rescued the Kampuchean people from total destruction." This was one of the few occasions when any state clearly supported the view that the use of military force could be legitimate if it had the humanitarian objective of preventing substantial loss of life of people who were not the intervening state's own nationals.[106]

Approximately 20 states participating in the General Assembly debate directly addressed the issue of whether substantial human rights violations could provide a justification for intervention; and they argued that they could not. In the presidency, Ireland presented the viewpoint of the European Community. The members were aware that "basic human rights" were "grossly violated" by the Khmer Rouge regime, which behaved with "unparalleled brutality." Nonetheless, the violations did not justify Vietnam's intervention, which was "in contravention of fundamental principles of the Charter."[107] Austria, Bhutan, Pakistan, and Zaire agreed, as did the US and Australia, repeating views that they had expressed some months earlier in the Security Council.

On this occasion, the ASEAN states spoke more emphatically about intervention on human rights grounds than they had earlier in the Security Council. In the Council only Singapore had directly addressed human rights, and it had argued that intervention was not permissible, "however badly [the Kampuchean] Government may have treated its people."[108] Singapore was joined in this viewpoint by Indonesia, Malaysia, and the Philippines. Malaysia, for example, argued, "No country has the right to intervene in the affairs of another for whatever reason or on whatever excuse. Admittedly, there is evidence that the Pol Pot government had been committing large scale violations of human rights in Kampuchea." Although Vietnam relied on such claims, according to the delegate, "This is a justification that no self-respecting country could accept. If it were to be accepted, no country could feel secure."[109] If anything, the Philippines put the matter even more emphatically. Having first declared that the Khmer Rouge regime was "genocidal,"[110] the Philippine representative went on to argue,

> At the same time – and we underscore this point – we cannot accept any pretext that armed intervention is necessary, justified and desired on the basis of whatever is happening within a country or under a regime ... . Neither do we agree that a human rights justification, as in the universal

condemnation of Pol Pot and his regime, should be used as a basis to justify political action such as armed intervention and the conquest of a neighbouring State.[111]

At the conclusion of the debate, on November 14, the General Assembly adopted the ASEAN-inspired Resolution 34/22 by a vote of 91–21–29, calling for the immediate withdrawal of foreign forces from Cambodia and appealing to all states to cease interfering in its internal affairs. Although not mentioned by name, the intention was to censure Vietnam, the only country with forces in Cambodia. The resolution was supported by, in addition to ASEAN, all Western countries, most Latin American countries, and a range of others. It was opposed by Vietnam, the Warsaw Pact countries, and such Soviet political allies as Cuba and Ethiopia.[112]

## TANZANIA'S INTERVENTION IN UGANDA, 1979

By the time of his overthrow in April 1979, the government of President Idi Amin was believed to have been responsible for the murder of "at least 100,000 and possibly as many as half a million people."[113] His eight-year regime was marked from the very beginning by repression and brutality. In the early period, the victims were primarily soldiers from the Acholi and Langi ethnic groups because they were assumed to be in favour of the reestablishment of the government of Milton Obote, whom Amin had overthrown in the January 1971 coup d'état.[114] A number of massacres of Acholi and Langi occurred between 1971 and 1973, but in the ensuing years the lack of discipline of the army and other armed agents of the regime was such that by 1977 the violence "had become almost random."[115] As AI was later to report, "the absence of restraint on killings of political opponents and criminal suspects led to many other civilians being seized and killed by members of the security forces for criminal motives or simply quite arbitrarily."[116]

As the former colonial power, Britain maintained close political and economic relations with Uganda, and this led the British press to publish stories of human rights violations. Britain decided to request the 1977 session of the UN Commission on Human Rights to establish an international enquiry into Ugandan human rights violations, and the Commonwealth Heads of Government, meeting in London later, went to the unprecedented length of condemning Uganda on the grounds that the "massive violation of human rights … were so gross as to warrant the world's concern and to evoke condemnation by Heads of Government in strong and unequivocal terms."[117] The World Council of Churches also condemned the regime in 1977, occasioned by Amin's murder of an Anglican archbishop, the regime's harsh treatment of other clergy, and its harassment of Christians generally.[118] The chorus of rising condemnation was supported by a 1978 AI report cataloguing the broad and systematic violation of human rights in Uganda.[119]

Internal opposition also increased. In April 1978, Amin publicly denounced his own vice president and minister of defence, army chief-of-staff, and chief of police. Then, at the end of September and early in October, Amin was forced to suppress mutinies at a number of army bases. Loyal troops pursued some of the mutineering soldiers across the border into Tanzania. Some days later, Amin announced on Ugandan radio that Uganda was annexing the Kagera region of northwest Tanzania. President Julius Nyerere of Tanzania responded by declaring that Uganda's purported annexation of Tanzanian territory was "tantamount to an act of war."[120]

Tanzania began a counterattack in mid-November.[121] By early December, it had pushed the Ugandan forces back across the border into Uganda. In a number of public statements, Amin referred to a "Phase Two" of his operation to annex the Kagera region; and in mid-December Ugandan troops invaded Tanzania a second time. That attack was repulsed, but Ugandan forces once again attacked in January. Nyerere was later to claim that, at this point, a decision was made to pursue the Ugandan forces well into Uganda, back to the army bases at Masaka and Mbarra, and to destroy those bases but that no decision had been made to penetrate further into Uganda.[122]

The rapid advance of the invading Tanzanian troops and Ugandan rebel forces alarmed Amin to the point where, on February 23, he called on "friendly countries in Africa, the Third World, Arabs, socialist countries and the PLO" for support.[123] In an effort to prop up the regime, Libya's Colonel Muammar Ghaddafi sent Libyan troops to Uganda. In early March, the *Nairobi Times* reported that approximately 2,500 Libyan troops had arrived in Uganda.[124] On March 13, Amin publicly announced that Palestinian forces had also joined the struggle on his side. Amin's use of foreign troops convinced Nyerere that Tanzania would not enjoy security unless Amin himself was overthrown. Tanzanian forces were ordered to penetrate deeper into Uganda. Kampala, the capital, fell on April 10, and Amin fled into exile, first to Libya and ultimately to Saudi Arabia.

Despite the regime's egregious violations of human rights and responsibility for the murder of at least tens of thousands of people, at no time did Tanzania advance the claim that its military action was humanitarian. Rather, Nyerere continuously emphasized that there were two wars being fought: "First there are Ugandans fighting to remove the Fascist dictator. Then there are Tanzanians fighting to maintain national security."[125] By this logic, Tanzania was using force in self-defence[126] and Ugandan exiles were fighting in an attempt to overthrow Amin in an exercise of self-determination.

International reaction to Tanzania's intervention was surprisingly muted. Amin wrote to UN Secretary-General Waldheim to ask for a Security Council meeting, but the request was withdrawn some days later.[127] No other member state requested a Security Council meeting. As a result, there was no focused debate at the UN on the validity of the Tanzanian and Ugandan claims and counterclaims concerning the self-defence argument or humanitarian intervention issue.[128]

The OAU discussed the Tanzanian intervention on three separate occasions – the February and July meetings of the Council of Ministers, and then the July meeting of the Heads of State and Government – but with no condemnation of the Tanzanian action. Four front-line states (Angola, Botswana, Mozambique, and Zambia) argued that Tanzania had legitimately used force in self-defence. Only African states with substantial Muslim populations were prepared to offer some support to Uganda's interpretation of events.[129] Libya, Nigeria, and Sudan did not accept the Tanzanian claim of self-defence and accused the government of aggression.

It is a matter of considerable speculation as to why international reaction to the Tanzanian intervention was so muted. It was, after all, the first occasion in the continent's post-colonial history when one state invaded a neighbour and then overthrew its government. Further, the Tanzanian intervention in Uganda came only weeks after the Vietnamese intervention in Cambodia, which had occasioned substantial and acrimonious debate, both in the Security Council and later in the General Assembly. There were certainly a number of factors that might help explain the muted response. The contrast between Tanzania's and Uganda's presidents was striking. Nyerere enjoyed high prestige in Africa and elsewhere as an honourable politician and statesman. Amin, by way of contrast, was regarded in many circles as a liar, buffoon, and even a madman.[130] Tanzania enjoyed an especially high reputation in OAU circles and also at the UN. In addition to matters of reputation and esteem, Nyerere seemed to have given an honest, straightforward, and consistent account of Tanzania's actions. This stands in stark contrast to Vietnam's disingenuous account of its own intervention.

Furthermore, many states simply accepted the claim that Tanzania had acted in self-defence. Certainly, Tanzania was not seen as having greater designs on Uganda or in the region, whereas Vietnam's intervention in Cambodia might have been seen as a hegemonic move on Vietnam's part[131] or, even worse for some, as part of a greater Soviet design, with Vietnam as a surrogate.[132] This was certainly not the case with Tanzania's intervention in Uganda. At this particular stage in the Cold War strategic balance, Uganda was beyond the periphery of the East–West rivalry.

Finally, since African countries were silent, other states may have felt disinclined to raise the matter. Whatever the reasons, Tanzania's intervention met with little protest. States began to establish diplomatic relations with the new Ugandan Government relatively quickly, and it was accredited at the autumn session of the General Assembly, very much in contrast to the situation of the Heng Samrin regime in Cambodia, whose credentials were denied in favour of those of the odious, overthrown Pol Pot regime by a vote of 71–35–34.[133]

## FRANCE'S INTERVENTION IN CENTRAL AFRICA, 1979

On the night of September 20, 1979, French troops invaded the Central African Empire and overthrew the government of self-proclaimed Emperor Jean-Bedel Bokassa while he was on a state visit to Libya.[134] The government's human rights record was abysmal. Political rights as such were barely recognized, there was substantial censorship of the press, and political prisoners were commonly tortured. The murder of dissidents became increasingly commonplace.

The catalyst for the French intervention was the regime's murder of secondary-school children in January and again in April. In January, Bokassa had issued an imperial decree making it compulsory for secondary-school children to wear a special uniform, manufactured in a factory owned by one of Bokassa's wives. The children held a public demonstration, and rioting later ensued. The army moved in to quell the disturbances and ultimately opened fire on some of the demonstrators. It is estimated that 150 to 200 school children were killed. Opposition to the government intensified, and in April secondary and university students began a general strike. Bokassa ordered a roundup of dissidents, and the students were brought to Ngaragba prison, where approximately 100 of them were tortured and then murdered over the next few days. It was alleged that Bokassa had personally taken part in the torture and killings. AI released the news of the murders and set up a Commission of Inquiry, composed of judges from five African countries, which reported in mid-August that the murders had in fact occurred and that Bokassa himself had "almost certainly" participated in them.[135]

Bokassa had become an extreme embarrassment to France,[136] which had been the principal support of successive Central African governments since independence in 1960.[137] With the murder of school children, the government's deteriorating human rights record had assumed grotesque proportions. Sometime in the summer, Paris decided that Bokassa had to be removed.[138] Taking advantage of his absence, the French government engineered a bloodless coup. Eighteen hundred French troops flew in and took over Bangui, the capital, in a matter of hours. At first, France tried to make it appear that the troops were invited by the new government of David Dacko, the former president, whom Bokassa had himself overthrown by coup d'état in 1966. But it soon emerged that the new government had in fact been brought to power by the French intervention.

International reaction was muted. Neither the UN nor the OAU formally debated the intervention, and few states even issued public comments. Burundi issued a statement praising the intervention, while Benin, Chad, and Libya condemned it.[139] Although France's intervention occurred literally a few days before the General Assembly's opening, during the general debate only Libya raised the issue.[140] Twenty-five member states, however, took the opportunity to comment on Vietnam's intervention in Cambodia.[141]

The Central African Empire was a small and desperately poor country, with France, the former colonial power, believed to be providing more than half the annual budget. Moreover, Bokassa had an increasingly embarrassing human rights record and had few remaining political allies in Africa or elsewhere. The closest political supporter of the self-proclaimed emperor had been Idi Amin, who had been overthrown himself some months before.

## THE US'S INTERVENTION IN GRENADA, 1983

On October 13, 1983, a coup d'état occurred on the tiny Caribbean island of Grenada, and Prime Minister Maurice Bishop was put under house arrest, as were some of his cabinet colleagues two days later.[142] On October 17, a crowd of Grenadians rescued Bishop and then tried to rescue the detained members of his cabinet. In the ensuing melee, Bishop and three cabinet ministers were killed, along with more than a dozen others. A 96-hour shoot-on-sight curfew was imposed.[143] The coup itself, followed afterwards by the murder of the prime minister and members of his cabinet, sent shock waves throughout the Caribbean. Meeting in Barbados on October 21 to discuss the implications for regional security, the prime ministers of the Organization of Eastern Caribbean States (OECS) requested US assistance.[144]

Four days later, approximately 2,000 US troops and 300 from neighbouring Caribbean countries landed in Grenada and subdued the forces of the coup leaders, after three days of surprisingly stiff resistance. On the day of the invasion itself, the OECS countries issued a press statement setting out their justifications for the military action.[145] It indicated that the intervention had become necessary for a number of reasons: the fear that there would be "further loss of life" and a "general deterioration of public order," that the new ruling authorities would "further suppress the population of Grenada," and that the "disproportionate military strength" of the new ruling authorities "posed a serious threat to the security of the OECS countries." In the opinion of these OECS countries, well-founded fears justified a "pre-emptive defensive strike," the legality of which was grounded in an invitation from the Grenadian governor-general and in the provisions of Article 8 of the OECS Treaty dealing with collective defence.

Two of the justifications for the intervention – the need to prevent further loss of life and suppression of the rights of Grenadians – represent quintessentially humanitarian claims.[146] In fact, the rationale of responding to the suppression of the rights of Grenadians went much further than previous grounds for humanitarian intervention. Elements of this wider humanitarian rationale were later used by some of the intervening states in their statements to the Security Council and the General Assembly. For example, Jamaica argued at one stage before the Council that "we are there to assist the people of Grenada to free themselves from a military dictatorship and to establish conditions within which it might be possible for the will of the people to be displayed in free elections."[147] This humanitarian claim initially seemed to be endorsed by the US, when its permanent representative, Ambassador Jeane Kirkpatrick, argued the next day that "the prohibitions against the use of force in the Charter are contextual, not absolute. They provide justification for the use of force in pursuit of other values also inscribed in the Charter, such values as freedom, democracy, peace."[148] In the subsequent General Assembly debate, Kirkpatrick returned to the theme, arguing that the use of force was lawful because it was carried out "in the service of values of the Charter, including the restoration of the rule of law, self-determination, sovereignty, democracy and respect for the human rights of the people of Grenada."[149]

This broader humanitarian argument attracted no supporters other than the intervening states themselves. And Washington later backed away as well. A letter sent by the State Department's legal adviser to the American Bar Association stated that, "[W]e did not assert a broad new doctrine of 'humanitarian intervention.' We relied instead on the narrowest, well-established ground of protection of US nationals."[150]

The narrower version of the humanitarian claim by the OECS countries – intervention to prevent loss of life – was not accepted by the vast majority of UN member states. There had been approximately 18 deaths in the week following the coup, most of them after the attempt by Bishop's supporters to free the now-deceased prime minister and his cabinet colleagues. The harsh shoot-on-sight curfew had ensured that Grenada remained quiet, if tense, since that time. Whatever the claims about the need to guard against further loss of life, Security Council statements by most of the Caribbean countries made clear that the essential reason for the intervention was the perceived need to preempt a threat to the security of the region.[151]

In addition to supporting the OECS motivations, the US added a more precise one, the protection of its own nationals. Kirkpatrick said that her country was "deeply concerned" by the shoot-on-sight curfew, which "constituted a clear and present danger to the security, safety and well-being of … the Americans," and that the alarming circumstances of this additional concern also justified the US in taking military action.[152] Many legal commentators have cast doubt on the appropriateness of this justification.[153] While the political situation in post-coup Grenada was uncertain, there seemed to have been no real danger to US or other nationals.[154] Like the Grenadians themselves, they were subject to the strict curfew, but certainly no direct threats were made against them. Subsequent research has shown that senior policy makers in Washington saw the unsettled political situation as a tactical opportunity to influence the authority structure in Grenada, rather than as a desperate situation for US nationals.[155]

The US later vetoed a resolution condemning the intervention. Interestingly, it was supported by two NATO allies, France and the Netherlands. When an almost identical resolution was voted on in the General Assembly, Washington's isolation became even more apparent. The only states voting against Resolution 38/7, which called the intervention "a flagrant violation of international law" and called for the "immediate withdrawal of foreign troops," were the invading countries, plus Israel and El Salvador. The resolution was passed by a vote of 108–9–27. Nine NATO allies – Denmark, France, Greece, Iceland, Italy, the Netherlands, Norway, Portugal, and Spain – argued that the intervention was unlawful, while the other members abstained.

Debate in both the Security Council and the General Assembly did not clarify whether those condemning the intervention believed that a unilateral use of military force to rescue endangered nationals abroad (or for the broader, OECS–US-declared purpose of preventing the further suppression of the rights of Grenadians) was unlawful, or whether the situation in Grenada was an invalid exercise of such a right.[156] For instance, The Netherlands representative stated, "[M]y delegation is of the view that the action taken cannot be considered compatible with the basic principles of the Charter of the United Nations."[157] However, the General Assembly overwhelmingly condemned the Grenada intervention as unlawful. Apart from the intervening states, none spoke in favour of a right of humanitarian intervention.

## THE US'S INTERVENTION IN PANAMA, 1989

On December 20, 1989, a US invasion force of 24,000 troops intervened in Panama to dislodge the regime of General Manuel Noriega.[158] The fighting lasted only a few days, after which Noriega was overthrown and brought to the US to face prosecution on drug-trafficking charges. Independent human rights organizations, such as the Commission for the Defense of Human Rights in Central America, estimate that during the intervention between 1,000 and 4,000 Panamanian civilians were killed and thousands wounded.[159]

At the request of Nicaragua, the Security Council met on the evening of the invasion to consider Nicaragua's claim that the US action was an unlawful act of aggression.[160] In a letter to the Security Council's president earlier in the day, the US reported that its military action had been taken in self-defence, in response to what it claimed were repeated attacks by Panamanian armed forces on US nationals.[161] The last such incidents, on December 16, resulted in the death of a US serviceman, the wounding of another, and the beating of a third. In his opening remarks to the Security Council, US Permanent Representative Thomas Pickering said that "the action is designed to protect American lives as well as to fulfil the obligations of the United States to defend the integrity of the Panama Canal Treaties."[162]

During the invasion, Washington's policy makers presented a mix of legal justifications and motives for the military action. Legal commentators since have commingled justifications and motives as though they were one and the same.[163] Speaking on national television hours after the invasion had been launched, President George Bush declared that the military action had a number of objectives: to protect US nationals in Panama, to help fulfill obligations under the Panama Canal Treaties, and to combat drug trafficking by ensuring the prosecution of Noriega.[164] In addition, he also included helping to restore democracy in Panama. In his statements to the Security Council, Pickering endeavoured to distinguish US legal justifications and objectives. He declared that the US interest in restoring democracy was an important goal but not a legal basis for the military action. The legal adviser to the State Department later declared that it did provide a legal basis:

> The United States does not accept the notion that a State is entitled to use force to overthrow the dictator of another State, however mad or cruel. The substantial respect accorded the doctrine of humanitarian intervention, however, reflects the fact that the advancement of human rights and of democratic self-determination are legitimate objectives of our international system. Panama presented a strong case for humanitarian intervention.[165]

This claim appears bolder than the variant asserted by some of the intervening states in Grenada. An assertion of a right to use military force to promote democratic and human rights values is clearly a broader and more expansive claim than one to protect human life.

Whatever legal consequences might be said to arise from the difference between US legal justifications and goals, UN member states were in no mood to split hairs. Other than the US itself, of the 19 states that made statements in the Security Council, 14 condemned the intervention as unlawful on the basis of the peremptory character of international norms related to nonintervention and to the nonuse of force. Finland and France regarded the intervention as unjustified because the circumstances did not warrant it.[166] Only Canada and the UK spoke in support of the legitimacy of the intervention, but they were imprecise about which elements of the US argument they approved.[167] A draft Security Council resolution condemning the invasion as contrary to international law was vetoed by Washington. An almost identical resolution was put to the General Assembly some days later, which voted 75–20–40 to condemn the invasion as a "flagrant violation of international law."[168] With the exceptions of Austria, Finland, Spain, and Sweden – which voted with the majority to censure the US – the rest of the Western world either voted against the resolution or abstained. The Soviet Union and its political allies voted in favour of the resolution, as did almost every Latin American country.[169] All of the African and Asian states either voted with the majority in censuring the US or abstained. OAS disapproval was even more apparent than at the UN. The OAS voted to censure the intervention by a vote of 20–1–5, with only the US voting against the resolution.

## AN OVERVIEW OF PRE-1990 INTERVENTIONS

Striking paradoxes arise from an analysis of interventions during the first 45 years of the Charter regime. Humanitarian justifications were most robust in cases where purely humanitarian motives were weakest. The protection of one's nationals was less "humanitarian," or more overtly self-interested, than the protection of nationals from another state. In a number of cases, even the protection of nationals was more of a smoke screen than a genuine motivation. During this period, the outright abuse of humanitarian justifications seemed to be a common feature of state practice. A recent study by the Danish Institute of International Affairs concluded that "judging from the experience of more than 150 years of practice, in which humanitarian considerations have been invoked to justify intervention, it is obvious that the doctrine gives room for abuse. This raises the question of the justifiability of the doctrine as applied to real life."[170]

The cases from this period demonstrate that powerful states have a long history of fabricating and employing tendentious legal arguments to rationalize intervention in weaker states. The argument, therefore, that the promotion of an international regime of humanitarian intervention would give interveners a legal pretext ignores one fact. Strong states which are – for reasons good or bad – determined to intervene in a weak state have no shortage of legal rationalizations for their actions.

If most of the self-proclaimed humanitarian interventions were of dubious legitimacy, several interventions where self-defence was invoked could have just as easily been based on humanitarian grounds. Although the invocation of humanitarian claims in the most egregious of the episodes would have been appropriate – in East Pakistan's mass murders in 1971, in Idi Amin's Uganda throughout the 1970s, and in Pol Pot's Cambodia in the late 1970s – intervening states chose to frame the legitimacy of their respective interventions on the grounds of self-defence. Furthermore, few other states raised the issue in international debates. Certainly the strongest contemporary advocates – NATO members – categorically rejected the existence of a norm of humanitarian intervention. In fact, these countries continued to recognize the Khmer Rouge as the representative of Cambodia at the UN for another decade. Ironically, the modest support that did exist came from unlikely quarters: Afghanistan, Laos, and the German Democratic Republic.

In retrospect, these three cases have become clear examples of the necessity – and even legitimacy – of humanitarian intervention, even though few such arguments were made at the time. There may have been some reluctance to set a precedent that others could also use against weaker states. As one sceptic has summarized, "Although they bowed in the direction of humanitarianism, the interventionist leaders involved in these episodes justified their actions on conventional grounds of self-defence."[171]

These interventions were motivated by the "internal character of the regimes they acted against. And history has by and large ratified that verdict," according to UN Secretary-General Kofi Annan. However, "few would now deny that in those cases intervention was a lesser evil than allowing the massacres to continue."[172] Interestingly, each case also challenges the conventional wisdom that disinterested, multilateral humanitarian interventions necessarily produce greater benefits to populations in distress than ones that are self-interested and undertaken by a state acting alone.

The failure of intervening states and their supporters to make additional use of a humanitarian justification may suggest either that such a norm was not considered to exist or that it was regarded as so contentious that it was necessary to justify the conduct on entirely different grounds. The failure to raise the humanitarian argument directly should not be overstated. There were, after all, very few instances in which it could have been raised with any real possibility of successfully mobilizing support. For many episodes, the threshold requirement of the existence or likelihood of substantial loss of life, however ambiguous a criterion that might be, could not be said to have been reached.

On balance, state practice from 1945 to 1990 reveals little support for a right of humanitarian intervention. This survey of state practice thus adds support to the international legal commentators who argue that military intervention without Security Council approval, even on humanitarian grounds, was prohibited by the UN Charter during the Cold War.[173] Revisionist historians, however, might be tempted to pose a counterfactual: "What would have been the international reaction to these cases had they occurred in the 1990s rather than before?"

## NOTES

1   For a review of these cases and others, see Simon Chesterman, *Just War or Just Peace?: Humanitarian Intervention and International Law* (New York: Oxford University Press, 2001); Nicholas J. Wheeler, *Saving Strangers: Humanitarian Intervention in International Society* (Oxford: Oxford University Press, 2000); Francis Kofi Abiew, *The Evolution of the Doctrine and Practice of Humanitarian Intervention* (The Hague: Kluwer Law International, 1999); Fernando Tesón, *Humanitarian Intervention. An Inquiry into Law and Morality*, 2nd ed. (Irvington-on-Hudson: Transnational Publishers, 1997); and Sean D. Murphy, *Humanitarian Intervention: The United Nations in an Evolving World Order* (Philadelphia: University of Pennsylvania Press, 1996).

2   *Keesing's Contemporary Archives* (1960), pp. 17639–17650 and pp. 17753–17761. Also, see Catherine Hoskyns, *The Congo since Independence* (London: Oxford University Press, 1965), pp. 85–139; Ernest W. Lefever, *Crisis in the Congo* (Washington: Brookings Institution, 1965), pp. 6–20; and Georges Abi-Saab, *The United Nations Operation in the Congo, 1960–1964* (Oxford: Oxford University Press, 1978), pp. 6–14 and 21–24.

3   Lefever, *Crisis*, p. 11.

4   UN Document S/4382, July 13, 1960.

5   UN Document S/PV. 873, July 13, 1960, p. 34.

6   Ibid., p. 35.

7   UN Document, S/PV.877, July 20–21, 1960, pp. 22–23. Also, see UN Document, S/PV.873, pp. 18, 29; and UN Document S/PV.879, pp. July 21–22, 1960, p. 28. As Belgium emphasized the right to protect its own nationals, most commentators do not categorize this episode as one of humanitarian intervention. See, for example, Ronzitti, *Rescuing Nationals*, p. 3; and Christine Gray, *International Law and the Use of Force* (Oxford: Oxford University Press, 2000), pp. 1 and 108.

8   UN Document, S/PV.873, July 13, 1960, p. 28.

9   Ibid., pp. 25–26.

10  Ibid., pp. 23–24.

11  Ibid., p. 15.

12  For the Soviet Union, see UN Document S/PV.873, July 13, 1960, pp. 16–21 passim; and for Poland, see, for example, UN Document S/PV. 878, July 21, 1960, pp. 18–19.

13   "We have always defended strongly the principle that danger to life or property of foreign residents – even if it was real – cannot constitute any justification for military aggression from outside." UN Document, S/PV.878, July 21, 1960, p. 19.

14   See UN Document S/PV.878, July 21, 1960, p. 5; and UN Document S/PV.879, July 21–22, 1960, p. 17.

15   *Yearbook of the United Nations* 14 (New York: United Nations, 1960), p. 97. Nationalist China, France, and the UK abstained.

16   Hoskyns, *Congo since Independence*, p. 117.

17   For a discussion of the calculatedly ambiguous elements of the resolution, see ibid., pp. 117–119.

18   Alan James, *The Politics of Peacekeeping* (London: Chatto & Windus, 1969), p. 355.

19   *Keesing's Contemporary Archives* (1965), pp.20561–20566. See Fred E. Wagoner, *Dragon Rouge: The Rescue of Hostages in the Congo* (Washington, DC: Government Printing Office, 1980); and Peter J. Schraeder, *United States Policy toward Africa* (Cambridge: Cambridge University Press, 1994), pp. 59–74. For analysis of the claims and counterclaims regarding the legitimacy of the intervention, see Howard L. Weisberg, "Note: The Congo Crisis 1964: A Case Study in Humanitarian Intervention," *Virginia Journal of International Law* 12 (1972), p. 261; and Alain Gerard, "L'opération Stanleyville-Paulis devant le Parlement belge et les Nations Unies," *Revue Belge de Droit International* 3 (1967), p. 242.

20   See Wagoner, *Dragon Rouge*, p. 16.

21   See Schraeder, *United States Foreign Policy towards Africa*, p. 70.

22   Wagoner, *Dragon Rouge*, pp. 44–45 and 67–68.

23   These conditions were later discussed by Belgian Foreign Minister Paul-Henri Spaak, when he made his opening statement to the Security Council. See UN Document S/PV.1173, December 11, 1964, p. 8.

24   This was later to be contested angrily by the Organization of African Unity ad hoc Commission, chaired by the prime minister of Kenya, Jomo Kenyatta, which had been set up to try to secure a truce between the warring sides, as well as to negotiate the release of the hostages.

25   For the text of the Belgian letter, see S/6063. For the text of the American letter, see S/6062.

26   See Wagoner, *Dragon Rouge*, p. 198. This was also the view of many of the African countries participating in the Security Council debate. See the views of Ghana, UN Document S/PV.1170, December 9, 1964, p. 22; Sudan (quoting from the *New York Times*), ibid., pp. 29–30; Guinea, UN Document S/PV.1171, December 10, 1964, pp. 6–7; Algeria, UN Document, S/PV.1172, December 10, 1964, p. 3; and Egypt, UN Document S.PV.1174, December 14, 1964, pp. 5–6.

27   See UN Document S/6076 and Add. 1–5.

28   For a journalist's account of the acrimony of the debate, in the light of other debates in the Council's his-tory, see Andrew Boyd, *Fifteen Men on a Powder Keg* (London: Methuen, 1971), pp. 178–185.

29   See, for instance, the comment by Mali: "It is another piece of legalistic quibbling to speak to us about the legality of the Tshombe Government. Will we also be told one day about the legality of the fascist and racist States of southern Africa – whether it be Southern Rhodesia or South Africa?" UN Document S/PV. 1171, December 10, 1964, pp. 16–17.

30   UN Document S/PV.1174, December 14, 1964, p. 9. Also see, for example, the views of Mali, UN Document S/PV.1171, December 10, 1964, p. 14; and Algeria, UN Document S/PV. 1172, December 10, 1964, pp. 5–6.

31   See, for instance, the comments by Ghana, UN Document S/PV.1170, December 9, 1964, p. 18; Guinea, UN Document S/PV.1171, December 10, 1964, p. 6; Mali, UN Document S/PV.1171., December 10, 1964, p. 14; and Algeria, UN Document S/PV.1172, December 10, 1964, p. 3.

32   Algeria, UN Document S/PV.1172, December 10, 1964, p. 3.

33   See, for instance, the comment by Sudan: "We do not look with favour on this demonstration of distrust by Western Powers – distrust in the ability and the will of African organizations and African statesmen to ward off conflicts and violence." UN Document S/PV.1170, December 9, p. 30. Also see, for example, the comments by Guinea, UN Document S/PV.1171, pp. 3 and 6; and Mali, UN Document S/PV.1171, p. 9.

34   The seemingly racist undertone of the intervention clearly outraged many African countries. See the acid comment by the Guinean representative, UN Document, S/PV.1171, p. 6. "The Belgian, South African and Rhodesian mercenaries ... have massacred hundreds upon hundreds of defenseless Congolese civilians ... . The so-called civilized Government and countries which today denounce what they call rebel atrocities did not then express any indignation. Then, there was no question of humanitarian motives. Is it because the thousands of Congolese civilians who have been murdered by the South Africans, Rhodesians, Belgians and Cuban refugee adventurers had dark skins like the coloured United States citizens who were murdered in Mississippi?" See also the comments by the Congo (Brazzaville), UN Document S/PV.1170, December 9, 1964, p. 15; and Algeria, UN Document S/PV.1172, December 10, 1964, pp. 8–9.

35   UN Document S/PV.1173, December 11, 1964, p. 14.

36   UN Document S/PV.1174, December 14, 1964, p. 11.

37   UN Document S/PV.1173, p. 3.

38   UN Document S/PV.1174, p. 13.

39   UN Document S/PV.1173, p. 38.

40   See Abraham F. Lowenthal, *The Dominican Intervention* (Baltimore: The Johns Hopkins University Press, 1995 edition with new preface); Jerome Slater, *Intervention and Negotiation: The United States and the Dominican Revolution* (New York: Harper & Row, 1970); John Carey, ed., *The Dominican Crisis* (Dobbs Ferry: Oceana, 1967); and Richard J. Barnet, *Intervention and Revolution: The United States in the Third World* (New York: World Publishing Company, 1971), pp. 153–180.

41   As quoted in Abram Chayes, Thomas Ehrlich, and Andreas F. Lowenfeld, *International Legal Process* (Boston: Little, Brown & Co., 1968), p. 1161.

42   Slater, *Intervention and Negotiation*, p. 31, argues that, "There is not the slightest doubt that the primary, indeed the overwhelming, factor in the US decision to intervene was the belief in both the embassy and the State Department that the apparently imminent constitutionalist victory would pose an unacceptable risk of a Communist takeover." See also Barnet, *Intervention and Revolution*, p. 172.

43   Ibid., pp. 174–175.

44   UN Document S/6316.

45   UN Document S/PV.1196, May 3, 1965, p. 19.

46   UN Document S/PV.1202, May 6, 1965, p. 4.

47   UN Document S/PV.1198, May 4, 1965, p. 13 (Britain); and UN Document S/PV.1203, May 7, 1965, p. 2 (Netherlands).

48   For the first of the many Soviet statements in this regard, see UN Document S/PV.1196, May 3, 1965, pp. 2–11; for the first of the Cuban statements, see ibid., pp. 19–37.

49   UN Document S/PV.1200, May 5, 1965, p. 5.

50   The text of Johnson's statement can be found in Chayes et al., *International Legal Process*, pp. 1168–1170.

51   UN Document, S.PV.1198, May 4, 1965, p. 24.

52   Ibid., pp. 2–6.

53   When the Security Council debate on the Dominican crisis resumed later in May, the Soviet Union pressed for a vote on its draft resolution condemning the US intervention. The Soviet draft received virtually no support except from Jordan. *Yearbook of the United Nations 19* (New York: United Nations, 1965), p. 156.

54   For a brief account of the Indian intervention, see *Keesing's Contemporary Archives* (1971), pp. 24989–24996; and *Keesing's Contemporary Archives* (1972), pp. 25053–25058 and 25069–25074. For an account of the war and the diplomatic manoeuvres, see Richard Sisson and Leo E. Rose, *War and Secession: Pakistan, India, and the Creation of Bangladesh* (Berkeley: University of California Press, 1990); and Robert Jackson, *South Asian Crisis: India–Pakistan–Bangladesh* (London: Chatto & Windus, 1975). For an account of the human rights situation, see International Commission of Jurists, *The Events in East Pakistan* (Geneva: International Court of Justice Secretariat, 1972). For a shortened version of the study, see *The Review of the International Commission of Jurists* 8 (July 1972), pp. 23–62.

55    For the text of the Indian Parliament's resolution, see *Keesing's Contemporary Archives* (1971), p. 24597: "This House calls upon all peoples and Governments of the world to take urgent and constructive steps to prevail upon the Government of Pakistan to put an end immediately to the systematic decimation of people, which amounts to genocide." See also Leo Kuper, *Genocide: Its Political Use in the Twentieth Century* (New Haven: Yale University Press, 1981), pp. 78–80 and 173–174, especially p. 173: "one of the major genocides of the twentieth century."

56    "There is overwhelming evidence that Hindus were slaughtered and their houses and villages destroyed simply because they were Hindus … . In our view there is a strong prima facie case that the crime of genocide was committed against the group comprising the Hindu population of East Bengal." International Commission of Jurists, *The Events in East Pakistan*, p. 57.

57    Ibid., pp. 26–27.

58    See D.K. Palit, *The Lightning Campaign: The Indo-Pakistan War 1971* (Salisbury: Compton, 1972), p. 38; and Sisson and Rose, *War and Secession*, pp. 178–181 and 206.

59    By November 24 Prime Minister Gandhi reported to the Indian Parliament that "we have lodged 66 protests for border violations covering 890 incidents. For air violations we have lodged seventeen protests covering fifty incidents." *Keesing's Contemporary Archives* (1971), p. 24995.

60    *Keesing's Contemporary Archives*, ibid., p. 25053.

61    See the Indian representative's remarks during the opening debate in the Security Council on December 4: "This is the fourth time Pakistan has committed aggression against India … . We reserve our right to take … all appropriate and necessary measures to safeguard our security and defense against aggression from Pakistan." UN Document S/PV.1606, December 6, 1971, p. 32.

62    UN Document S/PV.1606, December 6, 1971, p. 17, 15. Many commentators agreed that the burden placed on India was intolerable. See, for instance, the assessment by the International Commission of Jurists, *The Review of the International Commission of Jurists*, pp. 58–59. "We consider that India's armed intervention would have been justified if she had acted under the doctrine of humanitarian intervention." Ibid., p. 96.

63    UN Document S/PV.1606, December 6, 1971, p. 25; and UN Document S/PV.1615, December 15, 1971, p. 5.

64    UN Document S/PV.1606, December 6, 1971, pp.17–18. India's essential justification of self-defence was not a little obscured by the fact that the Indian representative discussed it as the second consideration, after having first argued that "we shall not be a party to any solution that will mean continuation of oppression of the East Pakistan people … . So long as we have any light of civilized behaviour left in us, we shall protect them." He then went on to say: "Secondly, we shall continue to save our own national security and sovereignty." On a number of other occasions, too, the Indian representative made a brief self-defence claim, only after having spoken at much greater length about atrocities in East Pakistan. See, for example, UN Document S/PV.1608, December 6, 1971, pp. 27–28; and UN Document S/PV.1611, December 12, 1971, pp. 4–14.

65    See UN Document S/PV.1611, December 12, 1971, p. 9: "On 3 December … Pakistan carried out a pre-meditated and massive aggression against India … . The Pakistani Air Force had carried out an extensive and unprovoked air strike against our cities and major air bases in northern India … . We later learned that this was an air strike carried out … in the hope of destroying our air force as a prelude to launching a full-scale ground attack against us"; also see UN Document S/PV.1613, December 13, 1971, p. 22.

66    See the Indian representative's comments in the Security Council in UN Document S/PV.1607, December 5, 1971, p. 18; UN Document S/PV.1608, December 6, 1971, pp. 8–9; UN Document S/PV.1613, December 13, 1971, p. 21, 23; and UN Document S/PV.1621, December 21, 1971, pp. 11–12. Also see the General Assembly, GAOR, 26th Session, 2003rd meeting, December 7, 1971, pp. 13–17.

67    Only the Soviet Union and some Eastern-bloc countries (Bulgaria, Czechoslovakia, Hungary, and Poland), as well as a few Soviet allies (Cuba and Mongolia) and Bhutan, offered support for the Indian case.

68    For example, on December 5, the first day of the debate in the Security Council, the Indian representative read out an excerpt from the current issue of *Foreign Affairs*, where *New York Times* journalist, Sydney Schanberg, claimed that "at this time of writing, foreign diplomats estimate that the army has killed at least 200,000 Bengalis." UN Document S/PV.1607, December 5, 1971, p. 18.

69   See the comments made during the General Assembly debate by Argentina (pp. 4–5), Ghana (pp. 5–6), Indonesia (p. 7), and Turkey (p. 7). GAOR, 2002nd meeting, December 7, 1971. And also Algeria (p. 2), Ceylon (p. 3), Lebanon (p. 5), Sudan (p. 8), Togo (p. 19), Madagascar (p. 20), Tanzania (p. 22), Nepal (p. 22), and Burundi (p. 31). GAOR, 2003rd meeting, December 7, 1971.

70   The Iranian representative stated that "no matter how grave has been the situation in Pakistan with regard to the humanitarian question of the refugees, nothing can justify armed action against the territorial integrity of a Member State." GAOR, 26th Session, 2003rd Plenary Meeting, December 7, 1971, p. 5.

71   The Jordanian representative put the matter even more delicately still and argued that "regardless of the merits and origin of the present conflict, there can be no justification for the armed intervention of one State in the territory of another." Ibid., p. 12.

72   The Swedish representative was more direct. After referring to Swedish awareness of the background to the war and to refugees having fled "terror in East Pakistan," he went on to argue that "the Charter of the United Nations forbids the use of force except in self-defense. No other purpose can justify the use of military force by States." Ibid., p. 27.

73   The Mauritanian representative returned to delicacy, simply arguing that "it seems to us dangerous to condone the idea that one State, regardless of its reasons, can interfere in the domestic affairs of another State." Ibid., p. 28.

74   For instance, the Indian representative in the Security Council downplayed India's substantial assistance over many months to the Mukti Bahini. On support to the Mukti Bahini, see Palit, *The Lightening Campaign*, pp. 76–78; and Sisson and Rose, *War and Secession*, pp. 210–211.

75   Pakistan claimed that the war had broken out on November 21, when Indian forces launched a number of attacks along the Indian border with East Pakistan and (contrary to Indian claims) did not then withdraw. UN Document S/PV.1606, December 4, 1971, p. 7. See also Sisson and Rose, *War and Secession*, p. 213.

76   *Keesing's Contemporary Archives* (1978), pp. 29125–29131; *African Research Bulletin* (1978), pp. 4854-4862 and 4890-4895; X *Africa Contemporary Record* (1977–78), pp. A88 and B589–B591. For brief comments, see Ronzitti, *Rescuing Nationals*, pp. 79–80; Alain Manin, "L'intervention française au Shaba," *Annuaire français de droit international* 24 (1978), p. 159. Many legal commentators ignore the Shaba intervention, since Belgium and France intervened at the request of the Congolese Government.

77   *Keesing's Contemporary Archives* (1978), p. 29125.

78   Belgium was quick to put a cynical interpretation on France's more expansive interpretation of its objectives. Senior Belgian policy makers became convinced that France "was using its military intervention as a pretext for expanding its influence in Shaba, which is among the richest mineral areas of Africa." *New York Times*, May 23, 1978, p. A1.

79   Ibid., p. A14.

80   But the intervention occasioned a very substantial debate at the July meeting of the Organization of African Unity leaders in Khartoum over the increasing tendency of African leaders to invite non-African powers to help them resolve internal conflicts. For a detailed discussion, see Zdenek Cervenka and Colin Legum, "The Organisation of African Unity in 1978: The Challenge of Foreign Intervention," XI *Africa Contemporary Record* (1978–79), pp. A25–A39.

81   US commercial interest in Congo was not very substantial. The Stanleyville intervention was seen much more in the geopolitical light of Cold War rivalry.

82   Cervenka and Legum, "The Organization of African Unity in 1978," p. A34.

83   For a brief account of Vietnam's intervention in Cambodia, see *Keesing's Contemporary Archives* (1979), pp. 29613–29621. For accounts of the human rights situation during the Khmer Rouge regime, see Michael Vickery, *Cambodia, 1975–1982* (Chiang Mai: Silkworm Books, 1999); Ben Kiernan, *The Pol Pot Regime* (New Haven: Yale University Press, 1996); David Chandler, *The Tragedy of Cambodian History* (New Haven: Yale University Press, 1991); and Amnesty International, *Political Killings by Governments* (London: Amnesty International, 1983), pp. 38–43.

84 Ronzitti, *Rescuing Nationals*, p. 98, uses the figure of 2 million people. Arend and Beck, *International Law and the Use of Force*, p. 121, citing different sources, use the figure of 1 million people. The Amnesty International study, *Political Killings by Governments*, pp. 38–43, does not cite a total figure. Scholars of Cambodian history are in some dispute themselves concerning the actual number of deaths. In an exceptionally detailed analysis of the issue, Kiernan, *The Pol Pot Regime*, p. 460, uses a figure of 1.5 million and argues that "there is no reason to believe that the killing would have slowed, had it not been stopped by the Vietnamese army." Vickery, *Cambodia*, believes that the figure is approximately 750,000. Chandler, *Tragedy of Cambodian History*, p. 236, cites a figure of "over a million."

85 Amnesty International, *Political Killings by Governments*.

86 Ibid., p. 42.

87 See Kiernan, *The Pol Pot Regime*, passim. For a summary treatment, see Chandler, *Tragedy of Cambodian History*, pp. 236–272; and Grant Evans and Kelvin Rowley, *Red Brotherhood at War: Vietnam, Cambodia and Laos*, 2nd ed. (London: Verso, 1990), pp. 92–102.

88 "As regards the border war between Vietnam and Kampuchea, the Pol Pot–Ieng Sary clique started it very early, immediately after the liberation of Phnom Penh early in 1975." UN Document, S/PV.2108, January 11, 1979, p. 12.

89 Stephen J. Morris, *Why Vietnam Invaded Cambodia* (Stanford: Stanford University Press, 1999), pp. 12–13.

90 UN Document, S/PV. 2110, January 13, 1979, p. 9.

91 In fact, in his first statement to the Security Council, the Soviet representative referred to the Khmer Rouge claim that Vietnam had invaded Cambodia as "slanderous allegations." UN Document S/PV.2108, January 11, 1979, p. 2.

92 For statements by the Soviet Union, see UN Document S/PV.2108, pp. 14, 17; UN Document S/PV.2111, January 15, 1979, p. 14; and UN Document S/PV.2122, January 15, 1979. For statements by the German Democratic Republic, see UN Document S/PV.2109, January 12, 1979, p. 8; Czechoslovakia, ibid., p. 4; Hungary, ibid., p. 9; Poland, UN Document S/PV.2111, January 15, 1979, p. 8; and Bulgaria, ibid., p. 10. For similar statements by Cuba and Mongolia, see Cuba, UN Document S/PV.2108, January 11, 1979, p. 19; and Mongolia, UN Document S/PV.2111, January 15, 1979, p. 5.

93 The closest any Soviet-bloc country came to admitting the Vietnamese invasion of Cambodia during the Security Council debate was a German Democratic Republic comment that Vietnam "was obliged to take measures to guarantee its self-defense" because of Cambodian "border provocations." See UN Document S/PV.2109, p. 8.

94 UN Document S/PV.2109, January 12, 1979, p. 2.

95 Ibid., p. 4.

96 UN Document S/PV.2110, January 13, 1979, p. 3. The US, after making reference to the Khmer Rouge regime's violations of human rights as "some of the worst violations of human rights in recorded history," said that, nonetheless, the fact remained that the troops of one country were occupying the territory of another and that the Council's responsibility was to have Vietnam withdraw its troops. Ibid., p. 7.

97 Ibid., p. 6.

98 UN Document S/PV.2111, January 15, 1979, p. 3. The remaining two Western states to have participated in the debate were New Zealand and Japan. Each stated that the internal conduct of a country could not justify intervention. UN Document S/PV.2110, January 13, 1979, p. 6; and UN Document S/PV.2111, January 15, 1979, pp. 2–3.

99 UN Document S/PV.2110, January 13, 1979, p. 5.

100 UN Document S/PV.2111, January 15, 1979, p. 7.

101 For Malaysia, see its argument that "armed intervention by any country … , irrespective of its military or political justification, cannot be condoned." UN Document S/PV.2110, January 13, 1979, p. 4. The Philippines stated that "no outside Power in any circumstances should justify itself to interfere in the internal affairs of Kampuchea." See UN Document S/PV.2111, January 15, 1979, p. 10.

102 For Bolivia, see UN Document S/PV.2109, January 12, 1979, p. 7; and for Jamaica, see UN Document S/PV.2111, pp. 13–14.

103  For Nigeria, see UN Document S/PV.2111, January 15, 1979, p. 4; and for Yugoslavia, see ibid., p. 13.

104  For Bangladesh, see UN Document S/PV.2109, January 12, 1979, p. 6; for Kuwait, see ibid., p. 2; for Sudan, see ibid., p. 10; for Gabon, see UN Document S/PV.2110, January 13, 1979, p. 2; and for Zambia, see ibid., p. 11.

105  "The fact that the Vietnamese armed forces responded to the appeal of the National United Front … and helped the people and the armed forces of Kampuchea to overthrow … the Pol Pot–Ieng Sary clique was a just action, in keeping with morality and in keeping with international law." GAOR, 34th Session, 62nd Plenary Meeting, November 12, 1979, p. 1197.

106  GAOR, 34th Session, 64th Plenary Meeting, November 13, 1979, p. 1232. For Laos, see GAOR, 34th Session, 65th Plenary Meeting, November 13, pp. 1240–1241. For Afghanistan, see GAOR, 34th Session, 66th Plenary Meeting, November 14, p. 1262.

107  GAOR, 34th Session, 63rd Plenary Meeting, November 12, 1979, p. 1216.

108  UN Document S/PV.2110, January 13, 1979, p. 5.

109  GAOR, 34th Session, 62nd Plenary Meeting, November 12, 1979, p. 1194.

110  GAOR, 34th Session, 67th Plenary Meeting, November 14, p. 1278.

111  Ibid., p. 1279. For points of view from Indonesia, see GAOR, 34th Session, 65th Plenary Meeting, November 13, 1979, p. 1251.

112  The other recent intervenors, India and Tanzania and Uganda, abstained. Bangladesh, the beneficiary of India's intervention, supported the resolution, based on its belief in the central importance of the principles of nonintervention and the nonuse of force. See UN Document S/PV.2109, January 12, 1979, pp. 5–6.

113  Amnesty International, *Political Killings by Governments*, p. 44.

114  Kyemba, *State of Blood*, p. 44. See also Amnesty International, *Political Killings by Governments*, pp. 11–12.

115  Amii Omara-Otunnu, *Politics and the Military in Uganda, 1890–1985* (New York: St. Martin's Press, 1987), p. 138.

116  Amnesty International, *Political Killings by Governments*, p. 47.

117  *Keesing's Contemporary Archives* (1979), p. 28505.

118  X *Africa Contemporary Record* (1977–78), p. B433. For details, see Henry Kyemba, *State of Blood* (London: Corgi Books, 1977), pp. 179–192.

119  Amnesty International, *Human Rights in Uganda* (London: Amnesty International, 1978).

120  *Keesing's Contemporary Archives* (1979), p. 29669.

121  For accounts of the Tanzanian intervention, see *Keesing's Contemporary Archives* (1979), pp. 29837–29838 and 29669–29674; XII *Africa Contemporary Record* (1979–80), pp. A59–A63; and XI *Africa Contemporary Record* (1978–79), pp. B421–B40. See also Kyemba, *State of Blood*, an account by one of Amin's former cabinet ministers; Semakula Kiwanuka, *Amin and the Tragedy of Uganda* (Munich: Weltforum Verlag, 1979); David Gwyn, *Idi Amin: Death-Light of Africa* (Boston: Little, Brown and Co., 1977); and Amnesty International, *Human Rights in Uganda* (London: Amnesty International, 1978).

122  *Blue Book*, quoted in K. Mathews and Samuel S. Mushi, *Foreign Policy of Tanzania, 1961–1981* (Dar Es Salaam: Tanzania Publishing House, 1981), p. 310.

123  XI *Africa Contemporary Record* (1978–79), p. B431.

124  *Keesing's Contemporary Archives* (1979), p. 29673.

125  Quoted by Wheeler, *Saving Strangers*, p. 118.

126  At the July 1979 meeting in Monrovia of the Organization of African Unity Assembly of Heads of State and Government, Nyerere said, "The war between Tanzania and Idi Amin's regime in Uganda was caused by the Ugandan Army's aggression against Tanzania and Idi Amin's claim to have annexed part of Tanzanian territory. There was no other cause for it." See K. Mathews and S.S. Mushi, *Foreign Policy of Tanzania, 1961–1981* (Dar Es Salaam: Tanzania Publishing House, 1981), pp. 305–312.

127  Amin wrote to UN Secretary-General Kurt Waldheim on March 28 requesting a Security Council meeting, but the Security Council appeared in no hurry to meet. Amin wrote again on April 5, withdrawing the Ugandan request for a meeting, on the advice of African member states. See *Yearbook of the United Nations* 33 (1979), pp. 262–263.

128 At the next session of the General Assembly, while approximately 25 states chose to raise the issue of Vietnam's intervention in Cambodia in the general debate, only Libya (other than Tanzania and Uganda itself) raised the issue of Tanzania's intervention in Uganda.

129 XII *Africa Contemporary Record* (1978–79), pp. A59–A63.

130 With regard to his mendacity, Amin had on a number of previous occasions claimed that Tanzania had invaded Uganda, and the claims were exposed as complete fabrications. See, for example, the comment in XI *Africa Contemporary Record* (1978–79), p. B426. On Amin's reputation in Africa generally, see Olajide Aluko, "African Response to External Intervention in Africa since Angola," *African Affairs* 80 (1981), pp. 159, 172.

131 ASEAN states were worried about Vietnam's regional ambitions. See Evans and Rowley, *Red Brotherhood at War*, pp. 184–185.

132 This was precisely the viewpoint of China. See, for example, UN Document, S/PV.2108, January 11, 1979, p. 10.

133 The contrast between the General Assembly's treatment of the new Ugandan Government, which succeeded Amin after Tanzanian intervention, and the new Cambodian Government, which succeeded Pol Pot after Vietnamese intervention, is brought out in Wheeler, *Saving Strangers*, pp. 122–132.

134 A brief account of the intervention can be found in *Keesing's Contemporary Archives* (1979), pp. 29933–29935. Other accounts can be found in XII *Africa Contemporary Record* (1979–80), pp. A120–A121 and B400–B402; XI *Africa Contemporary Record* (1978–79), pp. B518–B520; *Africa Research Bulletin* (1979), pp. 5373–5374 and 5410–5411; and Charles Rousseau, "Chronique des faits internationaux," *Revue Générale de Droit International Public* 84 (1980), pp. 361–365. See also Thomas O'Toole, *The Central African Republic* (Boulder: Westview Press, 1986), pp. 48–56.

135 Quoted in *Keesing's Contemporary Archives* (1979), p. 29933.

136 "The French Government was doing all it could to find a way to make Bokassa step down before the African [Commission of Inquiry] established that a head of a Government to which France had given so much support was personally guilty of a mass killing." O'Toole, *Central African Republic*, p. 55.

137 "Almost totally reliant upon French support in both the public and private sectors, the CAR [Central African Republic] under Bokassa remained a French colony in all but name." O'Toole, *Central African Republic*, p. 51.

138 Rousseau places the date at the end of July, that is, even before the Commission of Inquiry had issued its report: Rousseau, "Chronique des faits internationaux," p. 364.

139 Ibid., p. 365.

140 Other than France and the Central African Empire itself (now the Central African Republic).

141 See the summary of the remarks in the General Debate in XVII *UN Monthly Chronicle* (January 1980), pp. 93–216.

142 See *Keesing's Contemporary Archives* (1985), pp. 32614–32618; Robert J. Beck, *The Grenada Invasion* (Boulder: Westview Press, 1993); and William C. Gilmore, *The Grenada Intervention* (London: Mansell Publishing, 1984). For an account of the thinking of the American decision makers, see Bob Woodward, *Veil: The Secret Wars of the CIA, 1981–1987* (New York: Simon & Schuster, 1987). Also see Christopher L. Joyner, "The United States Action in Grenada: Reflections on the Lawfulness of Invasion," *American Journal of International Law* 78 (1984), p. 131; John Norton Moore, "Grenada and the International Double Standard," ibid., p. 145; Detlev F. Vagts, "International Law under Time Pressure: Grading the Grenada Take-Home Examination," ibid., p. 169; and Louise Doswald Beck, "The Legality of the United States Intervention in Grenada," *Netherlands International Law Review* 31 (1984), p. 355.

143 *Keesing's Contemporary Archives* (1985), p. 32615.

144 Based on CIA sources, Woodward reports that "word was sent to [the Organization of Eastern Caribbean States prime ministers] that the likelihood of US military action would be substantially increased if they requested it." See Woodward, *Veil*, p. 290.

145 Quoted by Gilmore, *The Grenada Intervention*, pp. 97–98. The legal justification of an invitation from the governor-general was added two days later in the Security Council debate.

146 The third reason, the need for a preemptive strike to prevent a possible future Grenadian attack on Organization of Eastern Caribbean States countries, need not concern us here. But see Arend and Beck, *International Law*, pp. 71–79; and Gray, *International Law and the Use of Force*, pp. 111–115.

147 UN Document S/PV.2489, October 26, 1983, p. 6.

148  UN Document S/PV.2491, October 27, 1983, p. 6.

149  GAOR, 38th Session, 43rd Plenary Meeting, November 2, 1983, p. 701.

150  Quoted in Beck, *The Grenada Invasion*, p. 71. For an excellent account of the shifting sands of the US legal justifications, see pp. 49–90, 188–96.

151  See UN Document S/PV.2489, p. 2.

152  UN Document S/PV.2487, October 25, 1983, p.19.

153  See Gilmore, *The Grenada Intervention*, p. 63; Murphy, *Humanitarian Intervention*, p. 110; Joyner, "The United States Action in Grenada," p. 143; and Doswald Beck, "The Legality of the United States," p. 362. For the contrary view, see Moore, "Grenada and the International Double Standard," pp. 149–150; and Tesón, *Humanitarian Intervention*, p. 211.

154  The United States had received diplomatic note from the new authorities guaranteeing the safety of the American nationals. See Gilmore, *The Grenada Intervention*, p. 62.

155  See Woodward, *Veil*, pp. 289–290, who interviewed William Casey, the then director of the CIA and others.

156  Nor, for that matter, is it clear whether states took the view that an invitation to intervene could not properly emanate from the Grenadian governor-general, nor whether they took the view that Article 8 of the Organization of East Caribbean States Treaty could not provide a legal basis for the intervention.

157  UN Document S/PV.2491, pp. 33–34.

158  See Murphy, *Humanitarian Intervention*, pp. 111–115. For a detailed account of the invasion, see Thomas Donnelly, Margaret Roth, and Caleb Baker, *Operation Just Cause: The Storming of Panama* (New York: Lexington Books, 1991); and Independent Commission of Inquiry on the US Invasion of Panama, *The US Invasion of Panama: The Truth behind Operation Just Cause* (Boston: South End Press, 1991). Also see Simon Chesterman, "Rethinking Panama: International Law and the US Invasion of Panama, 1989," in Guy S. Goodwin-Gill and Stefan Talmon, eds., *The Reality of International Law: Essays in Honour of Ian Brownlie* (Oxford: Clarendon Press, 1999), pp. 57–94; Ved P. Nanda, "The Validity of United States Intervention in Panama under International Law," *American Journal of International Law* 84 (1990), p. 495; Tom J. Farer, "Panama: Beyond the Charter Paradigm," in ibid., p. 503; and Anthony D'Amato, "The Invasion of Panama Was a Lawful Response to Tyranny," in ibid., p. 516.

159  The actual number of civilian deaths became a much-disputed issue. For discussion, see Independent Commission of Inquiry on the US Invasion of Panama, *The US Intervention*, pp. 40–45 and 102–104.

160  UN Document S/21034.

161  UN Document S/21035. For an account of the incidents leading up to the US military action, see Donnelly, *Operation Just Cause*, pp. 39, 42–44, 50, and 93–96.

162  UN Document S/PV.2899, December 20, 1989, p. 31.

163  See Gray, *International Law and the Use of Force*, p. 43; Murphy, *Humanitarian Intervention*, p. 114, who regards all the US goals as claimed "legal bases" for action; and Nanda, "The Validity of United State Intervention," pp. 494–503 passim.

164  Quoted by Chesterman, *Just War*, p. 57. Pickering made a number of statements concerning the US objectives, which in fact rather varied in content, but see UN Document S/PV.2902, p. 12.

165  Abraham D. Sofaer, "The Panamanian Revolution: Diplomacy, War and Self-Determination in Panama," remarks to the 84th Convention of the American Society of International Law, as quoted in Thomas Ehrlich and Mary Ellen O'Connell, *International Law and the Use of Force* (Boston: Little, Brown and Co, 1993), p. 99.

166  Making, therefore a total of 16 countries. For the Finnish view, see UN Document S/PV.2900, December 21, 1985, pp. 14–15. For the French view, see UN Document S/PV.2899, December 20, 1985, pp. 22–25.

167  It is possible that the Canadian and British representatives offered at least an element of support for the US claim to have intervened, inter alia, to restore democracy. For the relevant Canadian observations, see UN Document, S/PV.2899, 20 December 1985, pp. 28–30; and for the British ones, see ibid., pp. 26–27.

168  For the text of the resolution, see *Yearbook of the United Nations* 43 (New York: United Nations, 1989), p. 175.

169  With the exceptions of El Salvador, which joined the US in voting against the resolution, and Costa Rica and Honduras, which abstained. The new Panamanian Government also joined the US in opposing the resolution.

170  Danish Institute of International Affairs, *Humanitarian Intervention* (Copenhagen: Danish Institute of International Affairs, 1999), p. 100. For a similar conclusion, see Thomas Franck and Nigel Rodley, "After Bangladesh: The Law of Humanitarian Intervention by Military Force, *American Journal of International Law* 67 (1973), pp. 275, 290. The authors argue that "in very few, if any, instances has the right been asserted under circumstances that appear more humanitarian than self-interested and power-seeking."

171  Robert Jackson, *The Global Covenant: Human Conflict in a World of States* (Oxford: Oxford University Press, 2000), p. 259.

172  Kofi Annan, "Reflections on Intervention," paper presented at Ditchely Park, June 26, 1998.

173  According to the recent survey by the Danish Institute of International Affairs, *Humanitarian Intervention*, p. 88, "State practice during the Cold War does not support the view that a right of humanitarian intervention without Security Council authorization has been established under customary international law." Similar perspectives can be found in Ronzitti, *Rescuing Nationals*, pp. 108–110; Murphy, *Humanitarian Intervention*, p. 143; and Chesterman, *Just War*, pp. 84–87. For the other side of the argument, see Abiew, *The Evolution of the Doctrine and Practice of Humanitarian Intervention*, pp. 131–135; and Tesón, *Humanitarian Intervention*, pp. 222–223. For the most detailed account of these and other matters, see Dennis Driscoll, ed., *Humanitarian Intervention* (Galway: Irish Centre for Human Rights, forthcoming, Winter 2001–2002), which comprehensively surveys the state practice of the period under review.

# 5. INTERVENTIONS AFTER THE COLD WAR

The focus of this essay is on military interventions conducted in the 1990s against the wishes of a government, or without meaningful consent, but with purported humanitarian justifications. Cases where both these criteria are met amount to "humanitarian interventions," which are classically seen as "coercive action by one or more states involving the use of armed force in another state without the consent of its authorities, and with the purpose of preventing widespread suffering or death among the inhabitants."[1]

Some commentators argue that the term "intervention" should cover the deployment of both "solicited" and "unsolicited" military force. Here, however, the emphasis is only on the unsolicited type, defined as the absence of effective consent. This absence is clearest when there is explicit opposition from the government (in Iraq, the former Yugoslavia, and Rwanda). Because "the existence of *de facto* control is generally the most important criterion in dealing with a regime as representing the state,"[2] consent was controversial and of little practical meaning in several cases (Liberia, Haiti, and Sierra Leone) and irrelevant in one case (Somalia). The case of East Timor is included because consent was ambiguous – it emanated from an illegal occupying power, after significant international pressure that verged on coercion.

The second general criterion is the prominence of a humanitarian justification employed by intervening states. The definition of "humanitarian" refers to the threat or actual occurrence of large scale loss of life (especially genocide), massive forced migration, and widespread abuses of human rights; it does not, however, include the overthrow of a democratically elected government, unless one of the results is large scale loss of life. As motivations are inevitably mixed, the humanitarian rationale need not be exclusive, but it should be explicit. In some of the cases, other justifications predominated – regional-security concerns in Liberia or the nature of the target regime in Haiti – but responding to the needs of populations at risk remained clearly evident.

Using these criteria, eight cases from the 1990s, summarized in Table 5.1, are treated chronologically. The table also distinguishes the nature of their authorization under three categories: those authorized by the United Nations (UN) Security Council under Chapter VII of the Charter, those authorizations delegated to regional arrangements under Chapter VIII, and those not authorized by the Security Council.[3] Of the military interventions that were undertaken between 1990 and 2000, all were accompanied by sanctions and embargoes. International criminal prosecution has also been employed in several of the more recent cases.

## TABLE 5.1
## AUTHORIZATIONS FOR MILITARY INTERVENTIONS IN THE 1990s

| Country | Chapter VII Authorization and UN Mission | Chapter VII Authorization Delegated | No Initial Security Council Authorization |
|---|---|---|---|
| Liberia 1990–1997 | | | ECOMOG |
| Northern Iraq 1991– | | Coalition | Coalition |
| Former Yugoslavia 1992– | UNPROFOR | IFOR and SFOR | |
| Somalia 1992–1993 | UNOSOM II | UNITAF | |
| Rwanda 1994–1996 | UNAMIR II | Opération Turquoise | |
| Haiti 1994–1997 | UNMH | MNF | |
| Sierra Leone 1997– | UNAMSIL | | ECOMOG |
| Kosovo 1999– | | KFOR | NATO |
| East Timor 1999– | UNAMET | INTERFET | |

Note: ECOMOG, ECOWAS Monitoring Group; IFOR, Implementation Force; INTERFET, International Force in East Timor; KFOR, Kosovo Force; MNF, Multinational Force; NATO, North Atlantic Treaty Organization; SFOR, Stabilization Force; UNAMET, UN Mission in East Timor; UNAMIR, UN Assistance Mission in Rwanda; UNAMSIL, UN Mission in Sierra Leone; UNITAF, Unified Task Force; UNMH, UN Mission in Haiti; UNOSOM, UN Operation in Somalia; UNPROFOR, UN Protection Force.

One or both of the criteria were absent in outside military operations in several countries in the 1990s, and these operations are therefore not included here. Meaningful consent, for example, was expressed and justified the Russian military efforts in Georgia and Tajikistan and the Commonwealth of Independent States (CIS) in Tajikistan. Furthermore, these efforts were not based on explicitly humanitarian justifications. Similarly, three interventions in Africa had the consent of democratically elected governments, and again humanitarian concerns were not paramount. These were as follows: in 1998, in Guinea-Bissau, the Senegalese, Guinean, and the Economic Community of West African States (ECOWAS) efforts; in 1997, in the Central African Republic, Inter-African Force to Monitor the Implementation of the Bangui Agreements (MISAB); and in 1998, in Lesotho, the South African and Botswanan efforts in accordance with agreements of the Southern African Development Community (SADC).[4] Italy intervened in Albania in 1996 for humanitarian reasons, but with Tirana's consent.

# LIBERIA, 1990–1997

Liberia has a remarkable democratic history; between 1847 and 1980, a series of 20 democratically elected presidents ruled the country. After long-term mass public discontent, William V.S. Tubman was assassinated on April 12, 1980, and his government was overthrown by a coup d'état conducted by junior elements of the Armed Forces of Liberia (AFL), led by Master Sergeant Samuel K. Doe. In 1989, Doe's autocracy was toppled by a popular but excessively destructive insurgency, spearheaded by the National Patriotic Front of Liberia (NPFL), led by Charles M.G. Taylor, who in 1997 was elected the 22nd president of Liberia.

The Liberian Civil War began in 1989, when Taylor and a group of so-called dissidents launched an attack against AFL security personnel in Nimba county (located on the Liberian–Côte d'Ivoire border) and advanced toward the capital city of Monrovia. The NPFL proceeded to crush then president Doe's AFL. By May 1990, the NPFL controlled significantly more territory than Doe, whose presidential authority was limited to the capital, Monrovia.

The ALF suffered enormous losses on the battlefield, which led Doe to appeal for assistance to the UN[5] and the United States (US) government.[6] Finally, on July 14, 1990, he appealed to ECOWAS to introduce a "peace-keeping force into Liberia to forestall increasing terror and tension."[7] However, at the time of the request, Doe's regime had collapsed, was clearly not in de facto control of the country, and lacked both domestic and international legitimacy.

On August 7, 1990, the ECOWAS Standing Mediation Commission – comprised of the Gambia, Ghana, Nigeria, and Togo – met in Banjul and agreed to establish the ECOWAS Cease-fire Monitoring Group (ECOMOG) in Liberia. The objectives were to institute a cease-fire, form an interim government, and hold democratic elections. Concern was also expressed about the wanton destruction of human life and property.[8] ECOMOG's force commander was mandated to "conduct military operations for the purpose of monitoring the cease-fire, restoring law and order to create the necessary conditions for free and fair elections."[9]

The ECOMOG intervention in Liberia was controversial. The majority of francophone members of ECOWAS were not enthusiastic – in particular, Côte d'Ivoire and Burkina Faso – and believed that "such a force could only prevent an imminent victory for the NPFL whose cause they had given implicit support."[10] Moreover, in consonance with historical anglophone–francophone divisions in the region, several ECOWAS members were concerned about Nigeria's domination of the initiative. President Ibrahim Babangida also came under fire in Nigeria, as many believed that he was attempting to divert attention from domestic issues and that the intervention required resources that the country could ill-afford.

The legal basis for ECOWAS's intervention in Liberia was dubious. There was obviously no Security Council authorization, and the decision to intervene made no mention of Doe's request. Furthermore, the ECOWAS Treaty of 1975 did not provide for a regional-security mechanism to deal with internal conflicts – nor did the 1978 Protocol on Non-Aggression. The 1981 Protocol on Mutual Assistance on Defence, came closest, indicating in Article 18 that internal armed conflict that is likely to endanger security and peace in the community would be dealt with by the authority of the member states concerned.

On August 24, 1990, approximately 2,000 ECOMOG forces landed in Liberia to forestall the state from descending further into anarchy. The bulk of the troops were from Nigeria; however, other states – including the Gambia, Ghana, Guinea, and Sierra Leone – also

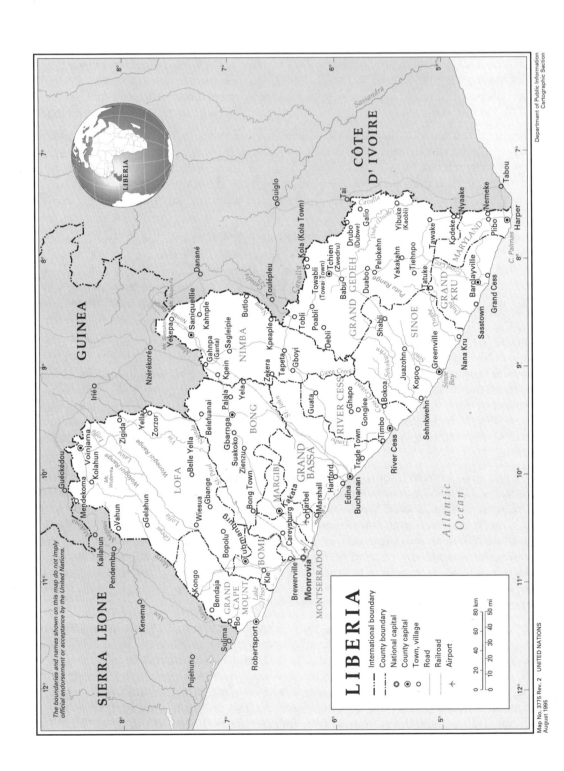

FIGURE 5.1:  MAP OF LIBERIA

contributed troops. The NPFL, which by then controlled approximately 90 percent of the country, attacked ECOMOG forces on their arrival. Although ECOMOG was able to push the rebels back into the bush and restore law and order in Monrovia, it was unable to establish authority in the interior.

After securing Monrovia, ECOWAS unsuccessfully resumed its efforts to negotiate a cease-fire and peace agreement between the NPFL, various splinter factions, and Doe's government. Consequently, on August 29, 1990, ECOWAS assisted Liberians to organize a National Conference of All Liberian Political Parties, Patriotic Fronts, Interest Groups and Concerned Citizens in Banjul. The purpose of the conference was to create an interim government, because of the total breakdown of law and order. Both Taylor and Doe boycotted the conference, and the former refused to recognize the new interim government. On September 9, 1990, nearly one week after the conference, members of the Independent National Patriotic Front of Liberia, an NPFL splinter group headed by Prince Yormie Johnson, ambushed and kidnapped Doe from ECOWAS headquarters and later murdered him.

In January 1991, five months after ECOMOG forces landed in Liberia, a Security Council presidential statement "commend[ed]" ECOWAS's efforts to promote peace in Liberia and "called upon all parties to the conflict to respect the cease-fire agreement." On October 30, 1991, the parties to the conflict signed an agreement at Yamoussoukro that called for the encampment and disarmament of warring factions and the establishment of transitional institutions to carry out free and fair elections.[11] It took nearly a year before ECOMOG was able to deploy troops in all areas held by the factions.

The disarmament plans fell apart on September 8, 1992, when the NPFL tortured and killed ECOMOG troops. In response, ECOMOG adopted a far more robust approach. At times, it "seemed less like a 'peace-making force' and more like an unintended party to the conflict."[12]

On November 19, 1992, the UN Security Council adopted Resolution 788, stating that the "deterioration of the situation in Liberia constitutes a threat to international peace and security, particularly in West Africa as a whole." Resolution 788 called for a complete weapons embargo against Liberia – authorizing ECOWAS to enforce its terms under Chapter VIII of the UN Charter. The ECOMOG enforcement action came to an end with the signing of the Cotonou Accord in July 1993, which ushered in another peacekeeping phase, including contingents from Tanzania and Uganda. On September 22, 1993, the Security Council adopted resolution 866, which called for the creation of the UN Observer Mission in Liberia (UNOMIL), stating that "this would be the first peace-keeping mission undertaken by the United Nations in cooperation with a peace-keeping mission already set up by another organization, in this case ECOWAS."[13] This operation was intended to complement the ECOMOG effort to restore order and disarm rival factions, by ensuring that the process was conducted impartially.

Therefore, "it can be said that Resolutions 788 and 866 placed a retroactive seal on the ECOWAS intervention," especially considering that, between January 22, 1991, and November 27, 1996, a series of Security Council resolutions and presidential statements commended ECOWAS for its efforts. The Secretary-General also created a Special Emergency Fund to assist countries that contributed to this ECOWAS operation.

It took ECOWAS another five years, until August 1995, to broker an agreement that was widely believed to have a chance of success. It was the 13th such accord, though it was also the first to involve all the factions, and it had the support of other local political and civic organizations.[14] On April 6, 1996, hopes for peace were dashed, however, when Monrovia erupted in bloody conflict after the police attempted to arrest Roosevelt Johnson, a former leader of a faction of the United Liberation Movement of Liberia for Democracy (ULIMO).

The human costs were overwhelming. Atrocities were committed against civilians, including children, which also led to the evacuation of virtually all humanitarian personnel from the former safe haven, where shelter had been provided for some 1.2 million internally displaced persons (IDPs). Warlords looted ECOMOG and UN offices and supplies. When ECOMOG troops eventually managed to separate the armed factions and gain a measure of control over the city in June 1996, health workers recovered more than 1,500 bodies from shallow graves.[15]

A subsequent rapprochement between Taylor and the Nigerian ruler, General Sani Abacha, paved the way for all-party peace talks and UN-observed elections in July 1997. Taylor amassed 75 percent of the vote. The UN welcomed the elections, and the Security Council called on all parties to abide by the results and cooperate in the formation of a new government. It also called on the government to protect the "democratic" system and promote human rights and fundamental freedoms under the rule of law.[16] Thereafter, UNOMIL began to withdraw from Liberia, a process completed by September 1997. The new government and ECOWAS agreed that ECOMOG should remain in the country to provide security, particularly during the repatriation of refugees.

Over the course of the conflict 785,000 of Liberia's 2.5 million citizens became refugees (420,000 in Guinea, 320,000 in Côte d'Ivoire, 20,000 in Ghana, 20,000 in Sierra Leone, and 5,000 in Nigeria). And at least 200,000 Liberians were killed between the start of the conflict in 1989 and the signing of the peace accord in August 1995. In total, ECOMOG operations cost Nigeria more than $1 billion, and 500 of its troops lost their lives. At the same time, it set a precedent for humanitarian intervention by an African subregional organization.

## NORTHERN IRAQ 1991–

On August 2, 1990, an Iraqi force of 120,000 troops invaded, illegally occupied, and annexed Kuwait. The invasion was met with universal disapproval. Just 11 hours later, the Security Council condemned the invasion in Resolution 660 (1990) and demanded Iraq's immediate and unconditional withdrawal. Four days later, the Council adopted Resolution 661 (1990), imposing comprehensive mandatory sanctions on Iraq. These included a ban on all trade, an oil embargo, the suspension of international flights, an arms embargo, a freeze of Iraqi Government financial assets, and a prohibition on financial transactions. On August 25, the Council called on member states to impose a sea blockade in consonance with Resolution 665 (1990). A month later, it decided in Resolution 670 (1990) that member states should block all aviation links with Iraq. Within days, a major humanitarian crisis arose, as some 850,000 third-country nationals and 300,000 Palestinians from Iraq and Kuwait fled, primarily to Jordan.

As sanctions were progressively tightened, the US and other countries began to deploy substantial military forces in the region. By late October 1990, Iraq had occupied Kuwait for more than two months, and a consensus was emerging between the US and the Soviet Union that some form of enforcement action might be authorized by the Security Council. In the course of negotiations, a senior US State Department official was quoted as saying that "[l]egally, our position and the position shared by others is that Article 51 provides a sufficient basis under international law for further action." A Council resolution authorizing some specific military action would, however, "provide a firmer political basis." There was little serious discussion of establishing an independent UN force; rather, the preferred action would put coalition forces under a UN "umbrella."

**FIGURE 5.2: MAP OF IRAQ (INCLUDING KUWAIT)**

On a visit to Moscow in November, US Secretary of State James Baker lobbied for such a resolution, pointing to Soviet President Mikhail Gorbachev's 1987 *Pravda* article on enhancing the UN's role.[17] Gorbachev suggested that the Council pass two resolutions: the first, adopted in late November, would authorize force after a six-week grace period; the second would provide the actual go-ahead. Baker proposed a single resolution, with a grace period before it would become operative. When he met the Soviet Foreign Minister Eduard Shevardnadze in Paris on November 18, Washington believed it had the votes for a resolution, but Moscow demurred. Among other concerns, Shevardnadze insisted that the actual word "force" not be used. Baker came up with five different euphemisms, finally settling on the phrase "all necessary means."[18]

On November 29, the Security Council adopted Resolution 678 (1990) by 12 votes to 2 (Cuba and Yemen), with China abstaining. In its operative paragraph, the Security Council "[a]uthorises Member States co-operating with the Government of Kuwait, unless Iraq on or before 15 January 1991 fully implements ... the foregoing resolutions, to use all necessary means to uphold and implement Resolution 660 (1990) and all subsequent relevant resolutions and to restore international peace and security in the area."

As the coalition commenced the air campaign that heralded Operation Desert Storm in January and February 1991, a number of states sought to bring about a last-minute peaceful resolution to the conflict. Under a plan proposed by the Soviet Union, the trade embargo on Iraq would have been lifted once two-thirds of Iraqi troops left Kuwait, with remaining sanctions to be lifted when the withdrawal was complete. The proposal was rejected by the US and the United Kingdom (UK), which asserted that they had the power to maintain sanctions for as long as they chose and to continue the war authorized by the Security Council until it adopted another resolution. As permanent members of the Council, they reserved the right to veto any such compromise.[19]

After a six-week air war that destroyed most of Iraq's military capabilities and much of the country's infrastructure, the ground war commenced on February 24, 1991. Some 500,000 coalition troops and personnel from 28 countries liberated Kuwait and occupied much of southern Iraq in only four days. Coalition forces entered Kuwait City on February 27; a cease-fire commenced at midnight on February 28.

Coalition aircraft had penetrated deep into Iraq, targeting bridges, electric plants, and infrastructure sites for other essential services. In all, they dropped more than 90,000 tons of explosives. The overwhelming superiority in air power contributed to wartime Iraqi military deaths, estimated at between 30,000 and 120,000, while several hundred died on the coalition side. Estimates suggest that 3,000 to 3,500 Iraqi civilians died during the conflict, with many more dying subsequently, owing to a combination of the damaged infrastructure and the harsh sanctions regime.[20] The costs of the operation are usually estimated at $60–70 billion.

One of the more controversial humanitarian aspects of international actions against Iraq results from more than 10 years of economic sanctions. They were designed to remain in effect until two conditions were met: Iraq's stockpiles of weapons of mass destruction were destroyed; and its treatment of minorities improved. Sanctions are still in place, as is the regime. As economic sanctions seemed to target the poor and vulnerable, without having any visible impact on the government and its policies, a new question arose: How much pain is the community of states willing to inflict on civilians in a quest for doubtful political gains?

During the military campaign against Iraq in 1991, US President George Bush publicly expressed his hope that Iraqi citizens would "take matters into their own hands" and remove Saddam Hussein from power. The apparently crushing defeat of the Iraqi Army and foreign support reignited the desire for independence among Kurds living in northern Iraq. Previous revolts had been brutally suppressed by Saddam Hussein's Ba'ath regime, with measures including the use of chemical weapons. On this occasion, Iraqi troops attacked Kurdish villages, forcing up to 2 million civilians to flee their homes, virtually overnight. By April 5, 1991, Turkey estimated that almost 1 million people were attempting to reach safety by crossing its borders.[21]

The Security Council expressed concern about the treatment of the Kurds in northern Iraq, along with the Shi'ites and Marsh Arabs in the south, at a meeting on April 3, 1991. Resolution 687 (1991) provided the terms of the cease-fire with Iraq and conditions for lifting sanctions, but conspicuously it failed to mention the plight of Iraq's civilian population. This absence subsequently has led to debate about the legality of measures under Council Resolution 688 (1991), which was agreed on only two days later.

Resolution 688 condemned the repression of the civilian population, demanded that Iraq end it, and insisted that the country allow international humanitarian organizations immediate access to all those in need of assistance in all parts of Iraq. The Council also appealed to all member states and aid organizations "to contribute to these humanitarian relief efforts." The strong language of the resolution was reminiscent of Chapter VII,[22] but none of the states voting for the resolution characterized it as such at the time. Washington noted that it planned to use military aircraft to drop food, blankets, clothing, tents, and other relief into northern Iraq. On the same day that the Security Council passed Resolution 688, Bush announced plans to commence aid drops to Kurds in northern Iraq in cooperation with France and the UK, emphasizing that the US would not intervene militarily in the conflict.[23]

As the diplomacy continued in New York, dramatic television images captured the plight of an exodus of some 2 million displaced persons exposed to the brutal conditions of winter in the mountains. An estimated 10,000 to 30,000 died of exposure and malnutrition in the squalid camps that sprouted virtually overnight. At least partially as a result of the images, governments reacted; observers began to point to the importance of the "CNN effect" or "BBC effect." Whatever the proximate trigger, President Bush reversed his previous policy and committed US troops to set up encampments in northern Iraq to ensure the safety of Kurdish refugees and coordinate relief supplies.

Turkey was one of the first states to propose the idea of safe havens for the Kurds.[24] The rationale behind its support for the creation of these safe havens was Ankara's concern for political stability in the southeast. In particular, the influx of additional Kurds threatened to exacerbate an already unstable political situation related to the separatist movement within Turkey. Secretary of State Baker affirmed the importance of the Kurds being free from threats and persecution but reiterated the US position that it would not "go down the slippery slope of being sucked into a civil war."[25]

European governments were less reticent in their support for more direct action. France had long advocated a bolder response to the Kurdish crisis, but the first concrete proposal came from the UK. Speaking at the Luxembourg summit meeting of the European Community (EC) on April 8, 1991, UK Prime Minister John Major proposed the creation of UN-protected Kurdish enclaves in northern Iraq. He stated that the proposal was intended to "build on" Resolutions 687 and 688: "We believe the rubric exists within 688 to avoid the need for a separate resolution but clearly we will need to discuss that in New York."[26]

The initial US response to the proposed safe havens was lukewarm, but it stressed its determination to protect the relief effort. On April 10, it demanded that the Iraqi Government cease all military activity north of the 36th parallel, to enable relief supplies to be delivered unimpeded and to prevent attacks on Kurdish refugees. The choice of this line excluded the oil-producing area around Kirkuk (a town claimed by Kurdish separatists), apparently in an attempt to avoid encouraging Kurdish secession.[27]

As it became clear that relief efforts were severely restricted by the geography of the Turkey–Iraq border, Bush stated on April 16 that, "consistent with" Resolution 688, US troops would enter northern Iraq: "Some might argue that this is an intervention into the internal affairs of Iraq. But I think the humanitarian concern, the refugee concern, is so overwhelming that there will be a lot of understanding about this."[28]

On April 18, twelve military relief flights (9 US, 2 UK, and 1 French) dropped almost 58 tons of relief supplies to refugees on the Turkey–Iraq border. This coincided with the signing of a Memorandum of Understanding (MOU) between the UN and Iraq, allowing the world organization to administer a civilian "humanitarian presence" throughout Iraq. In less than a week, nearly 6,000 tons of supplies had been dropped to the refugees. Toward the end of April, death rates among refugees had fallen from between 400 and 1,000 to about 60 deaths per day. By April 24, approximately 2,000 US Marines and several hundred British, French, and Dutch troops were stationed in northern Iraq. At the peak of the humanitarian operation, there were more than 20,000 soldiers from 13 states in the theatre.

These early efforts focused on the Turkey–Iraq border, in part as a result of Western and especially US reluctance to cooperate with Iran, even though the Islamic Republic had by then received more Kurdish refugees and spent more on them than any other state.[29]

By mid-July, most of the 1 million Kurds who had fled to Turkey in March had returned. With the withdrawal of coalition troops used as a bargaining chip, Iraq consented to the presence of the 500-strong lightly armed UN Guard Contingent in Iraq, signing an Annex to the MOU on May 25, 1991.[30] The last allied soldiers departed Iraq on July 15, 1991, leaving behind a multinational rapid-deployment force in Turkey, as a warning to Baghdad.

The US and its allies continued to police the no-fly zone and, on August 26, 1992, also declared a second air exclusion zone in southern Iraq, below the 32nd parallel. The US in particular justified its actions by referring to Resolution 688, which did not specifically mention southern Iraq.[31] This second zone was subsequently extended to the 33rd parallel in September 1996, a move that prompted France to refuse to patrol the extended area and later to withdraw entirely.

No consistent legal rationale was given for the no-fly zones, and many countries and observers have contested the actual legality of the enforcement effort, which continues as of this writing. Given the likelihood of a Chinese veto, no specific authorization measures were ever proposed in the Council. Later, when the objective was to transfer responsibility for the humanitarian effort to the UN, a Chapter VII resolution was not necessary. The second no-fly zone and subsequent air attacks seemed to have set a precedent, whereby new military measures took place without specific additional Security Council authorization.[32]

No Security Council member voting in favour of Resolution 688 publicly challenged the view that Operation Provide Comfort was "consistent with" the resolution.[33] The G-7's London Economic Summit Political Declaration on Strengthening the International Order expressed broad statements of support. As the months wore into years, however, calls for a reassessment of the policy became more frequent and widespread.

Throughout this period, Washington continued to assert its right to enforce the no-fly zones. Following the January 1993 air strike on Iraqi missile launchers, the UN Secretary-General issued an ambiguous statement that, "I can say that this action was taken and conforms to the resolutions of the Security Council and conforms to the Charter of the United Nations."[34] What status should be accorded a pronouncement by the Secretary-

General is unclear, particularly because it was inconsistent with the justifications proposed by the acting states (the UK claimed the incident was an act of self-defence, while France criticized the US for exceeding its mandate). By relying on the terms of the cease-fire resolution (which did not mention the Kurds), the Secretary-General's statement omitted any reference to the plight of Iraqi minorities that presumably provided the raison d'être for the no-fly zones.

Ultimately, the benefits of the safe havens are uncertain; Kurds in northern Iraq live precariously, as they did before the Gulf War. But at least they have returned home and enjoy some degree of protection from the brutish Iraqi regime. The innovation of safe havens remains a lasting legacy of the intervention in northern Iraq, though the significance is diminished because of the outright failure of safe havens elsewhere. In the eyes of many critics, there remains considerable cynicism about the motivations of the major powers. Again, colonial memories quickly come to the surface. Many developing countries question whether Security Council resolutions can be applied to pursue a different agenda than what many states actually had intended – in this case, a US–UK vendetta against the continued presence in power of Saddam Hussein.

## THE FORMER YUGOSLAVIA, 1992–

Following the Second World War and under the direction of Marshal Tito, the "People's Federal Republic of Yugoslavia" was formed from Serbia, Montenegro, Croatia, Slovenia, Bosnia and Herzegovina, and Macedonia. After Tito's death and the economic hardships and structural adjustments of the 1980s, strident nationalism tore the republic apart. Between June and October 1991, four of the six republics comprising Yugoslavia declared their independence. Croatia and Slovenia first made unilateral declarations on June 25, 1991, after internal referenda. War broke out almost immediately. In the early months of the fighting, the EC played a leading role; when it was unable to secure a cease-fire by mid-September, Austria, Canada, and Hungary requested a Security Council session, which adopted Resolution 713 (1991). It expressed concern that the "continuation of this situation constitutes a threat to international peace and security" and imposed a blanket arms embargo under Chapter VII of the UN Charter. Only Yugoslavia's consent to the resolution avoided a Chinese veto.[35]

A month later, Bosnia and Herzegovina proclaimed its independence, on October 15. Cease-fires were brokered and broken, and on December 15 the Council adopted Resolution 724 (1991), in which it strengthened the Chapter VII arms embargo and sought to lay the ground for a peacekeeping operation. December also saw the EC agree in principle to recognize the breakaway republics of the former Yugoslavia, with Germany formally recognizing Croatia and Slovenia on December 23 and the rest of the EC following suit on January 15, 1992. Bosnia and Herzegovina conducted a referendum and proclaimed its formal independence on March 3, 1992. On May 22, 1992, Croatia, Slovenia, and Bosnia and Herzegovina were extended UN membership.

The "birth" of the new states was painful. Only in Slovenia, where there were few Serbs, was the violence of a short duration. Within the former Republic of Croatia, there was a significant Serbian minority, which had bitter memories of internal repression by Croat fascists during the Second World War. Croatian Serbs held a referendum and declared the Serb Autonomous Region of Krajina accompanied by an expressed intention to join with Serbia. By the end of the year, some 6,000 to 10,000 civilians were dead, and another 10,000 were wounded. Croats were displaced by Serbs in the Krajina, and Croats displaced Serbs elsewhere. The siege and destruction of the Croatian town of Vukovar shocked the world's conscience and was viewed by many as a harbinger of the lengths to which Belgrade would

FIGURE 5.3: MAP OF THE FORMER YUGOSLAVIA

**FIGURE 5.4: MAP OF BOSNIA AND HERZEGOVINA**

go to establish "a Greater Serbia." It also produced an estimated 100,000 refugees. Months later, it was estimated that 250,000 Serbs and 100,000 Croats had been displaced by the initial round of fighting.

The cease-fire in Slovenia permitted the war in Bosnia to begin in earnest. A remarkable multiethnic fabric (about 45 percent Muslim, 18 percent Croat, and 32 percent Serb) was soon ripped into shreds. The Croats sided with Croatia, the Serbs with the remaining Federal Republic of Yugoslavia (FRY), and the Muslims were on their own. In military terms, they were particularly disadvantaged because most of the equipment (about 85 percent) of the former Yugoslav National Army went to the FRY, and the rest went to Croatia. Aided by its location on the sea, Croatia was able to avoid an arms embargo, procuring arms illegally.

Beginning in mid-1992, images of the pallid faces of emaciated people appeared behind the barbed-wire fences of concentration camps. This unsettled a continent, whose collective conscience recalled similar images of the Holocaust and the haunting slogan, "never again." The practice of ridding a territory of the unwanted members of another ethnic group – by threats of violence, as well as rape and murder – came to be known as "ethnic cleansing." While all sides engaged in atrocities, the Muslim population endured the brunt of such acts. The ethnic breakdown in victims can be somewhat accurately surmised from the ethnic breakdown of the first individuals indicted by the international tribunal in The Hague: about 70 percent Serb, 25 percent Croat, and 5 percent Muslim.

On May 30, the Council imposed, by Resolution 757 (1992), broad sanctions on the FRY (Serbia and Montenegro). The resolution banned all international trade, prohibited air travel, blocked financial transactions, banned sporting and cultural exchanges, and suspended scientific and technical cooperation. In November, this was extended to prohibit transshipment of goods through the FRY, by Resolution 787 (1992). Resolution 820, of April 17, 1993, further tightened the sanctions.

The UN Protection Force (UNPROFOR) for the former Yugoslavia was initially established by the Security Council in February 1992, as a peacekeeping operation with the consent of the FRY and other governments, in Resolution 743 (1992). As the situation deteriorated, its mandate was expanded from monitoring demilitarization in so-called UN protected areas in Croatia to conducting more complex security operations and protecting aid workers and convoys in Croatia and Bosnia and Herzegovina.

Then, in 1993, the Security Council established "safe areas" around five Bosnian towns and the city of Sarajevo in Resolutions 819 (1993) and 824 (1993). The original proposal to create such havens, made in August 1992 by then president of the International Committee of the Red Cross (ICRC), Cornelio Sommaruga, contained numerous provisions that were ignored in the actual implementation: demilitarization, continued negotiations, and well-defined geographic areas adequately protected with military force. UNPROFOR was given an ambitious but ambiguous mandate to protect them in Resolution 836 (1993):

> The Security Council authorizes [UNPROFOR] acting in self-defence, to take the necessary measures, including the use of force, in reply to bombardments against the safe areas by any of the parties or to armed incursion into them or in the event of any deliberate obstruction in or around those areas to the freedom of movement of UNPROFOR or of protected humanitarian convoys.

While UNPROFOR operated on the ground, an apparently general authorization was given to member states to take "all necessary measures, through the use of air power" to support ground forces in and around designated safe areas. Though unclear in the text itself, the decision to initiate the use of air power was to be taken by the Secretary-General, in consultation with the members of the Security Council.[36]

This served to deter attacks in the short term, but air power was ultimately ineffective because Western states were unwilling to put their vulnerable peacekeepers at risk. Moreover, "dual-key" decision making meant that the Special Representative of the Secretary-General (SRSG) and the force commander had to agree to initiate coercive military responses. When Srebrenica was overrun by the Bosnian Serbs in 1995, it became synonymous with the disparity between Council rhetoric and resolve.[37]

Another enforcement tack was taken in Resolution 827 of May 25, 1993, which established an international criminal tribunal to prosecute persons responsible for serious violations of international humanitarian law (IHL) committed in the territory of the FRY between January 1, 1991, and "a date to be determined by the Security Council upon the restoration of peace." The Yugoslav tribunal's indictments of the two most visible and notorious Bosnian Serb personalities – the politician, Radovan Karadzic, and the military leader, Ratko Mladic – at least served to exclude indicted war criminals from subsequent peace negotiations in Dayton, Ohio, in 1995.[38] Nonetheless, they have not yet been brought to trial, or even arrested, along with 25 other indicted war criminals hiding or even living openly either in Bosnia or Serbia. However, Bosnian Serb General Radislav Krstic, who was responsible for Europe's worst massacres since the Second World War, the systematic execution of more than 7,000 unarmed men and boys near Srebrenica, was the first convicted on a charge of genocide in the wars that broke up the former Yugoslavia.

Impartiality was the bedrock for successful peacekeeping operations during the Cold War, but such principles and the accompanying UN culture and command structures were particularly ill-suited when there was no peace to keep. The return of concentration camps and large scale human displacement in Europe provided graphic evidence of the frailty of multiethnic states and the need to apply deadly force to halt violence against civilians. The UN's mixing of consensual and nonconsensual activities was unworkable. The world organization had no comparative advantage in warfare or even the robust use of military force. The apparent success of North Atlantic Treaty Organization (NATO) air strikes and the Croatian military offensive in August and September 1995 reinforced this view, when they succeeded in coercing the parties to negotiate at Dayton, Ohio, in November 1995. The subsequent Dayton Peace Agreement was implemented and maintained by the Implementation Force (IFOR) and Stabilization Force (SFOR).

IFOR was deployed in Bosnia six days after the signing in Paris of the Dayton Peace Accords, on December 14, 1995. Earlier resolutions on Bosnia had authorized member states to act nationally or "through regional arrangements," but this was the first delegation *stricto sensu*. Under the Dayton agreement, the parties "invited" the Security Council to adopt the resolution to establish IFOR.[39] Resolution 1031 (1995) authorized member states "acting through or in co-operation with the organization referred to in Annex 1-A of the Peace Agreement [sc. NATO] ... under unified command and control" to take "all necessary measures to effect the implementation of and to ensure compliance with Annex 1-A of the Peace Agreement." NATO was not explicitly mentioned in the text of the resolution, nor in Resolution 1088 (1996) establishing SFOR as IFOR's legal successor.

Ultimately, protection for affected populations was problematic, to say the least. As many as 200,000 to 230,000 people died during UNPROFOR's watch, prior to Dayton. At the same time, there were positive results. Humanitarian succour was provided over the four years to some 4.3 million victims – more than 850,000 refugees, 1.6 million IDPs, and 1.8 million additional war-affected people. Despite the clear incompatibility between consensual and nonconsensual operations, at least the war aims of the Bosnian Serbs and of the FRY for a "Greater Serbia" were frustrated. The mission also pointed to the difficulty in protecting safe areas without the deployment of significant ground forces and a genuine willingness to use air power.

## SOMALIA, 1992–1993

The cumulative costs of poverty and a pattern of corrupt rule came together in tragedy shortly after the end of the Cold War in Somalia. In the power vacuum that followed the January 1991 ousting of President Mohammed Siad Barre, this ethnically, linguistically, and religiously homogeneous country imploded into clan-based civil war. Talks held in June and July 1991 led to the Djibouti Accords and the appointment of Ali Mahdi Mohamed as interim president. But the leader of a rival faction, General Mohamed Farah Aideed, rejected the accords. From November 1991 onward, heavy fighting persisted in the capital, Mogadishu.

On December 23, 1991, ICRC President Cornelio Sommaruga wrote to outgoing UN Secretary-General Javier Pérez de Cuéllar, requesting UN action, and followed it up with a visit to newly elected Secretary-General Boutros Boutros-Ghali early in January. In mid-January, the ICRC publicly reported that hundreds of thousands of refugees from the conflict were on the brink of starvation in camps south of the capital. The office of the UN High Commissioner for Refugees (UNHCR) reported in late January that 140,000 Somali refugees had reached Kenya, with another 700 arriving each day.

On January 23, 1992, the Security Council imposed Resolution 733, a Chapter VII arms embargo against Somalia. By March, an effective cease-fire had not been implemented. In light of the immediate threat posed by severe food shortages to a large proportion of Somalia's population, the Secretary-General reported that implementation of a planned relief programme should proceed, with the consequences of obstructing it made clear to the leaders of the two main armed factions.[40] On March 17, 1992, the Security Council unanimously adopted Resolution 746 (1992), which – though not under Chapter VII – stated that the Council was "deeply disturbed by the magnitude of the human suffering caused by the conflict and concerned that the continuation of the situation in Somalia constitutes a threat to international peace and security." In the discussion on Resolution 746, the Council's primary concern appears to have been the effect of the war on the provision of humanitarian assistance to the starving population, with only passing reference to the massive flow of refugees.[41]

The situation continued to deteriorate throughout 1992. The first UN Operation in Somalia (UNOSOM I) was deployed with the consent of the two leading factions in April. Because the force was comprised of only 500 soldiers and there existed no governing authority capable of maintaining law and order, the force was unable to implement its basic peacekeeping mandate. The provision of 3,500 UNOSOM security personnel for the protection of humanitarian relief efforts was approved in August, through Resolution 775 (1992), but deployment was slow and the situation worsened by the day. By October 1992, the Secretary-General reported that almost 4.5 million of Somalia's 6 million population were threatened by severe malnutrition and related diseases. Of those, at least 1.5 million were at immediate mortal risk. An estimated 300,000 had already died in the preceding 11 months.[42]

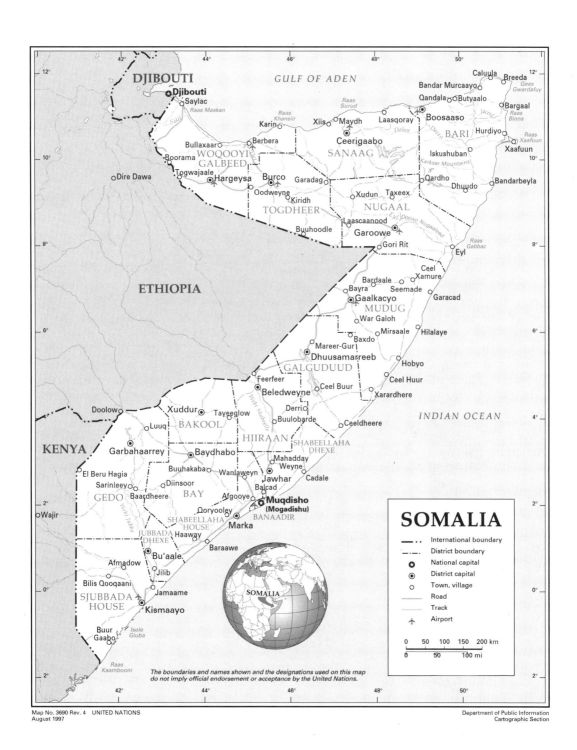

**FIGURE 5.5: MAP OF SOMALIA**

On November 29, Secretary-General Boutros Boutros-Ghali advised the Council that the only way that relief operations could continue was through resort to enforcement provisions under Chapter VII of the Charter, combined with parallel action to promote national reconciliation and remove the main factors that created the human emergency.[43] This recommendation came four days after an offer from the US to provide 20,000 troops as part of a multinational force authorized by the UN, owing in some part to the unprecedented media exposure given to the humanitarian disaster.[44]

On December 3, 1992, the Council unanimously adopted Resolution 794 (1992). Though recognizing the "unique character" of the situation, it stated that the "magnitude of the human tragedy caused by the conflict in Somalia, further exacerbated by the obstacles being created to the distribution of humanitarian assistance, constitutes a threat to international peace and security." In response, the Council, "*[a]cting* under Chapter VII … *authorises* the Secretary-General and Member States cooperating to implement the offer [by the United States to organize and lead an operation] to use all necessary means to establish as soon as possible a secure environment for humanitarian relief operations in Somalia."

Twenty-four hours later, outgoing US President George Bush ordered 28,000 troops into Somalia in Operation Restore Hope (also known as Unified Task Force, or UNITAF) to ensure the safe delivery of international assistance. The primary concern of the Security Council, as expressed in statements before and after the vote, was the delivery of humanitarian aid. In explanation of its vote, Washington stressed the essentially peaceful and limited character of the operation and that the action represented an important step toward a "post-Cold War world order."[45] China – which had cast its first affirmative vote for an enforcement resolution – and the Non-Aligned Movement (NAM) emphasized the unique character of the crisis and the role given to the Secretary-General and the Security Council.[46] Secretary-General Boutros-Ghali later stated that the Security Council had "established a precedent in the history of the United Nations: it decided for the first time to intervene militarily for strictly humanitarian purposes."[47]

On May 4, 1993, the US formally handed over to a second UN operation, UNOSOM II. The prior military operation, led by the remaining superpower, had been narrowly conceived. Now the UN's expanded mandate in Resolution 814 (1993) specified a host of activities categorically rejected by the US, including nation-building, disarming the factions, and arresting leaders such as General Aideed. Twenty-four Pakistani soldiers were killed on June 5 while inspecting weapons dumps in accordance with the expanded mandate. The next day, the Security Council passed Resolution 837 (1993), reaffirming that the Secretary-General was authorized to "take all necessary measures against those responsible for the armed attacks … to establish the effective authority of UNOSOM II throughout Somalia, including to secure the investigation of their actions and their arrest and detention for prosecution, trial and punishment."

This was tantamount to a declaration of war against Aideed's militia. A series of confrontations between a heavily reinforced UNOSOM II and the militia continued through the summer. The most infamous was the "Olympic Hotel battle" on October 3, 1993, when US Rangers and Delta commandos, who remained under US command and control, made an unsuccessful attempt to capture Aideed. Three US Black Hawk helicopters were downed and 18 Americans died, as did one of the Malaysians who came to extract them. At least 500 and as many as 1,000 Somalis – many of them civilians – were killed in the firefight. The dead US pilots being dragged through the streets to jeering crowds of onlookers became an enduring image of the risks of humanitarian impulses. Those who saw a "CNN effect" encouraging intervention also saw the impacts of unpalatable images forcing the withdrawal of military forces.

Within days, President Clinton set a pullout date for US troops for the following March. UNOSOM II was more ambitious than the earlier US-led UNITAF effort, but it had fewer warfighting resources. And by March 28, 1995, the complete withdrawal of UN troops had been completed, although few of UNOSOM II's mandated objectives had, in fact, been achieved.[48]

The mission was not without its successes. The impact of the famine was alleviated, as probably only 50,000 to 100,000 of the 1.5 million menaced by starvation actually died. Virtually the entire population of 5 million people received assistance. Half of the 1.5 million people driven from their homes returned a year later. The estimated 400–500,000 who died in the two years preceding the UNITAF intervention at least were not replicated, although there were an estimated 10,000 Somali casualties during the UNITAF and UNOSOM II operations.

But the post-1995 country remained for many the epitome of a failed state, essentially without a functioning central government and a breakaway quasi-independent Somaliland to the north. A former SRSG, Mohamed Sahnoun, argues that Somalia provides ample evidence "of how the failure of the international community to intervene in different phases of a crisis can be detrimental and lead to further deterioration."[49] Moreover, from a humanitarian point of view a paradox emerged: the costs of the military intervention ($1 billion for UNITAF and $1.6 billion for UNOSOM II) dwarfed humanitarian and development efforts by at least 10 to 1.

In macro-political terms, the "Somalia syndrome" became shorthand for the growing reluctance of Western countries to sustain military casualties in distant lands in the pursuit of fundamentally humanitarian objectives. Other "dirty words" entered the international public policy lexicon, including the difficulty of "nation-building," wariness about "mission creep," and the emphasis on a predetermined "exit strategy."

## RWANDA AND EASTERN ZAIRE, 1994–1996

Since Rwandan independence, serious tensions existed between the minority Tutsi population (15 percent) – which had constituted the pastoral monarchy that the ruling class favoured during the colonial period – and the majority Hutus. Previous instances of massive ethnic violence began shortly after independence in Rwanda. Some commentators have used the term "genocide" to describe the violence that took place in 1963, 1966, and 1973. As many as 20,000 Tutsi victims were killed in the first case, and thousands in the other two.

The horrors beginning in April 1994, however, completely overshadowed these previous events. On April 6, a surface-to-air missile shot down the plane carrying Rwandan President Juvénal Habyarimana and his Burundian counterpart, Cyprien Ntaryamira. Fighting broke out within hours in Rwanda, and a pre-planned strategy of genocide was put into effect. By the end of the following day militant Hutus, claiming that Habyarimana had been assassinated by Tutsi rebels, retaliated by killing Prime Minister Agathe Uwilingiyimana and seizing control of the government. This provoked rampages against Tutsis and moderate Hutus by security forces and armed gangs loyal to the government. Most notorious among the killers were the *Interhamwe* (those who stand together) and *Impuzamugambi* (the single-minded ones) – predominantly Hutu militias trained by the national army and organized as the youth wings of the major Hutu parties. The Rwandan Patriotic Front (RPF), led by Paul Kagame, recommenced its civil war with the Rwandan government from its bases in nearby Uganda.

At the time of Habyarimana's death, there were 2,500 UN peacekeepers stationed in Rwanda as part of the UN Assistance Mission in Rwanda (UNAMIR), a lightly armed peacekeeping mission designed to monitor the Arusha Accords, which had been signed the previous August. After 10 Belgian troops assigned to guard the prime minister were killed and mutilated on April 7, Belgium stated its intention to withdraw its 440 troops from UNAMIR.[50] The Secretary-General reported to the Council that UNAMIR's position had become untenable. He outlined alternatives: a massive reinforcement of UNAMIR to coerce the sides into a cease-fire; reduction of the UN's commitment to a small group, headed by the force commander and supported by a staff of about 270, which would attempt to bring about an agreement on a cease-fire; or complete withdrawal.[51]

Resolution 912 (1994) stated that the Council decided to "adjust the mandate of UNAMIR." On April 21, in the middle of the crisis, the Security Council voted to reduce that number to 270. By withdrawing the force as the bloodbath was gathering speed, the UN sent an unmistakable message to the genocidal forces that there was little or no international resolve to stand in their way. Even two weeks after the onset of the killings, Security Council members and UN officials were unwilling to use the term "genocide" and continued to call for a cease-fire among the warring factions.

One dissenting voice in the military wilderness was Major General Romeo Dallaire who, as UNAMIR's force commander, pleaded for 5,000 well-trained soldiers. In his view, they could have slowed the pace of the killings and perhaps turned the tide. He also requested an expansion of rules of engagement to incorporate the protection of civilians. Both requests were denied. Although some dispute whether 5,000 soldiers could have really stopped the genocide,[52] the appalling number of deaths may have been reduced substantially. Illustrative examples were the protection of some 10,000 civilians in Kigali's Amahoro Stadium and others at the King Faisal Hospital, both with only a handful of dedicated UN soldiers.

Although the remaining troops deterred some abuse, they were clearly inadequate to the task. From April to July 1994, Hutu extremists systematically murdered hundreds of thousands (estimates range as high as 800,000) of Tutsis, as well as Hutu moderates.[53] Women and children suffered in the aftermath of the genocide, with an estimated 47,000 children orphaned; 250,000 to 500,000 women raped; and 2,000 to 5,000 children outcast because they were conceived as a result of rape.[54]

Despite hypothetical offers from some 50 potential troop-contributing countries, there was little genuine willingness to intervene. By the third week of April, the Secretary-General put three options before the Council: strengthen UNAMIR by several thousand troops, reduce its strength, or withdraw completely. Of the three, he advocated the plan calling for 5,500 troops to be deployed in Kigali under an expanded UNAMIR mandate to provide security to humanitarian organizations for the distribution of relief supplies and to establish access to sites where displaced persons and refugees were concentrated and ensure their protection.[55]

This plan was resisted by the US, which questioned the UN proposal, arguing for more restructuring of the plan before going into Kigali. Part of the constraint was the early May issuance of Presidential Decision Directive 25, issued by President William J. Clinton, which made US funding and participation less likely. Following on the decisive 1993 public reactions to the debacle in Somalia and the aborted mission to Haiti, this document effectively rang the death knell for the policy announced, with much fanfare, by the incoming Clinton administration, as "assertive multilateralism."

The lassitude was condemned by the Organization of African Unity (OAU) and aid agencies, which accused the Council of applying different standards in Africa than in Europe. Massacres continued, and finally, on April 29, the Secretary-General urged the Council to reconsider its position and take "forceful action to restore law and order."[56]

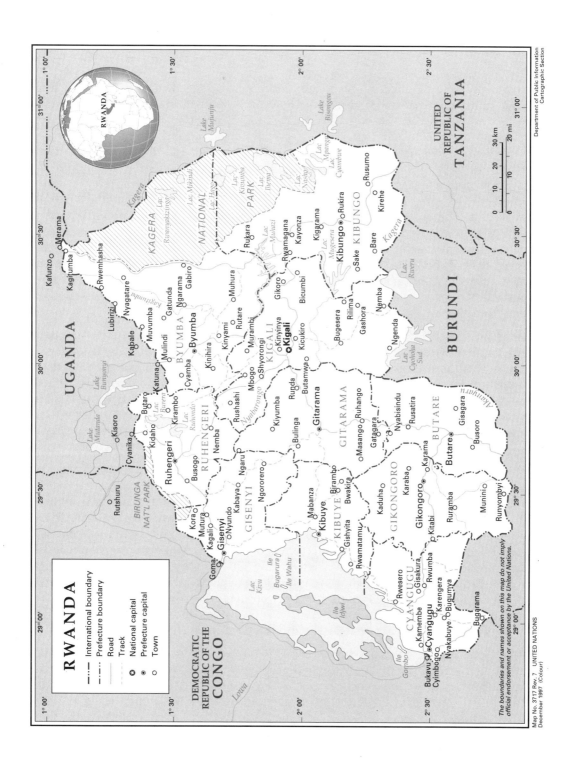

**FIGURE 5.6: MAP OF RWANDA**

Early UN reports systematically understated the scale of the carnage. By late May, Secretary-General Boutros-Ghali estimated that between 250,000 and 500,000 Rwandans, mostly Tutsi, had already been killed. He concluded that "the magnitude of the human calamity that has engulfed Rwanda might be unimaginable but for its having transpired. On the basis of the evidence that has emerged, there can be little doubt that it constitutes genocide."[57]

On May 17, the Council adopted Resolution 918 (1994), which imposed an arms embargo and authorized an expansion of UNAMIR. Washington argued that this should take place in two phases, however, with the first comprising only 150 unarmed observers and an 800-strong Ghanaian battalion to secure the Kigali airport. Despite the Secretary-General's report, governments resisted using the term "genocide," as it would have made their policies of inaction untenable in light of the 1948 convention.[58] Resolution 918 avoided the term, referring instead to "the killing of members of an ethnic group with the intention of destroying such a group in whole or in part."[59] It was not until June 8 that the Council, in Resolution 925 (1994), noted "with the gravest concern the reports indicating that acts of genocide have occurred in Rwanda." Although this resolution was intended to accelerate the deployment of the expanded UNAMIR, 10 days later the UNAMIR force still consisted only of about 500 troops under the command of Dallaire. The Secretary-General estimated that UNAMIR would be unable to undertake its full mandate for another three months.[60]

In a letter to the Secretary-General, dated June 20, 1994, France announced that it was prepared to intervene in Rwanda, "with its main European and African partners," to put an end to the massacres and protect groups threatened with "extinction." France requested Chapter VII authorization "in the spirit of resolution 794" (which had authorized the US-led UNITAF operation in Somalia) for itself and Senegal "to send a force in without delay, so as to maintain a presence pending the arrival of the expanded UNAMIR."[61] This offer met widespread suspicion, owing to France's close ties to the ousted Hutu regime and particularly its role in arming and training the predominantly Hutu government forces.

Despite the serious misgivings expressed by a number of Council members and an outright rejection by the RPF, the Security Council adopted Resolution 929 (1994) on June 22, 1994. The text recognized that the situation "constitutes a unique case which demands an urgent response by the international community" and "that the magnitude of the humanitarian crisis in Rwanda constitutes a threat to peace and security in the region." The Council authorized France to conduct an operation under national command and control to improve security and protect displaced persons, refugees, and civilians at risk. Under Chapter VII, France was authorized to use "all necessary means" to achieve these objectives. References to impartiality and humanitarian goals, as well as a two-month time limit, were added to the resolution during brief but intensive consultations.[62] Five abstentions to the resolution (Brazil, China, New Zealand, Nigeria, and Pakistan) suggested deep divisions within the Council about authorizing a French intervention.

While expressing its strong opposition, the RPF did not seek a confrontation with French forces, and on July 18 the RPF unilaterally declared a cease-fire, which effectively ended the civil war. The presence of the French seemed to have two results. It slowed the advance of the RPF and thereby permitted the former government forces to escape, and it helped to avert a massive outflow of refugees into Zaire, which many had predicted might rival the earlier flood of almost 1 million to the camps in Goma. In the eyes of critics, the intervention seemed designed primarily to secure French interests in the area, including preserving the remnants of the Hutu leadership that had fomented genocide.[63] On July 19, a government of national unity was formed, two weeks ahead of the scheduled French withdrawal from Rwanda.

The UNAMIR II mission never really got off the ground. On August 1, 1994, it still had fewer than 500 soldiers. The RPF had established military control over most of the country, and about 1.5 million (mainly Hutu) Rwandans had sought refuge in Zaire, out of fear of retribution. Of a total population of approximately 7 million, 3 million had been internally displaced, more than 2 million had fled to neighbouring countries, and roughly 800,000 had been killed. The inability of the UN force to protect civilians (including national UN staff) was subsequently described in the understated but scathing conclusions of the independent inquiry as "one of the most painful and debated issues of this period."[64]

On November 8, 1994, the Security Council adopted Resolution 955 (1994), providing for the establishment of the International Criminal Tribunal for Rwanda. Modelled after the one for the former Yugoslavia, the Rwandan counterpart was tasked with "prosecuting persons responsible for genocide and other serious violations of international humanitarian law committed in the territory of Rwanda and Rwandan citizens responsible for genocide and other such violations committed in the territory of neighbouring States, between January 1, 1994 and December 31, 1994."

The tribunal is located in Arusha, Tanzania, and has been plagued by corruption, mismanagement, and delays. More than $500 million has been spent, but only nine persons have been convicted. Nonetheless, of the 63 people who have been indicted, 49 are in custody (including the 9 who have been convicted). Two-thirds of the government ministers in office in April 1994 are in custody. What is more, the tribunal has recorded some historical breakthroughs, including the conviction of a former prime minister; the first conviction for genocide; and the first conviction for which rape was considered an integral component of genocide. At the same time, more than 100,000 Rwandans accused of participating in the genocide are also in custody inside Rwanda, most living under appalling conditions. The Arusha tribunal seems to represent the best hope for dealing with the persons responsible for the genocide and helping to set standards for international accountability, although some argue that local accountability would better facilitate longer term reconciliation.[65]

One outcome of the Rwandan genocide, and the subsequent mass exodus of Rwandans into Zaire, was the destabilization of eastern Zaire. The ongoing conflict involves troops from five neighbouring countries and has been dubbed "Africa's World War." The million refugees from Rwanda who gathered in eastern Zaire had by 1996 exacerbated ongoing problems of political and ethnic friction in the African Great Lakes region. Among the refugees were an estimated 100,000 to 150,000 members of the *Interhamwe* and other Hutu militant groups. Intense fighting in Zaire in November forced all international humanitarian workers to evacuate and caused 600,000 displaced Zairians to flee into Rwanda.[66] Rwanda and Zaire were mutually suspicious about each other's motives – Rwanda felt threatened by the *Interhamwe* and Zaire by the new government in Rwanda itself.

On November 7, 1996, the Secretary-General proposed to the Council that a multinational force be dispatched to eastern Zaire.[67] Kinshasa agreed to the deployment of such a force the next day,[68] and on November 9 the Council passed Resolution 1078 (1996). Chapter VII was invoked because the "magnitude of the present humanitarian crisis" constituted a threat to international peace and security. The Council clearly was not aiming to mount a UN operation, but rather appealed to a coalition of the willing. Canada offered to lead a temporary and strictly humanitarian operation,[69] which was duly authorized to use "all necessary means" by Resolution 1080 (1996). But the proposed intervention never materialized. Again, there was no enthusiasm to jump into the fray in the African Great Lakes. Good intentions were in greater supply than operational capacities or political will.

By December 5, the crisis in eastern Zaire appeared to have abated. The voluntary repatriation of many Rwandan refugees and the increased access of humanitarian organizations had partially achieved the proposed mission's objectives. And with the dispersal of the remaining refugees over large areas of eastern Zaire, the multinational force would have been of little utility at its approved level. In a letter, dated December 13, Canada decided to withdraw its command and forces by December 31.[70]

## HAITI, 1994–1997

Following a successful military ouster of "Baby Doc" Duvalier, a new constitution was approved in 1987, and in 1990 Jean-Bertrand Aristide was elected president of Haiti, with 67 percent of the popular vote during an internationally monitored election. As the first democratically elected government in the poorest country of the Western hemisphere, there was widespread international opprobrium when Aristide was removed from office by a coup d'état on September 30, 1991.

The OAS swiftly condemned the overthrow and recommended the imposition of diplomatic and, later, economic sanctions.[71] The Security Council failed to adopt a resolution on the issue, reportedly because China and certain NAM states were concerned about increased Security Council activism.[72] The General Assembly, by contrast, strongly condemned in Resolution 46/7 (1991) the "illegal replacement of the constitutional President of Haiti," affirming that "any entity resulting from that illegal situation" was unacceptable.

The refusal of Haiti's military dictators to reinstate the Aristide government, combined with the continued persecution of his supporters, eventually led the Security Council to impose a mandatory economic embargo in June 1993. Resolution 841 (1993) was adopted explicitly under Chapter VII and listed a variety of factors that had led the Council to determine "that, in these unique and exceptional circumstances, the continuation of this situation threatens international peace and security in the region." These circumstances covered "the incidence of humanitarian crises, including mass displacements of population," and the "climate of fear of persecution and economic dislocation which could increase the number of Haitians seeking refuge in neighbouring Member States."

Indeed, Haiti had many of the attributes of a country enduring a deadly conflict – in particular, substantial forced displacement, massive human rights abuses, and a devastated economy – without actually having experienced a civil war. An estimated 60,000 to 100,000 refugees fled Haiti by small craft for the shores of Florida and the Dominican Republic between 1991 and 1994. At least as many went into hiding within Haiti.

The Security Council embargo led the Haitian military junta to accept the Governor's Island Agreement (GIA), which provided for President Aristide to return to power. Sanctions were lifted on August 27, 1993, but the agreement collapsed when violence against Aristide's supporters resumed in September and October. This corresponded with severe reservations in the US about the merits of sending US soldiers to a volatile country after the death of 18 in Mogadishu. The USS *Harlan County* arrived in Port-au-Prince harbour on October 11, only to be withdrawn the next day after crowds of protesters staged a rally on the docks.

The Security Council responded by reimposing sanctions in Resolution 873 (1993) and authorizing a naval blockade under Chapters VII and VIII of the Charter in Resolution 875 (1993). But the date set in the GIA for Aristide's return, October 30, 1993, passed with only a presidential statement warning that sanctions might be strengthened in the future.[73]

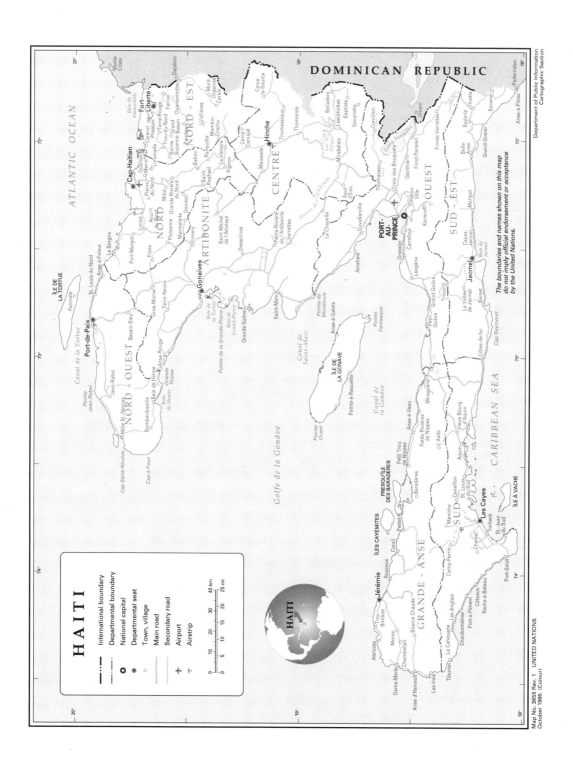

**FIGURE 5.7: MAP OF HAITI**

In February 1994, Aristide reversed his previous position and publicly signalled support for a surgical intervention to overthrow the de facto government and restore him to power.[74] On July 29, 1994, nearly three years after the coup, the Aristide government-in-exile formally requested "prompt and decisive action."[75] Two days later, the Security Council, acting under Chapter VII, passed Resolution 940 (1994), which authorized a multinational force to use

> all necessary means to facilitate the departure from Haiti of the military leadership, … the prompt return of the legitimately elected President and the restoration of the legitimate authorities of the Government of Haiti, and to establish and maintain a secure and stable environment that will permit implementation of the Governors Island Agreement.

Six weeks later, President Clinton delivered a televised speech advising Raoul Cédras and the "de factos" that their time was up and indicating that military action was imminent. An invasion was avoided when former US President Jimmy Carter, accompanied by former Senator Sam Nunn and former chair of the Joint Chiefs of Staff Colin Powell, secured an agreement with the Haitian military to return Aristide to power. By the end of September, more than 21,000 US soldiers and another 1,250 soldiers from 28 other nations were peacefully deployed in Haiti under the Multinational Force, or what the Pentagon called Operation Restore Democracy. There were no casualties among the interveners, though a number of Haitians died during violent demonstrations. International reaction to the events was generally positive, with only a few states expressing serious reservations.[76] Aristide returned to Port-au-Prince on October 15, 1994.

After a brief period, the US-led force began what many deem to have been a model handover from a coalition to a UN mission that followed after the election of René Préval in December 1995 and the peaceful transition in government in February 1996. The gradual handover to the UN Mission in Haiti (UNMIH) was completed by March 1996. Planning for the transition from the US-led enforcement to the UN peacekeeping mission, including the incorporation of UNMIH planning staff, began eight months prior to the actual transition. The presence of a US general as the first UNMIH commander and solid relations between him and the SRSG also facilitated this process. The mandate of the UN mission was not extended in December 1997, because China, citing Taiwan's links to Haiti, vetoed the resolution.

While the transition was successful, the overall impact of the intervention in the country does not appear to have been long lasting. The reforms of the police, the penal system, and the judiciary were not extensive or complete enough to ensure stability for Haiti's future. The shortcomings, however, were with the lack of follow-through on the nation-building side, rather than the military intervention itself.

## SIERRA LEONE, 1997–

Since the 1960s coups, countercoups, and thuggery were defining features of Sierra Leone's sociopolitical order.[77] By 1971, Sierra Leone's body politic had "been transformed into a de facto one-party government," with the Siaka Stevens regime using violence and political chicanery to stay in power.[78] In 1984, Stevens' chosen successor, Major-General Joseph Saidu Momoh, took over power "in a stage-managed election."[79]

As the civil war next door posed a serious security threat to Stevens' government, he permitted ECOMOG to use Sierra Leone territory to launch air strikes against NPLF strongholds. It has been suggested that former NPFL warlord Charles Taylor thereafter supported rogue elements inside Sierra Leone, which began a rebel movement in March 1991.[80] The rebels, who referred to themselves as the Revolutionary United Front (RUF), were led by a former army corporal of the Republic of Sierra Leone Military Forces (RSLMF), Foday Sankoh. The RUF remained a constant source of irritation for Momoh until he was ousted from power by a group of junior RSLMF officers led by army Captain Valentine Strasser in April 1992. Strasser and the other coup plotters established the National Provisional Revolutionary Council (NPRC) as the core governing structure for the country.

Under the Strasser regime, the RSLMF was unable to quell the RUF rebellion, which easily overran government forces and seized key diamond-producing areas. By 1992, more than 10,000 people, mostly women and children, had been killed, 300,000 had fled the country, and 400,000 were internally displaced. As the RUF insurrection gained momentum it became infamous for systematically raping women and children and hacking off limbs in order to terrorize and subjugate the local population.

By early 1995, RUF forces had effectively laid siege to the capital city of Freetown. Anarchic conditions soon prevailed. Thousands of civilians were slaughtered, raped, and maimed. As a result, Strasser, who was deposed in January 1996 by his deputy, Brigadier Julius Maada Bio, employed the services of a South African-based private military company, Executive Outcomes (EO). At the peak of operations against the RUF (January to March 1996), the EO force grew to about 250, before resuming a contracted level of human resources below 100 personnel from April 1996 to the termination of the contract at the end of January 1997. EO received an average monthly payment of about $1.7 million for the duration of its 21-month contract.[81]

EO assisted the NPRC to force RUF guerrillas back into the bush and establish the necessary conditions for elections in February and March 1996. EO trained company-sized contingents of the RSLMF and enlisted the support of the *Kamajors* (traditional hunters with exceptional bushcraft skills). They also provided the leadership, helicopters, and fire support necessary to pursue a successful small-scale war against the RUF. By late 1995, although the rebellion persisted, the siege of Freetown had been lifted and the RUF's headquarters had been destroyed. The Koindu diamond area and the Sierra Rutile area had been liberated and mining operations had been resumed.[82] There were, however, allegations of human rights abuses by EO, and the government reacted to international pressure by terminating the company's contract.

In February and March of 1996, Sierra Leone held presidential and parliamentary elections. The Sierra Leone Peoples Party, led by Ahmed Tijan Kabbah, was elected to power. However, warring between the government and RUF, which contested the elections, continued unabated. On November 30, 1996, the government of Côte d'Ivoire, ECOWAS, the UN, the OAU, and the CIS facilitated peace talks that culminated in the Abidjan Accord, ending the war.

On May 25, 1997, approximately six months after the war, several junior military officers, led by Major Johnny Koromah, and the RUF carried out a successful coup d'état against President Kabbah's democratically elected government, forcing him to flee to Guinea.[83] Though no longer in de facto control of the country, before leaving Kabbah requested that Nigeria and ECOWAS intervene to forestall the conflict and restore constitutional order to the country.[84]

There was universal condemnation of the coup, including a rebuke by the president of the Security Council.[85] The reaction of the OAU, during its Council of Ministers Sixty-Sixth Ordinary Session in Harare in May 1997, strayed far away from its historically strict adherence to the principles of nonintervention in the internal affairs of a country, stating that it

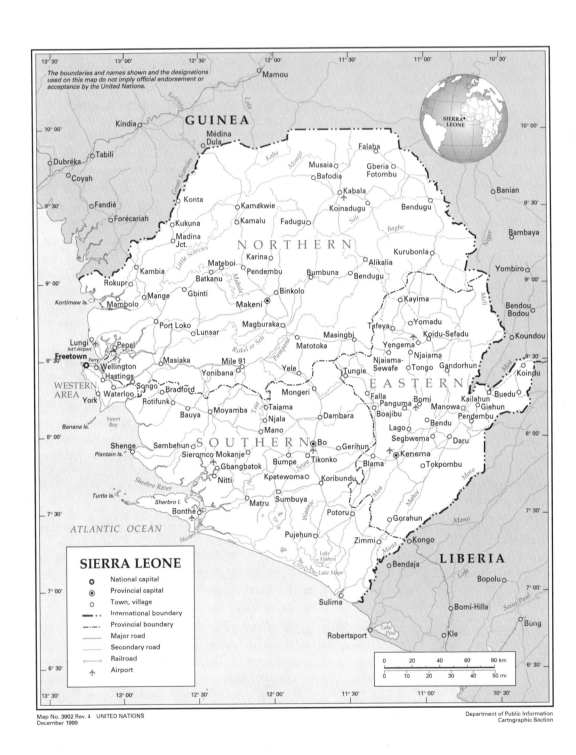

FIGURE 5.8: MAP OF SIERRA LEONE

"strongly and unequivocally condemns, the coup d'état ... and calls for the immediate restoration of constitutional order [and] appeals to the leaders of ECOWAS to assist the people of
Sierra Leone to restore constitutional order to the country."[86] This was one of the first times
that the OAU publicly took a stand in the name of human suffering and democracy against an
illegal coup and seizure of power.

In response to Kabbah's request of May 26, 1997, Nigeria sent forces to Sierra Leone to
protect Nigerian citizens, prevent further bloodshed, and restore law and order.[87] Nigeria
also based its decision to intervene on Article 58 of the ECOWAS Revised Treaty of 1993,
obliging member states "to work to safeguard and consolidate relations conducive to the
maintenance of peace, stability and security within the region."[88]

In early August 1997, pursuant to requests by the member states of ECOWAS, General
Sani Abacha, Nigeria's head of state and ECOWAS chair, issued an "executive directive"
authorizing an economic blockade against Sierra Leone, to be enforced by ECOMOG. On
August 30, 1997, during the Twentieth Summit of ECOWAS, in Abuja, ECOWAS officially
mandated ECOMOG to enforce sanctions and restore law and order to the country. There
were two separate interventions in Sierra Leone: the first under the authority of the Republic
of Nigeria and the second under ECOWAS.[89]

Although there was no Security Council authorization, considerable support was offered
from other quarters. OAU member states justified the intervention on humanitarian and
prodemocratic grounds. UN Secretary-General Kofi Annan affirmed this perspective when
he stated, "Africa can no longer tolerate, and accept as fait accompli, coups against elected
governments, and the illegal seizure of power by military cliques, who sometimes act for
sectional interests, sometimes simply for their own."[90]

Finally, on October 8, 1997, the Security Council supported these endeavours by adopting Resolution 1132, which determined that the situation constituted a threat to international peace and security. The Council imposed arms and oil embargoes and a freeze on
travel by, and financial assets of, members of the military junta. And the Council expressly
authorized ECOWAS, under Chapter VIII, to cut off the Armed Forces Revolutionary
Council's (AFRC's) foreign military supplies.

Similar to Resolution 788 on Liberia, Resolution 1132 served as a *post de jure* authentica-
tion of ECOMOG. Embargoes had been in force since August 1997, and ECOWAS forces
had engaged in sporadic attacks over the following months. Despite the reference to
Chapter VIII, ECOWAS continued to operate in advance of its Council mandate – Nigerian
ECOMOG forces launched a major military assault in February 1998, an action subsequently welcomed in a presidential statement and later in Resolution 1162 (1998).[91]

On February 5, 1998, "responding to an attack by junta forces on its position at Lungi,
ECOMOG launched a military attack on the junta," which led to the removal of the junta
from power and expulsion from Freetown on February 12, 1998.[92] By early March 1998,
"ECOMOG [had] established itself successfully across most of the country." On March 10,
1998, President Kabbah returned to Freetown to resume his position as president of Sierra
Leone. The leaders of Nigeria, Guinea, Mali, and Niger and the vice-president of the Gambia
accompanied him. On April 17, 1998, the Security Council adopted Resolution 1162, which
commended ECOMOG for restoring peace to Sierra Leone.

ECOMOG expanded in an attempt to secure the rest of the country. However, the force
was not able to stamp its authority on the hinterland much beyond Freetown, and rebels
continued to terrorize and brutalize the civilian population. This situation reached a bloody
climax on January 6, 1999, when AFRC and RUF rebels overwhelmed ECOMOG forces and

swept into Freetown, killing thousands of civilians and systematically dismembering and raping tens of thousands of others. The fighting resulted in the deaths of some 5,000 people, including rebel fighters, ECOMOG soldiers, and large numbers of civilians. Up to 150,000 people were displaced in and around Freetown, and buildings and homes were razed before ECOMOG forces eventually managed to expel the rebels and regain control of the city.[93]

Fighting between government and rebel forces continued, and the Council established, by Resolution 1181 (1998), the UN Observer Mission in Sierra Leone (UNOMSIL) to monitor the security situation, disarmament, and observance of IHL. Subsequently, an ill-fated peace agreement – providing for an immediate cease-fire, power-sharing between the government and the RUF, and national reconciliation – was signed in Lomé on July 7, 1999.

In October 1999, UNOMSIL's mandate was taken over by the UN Mission in Sierra Leone (UNAMSIL), with a more robust mandate to "afford protection to civilians under imminent threat of physical violence." Security Council Resolution 1270 (1999) provided for a maximum authorized strength of 6,000 military personnel, with an ambitious mandate, including disarmament, demobilization, and reintegration. In early December 1999, the first company of 133 Kenyan soldiers arrived as the advance unit of the first new UNAMSIL battalion, to join some 223 UN military observers already on the ground. Four ECOMOG battalions already in Sierra Leone (composed of troops from Ghana, Guinea, and Nigeria) were "rehatted" as UN blue helmets. Deployment of the remaining units was painfully slow. From the outset, UN peacekeepers were denied freedom of movement, amid frequent cease-fire violations that included ambushes against civilians and UN personnel, the maintenance of illegal roadblocks, and RUF troop movements.[94]

UNAMSIL was directly challenged in January 2000, when peacekeepers from Kenya and Guinea surrendered assault rifles, several rocket-propelled grenade launchers, four armored personnel carriers, communications equipment, and other military gear in at least three ambushes by the RUF. The failure to respond caused US, UK, and some UN officials to worry that the rebels would be enticed to step up their armed challenges to UN forces as they took over from the departing ECOMOG troops.[95]

On February 7, 2000, the Security Council unanimously approved the Secretary-General's plans for strengthening UNAMSIL, by raising the maximum authorized strength from 6,000 to 11,000, and it granted the mission an expanded mandate under Chapter VII. Resolution 1289 provided a legal framework for coercive action, but this was not translated into assertive and credible action on the ground.

The force commander, General Vijay Jetley, continued to defend the peacekeepers' soft approach, saying that while the RUF was "not as fully committed to disarmament as it would like people to believe," patience was necessary. He stressed that UNAMSIL was a "peacekeeping force, not a combat force."[96] However, restraint and neutrality did not impress the RUF. Human Rights Watch reported in March 2000 that the RUF was regularly committing atrocities, including rapes, abductions, and looting near locations where UN forces were stationed. Intelligence sources also warned that despite Sankoh's public pledges to disarm, he had told his commanders that there would be no disarmament until the RUF had achieved a victory at the polls.

Sankoh, pardoned in the Lomé agreement, was participating in the transitional govern-ment even while keeping his war options open. The UN came under increasing pressure to end the charade by the RUF, which included new camps and deployment to Koidu (the seat of the RUF diamond-mining centre).[97] A direct challenge to Sankoh resulted in a crisis on May 1, 2000, when drunken rebels demanded that UNAMSIL return 10 RUF fighters who had turned over their weapons. When the peacekeepers refused, the rebels took 10 Kenyans hostages. On the same day, seven Indian peacekeepers were captured, along with their helicopters.[98] Significantly, these incidents coincided with the final departure of the last of four battalions of Nigerian ECOMOG troops.

Emboldened RUF forces again attacked UNAMSIL positions the next day, and the Kenyan battalion returned fire, which resulted in the death of four of their soldiers. Three more Kenyans were wounded, and about 50 other UNAMSIL personnel were captured. By May 5, the number of UN hostages had increased to 92 and then to more than 500, with the "disappearance" of a second Zambian contingent, which also lost 13 armored personnel carriers, which were used afterwards by the rebels in an assault on Freetown.

On May 7, the UK Ministry of Defence announced that it was sending a battalion of paratroopers and five warships to protect British nationals. News reports suggest that Freetown might have fallen to the RUF without the deployment of more than 1,000 British troops. In fact, the British force kept UNAMSIL from totally disintegrating. According to a UN official, "They stiffened the spines of everyone around by coming in, taking charge and simply stating that the RUF would not be allowed to succeed."[99] By securing the airport, they ensured the safe departure of expatriates, enabled UNAMSIL troops to be redeployed elsewhere in Freetown, and facilitated the arrival of thousands of additional peacekeepers. British forces also provided training to the Sierra Leone armed forces.

At the end of 2000, however, UNAMSIL still lacked direction and continued to languish in Freetown awaiting more troops. Major-General Vijay Jetley left after a disastrous political confrontation with his Nigerian lieutenants, but he was forthright:

> Most units under my command other than India, Kenya and Guinea have very little or no equipment with them. They have not been properly briefed in their country about the application of chapter VII in this mission for certain contingencies. It is for this precise reason that the troops do not have the mental aptitude or the will to fight the rebels when the situation so demanded.[100]

Currently, UNAMSIL continues to seek a negotiated settlement that would give the rebels a share of power. Until recently this has resulted in a pervasive unwillingness to deploy troops into rebel-held territory and derision among the inhabitants of Freetown.[101] UNAMSIL is being reinforced up to the authorized level of 11,000 troops, with training provided by the UK. And in July 2001, a tribunal was created and a planning team was sent to Sierra Leone.

Although prospects are now improving, the various missions to Sierra Leone have done little to reduce the civilian suffering or regional instability. Poorly armed and ill-disciplined UN troops were an inadequate response in the face of atrocities in Sierra Leone. At various times, private mercenaries, ECOMOG forces, and British soldiers proved more effective in employing the necessarily robust use of force.

## KOSOVO, 1999–

On June 28, 1989, Serbian President Slobodan Milosevic set the stage for the contemporary clash of nationalisms in the Balkans by inflaming Serbian fears of ethnic domination. His jingoistic speech invoked memories of the Serbs' defeat at the hands of the Turks precisely six centuries earlier. That same year, President Milosevic removed Kosovo's autonomy and replaced it with direct rule from Belgrade. Ethnic Albanian politicians in Kosovo responded by declaring independence in July 1990. They established parallel institutions that Serbia, in control of government in the formerly autonomous province, refused to recognize. Unrest continued through the decade, but international attention was focused elsewhere in the Balkans – Kosovo was not included in the Dayton Peace Accords.[102] Nonetheless, outgoing US President Bush issued a warning to President Milosevic on December 24, 1992, that "[i]n the event of conflict in Kosovo caused by Serbian action, the United States will be prepared to employ military force against the Serbs in Kosovo and in Serbia proper."[103]

The Kosovo cauldron simmered, until boiling over early in 1998, when dozens of suspected Albanian separatists were killed by Serb police. On March 31, 1998, Security Council Resolution 1160 (1998) condemned the use of excessive force by Serbian police and terrorist action by the Kosovo Liberation Army (KLA), imposed an arms embargo, and expressed support for a solution based on the territorial integrity of the FRY, but with a greater degree of autonomy for the Kosovar Albanians. Fighting continued and US-sponsored peace talks between Milosevic and the unofficial president of Kosovo, Ibrahim Rugova, broke down in May.

On September 23, 1998, Security Council Resolution 1199 (1998) "affirm[ed] that the deterioration of the situation in Kosovo constitutes a threat to peace and security in the region" and, under Chapter VII, demanded a ceasefire and action to improve the humanitarian situation. It further demanded that the FRY take concrete steps to implement the Contact Group demands of June 12, 1998 – including a cessation of action by security forces, the return of refugees and displaced persons, and free and unimpeded access for humanitarian organizations and supplies. The Council also decided that if these measures were not implemented, it would "*consider further action* and additional measures to maintain or restore peace and stability in the region."[104]

In the following week, reports of two massacres by Serbian forces of about 30 Kosovar Albanians strengthened NATO resolve. In a press conference on October 8, 1998, US Secretary of State Madeleine Albright said that the time had come to authorize military force if Milosevic failed to comply with existing resolutions. When questioned as to the need for a further Security Council resolution, she replied that "the United Nations has now spoken out on this subject a number of times."[105] *The Times* (of London) captured the curious mix of law and politics that underpinned this view:

> Diplomatic sources said yesterday that alliance members were approaching consensus on the legal basis for airstrikes. Although several countries, including Greece, Spain, Germany and Italy, had previously favoured seeking authorization from the United Nations Security Council, they now realized that was no longer realistic because of Moscow's pledge to veto military action.[106]

On October 13, 1998, the North Atlantic Council issued activation orders for a phased air campaign. NATO Secretary-General Javier Solana stated that execution of limited air operations would not begin for at least four days, to permit negotiations, but at the same time continued: "The Allies believe that in the particular circumstances with respect to the present crisis in Kosovo as described in UNSC [UN Security Council] Resolution 1199, there are legitimate grounds for the Alliance to threaten, and if necessary, to use force."[107]

An agreement signed on October 15, 1998, by the FRY's Chief of General Staff and General Wesley Clark, NATO's Supreme Allied Commander in Europe, provided for the establishment of an air verification mission over Kosovo.[108] The next day, an agreement

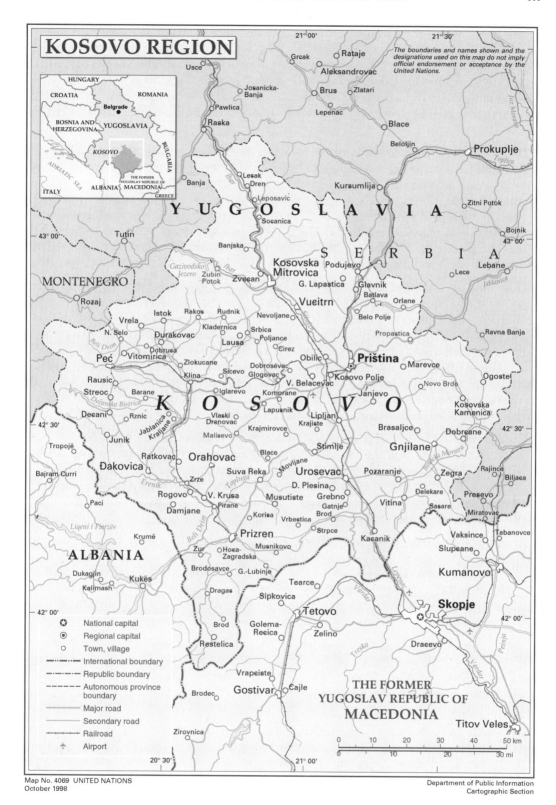

FIGURE 5.9: MAP OF THE KOSOVO REGION

signed by the FRY foreign minister and the chair-in-office of the Organization for Security and Co-operation in Europe (OSCE) provided for a verification mission in Kosovo, including undertakings by the FRY to comply with Security Council Resolutions 1160 (1998) and 1199 (1998).[109] On October 25, Clark and General Klaus Naumann negotiated an agreement with Belgrade concerning the withdrawal of Yugoslav forces and police. According to some analysts, the FRY complied with this call until there was renewed provocation from the KLA.

There were differences of opinion as to what, precisely, was authorized by Resolution 1203 (1998), other than demanding that both the FRY and the Kosovar Albanians comply with previous resolutions.[110] In statements made after they abstained from voting on Resolution 1203 (1998), both Russia and China – which had threatened to veto any resolution authorizing the use of force – made it clear that they did not see the resolution as authorizing military intervention.[111] The US representative, by contrast, said, "The NATO allies, in agreeing on October 13 to the use of force, made it clear that they had the authority, the will and the means to resolve this issue. We retain that authority."[112]

This resolution marked the Council's final substantive involvement in Kosovo until NATO's air operations ceased on June 10, 1999.[113] The issue simmered for some months, until the massacre of 45 civilians in Racak in January 1999 led to a NATO warning that it remained willing to take military action. Negotiations in Rambouillet from February 6 to 23 and in Paris from March 15 to 18 concluded with the FRY's refusing to sign the agreement that required freedom of movement for NATO throughout the whole of the FRY and a referendum on Kosovo's independence in three years. The draft agreement included a clause comparable to the Dayton agreement, in which the parties "invited" NATO to constitute and lead a military force authorized under a Chapter VII Security Council resolution.[114]

On March 24, 1999, NATO commenced air strikes against the FRY. NATO Secretary-General Solana stated that the military alliance acted because all diplomatic avenues had failed.[115] President Clinton emphasized that US interests in preventing a potentially wider war if action were not taken, as well as the humanitarian concerns, led the allies to act.[116] UK Prime Minister Blair stressed the need to protect Kosovar Albanian citizens and argued that the choice was to do something or do nothing.[117]

In an emergency session of the Security Council on March 24, Russia, China, Belarus, and India opposed the action as a violation of the Charter.[118] Of those states that supported the action, few asserted a clear legal basis for it. The US, Canada, and France stressed that the FRY was in violation of legal obligations imposed by Resolutions 1199 and 1203.[119] Only The Netherlands and the UK argued that the action was a legal response to a "humanitarian catastrophe"[120] and was "the minimum judged necessary for that purpose."[121]

Other states expressed concerns about the humanitarian situation and the failure of diplomacy. The Slovenian representative alluded to the studied ambiguity of earlier Council resolutions: "Because of differences of views among permanent members, it was not possible to provide in those resolutions a sufficiently complete framework to allow for the entire range of measures that might be necessary to address the situation in Kosovo with success."[122]

On March 26, 1999, a draft resolution demanding an end to the air strikes was rejected by 12 votes to 3.[123] Russia, China, and Namibia supported it, but 12 others (including 5 NATO members) did not. Few states opposing the draft advanced any legal basis for the action. The UK echoed its justification for the no-fly zones in Iraq, stating that military intervention was justified as an exceptional measure to prevent a humanitarian catastrophe. France and the Netherlands noted that previous resolutions had been adopted under Chapter VII of the Charter, thus implying that the coercive powers of the Council already had been invoked. For the most part, the resolution was simply seen as an inappropriate response to the situation, and one that might actually benefit Milosevic more than anyone else.[124]

In any event, the bombing initially exacerbated humanitarian problems. Ethnic cleansing began with a vengeance in Kosovo. Prior to the bombing, UNHCR estimated that there were 410,000 ethnic Albanians internally displaced as a result of Serb operations, and another 90,000 across the border. Within a matter of days, there were 750,00 refugees in Albania and Macedonia, as well as 250,000 IDPs at the border. UNHCR had prepared contingency plans for 100,000 refugees and was soon overwhelmed.

The 78-day bombing campaign was a textbook example of escalation theory and high-tech, low-risk military warfare. Initial targets were military, but after a month the bombing extended to dual-use targets, including mass media and power grids. The war was also extended to FRY territory, including the bombing of Belgrade. Many observers are of the opinion that the destruction of Serbia's infrastructure – for instance, 70 percent of bridges and 100 percent of refining capacity – and the threat of ground forces ended the war. The European Union (EU) estimated the cost of reconstruction at some $30 billion; the FRY, at $100 billion.

The FRY brought proceedings against 10 NATO members in the International Court of Justice (ICJ). In the course of hearings on the FRY's requests for provisional measures, Belgium presented the most elaborate legal justification for the action. In addition to relying on Security Council resolutions, Belgium claimed that a doctrine of humanitarian intervention was compatible with Article 2 (4) of the UN Charter, in addition to making an argument founded on humanitarian necessity.[125] The US also emphasized the importance of Security Council resolutions, and together with four other delegations (Germany, the Netherlands, Spain, and the UK) made reference to the existence of a "humanitarian catastrophe."[126] Four delegations did not offer any clear legal justification (Canada, France, Italy, and Portugal).

Yugoslavia had requested the ICJ to issue an injunction, based in part on provisions of the Genocide Convention, calling for an immediate cessation of bombing. However, the ICJ found that it did not have *prima facie* jurisdiction to issue what it termed "interim measures," based on those provisions. [127] The ICJ declined to grant the relief sought, for technical reasons to do with the FRY's accession to the jurisdiction of the ICJ during the conflict. Decision on the jurisdiction of the ICJ on other dimensions and a possible ruling on the merits of the case have been postponed at the request of Yugoslavia until April 2002.

Immediately following the end of hostilities, NATO deployed a 20,000-strong Kosovo Force to provide security within the war-torn society, which operated within the UN Interim Administration Mission in Kosovo. The security force was designed to complement the division of labour with four other intergovernmental organizations. The UN was charged with interim civil administration and capacity building. The UNHCR was given responsibility for humanitarian affairs. The EU took the lead in rehabilitation, reconstruction, and post-war peace building. And the OSCE pursued more elusive longer-term institution-building.

As Kosovo is a region of the FRY, and it was treated as such by NATO, the massive post-intervention effort constitutes a military "protectorate." The desire to avoid setting a precedent was evident in subsequent statements by NATO members. US Secretary of State Albright stressed in a press conference after the air campaign that Kosovo was "a unique situation sui generis in the region of the Balkans."[128] UK Prime Minister Tony Blair appeared to suggest at one point that such interventions might become more routine, stating that, "The most pressing foreign policy problem we face is to identify the circumstances in which we should get actively involved in other people's conflicts."[129] He subsequently retreated somewhat from this position, however, and emphasized the exceptional nature of the air campaign.[130] This was consistent with one of the more considered UK statements, by Baroness Symons in the House of Lords, made on November 16, 1998, and reaffirmed on May 6, 1999:

> There is no general doctrine of humanitarian necessity in international law. Cases have nevertheless arisen (as in northern Iraq in 1991) when, in the light of all the circumstances, a limited use of force was justifiable in support of purposes laid down by the Security Council but without the council's express authorization when that was the only means to avert an immediate and overwhelming humanitarian catastrophe. Such cases would in the nature of things be exceptional.[131]

The UK Foreign Affairs Committee, as part of its inquiry into the legal merits of the Kosovo intervention, concluded "that NATO's military action, if of dubious legality in the current state of international law, was justified on moral grounds."[132] Similarly, the Independent International Commission on Kosovo held that NATO's military intervention was "illegal but legitimate."[133]

The Kosovo case has important implications for the employment of international criminal prosecution. In May 1999, the chief prosecutor of the International Criminal Tribunal for the former Yugoslavia indicted Slobodan Milosevic and four senior FRY officials for crimes in Kosovo. In mid-June 2001, the new government in the FRY issued a decree that permitted the extradition of these indicted criminals to The Hague, despite the fact that the constitution did not permit it. Under considerable pressure from international donors, especially the US, the government contended that international covenants outweighed national law. The symbolism of Milosevic's transfer to The Hague on June 27, 2001, was noteworthy in itself – St Vitus's Day, the date in 1389 that the Serbs had lost a key battle in Kosovo, the day that he had unleashed the passionate jingoism in 1989, and the day 10 years after the Balkan wars erupted in Slovenia and Croatia.

One of the persistent criticisms, even among supporters of the intervention,[134] was the unwillingness of the NATO coalition to put ground troops into the equation. According to this view, the presence of and the threat to use ground troops would have averted the mass exodus of refugees. It would also have helped make a more credible moral stance, in that humanitarian intervention would have been worth the lives of Westerners as well as Yugoslavs. By remaining at 15,000 feet, there were no NATO casualties, and public support was sustained in the West.[135] But the moral high ground was less firm.

The NATO intervention in Kosovo remains highly controversial. The moral, legal, operational, and political dimensions of humanitarian intervention have never come under such sustained and sometimes vitriolic scrutiny. The establishment of what is, in effect, a UN protectorate is also controversial, particularly given the retaliatory attacks against the remaining Serb minority. Finally, however unwittingly, intervention on behalf of the repressed Kosovo Albanians played into the hands of the insurgents striving for independence. Despite NATO and UN protests that they do not support Kosovo's drive for independence, that is the most likely outcome.

## EAST TIMOR, 1999–

In 1975, Indonesia invaded the former Portuguese colony of East Timor in order to annex it as an integral part of Indonesia. The eastern half of the island of Timor was to become the 27th province. Both the Security Council and the General Assembly called for Indonesia to withdraw and respect East Timor's territorial integrity and the inalienable right of its people to self-determination. The Indonesian government ignored such calls, and its occupation resulted in some 200,000 to 300,000 dead and a long-standing insurgency.

The annexation of East Timor was not formally recognized by the vast majority of UN member states; Australia was the main exception. Despite this groundswell of world opinion, East Timor's independence only became possible following the replacement of Indonesian President Suharto by B.J. Habibie, who offered to hold a plebiscite on the territory's future. An agreement dated May 5, 1999, between Indonesia and Portugal (as the administering power of a non-self-governing territory), provided for a "popular consultation" on East Timor's future, to be held on August 8.[136] The agreement left security arrangements in the hands of Indonesia's military, which had actively suppressed the East Timorese population for the previous quarter century.

On June 11, Security Council Resolution 1246 (1999) established the UN Mission in East Timor (UNAMET) to organize and conduct the electoral consultation. Some 900 UN staff, 270 civilian police, and 4,000 local staff comprised this operation. A month later, with the consultation postponed because of security concerns until the end of August, the Secretary-General reported to the Council that "the situation in East Timor will be rather delicate as the Territory prepares for the implementation of the result of the popular consultation, whichever it may be."[137] Despite threats of violence, 98 percent of registered East Timorese voted in the referendum, with 78.5 percent opting for independence.

In the wake of the vote for independence, however, widespread violence and looting took place under the direction of the Indonesian military.[138] While the UN Secretary-General was engaged in negotiations about a possible security force, the headquarters of the ICRC was attacked, several local UNAMET personnel were killed, and the UN began to withdraw its civilian staff in the face of a rampage by the military-backed militias.

The humanitarian crisis was severe. For a tiny half of an island whose population was estimated to be only just more than 1 million, two-thirds had fled their homes and were totally dependent on international aid. The World Food Progam estimated a 6-month bill of about $135 million for some 750,000 IDPs.

There was some reluctance to intervene, despite the massive international response in Kosovo only months earlier, largely because of the political and economic importance of Indonesia. Nonetheless, Australia instigated discussions, driven by domestic political pressure, concern about a refugee crisis and regional stability, and some measure of contrition for its previous policies on East Timor; and the likely negative impact on UN credibility of remaining inactive loomed large. With many of the same motivations, members of the Security Council authorized, on September 15, an Australian-led multinational force under Chapter VII to restore peace and security to East Timor.

The legal necessity for requiring Indonesia's consent was doubtful to say the least.[139] But as a practical political matter, an outside military operation was inconceivable without Indonesian consent. No one was prepared to run the risk of serious resistance from Indonesian troops. After substantial arm-twisting – including pressure from international financial institutions and bilateral programmes of military and development assistance – consent came from Jakarta. Resolution 1264 (1999) welcomed a September 12 statement by the Indonesian president that expressed readiness to accept an international force in East Timor.

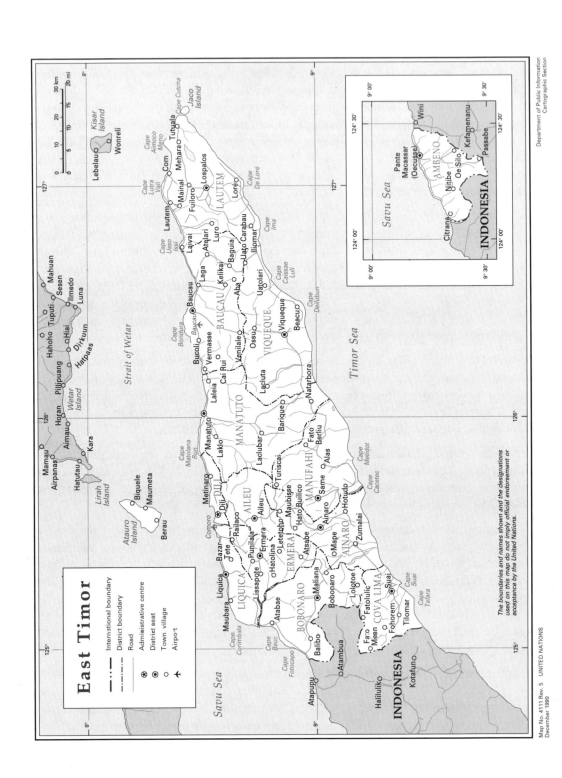

FIGURE 5.10: MAP OF EAST TIMOR

On September 20, roughly 2,500 soldiers, with helicopters and armoured personnel carriers, arrived in the smouldering ruins of the capital, Dili. Countries contributing troops included Australia, the UK, Canada, France, New Zealand, the Philippines, Thailand, and the US. At the outset, it was unclear how the Indonesian forces and the militias whom they controlled would respond. Yet, over the next few weeks, skirmishes with these forces were infrequent, and the International Force in East Timor (INTERFET) ultimately supervised the largely peaceful withdrawal of Indonesian soldiers. Control over the territory, however, did not mean that the victims were safe. As many as 200,000 people had been pushed out of the territory – most expelled at gunpoint by militias. They were subsequently forced into militia-controlled camps in West Timor, well beyond the range of the multinational force.

The resolution authorizing the Australian-led INTERFET noted that the multinational force should be replaced "as soon as possible" by a UN peacekeeping force. On October 25, the Council voted in Resolution 1272 (1999) to establish the UN Transitional Administration in East Timor (UNTAET). INTERFET transferred military control of the territory to UNTAET on February 23, 2000, and initiated an ambitious programme of police and civilian administration. Their mandate was to provide security and maintain law and order, establish an effective administration, assist in the development of civil and social services, and ensure the coordination and delivery of humanitarian aid, rehabilitation, and development assistance. This was to be accomplished by a military force of more than 8,000 troops and more than 1,500 civilian specialists, including police.

There are strong parallels between the ultimate outcomes in East Timor and Kosovo. As East Timor is to be an independent state, this post-intervention effect constitutes a "trusteeship." The administration of an area following an intervention – that is, comprehensive state-building with the UN in the role of quasi government – appears to be a necessary step in some post-intervention cases, regardless of the paternalistic connotations. Despite the unique international legal circumstances of East Timor, the intervention has also had an undeniable demonstration effect elsewhere within the Indonesian archipelago, with other insurgents seemingly empowered to confront Jakarta.

## RECENT TRENDS IN INTERVENTION

The concluding overview in the preceding essay about pre-1990 humanitarian interventions contained generalizations about the motives, justifications, and interests emanating from 10 historical cases. The present essay has reviewed the historical details of 9 of the more recent cases; the moral, legal, operational, and political implications will be dissected in detail in Section C of this part of the volume.

It is worth noting at this juncture, however, that all of the military interventions of the 1990s were, according to virtually everyone's definition, more legitimate than the earlier cases. Rather than remaining on the sidelines, the Security Council was seized by each of them and made decisions authorizing coercion. Unlike the earlier cases, in which the rescue of nationals and self-defence were the prominent justifications, the conscience-shocking and truly "humanitarian" elements of the post-1990 cases were explicitly recognized as important justifications for international action. Instead of single-state military operations, the interventions of the 1990s were also genuinely multilateral.

During this period, the balance between three forms of nonconsensual action shifted. The decade ended as it began, with multinational coalitions undertaking extremely high-intensity military interventions – yet the intervening years were characterized by considerable scepticism as to the utility of military force for humanitarian purposes, particularly as a result of experiences in Somalia and the Balkans.

It was a decade of profound change for two other forms of intervention – sanctions and international criminal prosecutions – as well. The 1990s have been labelled the "sanctions decade" because the Security Council imposed 12 sanctions regimes, several times more than in the previous 40 years combined. As well as being used more frequently, sanctions were also applied more widely, including against nonstate actors in Angola and Cambodia.[140] The frequent resort to sanctions occurred despite the fact that most observers criticized their political inefficacy, and an even larger number of critics lamented their humanitarian consequences.[141] Particularly as a result of the painful human suffering in Iraq, the view that sanctions represent a kinder and gentler alternative to deadly force seems unsustainable. Ultimately, the Charter's call to use nonforcible before forcible measures may have a less than optimal humanitarian result. Some advocate moving toward "smart sanctions" designed to target regime leaders while minimizing the impact on the general population,[142] while others call for the application of deadly force sooner rather than later.

International criminal prosecution was another type of intervention that, for the first time since the immediate aftermath of the Second World War, was employed to bring to justice those who had committed crimes against humanity. A number of recent legal decisions suggest considerable erosion of the rules relating to the immunity of states and their leaders. These have long provided that leading officials (including retired ones) of a state cannot be tried in courts in another country for acts committed in their own state and in the exercise of their official duties.[143] Although the Genocide Convention specifically calls for punishing perpetrators "whether they are constitutionally responsible rulers, public officials or private individuals," state practice over decades had overwhelmingly supported the notion of sovereign immunity. This is one reason why states avoided calling the Rwanda genocide a "genocide."[144]

The fight to establish limits to impunity received a boost with the establishment of the international criminal tribunals for the former Yugoslavia and Rwanda in 1993 and 1994, respectively. More recent violence in Burundi, the Congo, and East Timor has led to calls for additional ad hoc tribunals. And the Khmer Rouge's atrocities of the 1970s have long been a topic that has led to a similar call, although legislation to establish a tribunal is stalled in the Cambodian parliament. A more likely third tribunal may be for Sierra Leone, where rebels have committed horrible cruelties against civilians, and a planning delegation was authorized by the Security Council in July 2001, about a year after the decision to establish such a mechanism. While the tribunals for Rwanda and the former Yugoslavia are entirely international, the ones proposed for Cambodia and Sierra Leone would each have an international prosecutor but a mix of local and foreign judges.

Dissatisfaction with early institutional shortcomings for both the Rwandan and the former Yugoslavian tribunals demonstrated to many observers the need for a permanent court. The creation of the ICC awaits the 60th ratification of the 1998 Rome Statute. However, international agreement on the independence of the prosecutor and the court's jurisdiction over internal conflicts and disturbances suggests that criminal prosecution could become a common, rather than an ad hoc, response in the face of large scale atrocities.

Questions related to the legality of armed military intervention for humanitarian purposes are also relevant to nonmilitary intervention. The Security Council has the legal capacity both to authorize intervention and to delegate needed authority to regional bodies. Sanctions and embargoes have been imposed without Council authorization, by regional bodies or unilaterally.

The most substantive departure in the post-Cold War era, however, remains the Security Council's willingness to authorize military actions in response to matters thought previously to be solely within the domestic jurisdiction of states. The decade witnessed serious second thoughts about humanitarian intervention. Euphoria after the Gulf War and the rescue of the Kurds in 1991 gave way, three brief years later, to the nihilism of the international nonresponse to Rwanda's genocide. The last year of the millennium conjured up, depending on one's point of view, optimism or pessimism about humanitarian intervention, because of the visible and costly international efforts in Sierra Leone, Kosovo, and East Timor.

Two major trends in the nature of Security Council authorizations should be highlighted. The first relates to the expansion of what constitutes "threats to international peace and security." And the second relates to organizational limitations of the UN and the concomitant use of multinational forces and the dependency of the Council on such coalitions of the willing for the application of deadly force.

The most basic transformation in the use of Security Council powers is that civil war and internal strife have been described as threats to international peace and security and may therefore be the basis for Chapter VII enforcement action. This development was virtually inconceivable during the Cold War, when similar conflicts were not considered to constitute such threats. Yet, by 1995, the Appeals Chamber of the International Criminal Tribunal for the Former Yugoslavia summarized that it is the "settled practice of the Security Council and the common understanding of the United Nations membership in general" that a purely internal armed conflict may constitute a "threat to the peace."[145] In fact, when the Security Council considered the civil war in Angola, it was even prepared to locate such a threat specifically within a rebel movement.

Substantial flows of refugees have been deemed by the Security Council to constitute a threat to international peace and security. This has enabled them to justify Chapter VII actions to create safe havens in the Balkans and Rwanda. The Council also determined that "serious" or "systematic, widespread and flagrant" violations of IHL within a country also threaten international peace and security. This undoubtedly represents a considerable stretch for those who are familiar with the convictions of the framers of the UN Charter. But resolutions establishing the international criminal tribunals for Rwanda and the former Yugoslavia did not indicate that violations of IHL were a threat to international peace and security, a position strongly supported by the ICRC and other humanitarian agencies.[146] There has been, therefore, a gradual shift away from strict reliance on the transboundary implications of a humanitarian situation as the determining factor.

Some have argued that the ever-widening definition of international peace and security is artificial and unsustainable and that more explicit grounds for intervention to protect civilians should be developed. For example, the Independent Commission on Global Governance proposed "an appropriate Charter amendment permitting such intervention but restricting it to cases that constitute a violation of the security of people so gross and extreme that it requires an international response on humanitarian grounds."[147]

If humanitarian and human rights tragedies can be squeezed under the rubric of international peace and security, the restoration of democracy within a country demands even more leeway. In this light, Operation Restore Democracy in Haiti can be seen as a high watermark of Council activism in the 1990s. The unprecedented authorization called for the use of force to remove one regime and install another. It has been argued that this foreshadows the emergence of a more general norm of intervention in support of democracy, a proposition that finds limited support in the amended OAS Charter.[148] ECOWAS's intervention into Sierra Leone further supports the argument that an international norm of "prodemocratic" intervention is developing. While it can be seen neither as a literal interpretation of Chapter VIII nor as involving a threat to international peace and security, the Council's post hoc ratification of ECOWAS's intervention may be best understood as an example of prodemocratic intervention.

Three other cases of prodemocratic intervention are not discussed here because they do not fall under the humanitarian heading defined at the outset. However, the outside military efforts in Guinea-Bissau (by Senegal, Guinea, and ECOWAS), in the Central African Republic (by MISAB), and in Lesotho (by South Africa and Bostswana under SADC agreements) suggest that democratic governance is in the forefront of African "interventions." As one analyst notes, "While in theory, Western nations purport to have the strongest democratic traditions, in *practice*, this emerging norm is taking firmer root in Africa than in any other region."[149]

In addition, the expansion of situations that come generally under the rubric of "threats to international peace and security" has had another result, considered by many in a less positive light. A series of ambiguous resolutions and conflicting interpretations have arisen over the extent and duration of the authority conferred by the Security Council. These were most notable in the operations against Iraq throughout the 1990s and in the Kosovo War in 1999. The weakening of formal requirements may have undermined the substantive provisions of the Charter's collective security system and contributed to facilitating actions in advance of Council authorization, or indeed without it.

This reflects a second trend in the expanding activities of the Security Council in the 1990s. The absence of any real UN operational capacities to meet the growing demands of a responsibility to protect civilians has led to a delegation of authority. The provisions in Article 43 concerning Security Council military enforcement presume the existence of agreements with member states to make forces available to the Council "on its call." Such agreements have never been concluded, and Chapter VII has never been applied according to the strict terms of Article 42. Yet, the Security Council has repeatedly authorized states to use "all necessary means" (or similar language), and this appears to be accepted as a legitimate application of its Chapter VII powers. The same language appears relevant for the delegation of authority under Chapter VIII.

Security Council military enforcement actions were limited to situations where states had the political will to bear the financial and human costs. For humanitarian interventions, the division of labour resulting from the experience of the 1990s highlights the chasm between peacekeeping and peace enforcement. These enforcement actions make it clear that the military protection functions do not squarely fall under either Chapters VI or Chapter VII. Some argue that these challenges can be accommodated by a slightly more robust form of peacekeeping. But the evidence suggests that demilitarizing refugee camps and creating safe havens that are truly safe require scaling back combat-capable troops willing to employ deadly force, rather than scaling up blue helmets. Distinctions that were fuzzy in the 1992 *An Agenda for Peace* became clearer in the 1995 *Supplement to An Agenda for Peace*.[150] They have subsequently become clearer still in the recommendations from the 2000 Panel on UN Peace Operations: the UN should concentrate on peacekeeping and civilian administration – others should undertake robust military deployments.

Yet, the loose connections between UN authorization and member-state enforcement is not without its problems. In particular, the delegation of authority – or "subcontracting" to coalitions of the willing and able or to regional arrangements or agencies – has raised concerns about the use of Security Council authority to give legitimacy to the foreign policy objectives of powerful states.[151]

## NOTES

1    Adam Roberts, "The So-Called 'Right' of Humanitarian Intervention," *Yearbook of International Humanitarian Law 2001* (The Hague: T.M.C. Asser, forthcoming).

2    Louise Doswald-Beck, "The Legal Validity of Military Intervention by Invitation of the Government," *1985 British Yearbook of Interntional Law* (Oxford: Clarendon Press, 1985), p. 194.

3    This categorization is based on Simon Chesterman, *Just War or Just Peace? Humanitarian Intervention and International Law* (Oxford: Oxford University Press, 2001).

4    For an overview of this subject, see Jeremy Levitt, "African Interventionist States and International Law," in Oliver Furley and Roy May, eds., *African Interventionist States: The New Conflict Resolution Brokers* (Aldershot: Ashgate, forthcoming).

5    Attempts to bring the matter before the UN Security Council, in May 1990, were frustrated by Côte d'Ivoire and Burkina Faso, both Economic Community of West African States member states, which allegedly supported the National Patriotic Front of Liberia. Likewise, Zaire opposed Security Council involvement, fearing that intervention in Liberia might serve as a precedent elsewhere on the continent.

6    Consistent with its historically ambivalent policy toward Liberia, the US viewed the Liberian conflict as an internal affair, to be solved by Liberians themselves. See "Statement of Hon. Herman J. Cohen, Assistant Secretary of State, Bureau of African Affairs," US House of Representatives, Sub-Committee on Africa of the Committee on Foreign Affairs, 101st Congress, 2nd Session, Hearing on US Policy and the Crisis in Liberia, June 19, 1990.

7    Letter addressed by President Samuel K. Doe to the Chairman and Members of the Ministerial Meeting of the ECOWAS Standing Mediation Committee, July 14, 1990.

8    See ECOWAS Standing Mediation Committee, Decision A/DEC.1/8/90, on the Cease-fire and Establishment of ECOWAS Cease-fire Monitoring Groups for Liberia, Banjul, Republic of Gambia, August 7, 1990.

9    Jeremy Levitt, "Humanitarian Intervention by Regional Actors in Internal Conflicts: The Cases of ECOWAS in Liberia and Sierra Leone," *Temple International and Comparative Law Journal* 12, no. 2 (1998), p. 50.

10   Abiodun Alao, *The Burden of Collective Goodwill: The International Involvement in the Liberian Civil War* (Aldershot: Ashgate, 1998), p. 57.

11   At the peak of factionalization, the Cease-fire Monitoring Group of the Economic Community of West African States had to contend with some 10 factions.

12   Levitt, "Humanitarian Intervention by Regional Actors in Internal Conflicts," p. 350.

13   UN Document ST/DPI/1668, 52nd session, 41/1997, *The United Nations and the Situation in Liberia*.

14   Washington Office on Africa, "Liberia: More US Support Needed," October 22, 1995, www.sas.upenn.edu/Arican_Studies/Urgent_Action/DC_2210.html

15   Washington Office on Africa, "Liberia: WOA Update/Alert," July 29, 1996, www.sas.upenn.edu/Arican_Studies/Urgent_Action/DC_2210.html

16   UN Press Release, SC/6402.

17   Mikhail S. Gorbachev, "Reality and the Guarantees of a Secure World," *FBIS Daily Report: Soviet Union*, September 17, 1987, pp. 23–28, cited in David Malone, *Decision-making in the UN Security Council: The Case of Haiti, 1990–1997* (Oxford: Clarendon Press, 1998), p. 8.

18   Thomas L. Friedman, "Allies Tell Baker Use of Force Needs UN Backing," *New York Times*, November 8, 1990; Thomas L. Friedman, "How US Won Support to Use Mideast Forces," *New York Times*, December 2, 1990; Michael R. Beschloss and Strobe Talbott, *At the Highest Levels: The Inside Story of the End of the Cold War* (London: Little Brown, 1993) pp. 282–284.

19   UN Document S/PV.2977 (1991), p. 301 (US), p. 313 (UK).

20   United Nations, *Report to the Secretary-General on Humanitarian Needs in Kuwait and Iraq in the Immediate Post-crisis Environment by a Mission to the Area led by Mr. Martti Ahtisaari, Under-Secretary-General for Administration and Management, dated 20 March 1991* (New York: United Nations, 1991).

21   UN Document S/PV.2982 (1991), p. 6 (Turkey).

22   Nigel S. Rodley, "Collective Intervention to Protect Human Rights and Civilian Populations: The Legal Framework," in Nigel S. Rodley, ed., *To Loose the Bands of Wickedness: International Intervention in the Defence of Human Rights* (London: Brassey's, 1992), p. 31; and Sean Murphy, *Humanitarian Intervention: The United Nations in an Evolving World Order* (Philadelphia: University of Pennsylvania Press, 1996), pp. 196–197.

23   George H.W. Bush, remarks at a meeting with Hispanic business leaders and an exchange with reporters, April 5, 1991, in *Public Papers of the Presidents of the United States: George Bush*, vol. 1 (Washington, DC: US Government Printing Office, 1993), p. 379.

24   David Macintyre, "Major Gambles for High Stakes in the Mountains of Kurdistan," *Independent*, April 14, 1991.

25   Edward Lucas, Annika Savill, Will Bennett, and Anthony Bevins, "US Shifts Policy on Kurds," *Independent*, April 8, 1991.

26   Marc Weller, ed., "Iraq and Kuwait: The Hostilities and Their Aftermath," *Cambridge International Document Series*, vol. 3 (Cambridge: Grotius Publications Ltd., 1993), p. 715.

27   Lawrence Freedman and David Boren, " 'Safe Havens' for Kurds in Post-War Iraq," in Rodley, ed., *To Loose the Bands of Wickedness*, p. 53.

28   George Bush, remarks on assistance for Iraqi refugees and a news conference, April 16, 1991, *Public Papers of the Presidents of the United States: George Bush*, vol. 1, p. 379.

29   Freedman and Boren, " 'Safe Havens' for Kurds," p. 51.

30   UN Document S/22663 (1991).

31   George Bush, remarks on Hurricane Andrew and the situation in Iraq and an exchange with reporters, August 26, 1992, *Public Papers of the Presidents of the United States: George Bush*, vol. 2 (Washington, DC: US Government Printing Office, 1993), p. 1430.

32   Helmut Freudenschuss, "Article 39 of the UN Charter Revisited: Threats to the Peace and the Recent Practices of the UN Security Council," *Austrian Journal of Public International Law* 46, no. 1 (1993), p. 10.

33   Rodley, "Collective Intervention," p. 33.

34   Freudenschuss, "Article 39 of the UN Charter Revisited," pp. 10 and 9.

35   UN Document S/PV.3009 (1991), pp. 49–51 (China).

36   UN Document S/25939 (1993).

37   Report of the Secretary-General pursuant to General Assembly Resolution 53/35. "The Fall of Srebrenica," UN Document A/54/549 (November 15, 1999).

38   Simon Chesterman, "No Justice without Peace? International Criminal Law and the Decision to Prosecute," in Simon Chesterman, ed., *Civilians in War* (Boulder: Lynne Rienner, 2001), p. 151.

39   Annex 1A, Art. I (1)(a).

40   UN Document S/23693 (1992).

41   UN Document S/PV.3060 (1992).

42   UN Document A/47/553 (1992).

43   UN Document S/24868 (1992).

44   Walter Goodman, "Somalia: How Much Did TV Shape Policy?" *New York Times*, December 8, 1992.

45   UN Document S/PV.3145 (1992), p. 36 (US).

46   UN Document S/PV.3145 (1992), p. 7 (Zimbabwe), pp. 12–13 (Ecuador), pp. 16–18 (China), p. 46 (Morocco), pp. 49–50 (India).

47   *United Nations Year Book* 47 (New York: United Nations, 1993), p. 51.

48   Jarat Chopra, Å. Eknes, and T. Nordbø, "Fighting for Hope in Somalia," *Peacekeeping and Multinational Operations* 6 (Oslo: Norwegian Institute for International Affairs, 1995), p. 2.

49   Mohamed Sahnoun, *Somalia: Missed Opportunities* (Washington, DC: US Institute of Peace, 1994), p. xiii.

50   UN Document S/1994/446.

51   UN Document S/1994/470.

52  An intervention would have required more time and planning than most proponents admit. Given the terrifyingly rapid pace of the genocide, a major operation could probably have saved only a portion of the ultimate victims. See Alan J. Kuperman, "Rwanda in Retrospect," *Foreign Affairs* 79, no. 1 (January–February 2000), pp. 94–118.

53  All Africa Press Service, April 24, 1996.

54  According to extracts from a report by a UN special investigator published in *International Peacekeeping News* 2, no. 1 (March–April 1996), p. 7.

55  UN Document S/1994/728.

56  UN Document S/1994/518.

57  UN Document S/1994/640.

58  Fernando R. Tesón, *Humanitarian Intervention: An Inquiry into Law and Morality* (Dobbs Ferry: Transnational Publishers, 1997) p. 260; and Philip Gourevitch, *We Wish to Inform You That Tomorrow We Will Be Killed with Our Families* (London: Picador, 1999), pp. 152–154.

59  This is, of course, a partial definition of genocide. See also the Presidential Statement of April 30, 1994; UN Document S/PRST/1994/21.

60  UN Document S/1994/728.

61  UN Document S/1994/734.

62  Helmut Freudenschuss, "Between Unilateralism and Collective Security: Authorisations of the Use of Force by the UN Security Council," *European Journal of International Law* 46, no. 1 (1994), p. 521.

63  Ian Martin, "Hard Choices after Genocide: Human Rights and Political Failures in Rwanda," in Jonathan Moore, ed., *Hard Choices: Moral Dilemmas in Humanitarian Intervention* (Lanham: Rowman & Littlefield, 1998), p. 171.

64  United Nations, *Report of the Independent Enquiry into the Actions of the United Nations during the 1994 Genocide in Rwanda*, op. cit.

65  See José E. Alvarez, "Crimes of States/Crimes of Hate: Lessons from Rwanda, *The Yale Journal of International Law* 24 (1999), pp. 364–483.

66  *Keesing's Contemporary Archives* (1996), p. 41350.

67  UN Document S/1996/916.

68  UN Document S/1996/92.

69  UN Document S/1996/941.

70  *Keesing's Contemporary Archives* (1997), p. 41431.

71  OAS MRE/RES 1/91, MRE/RES 2/91, MRE/RES 3/91 (1991).

72  Malone, *Decision-making in the UN Security Council*, pp. 63–64.

73  UN Document S/26668 (1993).

74  UN Document A/48/867-S/1994/150 (1994).

75  UN Document S/1994/905, Annex.

76  Tesón, *Humanitarian Intervention*, p. 252; and Malone, *Decision-making in the UN Security Council*, p. 113.

77  See, for example, Richard West, *Back to Africa: A History of Sierra Leone and Liberia* (London: Jonathan Cape, 1970).

78  Alfred B. Zack-Williams, "Sierra Leone: The Political Economy of Civil War, 1991–98," *Third World Quarterly* 20, no. 1, (1999), p. 144.

79  Ibid., p. 143.

80  Alfred B. Zack-Williams and Stephen Riley, "Sierra Leone: The Coup and Its Consequences," *Review of African Political Economy* 20, no. 56 (1993), p. 93.

81  This compares favourably with the estimated $1–2 million per day to sustain the present UN Mission in Sierra Leone.

82   Ian Douglas, "Fighting for Diamonds," in Jakkie Cilliers and Peggy Mason, eds., *Peace, Profit or Plunder: The Privatisation of Security in War-Torn African Societies* (Johannesburg: Institute for Strategic Studies, 1999), pp. 182.

83   The junta referred to themselves as the Armed Forces Revolutionary Council.

84   *African Research Bulletin*, May 1997, p. 12695; see also, "Kabbah Urges ECOWAS Leaders to Restore Him to Power," *Panafrican News Agency*, September 2, 1997.

85   *Statement by the President of the Security Council*, UN SCOR, 52nd Session, UN Document S/PRST/1997/29 (1997).

86   Organization of African Unity Council of Ministers Sixty-sixth Ordinary Session May 28–30, 1997, Harare, Zimbabwe, Draft Decisions, CM/Draft/Dec.(LXVI) Rev.1, p. 18.

87   Given the circumstances on the ground in Sierra Leone, and the nature of the Nigerian mandate, it is clear that Nigeria intended to enforce the peace.

88   Economic Community of West African States Revised Treaty, Article 58 – Regional Security, July 24, 1993.

89   Portions of the aforementioned analysis were extracted from Levitt, "African Interventionist States and International Law" in Oliver Furley and Roy May, eds., *African Interventionist States: The New Conflict Resolution Brokers* (Aldershot: Ashgate, 2001).

90   *Secretary-General Pledges Support of United Nations in Helping Sierra Leone Leave behind Unfortunate Chapter in Country's History*, UNPR, 53rd Session, UN Document SG/SM/6481 – AFR/44 (1998).

91   UN Document S/PRST/1998/5.

92   *Fourth Report of the Secretary-General on the Situation in Sierra Leone*, UN SCOR, 53rd Session, UN Document S/1998/249 (1998).

93   S/1999/20, January 7, 1999, para. 10.

94   United Nation Security Council, Third Report of the Secretary-General on the United Nations Mission in Sierra Leone, UN Document S/2000/186, March 7, 2000, para. 10.

95   Ibid.

96   Douglas Farah, "Diamonds Help Fill Rebel Group's Arsenal," *Washington Post*, April 17, 2000.

97   Robert Block, "Diamonds Appear to Fuel the Fires in Sierra Leone," *Wall Street Journal*, May 12, 2000.

98   Reuters, May 2, 2000.

99   Douglas Farah, "Rebel Leader Exploited UN Weaknesses," *Washington Post*, Foreign Service, May 15, 2000.

100  Major-General Vijay Jetley, *Report on the Crisis in Sierra Leone*, May 2000, para. 9. Available at http://www.sierraleone.org/jetley0500.html

101  Doug Brooks, "Sierra Leone Burns While the UN Fiddles," *South African Institute of International Affairs Intelligence Update 21/2000*, November 16, 2000.

102  Richard Holbrooke, *To End a War* (New York: Random House, 1998), p. 357.

103  David Binder, "Bush Warns Serbs Not to Widen War," *New York Times*, December 28, 1992.

104  The *New York Times* described this as a "deliberate ambiguity" necessary to allow Russia to support the resolution: Barbara Crossette, "Security Council Tells Serbs to Stop Kosovo Offensive," *New York Times*, October 24, 1998.

105  Madeline Albright, press conference on Kosovo, Brussels, October 8, 1998, http://secretary.state.gov/www/statements/1998/981008.html

106  Michael Evans and Tom Walker, "NATO Bombers on Alert for Order to Hit Serbs," *Times*, October 12, 1998.

107  Javier Solana, press conference at NATO Headquarters in Brussels, October 13, 1998, http://www.nato.int/docu/speech/1998/s981013b.htm

108  UN Document S/1998/991, Annex.

109  UN Document S/1998/978.

110  UN Document S/PV.3937 (1998), pp. 14–15 (China).

111 Youssef M. Ibrahim, "UN Measure Skirts Outright Threat of Force against Milosevic," *New York Times*, October 25, 1998; and UN Document S/PV.3937 (1998), p. 12 (Russia), p. 14–15 (China).

112 UN Document S/PV.3937 (1998), p. 15 (US).

113 On May 14, 1999, the Security Council passed Security Council Resolution 1239 (1999) concerning assistance to refugees from the conflict. The only reference to the ongoing air operations was a paragraph urging "all concerned" to work toward a political solution along the lines of that proposed by the Meeting of G-8 Foreign Ministers on May 6, 1999, para. 5.

114 UN Document S/1999/648, Chapter 7, Art. I (1)(a).

115 North Atlantic Treaty Organization press release, March 23, 1999.

116 William Jefferson Clinton, President Clinton's address on air strikes against Yugoslavia, *New York Times*, March 24, 1999.

117 Tony Blair, text of British Prime Minister Tony Blair's statement on Kosovo bombing, *New York Times*, March 24, 1999.

118 UN Document S/PV.3988 (1999), pp. 12–13 (China), p. 13 (Russia), p. 15 (Belarus), pp. 15–16 (India).

119 UN Document S/PV.3988 (1999) p. 4 (US), pp. 5–6 (Canada), p. 9 (France). Germany, speaking as the Presidency of the European Union, stated that the members of the European Union were under a "moral obligation" to prevent a humanitarian catastrophe in the middle of Europe – UN Document S/PV.3988 (1999), p. 17.

120 UN Document S/PV.3988 (1999), p. 8 (The Netherlands).

121 UN Document S/PV.3988 (1999), p. 12.

122 UN Document S/PV.3988 (1999), pp. 19–20.

123 UN Document S/1999/328, sponsored by Belarus, India, and Russia.

124 UN Press Release SC/6659 (March 26, 1999).

125 *Legality of Use of Force Case* (Provisional Measures) (International Court of Justice, 1999), pleadings of Belgium, May 10, 1999, CR 99/15 (uncorrected translation).

126 For the US, see ibid., pleadings of the United States, May 11, 1999, CR 99/24, para. 1.7; for Germany, see May 11, 1999, CR 99/18, para. 1.3.1; for the Netherlands, see May 11, 1999, CR 99/20, para. 40 – cf. para. 38 ("remind[ing]" the International Court of Justice of certain Security Council resolutions); for Spain, see May 11, 1999, CR 99/22, para. 1; and for the UK, see May 11, 1999, CR 99/23, para. 17–18. The phrase "humanitarian catastrophe" appears in the pleadings of the United States, May 11 1999, CR 99/24, para. 1.7.

127 *Legality of Use of Force Case* (Provisional Measures) (ICJ, 1999), order of June 2, 1999.

128 Madeline M. Albright, press conference with Russian Foreign Minister Igor Ivanov, Singapore, July 26, 1999, http://secretary.state.gov//www//statements/1999/990726b.html

129 Colin Brown, "Blair's Vision of Global Police," *Independent*, April 23, 1999.

130 Tony Blair, UK parliamentary debates, Commons, April 26, 1999, col. 30.

131 Baroness Symons, UK parliamentary debates, Lords, November 16, 1998, WA 140.

132 Foreign Affairs Committee (UK), *Fourth Report: Kosovo*, HC 28-I, 2000.

133 Independent International Commission on Kosovo, *The Kosovo Report: Conflict, International Response, Lessons Learned* (Oxford: Oxford University Press, 2000), p. 4.

134 See, for example, Ivo. H. Daalder and Michael E. O'Hanlon, *Winning Ugly: NATO's War to Save Kosovo* (Washington, DC: Brookings Institution, 2000).

135 For a discussion, see Klaus Naumann, "NATO, Kosovo, and Military Intervention," *Global Governance* 8, no. 1 (January–March 2002), forthcoming.

136 UN Document S/1999/513, Annexes I–III.

137 UN Document S/1999/862, para. 5.

138 UN Document S/1999/976, Annex, para. 1.

139 Antonio Cassese, *Self-Determination of Peoples: A Legal Reappraisal* (Cambridge: Cambridge University Press, 1995), pp. 223–230.

140 In the case of Cambodia, the sanctions were not imposed under Chapter VII. On Angola, see United Nations, *Report of the Panel of Experts on Violations of Security Council Sanctions against UNITA*, UN Document S/2000/203, March 10, 2000.

141 See generally David Cortright and George A. Lopez, *The Sanctions Decade: Assessing UN Strategies in the 1990s* (Boulder: Lynne Rienner, 2000), Policy Brief Series.

142 For some of the literature, see Fourth Freedom Forum, *Towards Smarter, More Effective United Nations Sanctions* (Goshen: Fourth Freedom Forum, 1999); David Cortright, Alistair Millar, and George A. Lopez, *Smart Sanctions: Restructuring UN Policy in Iraq*; Kofi A. Annan, "We the Peoples": The Role of the United Nations in the 21st Century (New York: United Nations, 2000), pp. 49–50; *Expert Seminar on Targeting United Nations Financial Sanctions* (Interlaken: Swiss Federal Office for Foreign Economic Affairs, Department of Economy), March 17–19, 1998. UN Document S/1999/92, January 29, 1999; and UN Document S/2000/319, April 17, 2000.

143 The International Law Commission between 1977 and 1986 produced a "Draft Convention on the Jurisdictional Immunities of States and Their Property," which sought to change the previous rules, including by allowing legal actions against officials who committed crimes. However, the draft rules still required a nexus between where the crime was committed and the court in which the action was brought. More generally, moves to negotiate the draft Convention into existence failed.

144 Wheeler examines the deliberate decision by the Council and individual countries not to label the killings "genocide" to avoid having to take the action mandated by the Genocide Convention. See Nicholas J. Wheeler, *Saving Strangers: Humanitarian Intervention in International Society* (New York: Oxford University Press, 2000), pp. 226 and 229–230. He argues that, far from *not* having national interests at stake in Rwanda, stopping genocide should have been a national interest in its own right for states party to the Convention, such as the US and UK (p. 241). The Security Council established, by approving Resolution 1296 (2000), that targeting civilians in armed conflict and the denial of humanitarian access to civilian populations constitute threats to international peace and security, and hence they are triggers for Security Council action.

145 *Prosecutor v Tadic*, IT-94-1-AR72 (October 1995), para. 30.

146 International Committee of the Red Cross, "Report on the Protection of War Victims," *International Review of the Red Cross* 296 (September–October 1993), pp. 391–445.

147 The Commission on Global Governance, *Our Global Neighborhood* (Oxford: Oxford University Press, 1995), p. 90.

148 Chesterman, *Just War or Just Peace?*, p. 98. Some scholars argue that the absence of democracy may itself constitute a threat to international peace and security. This is an extreme form of the "democratic peace" thesis that authentic democracies do not fight each other, or, depending on the definition of "democracy" or "fighting," that such conflicts are exceptional. Depending on definitions, application of this thesis would mean that around one-third of the world's states could be deprived of the protection of Article 2 (7) of the UN Charter. See Tom J. Farer, "Collectively Defending Democracy in a World of Sovereign States: The Western Hemisphere's Prospect," *Human Rights Quarterly* 15 (November 1993), pp. 716–750; Michael E. Brown, Sean M. Lynn Jones, and Steven E. Miller, *Debating the Democratic Peace* (Cambridge, MA: Cambridge University Press, 1996).

149 Jeremy Levitt, "African Interventionist States and International Law," in Oliver Furley and Roy May, eds., *African Interventionist States: The New Conflict Resolution Brokers* (Aldershot: Ashgate, forthcoming); emphasis in original.

150 *Supplement to An Agenda for Peace: Position Paper of the Secretary-General on the Occasion of the Fiftieth Anniversary of the United Nations*, UN Document A/50/60-S/1995/1 (1995), paras. 77–80.

151 Chesterman, *Just War or Just Peace?*, pp. 219–36.

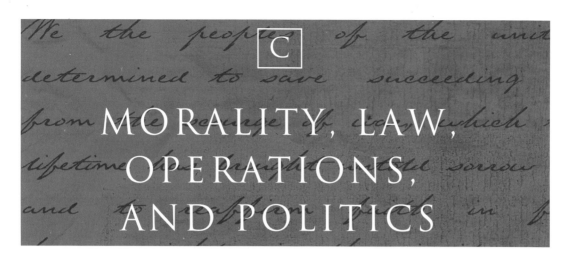

# MORALITY, LAW, OPERATIONS, AND POLITICS

The preceding descriptions of the main elements in the debate (sovereignty, intervention, and prevention), along with the brief history of post-1945 interventions, provide the building blocks to explore four overarching analytical areas: rights and responsibilities, legitimacy and authority, conduct and capacity, and domestic and international will. These are the topics for the third section of this part of the volume.

The existing literature devoted to these areas is vast. The main questions examined below – when is intervention justified, how is it authorized, how should it be conducted, and how can sufficient political will be mobilized – have all been extensively analyzed by scholars, policy analysts, and practitioners. The four essays here attempt to summarize the ongoing debate about these questions. The full breadth of contemporary discussion is set out, and the relative degree of support for the various positions is assessed.

These analyses also seek to add an additional perspective – how intervention affects, and is seen by, populations at risk. What are the rights to assistance and protection of affected local populations? Is an intervention legitimate or illegitimate, whether or not it is legal? Has the international response caused more good than harm? Have the views of affected local populations been actively sought and genuinely considered?

This section begins with ethical dimensions of the intervention debate. Essay 6, Rights and Responsibilities, opens with a discussion of the possible impact on world order of competing positions about intervention. Some argue that promoting justice beyond borders undermines international order and increases the likelihood of interstate war, while others maintain that humanitarian interventions can be undertaken under extreme circumstances without endangering international order. The essay then reviews the ethical traditions on the legitimate use of force – principally just war doctrine – and assesses how they apply to moral decision making about humanitarian intervention. The third part of the essay, covering the rights guaranteed to affected populations, suggests that while the range of rights is broad and detailed, there is as yet no right to protection from outside. This essay concludes with a discussion of the value of shifting from an emphasis on rights to responsibilities, which focuses attention on concrete measures that states might take to operationalize a meaningful right to protection for affected populations.

Essay 7, Legitimacy and Authority, focuses on the legal aspects of humanitarian intervention, beginning with the law relating to the UN Charter regime on the use of force. Despite opposing views, the bulk of scholarly and diplomatic opinion argues that only the Security Council can authorize intervention in the post-Cold War world. There follows an overview of the current status of customary international law. Few legal analysts argue that a customary norm of humanitarian intervention exists. At the same time, even the most conservative commentators do not completely dismiss the notion that this norm may be emerging. The final section explores the links between legality and legitimacy: it probes the declining legitimacy of the Security Council as the UN's supreme decision making body; and it identifies measures that could strengthen the legitimacy of interventions undertaken without Security Council authorization.

Essay 8, Conduct and Capacity, turns from questions of when and where interventions should be authorized to how they should be undertaken. Four conceptually distinct modes of international military operations are identified: peacekeeping, peace enforcement, coercive protection, and warfighting. Specific attention is given to the operational challenges of actually undertaking and sustaining the enforcement of peace and the provision of protection. While compelling peace is a formidable challenge that may not find sufficient international support when decade-long commitments seem untenable, one option may be to further develop the capacity to use military force to provide protection for populations at risk.

The fourth essay examines domestic and international will. Most accounts blame a lack of will for the failure of effective intervention in cases where it was deemed both necessary and legitimate. Yet relatively little analytical effort has been devoted to unpacking the dimensions of will – it is what social scientists call a "black box." If the so-called international community is responsible, too often no one actually is accountable. The question of will, either domestic or international, comes down to choices and decisions made by individuals and institutions. The discussion starts with the domestic dimensions of intervention, focusing on the importance of such factors as geographic proximity, cultural affinities, political culture, perceptions of national interests, and domestic decision making processes. The international components of political will follow, with particular attention given to multilateral leadership and the complex challenges of constructing and maintaining multinational coalitions.

# 6. RIGHTS AND RESPONSIBILITIES

A discussion of rights and responsibilities related to humanitarian intervention – global or national, individual, or collective – raises the most basic issues of moral philosophy. Thus, any expectation of a definitive statement about the normative dimensions of applying deadly force is likely to be frustrated. As one contemporary philosopher of war and peace notes, it is naive to think "that there is a solution to every moral problem with which the world can face us."[1]

Yet to avoid a discussion of responsibility for this reason would be irresponsible. The issues of humanitarian action are too urgent and the dilemmas of inaction too acute to wait for a magical moment of global philosophical consensus. We continually make and justify decisions that have inescapable moral implications, and the question of responsibility is intrinsic to this process. Having himself fled from tyranny, the philosopher Isaiah Berlin's views on this point are a good point of departure. In his last essay, he wrote:

> The whole of our common morality, in which we speak of obligation and duty, right and wrong, moral praise and blame – the way in which people are praised or condemned, rewarded or punished, for behaving in a way in which they were not forced to behave, when they could have behaved otherwise – this network of beliefs and practices on which all current morality seems to me to depend, presupposes the notion of responsibility, and responsibility entails the ability to choose between black and white, right and wrong, pleasure and duty; as well as, in a wider sense, between forms of life, forms of government, and the whole constellation of moral values in terms of which most people, however much they may or may not be aware of it, do in fact live.[2]

Choice and responsibility lie at the heart of human action. We begin with the premise that there are genuine choices about whether, when, and how to act in the face of particular circumstances. The notion of responsibility itself entails fundamental moral reasoning and challenges determinist theories of human behaviour and international relations theory. The behaviour of states is not predetermined by systemic or structural factors, and moral considerations are not merely after-the-fact justifications or simply irrelevant. Taking such a position about the role of responsibility also challenges postmodern views that deny the possibility of engaging in intelligible moral reasoning across cultures and across time.

International responses to humanitarian crises in the 1990s indicate that we do have choices, that they reflect a hierarchy of values, and that even without a universally accepted code of morality we can engage in a dialogue on the morality of intervention. Fundamentally, an ethical judgement is one that can plausibly take "a universal point of view" and presumes that "the notion of morals implies some sentiment common to all mankind, which recommends the same object to general approbation."[3] Even without agreement on the foundations of morality or on the universality of its content, those who make ethical judgements should be able to adopt this minimalist universal point of view.

Evidence of variations across the planet are obvious to anthropologist and casual tourist alike. The issue is not the existence of variations but their ethical implications. For relativism makes a leap from the description of differences to the normative assertion that "right" means "right for a given society" and that therefore "it is wrong for people in one society to condemn, interfere with, etc., the values of another society."[4] In this view, what is right for one society or culture may not be right for another; the moral claims of various societies or cultures hold equal validity.

The lengthy debates about the merits and demerits of various forms of relativist thought should not detain us here.[5] "If value relativism were to be accepted, in *extremis*, then no tyrant – Adolf Hitler, Josef Stalin, Idi Amin, Pol Pot – could be criticized by outsiders," as Ramesh Thakur reminds us. "Relativism is often the first refuge of repressive governments."[6] There exists a broad international consensus around the kinds of behaviour – prohibitions on genocide, crimes against humanity, and "ethnic cleansing" – that might lead to intervention. There is no society or culture anywhere that outwardly condones murder, let alone mass murder, or wanton violence against civilians. This lowest common denominator – or, perhaps, the highest common dimension of international consensus – prohibits the "arbitrary, unexpected, unnecessary, and unlicensed acts of force and habitual and pervasive acts of cruelty and torture performed by military, paramilitary, and police agents in any regime."[7] This claim to universality is compelling because its demands are so basic.

Different societies can establish different priorities of values and standards of happiness, but these differences do not render their understandings of an underlying moral code inherently, and forever, incompatible. What matters most, to return to Rwanda in April 1994 or Cambodia two decades earlier, is the development of international responsibility to protect civilians against mass atrocities.

Several other important ethical traditions are worth describing briefly, because they permeate the intervention debate and lead to starkly different conclusions. One debate in this field centres on the source of ethical value, for which there are two broadly competing interpretations: communitarian and cosmopolitan. Communitarians find the source of value in bounded political communities, most often states. From this approach, the right of specific communities to chart their own course on all matters, including the rights afforded individuals, is predominant. Obligations or duties are also limited to fellow citizens within a state. As such, communitarians tend to oppose external intervention in whatever form. In contrast, cosmopolitans identify the source of ethical value in human beings regardless of their geographic location or citizenship. According to this approach, the relevant political community spans the globe, as does the sense of moral obligation. States mainly serve an instrumental function of ensuring the provision of rights to their populations. Where they fail, outside actors have a responsibility to intervene.

Another important distinction among ethical traditions is the standard by which ethical action should be measured. Here, again there are two distinct schools of thought: deontology and consequentialism. Deontology is the notion that morally appropriate behaviour is based on adherence to moral laws or duties; actions are judged against preexisting standards. For deontologists, the good is in the act itself, and intentions matter. This approach underpins most rights-based approaches to ethics, and it highlights the moral imperative to act in defence of human rights in individual cases. Consequentialist theories, in contrast, suggest that right and wrong are determined not by what was intended but by what actually happens. Utilitarianism – commonly understood as the desire to produce the greatest good for the greatest number – is perhaps the most widely recognized form of consequentalist thought. The good lies not in the act itself but in securing desirable outcomes. Most positions in the debate on humanitarian intervention contain a heavy dose of consequentialist logic – they seek to secure the most desirable long-term outcome. However, the recurring call to "do something," as well as calls for consistency in interventions irrespective of the consequences, draw more on deontological approaches.

The analysis begins with a review of competing ethical approaches to world order – some favouring the stability associated with the norm of nonintervention, others favouring the pursuit of justice through the promotion of human rights. The second part of the essay reviews the various ethical bases developed to justify the use of force, including the just war tradition and more recent efforts to develop criteria for humanitarian intervention. The third part reverses the usual analytical lens, focusing not on outside interveners, but rather on the populations at risk and the rights afforded to them by international human rights law, international humanitarian law (IHL), and refugee law. The analysis concludes by exploring the implications of taking seriously international commitments to assist and protect those severely affected by deadly conflicts through the prism of "responsibilities."

## ETHICAL POSITIONS ON INTERVENTION

An honest account of the responsibility to protect civilians from the ravages of deadly conflicts should acknowledge competing ethical approaches to world order. For some, overall peace and security are best ensured through unwavering adherence to the principles of state sovereignty and nonintervention. They argue that attempts to promote justice beyond borders undermine interstate order and increase the likelihood of interstate war.

Alternatively, there are those who argue that sustainable peace and security cannot exist in a world where genocidal regimes are allowed to pursue their strategies with impunity. On the basis of humane values and hard-headed *Realpolitik*, these observers argue that humanitarian interventions can be undertaken in extreme circumstances without fundamentally undermining the existing interstate order. Supporters of intervention in principle, however, are divided on the legitimacy of state power. Some are deeply sceptical about the motivations of great powers that possess the capacity to undertake intervention. Others respond that motivations are secondary, and the real question is whether there are humanitarian benefits, even where motives are mixed.

Each of these approaches seeks to protect individuals from harm, but they make very different assumptions about the nature of world politics and the role of the state. These differing assumptions lead to starkly diverging conclusions about the efficacy of using military force to protect human beings.

### Maintenance of Order

The importance of defending the principles of state sovereignty and nonintervention are the mainstay of legal theory and diplomatic practice. But they also form the basis for an ethically based approach to the study of world politics. Strands of this thinking can be found in various writers of the realist tradition, but they are most closely associated with the so-called English School pioneered by Martin Wight and Hedley Bull. This perspective understands international order to rest on what Bull termed an "anarchical society." The basic idea is that the absence of a world government does not condemn states to coexist in a Hobbesian world, where brute power is the only ordering principle. Instead, states form a society by recognizing certain common interests, rules, and institutions.[8] In this international society, states agree on the need for order, despite having diverse conceptions of justice. The philosophy is "live and let live." Restraint and nonactivism are the norms behind what otherwise is a laissez-faire international system. The cardinal norm that furnishes order is the reciprocal recognition of sovereignty and its logical corollary, the rule of nonintervention.

The moral justification for this pluralist ethic of coexistence is that each state upholds multiple conceptions of the good. There is no point in having rules to regulate interstate relations if states are not morally valuable in themselves. Central to the argument is the belief that the rules and norms of international society are valued because they provide for the security of individuals. But what if states threaten rather than protect civilians? What happens when the norm of nonintervention protects a state that commits appalling crimes within its own borders? Can the state be intervened against in the name of protecting human rights?

The answer that they offer is a resounding "no," if the agent of intervention is a single state or a groups of states that have authorized themselves to act – if, that is, it is a "unilateral" or unauthorized intervention, no matter how many states participate. If, on the other hand, the agent of intervention is the UN, they are prepared to accept the legitimacy of an intervention to the degree that it genuinely expresses the collective will of the society of states. This normative rejection of unilateral action is justified by arguing that humanitarian intervention poses a grave threat to order, given the lack of consensus on questions of justice. The argument is that in the absence of an international consensus on the conditions that should trigger military intervention to protect human rights, states will act on their own moral principles. Such a possibility would thereby weaken an international order built on the principles of sovereignty, nonintervention, and nonuse of force.

They also argue that the normative language of human rights as enshrined in international agreements and instruments does not constitute a strong enough consensus to ground a right or duty of intervention. Reflecting on state practice during the Cold War, Bull argued, in 1984, that this objection underpinned the reluctance of state leaders to raise humanitarian claims to defend the use of force:

> As regards the future of the right of so-called humanitarian intervention …
> there is no present tendency for states to claim, or for the international
> community to recognize, any such right. The reluctance evident in the
> international community even to experiment with the conception of a right
> of humanitarian intervention reflects not only an unwillingness to jeop-
> ardize the rules of sovereignty and non-intervention by conceding such a
> right to individual states, but also the lack of any agreed doctrine as to what
> human rights are.[9]

This moral defence of the nonintervention rule is based on what philosophers call consequentialism. The well-being of all individuals is the ethical test, and they argue that it is better served by upholding a legal rule that prohibits humanitarian intervention in the absence of agreement over what principles should govern the operation of such a doctrine. Enabling individual states to decide when intervention is permissible issues a licence to the strong to impose their preferences and moral values on the weak.

This position is underpinned by a profound scepticism about the possibilities of realizing notions of universal justice. Bull writes that "the cosmopolitanist society which is implied and presupposed in our talk of human rights exists only as an ideal, and we court great dangers if we allow ourselves to proceed as if it were a political and social framework already in place."[10] Particular states setting themselves up as judges of what constitute universal human rights threaten the ethics of coexistence. In relation to the claim by the North Atlantic Treaty Organization (NATO) in the Kosovo War that its use of force was a legitimate action taken on behalf of the community of responsible states, Bull would reply that we should always be suspicious of the particular interests and values lurking behind such universal pretensions.

A similar argument about the risks of intervention undermining the interstate order has been raised by a host of countries. For example, speaking in the Security Council debate on the legality and legitimacy of NATO's use of force against the Federal Republic of Yugoslavia (FRY), the representative for the Russian Federation stated that while his government did not defend the FRY's violations of IHL, "[a]ttempts to apply a different standard to international law and to disregard its basic norms and principles create a dangerous precedent that could cause acute destabilization and chaos on the regional and global level."[11] Similarly, Chinese Foreign Minister Tang Jixuan stated in September 1999 that "[s]uch arguments as 'human rights taking precedence over sovereignty' and 'humanitarian intervention' seem to be in vogue these days. But respect for sovereignty and non-interference are the basic principles governing international relations and any deviation from them would lead to a gunboat diplomacy that would wreak havoc in the world."[12]    .

While commonly dismissed by critics as rationalizations for narrow national self-interests, those who challenge the norm of unilateral humanitarian intervention are not necessarily indifferent to the plight of war victims. Rather, they fear that even greater human suffering might result from an increased incidence of interstate war as a result of setting aside the norm of nonintervention. As Robert Jackson wrote in the wake of NATO's bombing of Kosovo:

> The debate on humanitarian intervention is not a debate between those who are concerned about human rights and those who are indifferent or callous about human suffering … . States who are in a position to pursue and preserve international justice have a responsibility to do that when-ever and wherever possible. But they have a fundamental responsibility not to sacrifice or even jeopardize other fundamental values in the attempt … the stability of international society, especially the unity of the great powers, is more important, indeed far more important, than minority rights and humanitarian protections.[13]

Certainly in situations like Kosovo, in which human rights imperatives and great-power relations clash, proponents of intervention argue that the former should be subordinated to the latter. The logical implication of this position is that there can be no basis for states acting to end human rights emergencies unless this has the assent of at least all the permanent members of the Security Council. But does this mean that states should never advance justice claims if there is any risk of disrupting interstate order? And does it not simply leave the victims of human rights abuses to their fate?

## Pursuit of Justice

The diplomatic rhetoric and state practice of many countries represents the humanitarian intervention debate as if the choice were stark – sovereign rights or human rights. This is also the position taken by those who believe that the sovereign state is a fundamental barrier to the realization of human rights. Theorists like Richard Falk and Ken Booth argue that the rules and values of a sovereignty-based world order are morally bankrupt because they have failed to protect individuals and groups from torture, ethnic cleansing, and genocide.[14] States may have signed international agreements to uphold human rights, but they are primarily responsible for gross and systematic violations.

These critics of the maintenance of a state-based international society ask whom this order serves. Is it protecting the victims of torture, ethnic cleansing, and genocide? Or the 40,000 children who die of preventable diseases daily? Or the millions of women subject to domestic violence and degrading treatment? From the perspective of the victims of world politics, the society of states is providing neither order nor justice. In a description that might well have been drafted in the foreign ministry of the most critical antiglobalization persuasion, Booth argues that international society "bears an uncomfortable resemblance to a global protection racket"[15] run by the G-8 to protect its wealth and power. The normative practices of international society leave untouched the structural causes of the economic and social injustice rooted in a deregulated capitalist world system. As protection rackets go, it is by no means the worst imaginable, but it refutes the claim that the society of states can act as an effective guardian of human rights.

How, then, do these so-called "antistatists" deal with the challenge posed by genocide and mass murder? They look to global social movements to undermine the legitimacy of statist elites, and they promote the values of human rights, healthy and balanced economic development, and environmental protection. The global human rights regime grew from an interactive process among individuals, nongovernmental organizations, and states. As early as 1929, the Institut de droit international (Institute for International Law) spelled out minimum rights for every person in every state, declaring that its work was a response "to the conscience of the civilized world which demands the recognition of the rights of individuals, rights that are beyond the reach of the state."[16] Three-quarters of a century later, the UN High Commissioner for Refugees (UNHCR), Mary Robinson, writes, "Universality is, in fact, the essence of all human rights; all people are entitled to them, all state and civil actors should defend them. The goal is nothing less than human rights for all."[17]

Belief in human rights may proceed on several different foundations, philosophical or religious. One can, but need not, be a foundationalist in ethical terms to believe in the idea of human rights. At their core, human rights are those rights that all individuals have by virtue of their very humanity.[18] For some, this humanity is grounded in deontological theories of natural law, or neo-Kantian variants that emphasize the exercise of reason through the categorical imperative that we treat all humans as ends and not means.[19] Starting from consequentialist moral reasoning, utilitarians also find the idea of human rights quite compatible with their general approach to ethics.[20] Even avowed antifoundationalists argue that their position is compatible with the development of a global human rights culture.[21]

The compelling normative claim that all individuals have inalienable human rights has spread far and wide. In a speech at the UN just after the adoption of the Universal Declaration of Human Rights, in December 1948, Eleanor Roosevelt predicted that "a curious grapevine" would spread the ideas contained in the Declaration far and wide.[22] This aspiration has proved prophetic, as the ideas embodied in the Declaration have become the weapons that the powerless have mobilized against the powerful in their quest to secure the most fundamental human rights.

Henry Shue defined basic rights as security from arbitrary violence and the provision of minimum subsistence rights. These rights are basic because they are "essential to the enjoyment of all other rights" and are "everyone's minimum reasonable demands upon the rest of humanity."[23] The language of basic rights directs attention to the ongoing, "chronic" violations of human rights that go beyond the emergencies of genocide, mass murder, and ethnic cleansing to encompass the daily suffering of millions facing slow death through poverty and malnutrition. *The Human Development Report 2000* argues that "assessments of human development, if combined with the human rights perspective, can indicate the duties of others in the society to enhance human development." The report sets out the links between human rights and human development in ways that speak to any attempt to define global interests. It reminds us that human rights violations may be "loud," as in Rwanda, or "silent," as in the cases of "about 790 million people not adequately nourished, 250 million children used as child labour, 1.2 million women and girls under 18 trafficked for prostitution each year ... 1.2 billion people ... income poor, about 1 billion adults illiterate, 1 billion without safe water and more than 2.4 billion without basic sanitation."[24]

In seeking to define global responsibilities, addressing these kinds of deprivations is as central as deploying military force to intervene in the midst of a bloody and lethal conflict. These observers would argue that we have the solemn responsibility, negatively, to avoid depriving others of these rights and, positively, to work to create the conditions in which it is possible for everyone to enjoy them. This means treating all people – and particularly those affected by deadly conflicts, whether they be refugees, internally displaced persons (IDPs), or the chronically malnourished and sick who remain behind in war zones – not merely as recipients of charity but as bearers of the same human rights as citizens of Mexico City, New York, or Moscow. Taking basic rights seriously means taking responsibility for their protection everywhere.

The impact of human rights in sweeping away communist governments in east-central Europe and the former Soviet Union is now obvious. Other momentous changes have also occurred since the end of the Cold War. They include the spread of democratic values to previously authoritarian governments, the growing acceptance of human rights norms by governments that had previously repudiated their legitimacy, and the growing emphasis on strengthening the UN's machinery for protecting the rights of civilians in armed conflicts. Critics of statist values and structures argue that protecting the victims of world politics depends on focusing on the deeply rooted structural causes of poverty, underdevelopment, and social exclusion that create the breeding ground for violent conflict. They may be right in asserting that one key to achieving a more peaceful world lies in addressing global economic and social inequalities. But the question here is how we should respond when reality fails to match theory. How should human rights be defended in cases where states are guilty of crimes against humanity or when the state has collapsed into interethnic violence?

Only in situations where vital national interests are believed to be at stake will state leaders incur the costs of intervention. Thus, the problem for many advocates of human rights is that killing, even on the scale of genocide, seems insufficient to move governments to risk their soldiers' lives. If governments do intervene with the claim of humanitarian purposes, antista-tists look for the selfish interests lurking behind the action. Richard Falk considers that, in theory, the use of force "can be an emancipatory instrument, at least in certain extreme situa-tions," but this requires governments "to commit significant numbers of lives and resources over a prolonged period, with the prospect of possibly heavy losses, and even then with no assurance of success." He argues that the challenge is to persuade and cajole governments into making a stronger moral commitment to humanitarian intervention. Without it, he concludes that "military action in an interventionary mode virtually always produces destructive and counterproductive results."[25]

Set against this critique of the state as a moral agent of intervention is the view that there are possibilities to civilize the state so that it enforces cosmopolitan values. This school of thought acknowledges that the society of states has failed to protect human rights, but it is more optimistic that state power can be harnessed for moral purposes. R.J. Vincent argued that international society has strengthened its own legitimacy by co-opting the doctrine of universal human rights. The claims of individual rights have forced themselves onto the agenda of international society, and states have accepted a relationship between internal and external legitimacy. However, in arguing that individuals have become legitimate subjects of international law, Vincent admits that their rights could only be truly enforced by states. This is especially evident for humanitarian intervention.

Having identified the protection of basic rights as the litmus test of the moral credentials of international society, Vincent argued that the duty to protect these rights "falls on us all as individuals, but that we may seek to discharge it most effectively through our governments."[26] The state remains the bedrock of human rights protection, as well as of international order. This is not to say that transnational social forces are not playing an important role in standard-setting and monitoring. Yet, the post-Cold War period is like preceding eras in at least one way. There is little reason to invest much hope that global civil society can systematically ensure human security. When facing supreme humanitarian emergencies in northern Iraq or southern Sudan, aid agencies have at best a limited capacity to deliver food or medical supplies. In the case of Somalia, armed escorts were vital to the delivery of relief aid, and the chronic insecurity even led the International Committee of the Red Cross (ICRC) and other agencies to hire armed guards, so-called technicals. The limits of NGOs as agents of rescue was recognized by Médecins sans Frontières (MSF, Doctors Without Borders) during the Rwandan genocide. The organization had never before called for military intervention, believing that the use of violence was always escalatory and that states are notoriously self-serving. In making a call for intervention, MSF had lost none of its suspicion of states as agents of humanitarianism, but it felt compelled to do so to end the horrors in Rwanda.

Where then does this leave us? If seeing the state as a civilizing rather than corrupting force is to gain normative ground and policy salience, it is necessary to demonstrate that states are indeed capable of acting as agents of common humanity. Rather than accept the view that all states are legitimate, there is an alternative one – namely, that states should only qualify as legitimate if they meet certain basic standards of common humanity. What if a state's legal and moral right to nonintervention were dependent on ensuring basic rights for its citizens? Human beings live in national communities. The state collectively concentrates, represents, and speaks for their rights and concerns as citizens.

The implication is plain. If by its actions and, indeed, crimes, a state destroys the lives and rights of its citizens, it forfeits temporarily its moral claim to be treated as legitimate. Its sovereignty, as well as its right to nonintervention, is suspended. The Special Representative of the Secretary-General for Internally Displaced Persons, Francis M. Deng, has called this approach "sovereignty as responsibility."[27] In brief, the three traditional characteristics of a state in the Westphalian system (territory, authority, and population) have been supplemented by a fourth, respect for human rights.

The state has, first and foremost, the responsibility to protect the rights of its citizens. But in those situations in which it is unwilling or unable to fulfill this responsibility – or is itself the perpetrator of abuse – there is then a residual responsibility for other states to take up the slack. They should protect the citizens of the irresponsible state, particularly when massive loss of life occurs or is imminent. UN Secretary-General Kofi Annan's speeches at the end of the 1990s can be viewed as reflecting important aspects of the sovereignty-as-responsibility doctrine: "The Charter protects the sovereignty of peoples. It was never meant as a license for governments to trample on human rights and human dignity. Sovereignty implies responsibility, not just power."[28]

## Justifying Interventions

The fundamental assumptions underlying this position are not only that intervention can be morally legitimate but also that protecting human rights can be justified on security grounds. The belief that democratic states have a long-term national interest in, as well as moral responsibility to promote, human rights was christened "good international citizenship" by Gareth Evans, as Australia's foreign minister in the late 1980s.[29] It is this vision that underpins Canada's human-security agenda, with its conviction that there is a relationship between the provision of basic rights and wider international security.[30] The challenge facing enlightened state leaders is to build an international consensus behind policies that address the underlying cause of human rights deprivations and that defend basic rights wherever and whenever they are threatened. For advocates of good international citizenship, the promotion of justice is the key to lasting order, even if they also "must convince others of their case, their competence, and their motives."[31]

In the long term, such a conception of ethical statecraft looks to the elimination of armed conflict. Even from an idealistic vantage point, however, a lengthy process of transition would exist. Cases can be expected to arise for which the use of force is believed to be the only means to end gross and systematic violations of basic rights. The use of violence poses an agonizing moral dilemma for the good international citizen. Michael Ignatieff captures it in the following manner: "How can you have a human rights doctrine that puts the right to life at the centre of that doctrine but simultaneously legitimizes violence to right human rights abuses either internally or externally?"[32]

A problem yet to be adequately addressed is how to ensure that intervention, where it occurs, is legitimate. Commentators like Jackson would argue that authorizing intervention should be the sole responsibility of the Security Council. It follows that opposition by one or more of the permanent members is sufficient to stop an intervention. However, this seems to fly in the face of the moral impulses behind the sovereignty-as-responsibility doctrine. Not only does it shield major powers from being subject to intervention, but it also leaves international decision making hostage entirely to the prerogatives of major powers whose own human rights records are suspect. Such an absolutist position would require states to refrain from acting in future cases of genocide, mass murder, war crimes, and ethnic cleansing.

To emphasize the moral consequences of too rigid an attachment to the nonintervention rule without Security Council imprimatur, the UN Secretary-General posed a haunting rhetorical question to the General Assembly in September 1999. Should a coalition of states willing to use force to end the Rwandan genocide have refrained from acting in the absence of express Council authorization? At the same time, he recognized the dangers to order of permitting powerful states to authorize themselves to act as enforcers of global humanitarian values. "To those for whom the Kosovo action heralded a new era when States and groups of States can take military action outside the established mechanisms for enforcing international law," Kofi Annan asked, rhetorically: "Is there not a danger of such interventions undermining the imperfect, yet resilient, security system created after the Second World War, and of setting dangerous precedents for future interventions without a clear criterion to decide who might invoke these precedents, and in what circumstances?"[33]

States are not ready to explicitly sanction an intervention for humanitarian purposes without Security Council authorization. But neither are they always willing to condemn it. There seems to be recognition that the fabric of world order can tolerate the occasional armed intervention justified on humanitarian grounds outside of the UN Charter. There is no enthusiasm for codifying a treaty on humanitarian intervention, because of the worry that this would lead to states' abusing it. Not incidentally, an additional problem for such a development is the fact that a legal right of this nature would generate obligations to act in situations where states might well prefer a policy of inaction.

The moral and legal responsibility falls on intervening states to explain why their action should be treated as a legitimate exception to the cardinal rules of nonintervention and nonuse of force. The plausibility of these justifications and the scale of the humanitarian disaster should be important factors in shaping the international response. At the same time, it would be naive to ignore power considerations in determining how far justice claims advanced by particular states are tolerated, excused, or even legitimated. The challenge facing the UN and states committed to protecting basic human rights is to devise strategies of anticipatory intervention that are legitimated by the society of states and the wider community of actors in the humanitarian arena.

## ETHICAL TRADITIONS IN THE USE OF FORCE

Contemporary debates commonly invoke *le droit d'ingérence*, the so-called right to interfere. First popularized by MSF, and later on by other members of the French doctors' movement in the early 1970s, this doctrine privileges the provision of humanitarian assistance to victims of war, irrespective of the sovereign rights of states.[34] In the first instance, it rejects the necessity of state consent for the provision of assistance by humanitarian agencies, but it has become associated with the legitimacy to intervene with deadly force to protect civilians. Questions of the legitimacy of the use of military force, however, are part of an older debate. Before exploring criteria for decision making about intervention when human catastrophes threaten, it is worth considering these older ethical traditions. Although the focus was largely on conflicts between states, recent commentators have highlighted the direct relevance of these traditions to questions of humanitarin intervention.

One ethical position is to adopt a pacifist stance and reject the application of deadly force in any form, on the basis of profound religious convictions. Conscientious objection to participation in the armed forces is one manifestation. Such groups as the Quakers and the Mennonites in the West and the Jains in the East reject out of hand the proposition that military force could or should be used to pursue humanitarian or any other objectives.

Other profoundly religious minds have struggled with the reality of the need to use force in the face of political oppression. For instance, liberation theology was developed by Catholic clergy in Latin American to justify an armed struggle against the ruling classes as part of a necessary effort to foster self-determination, redistribution of power and wealth, and liberation of the suffering masses.[35]

Although the discussion below focuses on the Western just war tradition, there is ample evidence that similar principles exist within other religious traditions as well. Ephraim Isaac, for instance, draws on theological and anthropological evidence that "humanitarianism" (or a visceral concern for, and benevolence toward, fellow human beings) "is a universal phenomenon manifested globally and throughout the ages."[36] A number of scholars have pointed to a concept in Islamic theology comparable to just war doctrine,[37] while others have illustrated that Islam was among the first civilizations to establish clear constraints against inhumane acts.[38]

## Just War Tradition

The most thoroughly developed tradition of inquiry into the ethics of recourse to the use of lethal force is just war doctrine.[39] Beginning in the early medieval period, it attempted to identify the circumstances under which a resort to the use of force is justified (*jus ad bellum*), as well as the means by which a war may be legitimately fought (*jus in bello*). The discussion below focuses on the former; the latter is discussed in more detail in the analysis of military conduct in the subsequent essay about conduct and capacity.

Within the just war tradition there is a broad range of views, with no single list of criteria being universally accepted. Nevertheless, it is possible to identify core elements.[40] Thomas Aquinas set out three: right authority, just cause, and right intentions. Three additional elements subsequently developed: last resort, proportionality, and reasonable hope.

The notion of right authority is firmly rooted in the sovereignty of states. Prior to the general legal prohibition on the use of force in 1945, the just war tradition understood right authority to rest with the sovereign state, though over time the emphasis shifted from a sovereignty granted by a divine source to one of popular consent. The prohibition on the use of force in the UN Charter and the designation of the Security Council as the ultimate arbiter fundamentally transformed the sources of right authority.

The criterion of just cause was most commonly understood to refer to self-defence, though a number of other circumstances were considered: defending allies, reclaiming territory lost in previous wars, and punishing transgressors. In general, then, it was understood to depend on the degree of harm inflicted. A further, though less well-developed, just cause was the defence of the innocent.

Right intentions concern the motives that lie behind the recourse to the use of force. In earlier times, the principal legitimate motivation for the resort to war was the creation of a just peace. The more general point here is that the ethical status of the use of force depends on intentions, and ulterior motives undermine that status. The pursuit of narrowly defined national interests would not meet this minimum threshold. In many respects, however, it is easier to recognize unacceptable motives than acceptable ones.

The use of force should be a last resort, though there is no agreement as to whether the full range of alternatives should have been pursued first, or whether serious analysis of options would suffice to dismiss as unrealistic those short of force. There is certainly an inherent preference for nonviolence, though some writers within the tradition argue that options should be pursued only when they have a strong likelihood of success. Taking this conclusion a step further, others argue that last resort is not a temporal distinction at all, but refers only to the fact that the use of force is the least preferred option. According to this logic, "last" does not mean that it is "ultimate" but that serious reflection and evaluation of other options indicate no likelihood of bringing the desired outcomes.

The final two principles, proportionality and reasonable hope, are related. The first refers to the need for means to be commensurate with the ends, as well as being in line with the magnitude of the initial provocation. The second constitutes an assessment of whether there are good grounds for believing in advance that the desired outcome can be achieved. Together they make the case that a sound basis for intervention cannot be determined independently of measures proposed and anticipated results.

The just war tradition sets out an ethical basis for the use of force in circumstances beyond mere self-defence. Although it is seldom acknowledged, many of the ethical questions that need to be considered before using deadly force to protect civilians can be found within this tradition. Indeed, much of the contemporary debate seems to call for a carefully circumscribed approach to humanitarian intervention that in fact amounts to a modified just war doctrine.

## Moral Criteria for Intervention

The connections between just war thinking and overarching criteria for humanitarian intervention are clear. A series of attempts to establish criteria have not resulted in an agreed set, but there are common elements. Gareth Evans, during a session on humanitarian intervention organized by the International Peace Academy, succinctly summarized them as gravity, urgency, objectivity, acceptability, practicality, proportionality, and sustainability.[41]

Early efforts originated in a desire to identify the potential legal grounds on which an intervention could be justified, and this rationale continues to be prominent. Criteria have also been developed to act as a checklist for political leaders to encourage sound decision making, although even some supporters are hesitant in that too stringent criteria could also provide yet another unwanted and unnecessary brake on justified intervention. A further purpose for criteria particularly relevant to the subject matter here is to assess the morality – the ethical dimensions – of humanitarian intervention. Six criteria are worth enumerating.

*Scale of the Crisis* – Criteria for intervention on humanitarian grounds begin with the question of the scale or gravity of a crisis. There is considerable agreement about two circumstances under which intervention might be justified: when the government of a state is the perpetrator of mass atrocities; and when a government is fundamentally unable to maintain law and order (or halt the descent into anarchy).

There is a wider range of views on the necessary threshold in terms of "the scale of the breaches of human rights and international humanitarian law including the number of people affected and the nature of the violations."[42] There is near universal agreement that the threshold for military intervention is very high. For all but the most serious of human rights violations, the use of force is morally indefensible. A number of authors suggest that genocide and crimes against humanity – both have agreed legal definitions – warrant intervention. Others argue that there are additional grounds, including mass forced displacement. All of these criteria usually entail the actual, or imminent, large scale loss of life.

*Purposes of Intervention* – Another common element in the debate about criteria relates to the motivations underlying humanitarian intervention. It is often argued that the overarching purpose should be to protect victimized populations. In many formulations, this criterion is extended to mean that the intervention should exclusively be "apolitical" or "disinterested." While this would create a relatively clear prohibition on the seizure of territory or the installation of a puppet regime under the guise of protecting innocent civilians, it also implies an unattainable purity of motives. A counterclaim is that there should be a predominantly humanitarian motive, while accepting that considerations of national interest will inevitably intrude. In fact, if risks and costs of intervention are high and interests are not involved, it is unlikely that states will enter the fray or stay the course. Those who advocate action to protect human rights must inevitably come to grips with the nature of political self-interest to achieve good ends.

Other commentators take a less stringent view of motives. The morality of interventions should be judged in terms of their outcomes. For example, Fernando Tesón argues that, "[t]he true test is whether the intervention has put an end to human rights deprivations.

That is sufficient to meet the requirement of disinterestedness, even if there are other, non-humanitarian reasons behind the intervention."[43] Nicholas J. Wheeler proposes a sliding scale of international legitimacy, whereby interventions that have significant humanitarian motives are praised, while those that lack any such credentials, but which produce a positive outcome, are excused.[44]

Suspicion and probing questions seem warranted where intervenors seem to be pursuing their own political or security objectives. Nonhumanitarian intentions could badly taint decisions about how to carry out an intervention and defeat humanitarian goals. A history of inconsistent interventions that primarily pursued political objectives would destroy the credibility of a system that claimed to intervene for humanitarian ends and could end up justifying the abuse of power. However, in assessing the moral and human rights legitimacy of interventions, we are primarily assessing the consequences of the *action*, not the moral worth of the *actor* (the intervening force). A one-off intervention not wholly motivated by humanitarian intentions could still be beneficial.[45] Similarly, a series of consistent interventions by countries that have the best intentions in the world could be morally unjustifiable if, for instance, the intervening forces commit serious human rights violations or are so inept that suffering increases. The point is that a nonhumanitarian intention does not in itself make the intervention contrary to human rights principles.

A further measure to address the underlying motivations for intervention has been the relatively rapid withdrawal of military forces once the humanitarian objectives of an intervention have been secured. A related indicator is that no attempt is made to subvert or to change a political regime in a target country. While a common element of earlier attempts to devise criteria, there is a growing recognition that the safety of vulnerable populations cannot necessarily be guaranteed through a short military campaign. Moreover, the evidence from the interventions by Tanzania and Vietnam in the 1970s that overthrew Idi Amin and Pol Pot, respectively, is that effective intervention may require a change of political regime.

In fact, the challenge for contemporary interventions is now more often discussed in terms of avoiding simplistic and myopic "exit strategies." In light of the increased use of protectorates, or temporary international administrations, oversight, and trusteeship – with overt political agendas and long-term timelines – a more generic interpretation of the purposes of intervention may be appropriate. That is, the meaning of "apolitical" would be that interveners do not gain selfish or short-term political or any other advantage, and the overriding agenda of both short- and long-term activities remains the safety and security of the affected local civilian populations.

*Multilateral Action* – In order to limit abuse and foster more disinterested calculations, many commentators have called for all humanitarian interventions to be multilateral. Echoing the earlier discussion, it is often argued that a Security Council imprimatur is a strict requirement. Others have gone further by arguing interventions should not be undertaken by hegemonic powers, whether global or regional. There is no doubt that multilateral interventions reduce the prospects for abuse, particularly if the range of involved countries is broad. But from an ethical standpoint, it does not follow that interventions by a single state are necessarily illegitimate. If a particular multilateral intervention is ethically sound, it is hard to see why it would not remain so if conducted by a single state. Similarly, hesitations about intervention by hegemonic powers are understandable and may be warranted. But they alone cannot discredit an otherwise justifiable intervention, especially as these are among the few countries with the power to project military force beyond their borders.

*Last Resort* – Those who develop lists of criteria for assessing the legitimacy of humanitarian intervention invariably include the notion of last resort. Recourse to the use of deadly force is permissible only when the doctrine of necessity has been satisfied – that is, force is the only remaining option. Other measures include fact-finding missions, mediation, statements of concern by intergovernmental bodies, condemnation, criminal prosecution of perpetrators, and measures limiting political, economic, and military relations, including embargoes and offers of peacekeeping.

The meaning of "last resort" can be understood to apply when "nothing short of the application of armed force would be sufficient to stop the human rights violations in question." Therefore, "except where delay would permit massive, irreparable harm, all measures short of armed force should be exploited before resort to such force."[46] Few, however, suggest that this notion must be taken literally and interpreted in purely sequential terms. It is certainly not the case that all other available options must actually have been pursued and failed, but rather that other options will have been considered seriously.

There are clear links here with prevention. Armed intervention would be unnecessary in most cases if governments took early action before violations and armed conflicts escalated beyond control. In addition to addressing root causes of violence, the techniques developed by many UN and regional organizations over the last half century underscore the range of options short of military intervention that could be employed.

However, the failure of states to act early and avoid the need for military intervention cannot morally justify refusing to intervene when abuses have escalated to crimes against humanity. Failures in prevention expose the mistakes and weaknesses of the intervenors and should be used to press for early action elsewhere. But it is clearly not a response to the urgent moral question: What should be done when genocide is occurring?

The relationship between last resort and chronology is complicated. Certainly the crisis should be imminent, but is it necessary or even desirable to wait for massive casualties before intervention can be justified? Does the scale of atrocities have to become cataclysmic before international responses become thinkable? The weight of opinion seems to be changing, with a number of commentators noting that the early use of force may often, in fact, hold out greater prospects for success and entail less total suffering.

*Proportionality* – While questions about the nature and degree of force are normally reserved for discussions of conduct, they are relevant to ethical decision making about the recourse to deadly force as well. The use of force must be appropriate, not excessive. Furthermore, military intervention should only be undertaken when the prospects for success are strong – when the intervention is likely to do more good than harm.

The aim of stopping massive human rights violations might justify armed intervention, but it surely cannot justify *any* means. The minimum amount of force should be used to achieve a humanitarian objective. Force should be used only to achieve the goal of stopping the atrocities, not pursuing political or strategic objectives.

*Impact* – In both the short and long term, it is notoriously difficult to predict whether an intervention will do more harm than good. In moral terms, the intervention should do the least possible harm to those being protected, to bystanders such as any civilians who are not taking part in fighting, to the perpetrators, and to the intervening party itself. An intervening force has a duty to abide scrupulously by the rules of IHL. These principles include the prohibitions on direct or indiscriminate attacks on civilians and disproportionate strikes on military targets that unjustifiably harm civilians.

In addition, the application of this precautionary principle would also preclude military action against the major powers. It is difficult to imagine the resolution of any conflict or success in any humanitarian objective if military action were mounted against such powers. Thus, even though many commentators argue that Russian violations of humanitarian law in Chechnya have exceeded those in the former Yugoslavia, on purely utilitarian grounds there has been no serious consideration of intervention. The possible repercussions from a major war, including nuclear weapons, outweigh any conceivable humanitarian concerns. At the same time, if the use of force to halt egregious violations of human rights does not challenge a major power's core values and is considered important to preventing an escalation of violence and large scale loss of life, it is difficult to justify giving the permanent members a veto over such interventions.

Calculations about costs and benefits are often easier ex post facto than prior to the actual use of coercion. Imponderables inevitably intrude and make such calculations problematic. This reality – along with the uncertainties of waging war and subjective judgements about what constitutes acceptable and unacceptable damage – make proportionality and impact among the most subjective of possible criteria.

## RIGHTS OF AFFECTED POPULATIONS

In an ICRC-sponsored public opinion poll, 66 percent of respondents in 12 war-torn countries said there should be more international intervention on behalf of threatened civilians, while 17 percent said there should be less, and only 10 percent said there should be no intervention.[47] It may not be surprising that affected populations favour intervention, but such overwhelming support from the victims reminds us that this debate is about the life and death of real people.

Affected local populations have fundamental rights. If their violation might be grounds for intervention, then it is important to understand the nature and breadth of these rights. The underlying concern here is with the victims – threatened and actual – and the body of human rights and humanitarian principles created to protect them. The question then is, what fundamental rights are guaranteed to all human beings? What are the commitments made by states to protect people, especially against gross and systematic abuses? Can victims legitimately expect that if all else fails, states will intervene militarily to protect them against massive violations in their own country?

### Rights under International Law

Protection of the right to life and physical integrity is found in three related but distinct bodies of international law: IHL, human rights law, and refugee law. IHL, or the laws of armed conflict, does not prohibit war but limits wanton cruelty in order to spare persons who are not or who are no longer engaged in armed conflict. Growing from an initial concern to provide for prisoners of war, it has grown to encompass broader concerns about methods of war and includes calls to both states and rebel groups to protect civilians, as codified in the four 1949 Geneva Conventions and the two Additional Protocols of 1977.[48]

The human rights concept of crimes against humanity and the concept of war crimes from IHL (as updated by the crimes included in the Statute of the International Criminal Court [ICC]) have certain prohibitions in common. In addition to outlawing arbitrary killing, they prohibit torture, unjustified medical experimentation, slavery, rape, and other sexual violence, such as enforced prostitution, forced pregnancy, and enforced sterilization. Both prohibit the forced displacement of populations, starvation as a deliberate tactic, or trying to destroy a population by preventing access to medicine or by destroying crops and livestock.

The laws of armed conflict contain some fundamental principles, including that civilians and others not taking part in hostilities (for example, wounded or captured soldiers) should never be the object of attack; only military objectives should be attacked. Indiscriminate attacks are prohibited, as are attacks that are disproportionate to any legitimate military objective and that therefore strike against civilians. Weapons that cause unnecessary suffering are prohibited, as is poison and methods of warfare that may cause widespread, long-term, and severe environmental damage. The 1997 landmine treaty prohibits the use, stockpiling, production, and transfer of antipersonnel mines.

Violations of most of these provisions amount to the worst breaches of humanitarian law, called war crimes. Article 8 of the ICC statute includes a long list of attacks on people or property committed in international or civil wars: willful killing, torture, unlawful deportation, taking of hostages, employing poison and asphyxiation, use of poisonous or other gases, sexual violence, intentional use of starvation, indiscriminate attacks on civilians. The laws of armed conflict are complex, and some of these prohibitions technically apply only in international wars that involve more than one state, not in civil wars.[49] However, one fundamental guarantee applies to all armed conflicts, whether intranational or international. Article 3, which is common to all the Geneva Conventions, prohibits "violence to life and person, in particular murder of all kinds, mutilation, cruel treatment and torture" of anyone not taking part in the hostilities, whether civilians or wounded or captured soldiers.

International human rights law tries to limit the unrestrained power of the state. Although much ink was spilled in the 1990s about weak states, historically excessive state power has been far more prominent as a source of human rights violations. The first article of the Universal Declaration of Human Rights states, "Everyone has the right to life, liberty and security of person." International law does not prohibit killing as such. What it does prohibit in broad terms is arbitrary killing (deprivation of life) and violence against the physical integrity of people.

Underlying all branches of international law is the principle of nondiscrimination between peoples. It is the only human right expressly mentioned in the UN Charter. Article 1 of the Charter includes "promoting and encouraging respect for human rights and for fundamental freedoms, for all without distinction as to race, sex, language or religion" – language that has been ratified by almost every country in the world. Nondiscrimination has perhaps the strongest claim to be a norm binding on all states. Discrimination against ethnic or other groups is often at the heart of violence that demands international coercion. Long-term discrimination in areas such as education or employment can trigger a spiraling cycle of bloodshed.

Genocide and ethnic cleansing are the most egregious expressions of discrimination, and the ones that entail large enough losses of life to constitute for many observers a trigger for humanitarian intervention. While ethnic cleansing is a relatively new concept, emerging most directly from the Balkan crises of the 1990s, the notion of genocide has a clear legal definition. In the wake of the Nazi Holocaust, an international convention was agreed on, specifically designed to prevent and punish perpetrators of genocide.[50]

Many of the rights described above are echoed in documents that seek to protect particularly vulnerable groups. Children are specifically guaranteed all the most basic rights, and many more, in the UN Convention on the Rights of the Child.[51] This is particularly important because it has been ratified by every country in the world except the US and Somalia and is therefore also legally binding as a peremptory norm.

Refugee law, especially the 1951 Convention Relating to the Status of Refugees and its 1967 Protocol, obliges countries to give asylum to refugees who cannot return home because they face a well-founded fear of persecution.[52] It prohibits host or asylum countries from returning (*refoulement*) them to a home country where they face these risks. At their most basic level, these bodies of international law seek to protect the rights to life and physical integrity when people are faced with the arbitrary power of their own state, when civilians are caught in armed conflict, and when refugees flee from war and persecution.

Ironically, people who have fled across borders as refugees are entitled to a better codified international protection than those who have fled from one part of their country to another. The internally displaced cross no international border and do not enjoy the same international protection afforded refugees. It is for this reason that states agreed in 1992 that the UN Secretary-General should appoint a special representative on IDPs and subsequently proposed a set of "Guiding Principles" that apply specifically to those who flee and are displaced within their own country.[53] These norms largely reaffirm that the internally displaced should enjoy the same rights as others. But they also underscore certain key rights found in human rights or humanitarian law, such as the right not to be discriminated against, the right not to be arbitrarily displaced, the right to freedom of movement, and the right to essential food, water, shelter, clothing, and medical care.

People often speak of human tragedies that accompany gross and systematic violations of human rights, especially in wars. Victims die or fall sick because they do not have enough food and lack basic shelter and health care. These deprivations are another way to kill or maim, deliberately or by neglect. They are also another way of describing the unacceptable violations of the human rights to food, shelter, and health.

The rights just described apply to all human beings. They are universal. Notwithstanding any lingering controversy about whether rights such as freedom of expression or assembly should be applied equally in all cultures, there can be no argument that the rights to freedom from arbitrary killing, genocide, and torture apply equally to all people in every situation in every corner of the globe.[54] Although controversial, some observers now argue that the range of "peremptory norms of international law" (*jus cogens*)[55] includes the prohibition of genocide; systematic racial, religious, and gender discrimination; slavery; crimes against humanity; war crimes; enforced disappearances; murder; torture (including sexual violence); prolonged arbitrary detention; and denial of the right to self-determination.[56]

## Rights to Protection?

Individuals and vulnerable groups are at the heart of these international legal provisions. Treaties and other standards create a dense and interlocking set of fundamental rights and freedoms. Many of the UN texts are echoed in treaties adopted by regional bodies in Africa, Asia, the Americas, and Europe. UN and regional standards are benchmarks against which the seriousness of the behaviour of governments and rebel groups should be judged when it comes to possible intervention.

These legal guarantees raise legitimate expectations that protection will be provided against a host of threats from unrestrained political and military power. State authorities carry the primary burden for delivering relief, as for the protection of rights. Yet, humanitarian organizations argue that people have a right to receive assistance; and if this cannot be fulfilled by the state, outsiders have a right of access to fill the gap. The programme of action from the 1993 Vienna World Conference on Human Rights most directly supported this approach by reaffirming in Article I.29 "the right of victims to be assisted by humanitarian organizations, as set forth in the Geneva Conventions ... and calls for the safe and timely access for such assistance."

Other documents related to armed conflict, IDPs, and the UN's coordination role affirm that humanitarian organizations have a right to *offer* their services.[57] Moreover, attacks on UN humanitarian workers delivering assistance to those in need are now recognized as international crimes.[58] The documents set up a presumption that a state should accept such offers and facilitate assistance for those suffering from lack of food or medical care. In other words, the offer of help should not be arbitrarily rejected, especially when the authorities are unable or unwilling to provide the necessary assistance. But in the end, access is "subject to consent" of the state concerned, limiting the ultimate value of the supposed "right."

For present and future victims paper rights are meaningless without ways to enforce compliance by recalcitrant states. Human rights and humanitarian law, however, say little about the role of other states in ensuring compliance. When the UN was created in 1945, the Charter prohibition against interference in the domestic affairs of a state certainly meant that other states and international bodies might create standards and promote human rights in the abstract, but there was little consensus about calling violating states to account, with or without their consent.

It is undoubtedly true, however, that human rights are no longer purely a domestic matter. Not only are internal respect for rights and external legitimacy linked, but human rights law and practice have themselves also raised certain expectations on the part of victims and their advocates. The 1993 World Conference on Human Rights laid to rest, although not without debate, the argument that respect for human rights is purely a domestic matter. The simple and straightforward statement in Article I.4 of the programme of action was "the promotion and protection of human rights is a legitimate concern of the international community."

UN member states themselves started the erosion of the principle of noninterference soon after the Charter was adopted. The 1948 Genocide Convention suggested the possibility of intrusive enforcement by providing that any state party could call on the UN to "take such action under the Charter … as they consider appropriate for the prevention and suppression" of genocide.[59] It also provided that an international court could try perpetrators. The 1973 Apartheid Convention contained similar provisions and set up a new reporting procedure.[60]

At its first session in 1947, the UN Commission on Human Rights timidly admitted that "it had no power to take any action in regard to any complaints concerning human rights."[61] Yet, over the next half century it developed a range of techniques – including expert fact-finding, public exposure, and condemnation – to hold states accountable. They are often applied inconsistently and weakly, but states under scrutiny nonetheless work hard to avoid bad publicity and condemnation. Governments that keenly reject coercive and intrusive methods used against them often simultaneously support similar methods being turned on another state.

Gradually, methods of enforcement are being developed to catch up with the long disappointed expectations of victims around the world. For example, the creation of the ICC and the landmark United Kingdom court decision that General Augusto Pinochet was not immune from prosecution for human rights crimes have propelled the debate about limits to impunity into a realm that was inconceivable 20 years ago. This form of intervention may become more prominent and effective, in itself and as a deterrent.

Because of the controversial nature of military intervention, it is not surprising that no human rights document explicitly approves it as an enforcement method. Nevertheless, human rights are not a pacifist doctrine. The Universal Declaration warns that, if human rights are not protected by the rule of law, people will "be compelled to have recourse, as a last resort, to rebellion against tyranny and oppression." This recognizes a moral right of resistance; that violence in self-defence is a legitimate last resort to end massive human rights violations. Some commentators argue that applying deadly force to come to the rescue of others is a logical next step.

Existing treaties and conventions can be interpreted together as evidence that we are moving toward the notion that governments do not just have a negative duty to respect human rights by refraining from committing acts such as arbitrary killings. They also have a positive duty to fulfill the rights, such as taking steps to preserve life, as well as to protect people from having their rights violated by others. But what is the nature, character, and extent of these duties that transcend borders? If, as seems to be the case for an increasing number of state and nonstate observers, sovereignty has been infused with responsibility, what is the positive duty of the community of responsible states when one of its members acts so irresponsible as to inflict egregious suffering on its own population?

## FROM RIGHTS TO RESPONSIBILITIES

Most contemporary accounts of rights focus on the entitlements of individuals and consider obligations or duties secondary. An alternative approach is to complement the perspective of an individual's right to protection with the nature of the responsibilities that others may have to provide that protection. Attention to responsibilities is particularly important for those who conclude that the problem is less "unjustified interventions" than "unjustified refusals to intervene."[62] Although it may be clear that someone ought to provide protection, are specific states morally bound to do so?

A focus on rights tends to draw attention away from agency and from the duties of specific actors. But, as Vincent pointed out, rights presuppose "the bearer of the correlative duty"[63] against whom the right can be exercised. For rights to be realized, it is necessary to identify not only counterpart obligations but also specific obligation-bearers.

There is a fundamental difference between those rights that demand *noninterference* (negative rights) and those that demand specific *performance* (positive rights).[64] Obligations for negative rights are universal. The right not to be tortured, for example, is one that everyone has a duty not to violate. And the violation of that right is an act of commission. Obligations are much less clear for positive rights. For example, making good on the right to food for people starving half-way around the world requires taking positive steps to overcome food shortages there. But who is specifically obligated? A violation – that is, a failure to act – is only an act of omission.

Positive universal rights can only be met "distributively," where institutions are established that define the specific relationships between right-holder and obligation-bearer. These institutions commonly exist within particular states or communities. The right to protection within a state is ideally ensured by the police and judiciary. In some cases, as with the European Court on Human Rights, these institutions span state borders. At the global level, they are far less common; and where they exist, they are far less robust.

Consequently, genuine and specific counterpart duties do not really exist at the global level for most positive rights. And nothing better illustrates this institutional lacuna than the protection of the rights of individuals caught in the throes of deadly conflicts. For example, there is no international institution currently responsible for providing protection for IDPs. Furthermore, even where institutions exist for war victims, such as UNHCR or ICRC, their legal authority is often questioned or circumscribed. Moreover, they certainly lack the capacity to compel the implementation of international norms. "Naming and shaming" are not the same as enforcing protection. "Seeking consent" is, by definition, a recognition that there is no institutional mechanism to translate the positive duty to protect civilians into a meaningful reality.

The preceding discussion outlines the full range of measures that should be afforded to civilians at risk in deadly conflicts. These are clearly negative rights that all are obligated to respect. But there is as yet no accepted obligation to protect those at risk in other countries. It is, nevertheless, worth considering how such an obligation may emerge. For although the language of "duties," "obligations," and "responsibilities" may not have the same resonance as "rights," it may be a more effective basis to encourage state action. Individuals and states may well "have a duty to help those that have no right to expect it."[65] It would also clarify some of the tasks ahead. Those with responsibilities should set out in more specific terms the nature of their obligations: Which are the specific counterpart rights? To whom are they owed? And what institutional mechanisms could make good on them?

By beginning with responsibilities, attention turns to the practical measures that can be pursued by states and people who feel such an obligation. The questions are not just about protecting individuals against whom violence is committed; they also concern those even threatened by violence. This perspective focuses not on what to do with the violator, but on what to do for actual or threatened victims. The corresponding questions focus, not on retribution, but on practical steps to prevent or halt lethal conflicts and protect the basic rights of affected local populations. They raise questions about ethical rather than legal responsibility, both for interveners and for the targeted beneficiaries. They are about the types of actions that we are obligated to take and the ensuing moral responsibility.

With respect to exploring the responsibility to protect civilians, we should be in a position to answer two questions: Who has the responsibility to intervene? And for whom?

### Who Is Responsible?

Answers to the question of who holds ethnical responsibility are, paradoxically, both clear and obscure. As mentioned several times, in the first instance the responsibility to protect human rights resides in the state. A fundamental problem arises when the first line of defence breaks down. This occurs when a state is unwilling or unable to protect the lives of its citizens or, worse still, is the perpetrator of mass abuse. In such cases, the community of responsible states has the residual responsibility.

Do different states have different degrees of responsibility relative to their power, the authority that they wield, their proximity to an armed conflict, and their interests relative to the situation? Three positions are generally taken. The first is that states with the greatest wealth and military power, those with the greatest clout, have the greatest responsibility (for example, the five permanent members of the Security Council). A second position claims that states are equally responsible but that the execution of that responsibility should be proportionate to their means (for example, regional powers, such as Nigeria in West Africa or South Africa in southern Africa). In a third view, states have different responsibilities that are reinforced by moral decisions. Past actions that may have contributed, wittingly or unwittingly, to the emergence of a humanitarian crisis affect the weight of moral responsibility (for example, Australia on East Timor).

Responsibility lies not only with state institutions, but also with multilateral bodies. For a global approach, it would seem logical to make better use of the UN. Such a call would have to be tempered, however, by a realistic assessment of the capacities at the disposal of the world organization. At present, and many would say for the forseeable future, UN capacities are in no way equal to the magnitude of likely needs. In the realm of the protection of human rights by global actors or institutions, effectiveness and consistency seem to be distant prospects. The same applies for regional or subregional organizations, though it would appear that they are increasingly assuming primary responsibility for dealing with conflicts within their own geographic area.

Under a cosmopolitan view, it is not just state leaders who possess the responsibility to protect – the net of responsibility is cast much wider, although our capacities and the ways in which we fulfill these duties differ. Indeed, when the club of states has been reluctant to endorse the legitimacy of humanitarian claims, those motivated by a cosmopolitan ethical perspective have acted individually and collectively, either to help change state policies or to defy them. More often they have worked through NGOs, and in the face of considerable opposition, to combat cruelty, inhumanity, and injustice.

The answer to the question of who is responsible is ultimately "everyone." Vincent argued in his challenging defence of basic rights that "a duty to respect the right to life of others falls on us all as individuals."[66] Kofi Annan echoed this sentiment in issuing his own clarion call:

> So when we recall tragic evens such as those of Bosnia or Rwanda and ask: "why did no one intervene?," the question should not be addressed only to the United Nations, or even to its Member-States. Each of us as an individual has to take his or her share of responsibility. No one can claim ignorance of what happened. All of us should recall how we responded, and ask: What did I do? Could I have done more? Did I let my prejudice, my indifference, or my fear overwhelm my reasoning? Above all, how would I react next time?[67]

## Responsible for Whom?

The question of where responsibility is directed is challenging. Are states equally responsible for all others who are denied freedom and oppressed by the absence of the rule of law? Or do states have different responsibilities depending on their prior relations?

Ultimately, the responsibility to protect ought not to be driven by proximity, but rather by the severity of a crisis for victims. In some ways, since the founding of the ICRC in 1864, humanitarians have been steadily pushing out the geographical boundaries for concern from the state, to the region, to the globe.

One way to approach universal obligations is to conclude that they relate not to particular judgements of conscience but to conscientiousness. Ideally, the community of states would share responsibility to protect the rights of all civilians in the territory of all its members, but as a minimum at least its weakest members. One analyst, for example, summarizes that "the power of obligation varies directly with the powerlessness of the one who calls for help."[68] Which acts are correct may depend on circumstances, but there is an absolute obligation to decide and act. Remaining on the sidelines is not an option. As another observer explains, "Our obligation is relative to the situation, but obligation in the situation is absolute."[69] Personal and institutional resources are far from unlimited. At the same time, egregious suffering, wherever it is located, morally requires similar responses.

Commentators – both proponents and critics of intervention, alike – often criticize double standards. They argue that intervening states and international organizations should be consistent. At the same time, the Cold War's "single standard" – to do nothing everywhere – is hardly preferable to acting at least some of the time.

The universality of human rights certainly demands consistency in responding to massive violations. Yet, interventions in countries to stop massive human rights violations are rare and highly selective. Why act in Kosovo but not in Rwanda? Why protect the Kurds in northern Iraq but not in Turkey? Why emphasize a crisis in Somalia and not a three-decade-long emergency in neighbouring Sudan? Why intervene against smaller states but ignore Russian actions in Chechnya?

The human rights of some populations still seem to be worthier of defence than those of others. The foreign policy of states and their decisions about humanitarian intervention are dictated in most cases, not merely by humanitarian objectives, but also by economic, political, territorial, and military self-interests. In brief, humanitarian interventions may be only partially motivated by humanitarian intentions.

The legitimacy of a principle is certainly undermined by the erratic – or, worse, demonstrably selective – application of that principle. For it conveys the impression that "some are more worth protecting than others."[70] This is a huge problem internationally, but it exists within domestic jurisdictions as well. Strict consistency in law enforcement remains more or less elusive everywhere.

To expect states to intervene in every worthy case and have pure humanitarian motivations is undoubtedly to demand the impossible.[71] The world presents far too rich an array of human rights violations, as attested by voluminous annual reports from such groups as Amnesty International and Human Rights Watch. There is already difficulty enough in mobilizing against documented acts of genocide, and so it seems myopic to pretend that wholesale interventions in cases at lower levels of violation are even remotely plausible. Hard-headed judgements are required about the scale of evil and the scale of international capacities. However, it is feasible to aim to avoid such maximum evils as genocide and ethnic cleansing, except when a major power is responsible and intervention would undoubtedly result in more harm than good.

National and world politics will never be consistent or pure in heart. The ideal should not be the enemy of the good. Yet, what is the price of recognizing this standard reality? Should selective military interventions be condemned as immoral and in violation of the bedrock principle of the universality of human rights? The issues of consistency and capacity to act are important to any definition of interests and responsibilities. A settled principle of ethical reasoning is that "ought implies can." At the same time as ethical principles should ideally be applied uniformly, it would be foolish to ignore the reality that such an obligation ultimately depends on the operational ability to carry it out. Because of the difficulty in saving all victims all the time, should we not resort to trying to save some of the victims some of the time? In the context of a pragmatic affirmative response to this question, the issue of "hard choices," and even triage, cannot be avoided. Or, as the Secretary-General wrote in his report to the Millennium Assembly, "The fact that we cannot protect people everywhere is no reason for doing nothing when we can."[72]

While aspiring to the ideal of consistency as a long-term objective, most commentators would say that the inability to intervene everywhere is not an excuse not to intervene when necessary and possible and where it can make a difference. The inevitable double standards of state practice should not be an excuse for paralysis. We should not abandon the aspiration for coherent responses to international humanitarian crises, but even occasionally doing the right thing well is certainly preferable to doing nothing routinely.

## NOTES

1   Thomas Nagel, *Moral Questions* (New York: Cambridge University Press, 1979), pp. 4–5.

2   Isaiah Berlin, "My Intellectual Path," *New York Review of Books* XLV, no. 8 (1998), p. 60.

3   William K. Frankena, *Ethics: An Introduction*, 2nd ed. (Englewood Cliffs: Prentice-Hall, 1973), p. 109.

4   Bernard Arthur Owen Williams, *Morality: An Introduction to Ethics* (New York: Harper & Row, 1972), pp. 20–21.

5   See, for example, Shashi Tharoor, "The Future of Civil Conflict," *World Policy Journal* 16, no. 1 (Spring 1999), pp. 1–11.

6   Ramesh Thakur, "Global Norms and International Humanitarian Law," *International Review of the Red Cross* 83, no. 841 (March 2001), pp. 28–29.

7   Judith N. Shklar, *Political Thoughts and Political Thinkers* (Chicago: University of Chicago Press, 1986), p. 9, 11.

8   Hedley Bull, *The Anarchical Society: A Study of Order in World Politics* (London: Macmillan, 1977).

9   Hedley Bull, ed., *Intervention in World Politics* (Oxford: Oxford University Press, 1984), p. 193.

10  Hedley Bull, *Justice in International Relations, Hagey Lectures* (Waterloo: University of Waterloo, 1984), p. 13.

11  UN Document S/PV.3988, March 24, 1999, p. 3.

12  Quoted by Barbara Crosette, "General Assembly Opens Debate," *New York Times*, September 23, 1999, p. A5.

13  Robert Jackson, *The Global Covenant: Human Conduct in a World of States* (Oxford: Oxford University Press, 2000), p. 291.

14  See Richard Falk, *Human Rights and State Sovereignty* (New York: Holmes and Meier, 1981); Richard Falk, "The Challenge of Genocide and Genocidal Politics in an Era of Globalization," in Tim Dunne and Nicholas J. Wheeler, eds., *Human Rights in World Politics* (Cambridge: Cambridge University Press, 1999), pp. 177–194; and Ken Booth, "Human Wrongs in International Relations," *International Affairs* 71, no. 1 (1995), pp. 103–126.

15  Ken Booth, "Duty and Prudence," in Lawrence Freedman, ed., *Military Intervention in European Conflicts* (Oxford: Blackwell, 1994), p. 57.

16  Quoted in Dorothy V. Jones, *Code of Peace: Ethics and Security in the World of the Warlord States* (Chicago: University of Chicago Press, 1991), p. 154.

17  Mary Robinson, "Universality and Priorities," cited by Frankena, *Ethics*, pp. 109–110.

18  R.J. Vincent, *Human Rights in International Relations* (Cambridge: Cambridge University Press, 1986), p. 13.

19  See, for example, Henry Shue, *Basic Rights: Subsistence, Affluence and US Foreign Policy*, 2nd ed. (Princeton: Princeton University Press, 1996); Ronald Dworkin, *Taking Rights Seriously* (London: Duckworth, 1977); John Finnis, *Natural Law and Natural Rights* (Oxford: Oxford University Press, 1980); and Alan Donagan, *The Theory of Morality* (Chicago: University of Chicago Press, 1977).

20  Anthony Ellis, "Utilitarianism and International Ethics," in Terry Nardin and David Mapel, eds., *Traditions of International Ethics* (Cambridge: Cambridge University Press, 1992), pp. 158–170.

21  Richard Rorty, "Human Rights, Rationality, and Sentimentality," *Yale Review* 18, no. 4 (1993), pp. 1–20.

22  Quoted in William Korey, *NGOs and the Universal Declaration on Human Rights: "A Curious Grapevine"* (New York: St. Martin's Press, 1998), p. 9.

23  Shue, *Basic Rights*, p. 19.

24  United Nations Development Programme, *Human Development Report 2000* (New York: Oxford University Press, 2000), pp. 21, 30.

25  Richard Falk, "Hard Choices and Tragic Dilemmas," *The Nation*, December 20, 1993, p. 758.

26  Vincent, *Human Rights and International Relations*, p. 127.

27  Francis M. Deng, *Protecting the Dispossessed: A Challenge for the International Community* (Washington, DC: Brookings Institution, 1993); Francis M. Deng et al., *Sovereignty as Responsibility* (Washington, DC: Brookings Institution, 1995); Francis M. Deng, "Frontiers of Sovereignty," *Leiden Journal of International Law* 8, no. 2 (1995), pp. 249–286.

28  Kofi Annan, "Reflections on Intervention," 35th annual Ditchley Foundation Lecture, June 26, 1998, reprinted in *The Question of Intervention: Statements by the Secretary-General* (New York: United Nations, 1999), p. 6.

29  See Nicholas J. Wheeler and Tim Dunne, "Good International Citizenship: A Third Way for British Foreign Policy," *International Affairs* 74, no. 4 (1998), pp. 847–870.

30  Lloyd Axworthy, "Human Security and Global Governance: Putting People First," *Global Governance* 7, no. 1 (2001), pp. 19–23.

31  See Andrew Linklater, "The Good International Citizen and the Crisis in Kosovo," in Ramesh Thakur and Albrecht Schnabel, eds., *Kosovo and the Challenge of Humanitarian Intervention: Selective Imagination, Collective Action, and International Citizenship* (Tokyo: UN University Press, 2000), p. 493.

32  Michael Ignatieff, "Human Rights, Sovereignty and Intervention," lecture delivered to Amnesty International, Oxford University, February 2, 2001.

33  Kofi Annan, "Two Concepts of Sovereignty," September 20, 1999, reprinted in *The Question of Intervention*, p. 39.

34  See, for example, Mario Bettati and Bernard Kouchner, *Le devoir d'ingérence* (Paris: Denoël, 1987); and Mario Bettati, *Le droit d'ingérence: Mutation de l'ordre international* (Paris: Odile Jacob, 1996).

35  See, for example, Gustavo Gutierrez, *A Theology of Liberation: History, Politics, and Salvation* (Maryknoll, NY: Orbis Books, 1973); and Paulo Freire, *Pedagogy of the Oppressed* (New York: Continuum, 1970).

36  Ephraim Isaac, "Humanitarianism across Religions and Cultures," in Thomas G. Weiss and Larry Minear, eds., *Humanitarianism across Borders: Sustaining Civilians in Times of War* (Boulder: Lynne Rienner, 1993), p. 13.

37  Oliver Ramsbotham, "Islam, Christianity, and Forcible Humanitarian Intervention," *Ethics and International Affairs* 12 (1998), pp. 81–102; and Richard C. Martin, "The Religious Foundations of War, Peace and Statecraft in Islam," in John Kelsey and James Turner, eds., *Just War and Jihad: Historical and Theoretical Approaches on War and Peace in Western and Islamic Traditions* (New York: Greenwood Press, 1991), pp. 91–117.

38  Marcel A. Boisard, *L'Humanisme de l'Islam* (Paris: Albin Michel, 1979).

39  For a thorough review of the applicability of just-war doctrine to humanitarian intervention, see Moa Fixdal and Dan Smith, "Humanitarian Intervention and Just War," *Mershon International Studies Review* 42 (1998), pp. 283–321.

40  James Turner Johnson, *Just War Tradition and the Restraint of War* (Princeton: Princeton University Press, 1981); James Turner Johnson, *Can Modern War Be Just?* (New Haven: Yale University Press, 1984); William V. O'Brien, *The Conduct of Just and Limited War* (New York: Praeger, 1981).

41  International Peace Academy, *Humanitarian Action: A Symposium Summary*, IPA Conference Report (New York: International Peace Academy, 2000).

42  *Report of the Secretary-General to the Security Council on the Protection of Civilians in Armed Conflict*, UN Document S/1999/957, September 8, 1999.

43  Fernando Tesón, *Humanitarian Intervention: An Inquiry into Law and Morality* (Dobbs Ferry: Transnational Publishers, 1988), pp. 106–107.

44  Nicholas J. Wheeler, *Saving Strangers: Humanitarian Intervention in International Society* (Oxford: Oxford University Press, 2000).

45  Some commentators even argue that military intervention should not be undertaken *unless* states are motivated by self-interest, because otherwise they would not stay the course. See Richard Falk, *American Society of International Law* 93, no. 4 (October 1999), http://www.asil.org/kosovo.htm

46  Nigel Rodley, "Collective Intervention to Protect Human Rights and Civilian Populations: The Legal Framework," in Nigel Rodley, ed., *To Loose the Bands of Wickedness* (London: Brassey's, 1992), p. 37.

47  International Committee of the Red Cross (and Greenberg Research Inc.), *The People on War*. Report, accessed by Internet, http://nt.oneworld.org/cfdocs/icrc/pages/reports/globalreport.html

48    International Committee of the Red Cross, *The Geneva Conventions of August 12, 1949* and *Protocols Additional to the Geneva Conventions of 12 August 1949* (Geneva: International Committee of the Red Cross, 1977).

49    The Statute of the International Criminal Court has softened the distinction by outlawing in civil wars many (but not all) of the acts which the Geneva Conventions of 1949 and the two Additional Protocols of 1977 only prohibit in international conflicts.

50    United Nations, *Convention on the Prevention and Punishment of the Crime of Genocide*, adopted by Resolution 260 (III) A, UN General Assembly, December 9, 1948.

51    A recent Protocol to the Convention on the Rights of the Child deals with child soldiers. It raises from 15 to 18 the minimum age for conscription into armed forces, sets at 15 the minimum age for voluntary recruitment into the armed forces of a state (provided 15–18 year olds do not directly fight) and prohibits armed groups from recruiting or using people under the age of 18 in hostilities in any way. The Optional Protocol to the Convention on the Rights of the Child on the involvement of children in armed conflict was adopted by the UN General Assembly, Resolution 54/263, May 16, 2000.

52    UN High Commissioner for Refugees, *Convention and Protocol Relating to the Status of Refugees* (Geneva: UN High Commissioner for Refugees, 1996). For texts of treaties and other documents on refugees, see Guy S. Goodwin-Gill, *The Refugee in International Law*, 2nd ed. (Oxford: Oxford University Press, 1996). See also Gil Loescher, *Beyond Charity: International Cooperation and the Global Refugee Crisis* (New York: Oxford University Press, 1993); and UN High Commissioner for Refugees, *The State of the World's Refugees 2000: Fifty Years of Humanitarian Action* (New York: Oxford University Press, 2000).

53    The *Guiding Principles on Internal Displacement* (New York: Office for the Coordination of Humanitarian Affairs, no date) does not have the same status as other human rights or humanitarian-law norms. Francis M. Deng, the Representative of the Secretary-General on IDPs, put them together. The UN Commission on Human Rights only took note of the document, but did not object to his stated intention to use them in his dealings with governments. Since then they have been widely distributed and used by UN agencies, governments, and NGOs.

54    The controversy in the early 1990s about the universality of human rights has been muted, if not ended, by the agreement at the Vienna World Conference on Human Rights that "[a]ll human rights are universal … . While the significance of national and regional particularities and various historical, cultural and religious backgrounds must be borne in mind, it is the duty of States, regardless of their political, economic and cultural systems, to promote and protect all human rights and fundamental freedoms." The Vienna Declaration and Programme of Action was adopted by the World Conference on Human Rights, Vienna, June 23, 1993, para. I.5.

55    Also called *jus cogens* norms. See Article 53, Vienna Convention on the Law of Treaties. The International Court of Justice has referred to them as "elementary considerations of humanity." See *Barcelona Traction* case (Second Phase), *ICJ Reports* 3 (1970), p. 32.

56    Restatement (Third) of the Foreign Relations Law of the US, 1987, Section 702, contains several of the rights in this list, but not war crimes, religious and gender discrimination, denial of self-determination, and crimes against humanity.

57    For international armed conflicts, see Article 70, Additional Protocol I to the Geneva Conventions; for non-international armed conflicts, see Article 18 (2) of Additional Protocol II; for the internally displaced, see Principle 25 of the Guiding Principles on Internal Displacement; for the UN's humanitarian coordination role, see the General Assembly resolution that authorized the setting up of the Department of Humanitarian Affairs – General Assembly Resolution 46/182, December 19, 1991, Clauses 3 and 6.

58    See the UN Convention on the Safety of United Nations and Associated Personnel, adopted by UN Resolution 49/59, December 9, 1994.

59    Article VIII, Convention on the Prevention and Punishment of the Crime of Genocide, adopted by the UN General Assembly, Resolution 260 A (III), December 9, 1948.

60    International Convention on the Suppression and Punishment of the Crime of Apartheid, adopted by the UN General Assembly, Resolution 3068 (XXVIII), November 30, 1973.

61    Report of the first session, E/259 (1947), paras. 21 and 22, quoted by Tom J. Farer and Felice Gaer, "The UN and Human Rights: At the End of the Beginning," in Adam Roberts and Benedict Kingsbury, eds., *United Nations, Divided World*, 2nd ed. (Oxford, Clarendon Press, 1993), p. 247.

62    Michael Walzer, *Just and Unjust Wars: A Moral Argument with Historical Illustrations*, 3rd ed. (New York: Basic Books, 2000), p. xiii.

63   Vincent, *Human Rights and International Relations*, p. 8.

64   Onora O'Neill, *Towards Justice and Virtue: A Constructive Account of Practical Reasoning* (Cambridge: Cambridge University Press, 1996), pp. 136–141.

65   Fixdal and Smith, "Humanitarian Intervention and Just War," p. 300.

66   Vincent, *Human Rights and International Relations*, p. 127.

67   Annan, "Reflections on Intervention," reprinted in *The Question of Intervention*, p. 14.

68   Catherine Lu, "Cosmopolitanism and Humanitarian Intervention," unpublished, Washington, DC, International Studies Association, February 16–20, 2000, p. 5.

69   Joseph Fletcher, *Situation Ethics: The New Morality* (Philadelphia: Westminster Press, 1966), p. 2.

70   Christine M. Chinkin, "Kosovo: A 'Good' or 'Bad' War?" *American Journal of International Law* 93 (1999), p. 846.

71   For a discussion, see Lori Fisler Damrosch, "The Inevitability of Selective Response? Principles to Guide Urgent International Action," in Thakur and Schnabel, eds., *Kosovo*, pp. 405–419.

72   Kofi A. Annan, *"We the Peoples": The Role of the United Nations in the 21st Century* (New York: United Nations, 2000), p. 48.

# 7. LEGITIMACY AND AUTHORITY

In exploring the nexus between humanitarian intervention and state sovereignty, one of the crucial dimensions – indeed, for some commentators the only valid starting point – is public international law. The key question revolves around authority: Who has the right – and under what circumstances – to authorize the use of deadly force in the pursuit of humanitarian objectives?

This question has been controversial for decades, and the principal positions in the debate are clear. One side argues that there is no exception to the requirement of a Security Council mandate. If approval is not forthcoming for whatever reason, then the intervention should not proceed. Should an intervention occur without such approval, it is illegal. Even the strongest proponents of relatively unfettered humanitarian intervention accept that states planning to intervene should systematically seek Security Council authorization prior to the intervention. However, some then argue that this requirement can be superseded in cases of supreme humanitarian emergency, an exceptional necessity when legal norms clash.

These alternative perspectives, articulated in bold relief around Kosovo within the United Nations (UN) Secretary-General Kofi Annan's statements before, during, and after the Kosovo War, capture the tensions between responding to an unfolding catastrophe and the importance of not bypassing the Security Council. On March 24, 1999, as cruise missiles and high-altitude bombing began, he stated,

> I deeply regret that, in spite of all of the efforts made by the international community, the Yugoslav authorities have persisted in their rejection of a political settlement, which would have halted the bloodshed in Kosovo and secured an equitable peace for the population there … . It is indeed tragic that diplomacy has failed, but there are times when the use of force may be legitimate in the pursuit of peace.

However, the Secretary-General also explicitly regretted the Security Council's inability to act. Russia and China, meanwhile, unconditionally condemned the campaign by the North Atlantic Treaty Organization (NATO) as illegal and contrary to the UN Charter.

It might be expected that a detailed review of the main international legal instruments, particularly the UN Charter,[1] would provide clear guidance about the conditions under which humanitarian intervention is legal and illegal.[2] While this supposition is accurate on some points, in many other respects the range of legal interpretations and opinions is very broad.[3]

In the first instance, inconsistencies apparent in the Charter and other key legal instruments prohibit drawing simple conclusions. Perhaps more importantly, law is not static; it evolves on the basis of changing state practice. Changing experiences shape principles and norms, just as principles and norms influence policies, decisions, and operations. As a result, and in addition to codified international law, custom also determines what is legal and illegal. To complicate matters, some observers argue that the intensity and quantity of rapid international interactions combine with activities by intergovernmental bodies to increase dramatically the rate at which customary law is being created.[4]

The term "unilateral" is avoided for the most part in this volume because of the differences between its use by international lawyers and by most social scientists. Whereas the latter often use the term to signify a decision or action by a single state (in juxtaposition to "bilateral," by two states, and to "multilateral," by more than two states), the former employ the term as a synonym for "nonauthorized" and hence of dubious legality no matter how many states have approved.

The analysis that follows does not stop with the current status of public international law. If there are significant gray areas relating to the authorization of humaitarian intervention, then questions of legitimacy become as important as questions of law. Legitimacy is an important dimension even when legality is clear. The Independent International Commission on Kosovo, for example, concluded that "the NATO military intervention was illegal but legitimate."[5] And certain factors – credible evidence of the scale of the human crisis, a genuine internal call for assistance, the conduct of the intervening states and agencies, and longer term outcomes – enhance the broader sense of legitimacy. In extreme cases, outcomes that undermine the legality of an intervention – an isolated veto in the Security Council or a supporting vote in the General Assembly that secures a majority but not two-thirds – may, in fact, strengthen its legitimacy.

This discussion begins with an examination of the legal bases for intervention. It first focuses on the UN Charter legal regime governing coercive intervention, and whether there are any other existing legal grounds for humanitarian intervention. The essay then turns to the question of customary international law and examines the impact of changing state practice, particularly in the 1990s, on Charter prohibitions. Given the degree of legal controversy, it concludes with an exploration of the growing importance of the legitimacy of the institutions that authorize interventions and of the interventions themselves.

## INTERVENTION AND THE UN CHARTER

The prohibition on the use of force by states is widely regarded as one of the central building blocks in the foundation of the UN Charter. Scholars classify this norm as *jus cogens*, or a peremptory norm, that cannot be modified by subsequent or inconsistent norms, treaties, or actions. Nevertheless, controversy persists about the intended breadth of this prohibition and whether it has been undermined by UN failures to uphold global security and by the rise of support for human rights and antigenocide initiatives.

States are assured by the domestic jurisdiction limitation of Article 2 (7) that "[n]othing contained in the present Charter shall authorize the UN to intervene in matters which are essentially within the domestic jurisdiction of any state." On the face of it, this provision accepts a sharp separation of internal and international conflict, restricting UN action to the latter. Reality is quite different, as the earlier discussion of the expanding definition of threats to international peace and security has made clear. Moreover, even within this article itself, there is an exception through the commitment that "this principle shall not prejudice the application of enforcement measures under Chapter VII." There is also a provision that exempts individual or collective self-defence (Article 51). Hence, both Security Council authorizations for coercion and legitimate self-defence trump the domestic jurisdiction restriction.

The whole tenor and context of the Charter is an effort, as stated at the outset of the Preamble, to "save succeeding generations from the scourge of war." As such, the UN itself is subject to this regime and is entrusted with the mission of minimizing the role of force in international affairs. This directive is articulated in Articles 2 (3) and 33, instructing states to settle their disputes by peaceful means. It is also implicit in the relation between Articles 41 and 42, mandating the Security Council to rely, to the extent possible, on non-military measures in carrying out its responsibilities.

Thus, the limits on UN authority with respect to responding to human catastrophes are essential to understanding contemporary humanitarian action. But so, too, are the concrete provisions that facilitate justified responses. The UN Charter provides the highest source of legal and constitutional authority in relation to claims relating to the use of force.

Yet, the authority of the Charter remains obscure in specific instances. It contains inconsistent norms and principles (for example, to promote human rights and respect domestic jurisdiction). It also has dormant provisions, especially in Chapter VII, that give a differing impression if the Charter is read literally or interpreted in light of subsequent events. The nonfunctioning Military Staff Committee is one clear-cut illustration. There is continual evolution and innovation in norms and principles through interpretation and practice. A dramatic example is the evolution of international human rights standards from a vague aspiration to a basis for judging conduct and seeking implementation and protection. As such, the Charter regime blurs the distinction between what is subject to international authority and what falls within domestic jurisdiction.

Finally, the Security Council appears to be at liberty to determine its modes of operation and perhaps even its mandate, irrespective of what the Charter says. For instance, the absence or abstention by permanent members is not treated as preventing a Security Council decision, despite the language of Article 27 (3), which requires the "affirmative vote of nine members including the concurring votes of the permanent members." Actions taken by the Security Council regarding the use of force may therefore become precedents, even if they seem inconsistent with the Charter.

In detailing the Charter's approach to the use of force in response to deadly conflicts with catastrophic human consequences, the discussion here begins with the Charter provisions dealing with armed conflict and Security Council responsibilities (Chapters VI, VII, and V). It continues with the relevant role of the General Assembly (Chapter IV) and "other" bases in the Charter, including Chapter VIII.

## Security Council

The Security Council's legal capacity to respond to crises that give rise to human catastrophes are set out in Chapters VI and VII of the UN Charter. Although entitled "Pacific Settlement of Disputes," Chapter VI sets out the decision making framework for UN responses to human catastrophes. There need not be a "dispute" to generate UN competence to respond. Article 34 states that the Security Council may investigate "any dispute, or any situation" that may cause "international friction." There is no doubt that these provisions were designed for international rather than intranational disputes. Nevertheless, the evolutionary practice of the UN has eroded this distinction, empowering the Security Council to regard internal situations that give rise to broader security concerns as legitimate subjects for consideration and response.

During the Dag Hammarskjöld era, an "innovation" in the interpretation of Chapter VI led to the development of UN peacekeeping that presupposed consent by the relevant state and a very limited role for UN personnel. At the outset, they were confined to the use of force only in self-defence, while this was later extended to protection of an operational mission's mandate. This expansion beyond dispute settlement had the significant incidental effect of bringing UN authority to bear on essentially internal situations. Thus, if a particular territorial government gives its consent, the Security Council can authorize a military presence that is designed to avert, mitigate, or overcome an incipient or ongoing human disaster. Traditional UN peacekeeping activities are an original and important contribution to international peace and security, and they have grown substantially in the post-Cold War era.[6]

Under the terms of Chapter V, the Security Council has primary jurisdiction over international peace and security and is empowered to make decisions binding on UN member states. Article 24 was formulated "to ensure prompt and effective action." The article obliges members of the Council to execute their mandate consistent with the principles and objectives of the UN. Some commentators have argued that Council therefore has not only the right, but also the responsibility, to act in the face of extraordinary humanitarian crises. Although the Charter may be read as *allowing* the Council to take such action, for most analysts no such obligation exists in Article 24 or elsewhere.

According to Article 27, Security Council decisions about nonprocedural matters, including the use of force, require support from 9 of its 15 members without a veto being cast by any of the five permanent members of the Security Council: China, France, Russia, the United Kingdom (UK), and the United States (US).

The sharp edge of the Council's powers are spelled out in Chapter VII, which provides the contours of the Charter approach to collective security, again designed for international armed conflict. The primary concern in 1945 was to provide member states with an assurance that their territorial integrity and political independence would be protected in the event of "threats to the peace, breaches of the peace or acts of aggression."

The Security Council was therefore empowered in Article 39 to "decide what measures shall be taken ... to maintain or restore international peace and security." Article 41 indicates that nonmilitary measures should be used to the extent possible to address such threats or breaches, as well as acts of aggression. In the event that nonmilitary measures prove largely unresponsive to humanitarian concerns, Article 42 authorizes the Security Council to decide on military measures "as may be necessary ... to maintain or restore international peace and security."

As a result of the Cold War, the Security Council was largely inactive as far as humanitarian aspects were concerned. There was a humanitarian *tabula rasa* – no resolution mentioned the humanitarian aspects of any conflict from 1945 until the Six Day War of 1967.[7] The first mention of the International Committee of the Red Cross[8] was not until 1978, and in the 1970s and 1980s, "[t]he Security Council gave humanitarian aspects of armed conflict limited priority ... but the early nineteen-nineties can be seen as a watershed."[9] During the first half of the decade, twice as many resolutions were passed as during the first 45 years of UN history. They contained repeated references, in the context of Chapter VII, to humanitarian crises amounting to threats to international peace and security, as well as repeated demands for parties to respect the principles of international humanitarian law (IHL).

Over the past decade, the Security Council has broadened its mandate considerably. In the aftermath of the Gulf War, it authorized protective action for the Kurdish minority in Iraq, and this authority has been interpreted by the US, the UK, and France as justifying the establishment and maintenance of no-fly zones, as well as attacks on Iraqi radar and antiaircraft sites. During the wars in Bosnia and Herzegovina, the Security Council authorized a robust form of peacekeeping, including safe havens to protect the Muslim civilian population of Bosnia from Serbian ethnic cleansing.

Together with the failure of the UN peacekeeping force in Rwanda to prevent genocide in 1994 and the world organization's abandonment of a nation-building role in Somalia, the Bosnian experience cast a dark shadow over the effectiveness of the Security Council to respond to the most calamitous human tragedies. In these cases, however, the limitations were less about legal competencies and more about political and operational weaknesses. Some commentators have concluded that a narrower view of the Security Council's legal authority would help the UN avoid the embarrassments associated with political and operational overextension.

An important and unresolved question is whether the Security Council can exceed its own authority by violating the constitutional restraints embedded in the Charter, particularly the inhibition on UN intervention contained in Article 2 (7). This issue has only been tangentially considered by the International Court of Justice (ICJ) in the *Lockerbie* case. The 1998 decision on preliminary objections affirmed that the Security Council is bound by the Charter. At the same time, there is no provision for judicial review of the Council's decisions, and therefore no way that a dispute over Charter interpretation can be resolved. With specific reference to Council-authorized intervention, there appear to be no theoretical limits to the ever-widening interpretation of international peace and security.

### General Assembly

The General Assembly's role in matters of peace and security is subordinate to the Security Council's.[10] Should the Council be unable or unwilling to authorize action, the matter can be considered by the Assembly. Article 11 provides that the General Assembly may consider and make recommendations (though not decisions) about matters relating to the maintenance of international peace and security. However, under Article 12, it is constrained from making such recommendations (though not specifically from considering the matter) "while the Security Council is exercising in respect of any dispute or situation the functions assigned to it in the present Charter ... unless the Security Council so requests."

Furthermore, the "Uniting for Peace" Resolution of 1950 specifically authorizes the Assembly to make recommendations on enforcement action when the Security Council is unable to take a decision. As a result, the General Assembly is a potential source of authorization when the Security Council is incapable of acting.

Moreover, widespread concerns about the slowness of General Assembly decision making seem unwarranted. Although it is not perpetually "on call," like the Security Council, the "Uniting for Peace" Resolution provided for holding an Emergency Special Session. Convened within 24 hours of a request being made, an Emergency Special Session must also "convene in plenary session only and proceed directly to consider the item proposed for consideration in the request for the holding of the session, without previous reference to the General Committee or to any other Committee."[11] Such sessions, however, are comparatively rare, having been convened only 10 times in the UN's history. The fact that this procedure has been used only three times to authorize a military operation – the last in the early 1960s, over the crisis in the Congo – reduces its relevance in the eyes of many commentators.

The main hurdle, once the matter has been brought before the Assembly, is the requirement in Article 18 (2) that any resolution relating to the maintenance of international peace and security have a two-thirds majority of UN members present and voting (that is, not abstaining). If all 189 are present and none abstains, then 126 affirmative votes are required. Given the significant opposition to a variety of past military interventions, the politics that produce deadlock among the Security Council would tend to produce similar vexing results in the General Assembly.

An intervention that took place with the necessary two-thirds backing or more in the General Assembly would almost certainly have a moral and political force sufficient to categorize it as "legal," even without Security Council endorsement. It would certainly be regarded as legitimate. Indeed, a vote in the Assembly that came close to the required majority would probably be sufficient to confer additional legitimacy on an ensuing humanitarian intervention.

## Regional Organizations

Another potential source of authorization for interventions is regional organizations. Chapter VIII of the Charter assigns a possible role in the maintenance of international peace and security to "regional arrangements or agencies," though with the caveat that the actions are consistent with the UN's purposes and principles. Article 52 (1) makes regional arrangements or agencies the first place where efforts should be made to "achieve pacific settlement of local disputes ... before referring them to the Security Council."

In terms of enforcement action, the relationship is set forth in clear language in Article 53 (1), which empowers the Security Council to "utilize such regional arrangements or agencies for enforcement action under its authority." The next sentence makes clear that regional organizations lack an independent authority with respect to enforcement undertakings because "no enforcement action shall be taken under regional arrangements or by regional agencies without the authorization of the Security Council." Article 54 imposes an obligation that the "Security Council shall at all times be kept fully informed of activities undertaken or in contemplation under regional arrangements" with respect to "the maintenance of peace and security."

Many international human catastrophes have direct effects on neighbouring countries, including massive refugee flows and use of territory as a base by rebel groups. Thus, states bordering on a war zone usually have strong interests, only partly humanitarian, for dealing swiftly and effectively with a large scale human catastrophe. Moreover, they may be better placed to act than the UN because of their familiarity with the intricacies of the local situation and actors. But regional organizations are only allowed to take action up to and including peacekeeping and are precluded from exercising Chapter VII powers, unless the Security Council has authorized them to do so.

## Other Grounds for Intervention

In addition to the powers granted to the Security Council, the General Assembly, and regional organizations, there are other potential legal grounds on which intervention for broadly humanitarian purposes might be based within the overall parameters of the Charter regime. Among the most important is the right of self-defence, the Genocide Convention, IHL, human rights law, and restoring democracies.

The "inherent right of individual or collective self-defence," provided for under Article 51, is one possible justification for the legal use of force with substantial humanitarian implications.[12] This right, however, has been restrictively interpreted by the ICJ as being available only in response to "an armed attack."[13] Nevertheless, some legal scholars, especially in North America and Europe, have for several reasons viewed it in more expansive terms. First, the narrowing of the inherent right was based on the expectation that the UN would establish an effective mechanism for collective security. The obvious failure to realize this goal, they argue, may effectively place the community of states in a pre-Charter legal setting. Second, in a number of instances, states using force beyond the bounds of Article 51 have not been censured by the Security Council if their acts have been viewed as reasonable exceptions. This has been particularly true of unilateral responses to international terrorism. A number of past interventions undertaken at least in part for humanitarian reasons or with significant humanitarian benefits – East Pakistan, Uganda, and Cambodia – were justified on the grounds of self-defence.

The 1948 Genocide Convention and the four Geneva Conventions of 1949 and their two Additional Protocols of 1977 impose obligations on warring parties.[14] Yet, both are explicit that they do not provide an independent foundation for intervention – responses must be undertaken within the context of the UN Charter. Article 1 of the Genocide Convention contains specific obligations both to prevent and to punish perpetrators of that crime, but Article 8 refers to calling on the competent organs of the UN to take such action under the Charter as they consider appropriate.

Similarly, IHL provides for measures that may be taken in the event of "grave breaches." Article 89 of Additional Protocol I is clear: "In situations of serious violations of the Conventions or of this Protocol, the High Contacting Parties undertake to act, jointly or individually, in cooperation with the UN and in conformity with the UN Charter." The conclusion that these instruments cannot provide independent justification for intervention is further strengthened in light of UN Charter Article 103, which gives primacy to Charter obligations in the event of a conflict with other legal ones.

The Charter clearly advocates respect for, and the advancement of, human rights.[15] But this is done in a language and manner that defers both to the primacy of sovereignty and the prohibition on the use of force. Article 1 (3) indicates that a purpose of the UN is "promoting and encouraging respect for human rights." Article 55 (c) sets forth the conviction that "universal respect for, and observance of, human rights and fundamental freedoms" are essential for the establishment of the sort of stability that could underpin a peaceful world. Perhaps more relevantly, Article 56 asserts that "[a]ll Members pledge themselves to take joint and separate action in co-operation with the Organization." Generally, these provisions have been read as aspirations and not as giving rise to any legal foundation for enforcement action.

Since 1945 the development of human rights law and institutions has made impressive strides, especially since the 1993 Vienna Conference on Human Rights and Development. The Office of UN High Commissioner for Human Rights was established, thereby becoming a focal point within the UN system that has increased both the visibility and the international salience of official (that is, UN), rather than private (that is, led by non-governmental organizations), human rights advocacy. Some scholars have argued that human rights should now be viewed on an equivalent basis of authority when considering the use of force.[16] With such an outlook, the use of force to address severe deprivations of human rights would be legally permissible. Recent UN Secretaries-General have hinted at such sentiments, though this perspective remains controversial.

A further potential rationale for military intervention that could be grouped under the label of "humanitarian" is the restoration of a democratic regime,[17] following its illegitimate removal. The authorization of the use of force in Haiti, at the request of the elected government then in exile, has been cited as evidence of an emerging right of intervention in support of democracy. An overthrow of a democratically elected government could plausibly threaten international peace and security only indirectly, but nonetheless it has resulted in Security Council action. This logic builds on earlier precedents of enforcement against the white-majority regimes of Southern Rhodesia and the Republic of South Africa.

Actions in Sierra Leone – and perhaps in Guinea-Bissau, the Central African Republic, and Lesotho – may provide further evidence of a change in international legal norms pertaining to "prodemocratic" intervention. The Council's post hoc endorsement of the Economic Community of West African States's (ECOWAS's) intervention in Sierra Leone seems to add further weight to the relevance of restoring democratic governments as a new rationale for intervention. The Security Council in this case authorized action under Chapter VII against an "illegitimate" regime, without even taking refuge in assertions of "extraordinary," "exceptional," or "unique" circumstances. Indeed, some commentators have gone so far as to argue that coups against elected governments are now, per se, violations of international law and that regional organizations may be licensed to use force to reverse such coups in member states.[18]

## INTERVENTION OUTSIDE THE UN CHARTER

Some commentators and governments argue that a ground invasion or bombing of a target state necessarily violates its territorial rights and political independence, no matter what the provocation. And they reject out of hand the idea that an invader would act in the true interests of local populations.

These arguments are countered by those who take the view that there often is no alternative to intervention – military and nonmilitary – as a means of saving lives when human catastrophe arises. Truly repressive governments represent only the interests of corrupt elites and not of the vast majority of people. The question of state sovereignty is beside the point, because popular sovereignty is so clearly violated by such regimes.

In considering the potential legality of interventions undertaken outside the framework of the UN Charter, there is inevitably some repetition of the preceding analysis. If intervention for humanitarian purposes approved by the Security Council is a *sine qua non*, many argue that intervention without a mandate from the Security Council is simply illegal. In addition, many of the cases in which states have claimed to exercise a right of humanitarian intervention have involved some form of action by the Council, albeit decisions that fall short of the authorization of force or that occur after an actual military intervention.

The dispute over claims about the changing nature of state practice, including its impact on the current status of the law regarding the use of force, are at the heart of the debate on whether humanitarian intervention may proceed in the absence of explicit Security Council authorization. The interventions of the 1990s have led a number of states and commentators to argue that a basis already exists in customary international law to support such interventions, albeit seriously circumscribed – that is, only where there is a large scale threat to life, and even then only as a last resort. If an obligation to respond to human tragedy exists with the Council's blessing, it also does without one. Others have suggested that such a right is emerging as a rule of customary law, but it has not yet achieved that status.

As a group, developing countries have explicitly rejected the idea that any broader precedent was being set. By consensus, the final communiqué of the Meeting of Ministers for Foreign Affairs and Heads of Delegation of the 113-member Non-Aligned Movement, held in New York, on September 23, 1999, stated, "We reject the so-called 'right of humanitarian intervention' which has no legal basis in the UN Charter or in the general principles of international law."[19] The Group of 77 Summit in Havana, in April 2000, adopted by consensus the Declaration of the South Summit; this time, 133 countries agreed to include the same exact sentence.[20]

At the same time, the opposition among developing countries is not as solid as these statements might indicate. When the votes were cast on General Assembly Resolution 55/101 (debated during the bombing of Kosovo and calling for respect for the principles of non-intervention), there were 52 opposed. In addition, 33 developing countries either abstained or did not vote at all. There has been considerable support from individual developing countries and their regional associations for specific humanitarian interventions. These countries include not only the 16 African member states of ECOWAS, but also a majority of members of the Organization of African Unity (OAU) who called for intervention in Rwanda.

Thus, there are compelling policy considerations on both sides of the debate. On the one hand, those who argue against the existence of any right of humanitarian intervention without the authorization of the Security Council point to the priority the UN Charter gives to the maintenance of international peace. On the other hand, the Charter and modern human rights law place a high priority on the protection of the individual from widespread killing and the horrors of ethnic cleansing. Inaction by the Security Council, as in Rwanda in 1994, can lead to abuses of an even greater kind and make the Council liable to the charge of tragic ineffectiveness.

## Legal Framework

The principal argument against the legality of intervention without a Security Council mandate is that it is said to violate the prohibition on the use of force enshrined in Article 2 (4).[21] Since such a humanitarian intervention falls within neither of the exceptions specified in the Charter, the use or threat of force to pursue humanitarian objectives is said to be contrary to international law.

A second argument follows from the bedrock principle of international order. Since each state is sovereign within its own territory, what it does within that territory, even if it involves a violation of international law, cannot give rise to a right of intervention by other states. At one time, this argument was advanced to oppose any form of interference, even diplomatic representations regarding a state's human rights record. It is seldom heard today in that extreme form. However, it continues to enjoy considerable support as an argument against humanitarian intervention without the express authorization of the Security Council.

In support of these arguments, commentators also point to the fact that neither the Declaration on the Principles of Friendly Relations in General Assembly Resolution 2625 (1970) nor the Definition of Aggression in General Assembly Resolution 3314 (1974) contains any hint of the existence of such a right. On the contrary, the definition condemns all forms of military intervention and thereby appears to preclude the emergence of a concept of humanitarian intervention.[22]

Supporters of an emerging custom have a different interpretation. They argue that Article 2 (4) states only one of the principles on which the UN operates, and it must be contextualized. The Charter is a living instrument that has evolved over the years and will continue to do so. Moreover, the Charter declares, beginning with the Preamble and Article 1, that the world organization's purposes include the promotion of human rights. The development of international human rights law since 1945 – through global agreements such as the Genocide Convention, the 1966 covenants on civil-political and economic-social-cultural rights, and regional instruments in Africa, the Americas, and Europe – has reached the point at which important aspects of the treatment by a state of its own population can no longer be regarded as domestic affairs. In particular, widespread and systematic violations of human rights involving the loss of life (or threatened loss of life) on a large scale are now well established as a matter of international concern.

Proponents of intervention argue that neither the concept of state sovereignty nor the general duty of nonintervention can preclude military intervention in extreme cases. International law in general, and the UN Charter in particular, do not rest exclusively on the principles of nonintervention and respect for sovereignty. The values on which the international legal system rests also include the Preamble's call to respect "the dignity and worth of the human person." While virtually no one suggests that intervention is justified whenever a state violates human rights, it does not follow that international law invariably requires that respect for the sovereignty and integrity of a state should in all cases be given priority over the protection of human rights – especially the most basic, the right to life.

Faced with human rights violations that may entail large scale loss of life, international law cannot – despite concerns that this would result in the violation of the sovereignty of the targeted state – require that all states stand back and allow massacres and massive forced migrations to take place. Supporters of humanitarian intervention argue that the prohibition on the use of force in Article 2 (4) is not an absolute prohibition but one whose limits have to be determined by reference to the actual practice of states and UN organs. For example, self-determination as a concept has evolved over time, particularly in the context of decolonization, legitimizing armed struggle. Similarly, the prohibition on the use of force and the equilibrium between that principle and other fundamental Charter principles is not static and develops with state practice and actions by the UN system.

Nor, some argue, does the status of the prohibition on the use of force as a rule of *jus cogens* preclude the lawfulness of military intervention for humanitarian purposes. The issue is not whether a customary law on humanitarian intervention has overridden Article 2 (4), but rather what is the extent of the rule of *jus cogens* – that is, how should this prohibition be interpreted in light of state practice and any evolving trends in customary international law. It has even been suggested that it is only the prohibition of the aggressive use of force that enjoys that status. Hence, there may be no prohibition on the use of force that falls short of aggression.

Neither, they argue, can the absence of any mention of "humanitarian intervention" in the Declaration on the Principles of Friendly Relations or the Definition of Aggression be regarded as conclusive. These resolutions are not legally binding; at most, they represent the interpretation of the relevant provisions of the Charter when they were adopted over a quarter of a century ago. They cannot set that interpretation in stone for all time. Furthermore, they did not represent an unequivocal rejection of military intervention for humanitarian objectives when they were adopted.[23]

In order to assess the relative merits of these positions, the legal claims must be tested against state practice. Specific instances of intervention were examined earlier. While there were several cases in which states asserted a right of humanitarian intervention before 1945, these are of limited relevance today as they occurred against the background of a law regarding the use of force that permitted states a far greater latitude than under the Charter regime. Accordingly, the analysis here confines itself to quickly reviewing practice since 1945 and emphasizes the post-Cold War era, in particular the "hard" case of Kosovo.

### State Practice, 1945–1990

Most instances in which states referred to humanitarian objectives in justifying the use of force prior to the Cold War's demise actually turned on claims of self-defence or the consent of the government of the state on whose territory the intervention took place. The absence of any clear reliance on humanitarian intervention during this period does not, however, mean that the practice of this period rejects the existence of such a right, merely that there were no manifestations.

It is worth revisiting three key cases discussed earlier, where the humanitarian rationale was secondary but the humanitarian benefits were substantial. With regard to India's conflict with Pakistan, New Delhi did not rely on humanitarian intervention as a justification for its resort to force – it claimed to have acted in self-defence. Yet, India referred on several occasions to the plight of the local population (including at least 1 million dead) and of the 10 million refugees on its own territory.[24] Furthermore, its actions went beyond what some would have regarded as proportionate self-defence; and in retrospect, it is now widely accepted that India could have based the intervention on humanitarian grounds.

The Vietnamese intervention in Cambodia in 1978–1979 resulted in the overthrow of the genocidal Pol Pot regime. In the Security Council debate on Cambodia, Vietnam distinguished between its own border conflict with Cambodia and the rebellion against Pol Pot within Cambodia, basing its justification for the invasion on the former. The case was further complicated by two factors: an unconvincing reliance on an invitation said to have been extended to Vietnam by a rival Cambodian government which Vietnam had been responsible for creating; and a sustained period of occupation. Once again, this justification could not have covered the full extent of the action taken by Vietnam, and clear references were made to the horrors perpetrated by the Khmer Rouge.

After being attacked by Uganda in 1979, Tanzania resorted to force, though President Julius Nyerere denied his intention to change the government in Kampala. Nevertheless, the Tanzanian forces went on to do precisely that. While self-defence undoubtedly provided a justification for the initial resort to force, it is difficult to see how it could have justified the full extent of Tanzania's action. Ultimately this use of force could have been justified in large measure by a right to protect the population of Uganda suffering under the rule of Idi Amin. At the time, and in retrospect, the intervention was widely seen as legitimate, and the humanitarian benefits were praised.

International reaction to these three cases was mixed. There was virtually no support from states for the notion of humanitarian intervention, yet the salutary impact was clear in all three instances. There was general acceptance of Tanzania's action in Uganda; and the effects of India's action were swiftly recognized, as Bangladesh was admitted to the UN, the Commonwealth, and other international institutions. Only in Cambodia – where Cold War and Sino-Soviet rivalries were prominent and numerous governments were highly suspicious of Vietnam's motives and intentions – was there a concerted attempt to deny recognition to the government created as a result of the intervention and to censure Vietnam for the invasion and the occupation.

The fact that India, Vietnam, and Tanzania did not make more of the argument that their actions were justified on humanitarian grounds suggests that this was not perceived as a strong legal argument at the time. But the general acquiescence at the UN in the Tanzanian and Indian cases, as well as a subsequent drop of relief in Sri Lanka by the Indian Air Force, was undoubtedly facilitated by a general acceptance of outcomes with such substantial and beneficial humanitarian effects.[25]

State practice during the period of 1945–1990 is inconclusive. It is insufficient to sustain either a right of humanitarian intervention or an unequivocal rejection of the concept. It is not surprising, therefore, that most studies of the subject during this period are cautious in reaching conclusions.[26]

## Contemporary State Practice

Four interventions undertaken in the 1990s provide evidence in support of the argument that a legal custom related to humanitarian intervention without Security Council authorization is at least emerging. The four interventions include ECOWAS's intervention in Liberia in 1990 and in Sierra Leone in 1997, the establishment and enforcement of no-fly zones in northern Iraq in 1991, and NATO's operation in Kosovo and the Federal Republic of Yugoslavia (FRY) in 1999. These interventions occurred in three geographic areas – Africa, the Middle East, and Europe – and together included military contingents from several continents.

In August 1990, ECOWAS's Cease-fire Monitoring Group (ECOMOG) intervened in Liberia to impose a ceasefire, restore democracy, and stop the senseless killing of innocent civilians.[27] Again in May 1997, Nigeria intervened in Sierra Leone to restore law and order, reverse the coup d'état, and protect human rights. In August 1997, ECOWAS mandated ECOMOG to enforce an economic embargo against the country and restore law and order there. Although presidents Doe and Kabbah both publicly requested external intervention, the unstable state of affairs inside each country raises questions as to whether such requests indicated genuine consent. At the time of the requests, neither Doe nor Kabbah was a de facto ruler of the state. Without local consent or a Security Council authorization, both military actions can be seen as involving the assertion of a right of humanitarian intervention.

International reaction to both interventions was generally supportive. The president of the Security Council issued statements supporting both interventions, and acting under Chapter VII of the UN Charter adopted several resolutions that deemed the situation in both countries a threat to international peace and security.[28] Resolutions 788 (1992) and 866 (1993) imposed a weapons embargo against rebel factions in Liberia and established the UN Observer Mission in Liberia, which was co-deployed side by side with ECOMOG forces. Resolution 1132 (1997) imposed an arms and petroleum embargo and travel restriction against the junta and the Revolutionary United Front in Sierra Leone. Resolutions 788 and 1132 sanctioned ECOWAS to enforce their terms. Security Council action in these cases effectively provided a retroactive *de jure* seal of approval on the interventions.

In April 1991, the UK, the US, France, and the Netherlands intervened in northern Iraq to create "safe havens" to enable the large numbers of refugees and displaced persons to return home in safety. While the Security Council had earlier condemned Iraqi repression of the civilian population as a threat to international peace and security, the actual authorization was not adopted under Chapter VII and did not specifically authorize the application of military force. The action taken by the intervening states was described by them as "being in support of Resolution 688," but it was not authorized specifically by that resolution. Nor could it be regarded as bound up with the self-defence of Kuwait. If it was lawful, therefore, the intervention had to be based on humanitarian justifications. That argument was not, however, fully articulated until the following year.

In 1992, a "no-fly zone" was imposed in southern Iraq by London and Washington to protect the civilian population. The UK defended these actions as the exercise of an exceptional right to intervene on humanitarian grounds. Speaking in 1992, after the imposition of the "no-fly zone" in southern Iraq, British Foreign Secretary Douglas Hurd said, "Not every action that a British government or an American government or a French government takes has to be underwritten by a specific provision in a UN resolution provided we comply with international law. International law recognizes extreme humanitarian need." He continued, "We are on strong legal as well as humanitarian ground in setting up this 'no-fly zone'."[29] With the exception of Iraq, very few states challenged the assertion of the need for military intervention in this case or challenged the underlying claim that a right of intervention existed for such extreme humanitarian cases.

There is no need to repeat the details of this well-documented case, but it is necessary to note that for proponents of a right to humanitarian intervention in emerging customary international law, the Iraqi case is similar to the Liberian one. They are important because states that intervened militarily implied a "humanitarian" justification for intervention. One involves a group of developing countries and the other major Western powers. The reaction of the rest of the community of states was general acquiescence. Protests at the time against the interventions on the grounds that they were unlawful were rare.

Of the interventions of the 1990s, Kosovo posed in the starkest terms the question of legitimacy and authority in the context of evolving state practice and customary international law. The action in Kosovo was justified in humanitarian terms. It was clearly not self-defence, nor was it authorized by the Security Council.

As the Kosovo situation deteriorated in the late 1990s, the Security Council indicated its competence to authorize forcible action in a series of resolutions; but it failed to do so, because of the presumed political opposition of China and Russia. NATO governments bypassed the Security Council, although Resolution 1244 (1999) in effect ratified the outcome of the NATO campaign, and the UN then took over a lead role in a peace building process, leaving military functions in the hands of NATO's Kosovo Force.

The legal justifications for NATO's intervention were not always expressly articulated, but they necessarily rested on some assertion of a right of humanitarian intervention or at least humanitarian "necessity." Although the Security Council did not authorize the bombing, three Chapter VII resolutions were adopted prior to the intervention (numbers 1160, 1199, and 1203). Legally binding on all states, including the FRY, these resolutions determined that the situation in Kosovo was a threat to international peace and security. They also established that the crisis in Kosovo involved serious violations of fundamental rights and an impending human catastrophe well before the NATO action began. But as critics correctly point out, they did not explicitly authorize the use of force.

Of the Western governments involved, the UK took the most consistent and overtly humanitarian position that the NATO action was justified because international law recognizes a right to take military action in a case of overwhelming humanitarian necessity. In October 1998, the Foreign and Commonwealth Office circulated a note among NATO member states arguing that, "Security Council authorization to use force for humanitarian purposes is now widely accepted (Bosnia and Somalia provide firm legal precedents). A UNSCR [UN Security Council resolution] would give a clear legal base for NATO action, as well as being politically desirable." It continued, "but force can also be justified on the grounds of overwhelming humanitarian necessity without a UNSCR."[30]

When the military action actually started, the UK Permanent Representative to the UN told the Security Council that "[t]he action being taken is legal. It is justified as an exceptional measure to prevent an overwhelming humanitarian catastrophe." He continued, "Every means short of force has been tried to avert this situation. In these circumstances, and as an exceptional measure on grounds of overwhelming humanitarian necessity, military intervention is legally justifiable. The force now proposed is directed exclusively to averting a humanitarian catastrophe, and is the minimum judged necessary for that purpose."[31]

A number of other NATO member states also invoked a right of humanitarian intervention. This is perhaps clearest in Belgium's submissions to the ICJ in the provisional-measures phase of the *Case Concerning Legality of Use of Force* brought by the FRY against 10 NATO member states in 1998.[32]

Some states – most notably Russia and China – were sharply critical of the legality of NATO's actions. And there were numerous other loud rejections of the right to humanitarian intervention without Security Council authorization. For example, the representative of India remarked that by ignoring the view of Russia, China, and India, NATO was acting contrary to the wishes of the "representatives of half of humanity."[33]

Proponents of an emerging custom, however, point to the firm rejection of a Russian proposal submitted to the Security Council on March 26, 1999. The draft resolution that would have condemned the NATO action as a breach of international law was defeated by 12 votes from a wide variety of countries (Argentina, Bahrain, Brazil, Canada, France, Gabon, the Gambia, Malaysia, the Netherlands, Slovenia, the UK, and the US) to 3 (China, Russia, and Namibia).

Since the end of the Cold War, state practice has shifted on issues of intervention and state sovereignty.[34] The Western states' reaction to both Iraq and Kosovo suggests a preoccupation with the humanitarian justification for intervention by ad hoc coalitions and regional organizations. African states, which as former colonies have historically been among the most vociferous defenders of absolute state sovereignty, have more recently been at the forefront of challenging traditional prohibitions on the use of force in internal conflicts. The African examples also suggest a growing consensus that state sovereignty is no longer inviolable when there is mass human suffering and democratic or legitimate governments are toppled.

## Regional Organizations

In the mid-1940s, regional organizations were unquestionably subordinated to the authority of the UN Security Council. At the turn of the century, it is less certain whether the text of the Charter remains definitive on the issue of regional authority. Specifically, there are questions as to whether regional enforcement action under all circumstances continues to fall under the subordinate status of the Security Council covered by Article 53 (1).

Some argue that prevention of genocide, crimes against humanity, "ethnic cleansing," and severe patterns of human rights violations have now generated legal authority to engage in intervention independently of the UN system. Having been neither acknowledged nor repudiated by the UN, such a legal right must be regarded as falling into a contested domain. Security Council practice provides a qualified endorsement for these claims of regional authority, especially in the setting of sub-Saharan Africa, but to some extent elsewhere, if the intervention claim is carried out in a context of a human tragedy resulting from a deadly conflict or in relation to a collapsed internal political order. The form of this endorsement, together with the absence of censure for uses of force that would appear to have contravened Charter constraints, has been a retrospective validation, either directly or indirectly, of initiatives of ECOWAS, NATO, and the Organization of American States.

One threshold question is whether regional alliances are subject to the Chapter VIII framework governing "Regional Arrangements." The issue relates particularly to the controversy regarding NATO's authority to act without an explicit mandate from the UN Security Council. Since its establishment on April 4, 1949, NATO has contended systematically that it is an organization dedicated to "collective self-defence" and thus not a regional arrangement in the sense intended by the Charter. In fact, Article 5 of the treaty explicitly distances NATO from Chapter VIII of the Charter because the Western Alliance is an entity exclusively concerned with bolstering "the right of individual and collective self-defence."

Those who argue that humanitarian intervention cannot be an application of self-defence would also question whether NATO could expand its scope of activity to encompass a broader range of claims without running afoul of Article 53's constraint on unauthorized regional enforcement. Article 1 of the NATO treaty commits the parties themselves to refrain from the use of force "in any manner inconsistent with the purposes of the UN." By virtue of the 1997 Madrid Declaration and other formal pronouncements of the 1990s, NATO attempted to adapt its mission to the conditions of post-Cold War Europe, stating that "[o]ur aim is to reinforce peace and stability in the Euro-Atlantic area." The Madrid Declaration includes the following suggestive language in paragraph 3: "While maintaining our core function of collective defence, we have adapted our political and military structures to improve our ability to meet the new challenges of regional crisis and conflict management." Paragraph 2 declares, "We are moving towards the realization of our vision of a just and lasting order of peace for Europe as a whole, based on human rights, freedom and democracy."

The constitutional issue posed is whether NATO's redefinition of its mission departs so much from its earlier identity as an organization devoted to Article 51 self-defence that in effect it has become a Chapter VIII regional organization dependent on Security Council authorization whenever it purports to use force to support a claim that is other than collective self-defence. Although the former Yugoslavia is "out of area" and beyond the scope of self-defence, its borders are contiguous with those of NATO countries. Hence, the argument of self-defence is considered plausible by some observers.

In contrast to NATO, where action has been based on a reinterpretation of the existing legal framework, African regional organizations have actually begun to codify a norm of humanitarian intervention.[35] In October 1998, in the wake of its experiences in Liberia and Sierra Leone, the ECOWAS heads of government in Abuja adopted and ratified the Framework for the Mechanism for Conflict Prevention, Management, Resolution, Peace and Security.

The framework empowers ECOWAS to deploy peacekeeping forces into internal conflict situations that threaten to trigger a humanitarian disaster, pose a serious threat to peace and security in the subregion, and erupt following the overthrow of a democratically elected government. In December 1999, they also adopted a protocol to the framework that recognizes it as binding on all issues related to conflict prevention, management, and resolution.

The principal goal of the Southern African Development Community (SADC) Organ for Politics, Defence, and Security is to protect the people of Southern Africa and safeguard the development of the region against instability arising from the breakdown of law and order, intrastate conflict, and external aggression. It explicitly seeks to encourage the observance of universal human rights, as enumerated in the charters of the OAU and UN. To complement the aims of the Organ, in June 1995 SADC adopted a Protocol on Peace, Security and Conflict Resolution,[36] which empowers it to establish peacekeeping forces in certain internal conflict situations. These include large scale violence between sections of the population of a state or between the state and (or) its armed or paramilitary forces and sections of the population, a threat to the legitimate authority of the government (such as a military coup by armed or paramilitary forces), a condition of civil war or insurgency, and any crisis that could threaten the peace and security of other member states.

There are, thus, now two regional organizations that have developed an explicit legal basis for the imposition of the use of force in internal conflicts for humanitarian ends and to restore democratic regimes that have been overthrown. ECOWAS and SADC structures and guiding criteria for intervention are nearly identical. However, from a legal perspective, SADC's security mechanism differs from ECOWAS's in one key respect: in an internal crisis, SADC may only respond to an invitation by a member country. ECOWAS, on the other hand, dispenses with even this limitation. Some would argue that this amounts to the codification of a doctrine of humanitarian intervention; others would suggest that it represents an expanded understanding of the right to self-defence, coupled with members of a regional organization granting "anticipatory" consent.

Regional organizations are becoming more assertive in authorizing their own interventions without prior approval from the Security Council. There is also growing opinion that to be regarded as "legitimate," such interventions need only be preceded by a credible account of an incipient or actual humanitarian catastrophe, demonstrate that reasonable efforts to reach a diplomatic or peaceful resolution have failed, and carry out the operation in accordance with IHL. Such a conception of legitimacy suggests that a literal reading of Chapter VIII of the Charter is no longer an accurate reflection of contemporary international law.

## LEGALITY AND LEGITIMACY

If a right to intervene on humanitarian grounds exists in customary international law (or if it is an emerging norm), it seems limited to cases where three conditions apply: there is widespread loss of life or such loss of life appears imminent; the existence of such a situation has been objectively determined (for example, by a resolution of the Security Council); and the Security Council has not explicitly rejected such an intervention.

There can be little doubt that a "gray sector" exists in international law, neither approving nor disapproving of a use of deadly force to protect people from severe forms of abuse. Russia, China, and many developing countries argue for what might be called a "green-light" interpretation: countries may proceed with military enforcement only if the Security Council has specifically authorized it. The West and some developing countries seem to be arguing for a "red light": countries may proceed unless the Security Council specifically votes to halt military enforcement. The legal status of humanitarian intervention under customary international law and independently of the UN Charter remains contested. A juridical stalemate exists.

Legality and legitimacy are linked but not synonymous. In the blurred area where international custom is evolving or unclear, the notion of legitimacy takes on greater significance. This is presently the case for actions taken both within and outside the framework of the UN Charter.

For many countries, the problem of democratic legitimacy within the Charter regime permeates all aspects of the humanitarian intervention debate. From their perspective, the ever-widening scope of Security Council action is nothing more than an abuse of the constitutional provisions of the UN. These, as well as other sceptics of humanitarian intervention, usually argue that the Security Council represents the distribution of power in 1945, rather than in today's world. It totally excludes from permanent membership major powers from Africa, Latin America, and the Middle East, and it also fails to acknowledge others in Asia and Europe, whose size and influence are comparable to those of other permanent members. Thus, the legitimacy of bona fide decisions is questionable on representational grounds alone.

They point out that the only previous Charter revision took place in 1965 to better reflect rapid decolonization and the vast increase in newly independent countries in the composition of the Security Council. In addition to the need to increase the numbers in the Council again, critics also point out that the veto is a historical relic, shielding human rights violators and guaranteeing impunity for the pursuit of narrow self-interests by the major powers.

At the same time, many developing countries are unwilling to accept as legitimate any intervention not explicitly authorized by the Security Council. The logic is straightforward, if somewhat paradoxical. There is no better or more appropriate body. Council decisions are authoritative because they result from an international political process that, even if flawed, is at least regulated.

In the debate over Kosovo, China and Russia were also reacting to concerns that the US and its close allies were converting the Security Council into an instrument of their foreign polices. The veto power was seen as a vital protection from other powerful states and as a means to neutralize Western geopolitical machinations. States that insist on maintaining the right to the veto are in a poor position to claim the need to act outside of the Charter framework when paralysis results from another permanent member's veto. The evasion of veto power in the case of Kosovo was interpreted as proof of efforts to undermine this legitimate sphere of UN authority. Suggestions have since surfaced that the permanent members should consider a pledge not to veto any intervention for humanitarian purposes when their own vital interests are not directly threatened. It seems aberrant that a veto could override the claims of the rest of humanity.[37]

Avoiding the Security Council poses one set of problems, but assertive leadership by the major powers poses others. Hence, in relation to the Gulf War and with respect to the imposition and retention of sanctions against Libya and Iraq, many developing countries have criticized efforts by Western states, and especially by the US, to widen the scope of acceptable multilateral authority and legitimacy. In effect, such critics have argued that the Charter conception of UN authority has been subjected to "geopolitical hijacking" and that such practice has imperiled the legitimate sovereign rights of many countries.

Legitimacy is also an increasingly important notion for those who accept that in certain circumstances humanitarian interventions should be undertaken even in the absence of clear Security Council authorization. Within segments of global civil society and for a significant number of governments, there exists a "legal" basis for intervention provided the facts of abuse are authenticated. If a human catastrophe related to a deadly conflict occurs, there is need to act whether or not the Security Council is seized by a crisis. Much of the debate in the West focuses on the difficulties of securing the necessary authority to undertake interventions and on operational shortcomings within the international system.

In the absence of a Council authorization to use force, observers have identified additional factors that could affect the perceived legitimacy of an intervention in response to situations that shock the conscience. Two possibilities were discussed earlier, namely, the Council's authorizing Chapter VII action, though not the use of force; and a two-thirds majority in the General Assembly. Other ideas have emerged that might be helpful in enhancing legitimacy, if not the legality, of an enforcement action. For instance, a strong majority on a Council vote, even with a veto, could suggest broad approval for enforcement action. In fact, even securing a solid majority in the Council or the General Assembly would indicate a certain degree of legitimacy. To return to the earlier image, these kinds of approval might provide an "amber light." Moreover, a truly cosmopolitan coalition of troop contributors could also provide substantial evidence of a widespread commitment among countries that are sufficiently persuaded by the justness of their cause to commit soldiers and risk international criticism.

Two other suggestions for enhancing legitimacy relate to independent judgements about the feasibility of humanitarian intervention claims, with or without Security Council approval. Some commentators have suggested that the ICJ review all cases of intervention as a way of checking abuse.[38] Most observers are doubtful about the utility of such a procedure because of the protracted time necessary for deliberations and because compulsory jurisdiction is lacking for most countries for this type of issue.[39] A second suggestion is that independent verification could be helpful in determining legitimacy. The possibility for fact-finding missions exists within the Geneva Conventions; and while this provision entered into force in the early 1990s, it has not yet been used. Alternatives include fact-finding authorized by the Security Council or the UN Secretary-General, or the establishment of an independent expert panel composed of eminent persons.

In the face of legal ambiguity, lists of possible thresholds and criteria assume increasing importance. The establishment of a set of criteria has been offered as one way to mitigate the potential for abuse. While not legally binding, they could nevertheless provide a benchmark against which the legitimacy of an intervention could be measured. As mentioned above, such lists of principles commonly reflect the essence of just war doctrine.

Developing criteria for humanitarian intervention is by no means a new idea. An extended effort in the early 1970s by the International Law Association was abandoned because of the dim prospects for securing consensus.[40] Yet, as discussed earlier in the volume, there remains remarkable consistency among the proposed criteria. The obvious difficulties in securing consensus aside, many commentators still oppose the codification of such criteria. They favour a more ad hoc and common-law approach because criteria could do more to inhibit than foster intervention when it is warranted; the "checklist" could provide a rationale for political leaders not wanting to assume any risk.

Two final factors that have a profound effect on the legitimacy of an intervention are the manner in which it is conducted and the effectiveness and sustainability of protection. Even those who argue that a Security Council decision is a prerequisite for justified humanitarian intervention accept that such an authorization could be undermined by the actual conduct of an operation. In such circumstances, a legal intervention could become illegitimate.

The paramount consideration is the ultimate efficacy of humanitarian intervention. Does it work, or does it actually give rise to worse problems than it solves? One line of argument discounts the propriety of military intervention on humanitarian grounds because it is likely to lead to further loss of life. The range of negative consequences extends from facilitating flight by forced migrants to sustaining war economies and making post-conflict peace building a distant dream. The result has been a serious questioning of the use of military force to secure humanitarian objectives.[41]

Others argue that the measure of success is simply lives saved, in both the short and the longer term. While military intervention is inevitably a blunt instrument, they claim that the safety of the population in Kosovo is more secure today than if Milosevic had remained in control of the territory. They would also argue that almost any intervention force would have had a positive impact for the Tutsi population in Rwanda.

While counterfactual arguments are notoriously unreliable, many argue that it is unfair to not at least ask the question and attempt a calculation for a proverbial bottom line. Despite mistakes and shortcomings, were populations at risk better off than they would have been in the absence of intervention?

# NOTES

1   For reviews of the UN Charter, see Bruno Simma, ed., *The Charter of the UN: A Commentary* (Oxford: Oxford University Press, 1995); Jean-Pierre Cot and Alain Peillet, eds., *La Charte des Nations Unies: Commentaire article par article* (Paris: Economica, 1991); and Leland M. Goodrich, Edvard Hambro, and Anne Patricia Simmons, *Charter of the UN: Commentary and Documents*, 3rd ed. (New York: Columbia University Press, 1969).

2   For two sides of the argument, see Ian Brownlie, *International Law and the Use of Force by States* (Oxford: Clarendon Press, 1963); and Fernando Tesón, *Humanitarian Intervention: An Inquiry into Law and Morality*, 2nd ed. (Irvington-on-Hudson: Transnational Publishers, 1997). For a review of the legal and international-relations literatures, see Oliver Ramsbotham and Tom Woodhouse, *Humanitarian Intervention in Contemporary Conflict* (Cambridge: Polity Press, 1996). See also Richard A. Falk, "The Complexities of Humanitarian Intervention: A New World Order Challenge," *Michigan Journal of International Law* 17, No. 2 (1996), pp. 491–513; and Tom J. Farer, "Harnessing Rogue Elephants: A Short Discourse on Foreign Intervention in Civil Strife," *Harvard Law Review* 82 (1969), pp. 511–514.

3   For legal and historical overviews, see Francis Abiew, *The Evolution of the Doctrine and Practice of Humanitarian Intervention* (The Hague: Kluwer Law International, 1999); Mario Bettati and Bernard Kouchner, *Le devoir d'ingérence: Peut-on les laisser mourir?* (Paris: Denoël, 1987); Simon Chesterman, *Just War or Just Peace? Humanitarian Intervention and International Law* (Oxford: Oxford University Press, 2001); Richard Lillich, *Humanitarian Intervention and the UN* (Charlottesville: University Press of Virginia, 1973); Sean D. Murphy, *Humanitarian Intervention: The UN in an Evolving World Order* (Philadelphia: University of Pennsylvania Press, 1996); Nicholas J. Wheeler, *Saving Strangers: Humanitarian Intervention in International Society* (Oxford: Oxford University Press, 2000); R.J. Vincent, *Nonintervention and International Order* (Princeton: Princeton University Press, 1974); and Natalino Ronzitti, *Rescuing Nationals Abroad through Military Coercion and Intervention on the Grounds of Humanity* (Dordrecht: Martinus Nijhoff, 1985).

4   See, for example, Christopher Greenwood, *Humanitarian Intervention: Law and Policy* (Oxford: Oxford University Press, 2001); and Christopher C. Joyner, *The UN and International Law* (Cambridge: Cambridge University Press, 1997).

5   Independent International Commission on Kosovo, *Kosovo Report: Conflict, International Response, Lessons Learned* (Oxford: Oxford University Press, 2000), p. 4.

6   For a documentary account, see United Nations, *The Blue Helmets*, 3rd ed. (New York: United Nations, 1996). For an historical overview of the Cold War period, see Alan James, *Peacekeeping in International Politics* (London: Macmillan, 1990); and for the post-Cold War era, see William J. Durch, ed., *The Evolution of UN Peacekeeping* (New York: St. Martin's, 1993) and William J. Durch, *UN Peacekeeping, American Policy, and the Uncivil Wars of the 1990s* (New York: St. Martin's, 1996).

7   Christine Bourloyannis, "The Security Council of the UN and the Implementation of International Humanitarian Law," *Denver Journal of International Law and Policy* 20, no. 3 (1993), p. 43.

8   For more detail on the role of the International Committee of the Red Cross, see Richard A. Falk, ed., *The International Law of Civil War* (Baltimore: The Johns Hopkins University Press, 1971); David P. Forsythe, *Humanitarian Politics* (Baltimore: The Johns Hopkins University Press, 1977); Jean S. Pictet, *Humanitarian Law and the Protection of War Victims* (Leiden: A.W. Sijthoff, 1975); and Jean S. Pictet, *Commentary: IV Geneva Convention Relative to the Protection of Civilian Persons in Times of War* (Geneva: the International Committee of the Red Cross, 1958). For a compendium of relevant documents, with commentary, see Adam Roberts and Richard Guelff, eds., *Documents on the Laws of War*, 3rd ed. (Oxford: Oxford University Press, 2000). For an in-depth treatment of the status of refugees in international law, see Guy S. Goodwin-Gill, *The Refugee in International Law*, 2nd ed. (Oxford: Clarendon Press, 1996).

9   Th. A. van Baarda, "The Involvement of the Security Council in Maintaining International Law," *Netherlands Quarterly of Human Rights* 12, no. 1 (1994), p. 140.

10   For a more elaborate discussion of the General Assembly, see M.J. Peterson, *The General Assembly in World Politics* (Boston: Allen & Unwin, 1986).

11   Rule 65 of the *Rules of Procedure of the UN General Assembly*, added as a result of the "Uniting for Peace" resolution.

12   Derek W. Bowett, *Self-Defence in International Law* (New York: Praeger, 1958); Helmut Freudenschuß, "Between Unilateralism and Collective Security: Authorizations of the Use of Force by the UN Security Council," *European Journal of International Law* 5, no. 4 (1994), pp. 492–531; and Michael J. Glennon, "Sovereignty and Community after Haiti: Rethinking the Collective Use of Force," *American Journal of International Law* 89, no. 1, pp. 70–74.

13   International Court of Justice, *Military and Paramilitary Activities in and against Nicaragua* (*Nicaragua vs. United States* case), June 27, 1986. See, for example, Thomas M. Franck, "Some Observations on the ICJ's Procedural and Substantive Innovations (in Appraisals of the ICJ's Decision: Nicaragua vs. United State (Merits))," *American Journal of International Law* 81, no. 1 (1987), pp. 116–121.

14   W. Michael Reisman, "Legal Responses to Genocide and Other Massive Violations of Human Rights," *Law and Contemporary Problems* 59, no. 4 (1996), pp. 75–80; and Yves Sandoz, Christophe Swinarski, and Bruno Zimmerman, eds., *Commentary on the Additional Protocols of 8 June 1977 to the Geneva Conventions of 12 August 1949* (Geneva: International Committee of the Red Cross, 1987).

15   See, for instance, Richard A. Falk, *Human Rights Horizons: The Pursuit of Justice in a Globalizing World* (New York: Routledge, 2000); and W. Michael Reisman, "Sovereignty and Human Rights in Contemporary International Law," *American Journal of International Law* 84, no. 4 (1990), pp. 866–876.

16   See, for example, Julie Mertus, *Open Wounds: Human Rights Abuses in Kosovo* (Berkeley: University of California Press, 1997); and Julie Mertus, *Kosovo: How Myths and Truths Started a War* (Berkeley: University of California Press, 1999).

17   For a discussion, see Thomas M. Franck, "The Emerging Right to Democratic Governance," *American Journal of International Law* 86, no. 1 (1992), pp. 46–91; W. Michael Reisman, "Humanitarian Intervention and Fledgling Democracies," *Fordham International Law Journal* 18, no. 3 (1995), pp. 794–805; and Oscar Schachter, "The Legality of Pro-Democratic Invasion," *American Journal of International Law* 78, no. 3 (1984), pp. 645–650.

18   Brad R. Roth, *Governmental Illegitimacy in International Law* (Oxford: Clarendon Press, 1999), p. 407.

19   Available at http://www.nam.gov.za/ungamin/com2309.htm, para. 171.

20   Available at http://www.nam.gov.za/south/77south.htm, para. 54.

21   For a contemporary discussion of the legal framework, see Christine Gray, *International Law and the Use of Force: Foundations of Public International Law* (Oxford: Oxford University Press, 2001), especially chapters 1 and 2; Lori Fisler Damrosch and David J. Scheffer, eds., *Law and the Use of Force in the New International Order* (Boulder: Westview Press, 1991); W. Michael Reisman, "Coercion and Self-Determination: Construing Charter Article 2 (4)," *American Journal of International Law* 78, no. 3 (1984), pp. 642–645; Michel-Cyr Djiena Wembou, "Le droit d'ingérence humanitaire: Un droit aux fondement incertains, au contenu imprécis et géométrie variable," *African Journal of International and Comparative Law* 4, no. 3 (1992), pp. 570–591; Richard N. Gardner, "International Law and the Use of Force," in David J. Scheffer, ed., *Post-Gulf War Challenges to the UN Collective Security System: Three Views of the Issue of Humanitarian Intervention* (Washington, DC: US Institute of Peace, 1992); and Louis Henkin, Stanley Hoffmann, Jeane J. Kirkpatrick, Allan Gerson, William D. Rogers, and David J. Scheffer, eds., *Right v. Might: International Law and the Use of Force* (New York: Council on Foreign Relations Press, 1991). Thomas M. Franck and Louis Henkin articulated opposite sides of this controversy decades ago, but the issue remains unresolved. Thomas M. Franck, "Who Killed Article 2(4)? Or Changing Norms Governing the Use of Force by States," *American Journal of International Law* 64 (1970), pp. 809–837; and Louis Henkin, "The Reports of the Death of Article 2(4) Are Greatly Exaggerated," *American Journal of International Law* 65 (1971), pp. 544–548.

22   Some commentators also rely on a passage in the decision of the International Court of Justice in the *Nicaragua vs. United States* case, in which the International Court of Justice rejected an argument that human rights violations in Nicaragua could afford a justification for US military support for the Contra rebel movement. See para. 268.

23   Similarly, the passage in the *Nicaragua* case on intervention in cases of human rights violations has to be seen in the context of the facts of that case. The US had not argued its case in full, having withdrawn from the proceedings after the jurisdiction phase, but its submissions on this point referred to a broad range of human rights violations, rather than to violations involving or threatening extensive loss of life. It is said that the decision of the International Court of Justice cannot therefore properly be regarded as dealing with the legality of military action to prevent genocide or other human rights violations leading to extensive loss of life. It is argued that the fact that the International Court of Justice rejected the US argument on the facts of the *Nicaragua* case, where there was no threat of widespread loss of life, could not rule out the possibility that humanitarian intervention might be lawful in a case where such a threat existed. See para. 207 of ibid.

24   Thomas M. Franck and Nigel S. Rodley, "After Bangladesh: The Law of Humanitarian Intervention by Military Force," *American Journal of International Law* 67 (1973), p. 275.

25  In 1987, the Indian Air Force dropped relief supplies to the Tamil population in northern Sri Lanka. This action was undertaken against the wishes of the Sri Lankan Government. Although it involved no use of force, there was an implied threat to use force if Sri Lankan forces interfered with the Indian Air Force operation. The Indian action attracted little criticism at the time. This incident has to be distinguished from India's later action in sending ground troops to Sri Lanka, which was undertaken with the consent of the government.

26  See, for instance, the conclusion in the study entitled "Is Intervention Ever Justified?" prepared by the Planning Staff of the Foreign and Commonwealth Office, Foreign Policy Document 148, para. II.22. Humanitarian intervention "cannot be said to be unambiguously illegal." Parts of the document are reproduced in *British Yearbook of International Law* 57 (1986), p. 614. Contrary to what is sometimes suggested, the study was a discussion paper, not an instance of UK state practice (see para. II.2).

27  UN Document S/21485.

28  UN Documents S/22133 and S/23886.

29  Interview on radio 4, August 19, 1992; reproduced in *British Yearbook of International Law* 63 (1992), p. 824.

30  Quoted by Adam Roberts, "NATO's 'Humanitarian War' over Kosovo," *Survival* 41, no. 2 (1999), p. 106.

31  UN Document S/PV.3988, p. 12; March 24, 1999. Also, see the statement by the Secretary of State for Defence in the House of Commons on March 25, 1999.

32  The court did not indicate provisional measures in any of the 10 cases, holding that the FRY had failed to show that there was a *prima facie* basis for jurisdiction; report at http://www.icj-cij.org

33  UN Document S/PV.3989, March 26, 1999, p. 16.

34  Nigel S. Rodley, ed., *To Loose the Bands of Wickedness: International Intervention in Defence of Human Rights* (London: Brassey's, 1992).

35  For a more extensive discussion of this case, see Jeremy Levitt, "African Interventionist States and International Law," in Oliver Furley and Roy May, eds., *African Interventionist States: The New Conflict Resolution Brokers* (Aldershot: Ashgate, forthcoming).

36  As a result of geopolitical tensions between South Africa and Zimbabwe, Southern African Development Community member states have been slow to ratify the Protocol. Yet, they consider it the sole guiding framework for all Southern African Development Community interventions.

37  Such a proposal has been suggested by the French Foreign Minister, Hubert Védrine. See "La question de la crise du Kosovo est une exception," *Le Monde*, March, 25, 2000, p. 16.

38  Robert Jennings and Arthur Watts, eds., *Oppenheim's International Law* (London: Longmans, 1996), p. 439.

39  Justiciability occurs after the fact. Time is of the essence when massive human tragedy requires military intervention, but the International Court of Justice requires years to consider all aspects of a case. The requirement of consent to the jurisdiction of the International Court of Justice may not always guarantee that a matter concerning intervention will be determined on its merits – unless, of course, there were to be a radical change in contemporary international politics that would warrant compulsory International Court of Justice jurisdiction on matters of intervention. See Thomas M. Franck, "Powers of Appreciation: Who Is the Ultimate Guardian of UN Legality?," *American Journal of International Law* 86, no. 3 (July 1992), p. 519; and W. Michael Reisman, "The Constitutional Crisis in the UN," *American Journal of International Law* 87, no. 1 (January 1993), p. 83.

40  See Danish Institute for International Affairs, *Humanitarian Intervention: Legal and Political Aspects* (Copenhagen: Danish Institute for International Affairs, 1999), p. 105. This thorough legal analysis is a useful compendium, as is the Advisory Council on International Affairs and Advisory Committee on Issues of Public International Law, *Humanitarian Intervention* (The Hague: Advisory Council on International Affairs, 2000).

41  See Adam Roberts, "Implementation of the Laws of War in Late 20th Century Conflicts," Pts. I and II, *Security Dialogue* 29, nos. 2 and 3 (June and September 1998), pp. 137–150 and 265–280; Thomas G. Weiss, "Politics, Principles, and Humanitarian Action," *Ethics & International Affairs* XIII (1999), pp. 1–22, as well as "Responses" by Cornelio Sommaruga, Joelle Tanguy, Fiona Terry, and David Rieff, on pp. 23–42; a special issue on "Humanitarian Debate: Law, Policy, Action," *International Review of the Red Cross* 81, no. 833 (March 1999); and Michael Bryans, Bruce D. Jones, and Janice Gross Stein, *Mean Times: Humanitarian Action in Complex Emergencies – Stark Choices, Cruel Dilemmas* (Toronto: Centre for International Studies, 1999).

# 8. CONDUCT AND CAPACITY

The following analysis explores the operational challenges of military intervention in humanitarian crises. The record of the 1990s indicates few clear principles about the use of deadly force and provides only limited evidence of the ability of the military to provide physical protection to civilians in deadly conflicts or to compel warring factions to stop fighting. Modifying peacekeeping, however radically, appears to many specialists as a highly inadequate response that would be incapable of providing protection to targeted populations in extreme circumstances. A clear operational concept is required for legitimate, multinational intervention to end large scale loss of life and gross abuses of human rights by both governments and armed oppositions. Such a shift in orientation, however, has significant implications for the tasks of intervening forces, and it would require a form of intervention that has hitherto been rejected in the evolving military intervention doctrine.[1]

Some may question the narrow focus on the military component of multilateral and United Nations (UN) missions. It has become popular for analysts to argue that the military is but one element of an intervention or peace support operation, and then quickly to examine debates about refining the humanitarian and developmental components. Yet, despite the general consensus that the military's principal value-added is in providing a secure environment, the military – or, perhaps more accurately, their political masters – have tended to be unwilling to employ deadly force to protect civilians. According to an Organisation for Economic Co-operation and Development (OECD) report, the growing involvement of military forces in humanitarian operations has created the "strange situation of the military engaging in all the tasks but that task for which they are most directly trained."[2]

The lack of attention to the peculiar operational dimensions of humanitarian intervention is also apparent in the analytical literature. Adam Roberts, in one of the few sustained dedicated studies on the subject, argues that "there has been remarkably little serious thinking about military protection" for civilians and aid workers and that the "failure to develop serious policies regarding the security of humanitarian action, and of the affected peoples and areas, has been the principal cause of the setbacks of humanitarian action in the 1990s."[3]

There have been efforts by national militaries to develop doctrine and procedures related to this area; and where possible, citations to the existing literature are included. But based on an examination of dozens of the most widely cited documents, it appears that assessments of these dimensions remain inadequate.

The aim of this essay, then, is to identify the operational challenges in applying deadly military force for humanitarian ends. Unlike the review of intervention earlier in the volume, the cases referred to here are not limited to nonconsensual military operations. Whether they were mandated under Chapter VI or Chapter VII of the UN Charter, all suffered at one stage or another from an absence or withdrawal of consent by belligerents and can thus provide useful insights for future efforts to operationalize the responsibility to protect vulnerable civilian populations.

## USE OF FORCE IN HUMANITARIAN CRISES

At the beginning of the 1990s, international interventions were characterized by extremes in the use of force. There were either high-intensity enforcement operations (for example, the Gulf War) or traditional UN peacekeeping, reliant on the consent of belligerents (quintessentially on the Golan Heights or in the Sinai). As peace missions were deployed within states in internal conflicts, a range of tasks between these two extremes reflected a "second generation" of international military deployments.[4] These middle level tasks characterize the bulk of military activity in what became known in British and North Atlantic Treaty Organization (NATO) doctrine as "peace support operations" and in the United States (US) doctrine as "peace operations."[5]

During the past decade, the UN was called on to oversee the implementation of a number of detailed peace agreements, which required its field missions to engage in a wide variety of nonmilitary functions. The tasks of intervening agents typically included the full range of measures stored in UN Secretary-General Boutros Boutros-Ghali's conflict resolution "toolbox" and outlined in the much-discussed *An Agenda for Peace*.[6] These tasks went far beyond observing, monitoring, and reporting on cease-fire agreements or acting as an interpositional force, the traditional bill of fare of peacekeeping operations. Actual mission mandates during the 1990s covered such ambitious projects as running transitional civil administrations, disarming and demobilizing warring factions, transforming regular and irregular forces into a unified army, reorganizing and retraining the police, reestablishing or reforming the judiciary, facilitating the delivery of humanitarian assistance, and helping to organize national elections.

Where civilians were at grave risk, the Security Council has also given increased attention to measures designed explicitly for their protection – most notably through resolutions mandating the creation of "security zones," "safe havens," or "protected areas." By the end of the decade, explicit reference to the protection of civilians emerged in Security Council resolutions. Through its unanimous adoption of Resolution 1296 on April 19, 2000, the Security Council placed the protection of civilians in armed conflict at the heart of the UN's future agenda. The Security Council had thus reached the point where it was prepared to invoke Chapter VII in authorizing UN military forces to protect civilians at risk in deadly conflicts.

Four conceptually distinct objectives for which military forces might be deployed in response to humanitarian crises are set out in Figure 8.1. They are to monitor compliance, compel compliance, provide protection, and defeat opponents.

The two ends of the spectrum are relatively well understood. On the left is traditional peacekeeping, based on the principles of consent, neutrality, and the nonuse of force, except in self-defence. This form of military deployment is designed to create and maintain conditions in which political negotiations can proceed – in effect, to monitor compliance with an agreement that belligerents have committed themselves to implement. It involves patrolling buffer zones between hostile parties, monitoring cease-fires, and helping to defuse local conflicts. Examples of traditional peacekeeping include unarmed military observers in Western Sahara and armed infantry-based forces in Cyprus. On the right of the spectrum lies the equally well-understood concept of warfighting. Here the objective is to defeat a clearly defined adversary, and it is undertaken by fully combat-capable troops. NATO's air campaign in Kosovo falls under this category, as does the defeat of genocidal regimes in Cambodia and Uganda.

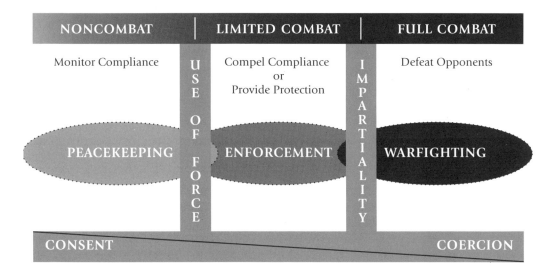

## FIGURE 8.1: FORMS OF INTERNATIONAL MILITARY OPERATIONS

Activities falling between these two extremes have, over the course of the 1990s, become the most common form of international military operations. Here it is useful to distinguish between two related but distinct sets of objectives: compelling compliance and providing protection. The first of these, commonly referred to as "peace enforcement," revolves around the search for comprehensive political settlements leading to sustainable peace. It involves traditional peacekeeping tasks, such as monitoring cease-fires, but it also involves complex tasks for which ultimate success requires a willingness and a capacity to use force. These include the "cantonment and demobilization of soldiers; the destruction of weapons; the formation and training of new armed forces; [and] monitoring existing police forces and forming new ones."[7] Examples of this form of military operation include the Implementation Force (IFOR) and the Stabilization Force (SFOR) organized by NATO in Bosnia, the US-led Multinational Force (MNF) in Haiti, and the UN Mission in Sierra Leone (UNAMSIL). A variant on this approach is the use of force to compel parties to the negotiating table. Examples here include the NATO air strikes preceding the signing of the Dayton agreement on Bosnia, and the early phase of intervention in Liberia, where the Economic Community of West African States (ECOWAS) deployed the ECOWAS Cease-fire Monitoring Group (ECOMOG), which fought Charles Taylor's rebels to secure a cease-fire and a secure environment to establish an interim government.

The other form of enforcement action consists of providing protection for civilians backed by the threat or use of military force. While "coercive protection" can take a variety of forms, the most common are the maintenance of humanitarian corridors, the protection of aid convoys, and the creation of safe havens or protected areas. Prominent examples include the no-fly zone in northern Iraq and the safe areas of Bosnia. A particularly important dimension of this kind of operation is the force posture of intervening troops. The previous three forms of military operations all have military forces oriented in relation to other military forces. Peacekeeping involves the monitoring of military cease-fires or the interposition of forces between armed parties to a conflict; compelling compliance involves the potential use of force against conflicting parties or spoilers; and warfighting involves combat against designated opponents. In contrast to these approaches, the provision of protection requires the interposition of forces between potential attackers (armies, militias, and gangs) and civilians. This is a contemporary task that is central to the challenging responsibility to protect civilians.

Compelling compliance and providing protection are often employed in the same mission. Where the political will exists to use military force to pressure the parties toward peace, there is usually also the will to use force to provide some degree of protection for civilians. In other cases, where compelling compliance is deemed unwise or too costly – for instance, the removal of Saddam Hussein from Baghdad to ensure the safety of the Kurds in the north – coercive protection measures may be employed on their own.

The conceptual distinctions in Figure 8.1 rarely match the complexities on the ground. As the considerable areas within the overlapping circles imply, many missions operate near the margins of these categories, often moving back and forth from one to the other. This makes the fundamental distinctions between the categories of the use of force and an impartial force posture all the more important. The principal distinction between peacekeeping and enforcement operations is the use of deadly force beyond self-defence. In contrast with the past, peacekeepers are now commonly armed and in many cases are deployed with some degree of combat equipment. But their rules of engagement (ROEs) invariably require that they be shot at before they can shoot back. In the case of enforcement action, ROEs explicitly allow for the use of force to lay the groundwork for a political settlement or to provide protection. The Australian-led International Force in East Timor (INTERFET) was authorized to do the former; the patrolling of the no-fly zone in northern Iraq clearly involved the latter.

Another fundamental distinction revolves around the complex notion of impartiality. Although sometimes thought to imply treating all sides alike, there is a growing appreciation that impartiality differs from neutrality. Impartiality is the even-handed application of mission mandates and international law. Hence, if a mission begins with the consent of the parties and then this is lost, outside military forces can employ violence against backsliding parties without the loss of impartiality. The report from the Panel on UN Peace Operations endorsed this approach when it argued that, "[I]mpartiality is not the same as neutrality or equal treatment of all parties in all cases for all time, which can amount to a policy of appeasement. In some cases, local parties consist not of moral equals but of obvious aggressors and victims, and peacekeepers may not only be operationally justified in using force but morally compelled to do so."[8]

When intervening forces determine that one of the factions is principally to blame, impartiality is inapplicable and the mission enters the realm of warfighting. This is clearly the case when the objective is to dislodge a genocidal regime. Other examples include NATO's bombing of Kosovo and the period during the second UN Operation in Somalia (UNOSOM II) when the US forces attempted to forcibly capture General Mohammed Farah Aideed. Important though the distinction between the partial and impartial use of force is to intervening forces, they share some of the same operational challenges. Belligerents invariably interpret the enforcement of mandates against them as practical actions in support of their opponents. Perception by warring parties may be quite distinct from the intentions of outside military forces, but these perceptions are frequently what counts on the ground.

As is evidenced by the robust interventions of the 1990s, the first half of the decade was characterized by the shift from peacekeeping to enforcement; and the latter half by the growing realization that there were circumstances under which even the impartial use of force was inadequate. A senior UN official, commenting on the publication of the Secretary-General's report on Srebrenica, admitted that the UN's failure was "in part rooted in a philosophy of neutrality and non-violence wholly unsuited to the conflict in Bosnia." He suggested that the report "breaks new ground by effectively damning the diplomatic nicety of trying to remain neutral and above the fray in civil conflict."[9]

A further conceptual point, before turning to explore the specific operational challenges of enforcement actions, involves the varying degree of consent across these various modes of operation. Although widely regarded as the fundamental difference between peacekeeping and peace enforcement, consent is rarely absolute and often evaporates. There are both quantitative and qualitative dimensions to the nature of consent.[10] Agreements may be reached on issues of fundamental importance to central actors, or on more peripheral matters. Once reached, however, agreements are notoriously vulnerable to a variety of interpretations.

Ultimately, consent is something that is given and thus may also be withdrawn when it seems advantageous to do so. This is not a new phenomenon, as the Egyptian withdrawal of consent for the presence of the first UN Emergency Force and the outbreak of war in 1967 illustrates. Much is made about consent in the 1990s, but once again history is important. However, the record of international military operations during the 1990s proves this point dramatically. Hence, it is unwise to count on the continuation of consent, particularly in collapsed states with no functional government structures and few factional leaders who respect any concept of the rule of law.[11] In reference to future operations, Kofi Annan commented while he was still head of the Department of Peacekeeping Operations (DPKO) that "the old dictum of 'consent of the parties' will be neither right [nor] wrong; it will be, quite simply, irrelevant."[12]

Having reviewed the various modes of military operations, the specific demands of effective enforcement action will now be discussed. In 2000, the Panel on UN Peace Operations reviewed the operational challenges facing UN missions. For the most part, however, that panel did not focus on the more robust use of military force. Their report confirmed that "the United Nations does not wage war. Where enforcement action is required, it has consistently been entrusted to coalitions of willing states."[13] At the same time, UN blue helmets are currently attempting to implement mandates with considerable enforcement dimensions in Sierra Leone and East Timor.

Dag Hammarskjöld once commented that, "Peacekeeping is not a job for soldiers, but only a soldier can do it." Enforcement action, whether to compel compliance or to provide protection, *is* a job for soldiers. This essay discusses enforcement objectives and strategies, the military dimensions of enforcement action, and the specific challenges of undertaking coercive protection and concludes with the tasks required to sustain both peace and protection.

## OBJECTIVES AND STRATEGIES

Virtually every report on traditional peacekeeping or military enforcement operations contains a straightforward recommendation to have clear and credible objectives with matching mandates and resources. This is easier to recommend than to follow. A central problem is that multilateral decision making bodies generally require consensus to succeed. Vagueness and incrementalism, rather than specificity and decisiveness, are inevitable outcomes of multilateral deliberations during which the limits and boundaries of intervention have become significantly obscured in order to secure agreement on deploying forces at all.

With regard to peace making initiatives, the UN Secretary-General has warned that "the failure of the major external actors to maintain a common political approach to an erupting or ongoing crisis is one of the principal impediments to progress towards a solution."[14] Decisions to intervene are usually based more on emergency impulses than strategic analyses of how to transform the target arena. Many interventions were triggered throughout the 1990s by an imperative to "do something." And this lack of strategic vision is usually disastrous. This was certainly the case with the UN Protection Force (UNPROFOR) in the former Yugoslavia because a large scale military force configured for peacekeeping was sent into an environment where all too often there was no peace to keep.[15] This lack of direction, despite the proliferation of resolutions, reflected the reality of political compromises and divisions among members of the Council.

However well or ill-defined the end-state of intervention, political vision should encompass what it will take to get there – conceptually as well as operationally. Without such calculations from the outset, there is little chance of mustering sufficient "political will" to see the intervention through to a successful conclusion. All too often, this vision has been limited to a commitment to verify, monitor, and report on circumstances in a mission area. Comprehensive and multidimensional peace processes militate against a stricter focus on the art of the possible during cease-fire and peace negotiations. Considerable issues of prestige are at stake in an intervention, which translates into reluctance among potential contributors to support a coalition that is tasked with a challenging mandate, especially where vital interests are **not** threatened.

### Peacekeeping and Enforcement

Although enforcement is a task for combat troops and not peacekeepers, the requirement for enforcement action often arises where peacekeepers have already been deployed. The need to be adaptable, have contingency plans and options, and be able to scale-up or scale-down, depending on challenges, should be obvious. Although this is standard for national military operations, it is not automatic within the UN. Financial allocations for UN operations (usually for only six months) suggest the tentative nature of national commitments to international operations. And countries that have approved the use of their soldiers as blue helmets cannot be assumed in advance to endorse the change of helmet colour to the olive green of warfighters.

Furthermore, the actual pattern of deployment of forces for peacekeeping may be counterproductive for enforcement operations. For instance, peacekeeping's success often relies on being highly visible in local communities and being exposed in ways that would be inappropriate if deadly force is employed and intervening soldiers become targets.[16] Hence, the deployment of the Dutch contingent around Srebrenica was patterned on successful interposition and observation missions elsewhere, but it was inappropriate to ensure the safety of the inhabitants or to prevent Dutch soldiers from being chained to bridges. Similarly, painting armoured personnel carriers white with black lettering may be appropriate for peacekeeping missions but obviously increases vulnerability.

One key problem with past UN operations has been the desire of governments, and the Secretariat, to get by on the cheap. Often, the UN Secretary-General has been asked not only to report on a given armed conflict, but also to formulate a concept of operations and to consult with potential troop contributors before the Security Council has agreed to a resolution authorizing the deployment of an intervention force. It is hard enough to get member states to commit troops and resources in the first place, and so best – rather than worst – case scenarios are usually the preferred planning device. In many cases, events on the ground quickly demonstrate the flaws in these assumptions, which are further exacerbated by media reporting and declining resolve among intervening states. According to the Panel on UN Peace Operations, this has led the Secretariat to tailor the proposed concept of operations and force level to fit within the perceived threshold of political will that the Council can muster.[17]

Realistic assessments of requirements – including a capacity to respond – consistently get lost in the political process. The ongoing debate about sending soldiers even to protect monitors in the Democratic Republic of the Congo is a case in point. "Wishful thinking" would be a generous characterization of the prospects of 5,000 lightly armed UN troops in a country that spans much of the lower part of the continent and has forces from six neighbouring countries mixed with the national army and numerous armed guerrilla movements. A genuine peace enforcement effort might require tens of thousands of troops. Because peacekeeping undoubtedly may prove to be inadequate or because a situation may deteriorate despite the presence of blue helmets, "the Secretariat must not apply best-case planning assumptions to situations where the local actors have historically exhibited worst-case behaviour."[18]

Deploying troops based on best case scenarios is not simply foolhardy or dangerous, it may even be counterproductive. In the Balkans and elsewhere, spoilers have exploited disunity among troop-contributing countries to neutralize the international presence or cause its withdrawal. At times, the weakness of the UN missions and the failure to establish authority and to provide a secure environment have led to the deployment of parallel enforcement missions in the middle of a process, such as the Unified Task Force's (UNITAF's) arrival amid UNOSOM I in Somalia, NATO's insertion of a rapid-reaction and bombing capacity amid UNPROFOR in the former Yugoslavia, and more recently the British Army in UNAMSIL in Sierra Leone.

## Exit and Entry Strategies

It has been widely advocated that intervention mandates should be converted into comprehensive campaign plans, supported by appropriate structures and the means for their implementation. Most UN peace enforcement operations are complex affairs, with a wide range of actors, including civilian administrators, international civilian police, humanitarian and development personnel, and nongovernmental organizations (NGOs). Comprehensive planning and coordination would require inputs from all the key implementing actors during the planning phase to enhance not only the overall concept of operations but also the commitment to effective implementation of those involved in the process. In reality, however, components of interventions of the 1990s have been planned in isolation. For example, during 1993–1994, mandates for conflict resolution in the Balkans were repeatedly negotiated and renegotiated within the Security Council, without a carefully developed resourcing plan. What *The Economist* ridiculed as "the confetti of resolutions" accurately summarized the discrepancy.[19]

Once an intervention is under way, there has been a tendency to adjust the vision (in terms of both scope and depth) through dialogue with a variety of international and local constituents. Some interpret this as a perfectly reasonable recognition of the "multifunctionality" of interventions and the self-evident need for post-conflict peace building. Detractors, however, are more likely to refer to the phenomenon as incrementalism and "mission creep."[20]

There are several dimensions to mission creep. Many military operations begin with fairly simple and straightforward mandates, including "benign" humanitarian ones, only to have them expanded to the pursuit of military, political, and developmental objectives as operational circumstances change or as new peace agreements and deals are struck. Mandates are inevitably adjusted in reaction to new demands during the course of an intervention. While the initial mandate may reflect a preoccupation with humanitarian actions, political and security concerns often predominate on the ground.

Furthermore, the more limited the initial vision in relation to the real problems at hand, the more likely that mission creep will take place. Somalia is a clear example where the initial response to insecurity and famine bore no relationship to longer term requirements. The follow-on UN operation (that is, UNOSOM II) included ambitious security and nation-building tasks but without commensurate means, military or otherwise, to realize them.

In traditional warfighting, military decision makers are expected to plan for the development of virtually any contingency; in international enforcement operations, they and their political masters complain or express surprise that circumstances change. Yet, mission creep has been the rule, not the exception, in the international military operations of the 1990s.

Clarity of purpose is both a prerequisite for mission success and an essential aid in judging where and when to intervene. It is also incompatible with the insistence by intervening countries and agencies to have an "exit strategy" implicitly linked to a fixed end-date. Human catastrophes, let alone war-to-peace transitions, involve long time horizons; and the desired end-states are redefined continually through active local debates, developments on the ground, and international political developments. The results are almost always different from those envisaged at the outset. This uncertainty is what drives many intervening countries and their militaries to define an exit strategy in terms of a target that is easiest to identify, namely an arbitrary date. This amounts to an exit "timetable," rather than a "strategy."

What is crucially important is having a clearly defined entry strategy that specifies the desired results, so that, once they are realized, the exit is a byproduct of success and not merely the elapse of a fixed time period. This requires detailed planning prior to military engagement, as well as the flexibility to adapt to changing circumstances in the operational theatre and internationally.

Ideally, the process of making a decision to intervene, the formulation of the mandate for the intervening agent (or combination of agents), and the allocation of structures and means for implementation should be related. For enforcement efforts, this procedure has rarely characterized the interactions between the Security Council, the Secretariat, and troop-contributing countries. It has somewhat more often characterized interactions within coalitions of the willing. However, here, too, harmonization involves welding considerably more complex interpretations of the facts on the ground and domestic interests than within a single government.

### Robust Capacity and Rules of Engagement

The common wisdom that has emerged from the past decade is that an effective intervention force should be credible and perceived as such. The credibility of operations, in turn, has depended on the belligerents' assessment of a force's capability to accomplish the mission.[21] Yet, Security Council resolutions have been strong on condemnation but weak in terms of instructions for intervening forces to deal with noncompliance by belligerents. The timorous approach of contingents deployed in the first crucial months of an intervention, more often than not, has damaged the credibility and future of UN operations and those undertaken by regional organizations. Examples range from Liberia and Somalia to Bosnia and Herzegovina.

UN-commanded operations have frequently been limited by national conceptions of command and control at the operational and tactical levels.[22] And most coalitions of the willing have been unwilling to unleash fully their warfighting capacities. Where contributions to international peace and security have required troop-contributors to pay a heavy price, multilateralism has given way to the more salient domestic political interests that usually dictate caution and risk-aversion.

Modalities for the proactive use of force have been determined more by military expediency than any sense of responsibility to protect humanitarian interests. In Bosnia, for example, those advocating military intervention typically used feasibility – meaning air strikes without casualties – as their prime argument, not moral or legal obligations. They rarely admitted the considerable risks associated with effective intervention on the ground. The real question, ultimately, was whether the West was willing to risk the lives of its soldiers in order to stop war crimes, crimes against humanity, human rights abuse, and forced migration.[23]

Shortcomings in strategy and objectives are even more apparent when it comes to coercive protection. Consider, for example, the creation of the safe areas in Bosnia in April 1992. The idea, first introduced by the president of the International Committee of the Red Cross in the summer of 1991, was to protect threatened communities in their place of residence in order to prevent armed attacks, forced population movements, harassment, and arbitrary arrests, and killings. The UN Secretary-General estimated that some 35,000 troops would be required for the protection of safe areas in Bosnia, but states approved one-fifth of that number, with results that are now infamous.[24] Far better, according to many commentators, to do nothing at all than to promise "protection" that lures victims to their death.

The Security Council has now reached the point that it is prepared explicitly to authorize UN military forces to protect civilians at risk in deadly conflicts. The first such resolution was adopted in February 2000 with reference to Sierra Leone, when the Council voted unanimously to approve the Secretary-General's plans for strengthening UNAMSIL. The resolution not only raised the maximum authorized strength from 6,000 to 11,000 in Sierra Leone, it also authorized the mission "to take the necessary action ... to afford protection to civilians under imminent threat of physical violence." Similarly, in the midst of a shaky cease-fire and highly volatile security environment in the Democratic Republic of the Congo, the Council mandated to "take the necessary action, in the areas of its deployment and as it deems within its capabilities, to protect ... civilians under imminent threat of physical violence."[25]

While these authorizations indicate that intervening forces have the right to use force to protect civilians, it is also clear that they are under no obligation to do so. And although broadening mandates and developing more robust ROEs have been welcomed in many quarters, some have argued that asking more of troops already underequipped for their existing tasks is a recipe for disaster. Indeed, the Panel on UN Peace Operations, while supporting the objective of protecting civilians, sounded a clear note of caution:

> [T]he Panel is concerned about the credibility and achievability of a blanket mandate in this area. There are hundreds of thousands of civilians in current United Nations mission areas who are exposed to potential risk of violence, and United Nations forces currently deployed could not protect more than a small fraction of them even if directed to do so ... . If an operation is given a mandate to protect civilians, therefore, it also must be given the specific resources needed to carry out that mandate.

This is wise counsel, for the record of implementation reveals that force and contingent commanders have often felt duty bound mainly to protect their own forces – at the expense of broader mission mandates and to the detriment of the safety of civilians. ROEs are critical to protecting populations at risk. They are the directions guiding the application of the use of force by soldiers in the theatre of operations. [26] The use of only minimal force in self-defence that characterizes traditional peacekeeping is clearly inappropriate for enforcers. Arresting common criminals and indicted war criminals, halting abuse, and deterring would-be killers and thugs require far more robust ROEs. The security of soldiers, aid workers, and the target population would improve if strong signals were sent to errant leaders and their supporters that mistreatment of local populations or foreign personnel would be met with deadly force. More precise ROEs for a multilateral intervention would help diminish the requirement for individual countries to issue individual clarifications for every item or exception – a serious impediment to effective joint operations.

## THE MILITARY AND ENFORCEMENT ACTION

As obvious as it sounds, well-trained and well-equipped troops are even more necessary for enforcement actions than for traditional peacekeeping. Sending poorly trained Bangladeshi troops to UNPROFOR, with inappropriate or no gear, was obviously misguided. At the same time, even the better-equipped Dutch were inappropriately deployed and supported when Srebrenica was overrun.

When Major General Romeo Dallaire requested 5,000 soldiers to help halt the genocide in Rwanda, he was not calling for seven different battalions from Bangladesh, The Netherlands, and five other countries. Setting aside for a moment the debate about the exact numbers that would have been required to make a difference, what he sought was a well-trained and well-equipped brigade. This raises the question of whether the military requirements for certain enforcement tasks would not be more readily available and reliable with a large military deployment by essentially a single state, rather than a multinational coalition. Although the approach would be potentially more open to abuse, there are cases that undoubtedly support this position, including India in East Pakistan, Tanzania in Uganda, and Vietnam in Cambodia during the 1970s; and the US in Haiti, the French in Rwanda, and the United Kingdom (UK) in Sierra Leone during the 1990s.

At the very least, it means that a multinational unit of this size should have had the kind of discipline, interoperability of first-rate equipment, and communications and transport capabilities that are now only available in NATO. Given the reductions in Western militaries since the end of the Cold War in most countries, the entire range of blue- to green-helmeted capacities necessary in April 1994 are not widely available now. Furthermore, the reluctance to sustain fatalities in humanitarian interventions complicated matters. Domestic spending priorities, the general expansion of peace operations, and the debacle in Somalia led to paralysis in the face of Rwanda's bloodshed in 1994.

The contributions of UN peacekeepers from the South have increased markedly as numbers from traditional Western troop-contributing countries have fallen. Although it is a politically sensitive subject, it is generally accepted that the effectiveness of troops from developing countries will need to be markedly improved if they are to play a prominent role in successful enforcement missions. Progress on this front is being made. There are also a number of initiatives to improve capacity, including the US effort to equip and train the African Crisis Response Initiative, the French Reinforcement of Capabilities of African Missions of Peacekeeping, and the British Military Advisory and Training Teams.

The challenges in this regard are clear; the question is whether the future will look any different from the past. The *Report of the Panel on United Nations Peace Operations* is worth citing at length:

> [T]he Secretary-General finds himself in an untenable position. He is given a Security Council resolution specifying troop levels on paper, but without knowing whether he will be given the troops to put on the ground. The troops that eventually arrive in theatre may still be underequipped: Some countries have provided soldiers without rifles, or with rifles but no helmets, or with helmets but no flak jackets, or with no organic transport capability (trucks or troops carriers). Troops may be untrained in peacekeeping operations, and in any case the various contingents in an operation are unlikely to have trained or worked together before. Some units may have no personnel who can speak the mission language. Even if language is not a problem, they may lack common operating procedures and have differing interpretations of key elements of command and control and of the mission's rules of engagement, and may have differing expectations about mission requirements for the use of force. This must stop.[27]

Not only do troops need to be well trained and well equipped, they also need to be in place quickly. The need for rapid deployment was central to the debate within the UN in the middle of the 1990s. Canada took a lead in discussions, arguing that the "critical lesson of the Rwandan experience is that modest but timely measures can make the difference between a situation which is stable or contained and one which spirals out of control."[28] Other like-minded governments joined the chorus – Denmark, The Netherlands, and Sweden also issued reports about the necessity for the UN to be in a position to have a speedy capacity to execute interventions.

Little concrete headway has been made since. A Rapidly Deployable Mission Headquarters was established at UN headquarters, but at the same time DPKO was stripped of gratis military personnel from Western countries as a result of a disagreement with developing countries over the geographical balance of military staff in New York. In the end, some would argue that DPKO is less capable now than it was some years ago.

At the same time, the standard by which rapid deployment is measured has itself deteriorated. The earliest UN operations deployed far more rapidly than contemporary ones. In the Congo, there was a mutiny against Belgian officers on July 5, 1960; and five days later, Belgium intervened to protect its nationals. The Security Council met on July 14, and the first contingents of UN troops arrived the next day; 3,500 UN troops were on the ground by July 17. Similarly for the Suez crisis, offers of assistance had been received before a General Assembly Special Session had actually mandated the peacekeeping force; the first troops were on the ground in 8 days, having been delayed somewhat by Egyptian concerns about the nature and composition of the force. Within 3 weeks, more than 2,500 UN troops were in place; and in 10 weeks, the force had reached its full strength of 6,000 troops drawn from 10 countries.[29]

In contrast, an assessment by the Carnegie Commission on Preventing Deadly Conflict claimed a two-week "window of opportunity" existed in mid-April, during which time a preventive deployment could have been successful in halting Rwanda's genocide.[30] However, the most detailed estimate, to date, about the time necessary for even a US unilateral effort in Rwanda was more than a month.[31]

## Conduct of Forces

A subject that has received relatively little attention is military conduct during humanitarian interventions. There is widespread agreement that intervening forces are subject to the rules of international humanitarian law (IHL), requiring that the use of force be discriminate and proportionate, that some types of weapons not be used, and that prisoners be treated properly.

An illustration of this principle in operation is the inquiry by the International Criminal Tribunal for the Former Yugoslavia into the conduct of NATO operations in 1999. The prosecutor decided that there was no basis on which to bring charges against anyone connected with that operation.[32] But the fact that the inquiry took place at all illustrates a concern about the legality of conduct by intervening forces. In fact, there is growing acceptance that the conduct of forces may have a decisive impact on the perceived legitimacy of an enforcement action.[33] As a result, some commentators have suggested that intervening armies and agencies may be subject to even more stringent standards than IHL,[34] though there does not seem to be support for this view in state practice.

Until recently, there was some question as to whether IHL was applicable to UN forces. Given that UN soldiers were confined to the role of traditional peacekeepers, this ambiguity was hard for many to understand. The issue was clarified, however, in a memorandum from the UN Secretary-General on August 12, 1999, explicitly extending the provisions of IHL to all UN personnel engaged in "enforcement actions, or in peacekeeping operations when the use of force is permitted in self-defence."[35] Whether the intervening forces have the legal status of "combatants" or not, it is now clear that these laws apply.

Where these norms are violated, however, there is still the challenge of enforcement. While the ad hoc tribunals – and, in the future, the International Criminal Court (ICC) – may be called on to assess the legality of military conduct, there is no common disciplinary procedure for troops that violate international norms. To date, it has been left to contributing nations to prosecute their own soldiers. While this can be done in good faith, it should be noted that if disciplinary action is not carried through, it can discredit an intervening force in the eyes of a local population and undermine civilian attempts to establish the rule of law.

## Military–Civilian Interactions

During the Cold War, there was a fair understanding of a simple division of labour whereby the UN mounted peace operations and observer missions, while regional organizations concentrated on political and diplomatic measures. The UN Transitional Authority in Cambodia, in conjunction with efforts by the Association of Southeast Asian Nations, is one example; as are a variety of UN operations in Central America, with efforts by the Contadora Group and other subregional diplomatic efforts. International enforcement simply was not an option, but this changed in the 1990s. A proliferation of devastating internal conflicts led to involvement by a number of diverse actors (governmental, intergovernmental, and nongovernmental) in attempts to resolve or ameliorate deadly conflicts at all levels.

The 1990s also marked a significant departure in humanitarian action. Warfighters and civilian humanitarians were working side by side to bring succour and protection to populations at risk. The coming together of the more hierarchical and disciplined military and the more horizontal humanitarian cultures was not without its problems. The mantra resulting from recent complex emergencies is for improved collaboration and perhaps integration among the "intervention trio" of the military, political–diplomatic elements, and humanitarian agencies.

Military decision making is based on clear and unequivocal communications and chains of command. Even for peacekeeping forces, the chain of command has been problematic, with the force commander rarely being totally in control of the behaviour of national contingents. Especially when dangerous conditions prevail, the commanders of national battalions contact their capitals before responding to so-called orders from the UN commander in the field or the Secretary-General in New York.

The requirement for clear command and control is unquestionably more important for enforcement than peacekeeping. Unity of purpose is essential when insecurity is high. Perhaps the clearest successful cases in this regard were the US leadership of coalitions of the willing in the Gulf War, Somalia, and Haiti or NATO's spearheading security efforts in post-Dayton Bosnia and Herzegovina and Kosovo. Politically the most disastrous illustration of problems resulting from a muddled chain of command occurred during the UNOSOM II operation, when the US contingent (which actually remained under American command and control) was ambushed in Mogadishu. The equivalent for air power was the dual-key operation in Bosnia, where the force commander needed the approval of the UN Special Representative Yasushi Akashi, which seldom came, in order to launch aerial attacks.

Ultimately, coordination is a topic that is a perpetual concern but about which little is actually done. Everyone is for coordination, but no one wishes to be coordinated. "Coordination" has become a hollow catchphrase to respond to fragmentation of international action in an operational area. At best, it has amounted to periodic meetings that focus on an exchange of information between international actors during the course of a mission. One official has described it as never "by command" but sometimes "by consensus" and usually "by default."[36] It seldom translates into integrated decision making on a regular basis, nor into genuine unity of effort. Coordination implies independent authorities' attempting to cooperate with each other. Despite much soul-searching, coordination has thus far amounted to little more than weak self-policing. When it works, most field-based personnel argue that coordination is based more on personalities than on standard operating procedures and structures.

The challenges here, however, may be less coordination and more a basic incompatibility of objectives. When enforcement begins, there are humanitarian consequences and tough choices about short- and long-term trade-offs. Humanitarian agencies are sensitive to the fact that political leaders have sometimes justified a failure to use deadly force in terms of the need to keep aid flowing. These agencies have been careful to reject this rationale by arguing that they do not wish to provide excuses for failure to end the causes of suffering. Moreover, even in the most insecure and unstable of circumstances, dedicated civilian humanitarians stay as long as possible. That the staff of the International Committee of the Red Cross remained in Kigali as Belgian soldiers departed or that numerous NGOs remained in Sarajevo despite snipers and rocket attacks indicates the level of commitment by many civilian humanitarian agencies to providing assistance and protection to affected local populations.

Yet, in seeking to apply deadly force, militaries may make it impossible for humanitarians to remain. Less humanitarian succour in the short run may be required in order to improve security and, ultimately, humanitarian action in the longer run. For instance, Bosnia demonstrated that "lift and strike" – eliminating the arms embargo on the Muslims and using NATO airpower against the Serbs – would have been incompatible with continued humanitarian operations. The same would have been true had it actually been possible to disarm the massive refugee camps controlled by *génocidaires* in eastern Zaire. Outside humanitarians would have been forced to abandon the camps while the mopping-up occurred.

Moreover, civilian humanitarians (like journalists) can become pawns and hostages. This line of reasoning has been used, for instance, to explain NATO's reluctance to round up prominent war criminals in post-Dayton Bosnia and Herzegovina.

### Politics and the Media

Compelling compliance with peace agreements and providing protection for civilians are relatively new tasks for the military in modern war zones. They therefore require calling into question typical procedures that have evolved in response to more traditional warfighting situations. According to the then Chair of NATO's Military Committee, General Klaus Naumann,

> [T]wo military sacred cows are on the slaughtering block. It will be virtually impossible to rely on secrecy and surprise or to make maximum use of the full and devastating power of modern weapons, traditionally key military assets. Moreover, democratic societies that are sensitive to human rights and the rule of law will no longer tolerate the pervasive use of overwhelming military power. Coalition operations will necessarily be characterised by gradualism and possibly delays in striking sensitive targets. These are lasting military disadvantages of coalition operations that are only partly compensated by the stronger political impact of such operations in comparison with those of a single country.[37]

Enforcement actions conducted by coalitions of the willing have to take into account the politics of member states and the impact of the media. While politics always intrudes on military efforts, coalition intervention in Kosovo demonstrated that the pace and intensity of military operations may be further affected by the lowest common political denominator among member states. As cohesion within in an intervening coalition is key, Greek and Italian reluctance played a role in constraining Washington and London in ways that would have been unthinkable for warfighting driven by truly vital interests. Furthermore, coalition warfare entails other restrictions on military conduct and political decision making that results from differing national legislation. In addition to the impact on the ground, the domestic conditions in 19 member states further reduced the preparedness of countries to conduct casualty-prone operations involving ground forces.

Political concerns are also important in that the use of military force may be as much about sending political messages as about securing military objectives. Many commentators point to NATO's bombing in 1995 as helping to move Belgrade closer to Dayton's negotiating table. Similarly, the 78-day campaign in the Kosovo War was designed not simply to destroy military targets but also to secure the political agreement negotiated at Rambouillet.

Modern communications and media coverage also influence enforcement in that there is a new capacity for the public to monitor the effectiveness of military operations and the impact of military action on civilians. Enforcement is likely to receive widespread public support if deadly force is applied in a way that can be, at least, tolerated by the majority of the populations in the countries of a coalition. The fallout from media coverage of civilian suffering as a result of sanctions in Iraq or of air strikes in Serbia is a new element in circumscribing military as well as political strategies.

Beyond contributing unevenly as a stimulus to intervene in a particular emergency (issues of where and when), television also has an impact on the question of how to intervene. The media are much better at focusing on the consequences of political decisions than on the rationale behind them. They are relatively incoherent when attempting to explain the political or diplomatic context in which humanitarian disasters, war crimes, crimes against humanity, or famine takes shape. Television has a tendency to focus on guns and bombs, rather than the operational plans and orders, and on the mutilated corpses, rather than the strategic goals of the "ethnic cleansers." In doing so, the media obscure the strategic context in which human suffering occurs.[38]

Television is thus something of a double-edged sword with regard to the protection of civilians in armed conflict. The media do not like to depict misery without also showing that someone is doing something about it. The presence of outside aid workers in zones of deadly conflict mitigates the horror, by suggesting that help is at hand, and affords the illusion that major powers are doing something. In this way, television coverage can also become an alternative to more serious political and military engagement, and it thus contributes to the illusion of effective engagement by Western governments. Traditional humanitarian aid sometimes precludes (and is often intended to preclude) any sort of intervention.

## COERCIVE PROTECTION

Civilians now constitute the majority of war casualties, an atrocious and alarming trend that has moved the UN Secretary-General to call for the creation of a "culture of protection" in dealing with situations of armed conflict.[39] In his March 2001 report on the protection of civilians in armed conflict, he emphasized that protection is a complex and multilayered process, involving a diversity of entities and approaches, including the delivery of humanitarian assistance, monitoring and reporting of violations of IHL and human rights law, institution-building, governance and development programmes, and ultimately the deployment of troops. Accepting the importance of all facets of the protection challenges,[40] this section nonetheless focuses on the potential role of intervening military forces.

The humanitarian missions of the 1990s are commonly seen as having been somewhat successful in the provision of material assistance to populations in need but inadequate in responding to their security needs. In far too many cases, those who received assistance ended up the "well-fed dead."[41] The words on a sign held by a Kurdish child fleeing the wrath of the Iraqi regime make the point eloquently: "We don't need food. We need safety."[42]

This critique is equally applicable to military operations in humanitarian crises. Anecdotal reports suggest that soldiers may have done more to provide protection than commonly believed. In many instances, they have pushed and even exceeded the limits of their ROEs rather than standing by and watching civilians being massacred. To cite only one example, some UNPROFOR troops were known to move into the line of fire when civilians were under attack, thereby enabling them to return fire supposedly within the bounds of self-defence. That said, the failures to provide adequate military protection to populations at risk in the 1990s are staggering.

The "safe havens" established in northern Iraq following the Gulf War represented one of the earliest efforts to implement coercive protection. The initial flight of the Kurdish population was a response to brutal suppression by Iraqi aircraft and helicopter gunships. The return of Kurdish refugees from the mountain camps along the border with Turkey depended on addressing these threats to their physical safety. In April 1991, Operation Provide Comfort created a security zone in northern Iraq. It was enforced through a no-fly zone banning Iraqi fixed-wing and helicopter flights north of the 36th latitude. Another no-fly zone was subsequently established in southern Iraq, below the 32nd parallel (and this was later expanded to the 33rd), to protect the Shi'ite population. Both no-fly zones remain in effect. While they continue to provide a modicum of protection for those living within them, they depend on deployment of US and British aircraft more than a decade after the outbreak of the crisis.

It was during the UN mission in Bosnia, however, that a much broader range of protective measures was attempted. In addition to a no-fly zone, UNPROFOR also used military force to protect aid convoys, create humanitarian corridors allowing civilians to flee areas of fighting, and establish so-called safe areas.

The air bridge established for Sarajevo allowed the population to receive essential supplies, despite the Serbian blockade – though it was repeatedly cut off by Serb fire. Convoys were escorted by UNPROFOR troops, but they could never impose access and were frequently stopped by Serb roadblocks. By deterring direct attacks, however, UNPROFOR did increase the physical safety of the convoys.[43]

Srebrenica became the first area declared "safe" in April 1993, and one month later Bihać, Goradže, Tuzla, Sarajevo, and Žepa were also included. Later resolutions authorized member states (implicitly NATO) to take all necessary measures to protect these areas. In particular, Resolution 836 (1993) included the use of air power to support UN forces on the ground. But the resolution eschewed the use of the terms "protect" or "defend," and linked the use of force instead to UNPROFOR's "acting in self-defence."[44]

UNPROFOR's overall record in protecting civilians was, at best, mixed. Although humanitarian aid reached hundreds of thousands of exposed people (more than 4 million received assistance), the creation of the security zones ultimately had perverse effects. The safe areas were almost all enclaves in Serb territory and were easy targets for aggression. At the same time, Muslim forces frequently used them to launch attacks on Serb forces, knowing that NATO could be provoked and might intervene against the Serbs in the event of return fire. Although Sarajevo was never overrun, the other safe areas fell to Serb forces. In the case of Srebrenica, at least 7,000 unarmed men and boys were murdered.

No other mission in the 1990s placed as much emphasis on protection as UNPROFOR, but several other cases are worth considering. In Liberia, following the execution of President Doe in September 1990, and with thousands of civilians trapped in Monrovia and hundreds dying daily, ECOMOG was mandated to clear the capital of rebels and make it safe. This task was accomplished by the end of December 1990, except for occasional infiltrations by the National Patriotic Front of Liberia.

Relative safety then prevailed in Monrovia until April 1996, when a bloody conflict erupted after police attempted to arrest Roosevelt Johnson, a former leader of a faction of the United Liberation Movement of Liberia for Democracy. The carnage involved civilians and children, and the widespread violence forced the evacuation of virtually all the humanitarian relief workers from the safe haven where protection had been provided for up to 1 million people. When ECOMOG troops eventually managed to separate the armed factions and gain a measure of control over the city in June 1996, health workers recovered more than 1,500 bodies from shallow graves.[45]

The prospects for coercive prevention have also been extensively debated in the context of the Rwandan genocide, especially the request by the force commander for an additional 5,000 troops only days into the genocide. With an ethnically mixed population and a bloodbath occurring in varying degrees of intensity throughout the country, there were no pre-existing "safe areas" to defend. Stopping the genocide therefore would have required halting mass displacements – many victims were identified as they passed through road-blocks. It would also have required protecting specific sites – churches, schools, stadiums – where threatened populations congregated. There is widespread acceptance that a brigade would have been able to slow or perhaps stop the genocide.[46] Although counterfactuals are hard to assess, even an assessment highly sceptical of Dallaire's claims concluded that the deployment of troops on a realistic schedule could have saved as many as 125,000 Tutsi lives.[47]

These examples from the 1990s suggest that there are a series of discrete measures to provide protection for targeted populations. Whether they actually provide much protection at all is a major point of controversy. One set of protective measures relates to the protection of humanitarian action and includes the defence of aid convoys and the maintenance of humanitarian corridors. It would also include the use of security forces to protect the storage and distribution of aid as with the controversial use of "technicals" in Somalia. A second set of measures relates to the physical protection of populations in discrete locations. Here it may be useful to distinguish between larger *safe zones*, where people remain in their homes and communities, and *safe havens*, where people from the surrounding area seeking protection congregate.[48] A related challenge is the protection of refugees in camps controlled by militants, as in eastern Zaire or West Timor.[49] Finally, there is the more complex task of providing protection in the midst of genocidal violence as in Rwanda or Sierra Leone.

Even if characterized by sufficient military force to ensure safety of civilians, the coercive protection option, by itself, does not provide a long-term political solution for those being protected. In the absence of such a solution, the commitment by outside forces to protection would need to be indefinite. This is particularly true of safe areas, which, by their very nature, represent a limited commitment in circumstances in which the intervening force lacks either the capacity or the will to alter the political situation (that is, the one giving rise to the fears of repression in the first place). That limitation is often reflected in the administration of, and the protection afforded to, such a safe area, which is why safe areas have often been so vulnerable. It is also why many advocates for the displaced have argued that flight from a country of persecution is preferable to border safe areas.

### Toward a Doctrine of Protection

National policy guidelines for participation in peace support operations continue to stress the need for a "comprehensive and lasting solution" as a precondition for involvement, but a more modest assessment of the attainable goals of military intervention to sustain humanitarian objectives is beginning to emerge. It revolves around the idea that military support can be used to create "humanitarian space" – including, but not limited to, security zones and safe corridors.

Doctrinal thinkers within the military have yet to create a systematic framework for intervention for the protection of civilian populations. The NATO manual on peace support operations includes a section entitled "The Protection of Humanitarian Operations and Human Rights" and another entitled "The Establishment and Supervision of Protected or Safe Areas." The NATO doctrine states that,

> Should the situation be such that humanitarian operations require wide spread protection and human rights abuses are endemic, then a PE [peace enforcement] profile will be more appropriate [than a peacekeeping profile]. The foremost task for the military force may be to restore the peace and create a stable and secure environment in which aid can run freely and human rights abuses are curtailed. Specific protection tasks may include Non-combatant Evacuation Operations … but will more normally apply to the protection of convoys, depots, equipment and those workers responsible for their operation.

This encapsulates the full spectrum of possible military tasks in support of humanitarian goals, from guarding and escorting to the stabilization of a whole area of operations. Yet, the manual does not actually address how these tasks are to be accomplished. Similarly, for establishing and supervising protected or safe areas, the NATO manual observes that,

> Unless those within the safe area are disarmed, it may be used as a base from which to sally out and conduct raids. Clear guidance should be given, therefore, as to what is demanded of any force that is tasked with establishing and supervising a protected or safe area … . The first stage in any PSO [peace-support operation] designed to protect or make an area safe is to demilitarize that area and this in itself may require enforcement actions.[50]

Others have also considered matters of protection in the revision of military doctrine. The British Army is involved in a continuous reappraisal of their peace support operations doctrine, based on their experience in low-level operations in support of the civilian power. Other European nations, such as Sweden, have also captured their recent military experiences in similar national doctrines. However, their doctrines still tend to be based on multifunctional peacekeeping, with its emphasis on multiple actors and the need for end-states defined as "sustainable peace."

While far more "robust" than any guidelines that have emanated from the UN Secretariat, accepting as it does a notion of enforcement, the doctrine still hinges on consent. Some analysts have suggested that the issue of consent be resolved on a situation-specific basis.[51] For example, if the military threat posed by noncooperating belligerents is limited to small-scale resistance, banditry, and looting and the principal parties to a conflict remain committed to an agreement, an intervention force may be empowered to confront such a marginal threat directly. Even against more effective forces, enforcement action does not necessarily increase the risk to intervening troops. There is evidence, for example, that the more robust stance taken by British and Danish UNPROFOR troops gained them increased respect from the warring factions.

Similarly, if threats to civilians come principally from private militias and isolated thugs, a more robust response by intervening forces to protect civilians may not encounter serious counterattacks. For instance, even in the horror of Rwanda's genocide, with virtually no military presence on the ground, a few UN peacekeepers managed to protect some 10,000 civilians in Kigali's Amahoro Stadium and King Faisal Hospital.

If consent is no longer a definitive and distinguishing feature of multilateral engagement in deadly conflicts, then current approaches are in need of urgent revision. Some analysts have suggested that the concept of legitimacy should replace consent as the foundation for intervention, arguing that it provides a more feasible doctrinal basis for interventions where the conditions for either supervising a peace agreement or compelling the parties to peace cannot be met.[52]

Another new point of departure for conceptualizing multilateral military interventions could be described as a "law-based" approach, rather than one based on the elusive notion of peace. There is clearly a difference between a temporary peace that may be achieved through coercion and a more durable peace that involves aspects of legitimacy, political participation, social integration, and economic development. However, it is difficult, if not impossible, to begin the long path to the higher, more dynamic aspects of peace before the lower aspects of law and order are met.[53] In addition, it may be politically more feasible for outside military forces and their political masters to commit themselves to providing a breathing space, rather than the peace that can ultimately only be ensured by local actors.

In some respects, the provision of protection can be likened to the enforcement of international legal instruments such as the Geneva Conventions. Military organizations worldwide remain extremely reluctant to engage in anything akin to policing functions, and crime remains an overlooked issue in military doctrinal thinking.[54] Nevertheless, the singular strand that would pull together various mission components dealing with protection, human rights, and security issues is a conception of intervention to enforce international law writ large.

This seemingly obvious but profound general principle was identified by the Joint Evaluation of Emergency Assistance to Rwanda: "[R]espect for international law and norms will tend to diminish conflict, whereas violations will tend to stoke it." The report continues, "[T]he behaviour of state and presumptive state actors was in this respect less than adequate, and mostly counter-productive." The evaluation identified the following shortcomings: international law and associated principles designed to uphold international order were repeatedly violated, including the sanctity of national borders and arms embargoes; international refugee law was not observed; the legal right and moral obligation to intervene to stop genocide were not acted on; human rights law was repeatedly and severely transgressed with impunity; and donors continued to give economic aid and even military assistance to a government linked to systematic violations of human rights.[55]

Olara Otunnu, the Special Representative of the Secretary-General (SRSG) for Children and Armed Conflict, has summarized the case for the logic of intervention to enforce international law in the following way:

> Over the past 50 years, the countries of the world have developed an impressive body of international human rights and humanitarian instruments … . The impact of these instruments remains woefully thin on the ground, however. Words on paper cannot save children and women in peril. The Special Representative believes that the time has come for the international community to redirect its energies from the juridical task of the elaboration of norms to the political project of ensuring their application and respect on the ground.[56]

If military intervention for humanitarian objectives is viewed as an exercise in enforcing international law, then the principles and practices for the conduct of military operations become clearer and logically more consistent. Reduced to its simplest terms, the law to be enforced during an intervention is defined by the mandate, but it would necessarily also include general tenets of IHL and human rights law. According to this line of argument, military intervention to enforce international law is a precursor to broader peace building.

The implications of a macro-strategic shift from peace enforcement to international law enforcement would no doubt provoke a vigorous debate among military practitioners and doctrinal thinkers, as well as humanitarian and human rights agencies. But by accepting, at the political level, the concept of intervention as the enforcement of international law, the military's desire for clear overarching strategic rationale could be satisfied.

## SUSTAINING PEACE AND PROTECTION

"Post-conflict peace building" has entered the working vocabulary of practitioners and analysts alike. Beginning with the call in *An Agenda for Peace*,[57] many bilateral and multi-lateral agencies, including the Washington-based financial institutions that formerly had avoided war zones, have moved closer to the coal face of active hostilities. The motivation is two-fold. First, there is a mammoth need to rebuild war-torn societies. And second, there is a preventive perspective. Successful humanitarian intervention may halt killing and provide temporary security. But in order to forestall a return to the status quo ante, it is necessary to provide enough breathing space for a local society to begin mending wounds and for the state to begin functioning again.

This is not the place to review the litany of challenges of post-conflict peace building. A section in the bibliography in Part II is devoted to the various dimensions of this complex subject. But two topics that are closely linked, both temporally and substantively, to compelling peace and to providing protection merit attention here. They provide distinct operational challenges for military forces engaged in international enforcement actions. The first involves the transition from coalitions of the willing during an enforcement phase to a less insecure phase in which the UN and other multilateral agencies may assume a range of responsibilities, including aspects of physical security. The second is the related topic of a comprehensive, if temporary, international takeover of responsibility for government functions.

## Post-Enforcement Transitions

One of the conclusive trends from the 1990s is the UN's devolution of authority for enforcement. During a humanitarian intervention, the UN usually takes a back seat in operations even if the Security Council is involved in authorizing and monitoring the effort. However, it is necessary to move toward post-conflict operations in which the world organization and other intergovernmental bodies have a more substantial role. States providing outside military forces are anxious to reduce their presence. Moreover, it is desirable to mobilize as many intergovernmental and nongovernmental resources as possible for what hopefully is the beginning of a post-conflict phase.

There have been four general types of transitions following the non-UN enforcement actions of the 1990s. All have substantial humanitarian dimensions that should be kept in mind in attempting to think about how best to sustain peace and protection.

The first is illustrated by the continuing effort by Washington and London to enforce the no-fly zone in northern Iraq – that is, there has been no transition. After the initial deployment of the UN Guards Contingent in Iraq, there has been no UN security presence on the ground. However, UN and NGO humanitarian and development agencies maintain modest activities.

The second type of transition involves an awkward and largely problematic transition to a UN operation. The end of the US-led United Task Force (UNITAF) led to the hasty handover to UNOSOM II, and this Chapter VII UN operation itself left the country without a functioning government in 1995. In Rwanda, after two months, the French Opération Turquoise handed over the international military portfolio to a renewed UN Assistance Mission in Rwanda, which itself was asked to leave by the government, a year later; but, in this case, the government was in a position to guarantee services and security. In Liberia, the transition from ECOMOG enforcement to the unarmed UN Observer Mission in Liberia was without incident, but it also left a fledgling new government without security on the ground.

A third type of transition represents a preferable scenario – the relatively smooth transition to a comprehensive UN mission. In Haiti, there was a relatively rapid if somewhat turbulent handover from the US's MNF, after six months, to a Chapter VI UN Mission in Haiti, which successfully helped oversee elections and the installation of a new government, as well as continued efforts to reform the security sector. The Australian-led enforcement effort through INTERFET smoothly handed over security and administrative responsibilities after four months to the UN Transitional Administration in East Timor. Similarly, although with less security as a result, in Sierra Leone there was a side-by-side presence of ECOMOG with UNAMSIL, with the remaining ECOMOG soldiers becoming part of UNAMSIL. Security deteriorated after the transition until bilateral assistance was provided by the UK, and subsequently, the UN's troop strength was doubled.

Finally, a fourth pattern occurred in the Balkans, in which coalition forces remained while the UN returned. With IFOR and SFOR in Bosnia, as well the Kosovo Force in Kosovo, NATO soldiers remained behind in great numbers to provide security while the UN and other intergovernmental organizations began administering the two areas.

Four analytically distinct kinds of protection tasks emerge from these post-enforcement experiences that are worth highlighting here. The first is the physical protection of minorities. This operational challenge is particularly important when civilians return to territories where another ethnic group is in the majority and there are antagonisms between or among them.

The relatively low number of refugees and internally displaced persons who have returned is telling in the Balkans. In Bosnia, the UN High Commissioner for Refugees reported that it

> faced enormous difficulties in trying to implement what has turned out to be one of the most contentious provisions of the Dayton Peace Agreement: the return of refugees and displaced people to their homes in Bosnia and Herzegovina... . Regrettably, the return of many other people was blocked by the leaders of Bosnia's divided communities, some of whom openly pursued in peace the same policy of ethnic separation which they had previously pursued during the war.[58]

The defence of the Serbian minority in post-war Kosovo is another striking recent example. In a June 2001 report to the Security Council, the UN Secretary-General reported that ethnic and political violence posed "a tangible threat to the fulfillment of the UNMIK [UN Interim Administration Mission in Kosovo] mandate." The increase in tensions in both predominantly Serb cities like Mitrovica and mixed ones like Pristina "have resulted in both loss of life and a severe limitation on freedom of movement, particularly for the Kosovo Serb community... . Largely as a result of the security situation, the number of returns remains minimal, and indeed in some areas more Kosovo Serbs are leaving Kosovo than returning."[59]

The second major protection task is security sector reform. The focus of such tasks has been to assist local authorities in their own process of security sector transformation. Bilateral and multilateral donors alike have sought to influence the direction of change, establish good practices, and transfer knowledge and insights to the new authorities. The importance as well as the difficulty of such efforts to recruit and train local police and reform the penal and judiciary systems has been evident in places as diverse as Haiti, Rwanda, and Bosnia. The problems are especially difficult in situations where trained personnel have been killed or fled in large numbers to avoid violence. Such reform is essential both to ensure public safety and to gain the confidence of the local population. As one first-hand observer has summarized, "Without accountable criminal investigative procedures, trained judges and lawyers, and prisons that adhere to fundamental human rights standards, police reform would be redundant."[60]

In this respect, an interim challenge concerns the use of civilian police. In fact, civilian police now number second only to soldiers in UN operations. In light of the post-war conflicts and need for impartiality, the Panel on UN Peace Operations notes that "[d]emand for civilian police operations dealing with intra-State conflict is likely to remain high on any list of requirements for helping a war-torn society restore conditions for social, economic and political stability."[61] The difficulty of recruiting international police is a central and crucial bottleneck, particularly in light of the need to reform and restructure local police forces in addition to advising, training, and monitoring new recruits.

Until recently, these efforts at security sector reform have been predicated on the ongoing consent of belligerents. In the case of Angola, for example, the third UN Angola Verification Mission was established by Resolution 976 (1995), which indicated that compliance by the parties was optional, or at least not compulsory. From the start, even this demand was patently ignored by the Union for the Total Independence of Angola, while no direct reference was made to the safety of local civilians.

The third main task concerns disarmament, demobilization, and reintegration (DD&R) of former warring factions. Reintegration is key to longer term peace building, and ultimately the resumption of the path to economic and social development. However, the focus here is on the shorter term, namely, on the security and protection of civilians. At the same time, an early, generous, vocal, and genuine commitment to reintegration and development can also have a beneficial short-term impact on the success of DD&R.

As reflected in Security Council resolutions and mission mandates, one key to stabilization has always been the demobilization of former combatants. Another aspect of the same challenge is to reconstitute, or create, a new national armed forces, which integrates, if possible, elements of the former armed forces with formerly competing factions or militias. The unstated purpose of stabilization measures has been to wrest power and the means of violence from local militias and warlords and recentralize it. In other words, the success of the whole intervention process has hinged on the degree to which warring factions can be effectively disarmed.[62] However, disarmament has been one of the most difficult tasks to implement. It has been extremely hard to collect all weapons, even at the end of an armed struggle, when the remaining conditions of insecurity create high incentives for the maintenance and acquisition of light weapons and small arms by the community at large. Physical security and economic needs have fuelled a trade in small arms long after withdrawals of intervention forces.

All disarmament commitments in peace processes have tended, at least at the outset, to be based on consent, regardless of whether external forces are deployed under a Chapter VI or VII mandate. However, the idea of voluntary disarmament is soon challenged by issues such as the security and economic livelihood of combatants thinking about turning in their weapons, along with the normally deficient number of peace support forces who are supposed to collect the arms. Faced with noncompliance with the disarmament provisions of the mandate, intervention forces have exhibited two basic reactions. The first is acquiescence in the face of local recalcitrance, combined with a shift in the mandate that allows the peace process to proceed regardless. The second approach has been to apply limited coercion to reluctant parties, while attempting to preserve the consensual nature of the intervention at the strategic level.

Cambodia and Angola provide classic examples of the acquiescent approach, while Somalia and, to an extent, Bosnia are examples of attempted coercion. Regional and UN operations in West Africa are characterized by a perplexing mixture of coercion and acquiescence, while the approach to disarmament and security challenges in Rwanda defies logic. None of these examples, however, provides positive conclusions about the ability of intervening military forces to improve the protection of civilians at risk by reducing arms available to local soldiers, militias, and gangs. In fact, the cases of Somalia and Srebrenica suggest that if this is not possible, it may be better not to pursue disarmament at all.[63] Intervention forces with a disarmament mandate have not been provided with the doctrinal, political, and military discretion to pursue an effective coercive strategy.

The fourth security task during the transition relates to the pursuit of war criminals. The details of the ongoing criminal proceedings for Rwanda and the former Yugoslavia were analyzed earlier. What is worth mentioning here is the possible new demand on military and police forces. Both during and immediately following enforcement actions, they may be required to locate and round up indicted war criminals without the consent of local political authorities. NATO commanders and politicians have been hesitant to pursue and arrest such criminals in the Balkans because of the possible hostility and violent reactions of local populations. Hence, some indicted criminals remain in hiding or are even allowed to live openly. According to the International Crisis Group, in many Republika Srpska municipalities,

> individuals alleged to have committed violations of international humanitarian law during the 1992–1995 war – mass murder, ethnic cleansing, and mass rape – remain in positions of power. They continue to work in the police force, hold public office, exercise power through the legal and illegal economy, or influence politics from behind the scenes. In eastern Republika Srpska in particular, many of these "small fish," who served in the local Serb wartime administrations and military units that carried out the policies of ethnic cleansing, remain a frightening force, often actively working to prevent refugee return and moves towards ethnic reconciliation.[64]

This operational challenge posed by the pursuit of war criminals is likely to grow with the establishment of additional country tribunals and burgeoning activities of the ICC.

### Protectorates and Nation-Building

During the mid-1990s, a proposal to address the longer term peace building challenges frequently made by academics – particularly in the context of failed states – was the reactivation of the UN Trusteeship Council. The idea was largely dismissed out of hand by donor and target countries alike. Because of the inherent paternalism and the daunting challenges of nation-building, the resurrection of trusteeship seemed as obvious as it was impossible.

Yet, by the end of the decade, following interventions in Kosovo and East Timor, similar approaches were not merely under discussion but were actually implemented. In both cases, the previous governmental authorities (the Federal Republic of Yugoslavia and Indonesia) withdrew their security forces. Their sovereign authority over the territories in question was suspended, but before functions of new local governments were in place.[65] The UN was therefore tasked, not only with constructing or reconstructing law and order, but also with a whole range of issues from day-to-day policing tasks to the long-term establishment of the criminal-justice triad of police, judiciaries, and penal systems, as well as the development of new legal codes. As one analyst has noted, "All of this points toward an international change comparable to decolonization, but operating in reverse gear, a counter-reformation of international trusteeship."[66]

Although elements of assistance to civilian authorities had been present in UN efforts in Namibia and Cambodia, the extensiveness and likely duration of the world organization's activities in Kosovo and East Timor are such that they are qualitatively different. Somewhat paradoxically, it was the Somalia experience that led to a realization that international responses to complex emergencies require substantially more than the use of force. The sources of deadly conflict are political, and a political capacity in the field is required to address them. In retrospect, there was hardly a better case for UN trusteeship than Somalia, because the state ceased to exist in anything but name. In contrast, bombing campaigns in the Balkans were eventually replaced by troops, civilian police, and administrators, as part of a massive effort to help mend societies and allow civil society and government authority to begin anew.

Historical analogies are always problematic, but analysts are naturally drawn to thinking about the Allied occupation of Germany and Japan immediately following the Second World War. The scale of destruction and displacement there would resemble that resulting from many internal armed conflicts of the 1990s. There were factors that facilitated progress in Germany and Japan that are missing from contemporary war zones – for instance, unconditional surrender gave more leeway; highly literate populations facilitated a rapid turnaround; and the Allied commitment to reestablish friendly state structures was serious and based on hard *Realpolitik* calculations. Nonetheless, today's thriving democracies and economies in Germany and Japan suggest the possibilities for, and payoff from, externally sponsored but temporary nation-building under appropriate circumstances. In addition to clear goals, cooperation among the allies, and substantial investments, according to one commentator the success can also be explained by "persistence in the face of inner doubts, resistance to external criticism, and acceptance of the glacial pace inherent to the process."[67]

Engagement in such a comprehensive peace building agenda is predicated on the assumption that military enforcement action has previously created a sufficiently secure macro-security environment for such projects to succeed. But the advent of multifunctional missions meant there were special command and control and harmonization problems, as separate elements functioned more independently than holistically to address the myriad problems. Therefore, a political capacity was required, not only to address the political sources of conflict on the ground, but also to unify the international efforts in the field – what has been labelled "peace maintenance."[68]

Coordination between these political entities and the military forces preparing to depart is particularly important. Informed by the experiences of Haiti and other complex crises, the US developed Presidential Decision Directive 56 on Managing Complex Contingency Operations. It was first used in Eastern Slovenia and Kosovo. The UK established a Joint Defence Centre to promote joint civil–military doctrine. NATO updated its peace operations doctrine along similar lines. And the Organization of African Unity has expressed interest in developing a comparable doctrine.[69]

Perhaps the most unusual aspect of transitional administration has been experiments to overcome serious previous shortcoming in interventions – namely links to local communities. In both Kosovo and East Timor, post-intervention efforts represent more of a longer term international commitment to helping the target areas and affected local populations to get back on their collective feet, a substantially new way to approach the responsibility to protect affected populations after an intervention. Criticized by some as "neocolonialist," nonetheless the necessary tasks of helping to mend war-torn societies have clearly emerged as an international, as well as local, priority.

The legitimate participation of local communities throughout a significant international transitional period is an old problem that seems to be emerging as a new international puzzle to solve. By the end of the 1990s, outside efforts to address human catastrophes began to include international missions to assume temporarily exclusive responsibility and administer an area directly in a governorship capacity. Or such transitional missions may assume responsibilities of a transitional process but not conduct all the tasks of governance directly. To date, there have been four categories of help:

❏ *Governorship* – The transitional authority assumes full responsibilities of government, as was done in Eastern Slovenia, Mostar, Brčko, Kosovo, and East Timor. This may occur after a collapse of state structures, either as the result of violent conflict or a natural disaster, or with the disappearance of structures imposed by a colonial or occupying power that has withdrawn.

❏ *Control* – A transitional authority may have been authorized under a mandate to exercise the powers of "direct control," as in Cambodia.

❏ *Partnership* – The local authority may be powerful and have adequate resources because it is a colonial power repatriating, another kind of occupation force withdrawing, or a totalitarian regime submitting itself to a democratizing process. In this case, the transitional authority behaves more as a partner of the local authority, as the UN did in Namibia.

❏ *Assistance* – The local administration may not be in complete disarray, and the transitional authority provides some overall coherence and an international standard for the development of governance structures.

Within such efforts, the international team's leadership – at national, regional, and district levels – is essential to the successful accomplishment of a mandate. The transitional administrator is the chief executive officer of an international mission and may be referred to as an SRSG (Somalia, Cambodia, and Haiti); High Representative (Bosnia); supervisor (Brčko); administrator (Mostar); or transitional administrator (Eastern Slovenia, Kosovo, and East Timor). In some essentially military cases, a force commander may also be the chief executive officer (UNITAF in Somalia, INTERFET in East Timor). In the structure of political authority and civil administration, one of the most important positions next to the national leader is the regional-level administrator. This individual may be referred to as a regional administrator (initially in Kosovo), provincial director (Cambodia), zone director (Somalia), district administrator (East Timor), or, in military areas, the sector commander (Bosnia). The next level is the district one, which is the base of the structure of political authority and civil administration, and here the transitional administrator is the district administrator, who is the frontline of administration and the one on whom the maintenance of law and order and the pacific settlement of disputes rests. Perhaps the most critical task requiring an alliance between the district office, international NGOs, and the local community is the use of force, either in a policing capacity to quell disorder, violence, or criminality or in a military capacity to ensure the delivery of food or respond to a challenge for a warring faction.

Past experience demonstrates that if the internal-security challenge is not handled early, "old" habits and structures will prevail and undermine other efforts to enhance post-conflict peace building. The immediate aftermath of any civil war spawns organized crime, revenge attacks, arms proliferation, looting, and theft. UN civilian police officers deployed alongside peacekeepers to assist in the resuscitation of national law enforcement agencies have not been equipped to address law enforcement in a "not crime–not war" environment. The military has remained the only feasible instrument, although this reality often has been obscured by the simplistic notion of peace as the antithesis of war.

Since 1999, the UN has experienced serious problems with law enforcement in Kosovo and East Timor, as a result of the absence of an "applicable law." The 2000 report from the Panel on UN Peace Operations thus recommended that, where such a situation arises, a model "UN interim criminal code" could fill the vacuum until there is an applicable law to be enforced by peacekeepers. The UN Secretary-General subsequently indicated that he has appointed a team of legal experts "to conduct a needs assessment of the areas in which it would be feasible and useful to draft a simple, common set of interim procedures," rather than a comprehensive criminal code.[70]

In order to provide an institutional framework for civilian personnel in Kosovo, the Special Representative, acting in terms of Resolution 1244, passes "laws" in the form of regulations to govern the province. These ad hoc regulations are intended to deal with specific situations ranging from policing, the appointment of judges, the arrest and detention of criminal offenders, taxes and custom duties, fiscal and monetary policies, among others. However, this arrangement, as well as the notion of an interim criminal code or interim policing procedures is delinked from the military deployment. At the same time, the UN Secretary-General has recognized that "[i]nternationally recognized standards of protection will be effectively upheld only when they are given the force of law, and when violations are regularly and reliably sanctioned."[71]

Limiting the adverse economic impact following interventions is also an emerging priority. Where situations of conflict have been severe enough to merit multinational humanitarian interventions, traditional economic practices and subsistence patterns will undoubtedly have been disrupted. In addition to understanding how those traditional patterns are reflected in the organization of disputing groups, peace operations should be conducted with a self-conscious sense of how their presence distorts local practices and values.

Peace operations introduce goods – like food supplies – that would be otherwise unavailable to local populations, and they inject foreign exchange that can distort the fragile local economy. In such a context, it is important to be sensitive to the effects of such infusions. Care should be taken that the relative abundance of goods and money in a peace operation does not get turned to socially destructive ends. Profiteering, exploitation, and illegal activities are all likely to accompany such distortions. Under "normal" circumstances business activities and patterns of reciprocity within the local society may be quite different from what members of peace operations are used to in their own countries and cultures. Hence, distinguishing between damaging distortions and appropriate activities presents a challenge. Understanding as fully as possible local business and economic practices is necessary in order not to reproduce situations of dependency and partisanship. There is a growing academic literature on these problems.[72]

### Peace or Protection?

Providing enough security and space for societies to mend themselves after a humanitarian intervention may be so overwhelming as to frighten even the most committed internationalists. The military costs alone of maintaining the no-fly zone in northern Iraq approach $500 million annually, and those of the 30,000-plus soldiers in Bosnia and 50,000 or so linked to Kosovo are estimated to be some $4 billion annually. The political will to maintain such security efforts – both financial and military – are, to say the least, a potent challenge for politicians and humanitarians alike. Sustaining accompanying efforts to administer a protectorate in Kosovo or a similar trusteeship in East Timor for as long as a generation adds to the burden of mobilizing will and resources to protect civilians following interventions elsewhere. "Donor fatigue" or "compassion weariness" are disputed by some, but the fact that they have such currency suggests at least some basis among publics and parliaments.

Humanitarians argued throughout the 1990s that humanitarian action is no substitute for politics, but how sustainable are such comprehensive transition efforts to maintain peace and protection? Undoubtedly other future cases will require protectorates, but will governments accept responsibility for enforcement efforts to compel compliance with a peace agreement? As there will undoubtedly be cases where the answer is "no," it is all the more important that coercive protection measures be considered. Even when vital interests are not engaged and comprehensive deployments are not possible, there may still be a chance that someone will act and make a difference to the lives of affected populations.

Providing protection entails a lower threshold of military resources and political commitment than compelling compliance with an imposed peace, but coercive protection can make a difference. This is not to underestimate the difficulties – the preceding analyses have demonstrated numerous operational problems for coercive protection. However, the modified "do something" approach can save lives and provide the chance that a functioning sovereign state reemerges as the provider of protection.

Here it may be useful to reconsider the case of Rwanda, the case that has framed assessments of humanitarian intervention. There was no robust intervention, and there certainly has been no substantial international protectorate. Nevertheless, a modicum of security and state services has returned, despite the tragic events of 1994. Would it not be possible to imagine the same outcome, but with slightly more robust and timely international responses in that fateful year that might have slowed the momentum of the genocide, prevented the flight of millions, and saved a few hundred thousand lives?

## NOTES

1   Pär Eriksson, "Civil–Military Co-ordination in Peace Support Operations – An Impossible Necessity?" *Journal of Humanitarian Assistance*, posted on September 16, 2000, http://www.jha.ac/articles/a061.htm, p. 2.

2   Organization for Economic Co-operation and Development, *Civilian and Military Means of Providing and Supporting Humanitarian Assistance during Conflict: Comparative Advantages and Costs* (Paris: Organization for Economic Co-operation and Development, 1998), Conflict, Peace, and Development Co-operation Report No. 1.

3   Adam Roberts, Humanitarian Action in War (New York: Oxford University Press, 1996), Adelphi Paper 305, pp. 8–9.

4   John Mackinlay and Jarat Chopra, "Second Generation Multinational Operations," *The Washington Quarterly* 15, no. 3 (1992), pp. 113–131; and John Mackinlay and Jarat Chopra, *A Draft Concept of Second Generation Multinational Operations* (Providence: Watson Institute, 1993).

5   UK Inspector General Doctrine and Training, *Wider Peacekeeping: Army Field Manual No. 5, Operations Other Than War* (London: Her Majesty's Stationery Office, 1995); Supreme Headquarters Allied Powers Europe, *NATO Doctrine for Peace Support Operations. Allied Command Europe* (Mons: Supreme Headquarters Allied Powers Europe, 1994); and US Army, *US Army Field Manual (FM) 100-23, Peace Operations* (Washington, DC: Department of the Army, 1994).

6   Boutros Boutros-Ghali, *An Agenda for Peace* (New York: United Nations, 1992).

7   For an overview of traditional peacekeeping, see Marrack Goulding, "The Evolution of United Nations Peacekeeping, " *Journal of International Affairs* 69, no. 3 (1993), pp. 451–464, quote at p. 457.

8   *Report of the Panel on United Nations Peace Operations*, UN Document A/55/305, S/2000/809, August 21, 2000, para. 50.

9   Barbara Crossette, "UN Details Its Failure to Stop '95 Bosnia Massacre," *New York Times*, November 16, 1999; and United Nations, *Report of the Secretary-General Pursuant to General Assembly Resolution 53/35: The Fall of Srebrenica*, A/54/549, November 15, 1999.

10  The judicious use of force entails a number of operational enforcement options, such as "graduated military power" escalations to deal with noncomplying belligerents. For a "menu" of escalation responses and discussion on the risks to credibility of graduating forceful responses, see Charles H. Swannack, Jr. and David R. Gray, "Peace Enforcement Operations," *Military Review* (November–December 1997), pp. 7–8.

11    John Mackinlay, "Improving Multifunctional Forces," *Survival* 6, no. 3 (Autumn 1994), pp. 150–151.

12    Kofi Annan, *Peace Operations and the United Nations: Preparing for the Next Century*, unpublished paper, February 1996.

13    *Report of the Panel on United Nations Peace Operations*, para. 53.

14    United Nations, *Report of the Secretary-General on the Causes of Conflict and the Promotion of Durable Peace and Sustainable Development in Africa*, UN Document A/52/871-S/1998/318, para. 20.

15    Paul Williams and Michael Scharf, "The Letter of the Law," in Ben Cohen and George Stamksoki, eds., *With No Peace to Keep … United Nations Peacekeeping and the War in the former Yugoslavia* (London: Grainpress Ltd., 1995), pp. 34–41.

16    John A. MacInnis, "The Rules of Engagement for U.N. Peacekeeping Forces in Former Yugoslavia: A Response," *Orbis* 39, no. 1 (Winter 1995), p. 99.

17    The Panel is quite frank on this issue, stating that, "The Secretariat must tell the Security Council what it needs to know, not what it wants to hear, when formulating or changing mission mandates, and countries that have committed military units to an operation should have access to Secretariat briefings to the Council on matters affecting the safety and security of their personnel, especially those meetings with implications for a mission's use of force." Ibid., p. x.

18    Ibid.

19    "In Bosnia's Fog," *The Economist*, April 23, 1994, p. 16.

20    Ericsson distinguishes between the interrelated concepts of "conflict creep" and "mission creep." Conflict creep occurs where the character of the conflict changes when the parties withdraw their consent to an intervention. Mission creep is experienced when the tasks of the intervening forces are expanded (often as a result of the withdrawal of consent) without a corresponding change in their mandate and resources. See Pär Eriksson, "Civil–Military Co-ordination in Peace Support Operations," p. 9.

21    Examining several peace support operations over the past nine years that "exemplify success," Daniel and Hayes conclude that, "The common thread throughout these examples is the quick deployment of robust forces which, possibly through shock effect, implicitly if not explicitly deliver the message that they mean business." Donald C.F. Daniel and Bradd C. Hayes, *Securing Observance of UN Mandates through the Employment of Military Forces* (Newport: US Naval War College, 1995). The Unified Task Force, Opération Turquoise, Provide Comfort, and Restore Democracy are cited as operations that succeeded in successfully inducing cooperation from belligerents.

22    Multilateralism implies a commitment to the principles governing the conduct of relations among states, as stipulated in the UN Charter. Inasmuch as it reflects a commitment to international principles, multilateralism tends to confer legitimacy on the military actions of nations – when the latter are authorized by the Security Council.

23    Tobias Vogel, "The Politics of Humanitarian Intervention," *Journal of Humanitarian Assistance*. Available at http://www-jha.sps.cam.ac.uk/a/a018.htm; posted on September 3, 1996.

24    United Nations, *Report of the Secretary-General Pursuant to General Assembly Resolution 53/35: The fall of Srebrenica*, UN Document A/54/549, November 15, 1999, pp. 17–18.

25    UN Document S/2000/1291.

26    Force commanders not only operationalize rules of engagement but usually dictate them. For example, this was the case for UN peacekeepers in Bosnia and Herzegovina. See both Bruce D. Berkowitz, "Rules of Engagement for UN Peacekeeping Forces in Bosnia," *Orbis* 38, no. 4 (Fall 1994), pp. 635–646; and John A. MacInnis, "The Rules of Engagement for UN Peacekeeping Forces in Former Yugoslavia: A Response," *Orbis* 39, no. 1 (Winter 1995), pp. 97–100.

27    *Report of the Panel on United Nations Peace Operations*, paras. 108–109.

28    Government of Canada, *Towards a Rapid Reaction Capability for the United Nations* (Ottawa: Government of Canada, September 1995), p. iv.

29    Alan James, *Politics of Peacekeeping* (London: Chatto and Windus, Ltd., 1969), pp. 355 and 99.

30    Carnegie Commission on Preventing Deadly Conflict, *Preventing Deadly Conflict – Final Report* (Washington, DC: Carnegie Commission on Preventing Deadly Conflict, 1997), p. 6.

31    Alan Kuperman, *The Limits of Humanitarian Intervention* (Washington, DC; US Institute of Peace, 2001), pp. 63–77.

32    The Report of the inquiry to the Prosecutor is published in *International Legal Materials* 39 (2000), p. 1257. The Prosecutor's conclusions are set out in her speech to the Security Council; Record of the 1450th Meeting of the UN Security Council, June 2, 2000; UN Document S/PV.4150, p. 3, col. 1.

33    Peter Baehr argues that the following conditions should be fulfilled within a legitimate humanitarian intervention: 1) the purpose is clear and public from the outset; 2) the use of force should be limited to what is necessary for the stated purpose; 3) IHL should be fully complied with; 4) the effects on the target country should be limited to the minimum necessary to attain the stated purpose; 5) full reporting to the Security Council; and 6) care to ensure transition to subsequent peace building. See International Peace Academy, *Humanitarian Action: A Symposium Study* (New York: International Peace Academy, 2000), pp. 4–5.

34    See Independent International Commission on Kosovo, *Kosovo Report: Conflict, International Response, Lessons Learned* (Oxford: Oxford University Press, 2000), p. 165.

35    Secretary-General's Bulletin, "Observance by United Nations Forces of International Humanitarian Law," UN Document ST/SGB/199/13, para. 1.

36    Antonio Donini, *The Policies of Mercy: UN Coordination in Afghanistan, Mozambique, and Rwanda* (Providence: Watson Institute, 1996), Occasional Paper #22, p. 14.

37    Klaus Naumann, "NATO, Kosovo, and Military Intervention," *Global Governance* 8, no. 1 (January–March 2002), forthcoming.

38    Michael Ignatieff, "The Stories We Tell: Television and Humanitarian Aid," in Jonathan Moore, ed., *Hard Choices: Moral Dilemmas in Humanitarian Intervention* (Lanham: Rowman & Littlefield, 1998), pp. 293–294.

39    United Nations, *Report of the Secretary-General to the Security Council on the Protection of Civilians in Armed Conflict*, UN Document S/2001/331, March 30, 2001.

40    For an overview of nonmilitary efforts that could be employed, specifically designed to provide protection for civilians, see Diane Paul, "Protection in Practice: Field-level Strategies for Protecting Civilians from Deliberate Harm," *RRN Paper* no. 30 (London: Overseas Development Institute, 1999).

41    Roberta Cohen and Francis M. Deng, "Exodus within Borders: The Uprooted Who Never Left Home," *Foreign Affairs* 77, no. 4 (July–August 1998), p. 15.

42    Roberts, *Humanitarian Action in War*, p. 39.

43    Médecins du Monde, *A Case by Case Analysis of Recent Crises Assessing 20 Years of Humanitarian Action*, working paper, April 1999.

44    Ibid., p. 24.

45    Anon., *Liberia: WOA Update/Alert*, Washington Office on Africa, 29 July 1996, www.sas.upenn.edu/Arican_Studies/Urgent_Action/DC_2210.html

46    See, for example, Scott R. Feil, *Preventing Genocide: How the Early Use of Force Might Have Succeeded in Rwanda* (New York: Carnegie Commission on Preventing Deadly Conflict, 1998).

47    Alan Kuperman, "Rwanda in Retrospect," *Foreign Affairs* 79, no. 1 (January–February 2000), p. 108.

48    Barry Posen, "Military Responses to Refugee Disasters," *International Security* 21, no. 1 (Summer 1996), p. 78. On safe areas, see also Claude Bruderlein, *Towards a New Strategic Approach to Humanitarian Protection and the Use of Protected Areas* (Cambridge, MA: Harvard Center for Population and Development Studies, 1999), Working Paper, including an accompanying "Review of the Literature on Protected Areas"; and Karin Landgren, "Safety Zones and International Protection: A Dark Grey Area," *International Journal of Refugee Law* 7, no. 3 (1995), pp. 436–458.

49    For Eastern Zaire, see UN Document S/1996/916; and James Apparthurai and Richard Lyshysyn, "Lessons Learned from the Zaire Mission," *Canadian Foreign Policy* 5, no. 2 (Winter 1998), pp. 93–105. For West Timor, see UN Document SC/2000/738.

50    North Atlantic Treaty Organization, *AJP-3.4.1 Peace Support Operations*, 2nd Study Draft, 1999, quotes from pp. 6–8.

51    Mats Berdal, "Armies in International Peacekeeping," paper presented at Taking the South African Army into the Future, Pretoria, November 15, 1993.

52    James Gow and Christopher Dandeker, "Peace-Support Operations: The Problem of Legitimation," *The World Today* 51 (August–September 1995), pp. 171–174.

53    Michael Doyle, "Peacebuilding in Cambodia," *IPA Policy Briefing Series*, December 1996, p. 3.

54    Robert J. Bunker, "Failed State Operational Environment Concepts," *Military Review* 77, no. 5 (September–October 1997), p. 90.

55    Howard Adelman and Astri Suhrke, "The International Response to Conflict and Genocide: Lessons from the Rwanda Experience," *Early Warning and Conflict Management* (Study 2), Steering Committee of the Joint Evaluation of Emergency Assistance to Rwanda, March, 1996, p. 72.

56    United Nations General Assembly, *Protection of Children Affected by Armed Conflict: Report of the Special Representative of the Secretary-General for Children and Armed Conflict*, A/54/30, New York, October 1, 1999, paras. 29–30.

57    Boutros-Ghali, *An Agenda for Peace*, especially paras. 55–59.

58    UN High Commissioner for Refugees, *The State of the World's Refugees: A Humanitarian Agenda* (Oxford: Oxford University Press), p. 170.

59    UN Document SC/565, June 7, 2001, paras. 6 and 17.

60    Karin von Hippel, *Democracy by Force: US Military Intervention in the Post-Cold War World* (Cambridge: Cambridge University Press, 2000), p. 194.

61    *Report of Panel on United Nations Peace Operations*, para. 118.

62    John MacKinlay, "Beyond the Logjam: A Doctrine for Complex Emergencies," in Max Manwaring and John Fishel, eds., *Toward Responsibility in the New World Disorder: Challenges and Lessons of Peace Operations* (London: Frank Cass, 1998), pp. 120–121.

63    Fred Tanner, "Consensual Versus Coercive Disarmament," in Estanislao A. Zawels et al., eds., *Managing Arms in Peace Processes: The Issues* (New York: United Nations, 1996), pp. 203–204.

64    International Crisis Group, "War Criminals in Bosnia's Republika Srpska: Who Are the People in Your Neighbourhood?," http://www.crisisweb.org/projects/balkans/bosnia/reports/A400001_02112000.pdf

65    There is a substantial difference, however, between the two cases. In the case of East Timor, a final status is envisaged (full independence). In the case of Kosovo, no such final status has been agreed on; and, in principle, the suspension of Yugoslav sovereignty over the province spelled out in UN Document S/1999/1244 is a temporary measure until a settlement has been found.

66    For a discussion, see Robert Jackson, *The Global Covenant: Human Conduct in a World of States* (Oxford: Oxford University Press, 2000), especially chapter 11, "Failed States, International Trusteeship," quote at p. 301.

67    Richard L. Merritt, *Democracy Imposed: US Occupation Policy and the German Public, 1945–1949* (New Haven: Yale University Press, 1995), p. xiii.

68    Jarat Chopra, *The Politics of Peace-Maintenance* (Boulder: Lynne Rienner, 1998); Jarat Chopra, *Peace-Maintenance: The Evolution of International Political Authority* (London: Routledge, 1999); and US Army, *US Army Field Manual (FM) 27–5* (Washington, DC: Department of the Army, 1940).

69    Tonya Langford, "Things Fall Apart: State Failure and the Politics of Intervention," *International Studies Review* 1, no. 1, 1999, pp. 59–79; and Tonya Langford, "Orchestrating Peace Operations: The PDD-56 Process" *Security Dialogue* 30, no. 2 (1999), pp. 137–149.

70    *Report of the Secretary-General on the Implementation of the Report of the Panel on United Nations Peace Operations*, para. 33.

71    *Report of the Secretary-General to the Security Council on the Protection of Civilians in Armed Conflict*, UN Document S/2001/331.

72    See, for example, a report by the International Committee of the Red Cross, *War, Money and Survival* (Geneva: International Committee of the Red Cross, 2000); David Keen, *The Economic Functions of Violence in Civil Wars* (Oxford: Oxford University Press, 1998), Adelphi Paper 320; Mats Berdal and David M. Malone, eds., *Greed and Grievance: Economic Agendas in Civil Wars* (Boulder: Lynne Rienner, 2000); and Mark Duffield, *Aid Policy and Post-Modern Conflict: A Critical Review* (Birmingham: University of Birmingham, 1998), Occasional Paper 19. On the phenomenon of so-called spoilers in peace processes, see Stephen John Stedman, "Spoiler Problems in Peace Processes," *International Security* 22, no. 1 (Fall 1997), pp. 5–53.

# 9. DOMESTIC AND INTERNATIONAL WILL

Although the international debate on humanitarian intervention has focused largely on questions of authority and capacity, the dearth of effective international responses has in most cases resulted from a lack of will. In neither Rwanda nor Srebrenica did a lack of authority or capacity stand in the way of action. In both cases, Chapter VII mandates existed. When Srebrenica was being overrun, military aircraft from the North Atlantic Treaty Organization (NATO) were in the air waiting only for the political order to strike. In Rwanda, there is now broad agreement that the necessary military forces could have been deployed to slow down or even halt the *génocidaires*, equipped with only light arms or even machetes.

The problem, as has been repeated in a litany of speeches and analyses, is a lack of will. But such a designation often does little more than obfuscate the central questions of motivation, decision making, and implementation among a range of disparate governments and intergovernmental bodies. Accepting that there will be circumstances in which interventions will be deemed both legal and legitimate, the objective here is to explore the challenges of mobilizing national governments and generating effective intergovernmental cooperation to act in the face of human catastrophes.

For prevention or intervention alike, the challenges of moving from words to deeds have much in common. Two points raised earlier are worth reiterating. First, for the notion of responsibility to be meaningful, it should ultimately reside in specific places and institutions, and with specific people. If everyone is responsible then no one is actually responsible. Second, mobilizing support for a specific instance of humanitarian intervention is first and foremost a challenge of leadership because there will always be a compelling rationale for inaction.

There is nothing unusual about the unwillingness of politicians and government officials to participate in high-risk interventions far from their borders in the absence of vital interests or of pressures from domestic constituencies. Caution is perhaps easiest to understand in two sets of countries: those with reason to worry about the possibility of future interventions on their own soil; and those in possession of military, economic, and political assets that are most in demand from international bodies for implementing intervention mandates. For the leaders of the second set of countries, votes in intergovernmental fora to authorize such interventions may well entail their constituents' bearing significant human, financial, and material costs.

Neither international nor domestic decision making processes operate independently. Domestic factors are often more influential, but domestic decision making is affected by international developments and deliberations. Domestic forces, like national interests and identities, are not immutable. They are subject to being redefined, and international crises and ensuing debates often directly influence the power profile and perspectives of domestic political actors. Mobilizing domestic political forces should be an integral part of international strategies. Too often, multilateral planning and decision making considers domestic constituencies as afterthoughts rather than as essential prerequisites.

The analysis below, therefore, examines motivation, decision making, and implementation in both domestic and international arenas. It begins by discussing a neglected subject – the mobilization of domestic support for humanitarian interventions. Leadership remains critical to mobilizing adequate national will to undertake potentially costly and risky military operations. However, certain contextual factors – such as geography, political culture, and understandings of national interest – define the parameters and the constraints within which national leaders operate; they are discussed in the second section.

Getting national governments to provide support for intervention is an important first step in moving from rhetorical commitments to international action, which forms the basis for the third section. The accompanying crucial step in operationalizing a responsibility to protect civilians in deadly conflicts is ensuring sufficient multilateral leadership to mobilize intergovernmental machinery and to construct broad-based and sustainable "coalitions of the willing." This step, ignored or underemphasized in analyses of the last decade, forms the substance of the fourth and concluding section.

## DOMESTIC POLITICS AND INTERVENTION

States remain the ultimate units of decision making about military interventions for humanitarian objectives within the United Nations (UN) and elsewhere. Accordingly, foreign-policy decision making processes – and not the workings of multilateral organizations or the provisions of international law – define and influence the limits circumscribing potential humanitarian interventions. Security Council resolutions, in that sense, should be seen as the tip of the decision making iceberg – the result of a chain of political outcomes, beginning with the governing structures and political dynamics of individual member states. For most countries, and certainly for the great powers, fundamental decisions are made by heads of state, ministers, and parliaments, not by diplomats in New York.

States do not possess a monopoly of the means of persuasion or coercion, but they do control the lion's share. They include political, financial, and legal carrots and sticks for bringing uncooperative state and nonstate actors into line – including intergovernmental institutions. International agencies rely on their member states for human, material, and financial resources, as well as for the political backing required for humanitarian interventions. International institutions are relatively strong and effective when their members value what they do, and these institutions have sufficiently broad common interests to permit decisive multilateral action. When their members are divided, ambivalent, or apathetic, little gets accomplished.

Whatever the circumstances, a key question concerns will: Does there exist, or can there be assembled, enough political support within key countries, not only to authorize and undertake a particular intervention to pursue humanitarian objectives, but also to sustain it even in the face of possible setbacks along the way? Consider, for example, the impact of the slaughter of Belgian peacekeepers in Kigali; the bodies of the United States (US) Rangers dragged through the dusty streets of Mogadishu; and UN peacekeepers chained to bridges in Bosnia and Herzegovina. Most evident in cases of military intervention in which soldiers may be put in harm's way, the same line of questioning is apt for efforts to invoke and implement such nonforcible intervention as economic sanctions, arms and oil embargoes, and international criminal prosecution.

The dynamics of domestic political forces are not the same from country to country. In many cases there have been, and will be, domestic pressures for, as well as against, intervention. Rarely is there a single, universally accepted, understanding of the nature and content of the national interest. Indeed, it is commonplace for groups that are for and against intervention to coexist. Ultimately, decisions reflect how attitudes are framed and communicated, how leaders choose to address competing domestic influences, how perceptions of the political dynamics within other countries are taken into account in shaping policy choices, and how international and local groups seek to influence this nexus of factors. Thus, the next section is devoted to the question of how leaders affect and even manipulate them on behalf of robust military intervention for humanitarian objectives.

## MOTIVATION

The end of the Cold War and the success of the Security Council-authorized collective security operation in Kuwait initially made the early 1990s look like the dawn of a new era – "renaissance" of the world organization was a frequent metaphor. In publicly justifying their decisions to participate in international efforts to enforce human rights norms, leaders customarily cited UN decisions and their national obligations under the Charter to carry out mandates. Council decisions, especially those taken under Chapter VII, were widely credited with adding both legal authority and political legitimacy to national action.

Activism within the Council's chambers, however, did not necessarily translate into effective action on the ground or into greater public credibility for the world organization. The number, variety, and size of UN peace operations reached historic heights in 1993. Yet, the relative successes of many of those early missions were overshadowed by failures in Bosnia, a wholesale retreat in Somalia, and the abandonment of defenceless civilians in Rwanda. In the US, these setbacks seemed only to confirm congressional scepticism, while feeble American leadership reinforced the caution already visible in many other capitals. As the 2000 *Report of the Panel on United Nations Peace Operations* underlined, many member states have become more prone to say "no" rather than "yes" to requests from the Secretary-General to provide forces for UN peacekeeping operations.[1] It is a tendency that is even more pronounced for missions of open-ended duration that involve significant risks and uncertainties.

Given the magnitude of present operations in the Balkans (about 80,000 troops), as well as shrinking military budgets in the post-Cold War era, there are real constraints on most Western militaries. By way of historical comparison, UN peacekeeping may have peaked in 1993 at 78,000 troops. But today, if both NATO and UN missions are included, the number of soldiers in international peace operations has soared by about 40 percent, to 110,000. States are not running away from foreign military commitments, but they are being compelled to make choices about how to use limited and strained military capabilities to meet a variety of international demands.

If interventions regarded as legal and legitimate fail to occur because domestic will is in short supply, then a key challenge is altering the nature of debate in those countries whose participation and support are essential. How this shift might occur can be considered by examining two sets of questions. First, what have been the key determinants of national policies toward intervention, how have they varied from country to country, and how different are national decision making processes and structures? Second, what might be done to encourage a convergence of transnational and humanitarian impulses with national nterests and decision making processes? Ultimately, why particular countries act where and when they do is subject to several factors. Among the variables that help explain a willingness to participate in multilateral humanitarian interventions are geographic proximity, domestic political culture, and understandings of national interests.

### Geographic Proximity and Cultural Affinity

States traditionally have found numerous reasons to intervene and justify intervention – some international, some domestic, and oftentimes a mix of both – with or without the UN's blessing. In general, geographic proximity – a feature that may have acute security, economic, political, and domestic dimensions – has played a crucial role. What happens nearby is more likely to endanger nationals, raise significant security concerns, and result in refugees, economic disruptions, and unwanted political spillovers. It is also likely to attract more comprehensive media coverage than events farther away. Such a crisis does not get lost as easily in the agenda of a regional organization as it does at the UN in New York.

Relatively few states, moreover, have the capacity to project military power far from home. Thus, options to intervene normally are more easily considered and implemented either in a neighbouring country or as part of a supporting role in an international coalition – whether led by the UN, a regional body, or a major power. Robust interventions are most frequently led by a regional power: Australia in East Timor, Nigeria in Liberia and Sierra Leone, South Africa in Lesotho, Russia in the former Soviet Union, and states of Western Europe in Bosnia and Herzegovina and Kosovo.

Only the great powers have the capacity to mount operations well beyond their borders. The US has frequently intervened within its own hemisphere (for example, Dominican Republic, Grenada, Panama, and Haiti), but it has also been indispensable in interventions elsewhere (Iraq, Somalia, and the Balkans). Long-distance military efforts have also been undertaken by others – the United Kingdom (UK), France, and Belgium – particularly in cases where there have been colonial ties.

Likewise, cultural affinity may play a role. During the Bosnian conflict, Iran regularly shipped arms to the Bosnians in contravention of the arms embargo. The justification was largely based on a shared Muslim heritage. It is thought that Secretary-General Boutros-Ghali's labeling significant efforts by the West in the Balkans as a "white man's war" had an impact in highlighting Somalia's relatively ignored position in 1992. The difficulty of applying such generalizations is evident from the fact that eventually, in both Bosnia and Kosovo, the Judeo-Christian West applied substantial military might in favour of largely Muslim populations and against states composed essentially of peoples with Catholic and Orthodox Christian backgrounds. The indictment and pursuit of war criminals also went against stereotypical cultural affinities in that the tribunal in The Hague had relatively few Muslims in the docket.

### Political Culture

Whether a state is likely to join an international coalition engaged in humanitarian intervention often appears to be related to its political culture, which is shaped by history and by public and elite views about their country's place in the contemporary world. Latin American countries are, for historical reasons, generally cautious about either backing or joining in any effort identified as an "intervention," though this hesitation seems to be easing in some parts of the region. Sanctions and military intervention in Haiti were unanimously backed by the Organization of American States (OAS). Argentina, for example, has become a prominent UN peacekeeping contributor and has provided forces to the NATO-led missions in Bosnia and Herzegovina and Kosovo.

Japan, for a combination of historical, constitutional, and cultural reasons, remains cautious about sending its self-defence forces overseas, even under the blue UN flag.[2] Germany, on the other hand, has shed some of its domestic legal restraints and political inhibitions, as demonstrated by its participation in Kosovo within the NATO framework. Thus, political cultures have evolved, especially over the past decade, to permit modest participation in international peacekeeping and even humanitarian interventions.

Other traditionally strong troop-contributing countries may have become somewhat more hesitant over that same period. Belgium, the Netherlands, and Canada faced some difficult national soul-searching following traumatic incidents involving their armed forces in UN operations during the 1990s.[3] At the outset of the 1994 genocide in Rwanda, Hutu militiamen slaughtered 10 Belgian peacekeepers, spurring the withdrawal of the remaining Belgian troops and opening the door to the killing frenzy that followed. The inability of Dutch peacekeepers to do anything to prevent the massacre at Srebrenica in 1995 triggered a deeply painful national debate about the responsibilities and obligations of peacekeepers. Canada's proud peacekeeping tradition was tarnished when a national inquiry publicized an incident in which its soldiers tortured a Somali prisoner.

Another pertinent element of political culture is how to ensure democratic accountability when military forces are used in internationally approved enforcement operations. For international missions other than the traditional monitoring, observation, and peacekeeping, there is a tendency for democratic countries to involve parliaments in decision making. Although the Security Council provides both international and domestic legitimacy, it does not ensure democratic accountability within countries. Although analyses have focused on the role of the US Congress in such decision making, a recent research project suggests that eight other democracies – Canada, France, Germany, India, Japan, Norway, the Russian Federation, and the UK – are not dissimilar.[4] Ensuring that military forces operate in accord with law and norms remains a national responsibility. Moreover, it is not impossible that in some future instance, a parliament could take a negative decision after a government makes a decision to participate in a Security Council-approved operation.

## National Interests

It is not surprising that where significant interests are not engaged, countries are hesitant to commit troops. Often, only countries with significant interests find sufficient motivation to consider joining an intervention force. This was not necessarily the case for traditional peacekeeping (that is, the permanent members of the Security Council almost never sent troops). It is certainly true for Chapter VII operations, and even more so for robust intervention involving greater firepower and greater risk. Recent examples that demonstrate this point include the British in Sierra Leone, the French in Rwanda and the Central African Republic, the Italians in Somalia and Albania, the North Americans in Haiti, Western Europeans throughout the former Yugoslavia, and the Russians in Georgia, Tajikistan, and Kosovo. This reality raises problems for those who often argue for only disinterested intervention. But the reality of the 1990s has been that humanitarian motives alone rarely suffice to sustain an intervention. Mixed motives are the norm, and many observers deem national interests as a necessary if insufficient condition for a successful humanitarian intervention.

Other kinds of interests also have an important impact on the willingness of countries to participate. For many countries, there is an interest in maintaining solidarity within regional groupings and military alliances. Whether the Rio Group, the OAS, NATO, or the Non-Aligned Movement, the views of "like-minded" countries can tip the balance in domestic decisio making processes. For other countries, international expectations and images remain influential. In the case of France and the UK, for instance, the benefits of displaying leadership on global issues seem to exert a significant pull toward activism in the Security Council, where their status as great powers with a claim on a veto is seen by some as questionable.

Moreover, differences in power are reflected in the multilateral flavour of a country's definition of national interests. Middle powers, for example, have modest leverage in foreign policy, resulting from a rule-bound multilateral system, but they have more than they would in one based purely on power. From this perspective, the traditional support for UN undertakings by Nordic countries, Canada, Australia, and New Zealand are logical and, in fact, self-interested. What many see as Washington's indifference or even hostility to multilateralism is also a reflection of power. The obsession with a definition of national interests that is circumscribed by a defence of the continental US and stable economic relations with allies is really only possible for such a dominant military and economic state.

The foreign policy strategies, priorities, and capacities of individual countries are key determinants in decisions by individual governments to participate in robust military missions. Humanitarian intervention is not an endeavour in which one size fits all. National political cultures matter, and the rationale for an intervention may need to be tailored to specific countries at particular historical junctures. Viewed in this optic, the unraveling of states and the need for outside intervention in such areas as the Balkans and Central Africa could take on a different perspective in Washington or Beijing, if the assumption is made that it is in no one's interest to have vacuums in state authority. Attitudes vary about sources of legitimacy, the use of force or economic coercion, sovereignty, and international law and organization, not to mention the implications of existing asymmetries in national power and wealth.

National interests are often thought of as fixed or given; they are viewed as simply a product of geographic, political, and military circumstances. In fact, national interests are based on particular perceptions and strategic calculations. Consequently, they are often subject to change, sometimes radical change.

The dynamic elements in the content of "national interest" offer the possibility of building a forward-looking message, one that aims to build a foundation of support for future efforts, not just for the crisis of the day.[5] Those who determine the politics of humanitarian responses are the leaders of states and state-like authorities. They act on the basis of calculations of political interests. These are anything except fixed and unchanging, as the 1990s amply demonstrated. Shaping calculations of interest requires conscious engagement in political processes, because the construction and redefinition of interest are products of learning that should take place after each humanitarian crisis.

## GOVERNMENTAL DECISION MAKING

The previous section examined several generic factors that condition the likely willingness of countries to participate in international military operations. The task now is to explore in more detail two related dimensions of national decision making processes that affect specific undertakings for particular countries. First, there are a range of additional actors that influence government decisions, some intentionally (for example, diaspora and nongovernmental organizations [NGOs]) and others inadvertently (the media). Second, particular forms and structures of government affect the relative influence of these other actors. They are also important in their own right, as they determine the relative ease with which troops can be committed.

Occasionally a distant event is so horrific and generates sufficient NGO and media attention as to elicit a broad public reaction, even calling for concerted and urgent action. If so, the event becomes a factor in domestic politics. It is sometimes suggested, for instance, that such empathetic humanitarian responses, spurred by the so-called CNN or BBC effect, could help explain the earlier Bush administration's decisions to intervene militarily in northern

Iraq in April 1991 and in Somalia in December 1992. Whatever its impact in these cases, the media evidently could not elicit action to counter the subsequent genocide in Rwanda, partly as a result of its inaccurate depiction of the challenges involved in halting what it characterized as an intractable intertribal conflict.

In this context, state decisions about engagement often juxtapose potentially contradictory impulses from the domestic political arena. Although one can overestimate the media's impact, there is no question that real time transmission of images of suffering has on occasion created domestic pressure to act.[6] The effects are most likely to be significant when governments are slow to react and indecisive with regard to a humanitarian crisis (that is, where the strategic imperative is weak). By focusing on human suffering, media attention tends to divert publics and policy makers from hard diplomatic and military decisions. Interviews with officials suggest that such pressure can be almost irresistible. In particular, time pressures sometimes push policy makers to become involved before serious analysis and planning occur. This was evident, for example, in the aborted Canadian-led multinational force initiative in eastern Zaire in 1996. Policy planners were told of the decision to deploy before any serious assessment had taken place of the problem and Canada's capacity to deal with it.[7]

Sometimes, pressure from particular domestic interest groups may help to persuade an ambivalent government to act despite substantial misgivings. The urgings of the US Congressional Black Caucus, TransAfrica (led by Randall Robinson), and many citizens in politically pivotal Florida, for example, may have finally convinced the Clinton administration to intervene in Haiti in September 1994. Similarly, it seems pressure from the Tamil population in southern India encouraged action in the Jaffna Peninsula in 1987. In other cases, however, the impact of such pressure offsets the lobbying of another group. Within the US and Canada, for example, members of the Albanian diaspora tend to push in one policy direction for Kosovo, while the Serbian one pushes in the opposite.

NGOs are significant advocates for cross-border humanitarian action, including in some cases military intervention. It is difficult to draw causal arrows, but most politicians and analysts acknowledge the importance of such voices for changes in government policy. A clear example was the call of a number of NGOs, but particularly Médecins sans Frontières, for military intervention into eastern Zaire in the aftermath of the Rwandan genocide. Another striking example of such influence was the case cited earlier in which International Committee of the Red Cross President Cornelio Sommaruga began lobbying in December 1991 and January 1992 with the outgoing and incoming Secretaries-General to move robust action in Somalia onto the international radar screen. Later in 1992, the Washington-based consortium of US NGOs, Inter-Action, organized a lobbying session with President Bush to urge military intervention in the Horn of Africa.

NGOs are relatively dynamic and flexible, and they are able to bring an incipient crisis to the attention of the public, media, and officialdom. Yet, they do have their limitations as advocates for humanitarian intervention. Government representatives, especially from developing countries, often question the status of NGOs with which they disagree, asking just whom and what they represent. Consequently, the drive to widen NGO participation in the UN has stalled, or at least slowed down, in recent years.

Furthermore, NGOs often lack policy making experience and are frequently divided over which precise policy course is optimal. They may also be skittish about the cynical world of politics or about the employment of military and economic coercion, steps that could alleviate or exacerbate humanitarian suffering but that smack of great-power dominance of weaker countries. Western NGOs, for instance, were as divided about whether and how to use military force in Kosovo as they had been in Somalia. These points of difference or ambivalence give policy makers considerable freedom of action, as NGOs generally are more successful at getting an issue moved up the ladder of priorities than at compelling a specific course of action once the problem is being addressed.[8]

Influence varies with the nature and structure of a particular society and a particular elected government. And, as mentioned at the outset, little in-depth research has been undertaken for most countries on the dynamics of influence regarding humanitarian intervention. The prime targets for pressure from civil society may vary from country to country. Nongovernmental actors are accorded greater latitude in the West than in China, Russia, and most developing countries.[9]

In addition to the importance of political culture discussed above, traditions, patterns, and structures of governance also affect the prospects for the commitment of troops. It has been argued that in traditional troop-contributing countries for UN peacekeeping operations, national cultures may be understood as permissive, rather than causal. As such, pressure to commit troops comes from the long-established organizational culture in foreign-ministry bureaucracies.[10] This pattern, however, might not hold in cases of Chapter VII enforcement missions or other high-risk operations with the possibility of substantial casualties.

Many of the key factors in national decision making are country specific. In France, the office of the president is reputed to hold considerable sway over a number of aspects of foreign policy, including the pursuit of French interests in its former African colonies.[11] In the UK, there would appear to be a recurrent clash between two traditions: automatic support for multilateral initiatives and Parliament's taste for vibrant debate. The result seems to be a relatively consistent set of policy outcomes, without Paris's centralized decision making process. Given the public caution and constitutional constraints that still hold in Japan and that have only recently been eased in Germany, it is inconceivable that either country would contemplate a significant role in a humanitarian intervention without serious parliamentary deliberations and public debate. In the US, the executive and legislative branches often hold quite different and sometimes contradictory views.[12] Few questions bring out the interbranch and interparty divisions, and even splits, within the major parties more vividly than those involving the deployment of US military forces. Washington's diplomats have limited flexibility and are necessarily cautious about playing the kind of leadership role and taking the sorts of initiatives that would otherwise be expected from a dominant power.

In some cases, changes in government can affect, and often decrease, support for military interventions. Although it has yet to be borne out in practice, the incoming Bush administration was explicit in its desire to reduce US military commitments in the Balkans. In some cases the effects of such changes are counterintuitive. When Nigeria was a military dictatorship, it was more easily able to support military interventions in Liberia and Sierra Leone than after it returned to democratic rule. With the election of Olusegun Obasanjo, the cost of maintaining olive-green-helmeted troops in Sierra Leone became unsustainable.

Useful indicators of whether a state will participate in a particular humanitarian intervention seem to be proximity, political culture, and national interest. These conclusions help to define the proverbial bottom-line, or primary policy challenge: What can be done so that countries are more likely to participate in humanitarian interventions that are widely considered to be legitimate and justified?

Obstacles relating to proximity and capacity cannot be overcome very quickly. In some countries – such as China, Japan, and much of Latin America – the political culture against intervention is so deeply engrained that it would take more than a generation to change it. In other countries, however, leanings in one direction or the other may evolve more quickly or from case to case. The most potentially malleable factor would appear to be how national interest and identity are defined or redefined.

## FROM DOMESTIC SUPPORT TO INTERNATIONAL ACTION

Unpacking the notion of political will demonstrates the significance, often overlooked, of domestic politics and national interests. But agreement in capitals is usually only one of the necessary components for effective multilateral intervention. Domestic will alone is inadequate to ensure protection for individuals from the ethnic cleansing in Croatia, widespread killings in Cambodia, dismemberments in Sierra Leone, or massive starvation in Sudan.

What happens during intergovernmental deliberations, and the statements and proposals of the UN Secretary-General and his organization, matter in capitals. For all but a few of the most powerful or recalcitrant countries, multilateral diplomacy has an impact on domestic decision making and thus on potential support for international initiatives. Furthermore, cooperation between and among states and other international actors is a necessary part of the chain linking political decisions to the actual deployment of military forces.

International will, then, is more than just the sum of attitudes and policies of individual countries. It also consists of leadership and coordination to convert material political commitments into effective international action on the ground. While broader political support and legitimacy are always helpful, they are vital where the interests of Western powers or regional hegemonic powers are not immediately threatened. Two international dimensions are crucial: multilateral leadership and coalition building.

### Multilateral Leadership

Though it is easy to overstate the importance of intergovernmental institutions in deciding when, where, and how to intervene, these bodies do play a critical role in facilitating the transition from domestic decision making to international action. An obvious starting point when looking for multilateral leadership is the UN Secretary-General and senior officials in the Secretariat. Although provisions in the Charter such as Article 99 are often discussed, it is the Secretary-General's international profile with governments and the media, as well as his routine activities and interactions with the Security Council, that give him a unique opportunity to mobilize international support. Furthermore, the Secretariat, particularly through reports and recommendations to the Security Council, shapes deliberations and may help determine the range of options considered.

Take, for example, the importance of leadership from the Secretary-General. Where it exists, the impact can be considerable. Dag Hammarskjöld's working with Canadian Foreign Minister Lester B. Pearson helped invent peacekeeping in the Suez Crisis of 1956. On the basis of Charter Article 99, he also forced the Security Council to consider the violence in the Congo in 1960. Similarly, Javier Pérez de Cuéllar's diligence helped bring an end to El Salvador's civil war in 1991–1992. These and other illustrations demonstrate that members of the international civil service are actors with some independent scope, and probably more than is commonly assumed.

By the same token, the failure to respond to the genocide in Rwanda in 1994 illustrates the importance of leadership within the UN and the effective functioning of the Secretariat. As the Independent Inquiry on Rwanda reiterates, blame for the failure to respond to the genocide in Rwanda is widespread. Yet, the report goes on to specifically highlight the shortcomings of the Secretary-General and the Secretariat:

> The Independent Inquiry finds that the response of the United Nations before and during the 1994 genocide in Rwanda failed in a number of fundamental respects. The responsibility for the failings of the United Nations to prevent and stop the genocide in Rwanda lies with a number of different actors, in particular the Secretary-General, the Secretariat, the Security Council, UNAMIR [UN Assistance Mission in Rwanda] and the broader membership of the United Nations.[13]

Criticisms of the UN's chief executive officer and his senior team included their "mistaken analysis which underpinned the recommendations to the Council, and for recommending that the mission be composed of fewer troops than the field mission had considered necessary"; their improper handling of the telegram of January 11, 1994, from the Force Commander reporting on the advanced state of planning for a premeditated slaughter of the Tutsi population; the Department of Peacekeeping Operations, unwillingness to argue forcefully for a more robust mandate and an increase in troop strength in the aftermath of the Belgian withdrawal; and their persistence in viewing the situation as a civil war, including their unwillingness until the end of April to use the term "genocide."

In contrast to the events in the spring of 1994, the Secretary-General and senior officials have in recent years been willing to take on controversial issues that surround humanitarian intervention. An obvious example is the hard-hitting self-analyses in investigations into Rwanda, Srebrenica, and UN peace operations. In fact, in response to the Rwanda report, Annan publicly stated that "[o]n behalf of the United Nations, I acknowledge this failure and express my deep remorse." He went on to say that,

> Both Reports – my own on Srebrenica, and that of the independent Inquiry on Rwanda – reflect a profound determination to present the truth about these calamities. Of all my aims as Secretary-General, there is none to which I feel more deeply committed than that of enabling the United Nations never again to fail in protecting a civilian population from genocide or mass slaughter. [14]

The call by the Secretary-General at the General Assembly's opening session in September 1999 further illustrates the significance of multilateral leadership in terms of ideas and norms. The debate on humanitarian intervention that has ensued, and indeed the launch of the International Commission on Intervention and State Sovereignty, would have been unlikely without Annan's prompting.

Leadership within the Security Council can also make the difference between impotent rhetoric and effective responses. One example is the invigoration of the Angola Sanctions Committee largely through the efforts of Robert Fowler, Canadian Permanent Representative to the UN. A sanctions committee on Angola was established by Resolution 864 (1994) on September 15, 1994, to supervise the imposition of an oil and arms embargo on the rebel group the Union for the Total Independence of Angola. These sanctions were subsequently extended on July 1, 1998, to include an embargo on unofficial diamonds. Despite their imposition, however, it was clear that "UNITA [Union for the Total Independence of Angola] was still able to procure what it needed for its war machine, and sell its diamonds. UNITA officials still traveled with little restriction, and UNITA continued to be active in international capitals through 'unofficial' offices and representatives."[15]

In January 1999, Fowler launched a series of new initiatives designed to improve their effectiveness. And that summer, following his extensive series of visits to Africa and Europe, the Security Council debated 19 concrete recommendations on what could be done to enhance the effectiveness of the sanctions regime.[16] According to a report by the *Angola Peace Monitor*, Fowler personally "injected new energy into the embargoes, through early recommendations about how they might be made to work better and by investigative visits to Southern Africa as well as the diamond dealing and arms trading capitals of Europe."[17] The launch of a series of expert panels ensured follow-up within the Security Council, while the overall initiative created a precedent for exploring the economic foundations of ongoing conflicts and paved the way for similar reports on Sierra Leone and the Congo.[18] The initiative also gave impetus to a subsequent international effort to control "conflict diamonds."

A similar example, though ultimately less successful, was the effort of Nigeria's Permanent Representative to the UN, Ibrahim Gambari, during the Rwanda crisis. Following the outbreak of genocide in early April 1994, he consistently and vocally advocated a strengthening of the mandate of the UN Assistance Mission in Rwanda (UNAMIR) in Rwanda and an increase in troop numbers. In mid-April, he presented a draft resolution to the Security Council on behalf of the nonaligned caucus, and one week later met with the Secretary-General in an effort to counter moves in the Security Council to withdraw UNAMIR completely. During the following month, as president of the Council, he argued that international credibility was at risk. And he recommended that the Council ask the Secretary-General to prepare the contingency plans for a robust intervention.

The need for multilateral leadership is clearly not limited to the various organs of the UN. Effective action also requires the active engagement of regional and subregional bodies, other multilateral organizations, and even individuals. For example, during the early part of the decade in the Balkans, the prospects for peace and the safety of civilians rested in the hands of various entities and leaders, including the Special Representative of the Secretary-General Yasushi Akashi, the peace envoys Cyrus Vance and David Owen, and the members of the "Contact Group." Later, it was the G-8 political directors who first set out the principles for ending the war over Kosovo, and G-8 foreign ministers in Bonn and Cologne who negotiated the Security Council resolution that ended the war.

## Coalition Building

A subset of the larger question of multilateral leadership that deserves special attention is the construction and maintenance of multinational coalitions. At the start of the 1990s, particularly with the publication of Boutros Boutros-Ghali's *An Agenda for Peace*, the UN initially seemed on the brink of playing an important and direct role in the mobilization and deployment of military forces. Yet, in light of the experiences in Bosnia, Somalia, and Rwanda, the emphasis on peace enforcement was greatly reduced in the 1995 *Supplement to An Agenda for Peace*. This trend was further confirmed when the *Report of the Panel on United Nations Peace Operations* (in 2000) concluded that the "consent of the local parties, impartiality and the use of force only in self-defence should remain the bedrock principles of peacekeeping."[19] In cases of military intervention, therefore, the UN's role will seemingly be limited to authorizing the use of deadly force. The actual mobilization and deployment of such power will normally be conducted by coalitions of the willing, even if blue helmets occasionally have important responsibilities for some aspects of peace enforcement (for example, at present in Sierra Leone and East Timor).

During the 1990s most interventions were undertaken by like-minded coalitions. A broad but potentially fragile coalition was brought together by the US in response to the Iraqi invasion of Kuwait. South Africa mobilized support from the Southern African Development Community to intervene in Lesotho. Nigeria led the coalition within the Economic Community of West African States (ECOWAS) in both Liberia and Sierra Leone, while Francophone members took the lead in Guinea-Bissau. And an ad hoc grouping of states intervened in the Central African Republic. In each case common problems and challenges were faced: mobilizing troops, securing resources, agreeing on legal and administrative arrangements, and maintaining internal solidarity. Yet, despite the importance of coalition building to the politics of the 1990s, there has been relatively little in-depth research on how coalitions develop and how they function under duress. Other than memoirs and anecdotes, there is little to guide prospective coalition builders.

One case that has been examined in some detail was the aborted mission to Zaire in late 1996. In response to the refugee crisis in eastern Zaire, Security Council Resolution 1080 of November 15, 1996, authorized a Multinational Force (MNF), under Canadian command, to ensure the effective provision of aid to refugees and local populations and the voluntary and orderly repatriation of the refugees. The coalition was first created by calls from the Canadian prime minister to his counterparts. It was subsequently managed by a steering group bringing troop-contributing countries, humanitarian agencies, and major financial supporters into the decision making process. Ultimately, Canada was the only country to actually commit troops to the mission, and changing circumstances on the ground led to the mission's being cancelled by the end of the year.

In the spring of the following year, the Canadian government began a consultative process seeking ways to improve the capacity of the international community to prepare and manage military interventions in humanitarian crises. One outcome was a lessons-learned paper that focused on the challenges of managing an ad hoc multinational coalition.[20] The study concluded that the improvisation required to develop a coalition wasted valuable time and energy and that generic procedures and decision making models should be formalized. It also suggested that the inclusive and consensus-based decision making model based on a large steering group was unwieldy and ultimately impractical. Although the interests of potential troop-contributing countries should be respected, overarching political direction should be decided by a much smaller group focused exclusively on meeting the primary objectives of a mission.

A further conclusion of this analysis was that so-called middle powers are well suited to lead an MNF, because they are more politically acceptable in the developing world, but that their modest political and military status simultaneously limits their ability to mount and direct such military interventions effectively. For an operation as logistically complex as the one in Zaire, the commitment of US ground troops was a prerequisite for most potential troop contributors. This reality led the authors to propose that like-minded countries should consider pooling resources and coordinating the procurement of logistical capacity to reduce dependence on any one state.

The Zaire mission faced more formidable coalition building challenges than others in the 1990s. The great powers were either unwilling to lead or were, as in the case of France, unacceptable to others. And the coalition lacked preexisting structures and procedures of a regional organization or a military alliance. These challenges were also faced by Australia in leading the multinational force to East Timor, but geographic proximity made the operation more feasible.

Many commentators point to the obvious shortcomings when major or former colonial powers are involved, which is one reason why the permanent members of the Security Council were shunned for traditional UN peacekeeping operations. At the same time, operational challenges are greatly reduced when the great powers are engaged. The US, and in many cases Britain and France, have the military capacity to undertake military interventions single-handedly, or at least play a prominent leadership role. In these cases, the coalition building challenge is largely political: maintaining solidarity among members during the course of the intervention, with occasional financial burden-sharing. Prominent examples where the great powers were fully engaged include the US-led coalition in the Gulf War and NATO in Kosovo.

In the case of the Gulf War, the coalition was created through intense diplomatic lobbying by the US, with strong support from the UK. This lobbying included an 11-day, nine-country trip by US Secretary of State James Baker in September 1990 to build support. The coalition of 28 countries was constructed from the outset to meet three overarching objectives: to demonstrate solid support in the Arab world (for example, Saudi Arabia, Egypt, and Syria), to ensure access to adjacent territory for staging military operations (for example, Turkey and Saudi Arabia), and to spread the financial burden among wealthier countries (for example, Japan, Germany, and Saudi Arabia). Israel was excluded from the outset, as its participation was incompatible with strong support from Arab countries. And intense pressure was exerted during the Scud missile strikes to avoid retaliatory measures by Israel that might have split the coalition.

In Kosovo, the coalition was limited to NATO members. Hence, the mechanisms for decision making and operational modes were well established, and in fact predetermined. The real challenge was securing and maintaining commitments among political leaders in NATO countries. Once again, Washington and London played leading roles in the process, seeking to ensure military commitments, political support, and financial resources. The challenges were greatest in southern Europe – ironically, those countries that had the most to lose from the potential spillover from the conflict. In addition, country-specific factors made the process more difficult. Greece was concerned about the implications that the Kosovo precedent might have for a future conflict in Cyprus and the risk of exacerbating ethnic tensions in neighbouring Macedonia. In Italy, strong economic relations with Yugoslavia and the strength of the Communist Party in the Italian parliamentary coalition contributed to the government's hesitations. There were even difficulties with one of the central members of the alliance, Germany, in terms of the constitutional prohibition on waging war and the strength of the traditionally pacifist Green Party in the ruling coalition. Finally, there was concern among all NATO leaders that mounting civilian casualties, and the extension of the air campaign to Belgrade, might undermine the Western public's support.

Given the disproportionate contributions among members, even where interventions are undertaken by alliances and regional organizations, they remain coalitions of the willing and able. For instance, the contributions among NATO countries to the war in Kosovo were very uneven, with US warplanes flying 85 percent of the sorties. Imbalances were perhaps even more evident in the case of the intervention in Liberia.[21] ECOWAS authorized the intervention in July 1990, but at the outset only 5 of the 16 member countries – the Gambia, Ghana, Guinea, Nigeria, and Sierra Leone – committed troops.[22] Nigeria dominated the operation, contributing the bulk of the troops over time and as much as 90 percent at times.

A Standing Mediation Committee – including the Gambia, Ghana, Mali, Nigeria, and Togo – was established to manage the decision making process. It was subsequently supported in 1991 by the Committee of Five (Côte d'Ivoire, Ghana, Guinea, Liberia, Nigeria), the Gambia, Guineau-Bissau, Senegal, and Togo.

The first Force Commander was a Ghanaian, and overall control rested with the Chair of ECOWAS, a position that revolved annually. In fact, the maintenance of the coalition over more than six years was based on effective Nigerian diplomacy. From the outset, two ECOWAS members – Burkina Faso and Côte d'Ivoire – strongly opposed the intervention. In fact, because of belligerents propelling the conflict in neighbouring Liberia, they had actively worked to keep Liberia off the Security Council's agenda. Yet, by 1992, both had come to accept the need for a political settlement and were included in ECOWAS's expanded Committee of Nine. And although the coalition was heavily anglophone at the outset, Nigeria consistently pressed for greater francophone involvement. In 1991, both Senegal and Gabon agreed to provide troops; and the following year, Senegal was also included in the Committee of Nine. Efforts were also made to broaden the coalition beyond West Africa. Troops from Tanzania and Uganda joined in late 1993, though earlier commitments from Zimbabwe and Egypt never materialized.

### Responsibility to Act

In retrospect, failure to respond to humanitarian crises is usually explained by inadequacies in the so-called international community. More often than not, the lack of political will is deemed the determining factor and is once again bemoaned. Yet, such conclusions explain little. If the "international community" is responsible, then no one really is. In the end, the question of political will, whether domestic or international, comes down to choices and decisions by individuals. To take just one case, the responsibility for not having responded to the April 1994 genocide in the African Great Lakes lies with particular governments and ultimately individual leaders who could have made a difference but chose not to.

The 1990s were a revolutionary decade for humanitarian action. At one time or another, crises on four different continents dominated the international agenda. The Security Council authorized more than a dozen Chapter VII operations in response to conscience-shocking human catastrophes; regional organizations were seized with these issues and responded; militaries and humanitarian agencies adopted new policies and practices.

For all the despair, it was also a decade in which the lives of literally hundreds of thousands were saved. Collective efforts assisted and protected human beings caught in the throes of deadly conflicts.

Political and institutional leaders now accept a moral responsibility for civilians whose lives are threatened, wherever they may be located. The obstacles to making good on this responsibility do not appear insurmountable. The Security Council is no longer fundamentally split. In the face of a veto, there are other multilateral measures, especially through regional organizations, that can provide legitimacy. After a decade of experiments, the operational challenges are apparent. A litany of reports have set out the changes necessary, and it is now a question of implementation.

In this new environment, the onus is truly on leadership. Responsibilities are allocated in the centres of power – whether in the capitals of major powers, the headquarters of international organizations, or wider stakeholder institutions. At the same time, military contingents, humanitarian agencies, and individuals are accountable in the field for decisions – those made and those avoided. Macro-level decisions are operationalized through a myriad of micro-level decisions and the actions that follow. When it comes to mobilizing the will to act, people matter.

Perversely, while the protection of civilians at risk has gained public attention in recent years, confidence in the ability of international law and the UN to deal with them has ebbed. The leadership challenge is to mobilize domestic and international support as a matter of basic human decency and hard-headed realism. At the beginning of the 21st century, there appear to be a growing number of parliamentarians and pundits, scholars and practitioners, citizens and humanitarians of all stripes who believe it possible and necessary to make good on the obligation to ensure protection for civilians threatened by war's worst horrors – ethnic cleansing, slaughter, and genocide.

## NOTES

1   *Report of the Panel on United Nations Peace Operations* (New York: United Nations, August 2000), p. 17, para. 103.

2   See Akihiko Tanaka, "The Domestic Context: Japanese Politics and UN Peacekeeping," in Selig S. Harrison and Masashi Nishihara, eds., *UN Peacekeeping: Japanese and American Perspective* (Washington, DC: Brookings Institution, 1995), pp. 89–105.

3   For Canada, see Commission of Inquiry into the Deployment of Canadian Forces to Somalia, *Dishonoured Legacy: The Lessons of the Somali Affair – Report of the Commission of Inquiry into the Deployment of Canadian Forces to Somalia* (Ottawa: Commission of Inquiry into the Deployment of Canadian Forces to Somalia, 1997). For the Netherlands, see a forthcoming report by Netherlands Institute for War Research. For Belgium, see Belgium Senate Session 1997–1998, *Le Rapport de la Commission d'enquête parlementaire concernant les événements du Rwanda* [Parliamentary commission of inquiry regarding the events in Rwanda] (December 6, 1997).

4   This research is being conducted by the American Society of International Law. See Charlotte Ku and Harold K. Jacobson, "Using Military Forces under International Auspices and Democratic Accountability," *International Relations of the Asia–Pacific* 1, no. 1 (2001), pp. 21–50.

5   See, for example, S. Neil MacFarlane and Thomas G. Weiss, "Political Interest and Humanitarian Action," *Security Studies* 10, no. 1 (Autumn 2000), pp. 112–142.

6   See Nik Gowing, *Media Coverage: Help or Hindrance in Conflict Prevention* (New York: Carnegie Commission on Preventing Deadly Conflict, 1997); Warren P. Stroble, *Late-Breaking Foreign Policy: The News Media's Influence on Peace Operations* (Washington, DC: US Institute of Peace Press, 1997); Edward R. Girardet, ed., *Somalia, Rwanda, and Beyond: The Role of the International Media in Wars and Humanitarian Crises* (Dublin: Crosslines Publications, 1995); Johanna Neuman, *Lights, Camera, War: Is Media Technology Driving International Politics?* (New York: St. Martin's Press, 1996); Colin Scott, Larry Minear, and Thomas G. Weiss, *The News Media, Humanitarian Action, and Civil War* (Boulder: Lynne Rienner, 1996); and Robert I. Rotberg and Thomas G. Weiss, eds., *From Massacres to Genocide: The Media, Public Policy, and Humanitarian Crises* (Washington, DC: Brookings Institution, 1996).

7   For a somewhat jaded account of Canadian decision making in this instance, see David Pugliese, "Nobel Fever," *Saturday Night* (May 1997), pp. 52–62 and 112.

8   See Andrew Natsios, "Illusions of Influence: The CNN Effect in Complex Emergencies," in Rotberg and Weiss, eds., *From Massacres to Genocide: The Media, Public Policy, and Humanitarian Crises*, pp. 149–168.

9   On China, see David M. Bachman, "Structure and Process in the Making of Chinese Foreign Policy," in Samuel Kim, ed., *China and the World: Chinese Foreign Policy Faces the New Millennium* (Boulder: Westview Press, 1998), pp. 34–54.

10  Kimberly M. Zisk, "Lending Troops: Canada, India, and UN Peacekeeping," paper presented at the Annual Convention of the International Studies Association, Los Angeles, March 17, 2000, p. 4.

11  Brigette Stern, ed., *United Nations Peace-keeping Operations: A Guide to French Policies* (Tokyo: UN University Press, 1998), p. 124.

12  Edward Luck, *Mixed Messages: American Politics and International Organization 1919–1999* (Washington, DC: Brookings Institution, 1999).

13  *Report of the Independent Inquiry into the Actions of the United Nations during the 1994 Genocide in Rwanda*, UN Document S/1999/1257, December 15, 1999. For another account of the shortcomings of the UN during the Rwandan genocide, see Michael N. Barnett, "The UN Security Council, Indifference, and Genocide in Rwanda," *Cultural Anthropology* 12, no. 4 (1998), pp. 551–578.

14  *Report of the Independent Inquiry into the Actions of the United Nations*; and *Srebrenica: Report on the Fall of Srebrenica*, UN Document A54/549, November 15, 1999.

15  *Final Report of the UN Panel of Experts on Violations of Security Council Sanctions against UNITA*, UN document S/2000/203, March 10, 2000.

16  "Letter from the Chair of the Security Council Committee Established Pursuant to Resolution 864 (1993) Concerning the Situation in Angola Addressed to the President of the Security Council," UN Document S/1999/644; and "Report on the Chairman's Visit to Europe and Participation in the Seventieth Ordinary Session of the Council of Ministers of the Organization of African Unity," UN Document S/1999/829, July 28, 1999.

17  Angola Peace Monitor, "Waiting on Empty Promises: The Human Cost of International Inaction on Angolan Sanctions," April 2000, http://www.anc.org.za/angola/actsareportv4.html

18  *See Report of the Panel of Experts Appointed Pursuant to Security Council Resolution 1306 (2000)*, UN Document S/2000/1195, December 20, 2000; and *Report of the Panel of Experts on the Illegal Exploitation of Natural Resources and Other Forms of Wealth of the Democratic Republic of Congo*, UN Document S/2001/357, April 12, 2001.

19  *Report of the Panel on United Nations Peace Operations*, p. 9. The report also expresses some hesitation about "extending additional protection to civilians in armed conflicts," owing to the dim prospects that sufficient resources would be provided. See p. 11.

20  James Appathurai and Ralph Lyshysyn, "Lessons Learned from the Zaire Mission," *Canadian Foreign Policy* 5, no. 2 (Winter 1998), pp. 93–105.

21  For an overview of the ECOMOG case, see Michael S. Lund and Ugo Solinas, "West Africa: Intervention Precedes Legitimacy," http://www.euforic.org/euconflict/sfp/part2/280_.htm; and Inter Press Service, "Chronology of Liberia's July Elections," http://ips.org/index.htm

22  Gabon and Senegal subsequently provided military forces as well. ECOWAS members include Benin, Burkina Faso, Cape Verde, Côte d'Ivoire, the Gambia, Ghana, Guinea, Guinea-Bissau, Liberia, Mali, Mauritania, Niger, Nigeria, Senegal, Sierra Leone, and Togo.

# PART II

# BIBLIOGRAPHY

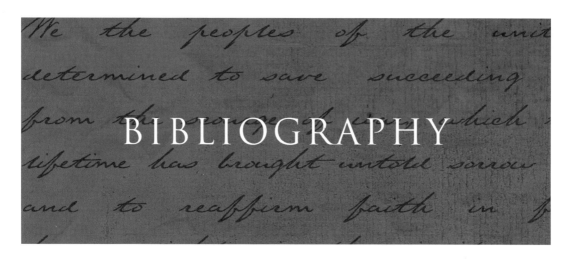

# BIBLIOGRAPHY

This extensive bibliography is designed to illustrate the range of material published on all aspects of humanitarian intervention and to provide a foundation for future research and policy development. The references are divided into 12 categories and roughly follow the structure of the main body of this supplementary volume. A short selection of key references – 10 to 12 – is listed, along with abstracts, at the beginning of each section.

The selection of titles for the bibliography is informed by several principles. An overarching objective was to include as wide a range of differing views as possible. In an attempt to be comprehensive, references were chosen not only through personal familiarity, but also on the basis of wide consultations with scholars and practitioners worldwide. The final section covers a selection of country cases. More than 20 specific interventions are covered in the historical overview, in the second part of the Research component of this volume. The cases from the post-1990 period were included, as were the three most important from the previous era – East Pakistan, Cambodia, and Uganda.

Given the overwhelmingly trans-Atlantic nature of the debate on humanitarian intervention, priority was given to seeking out non-Western views wherever possible. While examples appear throughout the bibliography, there is also a dedicated section on national and regional perspectives. A special effort was also made to cover not only the academic literature but also materials produced by governments, international organizations, and NGOs, including in some cases official documents. Many, though not all, of the citations in this volume also appear in the bibliography.

Difficult choices were required. Many of the selections could easily have been placed into more than one of the 12 subsections of the bibliography. It was difficult, for example, to separate neatly legal from ethical literatures. However, references were never duplicated. Where they would fit into different subsections, they were listed in the general category of humanitarian intervention or assigned to the category that seemed most directly relevant.

For edited collections and special issues of journals, the volume in question generally is cited, rather than each of the specific parts. However, where an article or a chapter in such a volume was deemed to be of particular significance, it figures separately in the appropriate section.

While this list of references will undoubtedly be useful, a fully key-worded and searchable electronic version is also available on CD-ROM and at the following website: http://www.iciss-ciise.gc.ca/

The bibliography is broken down into the following 12 categories:

1. Humanitarian Intervention
2. Sovereignty and Intervention
3. Conflict Prevention
4. Ethical Aspects
5. Legal Aspects
6. Interest and Will
7. National and Regional Perspectives
8. Nonmilitary Interventions
9. Operational Aspects of Military Interventions
10. Military Intervention and Humanitarian Action
11. Post-Conflict Challenges
12. Country Cases

# 1. HUMANITARIAN INTERVENTION

Advisory Council on International Affairs and Advisory Committee on Issues of Public International Law. *Humanitarian Intervention*. The Hague: Advisory Council on International Affairs, 2000.
Reassessment of the concept of humanitarian intervention and the issues raised by the experiences of the 1990s.

Annan, Kofi A. *The Question of Intervention: Statements by the Secretary-General*. New York: United Nations Department of Public Information, 1999.
Influential statements by the Secretary-General, including "Two Concepts of Sovereignty." Affirms the legitimacy of interventions in a world of sovereign states by placing the protection of human rights at the centre of the UN's work.

Bull, Hedley, ed. *Intervention in World Politics*. Oxford: Clarendon Press, 1984.
Classic collection, elucidating 1980s thinking on interventions and related issues. Contains widely cited essays, such as Stanley Hoffmann's "The Problem of Intervention," Rosalyn Higgins' "Intervention and International Law," and Michael Akehurst's "Humanitarian Intervention."

Danish Institute of International Affairs. *Humanitarian Intervention: Legal and Political Aspects*. Copenhagen: Danish Institute of International Affairs, 1999.
Explores political and legal aspects of humanitarian interventions and reviews four legal–political strategies, ranging from the status quo to the codification of a doctrine of humanitarian intervention.

Forbes, Ian and Mark Hoffman, eds. *Political Theory, International Relations, and the Ethics of Intervention*. New York: St. Martin's Press, 1993.
Assembles a variety of competing approaches and combines history and theory concerning the question of whether and when intervention may be justified.

Jackson, Robert H. *The Global Covenant: Human Conduct in a World of States*. Oxford: Oxford University Press, 2000.
Places the major armed interventions since the end of the Cold War into the pluralist framework of the international society approach.

Lyons, Gene M. and Michael Mastanduno, eds. *Beyond Westphalia? State Sovereignty and International Intervention*. Baltimore: The Johns Hopkins University Press, 1995.
Collection of essays dealing with the concepts of sovereignty and intervention, with an emphasis on transformations in their meaning and practice.

Nederveen Pieterse, Jan, ed. *World Orders in the Making: Humanitarian Intervention and Beyond*. Basingstoke: Macmillan in association with Institute of Social Studies, 1998.
Addresses the legal, military, sociological, and humanitarian aspects of intervention. Regards humanitarian intervention as part of the changing global architecture.

Ramsbotham, Oliver P. and Tom Woodhouse. *Humanitarian Intervention in Contemporary Conflict: A Reconceptualization*. Cambridge: Polity Press, 1996.
Review of the literature on humanitarian intervention, its essential concepts, and their evolution. Brings together perspectives of international relief organizations and the military.

Wheeler, Nicholas J. *Saving Strangers: Humanitarian Intervention in International Society*. Oxford: Oxford University Press, 2000.
Theoretically informed account of seven interventions, three in the 1970s and four in the 1990s. Claims that a customary norm of humanitarian intervention is emerging.

# References

Abiew, Francis Kofi. "Assessing Humanitarian Intervention in the Post-Cold War Period: Sources of Consensus." *International Relations* Vol. 14 No. 2 (1998): 61–90.

Académie du Royaume du Maroc, ed. *Le droit d'ingérence est-il une nouvelle légalisation du colonialisme?* Rabat: ARM, 1992.

Aroneau, Eugène. "La guerre internationale d'intervention pour cause d'humanité." *Revue Internationale de Droit Pénal* (1948): 173–244.

Ayoob, Mohammed, ed. *Conflict and Intervention in the Third World.* London: Croom Helm, 1980.

Bailey, Sydney D. *Humanitarian Intervention in the Internal Affairs of States.* Basingstoke: Macmillan, 1996.

Ball, M. Margaret. "Issue for the Americas: Non-Intervention v. Human Rights and the Preservation of Democratic Institutions." *International Organization* Vol. 15 No. 1 (1961): 21–37.

Beach, Hugo. *Just Intervention?* London: The Council for Arms Control, 1993.

Bennet, Andrew and Joseph Lepgold. "Reinventing Collective Security after the Cold War and Gulf Conflict." *Political Science Quarterly* Vol. 108 No. 2 (1993): 213–237.

Beyerlin, Ulrich. "Humanitarian Intervention." In *Encyclopedia of Public International Law*, edited by Rudolf Bernhardt, 211–215. Amsterdam: North-Holland Publishing Company, 1982.

Blechman, Barry M. "The Intervention Dilemma." *Washington Quarterly* Vol. 18 No. 3 (1995): 63–73.

Bonser, Michael. "Humanitarian Intervention in the Post-Cold War World: A Cautionary Tale." *Canadian Foreign Policy* Vol. 8 No. 3 (2001): 57–74.

Boutros-Ghali, Boutros. *An Agenda for Peace, 1995: With the New Supplement and Related UN Documents.* New York: United Nations, 1995.

Boutros-Ghali, Boutros. "An Agenda for Peace: One Year Later." *Orbis* Vol. 37 No. 3 (1993): 323–332.

Boutros-Ghali, Boutros. "Empowering the United Nations." *Foreign Affairs* Vol. 71 No. 5 (1992/1993): 89–102.

Boyé, Marc, Bernard Briand and René Coste et al. *Vous avez dit ingérence: nouveaux propos sur le droit et le devoir d'ingérence.* Boulogne: Editions du Griot, 1994.

Brilmayer, Lea. "What's the Matter with Selective Intervention?" *Arizona Law Review* Vol. 37 No. 4 (1995): 955–970.

Brown, Michael E., ed. *The International Dimensions of Internal Conflict.* Cambridge, MA: MIT Press, 1996.

Bruderlein, Claude. "People's Security as a New Means of Global Stability." *International Review of the Red Cross* Vol. 83 No. 842 (2001): 353–366.

Brunkhorst, Hauke, ed. *Einmischung erwünscht? Menschenrechte und bewaffnete Intervention.* Frankfurt am Main: Fischer, 1998.

Bugnion, François. "Le droit international humanitaire à l'épreuve des conflits de notre temps." *International Review of the Red Cross* Vol. 81 No. 835 (1999): 487–497.

Caballero Juárez, José Antonio. "La intervención humanitaria en el siglo XIX." In *Liber ad honorem Sergio García Ramírez*, edited by Universidad Nacional Autónomade México, 163–177. México: Universidad Nacional Autónoma, 1998.

Caplan, Richard. "Humanitarian Intervention: Which Way Forward?" *Ethics and International Affairs* Vol. 14 (2000): 23–38.

Cassidy, Robert. "Sovereignty versus the Chimera of Armed Humanitarian Intervention." *Fletcher Forum of World Affairs* Vol. 21 No. 2 (1997): 47–63.

Chakrabarti, Rhadanaman. *Intervention and the Problem of Its Control in the Twentieth Century*. New York: Sterling Publishers, 1974.

Charvet, John. "The Idea of State Sovereignty and the Right of Humanitarian Intervention." *International Political Science Review* Vol. 18 No. 1 (1997): 39–48.

Chemillier-Gendreau, Monique. "Portée et limites de l'ingérence humanitaire en Afrique." *Afrique Contemporaine* Vol. 180 (1996): 229–241.

Chestnut, Tricia and Ken Kohut, eds. *International Intervention: A Challenge to World Order?* Winnipeg: University of Manitoba Centre for Defence Studies, 1997.

Collins, Cindy and Thomas G. Weiss. *An Overview and Assessment of 1989–1996 Peace Operations Publications*. Providence: Thomas J. Watson Jr. Institute for International Studies, 1997.

Condorelli, Luigi. "Intervention humanitaire et/ou assistance humanitaire? Quelques certitudes et beaucoup d'intérrogations." In *International Legal Issues Arising under the United Nations Decade of International Law*, edited by Najeeb Al-Nauimi and Richard Meese, 999–1012. The Hague: Martinus Nijhoff, 1995.

Connaughton, Richard. *Military Intervention in the 1990s: A New Logic of War*. London: Routledge, 1992.

Cooper, Robert and Mats Berdal. "Outside Intervention in Ethnic Conflicts." *Survival* Vol. 35 No. 1 (1993): 118–142.

Cutler, Lloyd N. "The Right to Intervene." *Foreign Affairs* Vol. 64 No. 1 (1985): 96–122.

Dacyl, Janina W. "Sovereignty versus Human Rights: From Past Discourses to Contemporary Dilemmas." *Journal of Refugee Studies* Vol. 9 No. 2 (1996): 136–165.

Damrosch, Lori Fisler, ed. *Enforcing Restraint: Collective Intervention in Internal Conflicts*. New York: Council on Foreign Relations Press, 1993.

Debiel, Tobias. "Not und Intervention in einer Welt des Umbruchs: Zu Imperativen und Fallstricken humanitärer Einmischung." *Aus Politik und Zeitgeschichte* Vol. B 33–34 (1996): 29–38.

Debiel, Tobias and Franz Nuscheler, eds. *Der neue Interventionismus: Humanitäre Einmischung zwischen Anspruch und Wirklichkeit*. Bonn: J.H.W. Dietz, 1996.

Delpal, Marie-Christine. *Politique extérieure et diplomatie morale, le droit d'ingérence humanitaire en question*. Paris: Fondation pour les études de défense nationale, 1993.

Deyra, Michel. "'Initiative', 'assistance', 'ingérence': tentative de clarification de concepts parfois galvaudés." *Revue Québécoise de Droit International* Vol. 8 No. 1 (1993/1994): 88–94.

Diehl, Paul F. "United Nations Interventions and Recurring Conflict." *International Organization* Vol. 50 (1996): 683–700.

Dorman, Andrew M. and Thomas G. Otte, eds. *Military Intervention: From Gunboat Diplomacy to Humanitarian Intervention*. Aldershot: Dartmouth, 1995.

Driscoll, Dennis, ed., *Humanitarian Intervention*. Galway: Irish Centre for Human Rights, forthcoming Winter 2001/2002.

Duffield, Mark and John Prendergast. "Sovereignty and Intervention after the Cold War: Lessons from the Emergency Relief Desk." *Middle East Report* Vol. 24 No. 2/3 (1994): 9–15.

Dunér, Bertil. *Military Intervention in Civil Wars: The 1970s*. Aldershot: Gower, 1985.

Dunér, Bertil. "Proxy Intervention in Civil Wars." *Journal of Peace Research* Vol. 18 No. 4 (1981): 353–361.

Dupuy, Pierre-Marie. "Une évolution en quatre phases." *Défense Nationale* Vol. 56 No. 3 (2000): 27–31.

Eisemann, P.M. "Devoir d'ingérence et non-intervention: de la nécessité de remettre quelques pendules à l'heure." *Relations Internationales et Stratégiques* Vol. 1 No. 3 (1991).

Elfstrom, Gerard. "On Dilemmas of Intervention." *Ethics* Vol. 93 No. 4 (1983): 709–725.

Evans, Gareth. "Cooperative Security and Intrastate Conflict." *Foreign Policy* No. 96 (1994): 3–20.

Fennell, James. "Hope Suspended: Morality, Politics and War in Central Africa." *Disasters* Vol. 22 No. 2 (1998): 96–108.

Ferrari DaPassano, Paolo. "Quale diritto di ingerenza umanitaria?" *La civiltà cattolica* Vol. 150 No. 3583 (1999): 14–25.

Florescu, Octavian. "Sur l'intervention humanitaire." *Romanian Journal of International Affairs* Vol. 2 No. 1/2 (1996): 102–117.

Freedman, Lawrence, ed. *Strategic Coercion*. Oxford: Oxford University Press, 1998.

Freedman, Lawrence, ed. *Military Intervention in European Conflicts*. Oxford: Blackwell, 1994.

Friedling, Bernard. "Les forces interafricaines d'intervention pour le maintien de la paix." *Défense Nationale* Vol. 54 (1998): 117–123.

Friedmann, Wolfgang. "Interventionism, Liberalism, and Power Politics: The Unfinished Revolution in International Thinking." *Political Science Quarterly* Vol. 83 No. 2 (1968): 169–189.

Frye, Alton. *Humanitarian Intervention: Crafting a Workable Doctrine: Three Options Presented as Memoranda to the President*. New York: Council on Foreign Relations, 2000.

Garrett, Stephen A. *Doing Good and Doing Well: An Examination of Humanitarian Intervention*. Westport: Praeger, 1999.

Ghozali, Nacer Eddine. "Heurs et malheurs du devoir d'ingérence humanitaire." *Relations Internationales et Stratégiques* Vol. 1 No. 3 (1991).

Gillespie, Thomas R. "Unwanted Responsibility: Humanitarian Military Intervention to Advance Human Rights." *Peace and Change* Vol. 18 No. 3 (1993): 219–246.

Glennon, Michael J. "The New Interventionism: The Search for a Just International Law." *Foreign Affairs* Vol. 78 No. 3 (1999): 2–7.

Goldman, Steven E. "A Right of Intervention Based upon Impaired Sovereignty." *World Affairs* Vol. 156 (1994): 126–129.

Goodby, James E. "Collective Security in Europe after the Cold War." *Journal of International Affairs* Vol. 46 No. 2 (1993): 299–321.

Goodman, Louis. "Democracy, Sovereignty, and Intervention." *American University Journal of International Law* Vol. 9 No. 1 (1993): 27.

Griffin, Michèle. "Where Angels Fear To Tread: Trends in International Intervention." *Security Dialogue* Vol. 31 No. 4 (2000): 421–435.

Gustenau, Gustav, ed. *Humanitäre militärische Intervention zwischen Legalität und Legitimität: Tagungsband des Instituts für internationale Friedenssicherung, Wien*. Baden-Baden: Nomos, 2000.

Harff, Barbara. *Genocide and Human Rights: International Legal and Political Issues*. Denver: University of Denver Graduate School of International Studies, 1984.

Hayden, Robert M. "Humanitarian Hypocrisy." *East European Constitutional Review* Vol. 8 No. 3 (1999): 91–96.

Helton, Arthur C. "Forced Migration, Humanitarian Intervention, and Sovereignty." *SAIS Review* Vol. 20 No. 1 (2000): 61–86.

Hodges, Henry. *The Doctrine of Intervention*. Chicago: The Banner Press, 1915.

Hoffmann, Stanley, ed. *The Ethics and Politics of Humanitarian Intervention*. Notre Dame: University of Notre Dame Press, 1996.

Hoffmann, Stanley. "The Politics and Ethics of Military Intervention." *Survival* Vol. 37 No. 4 (1995/1996): 29–51.

Hopkinson, Nicholas. *Humanitarian Intervention?* London: Her Majesty's Stationery Office, 1995.

Jonge Oudraat, Chantal de. "Humanitarian Intervention: The Lessons Learned." *Current History* Vol. 99 No. 641 (2000): 419–429.

Jonge Oudraat, Chantal de. *Intervention in Internal Conflicts: Legal and Political Conundrums.* Washington, DC: Carnegie Endowment for International Peace, 2000.

Kamminga, Menno T. *Inter-State Accountability for Violations of Human Rights.* Philadelphia: University of Pennsylvania Press, 1992.

Kannyo, Edward. "Civil Strife and Humanitarian Intervention in Africa: A Preliminary Assessment." *African Yearbook of International Law* Vol. 4 (1996): 51–82.

Kervarec, Gaëlle. "L'intervention d'humanité dans le cadre des limites au principe de non-intervention." *Revue Juridique Thémis* Vol. 32 No. 1 (1998): 77–133.

Knudsen, Tonny Brems. "European Approaches to Humanitarian Intervention: From Just War to Assistance – and Back Again?" In *European Approaches to Crisis Management,* edited by Knud Erik Jørgensen, 171–199. The Hague: Kluwer Law International, 1997.

Knudsen, Tonny Brems. "Humanitarian Intervention Revisited: Post-Cold War Responses to Classical Problems." *International Peacekeeping* Vol. 3 No. 4 (1996): 146–165.

Kritsiotis, Dino. "Reappraising Policy Objections to Humanitarian Intervention." *Michigan Journal of International Law* Vol. 19 No. 4 (1998): 1005–1050.

Kuiper, Marcus A. "Keeping the Peace: Reflections on the Rules of the Game for International Intervention in the 1990s." *Journal of Slavic Military Studies* Vol. 6 No. 4 (1993): 562–575.

Kupchan, Charles A. and Clifford A. Kupchan. "Concerts, Collective Security and the Future of Europe." *International Security* Vol. 16 No. 1 (1991): 114–161.

Labouérie, Guy. "État et humanitaire." *Études* (1995): 475–484.

Lang, Anthony F. *Agency and Ethics: The Politics of Military Intervention.* Albany: State University of New York Press, 2001.

Legault, Albert, Craig Murphy and W. Ofuatey-Kodjoe. *The State of the United Nations.* Providence: Academic Council on the United Nations System, 1992.

Levite, Ariel, Bruce W. Jentleson and Larry Berman. *Foreign Military Intervention: The Dynamics of Protracted Conflict.* New York: Columbia University Press, 1994.

Lewy, Guenter. "The Case for Humanitarian Intervention." *Orbis* Vol. 37 No. 4 (1993): 621–632.

Luca, Donatella. "Intervention humanitaire: questions et réflexions." *International Journal of Refugee Law* Vol. 5 No. 3 (1993): 424–441.

Luttwak, Edward N. "Kofi's Rule: Humanitarian Intervention and Neocolonialism." *The National Interest* No. 58 (1999/2000): 57–62.

Madelin, Alain. *Le droit du plus faible: essai.* Paris: R. Laffont, 1999.

Malan, Mark. "The Principle of Non-Interference and the Future of Multinational Intervention in Africa." *African Security Review* Vol. 6 No. 3 (1997): 29–37.

Mariño Menendez, Fernando M., ed. *Los estados y las organizaciones internacionales ante el nuevo contexto de la seguridad en Europa.* Madrid: Universidad III de Madrid, 1995.

Martíne, R. "Conceptos actuales sobre soberania e intervención." *Revista de la Facultad de Derecho y Ciencias Sociales* Vol. 3 No. 2/3 (1952): 505–538.

Maynes, Charles W. "Relearning Intervention." *Foreign Policy* No. 98 (1995): 96–113.

McDermott, Anthony, ed. *Sovereign Intervention.* Oslo: International Peace Research Institute, 1999.

McDermott, Anthony, ed. *Humanitarian Force.* Oslo: International Peace Research Institute, 1997.

McWhinney, Edward. *The United Nations and a New World Order for a New Millennium: Self-Determination, State Succession and Humanitarian Intervention*. The Hague: Kluwer Law International, 2000.

Merino Birto, E. "Intervención y soberania." *Política Internacional* Vol. 10 (1966): 23–39.

Merle, Jean-Christophe and Alessandro Pinzani. "Rechtfertigung und Modalitäten eines Rechts auf humanitäre Intervention." *Vierteljahresschrift für Sicherheit und Frieden* Vol. 18 No. 1 (2000): 71–75.

Midlarsky, Manus I., ed. *The Internationalization of Communal Strife*. London: Routledge, 1992.

Mills, Kurt. "Sovereignty Eclipsed? The Legitimacy of Humanitarian Access and Intervention." *Journal of Humanitarian Assistance* (July 1997): http://www.jha.ac/articles/a019.htm

Minear, Larry and Thomas G. Weiss. *Mercy under Fire: War and the Global Humanitarian Community*. Boulder: Westview, 1995.

Nederveen Pieterse, Jan. "Sociology of Humanitarian Intervention: Bosnia, Rwanda and Somalia Compared." *International Political Science Review* Vol. 18 No. 1 (1997): 71–93.

Noel, Jacques. *Le principe de non-intervention: théorie et pratique dans les relations inter-américaines*. Bruxelles: Bruylant, 1981.

Paolini, Albert J., Anthony P. Jarvis and Christian Reus-Smit, eds. *Between Sovereignty and Global Governance: The United Nations, the State and Civil Society*. Basingstoke: Macmillan, 1998.

Pape, Matthias. *Humanitäre Intervention: Zur Bedeutung der Menschenrechte in den Vereinten Nationen*. Baden-Baden: Nomos, 1997.

Parekh, Bikhu. "Rethinking Humanitarian Intervention." *International Political Science Review* Vol. 18 No. 1 (1997): 49–69.

Pauer, Alexander. *Die humanitäre Intervention: Militärische und wirtschaftliche Zwangsmaßnahmen zur Gewährleistung der Menschenrechte*. Basel: Helbing and Lichtenhahn, 1985.

Peace Review. "Special Issue: Humanitarian Intervention?" Vol. 8 (1996): 459–576.

Pearson, Frederic S. "Foreign Military Interventions and Domestic Disputes." *International Studies Quarterly* Vol. 18 No. 3 (1974): 259–290.

Pease, Kelly Kate and David P. Forsythe. "Human Rights, Humanitarian Intervention, and World Politics." *Human Rights Quarterly* Vol. 15 No. 2 (1993): 290–314.

Pellet, Alain. "Droit d'ingérence ou devoir d'assistance humanitaire?" *Problèmes Politiques et Sociaux* No. 758/759 (1995): 1–133.

Perrot, Marie-Dominique, ed. *Dérives humanitaires: états d'urgence et droit d'ingérence*. Paris: Presses Universitaires de France, 1994.

Pons, Frédéric, Alain-Gérard Slama and Jean-Marc Varant. *Action humanitaire et politique internationale: politique et morale*. Paris: Centre d'analyse sur la sécurité européenne, 1993.

Rajan, Mannaraswamighala Sreeranga. "The New Interventionism?" *International Studies* Vol. 37 No. 1 (2000): 31–40.

Ramsbotham, Oliver P. "Humanitarian Intervention: 1990–1995. A Need to Reconceptualize?" *Review of International Studies* Vol. 23 No. 4 (1997): 445–468.

Reed, Laura W. and Carl Kaysen, eds. *Emerging Norms of Justified Intervention: A Collection of Essays from a Project of the American Academy of Arts and Sciences*. Cambridge, MA: Committee on International Security Studies, American Academy of Arts and Sciences, 1993.

Revista de Occidente. "Special Issue: Humanitarian Intervention." No. 236/237 (2001): 5–168.

Ritterband, Charles E. *Universeller Menschenrechtsschutz und völkerrechtliches Interventionsverbot*. Bern: Haupt, 1982.

Roberts, Adam. "The Road to Hell: A Critique of Humanitarian Intervention." *Current* No. 363 (1994): 24–28.

Roberts, Adam. "Humanitarian War: Military Intervention and Human Rights." *International Affairs* Vol. 69 No. 3 (1993): 429–449.

Rosas, Allan. "Focus on the Case for Intervention: Towards Some International Law and Order." *Journal of Peace Research* Vol. 31 No. 2 (1994): 129–135.

Rosenau, James N., ed. *International Aspects of Civil Strife*. Princeton: Princeton University Press, 1964.

Rudolf, Joseph R. "Intervention in Communal Conflicts." *Orbis* Vol. 39 No. 2 (1995): 259–273.

Rufin, Jean-Christophe. *L'aventure humanitaire*. Paris: Gallimard, 1994.

Rumpf, Helmut. *Der internationale Schutz der Menschenrechte und das Interventionsverbot*. Baden-Baden: Nomos, 1981.

Ryan, Christopher M. "Sovereignty, Intervention, and the Law: A Tenuous Relationship of Competing Principles." *Millennium* Vol. 26 No. 1 (1997): 77–100.

Ryniker, Anne. "Position du CICR sur l'intervention humanitaire." *International Review of the Red Cross* Vol. 83 No. 842 (2001): 521–526.

Sarooshi, Danesh. *Humanitarian Intervention and International Humanitarian Assistance: Law and Practice*. London: Her Majesty's Stationery Office, 1993.

Scheffer, David J., Richard N. Gardner and Gerald B. Helman. *Post-Gulf War Challenges to the UN Collective Security System: Three Views on the Issue of Humanitarian Intervention*. Washington, DC: United States Institute of Peace, 1992.

Schnabel, Albrecht. "Humanitarian Intervention: A Conceptual Analysis." In *Peacekeeping at a Crossroads*, edited by S. Neil MacFarlane, 19–44. Clemensport: Canadian Peacekeeping Press, 1997.

Schwarz, Urs. *Confrontation and Intervention in the Modern World*. Dobbs-Ferry: Oceana, 1970.

Semb, Anne-Julie. *The Normative Foundation of the Principle of Non-Intervention*. Oslo: International Peace Research Institute, 1992.

Senarclens, Pierre de. "Le 'droit d'ingérence' est inutile et sa rhétorique peut-être néfaste." *Défense Nationale* Vol. 56 No. 3 (2000): 6–13.

Simons, Penelope. *Humanitarian Intervention: A Review of the Literature*. Waterloo: Project Ploughshares, 2000.

Snow, Donald M. *Uncivil Wars: International Security and the New Internal Conflicts*. Boulder: Lynne Rienner, 1996.

Solarz, Stephen J. and Michael E. O'Hanlon. "Humanitarian Intervention: When Is Force Justified?" *Washington Quarterly* Vol. 20 No. 4 (1997): 3–14.

Sornarajah, M. "Internal Colonialism and Humanitarian Intervention." *Georgia Journal of International and Comparative Law* Vol. 11 (1981): 45–77.

Stack, John F. and Lui Hebron, eds. *The Ethnic Entanglement: Conflict and Intervention in World Politics*. Westport: Praeger, 1999.

Thakur, Ramesh. "Non-Intervention in International Relations: A Case Study." *Political Science* Vol. 42 No. 1 (1990): 27–61.

Thomas, Caroline. *New States, Sovereignty and Intervention*. Aldershot: Gower, 1985.

Thuan, Cao-Huy et al., eds. *Mutations internationales et évolution des normes*. Paris: Presses Universitaires de France, 1994.

Tilford, Earl H., ed. *Two Perspectives on Interventions and Humanitarian Operations*. Carlisle Barracks: US Army War College Strategic Studies Institute, 1997.

Tillema, H.K. and J.R. Van Wingen. "Law and Power in Military Intervention: Major States after World War II." *International Studies Quarterly* Vol. 26 No. 2 (1982): 220–250.

Tyagi, Yogesh K. "The Concept of Humanitarian Intervention Revisited." *Michigan Journal of International Law* Vol. 16 No. 3 (1995): 883–910.

Väyrynen, Raimo. *Enforcement and Humanitarian Intervention: Two Faces of Collective Action by the United Nations.* Notre Dame: Kroc Institute, 1995.

Verhoeven, Joe. "Human Rights, Intervention and Universality." In *Proceedings of the International Law Association First Asian–Pacific Regional Conference,* edited by Hungdah Chiu, 98–119. Taipei: Chinese Society of International Law, 1996.

Vincent, R.J. *Human Rights and International Relations.* Cambridge: Cambridge University Press, 1986.

Vogel, Tobias. "The Politics of Humanitarian Intervention." *Journal of Humanitarian Assistance* (September 1996): http://www.jha.ac/articles/a011.htm

Von Lipsey, Roderick K., ed. *Breaking the Cycle: A Framework for Conflict Intervention.* Basingstoke: Macmillan, 1997.

Wallensteen, Peter, ed. *International Intervention: New Norms in the Post-Cold War Era?* Uppsala, Sweden: Department of Peace and Conflict Research, Uppsala University, 1997.

Walter, Barbara F. and Jack L. Snyder, eds. *Civil Wars, Insecurity, and Intervention.* New York: Columbia University Press, 1999.

Weiss, Thomas G. "Triage: Humanitarian Interventions in a New Era." *World Policy Journal* Vol. 11 No. 1 (1994): 1–10.

Wheeler, Nicholas J. "Agency, Humanitarianism and Intervention." *International Political Science Review* Vol. 18 No. 1 (1997): 9–25.

Wheeler, Nicholas J. and Justin Morris. "Humanitarian Intervention and State Practice at the End of the Cold War." In *International Society after the Cold War: Anarchy and Order Reconsidered,* edited by Rick Fawn and Jeremy Larkins, 135–171. Macmillan: Basingstoke, 1996.

Whitman, Jim. "After Kosovo: The Risks and Deficiencies of Unsanctioned Humanitarian Intervention." *Journal of Humanitarian Assistance* (September 2000): http://www.jha.ac/articles/a062.htm

Whitman, Jim. "A Cautionary Note on Humanitarian Intervention."*Journal of Humanitarian Assistance* (September 1996): http://www.jha.ac/articles/a001.htm

Willame, Jean-Claude. "Le génocide et la communauté internationale." *Politique Africaine* Vol. 73 (1999): 164–171.

Williamson, Roger, ed. *Some Corner of a Foreign Field: Intervention and World Order.* Basingstoke: Macmillan, 1998.

Winters, Paul A., ed. *Interventionism: Current Controversies.* San Diego: Greenhaven Press, 1995.

Yusuf, A.A., E. Kwakwa, A. El Kadiri et al. *Nation-Building, Internal Conflicts and Humanitarian Intervention in Africa.* The Hague: Kluwer Law International, 1995.

# 2. SOVEREIGNTY AND INTERVENTION

Biersteker, Thomas J. and Cynthia Weber, eds. *State Sovereignty as Social Construct*. Cambridge: Cambridge University Press, 1996.
  Collection of essays arguing that the components of state sovereignty – recognition, territory, population, and authority – are socially constructed and vary in different historical circumstances.

Chopra, Jarat and Thomas G. Weiss. "Sovereignty Is No Longer Sacrosanct: Codifying Humanitarian Intervention." *Ethics and International Affairs* Vol. 6 (1992): 95–117.
  Early review of the legal and political dimensions of humanitarian intervention, arguing that the balance between sovereignty and human rights is shifting toward the latter.

Deng, Francis M., Sadikiel Kimaro, Terrence Lyons, Donald Rothchild and I. William Zartman, eds. *Sovereignty as Responsibility: Conflict Management in Africa*. Washington, DC: Brookings Institution, 1996.
  A set of essays arguing that sovereignty cannot be seen only as protection against outside interference. Suggests that sovereignty also implies that states are accountable to both domestic and external constituencies.

Hannum, Hurst. *Autonomy, Sovereignty, and Self-Determination: The Accommodation of Conflicting Rights*. Philadelphia: University of Pennsylvania Press, 1990.
  Argues that the legitimacy of states rests upon respect for human rights and the effective participation of all segments of populations in economic and political decision making.

Hinsley, F.H. *Sovereignty*. 2nd ed. Cambridge: Cambridge University Press, 1986.
  Classic study exploring sovereignty defined as the idea that there is a final and absolute political authority in a political community and that no final and absolute authority exists above the state.

Jackson, Robert H. *Quasi-States: Sovereignty, International Relations, and the Third World*. Cambridge: Cambridge University Press, 1990.
  Investigates the international normative framework that upholds sovereign statehood in the Third World, which in some cases is more judicial than empirical.

Krasner, Stephen D. *Sovereignty: Organized Hypocrisy*. Princeton: Princeton University Press, 1999.
  Historical inquiry into the theory and practice of state sovereignty, arguing that the principle of nonintervention is routinely ignored.

Vincent, R.J. *Nonintervention and International Order*. Princeton: Princeton University Press, 1974.
  Reviews doctrines of nonintervention held by individual states and points to the importance of the principle of nonintervention as the basis for order in the society of states.

Walker, R.B.J. and Saul H. Mendlovitz, eds. *Contending Sovereignties: Redefining Political Community*. Boulder: Lynne Rienner, 1990.
  Explores the implications of emerging political communities and the resulting structural transformations to the principle of sovereignty.

## References

Allott, Philip. *Eunomia: New Order for a New World*. Oxford: Oxford University Press, 1990.

Ashley, Richard K. "Untying the Sovereign State: A Double Reading of the Anarchy Problematique." *Millennium* Vol. 17 No. 2 (1988): 227–262.

Baev, Pavel K. "External Interventions in Secessionist Conflicts in Europe." *European Security* Vol. 8 No. 2 (1999): 22–51.

Barkin, Samuel J. "The Evolution of the Constitution of Sovereignty and the Emergence of Human Rights Norms." *Millennium* Vol. 27 No. 2 (1998): 229–252.

Barkin, Samuel J. and Bruce Cronin. "The State and the Nation: Changing Norms and the Rules of Sovereignty in International Relations." *International Organization* Vol. 48 No. 1 (1994): 107–130.

Baroch, Charles T. *The Soviet Doctrine of Sovereignty: The So-Called Brezhnev Doctrine.* Chicago: American Bar Association, 1970.

Bartelson, Jens. *A Genealogy of Sovereignty.* Cambridge: Cambridge University Press, 1995.

Beloff, Max. "Reflections on Intervention." *Journal of International Affairs* Vol. 22 No. 2 (1968): 198–207.

Bernard, Montague. *On the Principle of Non-Intervention.* Oxford: J.H. and J.A.S. Parker, 1860.

Bettati, Mario, R. Bottini, René-Jean Dupuy and Paul Isoart. *La souveraineté au XXe siècle.* Paris: A. Colin, 1971.

Bodin, Jean. *On Sovereignty: Four Chapters from the Six Books of the Commonwealth.* Cambridge: Cambridge University Press, 1992.

Brown, Peter and Henry Shue, eds. *Boundaries, National Autonomy and Its Limits.* Lanham: Rowman and Littlefield, 1981.

Calhoun, Frederick S. *Power and Principle: Armed Intervention in Wilsonian Foreign Policy.* Kent: Kent State University Press, 1986.

Camilleri, Joseph A. and Jim Falk. *The End of Sovereignty? The Politics of a Shrinking and Fragmenting World.* Aldershot: Edward Elgar, 1992.

Clapham, Christopher. "Degrees of Statehood." *Review of International Studies* Vol. 24 No. 2 (1988): 143–157.

Deng, Francis M. "Reconciling Sovereignty with Responsibility: A Basis for International Humanitarian Action." In *Africa in World Politics: Post-Cold War Challenges,* edited by John Harbeson and Donald Rothchild, 295–310. Boulder: Westview Press, 1995.

Denham, Mark E. and Mark Owen Lombardi, eds. *Perspectives on Third World Sovereignty: The Postmodern Paradox.* Basingstoke: Macmillan, 1996.

Donnelly, Jack. "Human Rights, Humanitarian Crisis, and Humanitarian Intervention." *International Journal* Vol. 48 No. 4 (1993): 607–640.

Doob, Leonard W. *Intervention: Guides and Perils.* New Haven: Yale University Press, 1993.

Duchhardt, Heinz. " 'Westphalian System': Zur Problematik einer Denkfigur." *Historische Zeitschrift* Vol. 269 No. 2 (1999): 305–315.

Duke, Simon. "The State and Human Rights: Sovereignty versus Humanitarian Intervention." *International Relations* Vol. 12 No. 1 (1994): 25–48.

Dyson, Kenneth H.F. *The State Tradition in Western Europe: A Study of an Idea and Institution.* New York: Oxford University Press, 1980.

Edkins, Jenny, Nalini Persram and Véronique Pin-Fat, eds. *Sovereignty and Subjectivity.* Boulder: Lynne Rienner, 1999.

Elazar, Daniel J. *Constitutionalizing Globalization: The Postmodern Revival of Confederal Arrangements.* Lanham: Rowman and Littlefield, 1998.

Eley, J.W. "Toward a Theory of Intervention: The Limitations and Advantages of a Transnational Perspective." *International Studies Quarterly* Vol. 16 No. 2 (1972): 245–256.

Falk, Richard A. "Intervention Revisited: Hard Choices and Tragic Dilemmas." *The Nation* Vol. 21 No. 257 (1993): 755–764.

Falk, Richard A. "Recycling Interventionism." *Journal of Peace Research* Vol. 29 No. 2 (1992): 129–134.

Falk, Richard A. *Human Rights and State Sovereignty.* New York: Holmes and Meier, 1981.

Fleiner-Gerster, Thomas and Michael A. Meyer. "New Developments in Humanitarian Law: A Challenge to the Concept of Sovereignty." *International and Comparative Law Quarterly* Vol. 34 (1985): 267–283.

Fowler, Michael Ross and Julie Marie Bunck. *Law, Power, and the Sovereign State: The Evolution and Application of the Concept of Sovereignty.* University Park: Pennsylvania State University Press, 1995.

Garigue, Philippe. "Intervention-Sanction and 'droit d'ingérence' in International Humanitarian Law." *International Journal* Vol. 48 No. 4 (1993): 668–686.

Gottlieb, Gidon. *Nation against State: A New Approach to Ethnic Conflicts and the Decline of Sovereignty.* New York: Council on Foreign Relations Press, 1993.

Gow, James. "A Revolution in International Affairs?" *Security Dialogue* Vol. 31 No. 3 (2000): 293–306.

Gross, Leo. "The Peace of Westphalia 1648–1948." *American Journal of International Law* Vol. 42 No. 1 (1948): 20–41.

Grovogui, Siba N'Zatioula. *Sovereigns, Quasi Sovereigns, and Africans.* Minneapolis: University of Minnesota Press, 1996.

Guelke, Adrian. "Force, Intervention and Internal Conflict." In *The Use of Force in International Relations,* edited by F.S. Northedge, 99–123. London: Faber and Faber, 1974.

Hampson, Fen Osler. *Madness in the Multitude: Human Security and World Disorder.* Oxford: Oxford University Press, 2001.

Hashmi, Sohail H., ed. *State Sovereignty: Change and Persistence in International Relations.* University Park: Pennsylvania State University Press, 1997.

Heiberg, Marianne, ed. *Subduing Sovereignty: Sovereignty and the Right To Intervene.* London: Pinter, 1994.

Helman, Gerald B. and Steven Ratner. "Saving Failed States." *Foreign Policy* No. 89 (1992/1993): 3–20.

Helms, Jesse. "American Sovereignty and the UN." *The National Interest* No. 62 (2000): 31–34.

Hendrickson, David C. "The Democratist Crusade: Intervention, Economic Sanctions, and Engagement." *World Policy Journal* Vol. 11 No. 4 (1994/1995): 18–30.

Hermann, Margaret G. and Charles W. Kegley. "Democracies and Intervention: Is There a Danger Zone in the Democratic Peace?" *Journal of Peace Research* Vol. 38 No. 2 (2001): 237–245.

Hermann, Margaret G. and Charles W. Kegley. "Ballots, a Barrier against the Use of Bullets and Bombs: Democratization and Military Intervention." *Journal of Conflict Resolution* Vol. 40 No. 3 (1996): 436–460.

Hinsley, F.H. "The Concept of Sovereignty and the Relations between States." *Journal of International Affairs* Vol. 21 No. 2 (1967): 242–252.

Inayatullah, Naeem and David L. Blaney. "Realizing Sovereignty." *Review of International Studies* Vol. 21 (1995): 3–20.

Ionescu, Ghita. *Between Sovereignty and Integration.* London: Croom Helm, 1974.

Jäckel, Hartmut, ed. *Ist das Prinzip der Nichteinmischung überholt?* Baden-Baden: Nomos, 1995.

Jackson, Robert H., ed. *Sovereignty at the Millennium.* Oxford: Blackwell, 1999.

Jackson, Robert H. "Armed Humanitarianism." *International Journal* Vol. 48 No. 4 (1993): 579–606.

Jackson, Robert H. and Alan James, eds. *States in a Changing World*. Oxford: Clarendon Press, 1993.

Jackson, Robert H. and Carl G. Rosberg. "Sovereignty and Underdevelopment: Juridical Statehood in the African Crisis." *Journal of Modern African Studies* Vol. 24 No. 1 (1986): 1–31.

Jahn, Beate. "Humanitäre Intervention und das Selbstbestimmungsrecht der Völker: Eine theoretische Diskussion und ihre historischen Hintergründe." *Politische Vierteljahresschrift* Vol. 34 No. 4 (1993): 567–587.

James, Alan. *Sovereign Statehood: The Basis of International Society*. London: Allen and Unwin, 1986.

Jaquet, Louis G.M., ed. *Intervention in International Politics*. The Hague: The Netherlands Institute of International Affairs, 1971.

Jouvenel, Bertrand de. *Sovereignty: An Inquiry into the Political Good*. Indianapolis: Liberty Fund, 1997.

Kegley, Charles W. and Margaret G. Hermann. "Putting Military Intervention into the Democratic Peace: A Research Note." *Comparative Political Studies* Vol. 30 No. 1 (1997): 78–107.

Kegley, Charles W. and Margaret G. Hermann. "How Democracies Use Intervention: A Neglected Dimension in Studies of the Democratic Peace." *Journal of Peace Research* Vol. 33 No. 3 (1996): 309–322.

Kegley, Charles W. and Margaret G. Hermann. "Military Intervention and the Democratic Peace." *International Interactions* Vol. 21 No. 1 (1995): 1–21.

Kegley, Charles W., Gregory A. Raymond and Margaret G. Hermann. "The Rise and Fall of the Nonintervention Norm: Some Correlates and Potential Consequences." *Fletcher Forum of World Affairs* Vol. 22 No. 1 (1998): 81–101.

Keller, Edmond J. and Donald Rothchild, eds. *Africa in the New International Order: Rethinking State Sovereignty and Regional Security*. Boulder: Lynne Rienner, 1996.

Kelsen, Hans. *Das Problem der Souveränität und die Theorie des Völkerrechts. Beitrag zur reinen Rechtslehre*. 2nd ed. Tübingen: Scientia Aalen, 1960.

Keohane, Robert. "Hobbes's Dilemma and Institutional Change in World Politics: Sovereignty in International Society." In *Whose World Order? Uneven Globalization and the End of the Cold War*, edited by Hans-Henrik Holm and Georg Sørensen, 165–186. Boulder: Westview Press, 1995.

Keohane, Robert. "Sovereignty, Interdependence, and International Institutions." In *Ideas and Ideals: Essays on Politics in Honor of Stanley Hoffmann*, edited by Linda B. Miller and Michael J. Smith, 91–107. Boulder: Westview Press, 1993.

Kingsbury, Benedict. "Sovereignty and Inequality." In *Inequality, Globalization, and World Politics*, edited by Andrew Hurrell and Ngaire Woods, 66–94. Oxford: Oxford University Press, 1999.

Korovin, Y. "Sovereignty and Peace." *International Affairs (Moscow)* No. 9 (1960): 7–12.

Krasner, Stephen D. "Compromising Westphalia." *International Security* Vol. 20 No. 3 (1995/1996): 115–151.

Krasner, Stephen D. "Westphalia and All That." In *Ideas and Foreign Policy*, edited by Judith Goldstein and Robert Keohane, 235–264. Ithaca: Cornell University Press, 1993.

Krasner, Stephen D. "Sovereignty: An Institutional Perspective." *Comparative Political Studies* Vol. 21 No. 1 (1988): 66–94.

Kratochwil, Friedrich. "Of Systems, Boundaries, and Territoriality: An Inquiry into the Formation of the State System." *World Politics* Vol. 39 No. 1 (1986): 27–52.

Langford, Tonya. "Things Fall Apart: State Failure and the Politics of Intervention." *International Studies Review* Vol. 1 No. 1 (1999): 59–79.

Lapidoth, Ruth. "Sovereignty in Transition." *Journal of International Affairs* Vol. 45 No. 2 (1992): 326–346.

Leurdijk, Henk J. *Intervention in International Politics*. Leeuwarden: Eisma B.V. Publishers, 1986.

Levin, D. "The Non-Interference Principle Today." *International Affairs (Moscow)* No. 11 (1966): 21–25.

Lingelbach, William F. "The Doctrine and Practice of Intervention in Europe." *Annals of the American Academy of Political and Social Science* Vol. 16 No. 1 (1900): 1–32.

Linklater, Andrew. "Citizenship and Sovereignty in the Post-Westphalian State." *European Journal of International Relations* Vol. 2 No. 1 (1996): 77–103.

Linklater, Andrew. *Men and Citizens in the Theory of International Relations*. London: Macmillan, 1990.

Little, Richard B. "Revisiting Intervention: A Survey of Recent Developments." *Review of International Studies* Vol. 13 No. 1 (1987): 49–60.

Little, Richard B. *Intervention: External Involvement in Civil Wars*. Totowa: Rowman and Littlefield, 1975.

Lugo, Luis E., ed. *Sovereignty at the Crossroads? Morality and International Politics in the Post-Cold War Era*. Lanham: Rowman and Littlefield, 1996.

MacFarlane, S. Neil. *Intervention and Regional Security*. London: The International Institute for Strategic Studies, 1985.

MacFarlane, S. Neil. "Intervention and Security in Africa." *International Affairs* Vol. 60 No. 1 (1984): 53–73.

Makinda, Samuel M. "Sovereignty and International Security: Challenges for the United Nations." *Global Governance* Vol. 2 No. 2 (1996): 149–168.

Mapel, David R. "Military Intervention and Rights." *Millennium* Vol. 20 No. 1 (1991): 41–55.

Maritain, Jacques. "The Concept of Sovereignty." *American Political Science Review* Vol. 44 No. 2 (1950): 343–357.

Mayall, James. "Intervention in International Society: Theory and Practice in Contemporary Perspective." In *International Society and the Development of International Relations Theory*, edited by Barbara Allen Robertson, 173–183. London: Pinter, 1998.

Mayall, James. "Non-Intervention, Self-Determination and the New World Order." *International Affairs* Vol. 67 No. 3 (1991): 421–429.

McMahan, Jeff. "Intervention and Collective Self-Determination." *Ethics and International Affairs* Vol. 10 (1996): 1–24.

Merriam, Charles E. *History of the Theory of Sovereignty since Rousseau*. New York: Columbia University Press, 1900.

Miliband, Ralph. "Military Intervention and Socialist Internationalism." *Socialist Register* (1980): 1–24.

Mill, John Stuart. "A Few Words on Non-Intervention." In *Dissertations and Discussions. Political, Philosophical, and Historical*, edited by John Stuart Mill, 153–178. London: Longmans, Green, Reader, and Dyer, 1867.

Mills, Kurt. *Human Rights in the Emerging Global Order: A New Sovereignty?* Basingstoke: Macmillan, 1998.

Mitchell, Timothy. "The Limits of the State: Beyond Statist Approaches and Their Critics." *American Political Science Review* Vol. 85 No. 1 (1991): 77–96.

Nincic, Djura. *The Problem of Sovereignty in the Charter and in the Practice of the United Nations*. The Hague: Martinus Nijhoff, 1970.

Onuf, Nicholas G. "Sovereignty: Outline of a Conceptual History." *Alternatives* Vol. 16 No. 4 (1991): 425–446.

Osiander, Andreas. "Sovereignty, International Relations, and the Westphalian Myth." *International Organization* Vol. 55 No. 2 (2001): 251–287.

Parvin, Manoucher and Maurie Sommer. "Dar al-Islam: The Evolution of Muslim Territoriality and Its Implications for Conflict Resolution in the Middle East." *International Journal of Middle East Studies* Vol. 11 No. 1 (1980): 1–21.

Paul, R.A. "Toward a Theory of Intervention." *Orbis* Vol. 16 No. 1 (1972): 105–118.

Pearson, Frederic S. "Geographic Proximity and Foreign Military Intervention." *Journal of Conflict Resolution* Vol. 18 No. 4 (1974): 432–460.

Pearson, Frederic S. and Robert Baumann. "International Military Interventions: Identification and Classification." *International Interactions* Vol. 14 (1988): 173–180.

Perez Casado, R. "The Scope and Objectives of Intervention." *Revista de Occidente* Vol. 236–37 (2001): 144–151.

Philpott, Daniel. *Revolutions in Sovereignty: How Ideas Shaped Modern International Relations.* Princeton: Princeton University Press, 2001.

Philpott, Daniel. "Sovereignty: An Introduction and Brief History." *Journal of International Affairs* Vol. 48 No. 2 (1995): 353–368.

Piradov, A. "The Principle of Non-Interference in the Modern World." *International Affairs (Moscow)* No. 1 (1966): 53–58.

Pogge, Thomas W. "An Institutional Approach to Humanitarian Intervention." *Public Affairs Quarterly* Vol. 6 No. 1 (1992): 89–103.

Prins, Gwyn. "The Politics of Intervention." *Pugwash Occasional Papers* Vol. 1 No. 1 (2000): 46–59.

Regan, Patrick M. *Outside Interventions and the Settlement of Internal Conflicts.* Ann Arbor: University of Michigan Press, 1999.

Regan, Patrick M. "Conditions of Successful Third-Party Intervention in Intrastate Conflicts." *Journal of Conflict Resolution* Vol. 40 No. 2 (1996): 336–359.

Rosas, Allan. "Focus on the Case for Intervention: Towards Some International Law and Order." *Journal of Peace Research* Vol. 31 No. 2 (1994): 129–135.

Rosenau, James N. "Intervention as a Scientific Concept." *The Journal of Conflict Resolution* Vol. 13 No. 2 (1969): 149–171.

Rosenau, James N. "The Concept of Intervention." *Journal of International Affairs* Vol. 22 No. 2 (1968): 165–176.

Ruggie, John G. "Territoriality and Beyond: Problematizing Modernity in International Relations." *International Organization* Vol. 47 No. 1 (1993): 139–174.

Sasser, Saskia. *Losing Control? Sovereignty in an Age of Globalization.* New York: Columbia University Press, 1996.

Schrijver, Nico. "The Changing Nature of State Sovereignty." In *The British Year Book of International Law 1999*, edited by James Crawford and Vaughan Lowe, 65–98. Oxford: Clarendon Press, 2000.

Schwarzenberger, Georg. "Hegemonial Intervention." *Yearbook of World Affairs* Vol. 13 (1959): 236–265.

Scott, Andrew. "Non-Intervention and Conditional Intervention." *Journal of International Affairs* Vol. 22 No. 2 (1968): 208–216.

Sellers, Mortimer, ed. *The New World Order: Sovereignty, Human Rights, and the Self-Determination of Peoples.* Oxford: Berg, 1996.

Sigelman, Lee. "Military Size and Political Intervention." *Journal of Political and Military Sociology* Vol. 3 No. 1 (1975): 95–100.

Sigelman, Lee. "Military Intervention: A Methodological Note." *Journal of Political and Military Sociology* Vol. 2 No. 2 (1974): 275–281.

Sikkink, Kathryn. "Human Rights, Principled Issue-Networks, and Sovereignty in Latin America." *International Organization* Vol. 47 No. 3 (1993): 411–441.

Singer, J. David and Melvin Small. *Resort to Arms: Intervention and Civil Wars 1816–1980*. Beverly Hills: Sage Publications, 1982.

Smith, Dan. "The Norm of Sovereignty in the Age of Intervention." In *Will World Peace Be Achievable in the 21st Century?*, edited by Young Seek Choue, 185–224. Seoul: Kyung Hee University, Institute of International Peace Studies, 2000.

Solarz, Stephen J. "When to Intervene." *Foreign Policy* Vol. 63 (1986): 20–39.

Soroos, Martin. *Beyond Sovereignty*. Columbia: University of South Carolina Press, 1986.

Spring, Dick. "New Forms of Intervention in World Politics: Opening Address." *Irish Studies in International Affairs* Vol. 5 (1994): 1–3.

Spruyt, Hendrik. *The Sovereign State and Its Competitors. An Analysis of Systems Change*. Princeton: Princeton University Press, 1994.

Stankiewicz, W.J., ed. *In Defense of Sovereignty*. New York: Oxford University Press, 1969.

Sulyok, Gábor. "Humanitarian Intervention: A Historical and Theoretical Overview." *Acta Juridica Hungarica* Vol. 41 No. 1/2 (2000): 79–109.

Tannahill, R. Neal. "A Methodological Note: Military Intervention in Search of a Dependent Variable." *Journal of Political and Military Sociology* Vol. 3 No. 2 (1975): 219–228.

Thomson, Janice E. "State Sovereignty in International Relations: Bridging the Gap between Theory and Empirical Research." *International Studies Quarterly* Vol. 39 No. 2 (1995): 213–233.

Thomson, Janice E. "Sovereignty in Historical Perspective: The Evolution of State Control over Extraterritorial Violence." In *The Elusive State*, edited by James Caporaso, 227–254. Newbury Park: Sage, 1989.

Thürer, Daniel. "The 'Failed State' and International Law." *International Review of the Red Cross* Vol. 81 No. 836 (1999): 731–760.

Tures, John A. "Addressing Concerns about Applying the Democratic Peace Arguments to Interventions." *Journal of Peace Research* Vol. 38 No. 2 (2001): 247–249.

Tures, John A. "Democracies as Intervening States: A Critique of Kegley and Hermann." *Journal of Peace Research* Vol. 38 No. 2 (2001): 227–235.

Ushakov, Nikolai A. "International Law and Sovereignty." In *Contemporary International Law: Collection of Articles*, edited by Grigorii I. Tunkin, 97–117. Moscow: Progress Publishers, 1969.

Van Tassell, G. Lane. "Intervention in International Politics: A Conceptual Model." *GPSA Journal* Vol. 2 No. 1 (1974): 51–71.

Van Wingen, J. and H. K. Tillema. "Law and Power in Military Intervention: Major States after World War II." *International Studies Quarterly* Vol. 26 No. 2 (1982): 220–250.

Varouxakis, Georgios. "John Stuart Mill on Intervention and Non-Intervention." *Millennium* Vol. 26 No. 1 (1997): 57–76.

Värrynen, Raimo, ed. *Globalization and Global Governance* (Lanham: Rowman and Littlefield, 1999).

Vattel, Emmerich de. *The Law of Nations or the Principles of Natural Law Applied to the Conduct and to the Affairs of Nations and of Sovereigns*. Washington, DC: Carnegie Institution of International Law, 1916.

Vincent, R.J. "Grotius, Human Rights, and Intervention." In *Hugo Grotius and International Relations*, edited by Hedley Bull et al., 241–256. Oxford: Clarendon Press, 1990.

Von Hippel, Karin. "The Non-Intervention Norm Prevails: An Analysis of the Western Sahara." *Journal of Modern Africa* Vol. 33 (1995): 67–81.

Weber, Cynthia. *Simulating Sovereignty. Intervention, the State and Symbolic Exchange.* Cambridge: Cambridge University Press, 1995.

Weber, Cynthia. "Reconsidering Statehood: Examining the Sovereignty/Intervention Boundary." *Review of International Studies* Vol. 18 (1992): 199–216.

Weede, Erich. "Some Simple Calculations on Democracy and War Involvement." *Journal of Peace Research* Vol. 29 No. 4 (1992): 377–383.

Wheeler, Nicholas J. "Pluralist or Solidarist Conceptions of International Society: Bull and Vincent on Humanitarian Intervention." *Millennium* Vol. 21 No. 3 (1992): 463–487.

Wicclair, Mark. "Human Rights and Intervention." In *Human Rights and US Foreign Policy*, edited by Peter G. Brown and Douglas Maclean, 141–157. Lexington: Lexington Books, 1979.

Wilks, Michael. *The Problem of Sovereignty in the Later Middle Ages.* Cambridge: Cambridge University Press, 1963.

Wriston, Walter. *The Twilight of Sovereignty.* New York: Scribners, 1992.

Young, Oran R. "Intervention and International Systems." *Journal of International Affairs* Vol. 22 No. 2 (1968): 177–187.

Zacher, Mark W. "The Territorial Integrity Norm: International Boundaries and the Use of Force." *International Organization* Vol. 55 No. 2 (2001): 215–250.

Zacher, Mark W. "The Decaying Pillars of the Westphalian Temple: Implications for International Order and Governance." In *Governance without Government: Order and Change in World Politics*, edited by James N. Rosenau and Ernst-Otto Czempiel, 58–101. Cambridge: Cambridge University Press, 1992.

Zartman, I. William. "Intervention among Developing States." *Journal of International Affairs* Vol. 22 No. 2 (1968): 188–197.

# 3. CONFLICT PREVENTION

Cahill, Kevin M., ed. *Preventive Diplomacy: Stopping Wars before They Start.* rev. ed. New York: Routledge and The Center for International Health and Cooperation, 2000.
Diplomats, physicians, humanitarians, and government officials explore the challenges of preventive diplomacy.

Carnegie Commission on Preventing Deadly Conflict. *Preventing Deadly Conflict: Final Report with Executive Summary.* Washington, DC: CCPDC, 1997.
Examination of the principal causes of ethnic, nationalist, and religious conflicts, the circumstances that foster or deter their outbreak, and the role of various international institutions in conflict prevention.

Crocker, Chester A., Fen Osler Hampson and Pamela R. Aall, eds. *Turbulent Peace: The Challenges of Managing International Conflict.* Washington, DC: United States Institute of Peace, 2001.
Collection of articles examining the complex causes of conflict and the instruments, actors, techniques, and policies for managing and resolving ethnic and civil conflicts.

Ginifer, Jeremy, Espen Barth Eide and Carsten Rønnfeldt, eds. *Preventive Action in Theory and Practice: The Skopje Papers.* Oslo: The Norwegian Institute of International Affairs, 1999.
Papers from a workshop on preventive diplomacy conducted in close collaboration with the Macedonian Ministry of Foreign Affairs.

Jentleson, Bruce W., ed. *Opportunities Missed, Opportunities Seized: Preventive Diplomacy in the Post-Cold War World.* Lanham: Rowman and Littlefield, 2000.
Assesses the feasibility of preventive diplomacy by concentrating on 10 major post-Cold War cases that all challenged the preventive diplomacy capacity of the international community.

Peck, Connie. *The United Nations as a Dispute Settlement System: Improving Mechanisms for the Prevention and Resolution of Conflict.* The Hague: Kluwer Law International, 1996.
Review of preventive diplomacy and UN's dispute-settlement repertoire in terms of interest-, rights-, and power-based approaches.

Stedman, Stephen John. "Alchemy for a New World Order: Overselling 'Preventive Diplomacy'." *Foreign Affairs* No. 74 (1995): 14–20.
Sceptical view of preventive diplomacy and conflict prevention.

Swedish Ministry of Foreign Affairs. *Preventing Violent Conflict: A Swedish Action Plan.* Stockholm: SMFA, 1999.
Focuses on the methods and efforts for peaceful management of conflicts and describes in what ways middle powers can engage in activities to prevent armed conflicts.

## References

Ackermann, Alice. *Making Peace Prevail: Preventing Violent Conflict in Macedonia.* Syracuse: Syracuse University Press, 1999.

Ackermann, Alice. "Managing Conflicts Non-Violently through Preventive Action: The Case of the Former Yugoslav Republic of Macedonia." *Journal of Conflict Studies* Vol. 19 No. 1 (1999): 5–21.

Adelman, Howard and Astri Suhrke. *Early Warning and Conflict Management.* Copenhagen: Steering Committee of the Joint Evaluation of Emergency Assistance to Rwanda, 1996.

Aklaev, Airat. "Causes and Prevention of Ethnic Conflict: An Overview of Post-Soviet Russian Language Literature": http://ccpdc.org/pubs/aklaev/aklaevframe.htm

Alao, Abiodun. *The Role of African Regional and Sub-Regional Organizations in Conflict Prevention and Resolution.* Geneva: United Nations High Commissioner for Refugees, 2000.

Annan, Kofi A. *Towards a Culture of Prevention: Statements by the Secretary-General of the United Nations*. Washington, DC: Carnegie Commission on Preventing Deadly Conflict, 1999.

Archer, Clive. "Conflict Prevention in Europe: The Case of the Nordic States and Macedonia." *Cooperation and Conflict* Vol. 29 No. 4 (1994): 367–386.

Bauwens, Werner and Luc Reychler, eds. *The Art of Conflict Prevention*. London: Brassey's, 1994.

Bercovitch, Jacob. "Understanding Mediation's Role in Preventive Diplomacy." *Negotiation Journal* Vol. 12 No. 3 (1996): 241–258.

Bildt, Carl. "Force and Diplomacy." *Survival* Vol. 42 No. 1 (2000): 141–148.

Bjork, James E. and Allan E. Goodman. *Yugoslavia, 1991–1992: Could Diplomacy Have Prevented a Tragedy?* Washington, DC: Georgetown University Institute for the Study of Diplomacy, 1992.

Björkdahl, Annika. "Conflict Prevention from a Nordic Perspective: Putting Prevention into Practice." *International Peacekeeping* Vol. 6 No. 3 (1999): 54–72.

Black, David R. and Susan J. Rolston, eds. *Peacemaking and Preventive Diplomacy in the New World (Dis)Order*. Halifax: Centre for Foreign Policy Studies, 1995.

Boudreau, Tom. *Sheathing the Sword: The UN Secretary General and the Prevention of International Conflict*. New York: Greenwood Press, 1991.

Boyce, James K. and Manuel Pastor. "Aid for Peace: Can International Financial Institutions Help Prevent Conflict?" *World Policy Journal* Vol. 15 (1998).

Brown, Michael E. and Richard Rosecrance, eds. *The Costs of Conflict: Prevention and Cure in the Global Arena*. Lanham: Rowman and Littlefield, 1999.

Carment, David and Karen Garner. "Conflict Prevention and Early Warning: Problems, Pitfalls and Avenues for Success." *Canadian Foreign Policy* Vol. 7 (1999): 103–118.

Carment, David and Frank Harvey. *Using Force to Prevent Ethnic Violence: An Evaluation of Theory and Evidence*. Westport: Praeger, 2001.

Carment, David and Patrick James, eds. *Peace in the Midst of Wars: Managing and Preventing International Ethnic Conflicts*. Columbia: University of South Carolina Press, 1998.

Carment, David and Albrecht Schnabel, eds. *Conflict Prevention: Path to Peace or Grand Illusion?* Tokyo: United Nations University Press, 2001.

Chayes, Abram and Antonia Handler Chayes, eds. *Preventing Conflict in the Post-Communist World: Mobilizing International and Regional Organizations*. Washington, DC: Brookings Institution, 1996.

Cohen, Jonathan. *Conflict Prevention in the OSCE: An Assessment of Capacities*. The Hague: The Netherlands Institute of International Relations Clingendael, 1999.

Conflict Management Group. *Preventive Diplomacy and Conflict Management in Europe: Methods and Strategies in Conflict Prevention*. Cambridge, MA: Conflict Management Group, 1994.

Cortright, David, ed. *The Price of Peace: Incentives and International Conflict Prevention*. Lanham: Rowman and Littlefield, 1997.

Council on Foreign Relations Center for Preventive Action. *Toward Comprehensive Peace in Southeast Europe: Report of the South Balkans Working Group of the Council on Foreign Relations*. New York: Twentieth Century Fund Press, 1996.

Coursen-Neff, Zama. "Preventive Measures Pertaining to Unconventional Threats to the Peace Such As Natural and Humanitarian Disasters." *New York University Journal of International Law and Politics* Vol. 30 No. 3/4 (1998): 645–707.

Creative Associates International. *Preventing and Mitigating Violent Conflicts: A Guide for Practitioners*. Washington, DC: Greater Horn of Africa Initiative and United States Agency for International Development, 1996.

Crocker, Chester A., Fen Osler Hampson and Pamela R. Aall, eds. *Herding Cats: Multiparty Mediation in a Complex World*. Washington, DC: United States Institute of Peace, 1999.

Crocker, Chester A., Fen Osler Hampson and Pamela R. Aall, eds. *Managing Global Chaos: Sources of and Responses to International Conflict*. Washington, DC: United States Institute of Peace, 1996.

Cross, Peter, ed. *Contributing to Preventive Action*. Baden-Baden: Nomos, 1998.

Cross, Peter and Guenola Rasaloelina, eds. *Conflict Prevention Policy of the European Union: Recent Engagements, Future Instruments*. Baden-Baden: Nomos, 1999.

Davies, John L. and Ted Robert Gurr, eds. *Preventive Measures: Building Risk Assessment and Crisis Early Warning Systems*. Lanham: Rowman and Littlefield, 1998.

Deacon, Bob. *Action for Social Change: A New Facet of Preventive Peacekeeping: The Case of UNPREDEP*. Helsinki: National Research and Development Center for Welfare and Health, 1996.

De Mars, William. "Waiting for Early Warning: Humanitarian Action after the Cold War." *Journal of Refugee Studies* Vol. 8 No. 4 (1995): 390–410.

Diamond, Louise and John McDonald. *Multi-Track Diplomacy: A Systems Approach to Peace*. 3rd ed. West Hartford: Kumarian Press, 1996.

Dixon, William J. "Third-Party Techniques for Preventing Conflict Escalation and Promoting Peaceful Settlement." *International Organization* Vol. 50 No. 4 (1996): 653–681.

Doom, Ruddy. "A Scientific Base for Conflict Prevention? Sustainable Peace, Development and Sciences." *Journal of Humanitarian Assistance* (March 1998): http://www.jha.ac/articles/a040.htm

Doom, Ruddy and Koen Vlassenroot. "Early Warning and Conflict Prevention: Minerva's Wisdom?" *Journal of Humanitarian Assistance* (July 1997): http://www.jha.ac/articles/a022.htm

Dorn, A. Walter. "Keeping Tabs on a Troubled World: UN Information-Gathering to Preserve Peace." *Security Dialogue* Vol. 27 No. 3 (1996): 263–276.

Elaraby, Nabil. "Preventive Diplomacy, Peacemaking and Peacekeeping in the Context of International Law." In *Perspectives on International Law*, edited by Nandasiri Jasentuliyana, 181–200. London: Kluwer Law International, 1995.

European Centre for Conflict Prevention, ed. *People Building Peace: 35 Inspiring Stories from around the World*. Utrecht: European Centre for Conflict Prevention, 1999.

Evans, Gareth. "Preventive Action and Conflict Resolution." In *Peacemaking and Peacekeeping for the New Century*, edited by Olara A. Otunnu and Michael W. Doyle, 61–87. Lanham: Rowman and Littlefield, 1998.

Evans, Gareth. *Cooperating for Peace: The Global Agenda for the 1990s and Beyond*. St. Leonards: Allen and Unwin, 1993.

Fein, Helen, Orlando Brugnola and Louise Spirer, eds. *The Prevention of Genocide: Rwanda and Yugoslavia Reconsidered*. New York: Institute for the Study of Genocide, John Jay College of Criminal Justice, 1994.

Franck, Thomas M. and Georg Nolte. "The Good Offices Function of the UN Secretary-General." In *United Nations, Divided World: The UN's Roles in International Relations*, edited by Adam Roberts and Benedict Kingsbury, 143–182. Oxford: Clarendon Press, 1993.

Furlong, Bob. "Powder Keg of the Balkans: The United Nations Opts for Prevention in Macedonia." *International Defense Review* Vol. 26 No. 5 (1993): 364–368.

George, Alexander L. and Jane E. Holl. *The Warning-Response Problem and Missed Opportunities in Preventive Diplomacy*. Washington, DC: Carnegie Commission on Preventing Deadly Conflict, 1997.

Ginifer, Jeremy and Espen Barth Eide. *An Agenda for Preventive Diplomacy: Theory and Practice*. Oslo: Norwegian Institute of International Affairs, 1997.

Greenberg, Melanie C., John H. Barton and Margaret E. McGuinness, eds. *Words over War: Mediation and Arbitration to Prevent Deadly Conflict.* Lanham: Rowman and Littlefield, 2000.

Gurr, Ted Robert. *Minorities at Risk: A Global View of Ethnopolitical Conflicts.* Washington, DC: United States Institute of Peace, 1993.

Gurr, Ted Robert and Barbara Harff. *Early Warning of Communal Conflict and Genocide: Linking Empirical Research to International Responses.* Tokyo: United Nations University Press, 1996.

Harff, Barbara and Ted Robert Gurr. "Systematic Early Warning of Humanitarian Emergencies." *Journal of Peace Research* Vol. 35 No. 5 (1998): 551–579.

Havermans, Jos. *Conflict Prevention and Peace Building in Africa: Report of the Conference Organized by the European Centre for Conflict Prevention.* The Hague: European Centre for Conflict Prevention, 1999.

International Security Information Service. *Restructuring for Conflict Prevention and Management: EU Restructuring Conference Report and Comments.* Brussels: ISIS Europe, 1999.

International Institute of Humanitarian Law. *Conflict Prevention: The Humanitarian Perspective.* San Remo: IIHL, 1994.

Jentleson, Bruce W. *Coercive Prevention: Normative, Political, and Policy Dilemmas.* Washington, DC: United States Institute of Peace, 2000.

Kaufman, Stuart J. "Preventive Peacekeeping, Ethnic Violence, and Macedonia." *Studies in Conflict and Terrorism* Vol. 19 No. 3 (1996): 229–246.

Kittani, Ismat. "Preventive Diplomacy and Peacemaking: The UN Experience." In *Peacemaking and Peacekeeping for the New Century,* edited by Olara A. Otunnu and Michael W. Doyle, 89–107. Lanham: Rowman and Littlefield, 1998.

Klugman, Jeni. *Social and Economic Policies to Prevent Complex Humanitarian Emergencies: Lessons from Experience.* Helsinki: UNU World Institute for Development Economics Research, 1999.

Koch, Jutta and Regine Mehl, eds. *Politik der Einmischung: Zwischen Konfliktprävention und Krisenintervention.* Baden-Baden: Nomos, 1994.

Krasno, Jean. *The Group of Friends of the Secretary-General: A Useful Diplomatic Tool.* Washington, DC: Carnegie Commission on Preventing Deadly Conflict, 1996.

Kuper, Leo. *The Prevention of Genocide.* New Haven: Yale University Press, 1985.

Kuroda, Michiko and Kumar Rupesinghe, eds. *Early Warning and Conflict Resolution.* Basingstoke: Macmillan, 1992.

Langille, H. Peter. "Conflict Prevention: Options for Rapid Deployment and UN Standing Forces." *International Peacekeeping* Vol. 7 No. 1 (2000): 219–253.

Leatherman, Janie, William DeMars, Patrick D. Gaffney and Raimo Väyrynen, eds. *Breaking Cycles of Violence: Conflict Prevention in Intrastate Crises.* West Hartford: Kumarian Press, 1999.

Lund, Michael S. *Preventing Violent Conflicts: A Strategy for Preventive Diplomacy.* Washington, DC: United States Institute of Peace, 1996.

Lund, Michael S. "Underrating Preventive Diplomacy." *Foreign Affairs* Vol. 74 No. 4 (1995): 160–163.

Lund, Michael S. and Guenola Rasamoelina, eds. *The Impact of Conflict Prevention Policy: Cases, Measures, Assessments.* Baden-Baden: Nomos, 2000.

Mares, David R. *Latin American Perspectives on the Causes, Prevention and Resolution of Deadly Intra- and Interstate Conflicts 1982–1996:* http://www.ccpdc.org/pubs/mares/mares.htm

Matthies, Volker. "Krisenprävention als Friedenspolitik: Zur Entstehung und Entwicklung eines neuen politischen Konzepts." *Entwicklung und Zusammenarbeit* Vol. 40 No. 4 (1999): 103–106.

Mekenkamp, Monique, J. Van Tongeren and Hans Van de Veen, eds. *Searching for Peace in Africa: An Overview of Conflict Prevention and Management Activities*. Utrecht: European Centre for Conflict Prevention, 1999.

Miall, Hugh. *The Peacemakers: Peaceful Settlement of Disputes since 1945*. New York: St. Martin's Press, 1992.

Miskel, James F. and Richard J. Norton. "Humanitarian Early-Warning Systems." *Global Governance* Vol. 4 No. 3 (1998): 317–329.

Munuera, Gabriel. *Preventing Armed Conflict in Europe: Lessons from Recent Experience*. Paris: Western European Union, Institute for Security Studies, 1994.

Ostrowski, Stephen T. "Preventive Deployment of Troops as Preventive Measures: Macedonia and Beyond." *New York University Journal of International Law and Politics* Vol. 30 No. 3/4 (1999): 793–880.

Ould Abdallah, Ahmedou. *Burundi on the Brink 1993–95: A UN Special Envoy Reflects on Preventive Diplomacy*. Washington, DC: United States Institute of Peace, 2000.

Peck, Connie. *Sustainable Peace: The Role of the UN and Regional Organizations in Preventing Conflict*. Lanham: Rowman and Littlefield, 1999.

Ramcharan, B.G. *The International Law and Practice of Early Warning and Preventive Diplomacy: The Emerging Global Watch*. Dordrecht: Martinus Nijhoff, 1991.

Ramcharan, B.G. *Humanitarian Good Offices in International Law: The Good Offices of the United Nations Secretary-General in the Field of Human Rights*. The Hague: Martinus Nijhoff, 1983.

Rotberg, Robert I. *Vigilance and Vengeance: NGOs Preventing Ethnic Conflict in Divided Societies*. Cambridge, MA: World Peace Foundation, 1996.

Rotberg, Robert I. and Theodore K. Rabb, eds. *The Origin and Prevention of Major Wars*. Cambridge: Cambridge University Press, 1989.

Rubin, Barnett R., ed. *Cases and Strategies for Preventive Action*. New York: Century Foundation Press, 1998.

Rupesinghe, Kumar. *Strategies for Conflict Prevention, Management, and Resolution*. Washington, DC: Winston Foundation, 1999.

Saferworld. *Preventing Violent Conflict: Opportunities for the Swedish and Belgian Presidencies of the European Union in 2001*. Saferworld and International Alert, 2000.

Schnabel, Albrecht and Nika Strazisar. "Conflict Prevention in the Former Yugoslavia: Missed Opportunities and Lessons for Post-Conflict Peacebuilding." In *The Southeast European Challenge: Ethnic Conflict and the International Response*, edited by Hans-Georg Ehrhart and Albrecht Schnabel, Baden-Baden: Nomos, 1999.

Sisk, Timothy D. *Power Sharing and International Mediation in Ethnic Conflicts*. Washington, DC: Carnegie Commission on Preventing Deadly Conflict, 1996.

Stockholm International Peace Research Institute. *Preventing Violent Conflict: The Search for Political Will, Strategies, and Effective Tools*. Stockholm: SIPRI, 2000.

Stremlau, John. *People in Peril: Human Rights, Humanitarian Action, and Preventing Deadly Conflict*. Washington, DC: Carnegie Commission on Preventing Deadly Conflict, 1998.

Stremlau, John and Francisco Sagasti. *Preventing Deadly Conflict: Does the World Bank Have a Role?* New York: Carnegie Commission on Preventing Deadly Conflict, 1998.

Thakur, Ramesh, ed. *International Conflict Resolution*. Boulder: Westview Press, 1988.

UN Secretariat. *Handbook on the Peaceful Settlement of Disputes between States*. New York: United Nations, 1991.

Uvin, Peter. *Aiding Violence: The Development Enterprise in Rwanda*. West Hartford: Kumarian, 1998.

Vance, Cyrus R. and David A. Hamburg. *Pathfinders for Peace: A Report to the UN Secretary-General on the Role of Special Representatives and Personal Envoys.* Washington, DC: Carnegie Commission on Preventing Deadly Conflict, 1997.

Van Tongeren, Paul, ed. *Searching for Peace in Africa: An Overview of Conflict Prevention and Management Activities.* Utrecht: African Centre for the Constructive Resolution of Disputes and European Platform for Conflict Prevention and Transformation, 2000.

Van Walraven, Klaas, ed. *Early Warning and Conflict Prevention: Limitations and Possibilities.* The Hague: Kluwer Law International, 1998.

Van Walraven, Klaas. *Conflict Prevention and Early Warning in the Political Practice of International Organizations.* The Hague: Netherlands Institute of International Relations, 1996.

Väyrynen, Raimo. "Preventive Action: Failure in Yugoslavia." *International Peacekeeping* Vol. 3 No. 4 (1996): 23–44.

Väyrynen, Raimo et al. *Inventive and Preventive Diplomacy.* Notre Dame: Joan B. Kroc Institute for International Peace Studies, University of Notre Dame, 1999.

Wallensteen, Peter, ed. *Preventing Violent Conflicts: Past Records and Future Challenges.* Uppsala: Department of Peace and Conflict Research, Uppsala University, 1998.

Wallensteen, Peter. "Prevention and Preventive Diplomacy: Lessons since the Cold War." In *The United Nations, Japan and Sweden, Achievements and Challenges,* edited by Bert Edström, 73–83. Stockholm: Swedish Institute of International Affairs, 1998.

Weiss, Thomas G. "The UN's Prevention Pipe-Dream." *Berkeley Journal of International Law* Vol. 14 No. 2 (1997): 501–515.

Williams, Abiodun. *Preventing War: The United Nations and Macedonia.* Lanham: Rowman and Littlefield, 2000.

Zartman, I. William, ed. *Preventive Negotiation: Avoiding Conflict Escalation.* Lanham: Rowman and Littlefield, 2001.

# 4. ETHICAL ASPECTS

Beitz, Charles R. *Political Theory and International Relations: With a New Afterword by the Author.* Princeton: Princeton University Press, 1999.
Treatment of normative problems in international relations. Proposes a principle of state autonomy based on the justice of a state's domestic institutions.

Elshtain, Jean Bethke. *New Wine and Old Bottles: International Politics and Ethical Discourse.* Notre Dame: University of Notre Dame Press, 1998.
Argues that ethics and politics are mutually constitutive and suggests the continued primacy of national sovereignty.

Fixdal, Mona and Dan Smith. "Humanitarian Intervention and Just War." *Mershon International Studies Review* Vol. 42 No. 2 (1998): 283–312.
Explores the application of the just war tradition and its main concepts to the current debate on humanitarian intervention, suggesting that these concepts, while seldom acknowledged, continue to provide the foundations for the ethical debate on the use of force.

Hashmi, Sohail H. "Is There an Islamic Ethic of Humanitarian Intervention?" *Ethics and International Affairs* Vol. 7 (1993): 55–73.
Exposition of Islamic discourse on humanitarian intervention, elaborating the ambiguous status of the nation-state in Islamic thought.

Hehir, Bryan J. "Intervention: From Theories to Cases." *Ethics and International Affairs* Vol. 9 (1995): 1–13.
Argues in favour of restraint on intervention, but accepts the need for exceptions to the norm of nonintervention based on ethical obligations.

Hoffmann, Stanley. *Duties beyond Borders: On the Limits and Possibilities of Ethical International Politics.* Lexington: D.C. Heath, 1981.
Classic text exploring the nature and character of ethical obligations in world politics.

Moore, Jonathan, ed. *Hard Choices: Moral Dilemmas in Humanitarian Intervention.* Lanham: Rowman and Littlefield, 1998.
Commissioned by the International Committee of the Red Cross, this wide-ranging collection of essays explores both operational and ethical challenges.

Nardin, Terry, ed. *The Ethics of War and Peace: Religious and Secular Perspectives.* Princeton: Princeton University Press, 1996.
Contributors discuss various traditions of ethical thought on the topic of ethics and the use of force, including natural law, political realism, Judaism, Islam, Christian pacifism, and feminism.

Tesón, Fernando. *Humanitarian Intervention. An Inquiry into Law and Morality.* 2nd ed. Irvington-on-Hudson: Transnational Publishers, 1997.
Argues that moral-philosophical analysis underpins international law and that significant violations of human rights justify, and even require, military intervention.

Walzer, Michael. *Just and Unjust Wars: A Moral Argument with Historical Illustrations.* 3rd ed. London: Basic Books, 2000.
Classic treatment of the legitimate use of force. Scepticism about military intervention in earlier editions qualified in light of the humanitarian crises of the 1990s.

## References

Adelman, Howard. "The Ethics of Humanitarian Intervention: The Case of the Kurdish Refugees." *Public Affairs Quarterly* Vol. 6 No. 1 (1992): 61–87.

Adeney, Bernard T. *Just War, Political Realism and Faith.* Metuchen: American Theological Library Association and Scarecrow Press, 1988.

Amstutz, Mark R. *International Ethics: Concepts, Theories, and Cases in Global Politics.* Lanham: Rowman and Littlefield, 1999.

Bacevich, A. J. "Just War II: Morality and High Technology." *The National Interest* No. 45 (1996): 37–47.

Barnett, Michael N. "The United Nations and Global Security: The Norm is Mightier than the Sword." *Ethics and International Affairs* Vol. 9 (1995): 37–54.

Barry, James A. *The Sword of Justice: Ethics and Coercion in International Politics.* Westport: Praeger, 1998.

Beach, Hugo. "Secessions, Interventions and Just War Theory: The Case of Kosovo." *Pugwash Occasional Papers* Vol. 1 No. 1 (2000): 11–36.

Beitz, Charles R. "Sovereignty and Morality in International Affairs." In *Political Theory Today*, edited by David Held, 236–254. Cambridge: Polity, 1991.

Beitz, Charles R. "Nonintervention and Communal Integrity." *Philosophy and Public Affairs* Vol. 9 No. 4 (1980): 385–391.

Beitz, Charles R. "Bounded Morality: Justice and the State in World Politics." *International Organization* Vol. 33 No. 3 (1979): 405–424.

Beitz, Charles R., Marshall Cohen and A. John Simmons, eds. *International Ethics.* Princeton: Princeton University Press, 1985.

Brewin, Christopher. "Liberal States and International Obligations." *Millennium* Vol. 17 No. 2 (1988): 321–338.

Brilmayer, Lea. *American Hegemony: Political Morality in a One-Superpower World.* New Haven: Yale University Press, 1994.

Brown, Chris. "Ethics of Coexistence: The International Theory of Terry Nardin." *Review of International Studies* Vol. 14 No. 3 (1988): 213–222.

Buchanan, Allen. "The Internal Legitimacy of Humanitarian Intervention." *Journal of Political Philosophy* Vol. 7 No. 1 (1999): 71–87.

Bull, Hedley. "Recapturing the Just War for Political Theory." *World Politics* Vol. 31 No. 4 (1979): 588–599.

Cady, Duane L. *From Warism to Pacifism: A Moral Continuum.* Philadelphia: Temple University Press, 1989.

Campbell, David and Michael J. Shapiro, eds. *Moral Spaces: Rethinking Ethics and World Politics.* Minneapolis: University of Minnesota Press, 1999.

Caney, Simon. "Human Rights and the Rights of States: Terry Nardin on Nonintervention." *International Political Science Review* Vol. 18 No. 1 (1997): 27–37.

Ceadel, Martin. *Thinking about War and Peace.* Oxford: Oxford University Press, 1987.

Childress, James F., ed. *Moral Responsibility in Conflicts: Essays on Nonviolence, War, and Conscience.* Baton Rouge: Louisiana State University Press, 1982.

Christopher, Paul. *The Ethics of War and Peace: An Introduction to Legal and Moral Issues.* 2nd ed. New York: Simon and Schuster, 1999.

Claude, Inis L. "Just Wars: Doctrines and Institutions." *Political Science Quarterly* Vol. 95 No. 1 (1980): 83–96.

Cohen, Marshall. "Moral Skepticism and International Relations." *Philosophy and Public Affairs* Vol. 13 No. 4 (1984): 299–346.

Cohen, Marshall, Thomas Nagel and Thomas Scanlon, eds. *War and Moral Responsibility.* Princeton: Princeton University Press, 1974.

Coicaud, Jean-Marc and Daniel Warner, eds. *Ethics and International Affairs: Extent and Limits*. Tokyo: United Nations University Press, 2001.

Cook, Martin L. "Immaculate War: Constraints on Humanitarian Intervention." *Ethics and International Affairs* Vol. 14 (2000): 55–65.

Davis, G. Scott, ed. *Religion and Justice in the War over Bosnia*. London: Routledge, 1996.

Dombrowski, D. *Christian Pacifism*. Philadelphia: Temple University Press, 1991.

Doppelt, Gerald. "Statism without Foundations." *Philosophy and Public Affairs* Vol. 9 No. 4 (1980): 398–403.

Doppelt, Gerald. "Walzer's Theory of Morality in International Relations." *Philosophy and Public Affairs* Vol. 8 No. 1 (1978): 3–26.

Dunn, John. "The Dilemma of Humanitarian Intervention: The Executive Power of the Law of Nature, after God." *Government and Opposition* Vol. 29 No. 2 (1994): 248–261.

European Commission Humanitarian Organization, ed. *Ethics in Humanitarian Aid*. Brussels: ECHO, 1996.

Elshtain, Jean Bethke, ed. *Just War Theory*. Oxford: Basil Blackwell, 1992.

Fisher, David. "The Ethics of Intervention." *Survival* Vol. 36 No. 1 (1994): 51–59.

Gordon, Joy. "A Peaceful, Silent, Deadly Remedy: The Ethics of Economic Sanctions." *Ethics and International Affairs* Vol. 13 (1999): 123–142.

Graham, Gordon. "The Justice of Intervention." *Review of International Studies* Vol. 13 No. 2 (1987): 133–146.

Hehir, Bryan J. "The Just-War Ethic Revisited." In *Ideas and Ideals: Essays on Politics in Honor of Stanley Hoffmann*, edited by Linda B. Miller and Michael Joseph Smith, 144–161. Boulder: Westview Press, 1993.

Hehir, Bryan J. "The Ethics of Intervention: Two Normative Traditions." In *Human Rights and US Foreign Policy: Principles and Applications*, edited by Peter G. Brown and Douglas Maclean, 121–139. Lexington: Lexington Books, 1979.

Held, Virginia, Sidney Morgenbesser and Thomas Nagel, eds. *Philosophy, Morality and International Affairs*. New York: Oxford University Press, 1974.

Hendrickson, David C. "In Defense of Realism: A Commentary on Just and Unjust Wars." *Ethics and International Affairs* Vol. 11 (1997): 19–53.

Himes, Kenneth R. "The Morality of Humanitarian Intervention: Notes on Moral Theology 1993." *Theological Studies* Vol. 55 No. 1 (1994): 82–105.

Holmes, R. *On War and Morality*. Princeton: Princeton University Press, 1989.

Johnson, James Turner. *The Holy War Idea in Western and Islamic Traditions*. University Park: Pennsylvania State University Press, 1997.

Johnson, James Turner. "The Broken Tradition." *The National Interest* No. 45 (1996): 27–36.

Johnson, James Turner. "Can Contemporary War Be Just? Elements in the Moral Debate." In *After the Cold War: Questioning the Morality of Nuclear Deterrence*, edited by Charles W. Kegley and Kenneth L. Schwab, 177–192. Boulder: Westview Press, 1991.

Johnson, James Turner. *Can Modern Wars Be Just?* New Haven: Yale University Press, 1984.

Johnson, James Turner. *Just War Tradition and the Restraint of War: A Moral and Historical Inquiry*. Princeton: Princeton University Press, 1981.

Johnson, James Turner. *Ideology, Reason, and the Limitation of War: Religious and Secular Concepts 1200–1740*. Princeton: Princeton University Press, 1975.

Johnson, James Turner and George Weigel. *Just War and the Gulf War*. Washington, DC: Ethics and Public Policy Center, 1991.

Johnson, Robert H. "Misguided Morality: Ethics and the Reagan Doctrine." *Political Science Quarterly* Vol. 103 No. 3 (1988): 509–529.

Jones, Dorothy V. *Code of Peace: Ethics and Security in the World of Warlord States*. Chicago: University of Chicago Press, 1991.

Kelsay, John. *Islam and War: A Study in Comparative Ethics*. Louisville: Knox, 1992.

Kelsay, John and James Turner Johnson, eds. *Just War and Jihad: Historical and Theoretical Perspectives on War and Peace in Western and Islamic Traditions*. New York: Greenwood, 1991.

Kleinig, John. "Good Samaritanism." *Philosophy and Public Affairs* Vol. 5 No. 4 (1976): 382–407.

Küng, Hans. "Politik aus Verantwortung: Plädoyer für eine ethisch-fundierte Außenpolitik." *Internationale Politik* Vol. 55 No. 2 (2000): 1–10.

Laberge, Pierre. "Humanitarian Intervention: Three Ethical Positions." *Ethics and International Affairs* Vol. 9 (1995): 15–35.

Lackey, D. *The Ethics of War and Peace*. Englewood Cliffs: Prentice-Hall, 1989.

Lackey, D. "A Modern Theory of Just War." *Ethics* (1982): 540–546.

Lewer, Nick and Oliver Ramsbotham. *Something Must Be Done: Towards an Ethical Framework for Humanitarian Intervention in International Social Conflict*. Bradford: University of Bradford, 1993.

Lillich, Richard B. "Kant and the Current Debate over Humanitarian Intervention." *Journal of Transnational Law and Policy* Vol. 6 (1997): 397–404.

Linklater, Andrew. *The Transformation of Political Community: Ethical Foundations of the Post-Westphalian Era*. Cambridge: Polity, 1998.

Lopez, George A. "More Ethical than Not: Sanctions as Surgical Tools." *Ethics and International Affairs* Vol. 13 (1999): 143–148.

Luard, Evan. *Human Rights and Foreign Policy*. New York: Pergamon Press, 1981.

Luban, David. "Just War and Human Rights." *Philosophy and Public Affairs* Vol. 9 No. 2 (1980): 160–181.

Luban, David. "The Romance of the Nation State." *Philosophy and Public Affairs* Vol. 9 No. 4 (1980): 392–397.

Lynch, Cecelia. "Acting on Belief: Christian Perspectives on Suffering and Violence." *Ethics and International Affairs* Vol. 14 (2000): 83–97.

Maxwell, Mary. "Toward a Moral System for World Society: A Reflection on Human Responsibilities." *Ethics and International Affairs* Vol. 12 (1998): 179–193.

McMahan, Jefferson. "The Ethics of International Intervention." In *Political Realism and International Morality*, edited by Kenneth Kipnis and Diana T. Meyers, 75–101. Boulder: Westview Press, 1987.

Melzer, Yehuda. *Concepts of Just War*. Leyden: Sijthoff, 1975.

Meron, Theodor. "Common Rights of Mankind in Gentili, Grotius and Suarez." *American Journal of International Law* Vol. 85 No. 1 (1991): 110–116.

Miller, David. "The Ethical Significance of Nationality." *Ethics* Vol. 98 No. 4 (1988): 647–663.

Miller, Lynn H. "The Contemporary Significance of the Doctrine of Just War." *World Politics* Vol. 16 No. 2 (1964): 254–286.

Miller, Richard B. "Humanitarian Intervention, Altruism, and the Limits of Casuistry." *The Journal of Religious Ethics* Vol. 28 No. 1 (2000): 3–35.

Miller, Richard B., ed. *War in the Twentieth Century: Sources in Theological Ethics*. Louisville: Westminster/John Knox Press, 1992.

Miller, Richard B. *Interpretations of Conflict: Ethics, Pacifism and the Just War Tradition*. Chicago: University of Chicago Press, 1991.

Myers, Robert J. "Notes on the Just War Theory: Whose Justice, Which Wars?" *Ethics and International Affairs* Vol. 10 (1996): 115–130.

Nardin, Terry. "International Ethics and International Law." *Review of International Studies* Vol. 18 No. 1 (1992): 19–30.

Nardin, Terry. *Law, Morality, and the Relations of States*. Princeton: Princeton University Press, 1983.

Nardin, Terry and David R. Mapel, eds. *Traditions of International Ethics*. Cambridge: Cambridge University Press, 1992.

Norman, Richard. *Ethics, Killing and War*. Cambridge: Cambridge University Press, 1995.

Nye, Joseph S. "Ethics and Intervention." In *Ideas and Ideals: Essays on Politics in Honor of Stanley Hoffmann*, edited by Linda B. Miller and Michael Joseph Smith, 127–143. Boulder: Westview Press, 1993.

O'Brien, William V. "Just-War Theory." In *The Ethics of War and Nuclear Deterrence*, edited by James P. Sterba, 30–44. Belmont: Wadsworth, 1985.

O'Brien, William V. *The Conduct of Just and Limited War*. New York: Praeger, 1981.

Orend, Brian. "Michael Waiter or Resorting to Force." *Canadian Journal of Political Science* Vol. 33 No. 3 (2000): 523–547.

Orend, Brian. *War and International Justice: A Kantian Perspective*. Waterloo: Wilfrid Laurier University Press, 2000.

Phillips, Robert Lester. *War and Justice*. Norman: University of Oklahoma Press, 1984.

Phillips, Robert Lester and Duane L. Cady. *Humanitarian Intervention: Just War versus Pacifism*. Lanham: Rowman and Littlefield, 1996.

Pierce, Albert C. "Just War Principles and Economic Sanctions." *Ethics and International Affairs* Vol. 10 (1996): 99–113.

Pogge, Thomas W. "Cosmopolitanism and Sovereignty." In *Political Restructuring in Europe: Ethical Perspectives*, edited by Chris Brown, 89–122. London: Routledge, 1994.

Pogge, Thomas W. "An Institutional Approach to Humanitarian Intervention." *Public Affairs Quarterly* Vol. 6 No. 1 (1992): 89–103.

Pogge, Thomas W. *Realizing Rawls*. Ithaca: Cornell University Press, 1989.

Quinn, Warren S. "Actions, Intentions and Consequences: The Doctrine of Double-Effect." *Philosophy and Public Affairs* Vol. 18 No. 4 (1989): 334–351.

Ramsbotham, Oliver P. "Islam, Christianity, and Forcible Intervention." *Ethics and International Affairs* Vol. 12 (1998): 81–102.

Ramsey, Paul. *The Just War: Force and Moral Responsibility*. New York: Charles Scribner's Sons, 1968.

Ramsey, Paul. "The Ethics of Intervention." *Review of Politics* Vol. 27 No. 3 (1965): 287–310.

Rawls, John. *The Law of Peoples: With "The Idea of Public Reason Revisited."* Cambridge, MA: Harvard University Press, 1999.

Rawls, John. "The Law of Peoples." In *On Human Rights: The Oxford Amnesty Lectures, 1993*, edited by Stephen Shute and Susan Hurley, 41–82. New York: Basic Books, 1993.

Regan, Richard J. *Just War: Principles and Cases*. Washington, DC: Catholic University of America, 1996.

Rosenthal, Joel H., ed. *Ethics and International Affairs: A Reader*. Washington, DC: Georgetown University Press, 1995.

Russell, Frederick. *The Just War in the Middle Ages*. Cambridge: Cambridge University Press, 1975.

Schmücker, Reinhold. "Gibt es einen gerechten Krieg?" *Deutsche Zeitschrift für Philosophie* Vol. 48 (2000): 319–340.

Sherman, Nancy. "Empathy, Respect, and Humanitarian Intervention." *Ethics and International Affairs* Vol. 12 (1998): 103–119.

Shue, Henry. *Basic Rights: Subsistence, Affluence, and US Foreign Policy.* 2nd ed. Princeton: Princeton University Press, 1996.

Slater, Jerome and Terry Nardin. "Nonintervention and Human Rights." *The Journal of Politics* Vol. 48 No. 1 (1986): 86–95.

Smith, Dan. "Just War, Clausewitz and Sarajevo." *Journal of Peace Research* Vol. 31 No. 2 (1994): 136–142.

Smith, Michael J. "Humanitarian Intervention: An Overview of the Ethical Issues." *Ethics and International Affairs* Vol. 12 (1998): 63–79.

Smith, Michael J. "Ethics and Intervention." *Ethics and International Affairs* Vol. 3 (1989): 1–26.

Smith, Tony. "Morality and the Use of Force in a Unipolar World: The 'Wilsonian Moment'?" *Ethics and International Affairs* Vol. 14 (2000): 11–22.

Steinweg, Reiner, ed. *Der gerechte Krieg: Christentum, Islam, Marxismus.* Frankfurt am Main: Suhrkamp, 1980.

Tanguy, Joelle and Fiona Terry. "Humanitarian Responsibility and Committed Action." *Ethics and International Affairs* Vol. 13 (1999): 29–34.

Tuck, Richard. *The Rights of War and Peace: Political Thought and the International Order from Grotius to Kant.* Oxford: Oxford University Press,

Valls, Andrew and Virginia Held, eds. *Ethics in International Affairs.* Lanham: Rowman and Littlefield, 2000.

Vetlesen, Arne Johan. "Genocide: A Case for the Responsibility of the Bystander." *Journal of Peace Research* Vol. 37 No. 4 (2000): 519–532.

Vincent, R.J. "Western Concepts of a Universal Moral Order." In *Moral Claims in World Affairs,* edited by Ralph Pettman, 52–78. London: Croom Helm, 1979.

Von Manz, Hans G. "Menschenrechtsschutz und Achtung staatlicher Souveränität: Eine Pflichtenkollision internationaler Politik? Ethische Überlegungen zu Bedingungen, Rechtfertigung und Notwendigkeit humanitärer Intervention." In *Prinzipien des Rechts,* edited by Giuseppe Orsi, 71–98. Frankfurt am Main: Lang, 1996.

Walzer, Michael. "The Politics of Rescue." *Social Research* Vol. 62 No. 1 (1995): 53–66.

Walzer, Michael. *Thick and Thin: Moral Argument at Home and Abroad.* Notre Dame: University of Notre Dame Press, 1994.

Walzer, Michael. *Spheres of Justice: A Defence of Pluralism and Equality.* New York: Basic Books, 1983.

Walzer, Michael. "The Moral Standing of States: A Response to Four Critics." *Philosophy and Public Affairs* Vol. 9 No. 3 (1980): 209–229.

Warner, Daniel. *An Ethic of Responsibility in International Relations.* Boulder: Lynne Rienner, 1991.

Wasserstrom, Richard, ed. *War and Morality.* Belmont: Wadsworth, 1970.

Weiss, Thomas G. "Principles, Politics, and Humanitarian Action." *Ethics and International Affairs* Vol. 13 (1999): 1–22.

Welch, David A. "Can We Think Systematically about Ethics and Statecraft?" *Ethics and International Affairs* Vol. 8 (1994): 23–37.

Welch, David A. *Justice and the Genesis of War.* Cambridge: Cambridge University Press, 1993.

Wells, Donald A. "How Much Can the 'Just War' Justify?" *The Journal of Philosophy* Vol. 66 No. 23 (1969): 819–829.

Wheeler, Nicholas J. "Guardian Angel or Global Gangster: A Review of the Ethical Claims of International Society." *Political Studies* Vol. 44 No. 1 (1996): 123–135.

Wicclair, Mark. "Rawls and the Principle of Non-Intervention." In *John Rawls' Theory of Social Justice*, edited by H. Gene Blocker and Elizabeth H. Smith, 289–308. Athens: Ohio University Press, 1980.

Wicker, Brian and Fred van Iersel, eds. *Humanitarian Intervention and the Pursuit of Justice: A Pax Christi Contribution to a Contemporary Debate*. Kampen: Kok Pharos, 1994.

Wright, Moorhead, ed. *Morality and International Relations: Concepts and Issues*. Aldershot: Avebury, 1996.

Wright, Moorhead. "An Ethic of Responsibility." In *The Community of States*, edited by James Mayall, 158–166. London: Allen and Unwin, 1982.

Zanetti, Véronique. "Global Justice: Is Interventionism Desirable?" *Metaphilosophy* Vol. 32 No. 1 (2001): 196–211.

Zohar, Noam J. "Boycott, Crime, and Sin: Ethical and Talmudic Responses to Injustice Abroad." *Ethics and International Affairs* Vol. 7 (1993): 39–53.

Zolo, Danilo. "La filosofia della 'guerra umanitaria' da Kant ad Habermas." *Iride: Filosofia e Discussione Pubblica* Vol. 12 No. 27 (1999): 249–253.

# 5. LEGAL ASPECTS

Abiew, Francis Kofi. *The Evolution of the Doctrine and Practice of Humanitarian Intervention*. The Hague: Kluwer Law International, 1999.
Review of historical precedents and contemporary developments. Defends the emergence of a right of humanitarian intervention and argues that it is not incompatible with state sovereignty.

Bettati, Mario and Bernard Kouchner. *Le devoir d'ingérence: peut-on les laisser mourir?* Paris: Denoël, 1987.
Influential statement arguing for the right to provide assistance to alleviate suffering caused by human-made disasters, without the consent of the state.

Brownlie, Ian. *International Law and the Use of Force by States*. Oxford: Clarendon Press, 1963.
Classic statement of the strict limitations on the use of force imposed by international law.

Chesterman, Simon. *Just War or Just Peace? Humanitarian Intervention and International Law*. Oxford: Oxford University Press, 2001.
Study of the legality of humanitarian intervention, examining the genealogy of the doctrine and arguing that as a legal concept it is incoherent. Appendix of relevant legal material.

Djiena Wembou, Michel-Cyr. "Le droit d'ingérence humanitaire: un droit aux fondement incertains, au contenu imprécis et géométrie variable." *African Journal of International and Comparative Law* Vol. 4 No. 3 (1992): 570–591.
Critical view of the right of humanitarian intervention, arguing that it has uncertain legal foundations.

Franck, Thomas M. "Who Killed Art. 2 (4)? Or: The Changing Norms Governing the Use of Force by States." *American Journal of International Law* Vol. 64 No. 4 (1970): 809–837.
States that the UN Charter's prohibition on the use of force remains weak as a result of the practical goals that nations are pursuing in defence of their national interest.

Lillich, Richard B., ed. *Humanitarian Intervention and the United Nations*. Charlottesville: University Press of Virginia, 1973.
Widely cited statements addressing the legal status of the doctrine of humanitarian intervention at the beginning of the 1970s.

Murphy, Sean D. *Humanitarian Intervention: The United Nations in an Evolving World Order*. Philadelphia: University of Pennsylvania Press, 1996.
Discusses the practice of states before and after the adoption of the UN Charter, including chapters on unilateral and regional organizations' interventions.

Rodley, Nigel S., ed. *To Loose the Bands of Wickedness: International Intervention in Defence of Human Rights*. London: Brassey's, 1992.
Early 1990s statement of the erosion of domestic jurisdiction in the light of human rights and its implications for Article 2 (7) of the UN Charter.

## References

Abib-Saab, R. *Droit humanitaire et conflits internes*. Geneva: Henry Dunant Institute, 1986.

*Aegean Sea Continental Shelf Case (Jurisdiction of the Court)* (December 19, 1978): http://www.icj-cij.org/icjwww.idecisions/isummaries/igtsummary781219.htm

Ajaj, Ahmad. "Humanitarian Intervention: Second Reading of the Charter of the United Nations." *Arab Law Quarterly* Vol. 8 (1993): 215–236.

Akehurst, Michael. "Enforcement Action by Regional Agencies with Special Reference to the Organization of American States." *British Year Book of International Law* (1967): 175–227.

Amer, Ramses. *The United Nations and Foreign Military Interventions: A Comparative Study of the Application of the Charter.* Uppsala: Department of Peace and Conflict Research, Uppsala University, 1992.

Andraos, A. "De l'intervention dans les affaires intérieures des États souverains." *Revue Égyptienne de Droit International* Vol. 10 (1954): 1–23.

Arend, Anthony Clark and Robert J. Beck. *International Law and the Use of Force: Beyond the UN Charter Paradigm.* London: Routledge, 1993.

Arnison, Nancy D. "International Law and Non-Intervention: When Do Humanitarian Concerns Supersede Sovereignty?" *Fletcher Forum of World Affairs* Vol. 17 No. 2 (1993): 198–211.

Baginjan, K.A. "Printsip nevmeshatel'sta i ustav OON." *Sovetskoe gosudarstvo i pravo* Vol. 6 (1957): 62–70.

Barrie, George N. "Forcible Intervention and International Law: Legal Theories and Realities." *South African Law Journal* Vol. 116 No. 4 (1999): 791–809.

Barry, Benjamin. "Unilateral Humanitarian Intervention: Legalizing the Use of Force to Prevent Human Rights Atrocities." *Fordham International Law Journal* Vol. 16 No. 2 (1991): 76–116.

Bedjaoui, Mohammed. *Nouvel ordre mondial et contrôle de la légalité des actes du conseil de sécurité.* Brussels: Bruylant, 1994.

Benjamin, Barry M. "Unilateral Humanitarian Intervention: Legalizing the Use of Force to Prevent Human Rights Atrocities." *Fordham International Law Journal* Vol. 16 (1992/1993): 120–158.

Benneh, E.Y. "Review of the Law of Non-Intervention." *African Journal of International and Comparative Law* Vol. 7 No. 1 (1995): 139–157.

Benvenuti, Paolo. "Recenti sviluppi in tema di osservanza del diritto internazionale umanitario da parte delle Forze delle Nazioni Unite: il bolletino del Segretario Generale." *La communità internazionale* Vol. 55 No. 3 (2000): 379–399.

Bermejo García, Romualdo. *El marco jurídico internacional en materia de uso de la fuerza: ambigüedades y límites.* Madrid: Civitas, 1993.

Best, Geoffrey. *War and Law since 1945.* Oxford: Clarendon Press, 1994.

Best, Geoffrey. *Humanity in Warfare: The Modern History of the International Law of Armed Conflict.* London: Methuen, 1983.

Bettati, Mario. *Le droit d'ingérence: mutation de l'ordre international.* Paris: Odile Jacob, 1996.

Bettati, Mario. "The International Community and Limitations of Sovereignty." *Diogenes* Vol. 44 No. 4 (1996): 91–109.

Bettati, Mario. "Ingérence, intervention ou assistance humanitaire?" In *International Legal Issues Arising under the United Nations Decade of International Law*, edited by Najeeb Al-Nauimi and Richard Meese, 935–962. The Hague: Martinus Nijhoff, 1995.

Bettati, Mario. "The Right of Humanitarian Intervention or the Right of Free Access to Victims?" *The Review: International Commission of Jurists* Vol. 49 No. 1 (1992): 1–11.

Bettati, Mario. "Un droit d'ingérence?" *Revue Générale de Droit International Public* Vol. 95 (1991): 639–670.

Beyerlin, Ulrich. *Die humanitäre Aktion zur Gewährleistung des Mindeststandards in nicht-internationalen Konflikten.* Berlin: Duncker und Humblot, 1975.

Bills, David. "International Human Rights and Humanitarian Intervention: The Ramifications of Reform on the United Nations Security Council." *Texas International Law Journal* Vol. 31 No. 1 (1996): 107–130.

Bin Cheng. "La jurimétrie: Sens et mesure de la souveraineté juridique et de la compétence nationale." *Clunet* (1991): 579–599.

Blanke, Hermann-Josef. "Menschenrechte als völkerrechtliche Interventionstitel." *Archiv des Völkerrechts* Vol. 36 No. 3 (1998): 257–284.

Blockmans, Steven. "Moving into UNchartered Waters: An Emerging Right of Unilateral Humanitarian Intervention?" *Leiden Journal of International Law* Vol. 12 No. 4 (1999): 759–786.

Boisson de Chazournes, Laurence and Luigi Condorelli. "Common Article 1 of the Geneva Conventions Revisited: Protecting Collective Interests." *International Review of the Red Cross* Vol. 82 No. 837 (2000): 67–87.

Boll, Alfred M. "The Asian Values Debate and Its Relevance to International Humanitarian Law." *International Review of the Red Cross* Vol. 83 No. 841 (2001): 45–57.

Boustany, Katia. "Intervention humanitaire et intervention d'humanité: évolution ou mutation en droit international." *Revue Québécoise de Droit International* Vol. 8 No. 1 (1993/1994): 103–111.

Bowett, Derek W., ed. *The Current Legal Regulation of the Use of Force.* Dordrecht: Martinus Nijhoff, 1986.

Bowett, Derek W. *United Nations Forces: A Legal Study of United Nations Practice.* London: Stevens, 1964.

Bowett, Derek W. *Self-Defence in International Law.* New York: Praeger, 1958.

Bowring, Bill. "The 'droit et devoir d'ingérence': A Timely New Remedy for Africa?" *African Journal of International and Comparative Law* Vol. 7 No. 3 (1995): 493–510.

Brenfors, Martha and Malene Maxe Petersen. "The Legality of Unilateral Humanitarian Intervention: A Defence." *The Nordic Journal of International Law* Vol. 69 No. 4 (2000): 449–499.

Brown, Bartram S. "Humanitarian Intervention at a Crossroads." *William and Mary Law Review* Vol. 41 No. 5 (2000): 1683–1741.

Brownlie, Ian. "Humanitarian Intervention." In *Law and Civil War in the Modern World*, edited by John Norton Moore, 217–228. Baltimore: The Johns Hopkins University Press, 1974.

Brownlie, Ian. "Thoughts on Kind-Hearted Gunmen." In *Humanitarian Intervention and the United Nations*, edited by Richard B. Lillich, 139–148. Charlottesville: University Press of Virginia, 1973.

Bula-Bula, Sayeman. "L'idée d'ingérence à la lumière du nouvel ordre mondial." *African Journal of International and Comparative Law* Vol. 6 No. 1 (1994): 14–44.

Burmester, Byron F. "On Humanitarian Intervention: The New World Order and Wars to Preserve Human Rights." *Utah Law Review* Vol. 1 (1994): 269–323.

Burton, Michael L. "Legalizing the Sub-Legal: A Proposal for Codifying a Doctrine of Unilateral Humanitarian Intervention." *Georgetown Law Journal* Vol. 85 No. 2 (1996): 417–454.

Butler, William E., ed. *The Non-Use of Force in International Law.* Dordrecht: Martinus Nijhoff, 1989.

Byers, Michael and Simon Chesterman. "'You, the People': Pro-Democratic Intervention in International Law." In *Democratic Governance and International Law*, edited by Gregory H. Fox and Brad R. Roth, 259–292. Cambridge: Cambridge University Press, 2000.

Canotilho, José J. Gomes. "Nova ordem mundial e ingerência humanitária." *Boletim da Faculdade de Direito* Vol. 71 (1995): 1–26.

Caron, David D. "The Legitimacy of the Collective Authority of the Security Council." *American Journal of International Law* Vol. 87 No. 4 (1993): 552–588.

Carpentier, Chantal. "La Résolution 688 (1991) du Conseil de Sécurité: quel devoir d'ingérence?" *Études Internationales* Vol. 23 (1992): 279–317.

*Case Concerning the Military and Paramilitary Activities in and against Nicaragua (Nicaragua v. United States of America) (Merits)* (June 27, 1986):
http://www.icjcij.org/icjwww/Idecisions/isummaries/inussummary860627.htm

Cassese, Antonio. "A Follow-Up: Forcible Humanitarian Countermeasures and Opinio Necessitatis." *European Journal of International Law* Vol. 10 No. 4 (1999): 791–800.

Cassese, Antonio. "Ex iniuria ius oritur: Are We Moving towards International Legitimation of Forcible Humanitarian Countermeasures in the World Community?" *European Journal of International Law* Vol. 10 No. 1 (1999): 23–30.

Cassese, Antonio, ed. *The Current Legal Regulation of the Use of Force*. Dordrecht: Martinus Nijhoff, 1986.

Concetti, Gino. *Il diritto di intervento umanitario*. Padova: Centro Editoriale Cattolico Carroccio, 1993.

Condorelli, Luigi, A. La Rosa and S. Scherrer, eds. *Les Nations Unies et le droit international humanitaire*. Paris: Éditions Pedone, 1996.

*Corfu Channel Case (Merits)* (April 9, 1949):
http://www.icj-cij.org/icjwww/idecisions/isummaries/Iccsummary490409.htm

Corten, Olivier. "Un renouveau du 'droit d'intervention humanitaire'? Vrais problèmes, fausse solution." *Revue Trimestrielle des Droits de l'Homme* Vol. 11 No. 44 (2000): 695–708.

Corten, Olivier and Pierre Klein. *Droit d'ingérence ou obligation de réaction? Les possibilités d'action visant à assurer le respect des droits de la personne face au principe de non-intervention*. Brussels: Bruylant, 1992.

Cot, Jean-Pierre and Alain Pellet, eds. *La Charte des Nations Unies: commentaire article par article*. Paris: Economica, 1991.

D'Amato, Anthony. "Trashing Customary International Law (in Appraisals of the ICJ's Decision: Nicaragua v. United States (Merits))." *American Journal of International Law* Vol. 81 No. 1 (1987): 101–105.

Damrosch, Lori Fisler. "Politics across Borders: Nonintervention and Nonforcible Influence over Domestic Affairs." *American Journal of International Law* Vol. 83 No. 1 (1989): 1–50.

Damrosch, Lori Fisler and David J. Scheffer, eds. *Law and Force in the New International Order*. Boulder: Westview, 1991.

Delbrück, Jost. "A Fresh Look at Humanitarian Intervention under the Authority of the United Nations." *Indiana Law Journal* Vol. 67 No. 4 (1992): 887–901.

Delbrück, Jost. "Menschenrechte im Schnittpunkt zwischen universalem Schutzanspruch und staatlicher Souveränität." *German Yearbook of International Law* Vol. 22 (1979): 384–402.

De Lima, F.X. *Intervention in International Law: With A Reference to the Organisation of American States*. The Hague: Uitgeverij Pax Nederland, 1971.

Delissen, A.J.M. and G.J. Tanja. *Humanitarian Law of Armed Conflict: Challenges Ahead: Essays in Honour of Frits Kalshoven*. Dordrecht: Martinus Nijhoff, 1991.

Diallo, J. *Traditions africaines et droit humanitaire*. Geneva: International Committee of the Red Cross, 1976.

Dinstein, Yoram. *War, Aggression and Self-Defence*. 3rd ed. Cambridge: Cambridge University Press, 2001.

Djiena Wembou, Michel-Cyr. "La répression des crimes de guerre et des autres violations graves du droit humanitaire." *African Journal of International and Comparative Law* Vol. 11 No. 3 (1999): 375–391.

Djiena Wembou, Michel-Cyr. "Validité et portée de la résolution 794 (1992) du Conseil de sécurité." *African Journal of International and Comparative Law* Vol. 5 (1993): 340–354.

Doehring, Karl. "Die humanitäre Intervention: Überlegungen zu ihrer Rechtfertigung." In *The Modern World of Human Rights: Essays in Honour of Thomas Buergenthal*, edited by Antonio Augusto Cançado Trindade, 549–565. San José: Instituto Interamericano de Derechos Humanos, 1996.

Domestici-Met, Marie-José. "Aspects juridiques récents de l'assistance humanitaire." *Annuaire Française de Droit International* (1989): 117–148.

Dowty, Alan and Gil Loescher. "Refugee Flows as Grounds for International Action." *International Security* Vol. 21 No. 1 (1996): 43–71.

Ehrlich, Thomas and Mary Ellen O'Connell. *International Law and the Use of Force*. Boston: Little, Brown and Co., 1993.

Ellerman, Christine. "Command of Sovereignty Gives Way to Concern for Humanity." *Vanderbilt Journal of Transnational Law* Vol. 26 No. 2 (1993): 341–371.

Erickson, Richard J. *International Law and the Revolutionary State: A Case Study of the Soviet Union and Customary International Law*. Dobbs Ferry: Oceana Publications, 1972.

Ermacora, Felix. "Human Rights and Domestic Jurisdiction (Art. 2 and 7 of the Charter)." *RCADI* Vol. 124 (1968): 371–451.

Essombe, Edimo Joseph. "Le droit d'ingérence humanitaire: une effectivité en mouvement." *African Journal of International and Comparative Law* Vol. 5 No. 3 (1993): 487–502.

Euzet, Christophe. "Le droit international d'intervention." *Annales de l'Université des Sciences Sociales de Toulouse* Vol. 46 (1998): 89–118.

Evans, Cedric E. "The Concept of 'Threat to Peace' and Humanitarian Concerns: Probing the Limits of Chapter VII of the UN Charter." *Transnational Law and Contemporary Problems* Vol. 5 No. 1 (1995): 213–235.

Evgenev, V.V. "Pravosub'ektivnost, suverenitet i nevmeshatel'stvo v mezhdunarodnom prave." *Sovetskoe gosudarstvo i pravo* Vol. 2 (1955): 75–84.

Fairley, H. Scott. "State Actors, Humanitarian Intervention and International Law: Reopening Pandora's Box." *Georgia Journal of International and Comparative Law* Vol. 10 No. 1 (1980): 29–63.

Falk, Mattias. *The Legality of Humanitarian Intervention: A Review of Recent UN Practice*. Stockholm: Juristförlaget, 1996.

Falk, Richard A. *Human Rights Horizons: The Pursuit of Justice in a Globalizing World*. New York: Routledge, 2000.

Falk, Richard A. "The United Nations, the Rule of Law and Humanitarian Intervention." In *Restructuring the Global Military Sector*, edited by Mary Kaldor and Basker Vashee, 108–133. London: Pinter, 1997.

Falk, Richard A. "The Complexities of Humanitarian Intervention: A New World Order Challenge." *Michigan Journal of International Law* Vol. 17 No. 2 (1996): 491–513.

Falk, Richard A. "The United Nations and the Rule of Law." *Transnational Law and Contemporary Problems* Vol. 4 No. 2 (1994): 611–642.

Falk, Richard A., ed. *The International Law of Civil War*. Baltimore: The Johns Hopkins University Press, 1971.

Falk, Richard A. *Legal Order in a Violent World*. Princeton: Princeton University Press, 1968.

Falk, Richard A., Gabriel Kolko and Robert Jay Lifton, eds. *Crimes of War: A Legal, Political-Documentary, and Psychological Inquiry into the Responsibility of Leaders, Citizens, and Soldiers for Criminal Acts in Wars*. New York: Random House, 1971.

Farer, Tom J. "Human Rights in Law's Empire: The Jurisprudence War." *American Journal of International Law* Vol. 85 No. 1 (1991): 117–127.

Farer, Tom J. "The Regulation of Foreign Intervention in Civil Armed Conflict." *Recueil des Cours* Vol. 142 No. 2 (1975): 291–406.

Farer, Tom J. "Harnessing Rogue Elephants: A Short Discourse on Foreign Intervention in Civil Strife." *Harvard Law Review* Vol. 82 (1969): 511–541.

Faundez, Julio. "International Law and Wars of National Liberation: Use of Force and Intervention." *African Journal of International and Comparative Law* Vol. 1 No. 1 (1989): 85–98.

Fauteux, Paul. "Droit d'ingérence et non-intervention: la quadrature de cercle?" In *Selected Papers in International Law. Contribution of the Canadian Council on International Law*, edited by Yves Le Bouthillier, 291–315. The Hague: Kluwer Law International, 1999.

Fenwick, Charles G. "Intervention: Individual and Collective." *American Journal of International Law* Vol. 39 No. 4 (1945): 645–663.

Ferencz, Benjamin B. *Defining International Aggression: The Search for World Peace*. Dobbs Ferry: Oceana, 1975.

Fidler, David P. "Caught between Traditions: The Security Council in Philosophical Conundrum." *Michigan Journal of International Law* Vol. 17 (1996): 412–453.

Fielding, Lois E. "Taking a Closer Look at Threats to Peace: The Power of the Security Council to Address Humanitarian Crises." *University of Detroit Mercy Law Review* Vol. 73 No. 3 (1996): 551–568.

Fleck, Dieter, ed. *The Handbook of Humanitarian Law in Armed Conflicts*. Oxford: Oxford University Press, 1995.

Fonteyne, Jean-Pierre L. "The Customary International Law Doctrine of Humanitarian Intervention: Its Current Validity under the UN Charter." *California Western International Law Journal* Vol. 4 (1974): 203–270.

Fox, Gregory H. and Brad R. Roth, eds. *Democratic Governance and International Law*. Cambridge: Cambridge University Press, 2000.

Franck, Thomas M. "The Emerging Right to Democratic Governance." *American Journal of International Law* Vol. 86 No. 1 (1992): 46–91.

Franck, Thomas M. "The 'Powers of Appreciation': Who Is the Ultimate Guardian of UN Legality?" *American Journal of International Law* Vol. 86 No. 3 (1992): 519–523.

Franck, Thomas M. "Some Observations on the ICJ's Procedural and Substantive Innovations (in Appraisals of the ICJ's Decision: Nicaragua v. United States (Merits))." *American Journal of International Law* Vol. 81 No. 1 (1987): 116–121.

Freeman, Mark. "International Law and Internal Armed Conflicts: Clarifying the Interplay between Human Rights and Humanitarian Protections." *Journal of Humanitarian Assistance* (July 2000): http://www.jha.ac/articles/a059.htm

Freudenschuß, Helmut. "Between Unilateralism and Collective Security: Authorizations of the Use of Force by the UN Security Council." *European Journal of International Law* Vol. 5 No. 4 (1994): 492–531.

Freudenschuß, Helmut. "Article 39 of the UN Charter Revisited: Threats to the Peace and the Recent Practice of the UN Security Council." *Austrian Journal of Public International Law* Vol. 46 (1993): 1–39.

Gabriel, Jürg Martin. "Die Gegenläufigkeit von Neutralität und humanitären Interventionen." *Schweizerische Zeitschrift für internationales und europäisches Recht* Vol. 10 No. 2 (2000): 219–236.

Gaja, Giorgio. "Use of Force Made or Authorized by the United Nations." In *The United Nations at Age Fifty: A Legal Perspective*, edited by Christian Tomuschat, 39–58. The Hague: Kluwer Law International, 1995.

Gallant, Judy A. "Humanitarian Intervention and Security Council Resolution 688: A Reappraisal in Light of a Changing World Order." *American University Journal of International Law* Vol. 7 No. 2 (1992): 881–920.

Gamio, José M. "Intervenciones humanitarias: balance de las experiencias recientes." In *Héctor Gros Espiell amicorum liber: persona humana y derecho internacional*, edited by Antonio Augusto Cançado Trindade and Christophe Swinarski, 405–428. Bruxelles: Bruylant, 1997.

Gardam, Judith, ed. *Humanitarian Law*. Aldershot: Ashgate, 1999.

Gardam, Judith. "Proportionality and Force in International Law." *American Journal of International Law* Vol. 87 No. 3 (1993): 391–413.

Gilmour, D.R. "The Meaning of 'Intervene' within Article 2 (7) of the United Nations Charter: An Historical Perspective." *International and Comparative Law Quarterly* Vol. 16 (1967): 330–351.

Glennon, Michael J. "Sovereignty and Community after Haiti: Rethinking the Collective Use of Force." *American Journal of International Law* Vol. 89 No. 1 (1995): 70–74.

Goodrich, Leland M., Edvard Hambro and Anne Patricia Simons. *Charter of the United Nations: Commentary and Documents*. 3rd ed. New York: Columbia University Press, 1969.

Goodwin-Gill, Guy S. *The Refugee in International Law*. 2nd ed. Oxford: Clarendon Press, 1996.

Gordon, Edward. "Article 2 (4) in Historical Context." *Yale Journal of International Law* Vol. 10 (1985): 271.

Gordon, Ruth. "Humanitarian Intervention by the United Nations: Iraq, Somalia, and Haiti." *Texas International Law Journal* Vol. 31 (1996): 43–56.

Gowlland-Debbas, Vera. "The Limits of Unilateral Enforcement of Community Objectives in the Framework of UN Peace Maintenance." *European Journal of International Law* Vol. 11 No. 2 (2000): 361–384.

Gowlland-Debbas, Vera. "Security Council Enforcement Action and Issues of State Responsibility." *International and Comparative Law Quarterly* Vol. 43 No. 1 (1994): 55–98.

Gravier, Bruno and Jean-Marc Elchardus, eds. *Le crime contre l'humanité*. Ramonville Saint-Agne: Erès, 1996.

Gray, Christine. *International Law and the Use of Force*. Oxford: Oxford University Press, 2000.

Greenwood, Christopher. *Humanitarian Intervention: Law and Policy*. Oxford: Oxford University Press, 2001.

Greenwood, Christopher. "International Humanitarian Law and United Nations Military Operations." *Yearbook of International Humanitarian Law* Vol. 1 (1998): 3–34.

Greenwood, Christopher. "Is There a Right of Humanitarian Intervention?" *The World Today* Vol. 49 No. 2 (1993): 34–40.

Greenwood, Christopher. "The Relationship between Jus ad Bellum and Jus in Bello." *Review of International Studies* Vol. 9 No. 4 (1983): 221–234.

Gros Espiell, Héctor. "El llamado 'derecho de injerencia humanitaria' en un mundo interdependiente." In *Las Naciones Unidas a los cincuenta años*, edited by Modesto Seara Vázquez, 200–220. México: Fondo de Cultura Económica, 1995.

Halderman, John W. "Legal Basis for United Nations Armed Forces." *American Journal of International Law* Vol. 56 No. 4 (1962): 971–996.

Halberstam, Malvina. "The Legality of Humanitarian Intervention." *Cardozo Journal of International and Comparative Law* Vol. 3 No. 1 (1995): 1–8.

Halberstam, Malvina. "The Copenhagen Document: Intervention in Support of Democracy." *Harvard International Law Journal* Vol. 34 No. 1 (1993): 163–175.

Helton, Arthur C. "Legal Dimensions of Responses to Complex Humanitarian Emergencies." *International Journal of Refugee Law* Vol. 10 No. 3 (1998): 533–546.

Helton, Arthur C. "The Legality of Providing Humanitarian Assistance without the Consent of the Sovereign." *International Journal of Refugee Law* Vol. 4 (1992): 373–375.

Henkin, Louis. "The Reports of the Death of Article 2 (4) Are Greatly Exaggerated." *American Journal of International Law* Vol. 65 No. 3 (1971): 544–548.

Henkin, Louis. *How Nations Behave: Law and Foreign Policy.* New York: Praeger, 1968.

Henkin, Louis. "Force, Intervention and Neutrality in Contemporary Law." *Proceedings of the American Society of International Law* Vol. 57 (1963): 147–173.

Henkin, Louis, Stanley Hoffmann, Jeane J. Kirkpatrick, Allan Gerson, William D. Rogers and David J. Scheffer, eds. *Right v. Might: International Law and the Use of Force.* New York: Council on Foreign Relations Press, 1991.

Higgins, Rosalyn. "Internal War and International Law." In *The Future of the International Legal Order,* edited by Cyril E. Black and Richard A. Falk, 81–121. Princeton: Princeton University Press, 1971.

Hoffman, Michael H. "Peace-Enforcement Actions and Humanitarian Law: Emerging Rules for 'Interventional Armed Conflict'." *International Review of the Red Cross* Vol. 82 No. 837 (2000): 193–203.

International Law Association. *Report of the Fifty-Seventh Conference.* Madrid: ILA, 1976.

International Law Association. *Report of the Fifty-Sixth Conference.* New Delhi: ILA, 1974.

International Law Association. *Report of the Fifty-Fifth Conference.* New York; London: ILA, 1972.

Jamart, Jean-Sébastien. "Le droit d'ingérence: mythe ou réalité?" *Actualités du Droit* Vol. 8 No. 2 (1998): 207–265.

Jesus, José Luís. "Intervention in the Domestic Affairs on Humanitarian Grounds and International Law." In *Liber amicorum Günther Jaenicke: Zum 85. Geburtstag,* edited by Volkmar Götz, 149–164. Berlin: Springer, 1998.

Jhabvala, Farrokh. "Unilateral Humanitarian Intervention and International Law." *Indian Journal of International Law* Vol. 21 No. 2 (1981): 208–230.

Jørgensen, Nina H.B. *The Responsibility of States for International Crimes.* Oxford: Oxford University Press, 2000.

Journal of Peace Research. "Special Issue on Humanitarian Law of Armed Conflict." Vol. 24 No. 3 (1987).

Kader, David. "Law and Genocide: A Critical Annotated Bibliography." *Hastings International and Comparative Law Review* Vol. 11 (1990): 381–390.

Kälin, Walter. "Humanitäre Intervention: Legitimation durch Verfahren? Zehn Thesen zur Kosovo-Krise." *Schweizerische Zeitschrift für internationales und europäisches Recht* Vol. 10 No. 2 (2000): 159–176.

Kalshoven, Frits and Yves Sandoz, eds. *Mise en œuvre du droit international humanitaire.* Dordrecht: Martinus Nijhoff, 1989.

Kelly, Michael J. *Restoring and Maintaining Order in Complex Peace Operations: The Search for a Legal Framework.* The Hague: Kluwer Law International, 1999.

Khare, Subhas Chandra. *Use of Force under the UN Charter.* New Delhi: Metropolitan, 1985.

Kimminich, Otto. "Der Mythos der humanitären Intervention." *Archiv des Völkerrechts* Vol. 33 No. 4 (1995): 430–458.

Klintworth, Gary. *"The Right to Intervene" in the Domestic Affairs of States.* Canberra: Strategic and Defence Studies Centre, 1991.

Komarnicki, Titus. "L'intervention en droit international moderne." *Revue Générale de Droit International Public* Vol. 60 No. 4 (1956): 521–568.

Koroma, Abdul G. "Humanitarian Intervention and Contemporary Law." *Schweizerische Zeitschrift für internationales und europäisches Recht* Vol. 5 No. 4 (1995): 409–416.

Kostenko, N.I. "Mezhdunarodnyi Ugolovnyi Sud (Iuridicheskie Aspekty)." *Gosudarstvo i Pravo* No. 3 (2000): 92–103.

Krylov, Nikolai. "Humanitarian Intervention: Pros and Cons." *Loyola of Los Angeles International and Comparative Law Journal* Vol. 17 No. 2 (1995): 365–407.

Lane, Eric. "Mass Killing by Governments: Lawful in the World Legal Order?" *New York University Journal of International Law and Politics* Vol. 12 No. 2 (1979): 239–280.

Leurdijk, Henk J. "Civil War and Intervention in International Law." *Netherlands International Law Journal* Vol. 24 No. 1/2 (1977): 143–159.

Lillich, Richard B. "The Role of the UN Security Council in Protecting Human Rights in Crisis Situations: UN Humanitarian Intervention in the Post-Cold War World." *Tulane Journal of International and Comparative Law* Vol. 3 No. 1 (1995): 2–17.

Lillich, Richard B. "Humanitarian Intervention through the United Nations: Towards the Development of Criteria." *Zeitschrift für ausländisches öffentliches Recht und Völkerrecht* Vol. 53 No. 3 (1993): 557–575.

Lillich, Richard B. "Forcible Self-Help by States to Protect Human Rights." *Iowa Law Review* Vol. 53 (1967): 325–351.

Lobel, Jules and Michael Ratner. "Bypassing the Security Council: Ambiguous Authorizations to Use Force, Cease-Fires and the Iraqi Inspection Regime." *The American Journal of International Law* Vol. 93 No. 1 (1999): 124–154.

Lowe, Vaughan. "The Principle of Non-Intervention: The Use of Force." In *The United Nations and the Principles of International Law: Essays in Memory of Michael Akehurst*, edited by Vaughan Lowe and C. Warbeck, 66–84. London: Routledge, 1994.

Magagni, Massimo. "L'adozione di misure coercitive a tutela dei diritti umani nella prassi del Consiglio di sicurezza." *Comunicazioni e studi–Istituto di Diritto Internazionale e Straniero della Università di Milano* Vol. 21 (1997): 653–726.

Mahalingam, Ravi. "The Compatibility of the Principle of Non-Intervention with the Right of Humanitarian Intervention." *UCLA Journal of International Law and Foreign Affairs* Vol. 1 No. 1 (1996): 221–263.

Malanczuk, Peter. *Humanitarian Intervention and the Legitimacy of the Use of Force*. Amsterdam: Het Spinhuis, 1993.

Mani, V.S. "International Humanitarian Law: An Indo-Asian Perspective." *International Review of the Red Cross* Vol. 83 No. 841 (2001): 59–75.

Mani, V.S. "Humanitarian Intervention and International Law." *Indian Journal of International Law* Vol. 33 (1993): 1–26.

Martin Martinez, Magdalena M. *National Sovereignty and International Organizations*. The Hague: Kluwer Law International, 1996.

McCoubrey, Hilaire. *International Humanitarian Law: The Regulation of Armed Conflicts*. Aldershot: Dartmouth, 1990.

McCoubrey, Hilaire and Nigel D. White. *The Blue Helmets: Legal Regulation of United Nations Military Operations*. Aldershot: Dartmouth, 1996.

McDougal, Myres S. and Florentino P. Feliciano. *Law and Minimum World Public Order: The Regulation of International Coercion*. New Haven: Yale University Press, 1961.

Mertus, Julie. "The Legality of Humanitarian Intervention: Lessons from Kosovo." *William and Mary Law Review* Vol. 41 No. 5 (2000): 1743–1787.

Miller, Linda B. *World Order and Local Disorder: The United Nations and Internal Conflict*. Princeton: Princeton University Press, 1967.

Ministerio de Defensa, ed. *El derecho de intervención en los conflictos.* Madrid: MDD, 1995.

Mitrovic, T. "The Principle of Non-Intervention in Contemporary International Law." *Jugoslov R. medun. Pravo* Vol. 11 No. 1 (1964): 29–42.

Monshipouri, Mahmood and Claude E. Welch. "The Search for International Human Rights and Justice: Coming to Terms with the New Global Realities." *Human Rights Quarterly* Vol. 23 No. 2 (2001): 370–401.

Moore, John Norton, ed. *Law and Civil War in the Modern World.* Baltimore: The Johns Hopkins University Press, 1974.

Moore, John Norton. "The Control of Foreign Intervention in Internal Conflict." *Virginia Journal of International Law* Vol. 9 (1969): 205.

Moreau Defarges, Philippe. *Un monde d'ingérence.* Paris: Presses des Sciences Politiques, 1997.

Morozov, Grigorii. *Mezhdunaronoye pravo i mezhdunarodniye otnosheniya.* Moscow: IMEMO, 1997.

Murphy, Sean D. "The Security Council, Legitimacy, and the Concept of Collective Security after the Cold War." *Columbia Journal of Transnational Law* Vol. 32 (1994): 201–288.

Murswiek, Dietrich. "Souveränität und humanitäre Intervention: Zu einigen neueren Tendenzen im Völkerrecht." *Der Staat* Vol. 35 No. 1 (1996): 31–44.

Mushkat, Rhoda. "When War May Justifiably Be Waged: An Analysis of Historical and Contemporary Legal Perspectives." *Brooklyn Journal of International Law* Vol. 15 (1989): 223–315.

Nafziger, James A.R. and Julie Jackson. "An Update on: Self-Determination and Humanitarian Intervention in a Community of Power." *Denver Journal of International Law and Policy* Vol. 26 No. 5 (1998): 917–932.

Nanda, Ved P., Thomas F. Muther and Amy E. Eckert. "Tragedies in Somalia, Yugoslavia, Haiti, Rwanda and Liberia: Revisiting the Validity of Humanitarian Intervention under International Law: Part 2." *Denver Journal of International Law and Policy* Vol. 26 No. 5 (1998): 827–869.

Niyungeko, Gérard. "La mise en œuvre du droit international humanitaire et le principe de la souveraineté des Etats." *International Review of the Red Cross* (1991): 113–141.

O'Connell, Mary Ellen. "The UN, NATO, and International Law after Kosovo." *Human Rights Quarterly* Vol. 22 No. 1 (2000): 57–89.

O'Connell, Mary Ellen. "Continuing Limits on UN Intervention in Civil War." *Indiana Law Journal* Vol. 67 (1992): 903–913.

O'Neill, William G. *A Humanitarian Practitioner's Guide to International Human Rights Law.* Providence: Thomas J. Watson Jr. Institute for International Studies, 1999.

Onuf, Nicholas G. "The Principle of Non-Intervention, the United Nations, and the International System." *International Organization* Vol. 25 No. 2 (1971): 209–227.

Österdahl, Inger. *Threat to the Peace: The Interpretation by the Security Council of Article 39 of the UN Charter.* Uppsala: Iustus Förlag, 1998.

Österdahl, Inger. "By All Means, Intervene! The Security Council and the Use of Force Under Chapter VII of the UN Charter in Iraq (to Protect the Kurds), in Bosnia, Somalia, Rwanda and Haiti." *Nordic Journal of International Law* Vol. 66 (1997): 241–271.

Ouchakov, N. "La compétence interne de l'État." *Recueil des Cours* Vol. 141 (1974): 5–85.

Palley, Claire. "Legal Issues Arising from Conflicts between UN Humanitarian and Political Mandates." In *The Problem of Refugees in the Light of Contemporary International Law Issues,* edited by Vera Gowlland-Debbas, 145–168. The Hague: Martinus Nijhoff, 1996.

Paye, Olivier. "Du droit à l'assistance humanitaire à l'ingérence humanitaire: un dérapage conceptuel dangereux." *Journal des Juristes démocrates* Vol. 80 (1991).

Pellet, Alain. "State Sovereignty and the Protection of Fundamental Human Rights: An International Law Perspective." *Pugwash Occasional Papers* Vol. 1 No. 1 (2000): 37–44.

Perez-Vera, Elisa. "La protection d'humanité en droit international." *Revue Belge de Droit International* (1969): 401–424.

Petersen, Frederick J. "The Façade of Humanitarian Intervention for Human Rights in a Community of Sovereign Nations." *Arizona Journal of International and Comparative Law* Vol. 15 No. 3 (1998): 871–904.

Pictet, Jean S. *Humanitarian Law and the Protection of War Victims*. Leiden: A.W. Sijthoff, 1975.

Pictet, Jean S. *Commentary: IV Geneva Convention Relative to the Protection of Civilian Persons in Time of War*. Geneva: International Committee of the Red Cross, 1958.

Pinelli, Cesare. "Sul fondamento degli interventi armati a fini umanitaria." *Diritto Publico* Vol. 5 No. 1 (1999): 61–87.

Ragazzi, Maurizio. *The Concept of International Obligations Erga Omnes*. Oxford: Oxford University Press, 2000.

Rajan, M. S. *United Nations and Domestic Jurisdiction*. 2nd ed. London: Asia Publishing House, 1961.

Ramón Chornet, Consuelo. *¿Violencia necesaria? la intervención humanitaria en derecho internacional*. Madrid: Trotta, 1995.

Reisman, W. Michael. "Unilateral Action and the Transformations of the World Constitutive Process: The Special Problem of Humanitarian Intervention." *European Journal of International Law* Vol. 11 No. 1 (2000): 3–18.

Reisman, W. Michael. "Legal Responses to Genocide and Other Massive Violations of Human Rights." *Law and Contemporary Problems* Vol. 59 No. 4 (1996): 75–80.

Reisman, W. Michael. "Humanitarian Intervention and Fledgling Democracies." *Fordham International Law Journal* Vol. 18 No. 3 (1995): 794–805.

Reisman, W. Michael. "Sovereignty and Human Rights in Contemporary International Law." *American Journal of International Law* Vol. 84 No. 4 (1990): 866–876.

Reisman, W. Michael. "Criteria for the Lawful Use of Force in International Law." *Yale Journal of International Law* Vol. 10 (1985): 279–285.

Reisman, W. Michael. "Coercion and Self-Determination: Construing Charter Article 2 (4)."*American Journal of International Law* Vol. 78 No. 3 (1984): 642–645.

Reisman, W. Michael. "Old Wine in New Bottles: The Reagan and Brezhnev Doctrines in Contemporary International Law and Practice." *Yale Journal of International Law* Vol. 13 No. 1 (1984): 171–198.

Remiro Brotóns, Antonio. "No intervención versus injerencia humanitaria y principio democrático." *Anuario Argentino de Derecho Internacional* Vol. 7 (1996/1997): 105–126.

Roberts, Adam. "The So-Called 'Right' of Humanitarian Intervention." *Yearbook of International Humanitarian Law* Vol. 3 (2001).

Roberts, Adam and Richard Guelff, eds. *Documents on the Laws of War*. 3rd ed. Oxford: Oxford University Press, 2000.

Roberts, Lawrence D. "United Nations Security Council Resolution 687 and Its Aftermath: The Implications for Domestic Authority and the Need for Legitimacy." *New York University Journal of International Law and Politics* Vol. 25 (1993): 612–613.

Robinson, Darryl. "Defining 'Crimes against Humanity' at the Rome Conference." *American Journal of International Law* Vol. 93 No. 1 (1999): 43–57.

Robinson, Nehemiah. *The Genocide Convention: A Commentary*. New York: Institute of Jewish Affairs, 1960.

Rodley, Nigel S. "Human Rights and Humanitarian Intervention: The Case Law of the World Court." *International and Comparative Law Quarterly* Vol. 38 No. 2 (1989): 321–333.

Ronzitti, Natalino. *Rescuing Nationals Abroad through Military Coercion and Intervention on Grounds of Humanity*. Dordrecht: Martinus Nijhoff, 1985.

Rougier, Antoine. "La théorie de l'intervention d'humanité." *Revue Générale de Droit International Public* Vol. 17 (1910): 468–526.

Ruddick, E.E. "The Continuing Constraint of Sovereignty: International Law, International Protection, and the Internally Displaced." *Boston University Law Review* Vol. 77 No. 2 (1997): 429–482.

Sahovic, Milan, ed. *Principles of International Law Concerning Friendly Relations and Cooperation*. Belgrade: Institute of International Politics and Economics, 1972.

Sandoz, Yves. " 'Droit' or 'devoir d'ingérence' and the Right to Assistance: The Issues Involved." *The Review: International Commission of Jurists* Vol. 49 (1992): 12–22.

Sandoz, Yves, Christophe Swinarski and Bruno Zimmermann, eds. *Commentary on the Additional Protocols of 8 June 1977 to the Geneva Conventions of 12 August 1949*. Geneva: International Committee of the Red Cross, 1987.

Sarooshi, Danesh. *The United Nations and the Development of Collective Security: The Delegation by the UN Security Council of Its Chapter VII Powers*. Oxford: Clarendon Press, 1999.

Sassòli, Marco and Antoine A. Bouvier. *How Does Law Protect in War? Cases, Documents and Teaching Materials on Contemporary Practice in International Humanitarian Law*. Geneva: International Committee of the Red Cross, 1999.

Schabas, William A. "Enforcing International Humanitarian Law: Catching the Accomplices." *International Review of the Red Cross* Vol. 83 No. 842 (2001): 439–460.

Schabas, William A. *Genocide in International Law: The Crime of Crimes*. Cambridge: Cambridge University Press, 2000.

Schachter, Oscar. "In Defense of International Rules on the Use of Force." *University of Chicago Law Review* Vol. 53 (1986): 113–136.

Schachter, Oscar. "The Legality of Pro-Democratic Invasion." *American Journal of International Law* Vol. 78 No. 3 (1984): 645–650.

Scheffer, David J. "Toward a Modern Doctrine of Humanitarian Intervention." *University of Toledo Law Review* Vol. 23 (1992): 253–293.

Schilling, T. "Zur Rechtfertigung der einseitigen gewaltsamen humanitären Intervention als Repressalie oder als Nothilfe." *Archiv des Völkerrechts* Vol. 35 No. 4 (1997): 430–458.

Schwebel, Stephan M. "The Roles of the Security Council and the International Court of Justice in the Application of International Humanitarian Law." *New York University Journal of International Law and Politics* Vol. 27 (1995): 731.

Schweigman, David. "Humanitarian Intervention under International Law: The Strife for Humanity." *Leiden Journal of International Law* Vol. 6 (1993): 91–111.

Simma, Bruno. "NATO, the UN and the Use of Force: Legal Aspects." *European Journal of International Law* Vol. 10 No. 1 (1999): 1–22.

Simma, Bruno, ed. *The Charter of the United Nations. A Commentary*. Oxford: Oxford University Press, 1995.

Singh, J. Nagendra. *Use of Force under International Law*. New Delhi: Harnam Publications, 1984.

Sinha, Manoj Kumar. "Is Humanitarian Intervention Permissible under International Law?" *Indian Journal of International Law* Vol. 40 No. 1 (2000): 62–71.

Sommaruga, Cornelio. "Le droit international humanitaire au seuil du troisième millénaire: bilan et perspectives." *International Review of the Red Cross* Vol. 81 No. 836 (1999): 903–924.

Stanger, Roland J., ed. *Essays on Intervention*. Columbus: Ohio State University Press, 1964.

Stone, Julius. *Aggression and World Order: A Critique of United Nations Theories of Aggression*. London: Stevens, 1958.

Stowell, Ellery C. "Humanitarian Intervention." *American Journal of International Law* Vol. 33 No. 4 (1939): 733–736.

Stowell, Ellery C. "La théorie et la pratique de l'intervention." *Recueil des Cours* Vol. 40 (1932): 91–151.

Stowell, Ellery C. *Intervention in International Law*. Washington, DC: John Byrne and Co., 1921.

Sunga, Lyal S. *Individual Responsibility in International Law for Serious Human Rights Violations*. Dordrecht: Martinus Nijhoff, 1992.

Tanca, Antonio. *Foreign Armed Intervention in Internal Conflict*. Dordrecht: Martinus Nijhoff, 1993.

Tesón, Fernando R. "Collective Humanitarian Intervention." *Michigan Journal of International Law* Vol. 17 No. 2 (2000): 323–371.

Tesón, Fernando R. "International Obligation and the Theory of Hypothetical Consent." *Yale Journal of International Law* Vol. 15 No. 1 (1990): 109–118.

Tesón, Fernando R. "Le Peuple, C'est Moi! The World Court and Human Rights (in Appraisals of the ICJ's Decision: Nicaragua v. United States (Merits))." *American Journal of International Law* Vol. 81 No. 1 (1987): 173–183.

Thiele, Terry Vernon. "Norms of Intervention in a Decolonized World." *New York University Journal of International Law and Politics* Vol. 11 No. 1 (1978): 141–174.

Thomas Van Wynen, Ann and A.J. Thomas. *The Concept of Aggression in International Law*. Dallas: Southern Methodist University Press, 1972.

Torrelli, Maurice. *Le droit international humanitaire*. Paris: Presses Universitaires de France, 1992.

Tsagourias, Nikolaos. "Humanitarian Intervention after Kosovo and Legal Discourse: Self-Deception or Self-Consciousness?" *Leiden Journal of International Law* Vol. 13 No. 1 (2000): 11–32.

Tsagourias, Nikolaos. *The Jurisprudence of International Law: The Humanitarian Dimension*. Manchester: Manchester University Press, 2000.

Tunkin, Grigorii I. *Law and Force in the International System*. Moscow: Progress, 1985.

Tunkin, Grigorii I., ed. *Contemporary International Law: Collection of Articles*. Moscow: Progress, 1969.

Turns, David. "War Crimes without War? The Applicability of International Humanitarian Law to Atrocities in Non-International Armed Conflict." *African Journal of International and Comparative Law* Vol. 7 No. 4 (1995): 804–830.

Tuzmukhamedov, Bakhtiyar. "The Legal Framework of CIS Regional Peace Operations." *International Peacekeeping* Vol. 6 No. 1 (2000): 1–6.

United Nations Educational, Scientific and Cultural Organization, ed. *International Dimensions of Humanitarian Law*. Geneva: Henri Dunant Institute, 1988.

Vargas Carreño, Edmundo. "La intervención humanitaria." In *Héctor Gros Espiell amicorum liber: persona humana y derecho internacional*, edited by Antonio Augusto Cançado Trindade and Christophe Swinarski, 1617–1648. Bruxelles: Bruylant, 1997.

Verwey, Wil D. "Humanitarian Intervention under International Law." *Netherlands International Law Review* Vol. 32 No. 3 (1985): 357–418.

Von Elbe, Joachim. "The Evolution of the Concept of the Just War in International Law." *American Journal of International Law* Vol. 33 No. 4 (1939): 665–688.

Wang, J. C. *Essai sur l'intervention en droit international, à la lumière de certaines pratiques récentes*. 1967.

White, Nigel D. "The Legality of Bombing in the Name of Humanity." *Journal of Conflict and Security Law* Vol. 5 No. 1 (2000): 27–43.

Wilson, Heather A. *International Law and the Use of Force by National Liberation Movements*. Oxford: Oxford University Press, 1988.

Winfield, P.H. "The History of Intervention in International Law 1922–23." *British Year Book of International Law* Vol. 3 (1922): 130–149.

Winters, Paul A., ed. *Interventionism: Current Controversies*. San Diego: Greenhaven Press, 1995.

Wippman, David. "Pro-Democratic Intervention by Invitation." In *Democratic Governance and International Law*, edited by Gregory H. Fox and Brad R. Roth, 293–327. Cambridge: Cambridge University Press, 2000.

Wolf, Daniel. "Humanitarian Intervention." *Michigan Year Book of International Legal Studies* Vol. 9 (1988): 333–368.

Wright, Quincy. "Intervention, 1956." *American Journal of International Law* Vol. 51 No. 2 (1957): 257–276.

Yang, Zewei. "Rendao-zhuyi-ganshe-zai-guojifa-zhong-de-diwei." *Faxue-yanjiu* Vol. 22 No. 4 (2000): 127–139.

Zarate, Carlos. *La no intervencion ante el derecho americano*. 2000.

Zorgbibe, Charles. *Le droit d'ingérence*. Paris: Presses Universitaires de France, 1994.

# 6. INTEREST AND WILL

Betts, Richard K. "The Delusion of Impartial Intervention." *Foreign Affairs* Vol. 73 No. 6 (1994): 20–33.
> Argues that traditional norms of impartiality, consent, and neutrality are difficult, or even impossible, to maintain in practice.

Finnemore, Martha. *National Interests in International Society.* Ithaca: Cornell University Press, 1996.
> Argues that the changing international normative context fundamentally shapes the interests of international actors.

Gowing, Nik. *Real-Time Television Coverage of Armed Conflicts and Diplomatic Crises: Does It Pressure or Distort Foreign Policy Decisions?* Cambridge, MA: Joan Shorenstein Barone Center, 1994.
> Examination of media stimulation of public concern over human tragedy and its influence on government officials' decisions.

Ignatieff, Michael. *The Warrior's Honor: Ethnic War and the Modern Conscience.* London: Chatto and Windus, 1998.
> Account of moral solidarity, the extent of Western commitments, and the dilemmas of contemporary humanitarian interventionism, including treatments of the media and the International Committee of the Red Cross.

MacFarlane, S. Neil. *Politics and Humanitarian Action.* Providence: Thomas J. Watson Jr. Institute for International Studies, 2000.
> Argues that humanitarian action is profoundly affected by states' perceived interests, which define the scope and the character of international engagement.

Morgenthau, Hans J. *Politics among Nations: The Struggle for Power and Peace.* 6th ed. New York: Knopf, 1985.
> Classic realist exposition regarding the state as a rational and unitary actor pursuing self-interest conceived as "the pursuit of power."

Natsios, Andrew S. *US Foreign Policy and the Four Horsemen of the Apocalypse: Humanitarian Relief in Complex Emergencies.* Westport: Praeger, 1997.
> Draws attention to the bureaucratic, security, political, and operational dimensions of complex emergencies. Asserts the need to redefine national interest to include complex humanitarian emergencies, even in the absence of geostrategic interests.

Nye, Joseph. "Redefining the National Interest." *Foreign Affairs* Vol. 78 No. 4 (1999): 22–35.
> Argues that for democracies it is not possible to distinguish between a morality- and an interest-based foreign policy.

Shawcross, William. *The Quality of Mercy: Cambodia, the Holocaust, and Modern Conscience.* New York: Simon and Schuster, 1984.
> Examines ethical imperatives for action and demonstrates that prevailing conceptions of national interest often preclude effective responses.

## References

Art, Robert J. "Geopolitics Updated: The Strategy of Selective Engagement." *International Security* Vol. 23 No. 3 (1998/1999): 79–113.

Barnett, Michael N. "The UN Security Council, Indifference, and Genocide in Rwanda." *Cultural Anthropology* Vol. 12 No. 4 (1997): 551–578.

Beard, Charles A. *The Idea of National Interest: An Analytical Study in American Foreign Policy.* New York: Macmillan, 1934.

Bettati, Mario. "Governments and (Unwarranted) Humanitarian Intervention." *Temps Modernes* Vol. 55 No. 610 (2000): 243–256.

Boniface, Pascal. "The Changing Attitude towards Military Intervention." *International Spectator* Vol. 32 (1997): 53–63.

Brands, H.W. "The Idea of the National Interest." *Diplomatic History* Vol. 23 No. 2 (1999): 239–261.

Carr, E.H. *The Twenty Years' Crisis, 1919–1939: An Introduction to the Study of International Relations.* 2nd ed. Basingstoke: Macmillan, 1991.

Clinton, W. David. *The Two Faces of National Interest.* Baton Rouge: Louisiana State University Press, 1994.

Clinton, W. David. "The National Interest: Normative Foundations." *The Review of Politics* Vol. 48 No. 4 (1986): 495–519.

Conversino, Mark J. "Sawdust Power: Perceptions of US Casualty Tolerance in the Post-Gulf War Era." *Strategic Review* Vol. 25 No. 1 (1997): 15–23.

Cushman, Thomas and Stjepan G. Mestrovic, eds. *This Time We Knew: Western Responses to Genocide in Bosnia.* New York: New York University Press, 1996.

Fierke, Karin M. *Changing Games, Changing Strategies: Critical Investigations in Security.* Manchester: Manchester University Press, 1998.

Fierke, Karin M. "Multiple Identities, Interfacing Games: The Social Construction of Western Action in Bosnia." *European Journal of International Relations* Vol. 2 No. 4 (1995): 467–497.

Finnemore, Martha. "Constructing Norms of Humanitarian Intervention." In *The Culture of National Security: Norms and Identity in World Politics,* edited by Peter J. Katzenstein, 153–185. New York: Columbia University Press, 1996.

Finnemore, Martha and Kathryn Sikkink. "International Norm Dynamics and Political Change." *International Organization* Vol. 52 No. 4 (1998): 887–917.

Franck, Thomas M. *The Power of Legitimacy among Nations.* New York: Oxford University Press, 1990.

Frankel, Joseph. *National Interest.* London: Pall Mall Press, 1970.

Fukuyama, Francis. "The Ambiguity of National Interest." In *Rethinking Russia's National Interests,* edited by Stephen Sestanovich, 10–23. Washington, DC: Center for Strategic and International Studies, 1994.

Gaubatz, Kurt Taylor. "Intervention and Intransitivity: Public Opinion, Social Choice, and the Use of Military Force Abroad." *World Politics* Vol. 47 No. 4 (1995): 534–554.

Girardet, Edward, Andrea Bartol and Jeffrey Carmel, eds. *Somalia, Rwanda, and Beyond: The Role of the International Media in Wars and Humanitarian Crises.* Geneva: Crosslines Communications, 1995.

Goertz, Gary and Paul F. Diehl. "International Norms and Power Politics." In *Reconstructing Realpolitik,* edited by Frank W. Wayman and Paul F. Diehl, 101–122. Ann Arbor: University of Michigan Press, 1994.

Goldstein, Judith and Robert O. Keohane, eds. *Ideas and Foreign Policy: Beliefs, Institutions, and Political Change.* Ithaca: Cornell University Press, 1993.

Gow, James. *Triumph of the Lack of Will: International Diplomacy and the Yugoslav War.* London: Hurst, 1997.

Gowing, Nik. *Media Coverage: Help or Hindrance in Conflict Prevention?* Washington, DC: Carnegie Commission on Preventing Deadly Conflict, 1997.

Hartigan, Kevin. "Matching Humanitarian Norms with Cold, Hard Interests: The Making of Refugee Policies in Mexico and Honduras, 1980–1989." *International Organization* Vol. 46 No. 3 (1992): 709–730.

Hawkins, Virgil. "The Price of Inaction: The Media and Humanitarian Intervention." *Journal of Humanitarian Assistance* (May 2001): http://www.jha.ac/articles/a066.htm

Herzfeld, Michael. *The Social Production of Indifference*. Chicago: University of Chicago Press, 1993.

Jakobsen, Peter Viggo. "National Interest, Humanitarianism or CNN: What Triggers UN Peace Enforcement after the Cold War?" *Journal of Peace Research* Vol. 33 No. 2 (1996): 205–215.

Jentleson, Bruce W. "The Pretty Prudent Public: Post-Vietnam American Opinion on the Use of Military Force." *International Studies Quarterly* Vol. 36 No. 1 (1992): 49–74.

Jentleson, Bruce W. and Rebecca Britton. "Still Pretty Prudent: Post-Cold War American Public Opinion on the Use of Military Force." *Journal of Conflict Resolution* Vol. 42 No. 4 (1998): 395–417.

Johansen, Robert C. *The National Interest and the Human Interest*. Princeton: Princeton University Press, 1980.

Johnson, Sterling. *Global Search and Seizure: The US National Interest vs. International Law*. Aldershot: Dartmouth, 1994.

Kassebaum, Nancy L. and Lee H. Hamilton. *Peacekeeping and the US National Interest*. Washington, DC: Henry L. Stimson Center, 1994.

Kratochwil, Friedrich. "On the Notion of 'Interest' in International Relations." *International Organization* Vol. 36 No. 1 (1982): 1–30.

Krauthammer, Charles. "The Short, Unhappy Life of Humanitarian War." *The National Interest* No. 57 (1999): 5–8.

Kritsiotis, Dino. "Reappraising Policy Objections to Humanitarian Intervention." *Michigan Journal of International Law* Vol. 19 No. 4 (1998): 1005–1050.

Kuper, Leo. *Genocide: Its Political Use in the Twentieth Century*. New Haven: Yale University Press, 1981.

Kuusisto, Riikka. "Framing the Wars in the Gulf and in Bosnia: The Rhetorical Definitions of the Western Power Leaders in Action." *Journal of Peace Research* Vol. 35 No. 5 (1998): 603–620.

Lekha Sriram, Chandra. "Intervention in a Troubled World: Moving beyond Shawcross and His Critics." *Ethics and International Affairs* Vol. 15 (2001): 151–158.

Luck, Edward C. "The United Nations, Multilateralism, and US Interests." In *US Foreign Policy and the United Nations System*, edited by Charles W. Maynes and Richard S. Williamson, 27–53. New York: W.W. Norton and Co., 1996.

Luttwak, Edward N. "Toward Post-Heroic Warfare." *Foreign Affairs* Vol. 74 No. 3 (1995): 109–122.

Luttwak, Edward N. "Where Are the Great Powers? At Home with the Kids." *Foreign Affairs* Vol. 73 No. 4 (1994): 23–28.

Lyons, Gene M. "International Organizations and National Interests." *International Social Sciences Journal* Vol. 144 (1995): 261–276.

MacFarlane, S. Neil and Thomas G. Weiss. "Political Interest and Humanitarian Action." *Security Studies* Vol. 10 No. 1 (2000): 120–152.

McGwire, Michael. "Why Did We Bomb Belgrade?" *International Affairs* Vol. 76 No. 1 (2000): 1–23.

Macleod, Alex and Stéphane Roussel, eds. *Intérêt national et responsabilités internationales: six états face au conflit en ex-Yugoslavie (1991–1995)*. Paris: Guérin universitaire, 1996.

Malnes, Raino. *National Interests, Morality and International Law*. Oslo: Scandinavian University Press, 1994.

Mandelbaum, Michael. "The Reluctance to Intervene." *Foreign Policy* No. 95 (1994): 3–18.

Maninger, Stephan. "The West, the Rest, and the Will to Project Power." *African Security Review* Vol. 6 No. 6 (1997): 34–45.

Mason, Andrew and Nicholas J. Wheeler. "Realist Objections to Humanitarian Intervention." In *The Ethical Dimensions of Global Change*, edited by Barry Holden, 94–110. Basingstoke: Macmillan, 1996.

Mastanduno, Michael and G. John Ikenberry. "Toward a Realist Theory of State Action." *International Studies Quarterly* Vol. 33 No. 4 (1989): 457–474.

Minear, Larry, Colin Scott and Thomas G. Weiss. *The News Media, Civil War, and Humanitarian Action.* Boulder: Lynne Rienner, 1996.

Minear, Larry and Thomas G. Weiss. *Humanitarian Politics.* New York: Foreign Policy Association, 1995.

Morgenthau, Hans J. "To Intervene or Not to Intervene?" *Foreign Affairs* Vol. 45 No. 3 (1967): 425–436.

Morgenthau, Hans J. *In Defense of the National Interest: A Critical Examination of American Foreign Policy.* New York: Knopf, 1952.

Morgenthau, Hans J. "The Mainsprings of American Foreign Policy: The National Interest vs. Moral Abstractions." *American Political Science Review* Vol. 44 No. 4 (1950): 833–854.

Neack, Laura. "UN Peace-Keeping: Community or Self?" *Journal of Peace Research* Vol. 32 No. 2 (1994): 181–196.

Newman, Johanna. *Lights, Camera, War.* New York: St. Martin's, 1996.

Nye, Joseph S. *National Interest in the Information Age.* New York: Carnegie Council on Ethics and International Affairs, 1999.

Olsen, Gorm Rye. "Europe and the Promotion of Democracy in Post Cold War Africa: How Serious Is Europe and for What Reason?" *African Affairs* Vol. 97 No. 388 (1998): 343–367.

O'Neal, John R. et al. "Are the American People 'Pretty Prudent'? Public Responses to the US Uses of Force, 1950–1988." *International Studies Quarterly* Vol. 40 No. 2 (1996): 261–280.

Orford, Anne. "Muscular Humanitarianism: Reading the Narratives of the New Interventionism." *European Journal of International Law* Vol. 10 No. 4 (1999): 679–711.

Osgood, Robert Endicott. *Ideals and Self-Interest in America's Foreign Relations: The Great Transformation of the Twentieth Century.* Chicago: University of Chicago Press, 1953.

Pearson, Frederic S., Robert A. Baumann and Jeffrey J. Pickering. "Military Intervention and Realpolitik." In *Reconstructing Realpolitik*, edited by Frank W. Wayman and Paul F. Diehl, 205–225. Ann Arbor: University of Michigan Press, 1994.

Rieff, David. "The Crusaders: Moral Principles, Strategic Interests, and Military Force." *World Policy Journal* Vol. 17 No. 2 (2000): 39–47.

Rieff, David. *Slaughterhouse: Bosnia and the Failure of the West.* New York: Simon and Schuster, 1995.

Roberts, Adam. "Willing the Ends but Not the Means." *World Today* Vol. 55 No. 5 (1999): 8–12.

Robinson, Piers. "The News Media and Intervention: Triggering the Use of Air Power during Humanitarian Crises." *European Journal of Communication* Vol. 15 No. 3 (2000): 405–414.

Robinson, Piers. "The CNN Effect: Can the News Media Drive Foreign Policy?" *Review of International Studies* Vol. 25 No. 2 (1999): 301–309.

Rosenau, James N. "The National Interest." In *International Encyclopedia of the Social Sciences*, New York: Crowell Collier, 1968.

Rotberg, Robert I. and Thomas G. Weiss, eds. *From Massacres to Genocide: The Media, Public Policy, and Humanitarian Crises.* Washington, DC: Brookings Institution, 1996.

Ruggie, John G. "Peacekeeping and US Interests." *Washington Quarterly* Vol. 17 No. 4 (1994): 175–184.

Schonberg, Karl K. "Traditions and Interests: American Belief Systems, American Policy, and the Bosnian War." *World Affairs* Vol. 162 No. 1 (1999): 11–21.

Shaw, Martin. *Civil Society and Media in Global Crises.* London: Pinter, 1996.

Shawcross, William. *Deliver Us from Evil: Peacekeepers, Warlords and a World of Endless Conflict*. London: Bloomsbury, 2000.

Sonderman, Fred A. "The Concept of the National Interest." *Orbis* Vol. 21 No. 1 (1977): 121–138.

Strobel, Warren P. *Late-Breaking Foreign Policy: The News Media's Influence on Peace Operations*. Washington, DC: United States Institute of Peace, 1997.

Suhrke, Astri. "Human Security and the Interests of States." *Security Dialogue* Vol. 30 No. 3 (1999): 265–276.

Terrif, Terry and James F. Keeley. "The United Nations, Conflict Management and Spheres of Interest." *International Peacekeeping* Vol. 2 No. 4 (1995): 510–535.

Thussu, D.K. "Legitimizing 'Humanitarian Intervention'? CNN, NATO and the Kosovo Crisis." *European Journal of Communication* Vol. 15 No. 3 (2000): 345–361.

Trent, John E. "Foreign Policy and the United Nations: National Interest in the Era of Global Politics." In *The United Nations System: The Policies of Member States*, edited by Chadwick F. Alger et al., 463–508. Tokyo: United Nations University Press, 1995.

Vertzberger, Yaacov Y.I. *Risk Taking and Decisionmaking: Foreign Military Intervention Decisions*. Stanford: Stanford University Press, 1998.

Von Hippel, Karin and Michael Clarke. "Something Must Be Done." *World Today* Vol. 55 No. 3 (1999): 4–7.

Weiss, Thomas G. "The Politics of Humanitarian Ideas." *Security Dialogue* Vol. 31 No. 1 (2000): 11–23.

Weiss, Thomas G. "Overcoming the Somalia Syndrome: 'Operation Rekindle Hope?'." *Global Governance* Vol. 1 No. 2 (1995): 171–187.

Weldes, Jutta. "Constructing National Interests." *European Journal of International Relations* Vol. 2 No. 3 (1996): 275–318.

# 7. NATIONAL AND REGIONAL PERSPECTIVES

Blair, Tony. "'Doctrine of the International Community': Speech by the Prime Minister to the Economic Club of Chicago" (April 1999): http://www.fco.gov.uk/news/speechtext.asp?2316
Major statement of the UK Government on the topic of humanitarian intervention.

Dickens, David and Guy Wilson-Roberts, eds. *Non-Intervention and State Sovereignty in the Asia–Pacific*. Wellington: Centre for Strategic Studies, 2000.
Papers presented at a Council for Security Cooperation in the Asia–Pacific Working Group on Comprehensive and Cooperative Security.

Guillot, Philippe. "France, Peacekeeping and Humanitarian Intervention." *International Peacekeeping* Vol. 1 No. 1 (1994): 30–43.
Examines the attempts by the French Government of 1988–1993 to promote a new norm of international law, establishing a "right to interfere."

Haass, Richard N. *Intervention: The Use of American Military Force in the Post-Cold War World*. Washington, DC: Brookings Institution, 1999.
Analysis of US military interventions largely from the post-Cold War period. Documentary appendix.

Luck, Edward C. *Mixed Messages: American Politics and International Organization, 1919–1999*. Washington, DC: Brookings Institution, 1999.
Traces the evolution of US ambivalent attitudes and policies toward the League of Nations and the UN.

Pugwash Study Group on Intervention, Sovereignty and International Security. *Pugwash Occasional Papers Vol. 2 No. 1: Papers from the Como Workshop: September 2000*. Como: PSGI, SIS, 2001.
Collection of essays including perspectives of states skeptical or critical of humanitarian interventions. Chapters devoted to Russia, China, Asia, and Africa.

Schnabel, Albrecht and Ramesh Thakur, eds. *Kosovo and the Challenge of Humanitarian Intervention: Selective Indignation, Collective Action, and International Citizenship*. Tokyo: United Nations University Press, 2000.
Analyses of the various aspects of the Kosovo War and its normative, operational and structural consequences for world politics. Includes numerous country perspectives.

Thakur, Ramesh. "Global Norms and International Humanitarian Law: An Asian Perspective." *International Review of the Red Cross* Vol. 841 (2001): 19–43.
Examines international humanitarian law in light of the Kosovo War. Points to the inconsistencies in the actions of Western countries and the need for a new consensus on external armed intervention.

Vales, Hernàn. "The Latin American View on the Doctrine of Humanitarian Intervention" *Journal of Humanitarian Assistance* (February 2001): http://www.jha.ac/articles/a064.htm
Describes how the principle of nonintervention has undergone a process of progressive relaxation in Latin America.

## References

AbuSulayman, AbdulHamid. *The Islamic Theory of International Relations: New Directions for Islamic Methodology and Thought*. Herndon: International Institute of Islamic Thought, 1987.

Adebajo, Adekeye and Chris Landsberg. "The Heirs of Nkrumah: Africa's New Interventionists." *Pugwash Occasional Papers* Vol. 2 No. 1 (2001): 65–90.

Adebajo, Adekeye and Chris Landsberg. "Pax Africana in the Age of Extremes." *South African Journal of International Affairs* Vol. 7 No. 1 (2000): 11–26.

African Centre for the Constructive Resolution of Disputes. *State, Sovereignty and Responsibility: African Solutions to African Problems*. Durban: African Conference on Peacemaking and Conflict Resolution, 1996.

Aguirre, Mariano and Francisco Rey. "Development Co-operation and Humanitarian Action in Spanish Foreign Policy." *Journal of Humanitarian Assistance* (July 2001): http://www.jha.ac/articles/a071.pdf

Ainsa, Fernando. "Droit d'ingérence: un point de vue latino-américain sur les justifications et les limites du droit d'ingérence." In *Les droits de l'homme à l'aube du XXIe siècle: Karl Vasak amicorum liber*, 47–61. Bruxelles: Bruylant, 1999.

Aluko, Olajide. "African Response to External Intervention in Africa since Angola." *African Affairs* Vol. 80 No. 319 (1981): 159–179.

Arangio-Ruiz, Gaetano. "Droits de l'homme et non intervention: Helsinki, Belgrade, Madrid." *La Communita Internazionale* Vol. 35 (1980): 453–507.

Aspen Strategy Group. *The United States and the Use of Force in the Post-Cold War Era*. Queenstown: Aspen Institute, 1995.

Ausink, John A. *Watershed in Rwanda: The Evolution of President Clinton's Humanitarian Intervention Policy*. Washington, DC: Institute for the Study of Diplomacy, School of Foreign Service, Georgetown University, 1997.

Axworthy, Lloyd. "The Hauser Lecture on International Humanitarian Law: Humanitarian Interventions and Humanitarian Constraints" (February 2000): http://www.un.int/canada/html/s-10feb2000axworthy.htm

Azrael, Jeremy R. and Emil A. Payin, eds. *US and Russian Policymaking with Respect to the Use of Force*. Santa Monica: RAND, 1996.

Baev, Pavel K. "Russia in the Caucasus: Sovereignty, Intervention and Retreat." In *The Russian Armed Forces at the Dawn on the Millennium*, edited by Michael Crutcher, 239–260. Carlisle Barracks: US Army War College, Center for Strategic Leadership, 2000.

Baev, Pavel K. "Intervention and Sovereignty in the CIS Area." In *Will World Peace Be Achievable in the 21st Century?*, edited by Young Seek Choue, 225–253. Seoul: International Institute of Peace Studies, Kyung Hee University, 1999.

Baev, Pavel K. "Russia's Stance against Secessions: From Chechnya to Kosovo." *International Peacekeeping* Vol. 6 No. 3 (1999): 73–94.

Baev, Pavel K. "Conflict Management in the Former Soviet South: The Dead-End of Russian Interventions." *European Security* Vol. 6 No. 4 (1997): 111–129.

Baginian. "Printsip nevmeshatel'stva i Ustav OON." *Sovetskoe gosudarstvo i pravo* Vol. 6 (1957): 62–70.

Bain, William W. "Against Crusading: The Ethic of Human Security and Canadian Foreign Policy." *Canadian Foreign Policy* Vol. 6 No. 3 (1999): 85–98.

Baranovsky, Vladimir. "Humanitarian Intervention: Russian Perspectives." *Pugwash Occasional Papers* Vol. 2 No. 1 (2001): 12–38.

Baranovsky, Vladimir. "Russia: Reassessing National Interests." In *Kosovo and the Challenge of Humanitarian Intervention: Selective Indignation, Collective Action, and International Citizenship*, edited by Albrecht Schnabel and Ramesh Thakur, 101–116. Tokyo: United Nations University Press, 2000.

Barnet, Richard J. *Intervention and Revolution: The United States in the Third World*. London: Paladin, 1972.

Barnett, Michael N. "Sovereignty, Nationalism, and Regional Order in the Arab States System." *International Organization* Vol. 49 No. 3 (1995): 479–510.

Beitz, Charles R. "The Reagan Doctrine in Nicaragua." In *Problems of International Justice*, edited by Steven Luper-Foy, 182–195. Boulder: Westview, 1988.

Beloff, Max. "Reflections on Intervention." *Journal of International Affairs* Vol. 22 No. 2 (1968): 198–207.

Ben Ashoor, Yadh. "Islam and International Humanitarian Law." *International Review of the Red Cross* No. 215 (1980): 59–69.

Benneh, E.Y. "Rules Constructed from the State Practice of African States Regarding Non-Intervention." *African Journal of International and Comparative Law* Vol. 7 No. 1 (1995): 184–186.

Bennet, Andrew. *Condemned to Repetition? The Rise, Fall, and Reprise of Soviet-Russian Military Interventionism, 1973–1996.* Cambridge, MA: MIT Press, 1999.

Bennis, Phyllis. *Calling the Shots: How Washington Dominates Today's UN.* New York: Olive Branch, 1996.

Berry, Nicholas. "The Conflict between United States Intervention and Promoting Democracy in the Third World." *Temple Law Quarterly* Vol. 60 (1987): 1015–1021.

Bing, Adotey. "Salim A. Salim on the OAU and the African Agenda." *Review of African Political Economy* Vol. 18 No. 50 (1991): 60–69.

Blaney, David L. "Equal Sovereignty and an African Statehood: Tragic Elements in the African Agenda in World Affairs." In *Contending Dramas: A Cognitive Approach to International Organizations*, edited by Martha L. Cottam and Chih-yu Shih, 211–226. New York: Praeger, 1992.

Boker-Szegö, Hanna. "The Attitude of Socialist States towards the International Regulation of the Use of Force." In *The Current Legal Regulation of the Use of Force*, edited by Antonio Cassese, 453–477. Dordrecht: Martinus Nijhoff, 1986.

Brown Firmage, Edwin. "The 'War of National Liberation' and the Third World." In *Law and Civil War in the Modern World*, edited by John Norton Moore, 304–347. Baltimore: The Johns Hopkins University Press, 1974.

Brune, Lester H. *The United States and Post-Cold War Interventions: Bush and Clinton in Somalia, Haiti and Bosnia, 1992–1998.* Claremont: Regina Books, 1998.

Butler, William E. "Soviet Attitudes toward Intervention." In *Law and Civil War in the Modern World*, edited by John Norton Moore, 380–398. Baltimore: The Johns Hopkins University Press, 1974.

Cabranes, José A. "Human Rights and Non-Intervention in the Inter-American System." *Michigan Law Review* Vol. 65 (1967): 1147–1182.

Caminos, Hugo. "Humanitarian Intervention and the Inter-American System." In *International Legal Issues Arising under the United Nations Decade of International Law*, edited by Najeeb Al-Nauimi and Richard Meese, 963–998. The Hague: Martinus Nijhoff, 1995.

Caraley, Demetrios James, ed. *The New American Interventionism: Lessons from Successes and Failures.* New York: Columbia University Press, 1999.

Cerna, Christina. "Human Rights in Conflict with the Principle of Non-Intervention: The Case of Nicaragua before the Seventeenth Meeting of Consultation of Ministers of Foreign Affairs." In *Derechos Humanos en las Américas*, edited by Comisión Interamericana de Derechos Humanos, 93–107. Washington, DC: Comisión Interamericana de Derechos Humanos, 1984.

Cervenka, Zdenek and Colin Legum. "The Organisation of African Unity in 1978: The Challenge of Foreign Intervention." *XI Africa Contemporary Record* (1978–79): A25–A39.

Chakste, Mintauts. "Soviet Concepts of the State, International Law and Sovereignty." *American Journal of International Law* Vol. 43 No. 1 (1949): 21–36.

Chimni, B.S. "Towards a Third World Approach to Non-Intervention: Through a Labyrinth of Western Doctrine." *Indian Journal of International Law* Vol. 20 (1980): 243–264.

Clinton, William J. *A National Security Strategy of Engagement and Enlargement: 1995–1996.* London: Brassey's, 1996.

Cohen, Jerome Alan. "China and Intervention." In *Law and Civil War in the Modern World*, edited by John Norton Moore, 348–379. Baltimore: The Johns Hopkins University Press, 1974.

Coning, Cedric de. "African Perspectives on Intervention: The Rising Tide of Neo-Interventionism." In *Sovereign Intervention*, edited by Anthony McDermott, 171–190. Oslo: International Peace Research Institute, 1999.

Daalder, Ivo H. "The United States and Military Intervention in Internal Conflict." In *The International Dimension of Internal Conflict*, edited by Michael E. Brown, 461–488. Cambridge, MA: MIT Press, 1996.

De Guttry, Andrea. *Le missioni delle forze armate italiane fuori area: profili giuridici della partecipazione nazionale alle "peace support operations."* Milano: Franco Angeli Libri, 2000.

De Muth, Christopher C. *The Reagan Doctrine and Beyond.* Washington, DC: American Enterprise Institute for Public Policy Research, 1988.

Deng, Yong. "The Chinese Conception of National Interests in International Relations." *The China Quarterly* No. 154 (1998): 308–329.

Department of Foreign Affairs and International Trade. *Human Security: Safety for People in a Changing World.* Ottawa: DFAIT, 1999.

Dihigo, Ernesto. "Legality of Intervention under the Charter of the Organization of American States." *Proceedings of the American Society of International Law* (1957): 91–100.

Doherty, Roisin. "Partnership for Peace: The Sine Qua Non for Irish Participation in Regional Peacekeeping." *International Peacekeeping* Vol. 7 No. 2 (2000): 63–82.

Donnelly, Jack. "Humanitarian Intervention and American Foreign Policy: Law, Morality, and Politics." In *Human Rights in the World Community: Issues and Action*, edited by Richard Pierre Claude and Burns H. Weston, 307–320. Philadelphia: University of Pennsylvania Press, 1992.

Donnelly, Jack. "Human Rights, Humanitarian Intervention and American Foreign Policy: Law, Morality and Politics." *Journal of International Affairs* Vol. 37 No. 2 (1984): 311–328.

Duke, Simon, Hans-Georg Ehrhart and Matthias Karádi. "The Major European Allies: France, Germany, and the United Kingdom." In *Kosovo and the Challenge of Humanitarian Intervention: Selective Indignation, Collective Action, and International Citizenship*, edited by Albrecht Schnabel and Ramesh Thakur, 128–148. Tokyo: United Nations University Press, 2000.

Dumas, Roland. "La France et le droit d'ingérence humanitaire." *Relations Internationales et Stratégiques* Vol. 1 No. 3 (1991): 55–66.

Dunér, Bertil. *The Bear, the Cubs and the Eagle: Soviet Bloc Interventionism in the Third World and the US Response.* Aldershot: Gower, 1987.

Elaigwu, J. Isawa. "Military Intervention in Politics: An African Perspective." *Genève-Afrique* Vol. 19 No. 1 (1981): 17–38.

Elsässer, Jürgen. *Nie wieder Krieg ohne uns. Das Kosovo und die neue deutsche Geopolitik.* Hamburg: Elefanten Press, 1999.

Evans, Rusty. "The Humanitarian Challenge: A Foreign Policy Perspective." *African Security Review* Vol. 6 No. 2 (1997): 28–32.

Falk, Richard A. "The United States and the Doctrine of Non-Intervention in the Internal Affairs of Independent States." *Howard Law Journal* Vol. 5 (1959): 163–189.

Farer, Tom J., ed. *Beyond Sovereignty: Collectively Defending Democracy in the Americas*. Baltimore: The Johns Hopkins University Press, 1996.

Farer, Tom J. "Collectively Defending Democracy in a World of Sovereign States: The Western Hemisphere's Prospect." *Human Rights Quarterly* Vol. 15 No. 4 (1993): 716–750.

Farer, Tom J. "Intervention and Human Rights: The Latin American Context." *California Western International Law Journal* Vol. 12 (1982): 503–507.

Fenwick, Charles G. "The Issues at Punta del Este: Non-Intervention v. Collective Security." *American Journal of International Law* Vol. 56 No. 2 (1962): 469–474.

Fernándo Arribas, Javier. *Casco azul, soldado español*. Madrid: Ediciones Temas de Hoy, 1994.

Frost, Mervyn. "Putting the World to Rights: Britain's Ethical Foreign Policy." *Cambridge Review of International Affairs* Vol. 12 No. 2 (1999): 80–89.

Furley, Oliver and Roy May, eds. *African Interventionist States: The New Conflict Resolution Brokers*. Aldershot: Ashgate, 2001.

Liu, Fu-Kuo and Linjun Wu. "The Antiquated Principle of Non-Intervention on the Verge of Transformation? Taiwan's Perspective." In *Non-Intervention and State Sovereignty in the Asia–Pacific*, edited by David Dickens and Guy Wilson-Roberts, 61–67. Wellington: Centre for Strategic Studies, 2000.

Franceschet, Antonio and W. Andy Knight. "International(ist) Citizenship: Canada and the International Criminal Court." *Canadian Foreign Policy* Vol. 8 No. 2 (2001): 75–93.

Funston, John. "ASEAN and the Principle of Non-Intervention: Practice and Prospects." In *Non-Intervention and State Sovereignty in the Asia–Pacific*, edited by David Dickens and Guy Wilson-Roberts, 5–18. Wellington: Centre for Strategic Studies, 2000.

Gacek, Christopher. *The Logic of Force: The Dilemma of Limited War in American Foreign Policy*. New York: Columbia University Press, 1994.

Gamba, Virginia. "Justified Intervention? A View from the South." In *Emerging Norms of Justified Intervention: A Collection of Essays from a Project of the American Academy of Arts and Sciences*, edited by Laura W. Reed and Carl Kaysen, 115–125. Cambridge, MA: Committee on International Security Studies, American Academy of Arts and Sciences, 1993.

Gause, Gregory F. "Sovereignty, Statecraft and Stability in the Middle East." *Journal of International Affairs* Vol. 45 No. 2 (1992): 441–469.

Gill, Bates and James Reilly. "Sovereignty, Intervention and Peacekeeping: The View from Beijing." *Survival* Vol. 42 No. 3 (2000): 41–59.

Girling, J.L.S. *America and the Third World: Revolution and Intervention*. London: Routledge and K. Paul, 1980.

Gomes, Solomon. "The OAU, State Sovereignty, and Regional Security." In *Africa in the New International Order: Rethinking State Sovereignty and Regional Security*, edited by Edmond J. Keller and Donald Rothchild, 37–51. Boulder: Lynne Rienner, 1996.

González Casanova, Pablo, ed. *No intervencion, autodeterminacion y democracia en America Latina*. 1983.

Graber, Doris A. *Crisis Diplomacy: A History of US Intervention Policies and Practices*. Washington, DC: Public Affairs, 1959.

Graber, Doris A. "The Truman and Eisenhower Doctrines in the Light of the Doctrine of Non-Intervention." *Political Science Quarterly* Vol. 73 No. 3 (1958): 321–334.

Greenwood, Christopher. "The United Nations as Guarantor of International Peace and Security: Past, Present and Future: A United Kingdom View." In *The United Nations at Age Fifty: A Legal Perspective*, edited by Christian Tomuschat, 59–75. The Hague: Kluwer Law International, 1995.

Haass, Richard N. *The Reluctant Sheriff: The United States after the Cold War.* New York: Council on Foreign Relations, 1997.

Haglund, David G. and Allen Sens. "Kosovo and the Case of the (Not So) Free Riders: Portugal, Belgium, Canada, and Spain." In *Kosovo and the Challenge of Humanitarian Intervention: Selective Indignation, Collective Action, and International Citizenship,* edited by Albrecht Schnabel and Ramesh Thakur, 181–200. Tokyo: United Nations University Press, 2000.

Halverson, Thomas. "Disengagement by Stealth: The Emerging Gap between America's Rhetoric and the Reality of Future European Conflicts." In *Military Intervention in European Conflicts,* edited by Lawrence Freedman, 76–93. Oxford: Blackwell, 1994.

Hancilova, Blanka. "Czech Humanitarian Assistance, 1993–1998." *Journal of Humanitarian Assistance* (April 2000): http://www.jha.ac/articles/a054.htm

Harris, Robin. "Blair's 'Ethical' Policy." *The National Interest* No. 63 (2000): 25–36.

Hashmi, Sohail H. "Sovereignty, Pan-Islamism and International Organization." In *State Sovereignty: Change and Persistence in International Relations,* edited by Sohail H. Hashmi, University Park: Pennsylvania State University Press, 1997.

Heinrich, William, Akiho Shibata and Yoshihide Soeya, eds. *United Nations Peacekeeping: A Guide to Japanese Policies.* Tokyo: United Nations University Press, 1999.

Helsinki Watch. *War or Peace? Human Rights and Russian Military Involvement in the "Near Abroad."* New York: Helsinki Watch, 1993.

Henkin, Louis. "The Use of Force: Law and US Policy." In *Right v. Might: International Law and the Use of Force,* edited by Louis Henkin et al., 37–69. New York: Council on Foreign Relations Press, 1989.

Hermann, Margaret G. and Charles W. Kegley. "The US Use of Military Intervention to Promote Democracy: Evaluating the Record." *International Interactions* Vol. 24 No. 2 (1998): 91–114.

Hermet, Guy. "L'humanitaire dans la politique française." *Projet* Vol. 237 (1994): 62–70.

Higham, Robin, ed. *Intervention or Abstention: The Dilemma of American Foreign Policy.* Lexington: University Press of Kentucky, 1975.

Holoboff, Elaine. "Russian Views on Military Intervention: Benevolent Peacekeeping, Monroe Doctrine or Neo-Imperialism?" In *Military Intervention in European Conflicts,* edited by Lawrence Freedman, 154–174. Oxford: Blackwell, 1994.

Honig, Jan Willem. "The Netherlands and Military Intervention." In *Military Intervention in European Conflicts,* edited by Lawrence Freedman, 142–153. Oxford: Blackwell, 1994.

Hourn, Kao Kim and Jeffrey A. Kaplan, eds. *Principles under Pressure: Cambodia and ASEAN's Non-Interference Policy.* Phnom Penh: Cambodian Institute for Cooperation and Peace, 1999.

Howorth, Jolyon. "The Debate in France over Military Intervention in Europe." In *Military Intervention in European Conflicts,* edited by Lawrence Freedman, 106–124. Oxford: Blackwell, 1994.

Ikenberry, G. John. "The Costs of Victory: American Power and the Use of Force in the Contemporary Order." In *Kosovo and the Challenge of Humanitarian Intervention: Selective Indignation, Collective Action, and International Citizenship,* edited by Albrecht Schnabel and Ramesh Thakur, 85–100. Tokyo: United Nations University Press, 2000.

Jakobsen, Peter Viggo. "The Danish Approach to UN Peace Operations after the Cold War: A New Model in the Making?" *International Peacekeeping* Vol. 5 No. 3 (1998): 106–123.

Jimenez, Amilcar Guido. *America Latina y la no intervencion.* 1984.

Joes, Anthony James, ed. *Saving Democracies: US Intervention in Threatened Democratic States.* Westport: Praeger, 1999.

Jones, Christopher D. "Soviet Hegemony in Eastern Europe: The Dynamics of Political Autonomy and Military Intervention." *World Politics* Vol. 29 No. 2 (1977): 216–241.

Jones, Robert A. *The Soviet Concept of "Limited Sovereignty" from Lenin to Gorbachev: The Brezhnev Doctrine*. New York: St. Martin's Press, 1990.

Jonson, Lena. "In Search of a Doctrine: Russian Interventionism in Conflicts in Its 'Near Abroad'." *Low Intensity Conflict and Law Enforcement* Vol. 5 No. 3 (1996): 440–465.

Joyner, Christopher C. *Intervention into the 1990s: US Foreign Policy in the Third World*. Boulder: Lynne Rienner, 1992.

Kanter, Arnold and Linton F. Brooks, eds. *US Intervention Policy for the Post-Cold War World: New Challenges and New Responses*. New York: Norton and Company, 1994.

Karabell, Zachary. *Architects of Intervention: The United States, the Third World, and the Cold War, 1946–1962*. Baton Rouge: Louisiana State University, 1999.

Karawan, Ibrahim A. "The Muslim World: Uneasy Ambivalence." In *Kosovo and the Challenge of Humanitarian Intervention: Selective Indignation, Collective Action, and International Citizenship*, edited by Albrecht Schnabel and Ramesh Thakur, 215–222. Tokyo: United Nations University Press, 2000.

Keal, Paul, ed. *Ethics and Foreign Policy*. Canberra: Allen and Unwin in association with Department of International Relations, 1992.

Keating, Tom and Nicholas Gammer. "The 'New Look' in Canada's Foreign Policy." *International Journal* Vol. 48 No. 4 (1993): 720–748.

Kervarec, Gaëlle. "L'intervention d'humanité dans le cadre des limites au principe de non-intervention." *Revue Juridique Thémis* Vol. 32 No. 1 (1998): 77–133.

Khadduri, Majid. *War and Peace in the Law of Islam*. Baltimore: The Johns Hopkins University Press, 1955.

Kim, Samuel S. "Sovereignty in the Chinese Image of World Order." In *Essays in Honor of Wang Tieya*, edited by John Macdonald, 425–445. Toronto: University of Toronto Press, 1993.

Kirkpatrick, Jeane J. and Allan Gerson. "The Reagan Doctrine, Human Rights, and International Law." In *Right v. Might: International Law and the Use of Force*, edited by Louis Henkin et al., 19–36. New York: Council on Foreign Relations Press, 1989.

Klare, Michael T. *Beyond the "Vietnam Syndrome": US Intervention in the 1980s*. Washington, DC: Institute for Policy Studies, 1981.

Konovalov, Alexander, Sergey Oznobistchev and Dmitry G. Evstafiev. "A Review of Economic Sanctions: A Russian Perspective." In *Economic Sanctions: Panacea or Peacebuilding in a Post-Cold War World?*, edited by David Cortright and George A. Lopez, 43–48. Boulder: Westview, 1995.

Korb, Lawrence J. "The Use of Force." *Brookings Review* Vol. 15 No. 2 (1997): 24–25.

Korostarenko. "Printsip nevmeshatel'stva v mezhdunarodnom prave (o vyskazyvaniiakh I.V. Stalina)." *Uchenye zapiski akademii obshchestvennykh nauk pri Tsk VPK (b)* (1950): 72–88.

Kostakos, Georgios. "The Southern Flank: Italy, Greece, Turkey." In *Kosovo and the Challenge of Humanitarian Intervention: Selective Indignation, Collective Action, and International Citizenship*, edited by Albrecht Schnabel and Ramesh Thakur, 166–180. Tokyo: United Nations University Press, 2000.

Kraft, Herman. "The Principle of Non-Intervention: Evolution and Challenges for the Asia–Pacific Region." In *Non-Intervention and State Sovereignty in the Asia–Pacific*, edited by David Dickens and Guy Wilson-Roberts, 19–37. Wellington: Centre for Strategic Studies, 2000.

Kumar, Radha. "Sovereignty and Intervention: Opinions in South Asia." *Pugwash Occasional Papers* Vol. 2 No. 1 (2001): 52–64.

Kummel, Gerhard. "United Nations Overstretch: A German Perspective." *International Peacekeeping* Vol. 1 No. 2 (1994): 160–178.

Kunig, Philip. *Das völkerrechtliche Nichteinmischungsprinzip: Zur Praxis der Organisation der afrikanischen Einheit (OAU) und des afrikanischen Staatenverkehrs*. Baden-Baden: Nomos, 1981.

Kwa, Chong Guan. "Intervention and Non-Intervention: A Singapore Comment." In *Non-Intervention and State Sovereignty in the Asia–Pacific*, edited by David Dickens and Guy Wilson-Roberts, 47–51. Wellington: Centre for Strategic Studies, 2000.

LaFeber, Walter. *Inevitable Revolutions: The United States in Central America*. 2nd ed. New York: W.W. Norton and Company, 1993.

Langan, John. "Le dilemme américain: intervenir sans principes." *Projet* Vol. 237 (1994): 71–76.

Langford, Tonya. "Orchestrating Peace Operations: The PDD-56 Process." *Security Dialogue* Vol. 30 No. 2 (1999): 137–149.

Lavrov, Sergej. "The Russian Approach: The Fight against Genocide, War Crimes, and Crimes against Humanity." *Fordham International Law Journal* Vol. 23 No. 2 (1999): 415–429.

Lee, Steve. "The Axworthy Years: Humanist Activism and Public Diplomacy." *Canadian Foreign Policy* Vol. 8 No. 1 (2000): 1–10.

Levenson, Joseph R. "Western Powers and Chinese Revolutions: The Pattern of Intervention." *Pacific Affairs* Vol. 26 No. 3 (1953): 230–236.

Levitt, Jeremy. "Conflict Prevention, Management, and Resolution: Africa: Regional Strategies for the Prevention of Displacement and Protection of Displaced Persons: The Strategies of the OAU, ECOWAS, SADC, and IGAD." *Duke Journal of Comparative and International Law* Vol. 11 No. 1: 39–79.

Lia, Brynjar. "Islamist Perceptions of the United Nations and Its Peacekeeping Missions: Some Preliminary Findings." *International Peacekeeping* Vol. 5 No. 2 (1998): 38–63.

Lillich, Richard B. "A United States Policy of Humanitarian Intervention and Intercession." In *Human Rights and American Foreign Policy*, edited by Donald P. Kommers and Gilburt D. Loescher, 243–245. Notre Dame: University of Notre Dame Press, 1979.

Liu, Fu-Kuo and Linjun Wu. "The Principle of Non-Intervention in the Asia–Pacific Region: A Chinese Perspective." In *Non-Intervention and State Sovereignty in the Asia–Pacific*, edited by David Dickens and Guy Wilson-Roberts, 53–59. Wellington, New Zealand: Centre for Strategic Studies, 2000.

Maclean, George. "Instituting and Projecting Human Rights: A Canadian Perspective." *Australian Journal of International Affairs* Vol. 54 No. 3 (2000): 269–276.

Maley, William. "Ethical Actors in Australian Foreign Policy: Political Parties, Pressure Groups and Social Movements." In *Ethics and Foreign Policy*, edited by Paul Keal, 81–97. Canberra: Allen and Unwin in association with Department of International Relations, 1992.

Manicacci, Raymond. "L'intervention extérieure vue par les Américains." *Défense Nationale* Vol. 50 (1994): 79–90.

Martin, Charles E. *The Policy of the United States as Regards Intervention*. New York: AMS Press, 1967.

Mas, Monique. *Paris-Kigali 1990–1994: lunettes coloniales, politique du sabre et onction humanitaire pour un génocide en Afrique*. Paris: L'Harmattan, 1999.

McRae, Rob and Don Hubert, eds. *Human Security and the New Diplomacy: Protecting People, Promoting Peace*. Montréal: McGill–Queen's University Press, 2001.

Meernik, James. "United States Military Intervention and the Promotion of Democracy." *Journal of Peace Research* Vol. 33 No. 4 (1996): 391–402.

Menon, Rajan. "Military Power, Intervention, and Soviet Policy in the Third World." In *Soviet Foreign Policy in the 1980s*, edited by R. Kanet, New York: Praeger, 1982.

Moïsi, Dominique. "Intervention in French Foreign Policy." In *Intervention in World Politics*, edited by Hedley Bull, 67–77. Oxford: Clarendon Press, 1984.

Møller, Bjørn. "The Nordic Countries: Whither the West's Conscience?" In *Kosovo and the Challenge of Humanitarian Intervention: Selective Indignation, Collective Action, and International Citizenship*, edited by Albrecht Schnabel and Ramesh Thakur, 151–165. Tokyo: United Nations University Press, 2000.

Moore, John Norton. "The Elephant Misperceived: Intervention and American Foreign Policy." In *Law and the Indo-China War*, edited by John Norton Moore, Princeton: Princeton University Press, 1972.

Morrison, Alex, ed. *Peacekeeping, Peacemaking or War: International Security Enforcement*. Toronto: Canadian Institute of Strategic Studies, 1991.

Mubiala, Mutoy. "African States and the Promotion of Humanitarian Principles." *International Review of the Red Cross* No. 269 (1989): 93–110.

Müller, Harald. "Military Intervention for European Security: The German Debate." In *Military Intervention in European Conflicts*, edited by Lawrence Freedman, 125–141. Oxford: Blackwell, 1994.

Muravchik, Joshua. *The Uncertain Crusade: Jimmy Carter and the Dilemmas of Human Rights Policy*. New York: Hamilton Press, 1986.

Murphy, Ray. "Ireland, the United Nations and Peacekeeping Operations." *International Peacekeeping* Vol. 5 No. 1 (1998): 22–45.

Nakayama, Toshihiro. "Principles of Non-Intervention: A Japanese Perspective." In *Non-Intervention and State Sovereignty in the Asia–Pacific*, edited by David Dickens and Guy Wilson-Roberts, 69–74. Wellington: Centre for Strategic Studies, 2000.

Nambiar, Satish. "India: An Uneasy Precedent." In *Kosovo and the Challenge of Humanitarian Intervention: Selective Indignation, Collective Action, and International Citizenship*, edited by Albrecht Schnabel and Ramesh Thakur, 260–269. Tokyo: United Nations University Press, 2000.

Nel, Philip. "South Africa: The Demand for Legitimate Multilateralism." In *Kosovo and the Challenge of Humanitarian Intervention: Selective Indignation, Collective Action, and International Citizenship*, edited by Albrecht Schnabel and Ramesh Thakur, 245–259. Tokyo: United Nations University Press, 2000.

Nichols, Bruce and Gil Loescher. *The Moral Nation: Humanitarianism and US Foreign Policy Today*. Notre Dame: University of Notre Dame Press, 1989.

Niquet, Valérie. "La participation du Japon aux opérations de maintien de la paix." *Défense Nationale* Vol. 53 (1997): 101–115.

O'Brien, William V. *US Military Intervention: Law and Morality*. Washington, DC: Center for Strategic and International Studies, Georgetown University; Sage Publications, 1979.

Ogden, Suzanne. "Sovereignty and International Law: The Perspective of the People's Republic of China." *New York University Journal of International Law and Politics* Vol. 7 (1974): 1–32.

Ortega, Martin. *Military Intervention and the European Union*. Paris: Institute for Security Studies, Western European Union, 2001.

Österdahl, Inger. *La France dans l'Afrique de l'après-guerre froide: interventions et justifications*. Uppsala: Nordiska Afrikainstitutet, 1997.

Otunnu, Olara A. "Maintaining Broad Legitimacy." In *Keeping the Peace in the Post-Cold War Era: Strengthening Multilateral Peace-Keeping*, edited by John Roper et al., 69–82. Washington, DC: Trilateral Commission, 1993. Trilateral Commission Report.

Owens, Heather and Barbara Arneil. "The Human Security Paradigm Shift: A New Lens on Canadian Foreign Policy?" *Canadian Foreign Policy* Vol. 7 No. 1 (1999): 1–12.

Papisca, Antonio. "La posizione della società civile europea sul tema della ingerenza umanitaria." *Pace* Vol. 7 No. 3 (1993): 125–131.

Pascallon, Pierre, ed. *Les interventions extérieure de l'armée française*. Bruxelles: Bruylant, 1997.

Pavlov, O. "Proletarian Internationalism and Defence of Socialist Gains." *International Affairs (Moscow)* (1968): 11–16.

Payne, Keith. "Are They Interested in Stability? The Soviet View of Intervention." *Comparative Strategy* Vol. 3 No. 1 (1981): 1–24.

Peceny, Mark. "Two Paths to the Promotion of Democracy during US Military Interventions." *International Studies Quarterly* Vol. 39 No. 3 (1995): 371–401.

Pellet, Alain. "The Road to Hell is Paved with Good Intentions: The United Nations as Guarantor of International Peace and Security: A French Perspective." In *The United Nations at Age Fifty: A Legal Perspective*, edited by Christian Tomuschat, 113–133. The Hague: Kluwer Law International, 1995.

Peters, Rudolph. *Islam and Colonialism: The Doctrine of Jihad in Modern History*. The Hague: Mouton, 1979.

Petras, James. "US Foreign Policy: The Revival of Interventionism." *Monthly Review* (1980): 15–27.

Pirrone, Pasquale. "The Use of Force in the Framework of the Organization of American States." In *The Current Legal Regulation of the Use of Force*, edited by Antonio Cassese, 223–240. Dordrecht: Martinus Nijhoff, 1986.

Piscatori, James P. *Islam in a World of Nation-States*. Cambridge: Cambridge University Press in ssociation with The Royal Institute of International Affairs, 1986.

Porter, Andrew. *European Imperialism 1860–1914*. Basingstoke: Macmillan, 1994.

*Presidential Decision Directive 25: The Clinton Administration's Policy on Reforming Multilateral Peace Operations: Executive Summary*. Washington, DC: Department of State Publications, 1994.

Putnam, Robert D. "Toward Explaining Military Intervention in Latin American Politics." *World Politics* Vol. 20 No. 1 (1967): 83–110.

Quigley, John. *The Ruses for War: American Interventionism since World War II*. Buffalo: Prometheus Books, 1992.

Quiles, Paul. "Le rôle du Parlement en matière d'interventions extérieures des forces armées." *Révue Internationale et Stratégique* (1998): 15–25.

Raevsky, Andrei and I.N. Vorob'ev. *Russian Approaches to Peacekeeping Operations*. New York: United Nations, 1994.

Rajaee, Farhang. *Islamic Values and World View: Khomeini on Man, the State and International Politics*. Lanham: University Press of America, 1983.

Robinson, William I. *Promoting Polyarchy: Globalization, US Intervention, and Hegemony*. Cambridge: Cambridge University Press, 1996.

Ross, Jennifer. "Is Canada's Human Security Policy Really the 'Axworthy' Doctrine?" *Canadian Foreign Policy* Vol. 8 No. 2 (2001): 75–93.

Said, Abdul Aziz, Nathan C. Funk and Ayse S. Kadayifci, eds. *Peace and Conflict Resolution in Islam: Precept and Practice*. Lanham: University of America Press, 2001.

Salmi, Ralph H., Cesar Adib Majul and George K. Tanham. *Islam and Conflict Resolution: Theories and Practices*. Lanham: University Press of America, 1998.

Scharping, Rudolf. "Der Stein auf unserer Seele. Deutschland und der gerechte Krieg." In *Der westliche Kreuzzug. 41 Positionen zum Kosovo-Krieg*, edited by Frank Schirrmacher, 129–136. Stuttgart: Deutsche Verlags-Anstalt, 1999.

Schmid, Alex P. *Soviet Military Interventions since 1945*. New Brunswick: Transaction Books, 1985.

Schraeder, Peter J., ed. *Intervention into the 1990s: US Foreign Policy in the Third World*. Boulder: Lynne Rienner, 1993.

Schrecker, John and Michael Walzer. "American Intervention and the Cold War." *Dissent* Vol. 12 No. 4 (1965): 431–446.

Scott, James M. *Deciding to Intervene: The Reagan Doctrine and American Foreign Policy.* Durham: Duke University Press, 1996.

Serrano, Mónica. "Latin America: The Dilemmas of Intervention." In *Kosovo and the Challenge of Humanitarian Intervention: Selective Indignation, Collective Action, and International Citizenship,* edited by Albrecht Schnabel and Ramesh Thakur, 223–244. Tokyo: United Nations University Press, 2000.

Shapiro, Harry H. *The United States and the Principle of Absolute Nonintervention in Latin America, with Particular Reference to Mexico.* Philadelphia: University of Pennsylvannia, 1949.

Shulong, Chu. "China, Asia and Issues of Intervention and Sovereignty." *Pugwash Occasional Papers* Vol. 2 No. 1 (2001): 39–51.

Smith, Anthony. "Intervention and East Timor: A New Zealand Perspective." In *Non-Intervention and State Sovereignty in the Asia–Pacific,* edited by David Dickens and Guy Wilson-Roberts, 75–85. Wellington: Centre for Strategic Studies, 2000.

Smith, Tony. "In Defense of Intervention." *Foreign Affairs* Vol. 73 No. 6 (1994): 34–46.

Snow, Donald M. "Peacekeeping, Peace-Enforcement, and Clinton Defense Policy." In *Clinton and Post-Cold War Defense,* edited by Stephen J. Cimbala, Westport: Praeger, 1996.

Spiry, Emmanuel. "Interventions humanitaires et interventions d'humanité: la pratique française face au droit international." *Revue Générale de Droit International Public* Vol. 102 No. 2 (1998): 407–434.

Spiry, Emmanuel. "La légalité des interventions extérieures de la France." *Défense Nationale* Vol. 54 (1998): 45–55.

Sredin, Vasilii. "To Defend Russia's Vital Interests." *International Affairs* (Moscow) Vol. 46 No. 1 (2000): 42–47.

Sreenivasa Rao, Pemmaraju. "The United Nations and International Peace and Security: An Indian Perspective." In *The United Nations at Age Fifty: A Legal Perspective,* edited by Christian Tomuschat, 143–184. The Hague: Kluwer Law International, 1995.

Stapleton, Augustus Granville. *Intervention and Non-Intervention: The Foreign Policy of Great Britain from 1790 to 1865.* London: J. Murray, 1866.

Stedman, Stephen John. "The New Interventionists." *Foreign Affairs* Vol. 72 No. 1 (1993): 1–16.

Stern, Brigitte, ed. *United Nations Peacekeeping Operations: A Guide to French Policies.* Tokyo: United Nations University Press, 1998.

Stevenson, Charles A. "The Evolving Clinton Doctrine on the Use of Force." *Armed Forces and Society* Vol. 22 (1996): 511–535.

Sukma, Rizal. "Indonesia and Non-Intervention: Debate in Southeast Asia." In *Non-Intervention and State Sovereignty in the Asia–Pacific,* edited by David Dickens and Guy Wilson-Roberts, 87–97. Wellington: Centre for Strategic Studies, 2000.

Tálas, Péter and László Valki. "The New Entrants: Hungary, Poland, and the Czech Republic." In *Kosovo and the Challenge of Humanitarian Intervention: Selective Indignation, Collective Action, and International Citizenship,* edited by Albrecht Schnabel and Ramesh Thakur, 201–212. Tokyo: United Nations University Press, 2000.

Tardy, Thierry. "French Policy towards Peace Support Operations." *International Peacekeeping* Vol. 6 No. 1 (1999): 55–78.

Thomas, Ann Van Wynen and A.J. Thomas. *Non-Intervention: The Law and Its Import in the Americas.* Dallas: Southern Methodist University Press, 1956.

Thomas, Caroline. "The Muslim Stance on Non-Intervention." In *New States, Sovereignty and Intervention,* edited by Caroline Thomas, 77–86. Aldershot: Gower, 1985.

Thomas, Caroline. "The Soviet Stance on Non-Intervention." In *New States, Sovereignty and Intervention*, edited by Caroline Thomas, 53–63. Aldershot: Gower, 1985.

Thomas, Caroline. "The Stand Adopted by the OAU." In *New States, Sovereignty and Intervention*, edited by Caroline Thomas, 63–77. Aldershot: Gower, 1985.

Tillema, Herbert K. *Appeal to Force: American Military Intervention in the Era of Containment.* New York: Thomas Y. Crowell Co., 1973.

Torrelli, Maurice. "Les missions humanitaires de l'armée française." *Défense Nationale* Vol. 49 No. 3 (1993): 65–78.

Touval, Saadia. "The OAU and African Borders." *International Organization* Vol. 21 No. 1 (1967): 102–127.

Towle, Philip. "The British Debate about Intervention in European Conflicts." In *Military Intervention in European Conflicts*, edited by Lawrence Freedman, 94–105. Oxford: Blackwell, 1994.

Travis, Martin B. "Collective Intervention by the Organization of American States." *Proceedings of the American Society of International Law* (1957): 100–110.

Treacher, Adrian. "A Case of Reinvention: France and Military Intervention in the 1990s." *International Peacekeeping* Vol. 7 No. 2 (2000): 23–40.

Tripodi, Paolo. "Concscripts and Humanitarian Intervention: An Italian Perspective." *International Relations* Vol. 14 No. 6 (1999): 1–12.

Tucker, Robert W. and David C. Hendrickson. *The Imperial Temptation: The New World Order and America's Purpose.* New York: Council on Foreign Relations, 1992.

UK House of Commons Foreign Affairs Committee. *Fourth Report: Kosovo, Vol.: Report and Proceedings of the Committee.* London: Stationery Office, 2000.

Utley, Rachel. "The New French Interventionism." *Civil Wars* Vol. 1 No. 2 (1998): 83–103.

Valenta, Jiri. "Revolutionary Change, Soviet Intervention, and 'Normalization' in East-Central Europe." *Comparative Politics* Vol. 16 No. 2 (1984): 127–151.

Valenton, Joel V. "Re-Examining the Principle of Non-Intervention in the Region: A Philippine Perspective." In *Non-Intervention and State Sovereignty in the Asia–Pacific*, edited by David Dickens and Guy Wilson-Roberts, 99–105. Wellington: Centre for Strategic Studies, 2000.

Van Der Stoel, Max. "The Political Aspects of Intervention in the Netherlands." In *Intervention in International Politics*, edited by Louis G.M. Jaquet, 99–114. The Hague: Netherlands Institute of International Affairs, 1971.

Van Dijk, P. and A. Bloed. "Conference on Security and Cooperation in Europe, Human Rights and Non-Intervention." *Liverpool Law Review* Vol. 8 (1983): 117.

Van Wingen, J. and H.K. Tillema. "British Military Intervention after World War II: Militance in a Second-Rank Power." *Journal of Peace Research* Vol. 17 No. 4 (1980): 291–303.

Vasconcelos, Alvaro. "L'intervention au Timor et le multilateralisme possible." *Politique Étrangère* Vol. 65 (2000): 135–149.

Villagran Kramer, Francisco. "Los derechos humanos y el principio de no intervencion: planteami-ento sobre reglas esclarecedoras y sanciones por violaciones a los derechos humanos." *Revista IIDH* Vol. 13 (1991): 87–124.

Vincent, R.J. "Soviet Doctrine and Practice." In *Nonintervention and International Order*, edited by R.J. Vincent, 145–187. Princeton: Princeton University Press, 1974.

Vincent, R.J. "United States Doctrine and Practice." In *Nonintervention and International Order*, edited by R.J. Vincent, 188–232. Princeton: Princeton University Press, 1974.

Von Hippel, Karin. *Democracy by Force: US Military Intervention in the Post-Cold War World.* Cambridge: Cambridge University Press, 2000.

Von Hippel, Karin. "The Non-Interventionary Norm Prevails: An Analysis of the Western Sahara." *Journal of Modern African Studies* Vol. 33 No. 1 (1995): 67–81.

Ware, Glenn T. "The Emerging Norm of Humanitarian Intervention and Presidential Decision Directive 25." *Naval Law Review* Vol. 44 (1997): 1–58.

Weggel, Oskar. "Chaos, Ratlosigkeit und Angst vor Präzedenzwirkungen: Chinas Haltung im Kosovo-Konflikt." *China Aktuell* Vol. 28 No. 3 (1999): 261–266.

Wheeler, Nicholas J. and Tim Dunne. "Good International Citizenship: A Third Way for British Foreign Policy." *International Affairs* Vol. 74 No. 4 (1998): 847–870.

Williams, Rocky. "From Peacekeeping to Peacebuilding? South African Policy and Practice in Peace Missions." *International Peacekeeping* Vol. 7 No. 3 (2000): 84–104.

Wilson, L.C. "El principio de no intervención en la política interamericana." *Política (Caracas)* Vol. 6 No. 63 (1967): 59–77.

Wolf, Alvin. *Foreign Policy: Intervention, Involvement, or Isolation?* Englewood Cliffs: Prentice-Hall, 1977.

Woodhouse, Tom. "The Gentle Hand of Peace? British Peacekeeping and Conflict Resolution in Complex Political Emergencies." *International Peacekeeping* Vol. 6 No. 2 (1999): 24–37.

Wyllie, James H. *The Influence of British Arms: An Analysis of British Military Intervention since 1956.* London: Allen and Unwin, 1984.

Yarmolinsky, Adam. "American Foreign Policy and the Decision to Intervene." *Journal of International Affairs* Vol. 22 No. 2 (1968): 231–235.

Yarmolinsky, Adam. *United States Military Power and Foreign Policy.* Chicago: University of Chicago Center for Policy Study, 1967.

Yoon, Mi Yung. "Explaining US Intervention in Third World Internal Wars, 1945–1989." *Journal of Conflict Resolution* Vol. 41 No. 4 (1997): 580–602.

Zhang, Yongjin. "China and UN Peacekeeping: From Condemnation to Participation." *International Peacekeeping* Vol. 3 No. 3 (1996): 1–15.

Zhang, Yunling. "China: Whither the World Order after Kosovo?" In *Kosovo and the Challenge of Humanitarian Intervention: Selective Indignation, Collective Action, and International Citizenship,* edited by Albrecht Schnabel and Ramesh Thakur, 117–127. Tokyo: United Nations University Press, 2000.

Zimmerman, William and Robert Axelrod. "The 'Lessons' of Vietnam and Soviet Foreign Policy." *World Politics* Vol. 34 No. 1 (1981): 1–24.

# 8. NONMILITARY INTERVENTIONS

Bass, Gary Jonathan. *Stay the Hand of Vengeance: The Politics of War Crimes Tribunals*. Princeton: Princeton University Press, 2000.
> Systematic and comparative account of the politics of international war crimes tribunals from St. Helena, Leipzig, and Constantinople to Nuremberg and The Hague. Asks what makes governments support international war crimes tribunals and what makes them abandon them.

Cassese, Antonio. "On the Current Trends Towards Criminal Prosecution and Punishment of Breaches of International Humanitarian Law." *European Journal of International Law* Vol. 9 No. 1 (1998): 2–17.
> Argues that international criminal tribunals are vital to upholding justice and the rule of law but that state sovereignty remains a major obstacle to the effective enforcement of international criminal justice.

Cortright, David and George A. Lopez. *The Sanctions Decade: Assessing UN Strategies in the 1990s*. Boulder: Lynne Rienner, 2000.
> Explores the effectiveness of the 12 cases of UN Security sanctions imposed during the 1990s and offers a broad range of future policy recommendations.

Crawford, Neta and Audie Klotz, eds. *How Sanctions Work: Lessons from South Africa*. Basingstoke: Macmillan, 1999.
> Discusses the efficacy of various kinds of sanctions as a tool of influence. Concludes that the South African experience demonstrates that international sanctions can play a constructive role in domestic political change.

Daniel, Donald C.F., Bradd C. Hayes and Chantal de Jonge Oudraat. *Coercive Inducement and the Containment of International Crises*. Washington, DC: United States Institute of Peace, 1999.
> Examines the resort to coercive diplomacy as a "middle ground" between peace enforcement and traditional peacekeeping.

Doxey, Margaret P. *International Sanctions in Contemporary Perspective*. Basingstoke: Macmillan, 1996.
> Summaries of important cases and analyses of the contexts and rationales for sanctions. Argues that the UN offers the most comprehensive and legitimate framework for sanctions.

Gutman, Roy and David Rieff, eds. *Crimes of War: What the Public Should Know*. London: W.W. Norton and Co., 1999.
> Concise encyclopedia for the lay reader, covering the main elements of the humanitarian debate of the 1990s.

Hufbauer, Gary Clyde, Jeffrey J. Schott and Kimberly Ann Elliott. *Economic Sanctions Reconsidered: History and Current Policy*. 3rd ed. Washington, DC: Institute for International Economics, 2001.
> Study of 170 cases of economic sanctions imposed since the Second World War, 50 of which were launched in the 1990s.

Lee, Roy S., ed. *The International Criminal Court: The Making of the Rome Statute – Issues, Negotiations, Results*. The Hague: Kluwer Law International, 1999.
> Collective work by a group of authors closely associated with the making of the Rome Statute, covering the substantive and procedural issues raised during the preparatory stages, as well as at the UN Conference in Rome.

Martin, Lisa L. *Coercive Cooperation: Explaining Multilateral Economic Sanctions.* Princeton: Princeton University Press, 1992.
> Situates economic sanctions in the broader theoretical framework of international cooperation. Develops a typology of cooperation problems and tests it against four case studies.

Pape, Robert A. "Why Economic Sanctions Do Not Work." *International Security* Vol. 22 No. 2 (1997): 90–136.
> Statement of the ineffectiveness of economic sanctions. Suggests that sanctions are not likely to achieve foreign policy goals.

Ratner, Steven R. and Jason S. Abrams. *Accountability for Human Rights Atrocities in International Law: Beyond the Nuremberg Legacy.* 2nd ed. Oxford: Clarendon Press, 2001.
> Appraisal of individual accountability for human rights atrocities in international law, focusing on individual responsibility. Includes a case study on the Khmer Rouge.

## References

Africa Research Centre. *The Sanctions Weapon.* Cape Town: Bucho Books, 1989.

Akhavan, Payam. "Justice in the Hague, Peace in the Former Yugoslavia? A Commentary on the United Nations War Crimes Tribunal." *Human Rights Quarterly* Vol. 20 No. 4 (1998): 737–816.

Akhavan, Payam. "Justice and Reconciliation in the Great Lakes Region of Africa: The Contribution of the International Criminal Tribunal for Rwanda." *Duke Journal of Comparative and International Law* Vol. 7 No. 2 (1997): 325–348.

Akhavan, Payam. "The International Criminal Tribunal for Rwanda: The Politics and Pragmatics of Punishment." *American Journal of International Law* Vol. 90 No. 3 (1996): 501–510.

Akhavan, Payam. "The Yugoslav Tribunal at a Crossroads: The Dayton Peace Agreement and Beyond." *Human Rights Quarterly* Vol. 18 No. 2 (1996): 259–285.

Akhavan, Payam. "Punishing War Crimes in the Former Yugoslavia: A Critical Juncture for the New World Order." *Human Rights Quarterly* Vol. 15 No. 2 (1993): 262–289.

Alvarez, José E. "Crimes of States/Crimes of Hate: Lessons from Rwanda." *Yale Journal of International Law* Vol. 24 No. 2 (1999): 365–483.

Alvarez, José E. "Nuremberg Revisited: The Tadic Case." *European Journal of International Law* Vol. 7 No. 2 (1996): 245–264.

Arsanjani, Mahnoush H. "The Rome Statute of the International Criminal Court." *American Journal of International Law* Vol. 93 No. 1 (1999): 22–43.

Baldwin, David A. *Economic Statecraft.* Princeton: Princeton University Press, 1985.

Baldwin, David A. "The Power of Positive Sanctions." *World Politics* Vol. 24 No. 1 (1971): 19–38.

Baldwin, David A. "Foreign Aid, Intervention, and Influence." *World Politics* Vol. 21 No. 425 (1969): , 447.

Baldwin, David A. and Robert A. Pape. "Evaluating Economic Sanctions." *International Security* Vol. 23 No. 2 (1998): 189–198.

Bantekas, Ilias. "The Interests of States versus the Doctrine of Superior Responsibility." *International Review of the Red Cross* Vol. 82 No. 838 (2000): 391–401.

Bantekas, Ilias. "The Contemporary Law of Superior Responsibility." *American Journal of International Law* Vol. 93 No. 3 (1999): 573–595.

Baram, Amatzia. "The Effect of Iraqi Sanctions: Statistical Pitfalls and Responsibility." *The Middle East Journal* Vol. 54 No. 2 (2000): 194–223.

Barber, James. "Economic Sanctions as a Policy Instrument." *International Affairs* Vol. 55 No. 3 (1979): 367–384.

Bassiouni, M. Cherif. *Crimes against Humanity in International Criminal Law.* 2nd ed. The Hague: Kluwer Law International, 1999.

Bassiouni, M. Cherif. *The Statute of the International Criminal Court: A Documentary History.* Ardsley: Transnational Publishers, 1998.

Bassiouni, M. Cherif. "International Crimes: Jus Cogens and Obligatio Erga Omnes." *Law and Contemporary Problems* Vol. 59 No. 4 (1996): 63–74.

Bassiouni, M. Cherif. "Searching for Peace and Achieving Justice: The Need for Accountability." *Law and Contemporary Problems* Vol. 59 No. 4 (1996): 9–28.

Bassiouni, M. Cherif and Peter Manikas. *The Law of the International Criminal Tribunal for the Former Yugoslavia.* Irvington-on-Hudson: Transnational Publishers, 1996.

Bassiouni, M. Cherif and Edward M. Wise. *Aut dedere aut judicare: The Duty to Extradite or Prosecute in International Law.* Dordrecht: Martinus Nijhoff, 1995.

Bayard, Thomas, Joseph Pelzman and Jorge Perez-Lopez. "Stakes and Risks in Economic Sanctions." *World Economy* Vol. 6 No. 1 (1983): 73–87.

Beigbeder, Yves. *Judging War Criminals: The Politics of International Justice.* Basingstoke: Macmillan, 1999.

Bellamy, Alex J. "Lessons Unlearned: Why Coercive Diplomacy Failed at Rambouillet." *International Peacekeeping* Vol. 7 No. 2 (2000): 95–114.

Benedetti, F. and J.L. Washburn. "Drafting the International Criminal Court Treaty: Two Years to Rome and an Afterword on the Rome Diplomatic Conference." *Global Governance* Vol. 5 No. 1 (1999): 1–38.

Berdal, Mats and David M. Malone, eds. *Greed and Grievance: Economic Agendas in Civil Wars.* Boulder: Lynne Rienner, 2000.

Bienen, Henry and Robert Gilpin. *Evaluation of the Use of Economic Sanctions to Promote Foreign Policy Objectives.* Seattle: Boeing Corp., 1979.

Blanchard, Jean-Marc and Norrin M. Ripsman. "Asking the Right Question: When Do Economic Sanctions Work Best?" *Security Studies* Vol. 9 No. 1/2 (2000): 219–253.

Boelaert-Suominen, Sonja. "The International Criminal Tribunal for the Former Yugoslavia and the Kosovo Conflict." *International Review of the Red Cross* Vol. 82 No. 837 (2000): 217–251.

Bolks, S. and D. Al Sowayel. "How Long Do Economic Sanctions Last? Examining the Sanctioning Process through Duration." *Political Research Quarterly* Vol. 53 No. 2 (2000): 241–265.

Bolton, John R. "The Risks and Weaknesses of the International Criminal Court from America's Perspective." *Law and Contemporary Problems* Vol. 64 No. 1 (2001): 167–180.

Bowett, Derek W. "Crimes of State and the 1996 Report of the International Law Commission on State Responsibility." *European Journal of International Law* Vol. 9 No. 1 (1998): 163–173.

Broomhall, Bruce. "Toward US Acceptance of the International Criminal Court." *Law and Contemporary Problems* Vol. 64 No. 1 (2001): 141–152.

Brown-John, C. Lloyd. *Multilateral Sanctions in International Law: A Comparative Analysis.* New York: Praeger, 1975.

Buchheit, Lee C. "The Use of Nonviolent Coercion: A Study in Legality under Article 2 (4) of the Charter of the United Nations." In *Economic Coercion and the New International Economic Order*, edited by Richard B. Lillich, 41–69. Charlottesville: Michie Co., 1976.

Carment, David and Dane Rowlands. "Threes Company: Evaluating Third Party Intervention in Intrastate Conflict." *Journal of Conflict Resolution* Vol. 42 No. 4 (1998): 572–599.

Cassette, Jacquie. "Towards Justice in the Wake of Armed Conflicts? The Evolution of War Crimes Tribunals." *African Security Review* Vol. 9 No. 5 (2000).

Cavare, Louis. "Les sanctions dans le cadre de l'ONU." RCADI Vol. 80 (1952): 191–291.

Cissé, Catherine. "The End of a Culture of Impunity in Rwanda? Prosecution of Genocide and War Crimes before Rwandan Courts and the International Criminal Tribunal for Rwanda." *Yearbook of International Humanitarian Law* Vol. 1 (1998): 161–188.

Cissé, Catherine. "The International Tribunals for the Former Yugoslavia and Rwanda: Some Elements of Comparison." *Transnational Law and Contemporary Problems* Vol. 7 No. 1 (1997): 103–118.

Clark, Roger S. and Madeleine Sann, eds. *The Prosecution of International Crimes.* New Brunswick: Transaction Publishers, 1996.

Clawson, Patrick. "Sanctions as Punishment, Enforcement, and Prelude to Further Action." *Ethics and International Affairs* Vol. 7 (1993): 17–37.

Combacau, Jean. *Le pouvoir de sanction de l'ONU: Etude théorique de la coercition non militaire.* Paris: A. Pedone, 1974.

Conlon, Paul. "The Humanitarian Mitigation of UN Sanctions." *German Yearbook of International Law* Vol. 39 (1996): 249–284.

Conlon, Paul. "The UN's Questionable Sanctions Practice." *Außenpolitik* Vol. 46 No. 4 (1995): 327–338.

Cortright, David and George A. Lopez. "Learning from the Sanctions Decade." *Global Dialogue* Vol. 2 No. 3 (2000): 11–24.

Cortright, David and George A. Lopez, eds. *Economic Sanctions: Panacea or Peacebuilding in a Post-Cold War World?* Boulder: Westview Press, 1995.

Cortright, David and George A. Lopez. "The Sanctions Era: An Alternative to Military Intervention." *Fletcher Forum of World Affairs* Vol. 19 No. 2 (1995): 65–85.

Cortright, David, Alistair Millar and George A. Lopez. *Smart Sanctions: Restructuring UN Policy in Iraq.* Goshen: Fourth Freedom Forum, 2001.

D'Amato, Anthony. "Peace vs. Accountability in Bosnia." *American Journal of International Law* Vol. 88 No. 3 (1994): 500–506.

Damrosch, Lori Fisler, ed. *The International Court of Justice at a Crossroads.* Dobbs Ferry: Transnational Publishers, 1987.

Daoudi, M.S. and M.S. Dajani. *Economic Diplomacy: Embargo Leverage and World Politics.* Boulder: Westview Press, 1985.

Daoudi, M.S. and M.S. Dajani. *Economic Sanctions: Ideals and Experience.* London: Routledge and Kegan Paul, 1983.

Dashti-Gibson, Jaleh, Patricia Davis and Benjamin Radcliff. "On the Determinants of the Success of Economic Sanctions: An Empirical Analysis." *American Journal of Political Science* Vol. 41 (1997): 608–618.

Doxey, Margaret P. *United Nations Sanctions: Current Policy Issues.* Halifax: Dalhousie University, 1999.

Doxey, Margaret P. "International Sanctions: Trials of Strength or Tests of Weakness?" *Millennium* Vol. 12 No. 1 (1983): 79–87.

Doxey, Margaret P. "International Sanctions: A Framework for Analysis with Special Reference to the UN and Southern Africa." *International Organization* Vol. 26 No. 3 (1972): 527–550.

Drezner, Daniel W. *The Sanctions Paradox: Economic Statecraft and International Relations.* Cambridge: Cambridge University Press, 1999.

Duke Journal of Comparative and International Law. "Symposium: Justice in Cataclysm: Criminal Trials in the Wake of Mass Violence." Vol. 7 No. 2 (1997): 319–598.

Dworkin, A. "War Crimes Tribunals: The World in Judgement." *Index on Censorship* Vol. 25 No. 5 (1996): 137–144.

Eaton, Jonathan and Maxim Engers. "Sanctions." *Journal of Political Economy* Vol. 100 No. 5 (1992): 899–928.

Edelenbos, Carla. "Human Rights Violations: A Duty to Prosecute?" *Leiden Journal of International Law* Vol. 7 (1994): 5–22.

Elliott, Kimberly Ann. "The Sanctions Glass: Half Full or Completely Empty?" *International Security* Vol. 23 No. 1 (1998): 50–65.

Elliott, Kimberly Ann, Gary Clyde Hufbauer and Jeffrey J. Schott. *Reforming Economic Sanctions.* Washington, DC: Institute for International Economics, 2001.

Farer, Tom J. "Restraining the Barbarians: Can International Criminal Law Help?" *Human Rights Quarterly* Vol. 22 No. 1 (2000): 90–117.

Fatic, Aleksandar. *Reconciliation via the War Crimes Tribunal.* Aldershot: Ashgate, 2000.

Fenrick, William J. "The Application of the Geneva Conventions by the International Criminal Tribunal for the Former Yugoslavia." *International Review of the Red Cross* Vol. 81 No. 834 (1999): 317–329.

Fenrick, William J. "International Humanitarian Law and Criminal Trials." *Transnational Law and Contemporary Problems* Vol. 7 No. 1 (1997): 23–44.

Ferencz, Benjamin B. *An International Criminal Court: A Step toward World Peace.* New York: Oceana, 1980.

Ferstman, Carla J. "Domestic Trials for Genocide and Crimes against Humanity: The Example of Rwanda." *African Journal of International and Comparative Law* Vol. 9 (1997): 857.

*Final Report of the Monitoring Mechanism on Angola Sanctions* (2000): http://www.un.org/Depts/dpa/docs/monitoringmechanism.htm

Forsythe, David P. "International Criminal Courts." In *Human Rights in International Relations,* edited by David P. Forsythe, 84–109. Cambridge: Cambridge University Press, 2000.

Forsythe, David P. "International Criminal Courts: A Political View." *Netherlands Quarterly of Human Rights* Vol. 15 No. 1 (1997): 5–19.

Forsythe, David P. "Politics and the International Tribunal for the Former Yugoslavia." *Criminal Law Forum* Vol. 5 No. 2/3 (1994): 401–422.

Fourth Freedom Forum. *Towards Smarter, More Effective United Nations Sanctions.* Goshen: FFF, 1999.

Franck, Thomas M. *Judging the World Court.* New York: Priority Press, 1986.

Friman, Håkan. "The International Criminal Court: Negotiations and Key Issues." *African Security Review* Vol. 8 No. 6 (1999): 3–14.

Gaeta, Paola. "Is NATO Authorized or Obliged to Arrest Persons Indicted by the International Criminal Tribunal for the Former Yugoslavia?" *European Journal of International Law* Vol. 9 No. 1 (1998): 174–181.

Galtung, Johan. "On the Effects of International Economic Sanctions, with Examples from the Case of Rhodesia." *World Politics* Vol. 19 No. 3 (1967): 378–416.

Garraway, Charles. "Superior Orders and the International Criminal Court: Justice Delivered or Justice Denied." *International Review of the Red Cross* Vol. 81 No. 836 (1999): 785–793.

Garten, Jeffrey. "Comment: The Need for Pragmatism." *Foreign Policy* No. 105 (1996/1997): 103–106.

George, Alexander L. *Forceful Persuasion: Coercive Diplomacy as an Alternative to War.* Washington, DC: United States Institute of Peace, 1991.

George, Alexander L. and William L. Simons, eds. *The Limits of Coercive Diplomacy*. Boulder: Westview Press, 1994.

Goldstein, Joseph et al., eds. *The My Lai Massacre and Its Cover-Up: Beyond the Reach of Law?* New York: Free Press, 1976.

Goldstone, Richard J. "Assessing the Work of the United Nations War Crimes Tribunal." *Stanford Journal of International Law* Vol. 33 No. 1 (1997).

Goldstone, Richard J. *Prosecuting War Criminals*. London: David Davies Memorial Institute of International Studies, 1996.

Graham-Brown, Sarah. *Sanctioning Saddam: The Politics of Intervention in Iraq*. London: I.B. Tauris, 1999.

Green, Robert and Kate Dewes. "The World Court Project: History and Consequences." *Canadian Foreign Policy* Vol. 7 No. 1 (1999): 61–83.

Greppi, Edoardo. "The Evolution of Individual Criminal Responsibility under International Law." *International Review of the Red Cross* Vol. 81 No. 835 (1999): 531–552.

Guillaume, G. "Enforcement of Decisions of the International Court of Justice." In *Perspectives on International Law*, edited by Nandasiri Jasentuliyana, 275–288. London: Kluwer Law International, 1995.

Haass, Richard N. "Sanctioning Madness." *Foreign Affairs* Vol. 76 No. 6 (1997): 74–85.

Haass, Richard N., ed. *Economic Sanctions and American Diplomacy*. Washington, DC: Brookings Institution, 1988.

Harhoff, Frederik. "Consonance or Rivalry? Calibrating the Efforts to Prosecute War Crimes in National and International Tribunals." *Duke Journal of Comparative and International Law* Vol. 7 No. 2 (1997): 571–595.

Hart, R. "Democracy and the Successful Use of Economic Sanctions." *Political Research Quarterly* Vol. 53 No. 2 (2000): 267–284.

Helms, Jesse. "What Sanctions Epidemic?" *Foreign Affairs* Vol. 78 No. 1 (1999): 2–8.

Hendrickson, David C. "The Democratist Crusade: Intervention, Economic Sanctions, and Engagement." *World Policy Journal* Vol. 11 No. 4 (1994/1995): 18–30.

Higgins, Rosalyn. "Respecting Sovereign States and Running a Tight Courtroom." *International and Comparative Law Quarterly* Vol. 50 No. 1 (2000): 121–132.

Highley, Albert E. *The First Sanctions Experiment: A Study of League Procedures*. Geneva: Geneva Research Centre, 1938.

Human Rights Watch. *Accountability for Past Human Rights Abuses*. New York: HRW, 1989. Special Issue No. 4.

Jakobsen, Peter Viggo. *Western Use of Coercive Diplomacy after the Cold War: A Challenge for Theory and Practice*. Basingstoke: Macmillan, 1998.

Jentleson, Bruce W. "The Reagan Administration and Coercive Diplomacy: Restraining More Than Remaking Governments." *Political Science Quarterly* Vol. 106 No. 1 (1991): 57–82.

Jones, John R.W.D., ed. *The Practice of the International Criminal Tribunals for the Former Yugoslavia and Rwanda*. Ardsley: Transnational Publishers, 2000.

Jonge Oudraat, Chantal de. "Making Economic Sanctions Work." *Survival* Vol. 42 No. 3 (2000): 105–128.

Joyner, Christopher C. *The United Nations and International Law*. Cambridge: Cambridge University Press, 1997.

Joyner, Christopher C. "Arresting Impunity: The Case for Universal Jurisdiction in Bringing War Criminals to Accountability." *Law and Contemporary Problems* Vol. 59 No. 4 (1996): 153–172.

Joyner, Christopher C. "Collective Sanctions as Peaceful Coercion: Lessons from the United Nations Experience." *Australian Year Book of International Law* Vol. 16 (1995): 241–270.

Joyner, Christopher C. "Enforcing Human Rights Standards in the Former Yugoslavia: The Case for an International War Crimes Tribunal." *Denver Journal of International Law and Policy* Vol. 22 No. 2/3 (1994): 235–274.

Kaempfer, William H. and Anton D. Lowenberg. *International Economic Sanctions: A Public Choice Approach.* Boulder: Westview Press, 1992.

Kastrup, Dieter. "From Nuremberg to Rome and Beyond: The Fight against Genocide, War Crimes, and Crimes against Humanity." *Fordham International Law Journal* Vol. 23 No. 2 (1999): 404–414.

Keen, David. *The Economic Functions of Violence in Civil Wars.* Adelphi Paper. Oxford: Oxford University Press, 1998.

Kerr, Rachel. "International Judicial Intervention: The International Criminal Tribunal for the Former Yugoslavia." *International Relations* Vol. 15 No. 2 (2000): 17–26.

Kirshner, Jonathan. *Currency and Coercion: The Political Economy of International Monetary Power.* Princeton: Princeton University Press, 1995.

Klip, André and Göran Sluiter, eds. *Annotated Leading Cases of International Criminal Tribunals. Vol. 2: The International Criminal Tribunal for Rwanda 1994–1999.* Antwerpen: Intersentia, 2001.

Klip, André and Göran Sluiter, eds. *Annotated Leading Cases of International Criminal Tribunals. Vol. 1: The International Criminal Tribunal for the Former Yugoslavia 1993–1998.* Antwerpen: Intersentia, 1999.

Kritz, Neil J. "Coming to Terms with Atrocities: A Review of Accountability Mechanisms for Mass Violations of Human Rights." *Law and Contemporary Problems* Vol. 59 (1996): 127.

Kunz, Josef L. "Sanctions in International Law." *American Journal of International Law* Vol. 54 No. 2 (1960): 324–347.

Lamb, Susan. "The Powers of Arrest of the International Criminal Tribunal for the Former Yugoslavia." In *The British Year Book of International Law 1999,* edited by James Crawford and Vaughan Lowe, 1–63. Oxford: Clarendon Press, 2000.

Landsman, Stephan. "Alternative Responses to Serious Human Rights Abuses: Of Prosecution and Trust Commissions." *Law and Contemporary Problems* Vol. 59 No. 4 (1996): 81–92.

Lavin, Franklin. "Asphyxiation or Oxygen? The Sanctions Dilemma." *Foreign Policy* No. 104 (1996): 139–154.

Lenway, Stefanie Ann. "Between War and Commerce: Economic Sanctions as a Tool of Statecraft." *International Organization* Vol. 42 No. 2 (1988): 397–426.

Lescure, Karine and Florence Trintignac. *Une justice internationale pour l'ex-Yugoslavie: mode d'emploi du Tribunal pénal international de La Haye.* Paris: L'Harmattan, 1994.

Leyton-Brown, David, ed. *The Utility of International Economic Sanctions.* New York: St. Martin's Press, 1987.

Li, Chien-Pin. "The Effectiveness of Sanctions Linkages: Issues and Actors." *International Studies Quarterly* Vol. 37 (1993): 349–370.

Lindsay, James. "Trade Sanctions as Policy Instruments: A Re-Examination." *International Studies Quarterly* Vol. 30 (1986): 153–173.

Lopez, George A. and David Cortright. "Economic Sanctions and Human Rights: Part of the Problem or Part of the Solution?" *International Journal of Human Rights* Vol. 1 No. 2 (1997): 1–25.

Losman, Donald L. *International Economic Sanctions: The Cases of Cuba, Israel, and Rhodesia.* Albuquerque: University of New Mexico Press, 1979.

Mack, Andrew and Asif Khan. "The Efficacy of UN Sanctions." *Security Dialogue* Vol. 31 No. 3 (2000): 279–292.

Malloy, Michael P. "The Many Faces of Economic Sanctions." *Global Dialogue* Vol. 2 No. 3 (2000): 1–10.

Mansfield, Edward D. "International Institutions and Economic Sanctions." *World Politics* Vol. 47 No. 4 (1995): 575–605.

Marks, Stephen P. "Economic Sanctions as Human Rights Violations: Reconciling Political and Public Health Imperatives." *American Journal of Public Health* Vol. 89 No. 10 (1999): 1509–1513.

Martin, Lisa L. and Jeff Laurenti. *The United Nations and Economic Sanctions.* New York: United Nations Association, 1997.

Mayall, James. "The Sanctions Problem in International Economic Relations: Reflections in the Light of Recent Experience." *International Affairs* Vol. 60 No. 4 (1984): 631–642.

McCormack, Timothy L. H. and Gerry J. Simpson, eds. *The Law of War Crimes: National and International Approaches.* The Hague: Kluwer Law International, 1997.

McCoubrey, Hilaire. "From Nuremberg to Rome: Restoring the Defence of Superior Orders." *International and Comparative Law Quarterly* Vol. 50 No. 2 (2001): 386–393.

McWhinney, E. "The Role and Mission of the International Court in an Era of Historic Transition." In *Perspectives on International Law,* edited by Nandasiri Jasentuliyana, 217–273. London: Kluwer Law International, 1995.

Meier Wang, Mariann. "The International Tribunal for Rwanda: Opportunities for Clarification, Opportunities for Impact." *Columbia Human Rights Law Review* Vol. 27 No. 1 (1995): 177–226.

Méndez, Juan E. "National Reconciliation, Transnational Justice, and the International Criminal Court." *Ethics and International Affairs* Vol. 15 (2001): 25–44.

Meron, Theodor. "Is International Law Moving towards Criminalization?" *European Journal of International Law* Vol. 9 No. 1 (1998): 18–31.

Meron, Theodor. "International Criminalization of Internal Atrocities." *American Journal of International Law* Vol. 89 No. 3 (1995): 554–577.

Meron, Theodor. "The Case for War Crimes Trials in Yugoslavia." *Foreign Affairs* Vol. 72 No. 3 (1993): 122–135.

Miller, Judith. "When Sanctions Worked." *Foreign Policy* No. 39 (1980): 118–129.

Minear, Larry, David Cortright, Julia Wagler, George A. Lopez and Thomas G. Weiss. *Toward More Humane and Effective Sanctions Management: Enhancing the Capacity of the United Nations System.* New York: UN Department of Humanitarian Affairs, 1997.

Minear, Richard H. *Victor's Justice: The Tokyo War Crimes Trial.* Princeton: Princeton University Press, 1971.

Minow, Martha, ed. *Between Vengeance and Forgiveness: Facing History after Genocide and Mass Violence.* Boston: Beacon Press, 1998.

Miyagawa, Makio. *Do Economic Sanctions Work?* New York: St. Martin's Press, 1992.

Morgan, T. Clifton and Valerie L. Schwebach. "Fools Suffer Gladly: The Use of Economic Sanctions in International Crises." *International Studies Quarterly* Vol. 41 No. 1 (1997): 27–50.

Morris, Madeline H. "High Crimes and Misconceptions: The ICC and Non-Party States." *Law and Contemporary Problems* Vol. 64 No. 1 (2001): 13–66.

Morris, Madeline H. "The Trials of Concurrent Jurisdiction: The Case of Rwanda." *Duke Journal of Comparative and International Law* Vol. 7 No. 2 (1997): 349.

Morris, Virginia and Michael P. Scharf. *The International Criminal Tribunal for Rwanda*. 2 vols. Irvington-on-Hudson: Transnational Publishers, 1998.

Morris, Virginia and Michael P. Scharf. *An Insider's Guide to the International Criminal Tribunal for the Former Yugoslavia*. Irvington-on-Hudson: Transnational Publishers, 1995.

Mubiala, Mutoy. "Le Tribunal international pour le Rwanda." *African Journal of International and Comparative Law* Vol. 7 No. 3 (1995): 610–619.

Mucor, Daryl A. "Improving the Operation and Functioning of the International Criminal Tribunals." *American Journal of International Law* Vol. 94 No. 4 (2000): 759–773.

Murphy, Sean D. "Progress and Jurisprudence of the International Criminal Tribunal for the Former Yugoslavia." *American Journal of International Law* Vol. 93 No. 1 (1999): 57–97.

Neier, Aryeh. *War Crimes: Brutality, Genocide, Terror, and the Struggle for Justice*. New York: Times Books, 1998.

Nelson, Joan M. and Stephanie J. Eglinton. *Encouraging Democracy: What Role for Conditioned Aid?* Washington, DC: Overseas Development Council, 1992.

Newman, Frank C. "Non-Military Intervention by International and Regional Organizations in Armed Conflict." *Georgia Journal of International and Comparative Law* Vol. 13 (1983): 341–433.

Nincic, Miroslav and Peter Wallensteen, eds. *Dilemmas of Economic Coercion: Sanctions in World Politics*. New York: Praeger, 1983.

Nossal, Kim Richard. "International Sanctions as International Punishment." *International Organization* Vol. 43 No. 2 (1989): 301–322.

Olson, Richard Stuart. "Economic Coercion in World Politics: With a Focus on North–South Relations." *World Politics* Vol. 31 (1979): 471–494.

Orford, Anne. "Locating the International: Military and Monetary Interventions after the Cold War." *Harvard International Law Journal* Vol. 38 No. 2 (1997): 443–485.

Paust, Jordan J. "Applicability of International Criminal Laws to Events in the Former Yugoslavia." *American University Journal of International Law and Policy* Vol. 9 No. 2 (1994): 499–525.

Pella, Vespasian V. "Towards an International Criminal Court." *American Journal of International Law* Vol. 44 No. 1 (1950): 37–68.

Pellet, Alain. "Can a State Commit a Crime? Definitely, Yes!" *European Journal of International Law* Vol. 10 No. 2 (1999): 425–434.

Pellet, Alain. "Le Tribunal criminel international pour l'ex-Yougoslavie: poudre aux yeux ou avancée décisive?" *Révue Générale de Droit International Public* Vol. 98 (1994): 7–60.

Perera, Rohan. "Towards the Establishment of an International Criminal Court." *Commonwealth Law Bulletin* Vol. 20 (1994): 298.

Pfaff, William. "Judging War Crimes." *Survival* Vol. 42 No. 1 (2000): 46–58.

Philpot, John. "Le Tribunal pénal international pour le Rwanda: la justice trahie." *Études Internationales* Vol. 27 No. 4 (1996): 827–840.

Politi, Mauro and Giuseppe Nesi, eds. *The Rome Statute of the International Criminal Court: A Challenge to Impunity*. Aldershot: Ashgate, 2001.

Pollins, Brian M. "Cannons and Capital: The Use of Coercive Diplomacy by Major Powers in the Twentieth Century." In *Reconstructing Realpolitik*, edited by Frank W. Wayman and Paul F. Diehl, 29–54. Ann Arbor: University of Michigan Press, 1994.

Popovski, Vesselin. "International Criminal Court: A Necessary Step towards Global Justice." *Security Dialogue* Vol. 31 No. 4 (2000): 405–419.

Renwick, Robin. *Economic Sanctions*. Cambridge, MA: Harvard University Center for International Affairs, 1981.

*Report of the Panel of Experts on Violations of Security Council Sanctions against UNITA* (2000): http://www.un.org/News/dh/latest/angolareport_eng.htm

Robertson, Geoffrey. *Crimes against Humanity: The Struggle for Global Justice.* London: Penguin, 1999.

Rogers, Elizabeth S. "Using Economic Sanctions to Control Regional Conflicts." *Security Studies* Vol. 5 No. 4 (1996): 43–72.

*Rome Statute of the International Criminal Court* (July 17, 1998): http://www.un.org/law/icc/statute/romefra.htm

Roth, Brad R. "Peaceful Transition and Retrospective Justice: Some Reservations: A Response to Juan E. Méndez." *Ethics and International Affairs* Vol. 15 (2001): 45–50.

Rottensteiner, Christa. "The Denial of Humanitarian Assistance as a Crime under International Law." *International Review of the Red Cross* Vol. 81 No. 835 (1999): 555–581.

Rubin, Alfred P. "The International Criminal Court: Possibilities for Prosecutorial Abuse." *Law and Contemporary Problems* Vol. 64 No. 1 (2001): 153–166.

Schabas, William A. *Genocide in International Law: The Crime of Crimes.* Cambridge: Cambridge University Press, 2000.

Schabas, William A. "Sentencing by International Tribunals." *Duke Journal of Comparative and International Law* Vol. 7 No. 2 (1997): 461.

Scharf, Michael P. "The ICC's Jurisdiction over the Nationals of Non-Party States: A Critique of the US Position." *Law and Contemporary Problems* Vol. 64 No. 1 (2001): 67–118.

Scharf, Michael P. *Balkan Justice: The Story behind the First International War Crimes Trial since Nuremberg.* Durham: Carolina Academic Press, 1997.

Scharf, Michael P. "The Letter of the Law: The Scope of the International Legal Obligation to Prosecute Human Rights Crimes." *Law and Contemporary Problems* Vol. 59 No. 4 (1996): 41–61.

Scheffer, David J. "International Judicial Intervention." *Foreign Policy* No. 102 (1996): 34–51.

Schoultz, Lars. *Human Rights and United States Policy towards Latin America.* Princeton: Princeton University Press, 1981.

Schuett, Olivier. "The International War Crimes Tribunal for the Former Yugoslavia and the Dayton Peace Agreement: Peace versus Justice?" *International Peacekeeping* Vol. 4 No. 2 (1997): 91–114.

Segall, Anna. "Economic Sanctions: Legal and Policy Constraints." *International Review of the Red Cross* Vol. 81 No. 836 (1999): 763–783.

Shraga, Daphna and Ralph Zacklin. "The International Criminal Tribunal for Rwanda." *European Journal of International Law* Vol. 7 No. 4 (1996): 501–518.

Shraga, Daphna and Ralph Zacklin. "The International Criminal Tribunal for the Former Yugoslavia." *European Journal of International Law* Vol. 5 No. 3 (1994): 360–380.

Simons, Geoff. *Imposing Economic Sanctions: Legal Remedy or Genocidal Tool?* London: Pluto Press, 1999.

Skogly, Sigrun I. "Structural Adjustment and Development: Human Rights – An Agenda for Change." *Human Rights Quarterly* Vol. 15 No. 4 (1993): 751–778.

Smith, Alistair. "The Success and Use of Economic Sanctions." *International Interactions* Vol. 21 No. 3 (1996): 229–245.

*Statute of the International Court of Justice:* http://www.icj-cij.org/icjwww/ibasicdocuments/ibasictext/ibasicstatute.htm

*Statute of the International Criminal Tribunal for Rwanda Annexed to SC Resolution 955* (1994): http://www.ictr.org/

*Statute of the International Criminal Tribunal for the Former Yugoslavia ADOPTED 25 MAY 1993 by Resolution 827 (AMENDED 13 MAY 1998 by Resolution 1166, and AMENDED 30 NOVEMBER 2000 by Resolution 1329)*: http://www.un.org/icty/basic/statut/stat2000_con.htm

Stohl, Michael, David Carleton and Steven Johnson. "Human Rights and US Foreign Assistance from Nixon to Carter." *Journal of Peace Research* Vol. 21 (1984): 215–226.

Stremlau, John. *Sharpening International Sanctions: Toward a Stronger Role for the United Nations.* Washington, DC: Carnegie Commission on Preventing Deadly Conflict, 1996.

Stroun, Jacques. "Juridiction pénale internationale, droit international humanitaire et action humanitaire." *International Review of the Red Cross* Vol. 79 No. 828 (1997): 665–676.

Swiss Federal Office for Foreign Economic Affairs. *2nd Interlaken Seminar on Targeting United Nations Financial Sanctions 29–31 March 1999.* Interlaken: SFOFEA in cooperation with the United Nations Secretariat, 1999.

Swiss Federal Office for Foreign Economic Affairs, Department of Economy. *Expert Seminar on Targeting UN Financial Sanctions March 17–19, 1998.* Interlaken: SFOFEA, Department of Economy, 1998.

Taylor, Telford. *The Anatomy of the Nuremberg Trials: A Personal Memoir.* London: Bloomsbury, 1993.

Thakur, Ramesh. "Sanctions: A Triumph of Hope Eternal over Experience Unlimited." *Global Dialogue* Vol. 2 No. 3 (2000): 129–141.

Thornberry, Cedric. "Saving the War Crimes Tribunal." *Foreign Policy* No. 104 (1996): 72–85.

Thune, Henrik, ed. *The Sanctions Debate: UN Sanctions in the 1990s.* Oslo: Norwegian Institute of International Affairs, 2000.

Urbina, Julio Jorge. "La protection des personnes civiles au pouvoir de l'ennemi et l'établissement d'une juridiction pénale internationale." *International Review of the Red Cross* Vol. 82 No. 840 (2000): 857–885.

Van Brabant, Koenraad. *Sanctions: The Current Debate: A Summary of Selected Readings.* London: Overseas Development Institute, 1999.

Volcansek, Mary L. *Law above Nations: Supranational Courts and the Legalization of Politics.* Gainesville: University Press of Florida, 1997.

Wallensteen, Peter. *A Century of Economic Sanctions: A Field Revisited.* Uppsala: Department of Peace and Conflict Research, Uppsala University, 2000.

Wallensteen, Peter. "Characteristics of Economic Sanctions." *Journal of Peace Research* Vol. 5 (1968): 248–267.

Warbrick, Colin. "The United Nations System: A Place for Criminal Courts?" *Transnational Law and Contemporary Problems* Vol. 5 No. 2 (1995): 237–262.

Waxman, Matthew C. "Coalitions and Limits on Coercive Diplomacy." *Strategic Review* Vol. 25 No. 1 (1997).

Wedgwood, Ruth. "War Crimes in the Former Yugoslavia: Comments on the International War Crimes Tribunal." *Virginia Journal of International Law* Vol. 34 No. 2 (1994): 267–275.

Weiss, Thomas G., David Cortright, George A. Lopez and Larry Minear, eds. *Political Gain and Civilian Pain: Humanitarian Impacts of Economic Sanctions.* Lanham: Rowman and Littlefield, 1997.

White, H. and O. Morrissey. "Conditionality When Donor and Recipient Preferences Vary." *Journal of International Development* Vol. 9 No. 4 (1997): 497–505.

Zarif, M. Javad and Saeid Mirazee. "US Unilateral Sanctions against Iran." *Iranian Journal of International Affairs* Vol. 9 (1997): 1–20.

# 9. OPERATIONAL ASPECTS OF MILITARY INTERVENTIONS

Berdal, Mats. *Whither UN Peacekeeping? An Analysis of the Changing Military Requirements of UN Peacekeeping with Proposals for Its Enhancement.* Adelphi Paper. London: Brassey's for the International Institute for Strategic Studies, 1993.
Argues that the distinction between peacekeeping and peace enforcement should be maintained. Analyzes options for strengthening the capacity of UN peacekeeping.

Durch, William J., ed. *UN Peacekeeping, American Politics, and the Uncivil Wars of the 1990s.* Basingstoke: Macmillan, 1997.
Case studies examining international military operations by the UN in the 1990s. Particular attention is given to US support and influence.

Feil, Scott R. *Preventing Genocide: How the Early Use of Force Might Have Succeeded in Rwanda.* Washington, DC: Carnegie Commission on Preventing Deadly Conflict, 1998.
Suggests that the rapid introduction of robust combat forces could have made a significant difference in Rwanda in April 1994.

Findlay, Trevor, ed. *Challenges for the New Peacekeepers.* Oxford: Oxford University Press, 1996.
Focuses on the political and constitutional challenges and experiences faced by states in the wake of their first participation in peacekeeping operations. Attention is also given to NATO and the Organization for Security and Co-operation in Europe as actual and potential new peacekeepers.

Goulding, Marrack. "The Evolution of United Nations Peacekeeping." *International Affairs* Vol. 69 No. 3 (1993): 451–464.
Analyzes what peacekeeping had become by the time the Cold War ended, classifies the various types of peacekeeping operations, and discusses the trend from peacekeeping to peace enforcement.

Mackinlay, John, ed. *A Guide to Peace Support Operations.* Providence: Thomas J. Watson Jr. Institute for International Studies, 1996.
Essays by practitioners about the challenges of multifunctional peace operations, including military forces, civilian police, and political and humanitarian actors.

Mayall, James, ed. *The New Interventionism 1991–1994: United Nations Experience in Cambodia, Former Yugoslavia and Somalia.* Cambridge: Cambridge University Press, 1996.
Early account of the move to interventionism in the 1990s. Concludes that there has been no structural change in the nature of international relations to allow humanitarian interventions.

Oakley, Robert B., Michael J. Dziedzic and Eliot M. Goldberg, eds. *Policing the New World Disorder: Peace Operations and Public Security.* Washington, DC: National Defense University Press, 1998.
Addresses the police functions in peace operations and draws attention to the importance of rebuilding feasible law enforcement capabilities for their success.

O'Hanlon, Michael. *Saving Lives with Force: Military Criteria for Humanitarian Intervention.* Washington, DC: Brookings Institution, 1997.
Military analysis of recent US interventions. Stresses that interventions require substantial efforts and involve considerable risks.

Ratner, Steven. *The New UN Peacekeeping: Building Peace in Lands of Conflict after the Cold War.* New York: St. Martin's Press, 1995.
Study of multidimensional peace operations and their political, historical, and legal basis, with special reference to Cambodia. Sees the UN as an administrator, mediator, and guarantor of political settlements.

*Report of the Panel on United Nations Peace Operations.* New York: United Nations, 2000.
> UN report on improving military operations. Argues that the UN should continue to focus on peacekeeping as traditionally understood, avoiding operations that require the robust use of force.

Thakur, Ramesh and Carlyle A. Thayer, eds. *A Crisis of Expectations: UN Peacekeeping in the 1990s.* Boulder: Westview, 1995.
> Provides case studies of the major UN peacekeeping operations and analyzes conceptual questions stemming from changes in UN peacekeeping.

Tharoor, Shashi. "Should UN Peacekeeping Go 'Back to Basics'?" *Survival* Vol. 37 No. 4 (1995–1996): 52–64.
> Account of multidimensional peacekeeping, arguing that success depends on a clear distinction between peacekeeping and peace enforcement.

## References

Adams, Paul D. "Rules of Engagement: Friend or Foe." *Marine Corps Gazette* Vol. 77 No. 10 (1993): 21–23.

Amer, Ramses. "The United Nations' Reactions to Foreign Military Interventions." *Journal of Peace Research* Vol. 31 No. 4 (1994): 425–444.

Andersson, Andreas. "Democracies and UN Peacekeeping Operations, 1990–1996." *International Peacekeeping* Vol. 7 No. 2 (2000): 1–22.

Annan, Kofi A. *"We the Peoples": The Role of the United Nations in the Twenty-First Century: Report of the Secretary-General to the Fifty-Fourth Session.* Geneva: United Nations, 2000.

Annan, Kofi A. "Peace-Keeping in Situations of Civil War." *New York University Journal of International Law and Politics* Vol. 26 No. 4 (1994): 623–631.

Arias, Inociencio F. "Humanitarian Intervention: Could the Security Council Kill the United Nations?" *Fordham International Law Journal* Vol. 23 No. 4 (2000): 1005–1027.

Barnes, Rudolph C. *Military Legitimacy: Might and Right in the New Millennium.* London: Frank Cass, 1996.

Berdal, Mats. "Boutros-Ghali's Ambiguous Legacy." *Survival* Vol. 4 No. 3 (1999): 172–181.

Berkowitz, Bruce D. "Rules of Engagement for UN Peacekeeping Forces in Bosnia." *Orbis* Vol. 38 No. 3 (1994): 635–646.

Berman, Eric and Katie Sams. *Peacekeeping in Africa: Capabilities and Culpabilities.* New York: United Nations, 2000.

Bettati, Mario. "L'ONU et l'action humanitaire." *Politique Étrangère* Vol. 58 No. 3 (1993): 641–658.

Biermann, Wolfgang, ed. *UN Peacekeeping in Trouble: Lessons Learned from the Former Yugoslavia.* Aldershot: Ashgate, 1998.

Boulden, Jane. *Peace Enforcement: The United Nations Experience in Congo, Somalia, and Bosnia.* Westport: Praeger, 2001.

Boutros-Ghali, Boutros. *Unvanquished: A US–UN Saga.* London: I.B. Tauris, 1999.

Brady, Christopher and Sam Daws. "United Nations Operations: The Political–Military Interface." *International Peacekeeping* Vol. 1 No. 1 (1994): 59–79.

Chayes, Abram and Antonia Handler Chayes. *Planning for Intervention: International Cooperation in Conflict Management.* The Hague: Kluwer Law International, 1999.

Cohen, Ben and George Stamksoki, eds. *With No Peace to Keep ... United Nations Peacekeeping and the War in the Former Yugoslavia.* London: Grainpress Ltd., 1995.

Collins, Cindy and Thomas G. Weiss. *An Overview and Assessment of 1989–1996 Peace Operations Publications.* Providence: Thomas J. Watson Jr. Institute for International Studies, 1997.

Connaughton, Richard M. *Peacekeeping and Military Intervention*. London: Her Majesty's Stationery Office, 1992.

Curtis, Willie. "The Inevitable Slide into Coercive Peacekeeping." *Defense Analysis* Vol. 10 No. 3 (1994): 305–321.

Damrosch, Lori Fisler. "The Role of the Great Powers in United Nations Peace-Keeping." *Yale Journal of International Law* Vol. 18 No. 1 (1993): 429–434.

Daniel, Donald C.F. and Bradd C. Hayes, eds. *Beyond Traditional Peacekeeping*. New York: St. Martin's Press, 1995.

Davis, Lynn E. *Peacekeeping and Peacemaking after the Cold War*. Santa Monica: RAND, 1993.

Day, Arthur D. and Michael W. Doyle, eds. *Escalation and Intervention: Multilateral Security and Its Alternatives*. Boulder: Westview Press, 1986.

Dedring, Jürgen. *Humanitarian Intervention by the United Nations*. New York: United Nations Department for Humanitarian Affairs, 1994.

Diehl, Paul F., Jennifer Reifschneider and Paul R. Hensel. "United Nations Intervention and Recurring Conflict." *International Organization* Vol. 50 No. 4 (1996): 683–700.

Diehl, Paul F. *International Peacekeeping*. Baltimore: The Johns Hopkins University Press, 1993.

Doel, Mark T. "Military Assistance in Humanitarian Aid Operations: Impossible Paradox or Inevitable Development." *RUSI Journal* Vol. 140 No. 5 (1995): 26–32.

Doll, William R. and Steven Metz. *The Army and Multinational Peace Operations: Problems and Solutions*. Carlisle Barracks: Strategic Studies Institute, 1993.

Donini, Antonio. *UN Coordination in Complex Emergencies: Lessons from Afghanistan, Mozambique and Rwanda*. Providence: Thomas J. Watson Jr. Institute for International Studies, 1996.

Doyle, Michael W., Ian Johnstone and Robert C. Orr, eds. *Keeping the Peace: Multidimensional UN Operations in Cambodia and El Salvador*. Cambridge: Cambridge University Press, 1997.

Driscoll, R.F. "'Partnership for Peace' and European Peacekeeping Operations: A Step Backwards." *European Security* Vol. 3 No. 4 (1994): 691–710.

Duffey, Tamara. "Cultural Issues in Contemporary Peacekeeping." *International Peacekeeping* Vol. 7 No. 1 (2000): 142–168.

Durch, William J., ed. *The Evolution of UN Peacekeeping: Case Studies and Comparative Analysis*. New York: St. Martin's Press, 1993.

Dworken, Jonathan T. "Rules of Engagement: Lessons from Restore Hope." *Military Review* Vol. 74 No. 9 (1994): 26–34.

Dworken, Jonathan T. "What's So Special about Humanitarian Operations?" *Comparative Strategy* Vol. 13 No. 4 (1994): 391–399.

Dworken, Jonathan T. *Military Relations with Humanitarian Relief Organizations: Observations from Restore Hope*. Alexandria: Center for Naval Analyses, 1993.

Dworken, Jonathan T. *Rules of Engagement (ROE) for Humanitarian Intervention and Low-Intensity Conflict: Lessons from Restore Hope*. Alexandria: Center for Naval Analyses, 1993.

Eriksson, Pär. "Civil–Military Co-ordination in Peace Support Operations: An Impossible Necessity?" *Journal of Humanitarian Assistance* (September 2000): http://www.jha.ac/articles/a061.htm

Ero, Comfort and Suzanne Long. "Humanitarian Intervention: A New Role for the United Nations?" *International Peacekeeping* Vol. 2 No. 2 (1995): 140–156.

Eyadema, Gnassingbe. "La force d'interposition africaine." *Défense Nationale* Vol. 55 No. 2 (1999): 5–9.

Ezejiofor, Edward Kofi and Quashigah. "The United Nations and Humanitarian Intervention in the Contemporary World Situation." *ASICL Proceedings*. Vol. 5 (1993): 36–63.

Fermann, Gunnar. *Bibliography on International Peacekeeping*. Dordrecht: Martinus Nijhoff, 1992.

Ferris, Elizabeth, ed. *The Challenge to Intervene: A New Role for the United Nations?* Uppsala: Life and Peace Institute, 1992.

Fetherston, A.B. *Towards a Theory of United Nations Peacekeeping*. Basingstoke: Macmillan, 1994.

Fisas, Vicenç. *Blue Geopolitics: The United Nations Reform and the Future of the Blue Helmets*. London: Pluto Press, 1995.

Freedman, Paul. "International Intervention to Combat the Explosion of Refugees and Internally Displaced Persons." *Georgetown Immigration Law Journal* Vol. 9 No. 3 (1995): 565–601.

Galen Carpenter, Ted, ed. *Delusions of Grandeur: The United Nations and Global Intervention*. Washington, DC: Cato Institute, 1997.

Gilpin, Michael D. *Exit Strategy: The New Dimension in Operational Planning*. Carlisle Barracks: US Army War College, 1997.

Goodpaster, Andrew J. *When Diplomacy Is Not Enough: Managing Multinational Military Intervention*. Washington, DC: Carnegie Commission on Preventing Deadly Conflict, 1996.

Gordon, Ruth. "Humanitarian Intervention by the United Nations: Iraq, Somalia, and Haiti." *Texas International Law Journal* Vol. 31 No. 1 (1996): 43–56.

Gordon, Stuart. "Understanding the Priorities for Civil–Military Co-operation (CIMIC)." *Journal of Humanitarian Assistance* (July 2001): http://www.jha.ac/articles/a068.htm

Goulding, Marrack. "The United Nations and Conflict in Africa since the Cold-War." *African Affairs* Vol. 98 No. 391 (1999): 155–166.

Goulding, Marrack. "The Use of Force by the United Nations." *International Peacekeeping* Vol. 3 No. 1 (1996): 1–18.

Gourlay, Catriona. "Partners Apart: Managing Civil–Military Cooperation in Humanitarian Interventions." *Disarmament Forum* Vol. 3 (2000): 33–44.

Grey, Robert T. "Strengthening the United Nations to Implement the Agenda for Peace." *Strategic Review* Vol. 21 No. 3 (1993): 20–32.

Grove, Eric. "United Nations Armed Forces and the Military Staff Committee." *International Security* Vol. 17 No. 4 (1993): 172–182.

Henkin, Alice H., ed. *Honoring Human Rights: From Peace to Justice*. Washington, DC: Aspen Institute, 1998.

Hillen, John F. "Policing the New World Order: The Operational Utility of a Permanent United Nations Army." *Strategic Review* Vol. 22 No. 2 (1994): 54–62.

Hillen, John F. "United Nations Collective Security: Chapter Six and a Half." *Parameters* Vol. 24 No. 1 (1994): 27–37.

Hippolyte, Muyingi. "L'intervention des Nations Unies." *Revue Française de Science Politique* Vol. 19 No. 2 (1969): 444–458.

Human Rights Watch. *The Lost Agenda: Human Rights and UN Field Operations*. New York: HRW, 1993.

International Peacekeeping. "Special Issue: Managing Armed Conflicts in the 21st Century." Vol. 7 No. 4 (2000).

International Peacekeeping. "Special Issue: Peacekeeping and Conflict Resolution." Vol. 7 No. 1 (2000).

International Peacekeeping. "Special Issue: The UN, Peace and Force." Vol. 3 No. 4 (1996).

Jablonsky, David and James S. McCallum. "Peace Implementation and the Concept of Induced Consent in Peace Operations." *Parameters* Vol. 29 No. 1 (1999): 54–70.

Jakobsen, Peter Viggo. "Overload, Not Marginalization, Threatens UN Peacekeeping." *Security Dialogue* Vol. 31 No. 2 (2000): 167–178.

Jakobsen, Peter Viggo. "The Emerging Consensus on Grey Area Peace Operations Doctrine: Will It Last and Enhance Operational Effectiveness?" *International Peacekeeping* Vol. 7 No. 3 (2000): 36–56.

James, Alan. *Peacekeeping in International Politics*. Basingstoke: Macmillan in association with the International Institute for Strategic Studies, 1990.

James, Alan. *The Politics of Peacekeeping*. London: Chatto and Windus, 1969.

Jones, Peter and Bradley Runions. *Peacekeeping: An Annotated Bibliography – Volume II*. Clementsport: Canadian Peacekeeping Press, 1999.

Klein, Pierre. "La protection de l'assistance humanitaire: un nouveau mandat pour les forces des Nations Unies." *Revue Québécoise de Droit International* Vol. 8 No. 1 (1993/1994): 95–102.

Knight, W. Andy. "Towards a Subsidiarity Model for Peacemaking and Preventive Diplomacy: Making Chapter VIII of the UN Charter Operational." *Third World Quarterly* Vol. 17 No. 1 (1996): 31–52.

Lake, David A. and Donald Rothchild. *Ethnic Fears and Global Engagement: The International Spread and Management of Ethnic Conflict*. La Jolla: Institute on Global Conflict and Cooperation, 1996.

Landgren, Karin. "Safety Zones and International Protection: A Dark Grey Area." *International Journal of Refugee Law* Vol. 7 No. 3 (1995): 436–458.

Leurdijk, Dick A. "Rapid Deployment: A Capacity Gap." In *Reflections on International Law from the Low Countries in Honour of Paul de Waart*, edited by Erik Denters, Nico Schrijver, and J.I.M Paul de Waart, 301–314. The Hague: Martinus Nijhoff, 1998.

Leurdijk, Henk J. "Proposals for Increasing Rapid Deployment Capacity: A Survey." *International Peacekeeping* Vol. 2 No. 1 (1995): 1–10.

Luttwak, Edward N. "From Vietnam to Desert Fox: Civil–Military Relations in Modern Democracies." *Survival* Vol. 41 No. 1 (1999): 99–112.

Luttwak, Edward N. "Give War a Chance." *Foreign Affairs* Vol. 78 No. 4 (1999): 36–44.

MacFarlane, S. Neil, ed. *Peacekeeping at a Crossroads*. Cornwallis: Canadian Peacekeeping Press, 1997.

MacKenzie, Lewis. "Military Realities of UN Peacekeeping Operations." *RUSI Journal* Vol. 138 No. 1 (1993): 21–24.

Mackinlay, John. "Improving Multifunctional Forces." *Survival* Vol. 36 No. 3 (1994): 149–173.

Mackinlay, John and Jarat Chopra. "Second Generation Multinational Operations." *Washington Quarterly* Vol. 15 No. 3 (1992): 113–131.

MacKinnon, Michael J. *The Evolution of US Peacekeeping Policy under Clinton: A Fairweather Friend?* London: Frank Cass, 2000.

Malan, Mark, ed. *Boundaries of Peace Support Operations: The African Dimension*. Johannesburg: Institute for Security Studies, 2000.

Malan, Mark. "Peacekeeping in the New Millennium: 'Fourth Generation' Peace Operations?" *African Security Review* Vol. 7 No. 3 (1998): 13–20.

Malan, Mark. "A Concise Conceptual History of UN Peace Operations." *African Security Review* Vol. 6 No. 1 (1997): 16–27.

Malan, Mark and C. Lord, eds. *Prague to Pretoria: Towards a Global Consensus on the Military Doctrine of Peace Support Operations*. Prague: Institute of International Relations, 2000.

Manwaring, Max G. and John T. Fishel, eds. *Toward Responsibility in the New World Disorder: Challenges and Lessons of Peace Operations*. London: Frank Cass, 1998.

Martin, Laurence. "Peacekeeping as a Growth Industry." *The National Interest* No. 32 (1993): 3–11.

Mazarr, Michael J. "The Military Dilemmas of Humanitarian Intervention." *Security Dialogue* Vol. 24 No. 2 (1993): 151–162.

McCarthy, Patrick A. "Building a Reliable Rapid-Reaction Capability for the United Nations." *International Peacekeeping* Vol. 7 No. 2 (2000): 139–154.

McDermott, Anthony. "The UN and NGOs: Humanitarian Interventions in Future Conflicts." *Contemporary Security Policy* Vol. 19 No. 3 (1998): 1–26.

Morozov, G. "Mirotvorchestvo I Prinuzhdenie k Miru." Mirovaya Ekonomika i Mezhdunarodnye Otnoshenia No. 2 (1999): 60–69.

Nathan, James. "On Coercive Statecraft: 'The New Strategy' and the American Foreign Affairs Experience." *International Relations* Vol. 12 No. 6 (1995): 1–30.

O'Brien, David. "The Search for Subsidiarity: The UN, African Regional Organizations and Humanitarian Action." *International Peacekeeping* Vol. 7 No. 3 (2000): 57–83.

Otunnu, Olara A. "Préserver la légitimité de l'action des Nations Unies." *Politique Étrangère* Vol. 58 No. 3 (1993): 597–610.

Otunnu, Olara A. and Michael W. Doyle, eds. *Peacemaking and Peacekeeping for the New Century.* Lanham: Rowman and Littlefield, 1998.

Parsons, Anthony. *From Cold War to Hot Peace: UN Interventions, 1947–1994.* London: Michael Joseph, 1995.

Patman, Robert G. "Disarming Somalia: The Contrasting Fortunes of United States and Australian Peacekeeping during United Nations Intervention, 1992–1993." *African Affairs* Vol. 96 No. 385 (1997): 509–533.

Pearson, Frederic S. and Robert Baumann. "Towards a Regional Model of International Military Intervention: The Middle Eastern Experience." *Arms Control* Vol. 4 (1983): 187–222.

Pirnie, Bruce R. and William E. Simons. *Soldiers for Peace: Critical Operational Issues.* Santa Monica: RAND National Defense Research Institute, 1996.

Popovski, Vesselin. "UN Security Council: Rethinking Humanitarian Intervention and the Veto." *Security Dialogue* Vol. 31 No. 2 (2000): 249–252.

Posen, Barry R. "Military Responses to Refugee Disasters." *International Security* Vol. 21 No. 1 (1996): 72–111.

Pugh, Michael. *From Mission Cringe to Mission Creep? Implications of New Peace Support Operations Doctrine.* Oslo: Institut for Forsvarsstudier, 1997.

Pugh, Michael. "Peacekeeping and Humanitarian Intervention." In *Issues in World Politics,* edited by B. White et al., 134–156. Basingstoke: Macmillan, 1997.

Pugh, Michael, ed. *The UN, Peace and Force.* London: Frank Cass, 1997.

Rivlin, Benjamin and Leon Gordenker, eds. *The Challenging Role of the UN Secretary-General: Making "The Most Impossible Job in the World" Possible.* Westport: Praeger, 1993.

Roberts, Adam. "From San Francisco to Sarajevo: The UN and the Use of Force." *Survival* Vol. 37 No. 4 (1995/1996): 7–28.

Ruggie, John G. "Wandering in the Void: Charting the UN's New Strategic Role." *Foreign Affairs* Vol. 72 No. 5 (1993): 26–31.

Salla, Michael. "Peace Enforcement vs Non-Violent Intervention." *Peace Review* Vol. 8 No. 4 (1996): 547–554.

Scheffer, David J. "UN Engagement in Ethnic Conflicts." In *International Law and Ethnic Conflict,* edited by David Wippman, 147–177. Ithaca: Cornell University Press, 1998.

Semb, Anne-Julie. "The New Practice of UN-Authorized Interventions: A Slippery Slope of Forcible Interference?" *Journal of Peace Research* Vol. 37 No. 4 (2000): 469–488.

Shearer, David. *Private Armies and Military Intervention*. Oxford: Oxford University Press, 1998.

Shelton, Garth. "Preventive Diplomacy and Peacekeeping: Keys for Success." *African Security Review* Vol. 6 No. 5 (1997): 3–14.

Simons, Geoff. *UN Malaise: Power, Problems and Realpolitik*. Basingstoke: Macmillan, 1995.

Stoft, William A. "Ethnic Conflict: The Perils of Military Intervention." *Parameters* Vol. 25 No. 1 (1995): 30–42.

Studer, Meinrad. "The ICRC and Civil–Military Relations in Armed Conflict." *International Review of the Red Cross* Vol. 83 No. 842 (2001): 367–392.

Thakur, Ramesh. "The UN and Human Security." *Canadian Foreign Policy* Vol. 7 No. 1 (1999): 51–59.

Thakur, Ramesh. *International Peacekeeping in Lebanon: United Nations Authority and Multinational Force*. Boulder: Westview, 1987.

Thakur, Ramesh. *Peacekeeping in Vietnam: Canada, India, Poland and the International Commission*. Edmonton: University of Alberta Press, 1984.

Thakur, Ramesh and Albrecht Schnabel, eds. *United Nations Peacekeeping Operations: Ad Hoc Missions, Permanent Engagement*. Tokyo: United Nations University, 2001.

Thornton, Rod. "The Role of Peace Support Operations Doctrine in the British Army." *International Peacekeeping* Vol. 7 No. 2 (2000): 41–62.

Tittemore, Brian D. "Belligerents in Blue Helmets: Applying International Humanitarian Law to United Nations Peace Operations." *Stanford Journal of International Law* Vol. 33 (1997): 61–118.

United Nations. *The Blue Helmets: A Review of United Nations Peace-Keeping*. 3rd ed. New York: United Nations Department of Public Information, 1996.

Urquhart, Brian. "The UN's Crucial Choice." *Foreign Policy* No. 84 (1991): 157–165.

Urquhart, Brian. "Beyond the Sheriff's Posse." *Survival* Vol. 32 No. 3 (1990): 196–205.

Waltz, Kenneth. "A Strategy for the Rapid Deployment Force." *International Security* Vol. 5 No. 4 (1981): 49–72.

Weiss, Thomas G., ed. *Beyond UN Subcontracting: Task-Sharing with Regional Security Arrangements and Service-Providing NGOs*. Basingstoke: Macmillan, 1998.

Weiss, Thomas G., ed. *The United Nations and Civil Wars*. Boulder: Lynne Rienner, 1995.

Weiss, Thomas G. "Intervention: Whither the UN?" *Washington Quarterly* Vol. 17 No. 1 (1994): 109–128.

Wesley, Michael. *Casualties of the New World Order: The Causes of Failure of UN Missions to Civil Wars*. London: Macmillan, 1997.

White, Nigel D. "United Nations Peacekeeping: Development or Destruction?" *International Relations* Vol. 12 No. 1 (1994): 129–158.

Whitman, Jim. "'If It's Right, It's Gotta Be Done': A Cautionary Note on UN Humanitarian Intervention." *Cambridge Review of International Affairs* Vol. 48 No. 4 (1994): 607–640.

Woodhouse, Tom, Robert H. Bruce and Malcolm Dando, eds. *Peacekeeping and Peacemaking: Towards Effective Intervention in Post-Cold War Conflicts*. Basingstoke: Macmillan, 1998.

Zartman, I. William. "Intervening to Prevent State Collapse: The Role of the United Nations." In *Multilateral Diplomacy and the United Nations Today*, edited by James P. Muldoon, 68–77. Boulder: Westview, 1999.

Ziccardi, P. "L'intervento collettivo delle Nazioni Unite e i nuovi poteri dell'Assemblea Generale." *Comunità* Vol. 12 No. 2 (1957): 221–236.

# 10. MILITARY INTERVENTIONS AND HUMANITARIAN ACTION

Anderson, Mary B. *Do No Harm: How Aid Can Support Peace – Or War.* Boulder: Lynne Rienner, 1999.
Argues that in some circumstances, aid may fuel conflict. Claims that international assistance given in the context of a violent conflict has political impacts and therefore cannot be neutral.

Cahill, Kevin M., ed. *A Framework for Survival: Health, Human Rights and Humanitarian Assistance in Conflicts and Disasters.* New York: Routledge and The Center for International Health and Cooperation, 1999.
Collection of essays dealing with health, legal, and economic issues during international humanitarian crises. Discusses the role of the UN and NGOs in humanitarian crises.

*Disasters.* Special Issue: "The Emperor's New Clothes: Charting the Erosion of Humanitarian Principles." Vol. 22 No. 4 (1998): 283–360.
Reviews the evolution of humanitarian principles, analyzes the changing role of the military, and includes case studies on Sierra Leone and Sudan.

Gallagher, Dennis, Michel Moussalli and David Bosco. *Civilian and Military Means of Providing and Supporting Humanitarian Assistance during Conflict: A Comparative Analysis.* Washington, DC: Refugee Policy Group, 1997.
Commissioned by the OECD, this work assesses the comparative advantage of military and civilian means of delivering and supporting humanitarian assistance in conflict environments.

Harriss, John, ed. *The Politics of Humanitarian Intervention.* London: Pinter in association with Save the Children Fund and the Centre for Global Governance, 1995.
Addresses problems of international humanitarian assistance and issues of human rights, sovereignty, and institutional capacity.

Macrae, Joanna and Anthony Zwi, eds. *War and Hunger: Rethinking International Responses to Complex Emergencies.* London: Zed Books, 1994.
One of the first attempts to analyze the experiences of NGOs and UN agencies working in the context of conflict and famine. Pays special attention to complex emergencies in African countries.

Omaar, Rakiya and Alex De Waal. *Humanitarianism Unbound? Current Dilemmas Facing Multi-Mandate Relief Operations in Political Emergencies.* London: African Rights, 1994.
Examines the implications of the expanding mandate of international relief organizations after the end of the Cold War. Argues that neutral humanitarian action is impossible and may even be counterproductive.

Roberts, Adam. *Humanitarian Action in War: Aid, Protection and Impartiality in a Policy Vacuum.* Adelphi Paper. London: Oxford University Press for the International Institute for Strategic Studies, 1996.
Addresses the dilemmas of humanitarian action in war, stressing the difficulty of maintaining impartiality and providing protection in highly politicized conflicts.

Weiss, Thomas G. *Military–Civilian Interactions: Intervening in Humanitarian Crises.* Lanham: Rowman and Littlefield, 1999.
Five case studies focusing on relations between the military and humanitarian agencies. Emphasizes the limits of both military coercion and civilian charity.

## References

African Rights. *Humanitarianism Unbound? Current Dilemmas Facing Multi-Mandate Relief Operations in Political Emergencies*. London: AR, 1994.

Arulanantham, Ahilan T. "Restructured Safe Havens: A Proposal for Reform of the Refugee Protection System." *Human Rights Quarterly* Vol. 22 No. 1 (2000): 1–56.

Bakewell, Oliver. *Refugee Aid and Protection in Rural Africa: Working in Parallel or Cross-Purposes?* Geneva: United Nations High Commissioner for Refugees, 2001.

Baldwin, David A. "Foreign Aid, Intervention, and Influence." *World Politics* Vol. 21 No. 3 (1969): 425–447.

Beigbeder, Yves. *The Role and Status of International Humanitarian Volunteers and Organizations: The Right and Duty to Humanitarian Assistance*. Dordrecht: Martinus Nijhoff, 1991

Belgrad, Eric A. and Nitza Nachmias, eds. *The Politics of International Humanitarian Aid Operations*. Westport: Praeger, 1997.

Bettati, Mario, Rony Brauman and Bernard Holzer. "L'humanitaire peut-il être neutre?" *Projet* Vol. 237 (1994): 77–86.

Bonard, Paul. *Modes of Action Used by Humanitarian Players: Criteria for Operational Complementarity*. Geneva: International Committee of the Red Cross, 1999.

Bradbury, Mark. "Normalising the Crisis in Africa." *Disasters* Vol. 22 No. 4 (1998): 328–338.

Bryans, Michael, Bruce D. Jones and Janice Gross Stein. *Mean Times: Humanitarian Action in Complex Political Emergencies – Stark Choices, Cruel Dilemmas*. Toronto: Program on Conflict Management and Negotiation, 1999.

Chesterman, Simon, ed. *Civilians in War*. Boulder: Lynne Rienner, 2001.

Chr. Michelsen Institute. *Humanitarian Assistance and Conflict*. Bergen: CMI, 1997.

Cilliers, Jakkie and Greg Mills, eds. *From Peacekeeping to Complex Emergencies: Peace Support Missions in Africa*. Johannesburg: The South African Institute of International Affairs and the Institute for Security Studies, 1999.

Cohen, Roberta and Francis M. Deng, eds. *Masses in Flight: The Global Crisis of Internal Displacement*. Washington, DC: Brookings Institution, 1998.

Condamines, Charles. *L'aide humanitaire entre la politique et les affaires*. Paris: L'Harmattan, 1989.

Curtis, Devon. *Politics and Humanitarian Aid: Debates, Dilemmas and Dissension: Report of a Conference Organised by ODI, POLIS at the University of Leeds and CAFOD*. London: Overseas Development Institute, 2001.

Cushing, Christopher. *Humanitarian Assistance and the Role of NGOs*. Halifax: Centre for Policy Studies, Dalhousie University, 1995.

Daniel, Donald C.F. and Bradd C. Hayes. *Securing Observance of UN Mandates through the Employment of Military Forces*. Newport: US Naval War College, 1995.

DeMars, William. "Mercy without Illusion: Humanitarian Action in Conflict." *Mershon International Studies Review* Vol. 40 No. 1 (1996): 81–90.

Deng, Francis M. *Protecting the Dispossessed: A Challenge for the International Community*. Washington, DC: Brookings Institution, 1993.

Deng, Francis M. and Larry Minear. *The Challenges of Famine Relief*. Washington, DC: Brookings Institution, 1992.

De Senarclens, Pierre. "L'humanitaire et la globalisation." *International Review of the Red Cross* Vol. 82 No. 838 (2000): 311–324.

Destexhe, Alain. *L'humanitaire impossible ou deux siècles d'ambiguïté*. Paris: A. Colin, 1993.

De Waal, Alex, ed. *Who Fights? Who Cares? War and Humanitarian Action in Africa.* Trenton: Africa World Press, 2000.

De Waal, Alex. *Famine Crimes: Politics and the Disaster Relief Industry in Africa.* Oxford: James Currey, 1997.

De Waal, Alex and Rakiya Omar. "Can Military Intervention Be 'Humanitarian'?" *Middle East Report* Vol. 41 No. 2/3 (1994): 3–8.

Donini, Antonio. "Asserting Humanitarianism in Peace-Maintenance." *Global Governance* Vol. 4 No. 1 (1998): 81–96.

Donini, Antonio. "Beyond Neutrality: On the Compatibility of Military Intervention and Humanitarian Assistance." *Fletcher Forum of World Affairs* Vol. 19 No. 2 (1995): 31–45.

Doyle, Michael W. and Ian Johnstone. *Conflict and Humanitarian Action: Report of a Conference at Princeton University, 22–23 October 1993.* New York: United Nations High Commissioner for Refugees, 1994.

Duffield, Mark. *Aid Policy and Post-Modern Conflict: A Critical Review.* Birmingham: University of Birmingham, 1998.

Duffield, Mark. "NGO Relief in War Zones: Towards an Analysis of the New Aid Paradigm." *Third World Quarterly* Vol. 18 No. 3 (1997): 527–542.

Duffield, Mark. "Sovereignty and Intervention after the Cold War: Lessons from the Emergency Relief Desk." *Middle East Report* Vol. 24 No. 2/3 (1994): 9–15.

European Commission Humanitarian Organization. *Towards a Human Rights Approach to European Commission Humanitarian Aid.* Brussels: ECHO, 1999.

Emmanuelli, Xavier. *Les prédateurs de l'action humanitaire.* Paris: Albin Michel, 1991.

Farer, Tom J. "Intervention in Unnatural Humanitarian Emergencies: Lessons of the First Phase." *Human Rights Quarterly* Vol. 18 No. 1 (1996): 1–22.

Fishel, John T. *Civil Military Operations in the New World.* London: Praeger, 1997.

Forsythe, David P. *UNHCR's Mandate: The Politics of Being Non-Political.* Geneva: United Nations High Commissioner for Refugees, 2001.

Forsythe, David P. "The International Committee of the Red Cross and Humanitarian Assistance: A Policy Analysis." *International Review of the Red Cross* No. 314 (1996): 512–531.

Forsythe, David P. "Choices More Ethical than Legal: The International Committee of the Red Cross and Human Rights." *Ethics and International Affairs* Vol. 7 (1993): 131–151.

Frohardt, Mark, Diane Paul and Larry Minear. *Protecting Human Rights: The Challenge to Humanitarian Organizations.* Providence: Thomas J. Watson Jr. Institute for International Studies, 1999.

Gnaedinger, Angelo. "Security Challenges for Humanitarian Action." *International Review of the Red Cross* Vol. 83 No. 841 (2001): 171–182.

Gordenker, Leon and Thomas G. Weiss, eds. *Soldiers, Peacekeepers and Disasters.* Basingstoke: Macmillan, 1991.

Gorlick, Brian. *Human Rights and Refugees: Enhancing Protection through International Human Rights Law.* Geneva: United Nations High Commissioner for Refugees, 2000.

Greenaway, Sean. "Post-Modern Conflict and Humanitarian Action: Questioning the Paradigm." *Journal of Humanitarian Assistance* (January 2000): http://www.jha.ac/articles/a053.htm

Gundel, Joakim. *Humanitarian Assistance: Breaking the Waves of Complex Political Emergencies: A Literature Survey.* Copenhagen: Centre for Development Research, 1999.

Harrell-Bond, Barbara E. *Imposing Aid: Emergency Assistance to Refugees.* Oxford: Oxford University Press, 1986.

Harroff-Tavel, Marion. "Neutrality and Impartiality: The Importance of these Principles for the International Red Cross and Red Crescent Movement and the Difficulties Involved in Applying them." *International Review of the Red Cross* No. 273 (1989): 536–552.

Hendrickson, Dylan. "Humanitarian Action in Protracted Crisis: An Overview of the Debates and Dilemmas." *Disasters* Vol. 22 No. 4 (1998): 283–287.

Hendrickson, Dylan. *Humanitarian Action in Protracted Crises: The New Relief Agenda and Its Limits.* London: Overseas Development Institute, 1998.

Hermet, Guy. "Triomphe ou déclin de l'humanitaire?" *Cultures et Conflits* No. 11 (1993): 13–27.

Hulme, David and Michael Edwards, eds. *NGOs, States, and Donors: Too Close for Comfort?* New York: St. Martin's Press in association with Save the Children, 1997.

Hutchinson, John F. *Champions of Charity: War and the Rise of the Red Cross.* Boulder: Westview, 1996.

Hybertsen, Bente, Astri Suhrke, Gro Tjore, Emery Brusset and Bruce Jones. *Humanitarian Assistance and Conflict: A-State-of-the-Art Report.* Fantoft: Chr. Michelsen Institute, 1998.

Independent Commission on International Humanitarian Issues. *Modern Wars: The Humanitarian Challenge.* London: Zed Books, 1988.

Ingram, James C. "The Politics of Human Suffering." *The National Interest* No. 33 (1993): 59–67.

International Review of the Red Cross. "Special Issue: Humanitarian Debate: Law, Policy, Action." Vol. 81 No. 833 (1999).

Jean, François, ed. *Populations in Danger 1995.* London: Médecins sans Frontières, 1995.

Jean, François, ed. *Life, Death and Aid: The Médecins sans Frontières Report on World Crisis Intervention.* London: Routledge, 1993.

Kalshoven, Frits, ed. *Assisting the Victims of Armed Conflict and Other Disasters.* Dordrecht: Martinus Nijhoff, 1989.

Keen, David. "Aid and Violence, with Special Reference to Sierra Leone." *Disasters* Vol. 22 No. 4 (1998): 318–327.

Kent, Randolph. *The Anatomy of Disaster Relief: The International Network in Action.* London: Pinter, 1987.

Kouchner, Bernard. *Le malheur des autres.* Paris: Odile Jacob, 1991.

Krähenbühl, Pierre. "Conflict in the Balkans: Human Tragedies and the Challenge to Independent Humanitarian Action." *International Review of the Red Cross* Vol. 82 No. 837 (2000): 11–29.

Kwakwa, Edward. "Internal Conflicts in Africa: Is There a Right of Humanitarian Action?" *African Yearbook of International Law* Vol. 3 (1995): 9–45.

Lattanzi, Flavia. *Assistenza umanitaria e intervento di umanità.* Torino: Giappichelli, 1997.

Laurence, Tim. *Humanitarian Assistance and Peacekeeping: An Uneasy Alliance?* London: Royal United Services Institute for Defence Studies, 1999.

Leader, Nicholas. *The Politics of Principle: The Principles of Humanitarian Action in Practice.* London: Overseas Development Institute, 2000.

Leader, Nicholas. "Proliferating Principles: Or How to Sup with the Devil without Getting Eaten." *Disasters* Vol. 22 No. 4 (1998): 288–308.

Leader, Nicholas and Joanna Macrae, eds. *Terms of Engagement: Conditions and Conditionality in Humanitarian Action.* London: Overseas Development Institute, 2000.

Loescher, Gil. *Beyond Charity: International Cooperation and the Global Refugee Crisis.* New York: Oxford University Press, 1993.

Loescher, Gil and Laila Monahan, eds. *Refugees and International Relations.* New York: Oxford University Press, 1989.

Lopez, George A. and Drew Christiansen, eds. *Morals and Might*. Boulder: Westview, 1993.

MacFarlane, S. Neil. *Humanitarian Action and Conflict*. Providence: Thomas J. Watson Jr. Institute for International Studies, 2001.

MacFarlane, S. Neil. "Humanitarian Action and Conflict." *International Journal* No. 4 (1999): 537–561.

Macrae, Joanna. "The Death of Humanitarianism? An Anatomy of the Attack." *Disasters* Vol. 22 No. 4 (1998): 309–317.

Macrae, Joanna and Nicholas Leader. *Shifting Sands: The Search for Coherence between Political and Humanitarian Responses to Complex Emergencies*. London: Overseas Development Institute, 2000.

Mandigui, Yokabdjim N. "L'aide au développement et les droits de l'homme." *African Journal of International and Comparative Law* Vol. 6 No. 1 (1994): 59–75.

Maren, Michael. *The Road to Hell: The Ravaging Effects of Foreign Aid and International Charity*. New York: Free Press, 1997.

Maynard, Kimberly A. *Healing Communities in Conflict: International Assistance in Complex Emergencies*. New York: Columbia University Press, 1999.

Menkhaus, Kenneth. "Complex Emergencies, Humanitarianism, and National Security." *National Security Studies Quarterly* Vol. 4 No. 4 (1998): 53–61.

Mertus, Julie A. *War's Offensive on Women: The Humanitarian Challenge in Bosnia, Kosovo and Afghanistan*. West Hartford: Kumarian, 2000.

Miller, Robert. *Aid as Peacemaker: Canadian Development Assistance and Third World Conflict*. Ottawa: Carleton University Press, 1992.

Minear, Larry. *Partnerships in the Protection of Refugees and Other People at Risk: Emerging Issues and Work in Progress*. Geneva: United Nations High Commissioner for Refugees, 1999.

Minear, Larry. *Humanitarianism under Siege: A Critical Review of Operation Lifeline Sudan*. Trenton: Red Sea, 1991.

Minear, Larry and Philippe Guillot. *Soldiers to the Rescue: Humanitarian Lessons from Rwanda*. Paris: Development Centre of the Organisation for Economic Co-operation and Development, 1996.

Minear, Larry and Thomas G. Weiss. *Humanitarian Action: A Transatlantic Agenda for Operations and Research*. Providence: Thomas J. Watson Jr. Institute for International Studies, 2000.

Minear, Larry and Thomas G. Weiss. *Mercy under Fire: War and the Global Humanitarian Community*. Boulder: Westview, 1995.

Minear, Larry and Thomas G. Weiss. *Humanitarian Action in Times of War: A Handbook for Practitioners*. Boulder: Lynne Rienner, 1993.

Mongin, Olivier. "De la compassion à la réciprocité: Droits de l'homme et impératif politique." *Projet* (1994): 87–95.

Monod, Jean-Michel. "The ICRC in Asia: Special Challenges?" *International Review of the Red Cross* Vol. 83 No. 841 (2001): 9–17.

Mooney, Erin D. "Presence, Ergo Protection? UNPROFOR, UNHCR and the ICRC in Croatia and Bosnia and Herzegovina." *International Journal of Refugee Law* Vol. 7 No. 3 (1995): 407–435.

Morgenthau, Hans J. "A Political Theory of Foreign Aid." *American Political Science Review* Vol. 56 No. 2 (1962): 301–309.

Mosley, Paul, Jane Harrigan and John Toye. *Aid and Power: The World Bank and Policy-Based Lending*. London: Routledge, 1991.

Munro, Alan. "Humanitarianism and Conflict in a Post-Cold War World." *International Review of the Red Cross* Vol. 81 No. 835 (1999): 463–475.

Nafziger, E. Wayne, Frances Stewart and Raimo Väyrynen, eds. *War, Hunger and Displacement: The Origins of Humanitarian Emergencies.* Oxford: Oxford University Press, 2000.

Natsios, Andrew S. "NGOs and the UN in Complex Emergencies: Conflict or Cooperation." *Third World Quarterly* Vol. 16 No. 3 (1995): 405–419.

Natsios, Andrew S. "Food through Force: Humanitarian Intervention and US Policy." *Washington Quarterly* Vol. 17 No. 1 (1994): 129–144.

Nicholson, Frances and Patrick Twomey, eds. *Refugee Rights and Realities: Evolving International Concepts and Regimes.* Cambridge: Cambridge University Press, 1999.

Organisation for Economic Co-operation and Development. *Civilian and Military Means of Providing and Supporting Humanitarian Assistance During Conflict: Comparative Advantages and Costs.* Paris: OECD, 1998.

Oxfam. *An End to Forgotten Emergencies.* Oxford: Oxfam, 2000.

Pasic, Amir and Thomas G. Weiss. "The Politics of Rescue: Yugoslavia's War and the Humanitarian Impulse." *Ethics and International Affairs* Vol. 11 (1997): 105–131.

Patrnogic, Jovica. "Humanitarian Assistance – Humanitarian Intervention." In *International Legal Issues Arising under the United Nations Decade of International Law*, edited by Najeeb Al-Nauimi and Richard Meese, 1013–1040. The Hague: Martinus Nijhoff, 1995.

Perrot, Marie-Dominique, ed. *Dérives humanitaires: états d'urgence et droit d'ingérence.* Paris: Presses Universitaires de France, 1994.

Pirotte, Claire, Bernard Husson and Francois Grunewald, eds. *Responding to Emergencies and Fostering Development: The Dilemmas of Humanitarian Aid.* London: Zed Books, 1999.

Porter, Toby. "The Partiality of Humanitarian Assistance: Kosovo in Comparative Perspective." *Journal of Humanitarian Assistance* (June 2000): http://www.jha.ac/articles/a057.htm

Pottier, Johan. "Relief and Repatriation: Views by Rwandan Refugees: Lessons for Humanitarian Aid Workers." *African Affairs* Vol. 95 No. 380 (1996): 403–429.

Prendergast, John. *Frontline Diplomacy: Humanitarian Aid and Conflict in Africa.* Boulder: Lynne Rienner, 1996.

Prendergast, John and Colin Scott. *Aid with Integrity: Avoiding the Potential of Humanitarian Aid to Sustain Conflict.* Washington, DC: United States Agency for International Development, 1996.

Pugh, Michael. "Military Intervention and Humanitarian Action: Trends and Issues." *Disasters* Vol. 22 No. 4 (1998): 339–351.

Quénivet, Noëlle. "Humanitarian Assistance: A Right or a Policy?" *Journal of Humanitarian Assistance* (January 1999): http://www.jha.ac/articles/a030.htm

Refugee Policy Group. *Civilian and Military Means of Providing and Supporting Humanitarian Assistance During Conflict: A Comparative Analysis: A Note by the Secretariat.* Paris: Organisation for Economic Co-operation and Development, 1998.

Rieff, David. "Moral Imperatives and Political Realities: Response to 'Principles, Politics, and Humanitarian Action'." *Ethics and International Affairs* Vol. 13 (1999): 35–42.

Rieff, David. "The Humanitarian Trap." *World Policy Journal* Vol. 12 No. 4 (1994/1995): 1–11.

Riemer, Neal, ed. *Protection against Genocide: Mission Impossible?* Westport: Praeger, 2000.

Roberts, Adam. "Humanitarian Issues and Agencies as Triggers for International Military Action." *International Review of the Red Cross* Vol. 82 No. 839 (2000): 673–698.

Roberts, Adam. "The Role of Humanitarian Issues in International Politics in the 1990s." *International Review of the Red Cross* Vol. 81 No. 833 (1999): 19–42.

Rosenblatt, L.A. and L. Thompson. "Humanitarian Emergencies: Ten Steps to Save Lives and Resources." *SAIS Review* Vol. 15 No. 2 (1995): 91–109.

Ruffin, Jean-Christophe. *Le piège humanitaire*. Lattès, 1993.

Scholdan, Bettina. "Addressing the Root Causes: Relief and Development Assistance between Peacebuilding and Preventing Refugee Flows." *Journal of Humanitarian Assistance* (June 2000): http://www.jha.ac/articles/a058.htm

Seiple, Chris. *The US Military/NGO Relationships in Humanitarian Interventions*. Carlisle Barracks: US Army War College, 1996.

Seybolt, Taylor B. "The Myth of Neutrality." *Peace Review* Vol. 8 No. 4 (1996): 521–527.

Slim, Hugo. "The Stretcher and the Drum: Civil–Military Relations in Peace Support Operations." *International Peacekeeping* Vol. 3 No. 2 (1996): 123–140.

Slim, Hugo. "Military Humanitarianism and the New Peacekeeping: An Agenda for Peace?" (September 1995): http://www.jha.ac/articles/a003.htm

Sommaruga, Cornelio. "Humanity: Our Priority Now and Always – Response to 'Principles, Politics, and Humanitarian Action'." *Ethics and International Affairs* Vol. 13 (1999): 23–28.

Sommaruga, Cornelio. *Azione umanitaria ed intervento umanitario: il parere del Comitato Internazionale della Croce Rossa*. Milano: Giuffré, 1998.

Sommaruga, Cornelio. "L'action humanitaire et l'action politico-humanitaire: Pour une complémentarité dans la gestion des conflits." In *Boutros Boutros-Ghali amicorum discipulorumque liber: paix, développement, démocratie*, 739–745. Bruxelles: Bruylant, 1998.

Stockton, Nicholas. "In Defence of Humanitarianism." *Disasters* Vol. 22 No. 4 (1998): 352–360.

Stockton, Nicholas. "Defensive Development? Re-Examining the Role of the Military in Complex Political Emergencies." *Disasters* Vol. 20 No. 2 (1996): 91–144.

Supreme Headquarters Allied Powers Europe. *NATO Doctrine for Peace Support Operations: Allied Command Europe*. Mons: SHAPE, 1994.

Swannack, Charles H. and David R. Gray. "Peace Enforcement Operations." *Military Review* (1997): 7–8.

Tiso, Christopher M. "Safe Haven Refugee Programs: A Method of Combatting International Refugee Crises." *Georgetown Immigration Law Journal* Vol. 8 No. 4 (1994): 575–601.

Torrelli, Maurice. "L'humanitaire: le retour au réalisme?" *Arès* Vol. 14 (1994): 71–81.

Torrelli, Maurice. "From Humanitarian Assistance to 'Intervention on Humanitarian Grounds'?" *International Review of the Red Cross* Vol. 288 (1992): 228–248.

UK Inspector General Doctrine and Training. *Wider Peacekeeping: Army Field Manual No. 5: Operations Other than War*. London: Her Majesty's Stationery Office, 1995.

US Army. *US Army Field Manual (FM) 100–23: Peace Operations*. Washington, DC: Department of the Army, 1994.

Uvin, Peter. *The Influence of Aid in Situations of Violent Conflict*. Paris: Organisation for Economic Co-operation and Development, 1999.

Vigny, Jean-Daniel and Cecilia Thompson. "Standards fondamentaux d'humanité: quel avenir?" *International Review of the Red Cross* Vol. 82 No. 840 (2000): 917–938.

Weil, Carola. "The Protection–Neutrality Dilemma in Humanitarian Emergencies: Why the Need for Military Intervention?" *International Migration Review* Vol. 35 No. 1 (2001): 79–116.

Weiss, Thomas G. "Military–Civilian Humanitarianism: The 'Age of Innocence' Is Over." *International Peacekeeping* Vol. 2 No. 2 (1995): 157–174.

Weiss, Thomas G. and Kurt M. Campbell. "Military Humanitarianism." *Survival* Vol. 33 No. 5 (1991): 451–465.

Weiss, Thomas G. and Cindy Collins. *Humanitarian Challenges and Intervention: World Politics and the Dilemmas of Help*. Boulder: Westview Press, 1996.

Weiss, Thomas G. and Larry Minear, eds. *Humanitarianism across Borders: Sustaining Civilians in Times of War*. Boulder: Lynne Rienner, 1993.

Weller, Marc. "Access to Victims: Reconceiving the Right to 'Intervene'." In *International Law and The Hague's 750th Anniversary*, edited by Wybo P. Heere, 353–370. The Hague: T.M.C. Asser, 1999.

Weller, Marc. "The Relativity of Humanitarian Neutrality and Impartiality." *Journal of Humanitarian Assistance* (February 1998): http://www.jha.ac/articles/a029.htm

Whitman, Jim and David Pocok, eds. *After Rwanda: The Coordination of United Nations Humanitarian Assistance*. Basingstoke: Macmillan, 1996.

Wiener, Myron. "The Clash of Norms: Dilemmas in Refugee Policies." *Journal of Refugee Studies* Vol. 11 No. 4 (1998): 1–21.

Wilkinson, Philip. "Sharpening the Weapons of Peace: Peace Support Operations and Complex Emergencies." *International Peacekeeping* Vol. 7 No. 1 (2000): 63–79.

Williams, Michael C. *Civil–Military Relations and Peacekeeping*. Oxford: Oxford University Press, 1998.

Wood, William B. "From Humanitarian Relief to Humanitarian Intervention: Victims, Interveners and Pillars." *Political Geography* Vol. 15 No. 8 (1996): 671–696.

Wriggins, Howard. "Political Outcomes of Foreign Assistance: Influence, Involvement, or Intervention?" *Journal of International Affairs* Vol. 22 No. 2 (1968): 217–230.

Zorbige, Charles. "Condamner l'action humanitaire?" *Revue Politique et Parlementaire* Vol. 984 (1996): 66–78.

# 11. POST-CONFLICT CHALLENGES

Adedeji, Adebayo, ed. *Comprehending and Mastering African Conflicts: The Search for Sustainable Peace and Good Governance*. London: Zed Books in association with African Centre for Development and Strategic Studies, 1999.
African scholars analyze the roots of African conflicts and investigate successful transitions from conflict to peace and good governance in a number of cases, including northern Mali, Nigeria, Somaliland, and Liberia.

Ball, Nicole and Tammy Halevy. *Making Peace Work: The Role of the International Development Community*. Washington, DC: Overseas Development Council, 1996.
Extracts lessons for future peace building efforts from the recent experiences of Cambodia, El Salvador, Mozambique, and Nicaragua and focuses on the implications of these lessons for development cooperation agencies.

Chopra, Jarat, ed. *The Politics of Peace-Maintenance*. Boulder: Lynne Rienner, 1998.
Traces the evolution of the political, military, legal, and judicial components for legitimate and effective peace maintenance and longer term institutional developments by international authority.

Ginifer, Jeremy, ed. *Beyond the Emergency: Development within UN Peace Missions*. London: Frank Cass, 1997.
Examines critical issues relating to the interface between development, relief and peacekeeping with particular reference to Africa and poses the question of how sustainable development fits within the post-conflict part of UN peace missions.

Kumar, Krishna, ed. *Rebuilding Societies after Civil War: Critical Roles for International Assistance*. Boulder: Lynne Rienner, 1997.
Essays on international assistance in the political, social, cultural, and economic rehabilitation of war-torn societies, examining the nature of these interventions, their problems, and their achievements.

Lederach, John Paul. *Building Peace: Sustainable Reconciliation in Divided Societies*. Washington, DC: United States Institute of Peace, 1997.
Presents an integrated framework for peace building, in which structure, process, resources, training, and evaluation are coordinated in an attempt to transform conflicts and effect reconciliation.

Moore, Jonathan. *The UN and Complex Emergencies: Rehabilitation in Third World Transitions*. Geneva: United Nations Research Institute for Social Development, 1996.
Examines the performance of the UN and donor agencies in providing rehabilitation assistance to Afghanistan, Cambodia, Mozambique, and Somalia and argues that rehabilitation is essential for sustainability.

Zartman, I. William, ed. *Collapsed States: The Disintegration and Restoration of Legitimate Authority*. Boulder: Lynne Rienner, 1995.
Analyzes ways of reconstituting structure, authority, law, and political order in collapsed states by looking at Africa's experience.

## References

Abiew, Francis Kofi and T. Keating. "Outside Agents and the Politics of Peacebuilding and Reconciliation." *International Journal* Vol. 55 No. 1 80–106.

Adibe, Clement E. "Accepting External Authority in Peace-Maintenance." *Global Governance* Vol. 4 No. 1 (1998): 107–122.

Anderson, Mary B. and Peter J. Woodrow. *Rising from the Ashes: Development Strategies in Times of Disaster*. Boulder: Westview, 1989.

Annan, Kofi A. *Report of the Secretary-General on the Work of the Organization: The Causes of Conflict and the Promotion of Durable Peace and Sustainable Development in Africa*. New York: United Nations, 1998.

Appleby, Scott. *The Ambivalence of the Sacred: Religion, Violence, and Reconciliation*. Lanham: Rowman and Littlefield, 2000.

Azimi, Nassrine, ed. *The United Nations Transitional Authority in Cambodia (UNTAC): Debriefing and Lessons*. The Hague: Kluwer Law International, 1995.

Bakewell, Oliver. *Refugee Aid and Protection in Rural Africa: Working in Parallel or Cross-Purposes?* Geneva: United Nations High Commissioner for Refugees, 2001.

Bakewell, Oliver. *Returning Refugees or Migrating Villagers? Voluntary Repatriation Programmes in Africa Reconsidered*. Geneva: United Nations High Commissioner for Refugees, 1999.

Bertram, Eva. "Reinventing Governments: The Promise and Perils of United Nations Peace Building." *Journal of Conflict Resolution* Vol. 39 No. 3 (1995): 387–418.

Byrne, Sean and Cynthia L. Irvin, eds. *Reconcilable Differences: Turning Points in Ethnopolitical Conflict*. West Hartford: Kumarian Press, 2000.

Carbonnier, Gilles. *Conflict, Postwar Rebuilding and the Economy: A Critical Review of the Literature*. Geneva: United Nations Research Institute for Social Development, 1998.

Carley, Michael and Ian Christie. *Managing Sustainable Development*. Minneapolis: University of Minnesota Press, 1992.

Castillo, Graciana del. "Post-Conflict Peace-Building: A Challenge for the United Nations." *CEPAL Review* No. 55 (1995): 27–38.

Chopra, Jarat. *Peace-Maintenance: The Evolution of International Political Authority*. London: Routledge, 1999.

Cousens, Elizabeth and Chetan Kumar, eds. *Peacebuilding as Politics: Cultivating Peace in Fragile Societies*. Boulder: Lynne Rienner, 2001.

Cousens, Richard P. "Providing Military Security in Peace-Maintenance." *Global Governance* Vol. 4 No. 1 (1998): 97–105.

Crocker, Chester A. and Fen Osler Hampson. "Making Peace Settlements Work." *Foreign Policy* Vol. 104 (1996): 54–71.

Daniel, Donald C.F. and Bradd C. Hayes. "Securing Observance of UN Mandates through the Employment of Military Force." *International Peacekeeping* Vol. 3 (1996): 107–127.

David, Charles-Philippe. "Does Peacebuilding Build Peace? Liberal (Mis)steps in the Peace Process." *Security Dialogue* Vol. 30 No. 1 (1999): 25–41.

Duffield, Mark. "Complex Emergencies and the Crisis of Developmentalism." *Institute for Development Studies Bulletin* Vol. 25 No. 4 (1994): 37–45.

Eijk, Ryan van. "The United Nations and the Reconstruction of Collapsed States in Africa." *African Journal of International and Comparative Law* Vol. 9 (1997): 573–599.

Ferrari-Bravo, Giuliano. "National and International Trusteeship: Some Notes on UN Intervention in the System of Chapters XII and XIII of the Charter." *Africa (Roma)* Vol. 34 No. 4 (1979): 391–416.

Ginifer, Jeremy. "Development and the UN Peace Mission: A New Interface Required?" *International Peacekeeping* Vol. 3 No. 2 (1996): 3–13.

Goodhand, Jonathan and David Hulme. "From Wars to Complex Political Emergencies: Understanding Conflict and Peace-Building in the New World Disorder." *Third World Quarterly* Vol. 20 No. 1 (1999): 13–26.

Gordon, Ruth E. "Saving Failed States: Sometimes a Neocolonialist Notion." *American University Journal of International Law and Policy* Vol. 12 No. 6 (1997): 903–974.

Gordon, Ruth E. "Some Legal Problems with Trusteeship." *Cornell International Law Journal* Vol. 28 No. 2 (1995): 301–347.

Green, Reginald H. and Ismail I. Ahmed. "Rehabilitation, Sustainable Peace and Development: Towards Reconceputalisation." *Third World Quarterly* Vol. 20 No. 1 (1999): 189–206.

Hampson, Fen Osler. *Nurturing Peace: Why Peace Settlements Succeed or Fail.* Washington, DC: United States Institute of Peace, 1996.

Han, Sonia K. "Building a Peace That Lasts: The United Nations and Post-Civil War Peace-Building." *New York University Journal of International Law and Politics* Vol. 26 No. 4 (1994): 837–892.

Hansen, Annika S. and Brynjar Lia. *Implementation of Peace Agreements: A Study of the Functions and Effectiveness of International Security Assistance in Peace Implementation.* Kjeller: Forsvarets Forskningsinstitutt, 1997.

Harvey, Paul. "Rehabilitation in Complex Political Emergencies: Is Rebuilding Civil Society the Answer?" *Disasters* Vol. 22 No. 3 (1998): 200–217.

Hegedus, Nicole F. and T.K. Rousseau. *Questions of Intervention: Post-Conflict Peacebuilding and Social Reconstruction.* Halifax: Centre for Foreign Policy Studies, 1995.

Helmick, Raymond G. and Rodney L. Petersen, eds. *Forgiveness and Reconciliation: Religion, Public Policy, and Conflict Transformation.* Philadelphia: Templeton Foundation Press, 2001.

International Peacekeeping. "Special Issue: Peacebuilding and Police Reform." Vol. 6 No. 4 (1999).

Irving, Karl J. "The United Nations and Democratic Intervention: Is 'Swords into Ballot Boxes' Enough?" *Denver Journal of International Law and Policy* Vol. 25 (1996): 41–70.

Jamal, Arafat. *Access to Safety? Negotiating Protection in a Central Asian Emergency.* Geneva: United Nations High Commissioner for Refugees, 2000.

Joint Assessment Mission. *East Timor: Building a Nation: A Framework for Reconstruction.* Washington, DC: World Bank, 1999.

Juergensen, Olaf Tataryn. *Repatriation as Peacebuilding and Reconstruction: The Case of Northern Mozambique, 1992–1995.* Geneva: United Nations High Commissioner for Refugees, 2000.

Knight, W. Andy. "Establishing Political Authority in Peace-Maintenance." *Global Governance* Vol. 4 No. 1 (1998): 19–40.

Kühne, Winrich. *Improving African and International Capabilities for Preventing and Resolving Violent Conflict: The Great Lakes Region Crisis.* Ebenhausen: Stiftung Wissenschaft und Politik, 1997.

Kühne, Winrich. *The Transition from Peacekeeping to Peacebuilding: Planning, Coordination and Funding in the Twilight Zone.* Ebenhausen: Stiftung Wissenschaft und Politik, 1997.

Kumar, Krishna, ed. *Postconflict Elections, Democratization and International Assistance.* Boulder: Lynne Rienner, 1998.

Landgren, Karin. "Safety Zones and International Protection: A Dark Grey Area." *International Journal of Refugee Law* Vol. 7 No. 4 (1995): 436–458.

Lederach, John Paul. *Preparing for Peace: Conflict Transformation across Cultures.* Syracuse: Syracuse University Press, 1995.

Lyon, Peter. "The Rise and Fall and Possible Revival of International Trusteeship." *Journal of Commonwealth and Comparative Politics* No. 31 (1993): 96–110.

Macrae, Joanna. *Aiding Peace ... and War: UNHCR, Returnee Reintegration, and the Relief-Development Debate.* Geneva: United Nations High Commissioner for Refugees, 1999.

Mani, Rama. "Conflict Resolution, Justice and the Law: Rebuilding the Rule of Law in the Aftermath of Complex Political Emergencies." *International Peacekeeping* Vol. 5 No. 3 (1998): 1–25.

Maxwell, Simon and Margaret Buchanan-Smith, eds. *Linking Relief and Development.* Brighton: Institute of Development Studies, 1994.

Miall, Hugh, Oliver Ramsbotham and Tom Woodhouse. *Contemporary Conflict Resolution: The Prevention, Management and Transformation of Deadly Conflicts.* Cambridge: Polity Press, 1999.

Mindua, Antoine. "De la légalité de la 'zone de sécurité' française au Rwanda." *African Journal of International and Comparative Law* Vol. 6 No. 4 (1994): 643–652.

Moore, David. *Humanitarian Agendas, State Reconstruction and Democratisation Processes in War-Torn Societies.* Geneva: United Nations High Commissioner for Refugees, 2000.

Morphet, Sally. "Organizing Civil Administration in Peace-Maintenance." *Global Governance* Vol. 4 No. 1 (1998): 41–60.

Paris, Roland. "Peacebuilding and the Limits of Liberal Internationalism." *International Security* Vol. 22 No. 2 (1997): 54–89.

Patrick, Ian. "East Timor Emerging from Conflict: The Role of Local NGOs and International Assistance." *Disasters* Vol. 25 No. 1 (2001): 48–66.

Pettifer, James, ed. *The New Macedonian Question.* Basingstoke: Palgrave, 2001.

Plunkett, Mark. "Reestablishing Law and Order in Peace-Maintenance." *Global Governance* Vol. 4 No. 1 (1998): 61–79.

Pouligny, Béatrice. "Promoting Democratic Institutions in Post-Conflict Societies: Giving Diversity a Chance." *International Peacekeeping* Vol. 7 No. 3 (2000): 17–35.

Pugh, Michael. "Post-Conflict Rehabilitation: Social and Civil Dimensions." *Journal of Humanitarian Assistance* (December 1998): http://www.jha.ac/articles/a034.htm

Pugh, Michael. "Peacebuilding as Developmentalism: Lessons from Disaster Research." *Contemporary Security Policy* Vol. 16 No. 3 (1995): 320–346.

Pungong, V.P. "The Theoretical Basis and Political Feasibility of the Trusteeship–Peacekeeping Connection." *Cambridge Review of International Affairs* Vol. 13/14 No. 1/2 150–161.

Ramsbotham, Oliver P. "Reflections on UN Post-Settlement Peacebuilding." *International Peacekeeping* Vol. 7 No. 1 (2000): 169–189.

Reisman, W. Michael. "Stopping Wars and Making Peace: Reflections on the Ideology and Practice of Conflict Termination in Contemporary World Politics." *Tulane Journal of International and Comparative Law* Vol. 6 (1998): 6–56.

Rothstein, R.L., ed. *After the Peace: Resistance and Reconciliation.* London: Lynne Rienner, 1999.

Rufini, Giovanni. "The Potential of Non-Governmental Organizations in Peacekeeping Negotiation and Mediation." *Peacekeeping and International Relations* Vol. 24 No. 2 (1995): 7–8.

Rupesinghe, Kumar, ed. *Conflict Transformation.* New York: St. Martin's Press, 1995.

Rupesinghe, Kumar. "Building Peace after Military Withdrawal." *Bulletin of Peace Proposals* Vol. 20 No. 3 (1989): 243–251.

Rupnik, Jacques. "The Dilemmas of the Protectorate in Kosovo." *Esprit* No. 5 (2000): 181–184.

Salem, Paul E. "A Critique of Western Conflict Resolution from a Non-Western Perspective." *Negotiation Journal* Vol. 4 No. 4 (1993): 361–369.

Shaw, Timothy M. "Beyond Post-Conflict Peacebuilding: What Links to Sustainable Development and Human Security?" *International Peacekeeping* Vol. 3 No. 2 (1996): 36–48.

Shultz, Richard H. "Peace Operations: Post-Conflict Reconstruction and Restoration-Assistance Missions." *Special Warfare* Vol. 7 No. 2 (1994): 2–6.

Sidiropoulos, Elizabeth. "Minority Protection in the Former Yugoslav Republic of Macedonia: Will It Preserve the State?" *Cambridge Review of International Affairs* Vol. 12 No. 2 (1999): 139–152.

Soto, Alvaro de and Graciana del Castillo. "Obstacles to Peacebuilding." *Foreign Policy* No. 94 (1994): 69–83.

Stedman, Stephen John. "Spoiler Problems in Peace Processes." *International Security* Vol. 22 No. 2 (1997): 5–53.

Stedman, Stephen John and Donald Rothchild. "Peace Operations: From Short-Term to Long-Term Commitment." *International Peacekeeping* Vol. 3 No. 2 (1996): 17–35.

Tellis, Ashley J. "Terminating Intervention: Understanding Exit Strategy and US Involvement in Intrastate Conflicts." *Studies in Conflict and Terrorism* Vol. 19 No. 2 (1996): 117–151.

Torelli, Maurice. "Les zones de sécurité." *Revue Générale de Droit International Public* Vol. 99 (1995): 787–848.

United Nations Development Programme. *Human Development Report.* New York: United Nations Human Development Report Office, 1994.

Vasquez, John A., James Turner Johnson, Sanford Jaffe and Linda Stamato, eds. *Beyond Confrontation: Learning Conflict Resolution in the Post-Cold War Era.* Ann Arbor: University of Michigan Press, 1995.

Walter, Barbara F. "Designing Transitions from Civil War: Demobilization, Democratization, and Commitments to Peace." *International Security* Vol. 24 No. 1 (1999): 127–155.

Weiss Fagen, Patricia. *After the Conflict: A Review of Selected Sources on Rebuilding War-Torn Societies.* Geneva: United Nations Research Institute for Social Development, 1995.

Zartman, I. William, ed. *Elusive Peace: Negotiating an End to Civil Wars.* Washington, DC: Brookings Institution, 1995.

Zartman, I. William and Lewis Rasmussen, eds. *Peacemaking in International Conflict: Methods and Techniques.* Washington, DC: United States Institute of Peace, 1997.

# 12. COUNTRY CASES

## East Pakistan

Ayoob, Mohammed and K. Subrahmanyam. *The Liberation War*. New Delhi: S. Chand, 1972.

"Documents: Civil War in East Pakistan." *New York University Journal of International Law and Politics* Vol. 4 (1971): 524.

Franck, Thomas M. and Nigel S. Rodley. "After Bangladesh: The Law of Humanitarian Intervention by Military Force." *American Journal of International Law* Vol. 67 No. 2 (1973): 275–305.

International Commission of Jurists. *The Events in East Pakistan 1971: A Legal Study*. Geneva: ICJ, 1972.

Jackson, Robert V. *South Asian Crisis: India, Pakistan, Bangla Desh: A Political and Historical Analysis of the 1971 War*. London: Chatto and Windus for the International Institute of Strategic Studies, 1975.

Misra, Kashi P. *The Role of the United Nations in the Indo-Pakistani Conflict*. Delhi: Vikas, 1973.

Nanda, Ved P. "A Critique of the United Nations Inaction in the Bangladesh Crisis." *Denver Law Journal* Vol. 49 (1972): 53.

Nanda, Ved P. "Self-Determination in International Law: The Tragic Tale of Two Cities: Islamabad (West Pakistan) and Dacca (East Pakistan)." *American Journal of International Law* Vol. 66 No. 2 (1972): 321–336.

Nawaz, M. "Bangla Desh and International Law." *Indian Journal of International Law* Vol. 11 (1971): 251–266.

Palit, D.K. *The Lightning Campaign: The Indo-Pakistan War 1971*. Salisbury: Compton, 1972.

Rizvi, Hasan-Askari. *Internal Strife and External Aggression: India's Role in the Civil War in East Pakistan (1971)*. Ann Arbor: University Microfilms International, 1981.

Salzberg, John. "UN Prevention of Human Rights Violations: The Bangladesh Case." *International Organization* Vol. 27 No. 1 (1973): 115–127.

Schanberg, Sydney H. "Pakistan Divided." *Foreign Affairs* Vol. 50 No. 1 (1971): 125–135.

Sisson, Richard and Leo E. Rose. *War and Secession: Pakistan, India, and the Creation of Bangladesh*. Karachi: Oxford University Press, 1992.

Talbot, Phillips. "The Subcontinent: ménage à trois." *Foreign Affairs* Vol. 50 No. 4 (1971–1972): 698–710.

## Cambodia

Amnesty International. *Political Killings by Governments*. London: AI, 1983.

Burchett, Wilfried. *The China–Cambodia–Vietnam Triangle*. London: Zed Books, 1981.

Chanda, Nayan. *Brother Enemy: The War after the War*. New York: Collier, 1986.

Chandler, David P. *The Tragedy of Cambodian History: Politics, War and Revolution since 1945*. New Haven: Yale University Press, 1991.

Evans, Grant and Kelvin Rowley. *Red Brotherhood at War: Vietnam, Cambodia and Laos since 1975*. rev. ed. London: Verso, 1990.

Jackson, Karl D., ed. *Cambodia: Rendezvous with Death 1975–1978*. Princeton: Princeton University Press, 1989.

Kiernan, Ben. *The Pol Pot Regime*. New Haven: Yale University Press, 1996.

Klintworth, Gary. *Vietnam's Intervention in Cambodia in International Law*. Canberra: Australian Government Publishing Group, 1989.

Morris, Stephen J. *Why Vietnam Invaded Cambodia*. Stanford: Stanford University Press, 1999.

Vickery, Michael. *Cambodia, 1975–1982*. Chiang Mai: Silkworm Books, 1999.

## Uganda

Amnesty International. *Human Rights in Uganda*. London: AI, 1978.

Avirgan, Tony and Martha Honey. *War in Uganda: The Legacy of Idi Amin*. Westport: Lawrence Hill, 1982.

Burrows, Noreen. "Tanzania's Intervention in Uganda: Some Legal Aspects." *The World Today* (1979).

Chatterjee, S.K. "Some Legal Problems of Support Role in International Law: Tanzania and Uganda." *International and Comparative Law Quarterly* Vol. 30 (1981): 755–768.

Farooq, Hassan. "Realpolitik in International Law: After the Tanzanian–Ugandan Conflict, Humanitarian Intervention Re-Examined." *Willamette Law Journal* Vol. 17 (1981): 859–912.

Gwyn, David. *Idi Amin: Death Light of Africa*. Boston: Little, Brown and Co., 1977.

Kiwanuka, Semakula. *Amin and the Tragedy of Uganda*. München: Weltforum Verlag, 1979.

Mathews, K. and S.S. Mushi. *Foreign Policy of Tanzania, 1961–1981*. Dar Es Salaam: Tanzania Publishing House, 1981.

Umozurike, U.O. "Tanzania's Intervention in Uganda." *Archiv des Völkerrechts* Vol. 20 (1982): 301–313.

Wani, Ibrahim J. "Humanitarian Intervention and the Tanzania–Uganda War." *Horn of Africa* Vol. 3 No. 2 (1980): 18–27.

## Liberia

Adeleke, Ademola. "The Politics and Diplomacy of Peacekeeping in West Africa: The ECOWAS Operation in Liberia." *The Journal of Modern African Studies* Vol. 33 No. 4 (1995): 569–593.

Alao, Abiodun. *The Burden of Collective Goodwill: The International Involvement in the Liberian Civil War*. Aldershot: Ashgate, 1998.

Alao, Abiodun, John Mackinlay and Funmi Olonisakin. *Peacekeepers, Politicians, and Warlords: The Liberian Peace Process*. Tokyo: United Nations University Press, 1999.

Colin, Scott. *Humanitarian Action and Security in Liberia 1989–1994*. Providence: Thomas J. Watson Jr. Institute for International Studies, 1995.

Ero, Comfort. "ECOWAS and Subregional Peacekeeping in Liberia." *Journal of Humanitarian Assistance* (September 1995): http://www.jha.ac/articles/a005.htm

Frenkel, M. "Grazhdanskaya Voina v Liberii (1989–1997)." *Mirovaya Ekonomika i Mezhdunarodnye Otnoshenia* No. 7 (1998): 102–109.

Howe, Herbert. "Lessons of Liberia: ECOMOG and Regional Peacekeeping." *International Security* Vol. 21 No. 3 (Winter 1996–1997): 145–176.

Huband, Mark. *The Liberian Civil War*. London: Frank Cass, 1998.

Levitt, Jeremy. "Humanitarian Intervention by Regional Actors in Internal Conflicts: The Cases of ECOWAS in Liberia and Sierra Leone." *Temple International and Comparative Law Journal* Vol. 12 No. 2 (1998): 333–375.

Lillich, Richard B. "Forcible Protection of Nationals Abroad: The Liberian 'Incident' of 1990." *German Year Book of International Law* (1992): 35.

Magyar, Karl and Earl Conteh-Morgan, eds. *Peacekeeping in Africa: ECOMOG in Liberia*. Macmillan, 1998.

Mindau, Antoine-Didier. "Intervention armée de la CEDEAO au Libéria: illégalité ou avancée juridique." *African Journal of International and Comparative Law* Vol. 7 No. 2 (1995): 257–283.

Ofodile, Anthony Chukwuka. "The Legality of ECOWAS Intervention in Liberia." *Columbia Journal of Transnational Law* Vol. 32 No. 2 (1994): 381–418.

Ofuatey-Kodjoe, W. "Regional Organizations and the Resolution of Internal Conflict: The ECOWAS Intervention in Liberia." *International Peacekeeping* Vol. 1 No. 3 (1994): 261–302.

Olonisakin, Funmi. "Humanitarian Intervention and Human Rights: The Contradictions in ECO-MOG." *International Journal of Human Rights* Vol. 3 No. 1 (1999): 16–39.

Oteng Kufuor, Kofi. "The Legality of the Intervention in the Liberian Civil War by the Economic Community of West African States." *African Journal of International and Comparative Law* Vol. 5 (1993): 525–560.

Outram, Quentin. "Cruel Wars and Safe Havens: Humanitarian Aid in Liberia 1989–1996." *Disasters* Vol. 21 No. 3 (1997): 189–205.

Sesay, Max A. "Civil War and Collective Intervention in Liberia." *Review of African Political Economy* Vol. 23 No. 67 (1996): 35–52.

Van Walraven, Klaas. *The Pretence of Peace-Keeping: ECOMOG, West Africa and Liberia (1990–1998)*. The Hague: Netherlands Institute of International Relations, 1999.

Vogt, Margaret, ed. *The Liberian Crisis and ECOMOG: A Bold Attempt at Regional Peacekeeping*. Lagos: Gabumo Publishing Company, 1993.

Weller, Marc, ed. *Regional Peacekeeping and International Enforcement: The Liberian Crisis*. Cambridge: Cambridge University Press, 1994.

Wippman, David. "Enforcing the Peace: ECOWAS and the Liberian Civil War." In *Enforcing Restraint: Collective Intervention in Internal Conflicts*, edited by Lori Fisler Damrosch, 157–203. New York: Council on Foreign Relations Press, 1993.

## Iraq and the Kurds

Adelman, Howard. "Humanitarian Intervention: The Case of the Kurds." *International Journal of Refugee Law* Vol. 4 No. 1 (1992): 4–38.

Akhavan, Payam. "Lessons from Iraqi Kurdistan: Self-Determination and Humanitarian Intervention against Genocide." *Netherlands Quarterly of Human Rights* Vol. 11 No. 1 (1993): 4–62.

Freedman, Lawrence and Efraim Karsh. *The Gulf Conflict 1990–1991*. Princeton: Princeton University Press, 1993.

Gow, James, ed. *Iraq, the Gulf Conflict, and the World Community*. London: Brassey's, 1993.

Gray, Christine. "After the Ceasefire: Iraq, the Security Council and the Use of Force." *British Year Book of International Law* Vol. 65 (1994): 135–174.

Johnstone, Ian. *Aftermath of the Gulf War: An Assessment of UN Action*. Boulder: Lynne Rienner, 1994.

Keen, David. *The Kurds in Iraq: How Safe Is Their Haven Now?* London: Save the Children, 1993.

Khadduri, Majid and Edmund Ghareeb. *War in the Gulf, 1990–1991: The Iraq–Kuwait Conflict and Its Implications*. Oxford: Oxford University Press, 1997.

Kirisci, Kemal. "Turkey and the Kurdish Safe-Haven in Northern Iraq." *Journal of South Asian and Middle Eastern Studies* Vol. 19 No. 3 (1996): 21–39.

Malanczuk, Peter. "The Kurdish Crisis and Allied Intervention in the Aftermath of the Second Gulf War." *European Journal of International Law* Vol. 2 No. 2 (1991): 114–132.

Merle, Marcel. *La crise du Golfe et le nouvel ordre international*. Paris: Economica, 1991.

Schachter, Oscar. "United Nations Law in the Gulf Conflict." *American Journal of International Law* Vol. 85 No. 3 (1991): 452–473.

Stopford, Michael. "Humanitarian Assistance in the Wake of the Persian Gulf War." *Virginia Journal of International Law* Vol. 33 (1993): 491.

Tavernier, Paul, ed. *Nouvel ordre mondial et droits de l'homme: la guerre du Golfe*. Paris: Centre de recherches et d'études sur les droits de l'Homme et le droit humanitaire, 1993.

United Nations Department of Public Information. *The United Nations and the Iraq–Kuwait Conflict, 1990–1996*. New York: UNDPI, 1996.

Villani, Ugo. *Lezioni su l'ONU e la crisi des Golfo*. Bari: Caccuci Editore, 1991.

Weller, Marc, ed. *Iraq and Kuwait: The Hostilities and Their Aftermath*. Cambridge: Grotius Publications, 1993.

Weston, Burns H. "Security Council Resolution 678 and Persian Gulf Decision Making: Precarious Legitimacy." *American Journal of International Law* Vol. 85 No. 3 (1991): 516–535.

White, Nigel D. "The Legality of the Threat of Force against Iraq." *Security Dialogue* Vol. 30 No. 1 (1999): 75–86.

White, Nigel D. "Commentary on the Protection of the Kurdish Safe-Haven: Operation Desert Strike." *Journal of Armed Conflict Law* Vol. 1 No. 2 (1996): 197–204.

## Bosnia

Burg, Steven L. and Paul S. Shoup. *The War in Bosnia–Herzegovina: Ethnic Conflict and International Intervention*. London: M.E. Sharpe, 2000.

Caplan, Richard. *Post-Mortem on UNPROFOR*. London: Brassey's for the Centre for Defence Studies, 1996.

Chandler, David. "The Bosnian Protectorate and the Implications for Kosovo." *New Left Review* No. 235 (1999): 124–134.

Chandler, David. "The Limits of Peacebuilding: International Regulation and Civil Society Development in Bosnia." *International Peacekeeping* Vol. 6 No. 1 (1999): 109–125.

Chinkin, Christine M. "The Legality of NATO's Action in the Former Republic of Yugoslavia (FRY) under International Law." *International and Comparative Law Quarterly* Vol. 49 No. 4 (2000): 910–925.

Clemens, Walter C. Jr. "Can Outsiders Help? Lessons for Third-Party Intervention in Bosnia." *International Journal* Vol. 48 No. 4 (1993): 687–719.

Daalder, Ivo H. and Michael B.G. Froman. "Dayton's Incomplete Peace." *Foreign Affairs* Vol. 78 No. 6 (1999): 106–113.

Glenny, Misha. *The Fall of Yugoslavia: The Third Balkan War*. London: Penguin, 1996.

Gnesotto, Nicole. *Lessons of Yugoslavia*. Paris: Institute for Security Studies, 1994.

Holbrooke, Richard. *To End a War*. New York: Random House, 1998.

Kaplan, Robert D. *Balkan Ghosts: A Journey through History*. New York: St. Martin's Press, 1993.

Kresock, David M. "'Ethnic Cleansing' in the Balkans: The Legal Foundations of Foreign Intervention." *Cornell International Law Journal* Vol. 27 No. 1 (1994): 203–239.

Malesic, Marjan. "International Peacekeeping: An Object of Propaganda in Former Yugoslavia." *International Peacekeeping* Vol. 5 No. 2 (1998): 82–102.

Mercier, Michele. *Crimes without Punishment: Humanitarian Action in Former Yugoslavia*. London: Pluto Press, 1995.

Minear, Larry, Jeffrey Clark, Roberta Cohen, Dennis Gallagher and Iain Guest. *Humanitarian Action in the Former Yugoslavia: The UN's Role 1991–1993*. Providence: Thomas J. Watson Jr. Institute for International Studies, 1994.

Pape, Robert A. "Partition: An Exit Strategy for Bosnia." *Survival* Vol. 39 No. 4 (1997/1998): 25–28.

Pasic, Amir and Thomas G. Weiss. "Humanitarian Recognition in the Former Yugoslavia: The Limits of Non-State Politics." *Security Studies* Vol. 7 No. 1 (1997): 193–227.

Pasic, Amir and Thomas G. Weiss. "The Politics of Rescue: Yugoslavia's War and the Humanitarian Impulse." *Ethics and International Affairs* Vol. 11 (1997): 105–131.

*Report of the Secretary-General pursuant to General Assembly Resolution 53/55: The Fall of Srebrenica*. New York: 1999.

Rubin, Alfred P. "Dayton, Bosnia, and the Limits of Law." *The National Interest* Vol. 46 (1996/1997): 41–46.

Sandoz, Yves. *A Consideration of the Implementation of International Humanitarian Law and the Role of the International Committee of the Red Cross in the Former Yugoslavia*. Geneva: International Committee of the Red Cross, 1993.

Snyder, Frank M. *Humanitarian Intervention: Effectiveness of UN Operations in Bosnia*. Washington, DC: General Accounting Office, 1994.

Thant, Myint-U and Elizabeth Sellwood. *Knowledge and Multilateral Interventions: The UN's Experience in Cambodia and Bosnia–Herzegovina*. London: RIIA, 2000.

Ullman, Richard H., ed. *The World and Yugoslavia's Wars*. New York: Council on Foreign Relations Press, 1996.

Weiss, Thomas G. "UN Responses in the Former Yugoslavia: Moral and Operational Choices." *Ethics and International Affairs* Vol. 8 (1994): 1–22.

Weller, Marc. "The International Response to the Dissolution of the Socialist Federal Republic of Yugoslavia." *American Journal of International Law* Vol. 86 No. 3 (1992): 569–607.

Williams, John. "The Ethical Basis of Humanitarian Intervention, the Security Council and Yugoslavia." *International Peacekeeping* Vol. 6 No. 2 (1999): 1–23.

Woodward, Susan L. *The Balkan Tragedy: Chaos and Dissolution after the Cold War*. Washington, DC: Brookings Institution, 1995.

## Somalia

Abdullahi, Mohamed Diriye. *Fiasco in Somalia: US–UN Intervention*. Pretoria: Africa Institute of South Africa, 1995.

Bartl, Jürgen. *Die humanitäre Intervention durch den Sicherheitsrat der Vereinten Nationen im "failed state": Das Beispiel Somalia*. Frankfurt am Main: Lang, 1999.

Chopra, Jarat. "Achilles' Heel in Somalia: Learning from a Conceptual Failure." *Texas International Law Journal* Vol. 31 No. 3 (1996): 495–526.

Clark, Jeffrey. "Debacle in Somalia." *Foreign Affairs* Vol. 72 No. 1 (1993): 109–123.

Clarke, Walter S. *Humanitarian Intervention in Somalia: Bibliography*. Carlisle Barracks: US Army War College, 1995.

Clarke, Walter S. and Jeffrey Herbst, eds. *Learning from Somalia: The Lessons of Armed Humanitarian Intervention*. Boulder: Westview, 1997.

Clarke, Walter S. and Jeffrey Herbst. "Somalia and the Future of Humanitarian Intervention." *Foreign Affairs* Vol. 75 No. 2 (1996): 70–85.

Compagnon, Daniel. "Somalie: les limites de l'ingérence humanitaire: l'échec politique de l'ONU." *L'Afrique Politique* (1995): 193–202.

Crocker, Chester A. "The Lessons of Somalia: Not Everything Went Wrong." *Foreign Affairs* Vol. 74 No. 3 (1995): 2–8.

Drysdale, John. *Whatever Happened to Somalia? A Tale of Tragic Blunders.* London: Haan Associates, 1994.

Farrell, Theo. "Sliding into War: The Somalia Imbroglio and US Army Peace Operations Doctrine." *International Peacekeeping* Vol. 2 No. 2 (1995): 194–214.

Ganzglass, Martin R. "The Restoration of the Somali Justice System." *International Peacekeeping* Vol. 3 No. 1 (1996): 113–138.

Gibbs, David N. "Realpolitik and Humanitarian Intervention: The Case of Somalia." *International Politics* Vol. 37 No. 1 (2000): 41–56.

Hirsch, John L. and Robert B. Oakley. *Somalia and Operation Restore Hope: Reflections on Peacemaking and Peacekeeping.* Washington, DC: United States Institute of Peace, 1995.

Hutchison, M.R. "Restoring Hope: UN Security Council Resolutions for Somalia and an Expanded Doctrine of Humanitarian Intervention." *Harvard International Law Journal* Vol. 34 No. 2 (1993): 624–640.

Kennedy, Kevin M. "The Relationship Between the Military and Humanitarian Organizations in Operation Restore Hope." *International Peacekeeping* Vol. 3 No. 1 (1996): 92–112.

Lewis, I.M. *Making History in Somalia: Humanitarian Intervention in a Stateless Society.* London: Centre for the Study of Global Governance, LSE, 1995.

Lyons, Terrence and Ahmed Samatar. *Somalia: State Collapse, Multilateral Intervention, and Strategies for Political Reconstruction.* Washington, DC: Brookings Institution, 1995.

Makinda, Samuel M. *Seeking Peace from Chaos: Humanitarian Intervention in Somalia.* Boulder: Lynne Rienner, 1993.

Makinda, Samuel M. "Somalia: From Humanitarian Intervention to Military Offensive." *The World Today* Vol. 49 No. 10 (1993): 184–186.

Marchal, Roland. "La militarisation de l'humanitaire: l'example somalien." *Cultures et Conflits* No. 11 (1993): 77–92.

Menkhaus, Kenneth. "International Peacebuilding and the Dynamics of Local and National Reconciliation in Somalia." *International Peacekeeping* Vol. 3 No. 1 (1996): 42–67.

Murphy, Sean D. "Nation-Building: A Look at Somalia." *Tulane Journal of International and Comparative Law* Vol. 3 (1995): 19.

Natsios, Andrew S. "Humanitarian Relief Interventions in Somalia: The Economics of Chaos." *International Peacekeeping* Vol. 3 No. 1 (1996): 68–91.

Pausewang, Siegfried. *Humanitarian Assistance during Conflict in a State-less Society: The Case of Somalia.* Bergen: Chr. Michelsen Institute, 1999.

Refugee Policy Group. *Lives Lost, Lives Saved: Excess Mortality and the Impact of Health Interventions in the Somalia Emergency.* Washington, DC: RPG, 1994.

Sahnoun, Mohamed M. "Prevention in Conflict Resolution: The Case of Somalia." *Irish Studies in International Affairs* Vol. 5 (1994): 5–13.

Sahnoun, Mohamed M. *Somalia: The Missed Opportunities.* Washington, DC: United States Institute of Peace, 1994.

Sommer, John G. and Carole C. Collins. *Humanitarian Aid in Somalia: The Role of the Office of US Foreign Disaster Assistance (OFDA) 90–94.* Washington, DC: Refugee Policy Group, 1994.

Sucin, Snjezana. "Somalia Operations: Lessons to Be Learned by the United Nations and the United States." *Zbornik radova Pravnog Fakulteta u Splitu* Vol. 32 No. 1/2 (1995): 171–185.

Thakur, Ramesh. "From Peacekeeping to Peace Enforcement: The UN Operation in Somalia." *The Journal of Modern African Studies* Vol. 32 No. 3 (1994): 387–410.

Tripodi, Paolo. *The Colonial Legacy in Somalia: Rome and Mogadishu: From Colonial Administration to Operation Restore Hope*. London: Macmillan, 1999.

## Rwanda

Adelman, Howard and Astri Suhrke, eds. *The Path of a Genocide: The Rwanda Crisis from Uganda to Zaire*. New Brunswick: Transaction Publishers, 1999.

African Rights. *Rwanda: Death, Despair, and Defiance*. 2nd ed. London: AR, 1995.

Bauman, Ronny. *Devant le mal: Rwanda, un génocide en direct*. Paris: Arléa, 1994.

Burkhalter, Holly J. "The Question of Genocide: The Clinton Administration and Rwanda." *World Policy Journal* Vol. 11 No. 4 (1994/1995): 44–54.

Clapham, Christopher. "Rwanda: The Perils of Peacemaking." *Journal of Peace Research* Vol. 35 No. 2 (1998): 193–210.

Des Forges, Alison. *Leave None to Tell the Story: Genocide in Rwanda*. New York: Human Rights Watch, 1999.

De Waal, Alex and Rakiya Omaar. "The Genocide in Rwanda and the International Response." *Current History* Vol. 94 No. 591 (1995): 156–161.

Eriksson, John, Tor Sellström, Howard Adelman and Astri Suhrke. *The International Response to Conflict and Genocide: Lessons from the Rwanda Experience. Synthesis Report*. Copenhagen: Steering Committee of the Joint Evaluation of Emergency Assistance to Rwanda, 1996.

Gourevitch, Philip. *We Wish to Inform You That Tomorrow We Will Be Killed with Our Families: Stories from Rwanda*. London: Picador, 1999.

Hindell, Keith. "An Interventionist Manifesto." *International Relations* Vol. 13 No. 2 (1996): 23–35.

Human Rights Watch. *"Leave None to Tell the Story": Genocide in Rwanda*. New York: HRW, 1999.

Jones, Bruce D. " 'Intervention without Borders': Humanitarian Intervention in Rwanda, 1990–1994." *Millennium* Vol. 24 No. 2 (1995): 225–248.

Keane, Fergal. *Season of Blood: A Rwandan Journey*. London: Penguin, 1996.

Klinghoffer, Arthur J. *The International Dimension of Genocide in Rwanda*. Basingstoke: Macmillan, 1998.

Kuperman, Alan J. *The Limits of Humanitarian Intervention: Genocide in Rwanda*. Washington, DC: Brookings Institution, 2001.

Kuperman, Alan J. "Rwanda in Retrospect." *Foreign Affairs* Vol. 79 No. 1 (2000): 94–118.

Kuperman, Alan J. "The Other Lesson of Rwanda: Mediators Sometimes Do More Damage than Good." *SAIS Review* Vol. 16 No. 1 (1996): 221–240.

Lanxade, Amiral Jacques. "L'Opération Turquoise." *Défense Nationale* Vol. 51 No. 2 (1995): 7–15.

Mbadinga, Moussounga Itsouhou. "Considérations sur la légalité des interventions militaires étatiques dans la crise du Rwanda (1990–1994)." *African Journal of International and Comparative Law* Vol. 10 No. 1 (1998): 1–30.

McNulty, Mel. "France's Role in Rwanda and External Military Intervention: A Double Discrediting." *International Peacekeeping* Vol. 4 No. 3 (1997): 24–44.

Melvern, Linda. *A People Betrayed: The Role of the West in Rwanda's Genocide*. London: Zed Books, 2000.

O'Halloran, Patrick. *Humanitarian Intervention and the Genocide in Rwanda*. London: Research Institute for the Study of Conflict and Terrorism,1995.

Omaar, Rakiya and Alex de Waal. *Rwanda: Death, Despair and Destruction*. London: African Rights, 1994.

Ouguergouz, Fatsah. "La tragédie rwandaise du printemps 1994: quelques considérations sur les premières réactions de l'Organisation des Nations Unies." *Revue Générale de Droit International Public* Vol. 100 No. 1 (1996): 149–177.

Prunier, Gérard. *The Rwanda Crisis: History of a Genocide.* New York: Columbia University Press, 1997.

Raj, Sushil. "The Failure of Humanitarian Intervention in Rwanda and the Need for Reconceptualisation." *Indian Journal of International Law* Vol. 39 No. 3 (1999): 470–482.

Seybolt, Taylor B. *Coordination in Rwanda: The Humanitarian Response to Genocide and Civil War.* Cambridge, MA: Conflict Management Group, 1997.

Shue, Henry. "Let Whatever Is Smouldering Erupt? Conditional Sovereignty, Reviewable Intervention, and Rwanda 1994." In *Between Sovereignty and Global Governance: The United Nations, the State and Civil Society,* edited by Albert J. Paolini et al., 60–84. Basingstoke: Macmillan, 1998.

United Nations. *Report of the Independent Inquiry into the Actions of the United Nations during the 1994 Genocide in Rwanda.* New York: UN, 1999.

Uvin, Peter. *Development, Aid and Conflict: Reflection from the Case of Rwanda.* Helsinki: World Institute for Development Economics Research, 1996.

Willum, Bjørn. "Legitimizing Inaction towards Genocide in Rwanda: A Matter of Misperception?" *International Peacekeeping* Vol. 6 No. 3 (1999): 11–30.

## Haiti

Bar-Yaacov, Nomi. "Haïti: la lutte pour les droits de l'homme dans un conflit entre l'État et la Nation." *Le Trimestre du Monde* No. 1er trimestre (1995): 135–159.

Beardslee, W.Q. "The United States' Haiti Intervention: The Dangers of 'Redefined' National Security Interests." *Denver Journal of International Law and Policy* Vol. 25 (1996): 189–197.

Bentley, David. *Operation Uphold Democracy: Military Support for Democracy in Haiti.* Washington, DC: National Defense University, 1996.

Corten, Olivier. "La résolution 940 du Conseil de Sécurité autorisant une intervention militaire en Haïti: l'émergence d'un principe de légitimité démocratique en droit international?" *European Journal of International Law* Vol. 6 No. 1 (1995): 116–133.

Harvard Center for Population and Development Studies. *Sanctions in Haiti: Crisis in Humanitarian Action.* Cambridge, MA: Harvard School of Public Health, 1993.

Lecce, D.J. "International Law Regarding Pro-Democratic Intervention: A Study of the Dominican Republic and Haiti." *Naval Law Review* Vol. 45 (1998): 247–262.

Maguire, Robert, Edwige Balutansky, Jacques Fomerand, Larry Minear, William G. O'Neill, Thomas G. Weiss and Sarah Zaidi. *Haiti Held Hostage: International Responses to the Quest for Nationhood 1986–1996.* Providence: Thomas J. Watson Jr. Institute for International Studies, 1996.

Malone, David. *Decision-Making in the UN Security Council: The Case of Haiti, 1990–1997.* Oxford: Clarendon Press, 1998.

Malone, David. "Haiti and the International Community: A Case Study." *Survival* Vol. 39 No. 2 (1997): 126–146.

Morris, Justin. "Force and Democracy: UN/US Intervention in Haiti." *International Peacekeeping* Vol. 2 No. 3 (1995): 391–412.

Perusse, Roland. *Haitian Democracy Restored, 1991–1995.* Lanham: University Press of America, 1995.

Reisman, W. Michael. "Haiti and the Validity of International Action." *American Journal of International Law* Vol. 89 No. 1 (1995): 82–84.

Sweeney, John. "Stuck in Haiti." *Foreign Policy* No. 102 (1996): 143–151.

## Sierra Leone

Conteh, A.O. "Sierra Leone and the Norm of Non-Intervention: Evolution and Practice." *African Journal of International and Comparative Law* Vol. 7 No. 1 (1995): 166–183.

Davies, V.A.B. "Sierra Leone: Ironic Tragedy." *Journal of African Economies* Vol. 9 No. 3 (2000): 349–369.

Francis, David J. "Torturous Path to Peace: The Lomé Accord and Postwar Peacebuilding in Sierra Leone." *Security Dialogue* Vol. 31 No. 3 (2000): 357–373.

Francis, David J. "Mercenary Intervention in Sierra Leone: Providing National Security or International Exploitation?" *Third World Quarterly* Vol. 20 No. 2 (1999): 319–338.

Hirsch, John L. *Sierra Leone: Diamonds and the Struggle for Democracy.* Boulder: Lynne Rienner, 2001.

Human Rights Watch. *Getting Away with Murder, Mutilation, and Rape: New Testimony from Sierra Leone.* New York: HRW, 1999.

International Alert. *Abidjan Peace Accord: Sierra Leone.* London: IA, 1998.

Keen, David. "Aid and Violence, with Special Reference to Sierra Leone." *Disasters* Vol. 22 No. 4 (1998): 318–327.

Lizza, Ryan. "Where Angels Fear to Tread: Sierra Leone, the Last Clinton Betrayal." *New Republic* Vol. 223 No. 4 (2000): 22–27.

McGregor, Andrew. "Quagmire in West Africa: Nigerian Peacekeeping in Sierra Leone (1997–98)." *International Journal* Vol. 54 No. 3 (1999): 482–501.

Nowrot, Karsten. "The Use of Force to Restore Democracy: International Legal Implications of the ECOWAS Intervention in Sierra Leone." *American University International Law Review* Vol. 14 No. 2 (1998): 321–412.

Reno, William. "The Failure of Peacekeeping in Sierra Leone." *Current History* Vol. 100 No. 646 (2001): 219–225.

Shearer, David. "Exploring the Limits of Consent: Conflict Resolution in Sierra Leone." *Millennium* Vol. 26 No. 3 (1997): 845–860.

Smillie, Ian, Lansana Gberie and Ralph Hazleton. *The Heart of the Matter: Sierra Leone, Diamonds and Human Security.* Ottawa: Partnership Africa Canada, 2000.

## Kosovo

Alexander, Klinton W. "NATO's Intervention in Kosovo: The Legal Case for Violating Yugoslavia's National Sovereignty in the Absence of Security Council Approval." *Houston Journal of International Law* Vol. 22 No. 3 (2000): 403–449.

Ali, Tariq, ed. *Masters of the Universe? NATO's Balkan Crusade.* New York: Verso, 2000.

Amnesty International. *Kosovo: After Tragedy, Justice?* London: AI, 1999.

Bellamy, Alex J. "Lessons Unlearned: Why Coercive Diplomacy Failed at Rambouillet." *International Peacekeeping* Vol. 7 No. 2 (2000): 95–114.

Betts, Richard K. "The Lesser Evil: The Best Way out of the Balkans." *The National Interest* No. 64 (2001): 53–65.

Bilder, Richard B. "Kosovo and the 'New Interventionism': Promise or Peril?" *Journal of Transnational Law and Policy* Vol. 9 No. 1 (1999): 153–182.

Blackburn, Robin. "Kosovo: The War of NATO Expansion." *New Left Review* No. 235 (1999): 107–123.

Brownlie, Ian. "Kosovo Crisis Inquiry: Memorandum on the International Law Aspects." *International and Comparative Law Quarterly* Vol. 49 No. 4 (2000): 878–905.

Caccamo, Domenico. "Kosovo: vincitori e vinti." *Rivista di studi politici internazionali* Vol. 66 No. 3 (1999): 361–406.

Caplan, Richard. "Kosovo: The Implications for Humanitarian Intervention." *Forced Migration Review* No. 5 (1999).

Charney, Jonathan. "Anticipatory Humanitarian Intervention in Kosovo." *American Journal of International Law* Vol. 93 No. 4 (1999): 834–841.

Chinkin, Christine M. "Kosovo: A 'Good' or 'Bad' War." *American Journal of International Law* Vol. 93 No. 4 (1999): 841–847.

Chomsky, Noam. *A New Generation Draws the Line: Kosovo, East Timor and the Standards of the West.* New York: Verso, 2001.

Chomsky, Noam. *The New Military Humanism: Lessons from Kosovo.* London: Pluto Press, 1999.

Cimmino, Letizia. "Diritti umani e uso della forza: l'intervento armato in Kossovo." *Rivista di diritto pubblico e scienze politiche* Vol. 10 No. 2 (2000): 247–257.

Daalder, Ivo H. and Michael E. O'Hanlon. *Winning Ugly: NATO's War to Save Kosovo.* Washington, DC: Brookings Institution, 2000.

Egorov, Sergey Alexeyevich. "The Kosovo Crisis and the Law of Armed Conflicts." *International Review of the Red Cross* Vol. 82 No. 837 (2000): 183–192.

Falk, Richard A. "Kosovo, World Order, and the Future of International Law." *American Journal of International Law* Vol. 93 No. 4 (1999): 847–857.

Freedman, Lawrence. "Victims and Victors: Reflections on the Kosovo War." *Review of International Studies* Vol. 26 No. 3 (2000): 335–358.

Galen Carpenter, Ted, ed. *NATO's Empty Victory: A Postmortem on the Balkan War.* Washington, DC: Cato Institute, 2000.

Gowan, Peter. "The NATO Powers and the Balkan Tragedy." *New Left Review* No. 234 (1999): 83–105.

Greenwood, Christopher. "International Law and the NATO Intervention in Kosovo." *International and Comparative Law Quarterly* Vol. 49 No. 4 (2000): 926–934.

Guicherd, Catherine. "International Law and the War in Kosovo." *Survival* Vol. 41 No. 2 (1999): 19–33.

Hammond, Philip and Edward S. Herman, eds. *Degraded Capability: The Media and the Kosovo Crisis.* Sterling: Pluto Press, 2000.

Henkin, Louis. "Kosovo and the Law of 'Humanitarian Intervention'." *American Journal of International Law* Vol. 93 No. 4 (1999): 824–828.

Hummer, Waldemar. "Der Kosovo Krieg vor dem Internationalen Gerichtshof." *Neue Justiz* Vol. 54 No. 3 (2000): 113–120.

Ignatieff, Michael. *Virtual War: Kosovo and Beyond.* London: Vintage, 2001.

Independent International Commission on Kosovo. *The Kosovo Report: Conflict, International Response, Lessons Learned.* Oxford: Oxford University Press, 2000.

Ipsen, Knut. "Der Kosovo-Einsatz: illegal? gerechtfertigt? entschuldbar?" *Die Friedenswarte* Vol. 74 No. 1–2 (1999): 19–32.

Judah, Tim. *Kosovo: War and Revenge.* New Haven: Yale University Press, 2000.

Kamp, Karl-Heinz. "L'OTAN après le Kosovo: ange de paix ou gendarme du monde?" *Politique étrangère* Vol. 64 No. 2 (1999): 245–256.

Kohen, Marcelo G. "L'emploi de la force et la crise du Kosovo: vers un nouveau désordre juridique international." *Revue Belge de Droit International* Vol. 32 No. 1 (1999): 122–148.

Kovács, Péter. "Intervention armée des forces de l'OTAN au Kosovo: fondement de l'obligation de respecter le droit international humanitaire." *International Review of the Red Cross* Vol. 82 No. 837 (2000): 103–128.

Kritsiotis, Dino. "The Kosovo Crisis and NATO's Application of Armed Force against the Federal Republic of Yugoslavia." *International and Comparative Law Quarterly* Vol. 49 No. 2 (2000): 330–359.

Littman, Mark. *Kosovo: Law and Diplomacy*. London: Centre for Policy Studies, 1999.

Lowe, Vaughan. "International Legal Issues Arising in the Kosovo Crisis." *International and Comparative Law Quarterly* Vol. 49 No. 4 (2000): 934–943.

Lutz, Dieter S., ed. *Der Kosovo-Krieg: Rechtliche und rechtsethische Aspekte*. Baden-Baden: Nomos, 2000.

Mandelbaum, Michael. "A Perfect Failure: NATO's War against Yugoslavia." *Foreign Affairs* Vol. 78 No. 5 (1999): 2–8.

McCoubrey, Hilaire. "Kosovo, NATO, and International Law." *International Relations* Vol. 14 No. 5 (1999): 29–46.

Merkel, Reinhard, ed. *Der Kosovo-Krieg und das Völkerrecht*. Frankfurt am Main: Suhrkamp, 2000.

Merkel, Reinhard. "Das Elend der Beschützten: Über die Grundlagen der Legitimität sog. humanitärer Interventionen und die Verwerflichkeit der Nato-Aktionen im Kosovo-Krieg." *Kritische Justiz* Vol. 32 No. 4 (1999): 526–542.

Minear, Larry, Ted Van Baarda and Marc Sommers. *NATO and Humanitarian Action in the Kosovo Crisis*. Providence: Thomas J. Watson Jr. Institute for International Studies, 2000.

Mitic, Miodrag. "Case Concerning NATO Aggression against Yugoslavia before the International Court of Justice: Yet Another Precedent of the International Community." *Review of International Affairs* Vol. 50 (1999): 9–13.

Momtaz, Djamchid. "'L'intervention d'humanité' de l'OTAN au Kosovo et la règle du non-recours á la force." *International Review of the Red Cross* Vol. 82 No. 837 (2000): 89–101.

Picone, Paolo. "La 'guerra del Kosovo' e il diritto internazionale generale." *Rivista di diritto internazionale* Vol. 83 No. 2 (2000): 309–360.

Pugh, Michael C. "Civil–Military Relations in the Kosovo Crisis: An Emerging Hegemony?" *Security Dialogue* Vol. 31 No. 2 (2000): 229–242.

Rieff, David. "Kosovo's Humanitarian Circus." *World Policy Journal* Vol. 17 No. 3 (2000): 25–32.

Roberts, Adam. "NATO's 'Humanitarian War' over Kosovo." *Survival* Vol. 41 No. 3 (1999): 102–123.

Schirrmacher, Frank, ed. *Der westliche Kreuzzug: 41 Positionen zum Kosovo-Krieg*. Stuttgart: Deutsche Verlags-Anstalt, 1999.

Schwabach, Aaron. "Yugoslavia vs. NATO, Security Council Resolution 1244, and the Law of Humanitarian Intervention." *Syracuse Journal of International Law and Commerce* Vol. 27 (2000): 77.

Sofaer, Abraham D. "International Law and Kosovo." *Stanford Journal of International Law* Vol. 36 No. 1 (2000): 1–21.

Solana, Javier. "NATO's Success in Kosovo." *Foreign Affairs* Vol. 78 No. 6 (1999): 114–120.

Swift, John. "The Kosovo War and the Doctrine of Humanitarian Intervention." *Administration* Vol. 48 No. 2 (2000): 57–76.

Tomuschat, Christian. "Völkerrechtliche Aspekte des Kosovo-Konflikts." *Die Friedenswarte* Vol. 74 No. 1–2 (1999): 33–37.

Toro Dávila, Juan Guillermo. "Kosovo: Contraposition of Interests between the United Nations and the North Atlantic Treaty Organisation." *Peace and Security* Vol. 31 (1999): 10–24.

Valki, László. "The Kosovo Crisis and International Law." In *Le droit international au tournant du millénaire: l'approche hongroise*, edited by Péter Kovács, 33–47. Budapest: Pázmány Péter Catholic University, 2000.

Valticos, Nicolas. "Les droits de l'homme, le droit international et l'intervention militaire en Yougoslavie: où va-t-on? Éclipse du Conseil de Sécurité ou réforme du droit de veto?" *Revue Genérale de Droit International Public* Vol. 104 No. 1 (2000): 5–18.

Vasconcelos, Á de. "Kosovo, ponto de viragem na intervenção humanitária." *Política internacional* Vol. 20 (1999): 17–22.

Williams, John. "The Ethical Basis of Humanitarian Intervention, the Security Council and Yugoslavia." *International Peacekeeping* Vol. 6 No. 2 (1999): 1–23.

Yannis, Alexandros. "Kosovo under International Administration." *Survival* Vol. 43 No. 2 (2001): 31–48.

Zappala. "Nuovi sviluppi in relazione alle vicende del Kosovo." *Rivista di diritto internazionale* (1999): 975–1004.

## East Timor

Chopra, Jarat. "The UN's Kingdom of East Timor." *Survival* Vol. 42 No. 3 (2000): 27–39.

Cotton, James. "Against the Grain: The East Timor Intervention." *Survival* Vol. 43 No. 1 (2001): 127–142.

Downer, Alexander. "East Timor: Looking back on 1999." *Australian Journal of International Affairs* Vol. 54 No. 1 (2000): 5–10.

Dupont, Alan. "ASEAN's Response to the East Timor Crisis." *Australian Journal of International Affairs* Vol. 54 No. 2 (2000): 163–170.

Emmerson, Donald K. "Moralpolitik: The Timor Test." *The National Interest* No. 58 (1999/2000): 63–68.

Gunn, Geoffrey. *East Timor and the United Nations: The Case for Intervention*. Lawrenceville: Red Sea Press, 1997.

Kelly, Michael J., Timothy L.H. McCormack, Paul Muggleton and Bruce M. Oswald. "Legal Aspects of Australia's Involvement in the International Force for East Timor." *International Review of the Red Cross* Vol. 83 No. 841 (2001): 101–138.

Levrat, Bertrand. "Le droit international humanitaire au Timor oriental: entre théorie et pratique." *International Review of the Red Cross* Vol. 83 No. 841 (2001): 77–99.

Rothert, Mark. "UN Intervention in East Timor." *Columbia Journal of Transnational Law* Vol. 39 No. 1 (2000): 257–282.

Salla, Michael. "East Timor and Australian Foreign Policy." *Australian Journal of International Affairs* Vol. 49 No. 2 (1995): 207–222.

Sebastian, Leonard C. and Anthony L. Smith. "The East Timor Crisis: A Test Case for Humanitarian Intervention." In *Southeast Asian Affairs 2000*, edited by Daljit Singh, 64–83. Singapore: Institute of Southeast Asian Studies, 2000.

United Nations Development Programme. *Conceptual Framework for Reconstruction, Recovery and Development of East Timor*. Geneva: UNDP, 1999.

Vasconcelos, Alvaro. "L'intervention au Timor et le multilatéralisme possible." *Politique Étrangère* Vol. 65 No. 1 (2000): 135–149.

# PART III

# BACKGROUND

# BACKGROUND

The background component of this volume consists of three parts. The first part of the background provides a brief description of the terms of reference and various activities of the International Commission on Intervention and State Sovereignty (ICISS) itself, as well as how it was organized and functioned. The second part of the background contains short biographical information about the 12 Commissioners. The third features a list of participants and summary reports for each regional roundtable and national consultation that was organized on behalf of the ICISS.

# 1. ABOUT THE COMMISSION

## Mandate

At the United Nations (UN) Millennium Assembly in September 2000, Canadian Prime Minister Jean Chrétien announced that an independent International Commission on Intervention and State Sovereignity (ICISS) would be established as a response to Secretary-General Kofi Annan's challenge to the international community to endeavour to build a new international consensus on how to respond in the face of massive violations of human rights and humanitarian law.

Launching ICISS on September 14, 2000, then Foreign Minister Lloyd Axworthy said that the mandate of ICISS would be to promote a comprehensive debate on the issues and to foster global political consensus on how to move from polemics, and often paralysis, toward action within the international system, particularly through the UN. Much as the Brundtland Commission on Environment and Development in the 1980s took the apparently irreconcilable issues of development and environmental protection and, through the process of an intense intellectual and political debate, emerged with the notion of "sustainable development," it was hoped that ICISS would be able to find new ways of reconciling the seemingly irreconcilable notions of intervention and state sovereignty.

It was proposed that ICISS complete its work within a year, enabling the Canadian Government to take the opportunity of the 56th session of the UN General Assembly to inform the international community of ICISS's findings and recommendations for action.

## Commissioners

The Canadian Government invited to head ICISS the Honourable Gareth Evans, AO QC, President of the International Crisis Group and former Australian Foreign Minister, and His Excellency Mohamed Sahnoun of Algeria, Special Advisor to the UN Secretary-General and formerly his Special Representative (SRSG) for Somalia and the Great Lakes Region of Africa. In consultation with the Co-Chairs, 10 other distinguished Commissioners were appointed, spanning between them an enormously diverse range of regional backgrounds, views and perspectives, and experiences and eminently able to address the complex array of legal, moral, political, and operational issues ICISS had to confront. A full list of the members of ICISS, with biographical summaries, is contained in the second part of the background component of this volume.

## Advisory Board

Canada's Minister of Foreign Affairs, the Honourable John Manley, appointed an international Advisory Board of serving and former foreign ministers and other eminent individuals to act as a political reference point for the ICISS. The Advisory Board was designed to help Commissioners ground their report in current political realities and assist in building the political momentum and public engagement required to follow up on its recommendations.

Members of the Advisory Board are the Honourable Lloyd Axworthy (Chair), Director and CEO of the Liu Centre for the Study of Global Issues at the University of British Columbia and former Canadian Minister of Foreign Affairs; Her Excellency María Soledad Alvear Valenzuela, Minister of Foreign Affairs of the Republic of Chile; Dr. Hanan Ashrawi, former Cabinet Minister of the Palestinian National Authority; Right Honourable Robin Cook,

President of the Council and Leader of the House of Commons, United Kingdom of Great Britain and Northern Ireland, and former British Foreign Secretary; Mr. Jonathan F. Fanton, President of the John D. and Catherine T. MacArthur Foundation; Professor Bronisław Geremek, Chair of the European Law Committee of the Sejm of the Republic of Poland; Her Excellency Rosario Green Macías, former Secretary of Foreign Relations, United Mexican States; Dr. Vartan Gregorian, President of the Carnegie Corporation of New York; Dr. Ivan Head, Founding Director of the Liu Centre for the Study of Global Issues, University of British Columbia; Honorable Patrick Leahy, United States (US) Senator; His Excellency Amre Moussa, Secretary-General of the League of Arab States and former Minister of Foreign Affairs of the Arab Republic of Egypt; His Excellency George Papandreou, Minister of Foreign Affairs of the Hellenic Republic; His Excellency Dr. Surin Pitsuwan, former Minister of Foreign Affairs of the Kingdom of Thailand; Dr. Mamphela Ramphele, Managing Director of The World Bank Group and former Vice-Chancellor of the University of Cape Town; and His Excellency Adalberto Rodríguez Giavarini, Minister of Foreign Relations, International Trade and Worship of the Argentine Republic.

The Advisory Board met with Commissioners in London on June 22, 2001, with the following members participating in what proved to be a highly lively and productive debate: former Canadian Foreign Minister, Lloyd Axworthy; Secretary-General of the Arab League, Amre Moussa; former British Foreign Secretary, Robin Cook; former Mexican Foreign Minister, Rosario Green; former Chilean Foreign Minister Juan Gabriel Valdés (also representing the current Chilean Foreign Minister); representatives of the foreign ministers of Argentina and Greece; President of the MacArthur Foundation, Jonathan Fanton; and Founding Director of the Liu Centre at the University of British Columbia, Ivan Head.

### Commission Meetings

Five full meetings of ICISS were held: in Ottawa on November 5–6, 2000; Maputo, March 11–12, 2001; New Delhi, June 11–12, 2001; Wakefield, Canada, August 5–9, 2001; and Brussels, September 30, 2001. There was also an informal Commission meeting in Geneva on February 1, 2001, involving a number of Commissioners in person and others by conference call, and multiple further meetings of small groups of Commissioners in the roundtables and consultations described below.

At their first meeting, Commissioners considered a series of central questions, identified the key issues and decided on a general approach. An early draft outline of the report was then developed and circulated. This outline was considered at the Geneva meeting in early February and expanded further at the Maputo meeting in March. A fuller draft was then produced in May, circulated to Commissioners for consideration and initial comment and considered in more detail at the New Delhi meeting in June. Significant changes to the substance and structure of the report were agreed on at that meeting. On this basis, a further draft was produced and circulated in early July, with Commissioners making specific written comments.

The final stage of the process involved the Co-Chairs themselves – meeting in Brussels over several days in July – producing a further full-length draft, with substantial written input from a number of other Commissioners. The Co-Chairs' draft, distributed to Commissioners a week in advance of the final Commission meeting in Wakefield, was then considered in exhaustive detail over four days. The final terms of the report were agreed on unanimously. A further meeting of the Commission was held in Brussels at the end of September to consider the implications for the report of the horrifying terrorist attacks on New York and Washington DC earlier that month: this resulted in a number of adjustments to the final text as published.

## Consultation

In order to stimulate debate and ensure that ICISS heard the broadest possible range of views during the course of its mandate, 11 regional roundtables and national consultations were held around the world between January and July 2001. In date order, they were held in Ottawa on January 15, Geneva on January 31, London on February 3, Maputo on March 10, Washington DC, on May 2, Santiago on May 4, Cairo on May 21, Paris on May 23, New Delhi on June 10, Beijing on June 14, and St Petersburg on July 16. Summaries of the issues discussed in these meetings, and lists of those participating in them, may be found in what follows.

At least one, and usually both, of the Co-Chairs attended each of these consultations, for the most part with some other Commissioners as well. A variety of national and regional officials, and representatives of civil society, nongovernmental organizations (NGOs), academic institutions and think-tanks were invited to each of the meetings. A paper setting out the main issues from ICISS's perspective was circulated to participants in advance of the meetings to stimulate discussion, and specific participants were invited in advance to prepare papers and make special presentations on various aspects of the issues. These papers formed an additional and extremely useful source of research material on which ICISS could draw. A further participant at each roundtable was selected to produce a summary report of the proceedings and outcomes of each of the roundtables. These various contributions are more fully acknowledged elsewhere in this volume.

Regular briefings were also given to interested governments in capitals, as well as to diplomatic missions in Ottawa and Geneva and most recently in New York on June 26–27, where the Commission met with representatives from a number of Permanent Missions as well as with Secretary-General Annan and key members of the UN Secretariat. Consultations were also held in Geneva on January 31 with the heads or senior representatives of major international organizations and UN agencies (UN Office Geneva, UN High Commissioner for Refugees, Commission on Human Rights, World Health Organization, International Organization for Migration [IOM], International Committee of the Red Cross and International Federation of Red Cross and Red Crescent Societies, and Office for the Coordination of Humanitarian Affairs).

## Research

An extensive programme of research was organized in support of ICISS's work. Aiming to build upon and complement the many efforts previously undertaken on these issues, Commissioners drew upon the record of debate and discussion generated at the UN and in regional and other forums; the vast body of already published scholarly and policy research on this topic, including a number of important independent and nationally sponsored studies; and a series of papers and studies specially commissioned for the ICISS.

To supplement and consolidate the intellectual dimension of ICISS's work, an international research team was created. This was led jointly by Thomas G. Weiss of the United States, Presidential Professor at The CUNY Graduate Center, where he is also director of the Ralph Bunche Institute for International Studies, and Stanlake J.T.M. Samkange, of Zimbabwe, a lawyer and former speechwriter to UN Secretary-General Boutros Boutros-Ghali. Tom Weiss, with research consultant Don Hubert of Canada, assumed primary responsibility for producing the research papers contained in this supplementary volume, while Stanlake Samkange's primary role was as rapporteur, assisting ICISS in the drafting of its report.

Other members of the research team played important roles. Kevin Ozgercin and Peter Hoffman of the Research Directorate, located at The CUNY Graduate Center, provided essential research and support in the writing of this volume. Carolin Thielking at Oxford University, with supervision from Professor S. Neil MacFarlane, had a principal role in the preparation of the bibliography contained in this volume.

It is hoped that the research material prepared for ICISS and contained in this supplementary volume, together with the report itself, will constitute an enduring legacy for scholars, specialists and policy makers in the field. This volume, as well as the report, have accordingly been produced and made available in CD-ROM form, with the Bibliography cross-referenced with key-words to enhance its utility as a research tool. These and other documents also appear on the special ICISS website – www.iciss-ciise.gc.ca – which will be maintained for at least the next five years.

### Administrative Support

The workplan of ICISS was administered by a small Secretariat, provided as part of the Canadian Government support for ICISS. Housed within the Department of Foreign Affairs and International Trade in Ottawa, the Secretariat undertook necessary fund-raising, organized the roundtable consultations and Commissioners' meetings, managed the publication and distribution of ICISS's report and background research, and spearheaded diplomatic efforts to engage governments and build political support for the debate. The Secretariat was led by Jill Sinclair, Executive Director, and Heidi Hulan, Deputy Director, and comprised Susan Finch, Manager of the Outreach Strategy; Tony Advokaat, Policy Advisor; Joseph Moffatt, Policy Advisor; Tudor Hera, Policy Analyst; Harriet Roos, Manager of Communications; and Carole Dupuis-Têtu, Administrative Assistant. Former Australian diplomat Ken Berry acted as Executive Assistant to the Co-Chairs, and staff at Canadian Embassies round the world and the International Development Research Centre in Ottawa provided additional support to the Secretariat.

### Funding

ICISS was funded by the Canadian Government, together with major international foundations, including the Carnegie Corporation of New York, the William and Flora Hewlett Foundation, the John D. and Catherine T. MacArthur Foundation, the Rockefeller Foundation, and the Simons Foundation. ICISS is also indebted to the governments of Switzerland and the United Kingdom for their generous financial and in-kind support to the work of ICISS.

# 2. ABOUT THE COMMISSIONERS

**Gareth Evans** *(Australia)*, *Co-Chair*, has been President and Chief Executive of the Brussels-based International Crisis Group since January 2000. He was an Australian Senator and Member of Parliament from 1978 to 1999 and a Cabinet Minister for 13 years (1983–1996). As Foreign Minister (1988–1996), he played prominent roles in developing the UN peace plan for Cambodia, concluding the Chemical Weapons Convention, founding the Asia Pacific Economic Cooperation forum and initiating the Canberra Commission on the Elimination of Nuclear Weapons. He is a Queen's Counsel (1983) and Officer of the Order of Australia (2001). His many publications include *Cooperating for Peace* (1993) and the article "Cooperative Security and Intrastate Conflict" (*Foreign Policy*, 1994), for which he won the 1995 Grawemeyer Prize for Ideas Improving World Order.

**Mohamed Sahnoun** *(Algeria)*, *Co-Chair*, is a Special Advisor to the UN Secretary-General and has previously served as Special Envoy of the Secretary-General on the Ethiopian–Eritrean conflict (1999); Joint UN–Organization of African Unity (OAU) Special Representative for the Great Lakes Region of Africa (1997); and SRSG for Somalia (March–October 1992). He was also a member of the World Commission on Environment and Development (the Brundtland Commission). A senior Algerian diplomat, he served as Ambassador to Germany, France, the US, and Morocco and as Permanent Representative to the UN in New York. He also served as Deputy Secretary-General of both the OAU and the Arab League.

**Gisèle Côté-Harper** *(Canada)* is a barrister and Professor of Law at Laval University, Quebec. She has been a member of, among numerous other bodies, the UN Human Rights Committee, the Inter-American Institute of Human Rights, and the Quebec Human Rights Commission. She was Chair of the Board of the International Centre for Human Rights and Democratic Development (Montreal) (1990–1996) and a member of the official Canadian delegation to the Fourth World Conference on Women, Beijing (1995). She was awarded the Lester B. Pearson Peace Medal in 1995 and in 1997 became an Officer of the Order of Canada, as well as receiving the Quebec Bar Medal. Among her published works is *Traité de droit pénal canadien* (4th ed., 1998).

**Lee Hamilton** *(US)* is Director of the Woodrow Wilson International Center for Scholars, Washington, DC, and Director of the Center on Congress at Indiana University. A member of the US Congress from 1965 to 1999, his distinguished record includes the chairships of the Committee on International Relations, the Permanent Select Committee on Intelligence, and the Joint Economic Committee. He has served on a number of commissions dealing with international issues, including the Task Force on Strengthening Palestinian Public Institutions, the Task Force on the Future of International Financial Architecture, and the Council of Foreign Relations Independent Task Force on US–Cuban Relations in the 21st Century, as well as numerous other panels, committees, and boards.

**Michael Ignatieff** *(Canada)* is currently Director of the Carr Center for Human Rights Policy at the Kennedy School of Government, Harvard University. He is also a Senior Fellow of the 21st Century Trust and served as a member of the Independent International Commission on Kosovo. Since 1984 he has worked as a freelance writer, broadcaster, historian, moral philosopher, and cultural analyst. He has written extensively on ethnic conflict and most recently on the various conflicts in the Balkans, including *Virtual War: Kosovo and Beyond*. He has also authored numerous other works, including a biography of the liberal philosopher Isaiah Berlin. *The Russian Album*, a family memoir, won Canada's Governor General's Literary Award and the Heinemann Prize of Britain's Royal Society of Literature in 1988. His second novel, *Scar Tissue*, was short-listed for the Booker Prize in 1993.

**Vladimir Lukin** *(Russia)* is currently Deputy Speaker of the Russian State Duma. He worked at the Institute of World Economics and International Relations, Moscow (1961–1965) and the Institute of US and Canadian Studies of the Soviet Academy of Sciences (1968–1987). He also served from 1965 to 1968 as an editor of the international journal *Problems of the World and Socialism*, in Prague, but was expelled for opposing the Soviet invasion of Czechoslovakia in 1968. He joined the Soviet Foreign Ministry in 1987 and served as Russian Ambassador to the US (1992–1993). He was elected a Deputy to the Supreme Soviet of the Russian Soviet Federated Socialist Republic in 1990 and to the State Duma of the Russian Federation in 1993. In that year, he helped found the Yabloko Faction, a party that he still represents. He served as Chair of the International Affairs Committee of the Duma (1995–1999).

**Klaus Naumann** *(Germany)* served as Chair of the North Atlantic Military Committee of the North Atlantic Treaty Organization (NATO) (1996–1999) and played a central role in managing the Kosovo crisis and in developing NATO's new integrated military command structure. He joined the German Bundeswehr in 1958. As a Colonel, he served on the staff of the German Military Representative to the NATO Military Committee in Brussels in 1981–1982. He was promoted to Brigadier General in 1986, followed by a two-star assignment as Assistant Chief of Staff of the Federal Armed Forces. He was promoted to Four Star General in 1991 and appointed, at the same time, Chief of Staff, a position he held until becoming Chair of the NATO Military Committee. After retirement, he served as a member of the Panel on UN Peace Operations.

**Cyril Ramaphosa** *(South Africa)* is currently Executive Chair of Rebserve, a major South African service and facilities management company. He was elected Secretary-General of the African National Congress in June 1991, but he left politics for business in 1996. He played a major role in building the biggest and most powerful trade union in South Africa, the National Union of Mineworkers, from 1982 onwards. A lawyer by training, his university years were interrupted by periods in jail for political activities. He played a crucial role in negotiations with the former South African regime to bring about a peaceful end to apartheid and steer the country toward its first democratic elections in April 1994, after which he was elected Chair of the new Constitutional Assembly. He received the Olaf Palme prize in October 1987 and was invited to participate in the Northern Ireland peace process in May 2000.

**Fidel V. Ramos** *(Philippines)* served as President of the Republic of the Philippines from 1992 to 1998 and has since 1999 been Chair of the Ramos Peace and Development Foundation, which deals with Asia–Pacific security, sustainable development, democratic governance, and economic diplomacy. Prior to becoming President, he had a long and distinguished military and police career, including service in both the Korean and Vietnam wars. He became Deputy Chief of Staff of the armed forces of the Philippines in 1981 and Chief of Staff in 1986 and subsequently served as Secretary of National Defence from 1988 to 1991. He played a central role in peace negotiations with Muslim rebels in the southern Philippines and wrote *Break Not the Peace*, a book about that peace process.

**Cornelio Sommaruga** *(Switzerland)* is currently President of the Caux Foundation for Moral Re-Armament, as well as President of the Geneva International Centre for Humanitarian Demining. He is, in addition, a member of the Board of the Open Society Institute, Budapest, and served as a member of the Panel on UN Peace Operations. Prior to that, he was President of the International Committee of the Red Cross (ICRC) (1987–1999). From 1984 to 1986, he served as Switzerland's State Secretary for External Economic Affairs. From 1960, he had had a long and distinguished career as a Swiss diplomat, including a period from 1973 as Deputy Secretary-General of the European Free Trade Association in Geneva. In 1977–1978, he served as President of the UN Economic Commission for Europe.

**Eduardo Stein Barillas** *(Guatemala)* is currently working with United Nations Development Programme in Panama and served as Head of the Organization of American States (OAS) Observer Mission to Peru's May 2000 general elections. He was Guatemalan Foreign Minister (1996–2000), a position in which he played a key role in overseeing the Guatemalan peace negotiations, particularly in marshalling international support. He lectured in universities in Guatemala and Panama from 1971 to 1980 and 1985 to 1987; and from 1982 to 1993, he was based in Panama and worked on various regional development projects within the Latin American Economic System and the Contadora Group. This involved cooperation with various Latin American countries, the European Community, and the Nordic countries. From December 1993 to 1995, he was Resident Representative in Panama of the Organization for Migration (IOM).

**Ramesh Thakur** *(India)* has been Vice-Rector of the United Nations University, Tokyo, since 1998, in charge of the university's Peace and Governance Program. Educated in India and Canada, he was a lecturer, then Professor of International Relations at the University of Otago (New Zealand) from 1980 to 1995. He was then appointed Professor and Head of the Peace Research Centre at the Australian National University in Canberra, where he was involved in the Non-Proliferation Treaty Review and Extension Conference, drafting of the Comprehensive Test Ban Treaty and the International Campaign to Ban Landmines. He was also a consultant to the Canberra Commission on the Elimination of Nuclear Weapons. He is the author of numerous books and articles, including *Past Imperfect, Future Uncertain: The United Nations at Fifty*, and in 2000 he co-edited *Kosovo and the Challenge of Humanitarian Intervention*.

# 3. REGIONAL ROUNDTABLES AND NATIONAL CONSULTATIONS

An integral part of the deliberations by the ICISS consisted of 11 regional roundtables and national consultations. The summaries of those deliberations along with participants who were invited by ICISS and attended the sessions are listed below.

## OTTAWA

## ROUNDTABLE CONSULTATION WITH NONGOVERNMENTAL AND OTHER INTERESTED ORGANIZATIONS

## JANUARY 15, 2001

PARTICIPANTS

John English, University of Waterloo (Co-Chair)
Steven Lee, Canadian Centre for Foreign Policy Development (Co-Chair)

Charlie Avendano, Mines Action Canada
Gerry Barr, Canadian Council for International Cooperation
Gerald Caplan, author
Jocelyn Coulon, Pearson Peacekeeping Centre
Jean Daudelin, North–South Institute

Pierre Duplessis, Canadian Red Cross
John Hay, Consultant
Roman Jakubow, Department of National Defence
Will Kymlicka, Queen's University at Kingston
Hunter McGill, Canadian International Development Agency
Errol Mendes, Human Rights Research and Education Centre, University of Ottawa
Mohammed Qazilbash, Oxfam Canada
Ernie Regehr, Project Ploughshares
Jean-François Rioux, Université du Québec à Montréal
Penelope Simons, Simons Foundation
Denis Stairs, Dalhousie University
Nečla Tschirgi, International Development Research Centre
A. John Watson, CARE Canada
Fergus Watt, Canadian Peacebuilding Coordinating Committee
Paul Wharram, Canadian Red Cross
James Wright, Department of Foreign Affairs and International Trade, Canada

# SUMMARY

### Terminology

There was broad support, particularly from the NGO community, for dissociating the term "humanitarian" from the concept of military intervention. It was noted that a change in terminology could also help to move the debate away from how it had traditionally been developed, though one participant argued that basing it on protection has a neocolonial ring to it. On the other hand, one member of the NGO community argued that the term "humanitarian" has a specific technical and legal meaning in the context of the intervention debate. The term "humanitarian intervention" refers to a very limited military emergency-response mechanism carried out according to humanitarian principles, such as universality, independence, impartiality, and humanity. Hence, there is value in retaining that term and distinguishing it from other types of collective military action.

### National Interest

The question was raised of how there could be serious nonselective intervention when it is the five permanent members of the Security Council (P-5) who determine whether there would be an intervention and who would participate. One participant argued that the major powers would support dictatorships abusive of their civilian population when it suits their interest. It was also noted that the Bush Administration would not favour intervention unless it is clearly in the national interest of the US.

National interest, rather than sovereignty, was identified as the most serious constraint on intervention, playing a key role in whether and where an intervention takes place. Thus, the real debate is not about the right of the international community to intervene and the target state's right of sovereignty, but about humanitarian imperatives and national interest. The need to reconceive the concept of national interest was emphasized. It is about economics and security, but it is also about reputation. There is a benefit in its own right in being, and being seen to be, a good international citizen. This may be a rationale that the Bush administration could understand.

It was suggested that we should assume that national interest is always present and that we should thus seek to harness it, instead of trying to distance it from the issue of intervention. This would mean focusing on states with an interest in the target state and working with those states for effective intervention. On this argument, intervention should be undertaken by the states of the region, which would more likely than not be in the South, with an interest in the target state. In this way, the responsibility for the intervention would move to the states with something at stake. The current investment of the Northern states in intervention could be used instead to monitor and follow up on the missions.

## Threshold Principles – Triggering Events and Measurement

Many of the participants suggested that the development of threshold principles – which, when met, would trigger international intervention – is important, particularly in making interventions more credible and helping to reassure states that the intervention is indeed legitimate and not abusive. However, it was also noted that some level of international consensus on threshold criteria for military intervention already exists and that the real challenge is finding an effective and timely way to *measure* when the criteria are met. It was suggested that there is a need for a disinterested but authoritative agency on the ground, with the resources and capacity to monitor and assess a humanitarian situation and determine whether the criteria for military intervention have been met. In addition, having criteria and a measurement mechanism would hopefully create a certain automaticity of action, so that when a crisis arises that has been determined as meeting the criteria, intervention of some kind would take place. One participant argued that the international community is not ready to codify the principles and criteria that would trigger intervention. Another pointed out that even if institutional mechanisms for intervention are established, the main challenge would be enabling such mechanisms to work effectively.

With respect to measurement, it was noted that the media, in particular CNN and the BBC, play a powerful role in determining whether or not a crisis situation exists, and the ensuing media and public pressure then helps to decide whether an intervention would take place.

## Institutional Reform – Middle Powers

One participant argued for a sustained commitment to the reform of the UN Charter (and of the Security Council) to make the human rights provisions operational, rather than aspirational. Another pointed out that it is important to remain broad-minded about the question of institutional reform. The development of new institutions may be the path of least resistance.

One suggestion, which was broadly discussed, was that middle-power states that have developed a level of expertise in humanitarian aid and protection should carry out the interventions, and that major powers should support the initiative from behind the scenes. It was noted, from a military perspective, that it is preferable to have the major-power support but not necessarily to have its presence in the field. One problem with middle-power intervention, however, is that these states did not always have the resources to carry out interventions. Canada, for example, often relies on US resources for such operations, thus constraining independent Canadian action.

The discussion of institutional reform included reform of the military. A military participant argued that the military requires a new set of skills to effectively carry out a humanitarian mandate and be effective in conflict resolution. This also means that the contract between the military and the nation needs to be revised. There must be a change in policy, so that troops are trained and prepared to die in missions aimed at restoring peace and stopping or preventing violations of fundamental rights in a state or region where the conflict may have nothing to do with the intervening nation's direct military security.

## Civil Society

There was a brief discussion of the role of civil society. It was suggested that a case needs to be made within civil societies, especially those of the P-5, that it is in the national interest to undertake both military intervention and missions for long-term conflict prevention and resolution. The question was raised whether it would be possible to gain the support of US civil society for such interventions.

## Preventive Measures – Conflict Resolution

The need to use forms of intervention other than Chapter VII was emphasized. There was broad support for intervention consisting of preventive measures, so human rights situations would not reach the critical point that, for example, the Rwandan crisis reached. At the same time, participants were challenged to think about International Monetary Fund-administered economic austerity packages as interventions in their own right. The West has to accept responsibility for the impact it has on social and economic structures.

The question of timing was deemed critical. It was argued that the earlier an intervention takes place, the greater chance it would have of being effective and the greater the possibility of rebuilding an inclusive society after the conflict. One participant stated that once people are being murdered and there is a need for military forces, the situation is already lost.

It was suggested that since the genocidal process usually begins within civil society, ICISS should look at some of the early symptoms of genocide and consider preventive measures, such as

- ❏ tracking the transfer of property and the traffic of conflict commodities;
- ❏ tracking the development of prejudice in the local language;
- ❏ taking steps to stop or prevent the dissemination of hate propaganda;
- ❏ educating the local population;
- ❏ promoting discussion of the protection of civilians and humanitarian workers in forums such as the Economic and Social Council;
- ❏ creating a stable environment within which civilians can live their lives and humanitarian workers can provide necessary assistance;
- ❏ promoting the humanitarian values of democratic principles, tolerance, and respect; and
- ❏ providing a security envelope for moderates from the perpetrators' side.

It was noted that there is a role for middle powers in conflict prevention and resolution, depending on their expertise. However, one NGO representative also made the point that the absence of a public perception of crisis is the primary impediment to effective preventive action. Another participant stated that it is necessary to employ small strategies, limited in scope, so that states would not shrink from undertaking legitimate interventions.

## Use of Force

On the question of whether it is appropriate to use force for humanitarian purposes, an NGO participant stated that it would be necessary to measure the true consequences of a military intervention. On the ground, military force can be as damaging as nonintervention and have long-term consequences. However, another NGO participant argued that there would be utility in identifying a category of intervention using military force that could be

true to a humanitarian mandate. Such a use of force would be very heavily circumscribed and designed to address humanitarian issues and not to advance the interest of the intervenors. Moreover, building international support for constrained humanitarian action would be possible only if it is genuinely different from warfighting.

A member of the military made the point that use of force in this context needs to be multidisciplinary. Thus, a mission must incorporate political, humanitarian, economic, military, and nation-building elements in one plan, and it must be designed for the long term. It was also noted that the kinds of problems that intervention seeks to deal with require a long-term commitment, substantial commitment of financial and personnel resources, and highly intrusive participation in governmental processes, if the issues are to be addressed in a responsible way. On the other hand, some participants argued that it is easier to sell the idea of short-term intervention to politicians. Another participant noted that states often pledge large resources for post-conflict–post-disaster reconstruction but rarely pay what they have pledged.

The question was raised whether intervention should also include operations aimed at reinstating a democratically elected government – a type of mission that has support among some African nations. However, there were no comments made in favour of this. One participant argued in favour of keeping the goal posts on the issue narrow, because of the difficulty in achieving international consensus on intervention for humanitarian purposes. Widening the possible rationales would open the door further to the possibility of abusive intervention.

## Nonmilitary Measures

Some participants raised the issue of nonmilitary measures to entice governments to change their behaviour or cease committing violations of fundamental human rights. Economic sanctions often adversely affect the civilian population, rather than the ruling elite. "Smart sanctions" should be examined that could effectively put a stranglehold on the resources of such ruling elites.

Another participant argued for enlarging the general view of what human suffering is, so as to include poverty, hunger, etc., and to be more creative in thinking about what measures would entice governments to change. Debt forgiveness may have more leverage than the use of force with governments that are perpetrating human rights abuses, and such measures may ultimately be more constructive than military intervention.

## UN Rapid-Reaction Force – Mercenary Forces

Several participants mentioned the need for a UN rapid-reaction force, which would give the UN greater capacity to act. The problem of who would command such a force and who would decide when and where it would be deployed was raised. A member of the military noted that it is unlikely that the P-5 would allow such a force to be effective.

The use of mercenary forces was discussed and deemed an important issue to consider. A member of the military noted that, from a soldier's perspective, it was not clear who would pay the troops, what their credibility would be after their first failure, and what loyalty they would have. Another participant pointed out that some UN missions already used mercenary forces. While some states donated their forces, for others it was a form of revenue. It was the mandate and the conduct of the force that was important, rather than the motive.

# GENEVA I

## ROUNDTABLE CONSULTATION WITH UNITED NATIONS AND INTERNATIONAL ORGANIZATIONS

### JANUARY 31, 2001

PARTICIPANTS

Gareth Evans, ICISS (Co-Chair)
Mohamed Sahnoun, ICISS (Co-Chair)

Gro Harlem Brundtland, World Health Organization
Annar Cassam, UN Educational, Scientific and Cultural Organization (Geneva)
Stephen Davey, International Federation of Red Cross and Red Crescent Societies
Jacques Forster, ICRC
Ruud Lubbers, UN High Commissioner for Refugees (UNHCR)
Brunson McKinley, International Organization for Migration
Ross Mountain, Office for the Coordination of Humanitarian Affairs
Vladimir Petrovsky, UN Office at Geneva
Mary Robinson, UN High Commissioner for Human Rights
Christopher Westdal, Canadian Mission to the UN, Geneva

# GENEVA II

## ROUNDTABLE CONSULTATION WITH NONGOVERNMENTAL AND OTHER INTERESTED ORGANIZATIONS

### JANUARY 31, 2001

PARTICIPANTS

Jovan Patrnogić, International Institute of Humanitarian Law (Chair)

Justice Georges Abi-Saab, Graduate Institute of International Studies, Geneva
Adrien Arena, International Commission of Jurists
Kofi Asomani, Centre for Humanitarian Dialogue
David Atwood, Quaker UN Office
Anatoli Ayissi, UN Institute for Disarmament Research
Rachel Brett, Quaker UN Office
William Canny, International Catholic Migration Commission
Andrew Clapham, Graduate Institute of International Studies, Geneva
Luigi Condorelli, Université de Genève
Marie-Anne Coninsx, European Union (EU)
Heiner Hanggi, Centre for Democratic Control of Armed Forces
Alexandre Kamarotos, Médecins du Monde
Keith Krause, Graduate Institute of International Studies, Geneva
Jennifer Milliken, Graduate Institute of International Studies, Geneva
David Petrasek, International Council on Human Rights Policy
Graciela Robert, Médecins du Monde

Ed Schenkenberg van Mierop, International Council for Voluntary Agencies
Jackie Seck, UN Institute for Disarmament Research
Matthias Stiefel, War-Torn Societies Project
Fred Tanner, Geneva Centre for Security Policy
Mark Vincent, Norwegian Refugee Council
Ivana Wagner, Ministry of Foreign Affairs, Switzerland
Christopher Westdal, Canadian Mission to the UN, Geneva

## SUMMARY

To help frame discussion, a discussion paper was presented that highlighted the following four issues.

The *problematic focus on military intervention* if the issue is to strengthen international means of protecting human rights. It could undermine the hard-won legitimacy of less coercive and intrusive actions to address human rights abuses (for example, economic and diplomatic sanctions, international criminal prosecutions) by making these seem the "slippery slope" to military intervention, as well as feeding the scepticism of many countries about the human rights agenda. Intervention has also been reserved for exceptional cases of human rights abuses – genocide, war crimes, and crimes against humanity – wherein political will to act exists.

*Countries' resistance to new interventionary norms is historically grounded* in the way that colonial conquests are justified by moral arguments about "doing good" for the "natives" and, more narrowly, the way that "humanitarian intervention" means selective and not universal protection (for example, intervention on behalf of coreligionists or ethnic kin).

*New institutions for military intervention are as important as new rules of international law.* Resistance to intervention on human rights grounds also arises because people rightly contest the legitimacy of the UN Security Council, an unrepresentative body that can include as members governments responsible for committing crimes against humanity, as well as those that have refused to ratify key international human rights treaties. Issues such as reform of the Security Council or creation of a UN standby military force to act as an impartial "police force" are very difficult ones, but they need to be part of the debate that ICISS is undertaking.

*The roles and responsibilities of the various actors needed to be rethought.* Along with the roles and responsibilities of intervening governments and leading NGOs, the role of affected populations (victims) is one that it would be crucial to rethink, not just when military intervention is being considered but also in the aftermath when a state is to be rebuilt. Only through actively involving an affected population in rebuilding institutions can legitimate and sustainable institutions emerge.

In the discussion that followed, participants broadly endorsed ICISS's possible approach of thinking of intervention in terms of a "responsibility to protect," as opposed to a "right to intervene." But doubts were still raised about ICISS's continued emphasis on military intervention. There was strong endorsement of the point made in the discussion paper about consulting the victims.

It was pointed out that the responsibility to protect extends to the Security Council and that in a case such as Rwanda, involving grave violations of international law, a failure of the Council to act represents a further violation of international law by the Council itself. Such violations need greater publicity.

## The Case for Military Intervention

A further paper was presented, making the case for military intervention. The main points were as follows:

*Intervention, rather than nonintervention, has been the norm during the Cold War* era, although the interventions have often been limited in scale, usually invited by the government of the target state, and rarely directed toward stopping violations of human rights or crimes against humanity.

*Given this, the abstract case for intervention on grounds of massive violations of human rights or genocide is easy to make.* The case for intervention would rest on sovereignty being treated as a conditional right acquired by states, granted by the international community on the basis of an acceptance that all individuals possess at least some inalienable human rights.

*Circumstances that make intervention on human rights grounds appropriate:*

❏   massive violations of human rights, and the government of the state in question is unable or unwilling to act to ameliorate the situation;

❏   after all nonmilitary means have been tried and found wanting, or when the urgency of the situation is such that nonmilitary means will not have time to take effect;

❏   when the use of military force has a high chance of stopping the massive violations of rights that are occurring;

❏   when the military means used is proportionate to the situation it faces; and

❏   when the military means does not cause a harm greater than it is intended to stop.

*In these circumstances, intervention needs to be decided upon multilaterally.* However, this does not mean that only the Security Council can authorize military intervention on human rights grounds generally, nor can it be presented as an absolute obstacle to intervention.

*Military intervention is only justified if accompanied by a serious commitment to foster political, social, and economic arrangements that would reduce the risk of future massive violations of human rights.* Intervention rarely "solves" the underlying problems that give rise to a massive violation of rights. A commitment to post-conflict state-building is also required.

*The rule of nonintervention has never prevented the strong from violating the rights of the weak.* A generalized right of intervention would not somehow create chaos in international relations, and it might actually save some lives and do some good.

In the ensuing discussion, it was noted that the difficulty remains of ensuring that the multilateral authorization of intervention is not dominated by developed countries. From a Western viewpoint, NATO is a democratic security community, but to others, it appears to be an ex-colonial club. Similarly, most international NGOs are from developed countries. Given this and the history of military intervention, people in developing countries might well say that intervention is never worth it.

## Constraints on Military Intervention

A further paper was presented on constraints on intervention that made the following points:

❏   Customary international law concerning military intervention has not changed just because there have been cases of humanitarian intervention in recent years. To make new legal rules, state agreement is required. This agreement clearly has been withheld, and opposition exists to changing existing law.

❏ International law allows for cases of necessity based on moral reasons. But the intervention should not make the humanitarian situation worse. If Security Council authorization is not forthcoming, some other institutional means for debate is still required. The General Assembly would appear to be the most appropriate forum.

❏ In cases such as Rwanda, the constraints on intervention appeared to have been more practical than legal. The UN should have a multilateral force for overcoming the practical constraints.

❏ In considering operational constraints, people give too much attention to constituencies within an intervening state. Conversely, they give too little attention to affected populations within the target state.

❏ The "humanitarian intervention" label is worrying from the standpoint of bodies working on human rights and makes it harder to talk to states about human rights abuses.

In the ensuing discussion, a participant emphasized that intervention is proscribed in international law, except for Article 42 of the Charter, and this could only be changed through Charter reform. The Non-Aligned Movement has three times since Kosovo stated that it does not recognize humanitarian intervention, so such change is unlikely to occur any time soon. Moreover, reform of the Security Council would still not guarantee authorization for future interventions. There is, however, a way around the Security Council blockage, which is the "Uniting for Peace" resolution.

When other possible grounds for intervention were discussed, such as intervention to protect or restore democracy, it was pointed out that the dilemmas of determining when intervention might be justifiable would only become greater. The essential constituency should be the victims, but while those in the outside world might have some clarity about their views if a democracy is overturned through a military coup, in other cases it is going to be much more difficult to determine.

A participant questioned whether the issue is really whether or not the UN could take on a full-fledged army. Humanitarian protection usually means helping people in immediate danger from what are quite lightly armed forces. However, as someone else pointed out, the size of the intervening force sometimes does matter, as has been clearly demonstrated in Rwanda.

It was noted that the international community has been doing little in the area of prevention. In this context, a participant drew attention to the Médecins sans Frontières (Doctors Without Borders) proposal to create a Humanitarian Commission in the UN – composed of independent experts appointed by the Secretary-General – to serve as an information-gathering site, a source of analysis of the vulnerability of civilian populations, and a body to create clear guidelines and recommendations for action.

## To Act or Not to Act

Another paper was then presented that differentiated between prevention, nonmilitary intervention, and military intervention. It was based on the target population's perspective and dealt with the impact of intervention, especially from a long-term perspective. The main points were the following:

❏ Rebuilding must be part of intervention.

❏ Solutions cannot be imported from the outside. External actors may at first play a major role, but if they must support, empower, moderate, or exert pressure then they should do so in a capacity made secondary to that of local actors.

❏ There are no quick fixes. It takes a generation or more after intervention to "fix" a society.

❏ Prevention should be brought to the fore, and greater attention should be paid to post-conflict peace building.

❏ Military intervention is the worst-case scenario: it means that all other solutions have failed, and it brings as many problems as it solves. In the long term, military intervention inevitably disempowers local actors.

In the discussion that followed, a participant agreed that consideration of an intervention should always take up issues of long-term state-rebuilding, particularly since a long-term intervention often amounts in practice to a neocolonial trusteeship. Others, however, noted that it would not be thus if local actors are made central. It was also noted that the issue of disempowerment is also emerging in humanitarian relief and development debates and that all solutions – short or long term, interventionary or less coercive – need to take this into account.

Another participant noted that the vast majority of Cold War interventions have been part of state-supporting practices and have included military aid and economic development assistance. Those state-supporting practices have failed, and the work of ICISS should be seen as part of the ongoing search for something to replace them. In this respect, it makes sense for ICISS to reflect on whether "state-rebuilding" is connected to intervention.

Continuing this theme, a participant observed that given the number of interventions that have occurred in recent years, ICISS should examine what has worked in order to draw a better picture of how interventions should be mounted. Another participant observed that there is increasing interest in regional interventionary forces (for example, the EU's rapid-reaction force), but there has been no strategic concept to guide its use – perhaps ICISS's work could help in this regard. Someone also suggested that when ICISS "has the solution," it should circulate its draft and allow comments in order to better develop the international consensus that ICISS hopes to create. Moreover, prevention has not been given much of a chance, and one role of ICISS could be to emphasize this. Reflecting on how to translate ICISS's work into lasting results, a participant suggested that it should focus on the victims and seek to change attitudes and build an awareness of what has been happening to victims and in this way start a dialogue.

# LONDON

## REGIONAL ROUNDTABLE CONSULTATION WITH NONGOVERN-MENTAL AND OTHER INTERESTED ORGANIZATIONS

### FEBRUARY 3, 2001

PARTICIPANTS

Peter Marshall, KCMG, University of Westminster (Chair)

Nabil Ayad, Diplomatic Academy of London, University of Westminster
Chaloka Beyani, London School of Economics and Political Science
Keith Bezanson, University of Sussex
Cees Flinterman, Advisory Council on International Affairs, Netherlands

Steven Haines, Oxford University
Jeremy Kinsman, Canadian High Commission in Great Britain and Northern Ireland
Mark Leonard, Foreign Policy Centre
Sverre Lodgaard, Norwegian Institute for International Affairs
Linda Melvern, University of Aberystwyth, Wales
Bjoern Moeller, Copenhagen Peace Research Institute, Denmark
Stephen Patison, British Foreign and Commonwealth Office
Veselin Popovski, University of Exeter
Gwyn Prins, Pugwash
Caroline Rees, British Foreign and Commonwealth Office
Simon Reich, Royal Institute for International Affairs
Adam Roberts, Oxford University
Malcolm Rodgers, Christian Aid
Irene Sage, Foundation for International Security
Nicholas J. Wheeler, University of Aberystwyth, Wales
Roger Williamson, Wilton House
Stan Windass, Foundation for International Security
Martin Wollacott, *The Guardian*

## SUMMARY

### A Right or Duty of Humanitarian Intervention

It was generally agreed that the "Charter is a mess," because both supporters and opponents of humanitarian intervention make appeals to its norms. The question is whether humanitarian intervention should be recognized as an exception to the *jus cogens* rules governing the use of force under the Charter. This led to a discussion of whether the Charter is a static or dynamic instrument. There was broad support for the latter interpretation, and it was pointed out that in the 1990s the Security Council was prepared to define humanitarian crises and human rights emergencies as constituting a threat to international peace and security under Article 39 of the Charter. This represents a major change when compared with the expansive interpretation given to the concept of "domestic jurisdiction" in Article 2 (7) during the Cold War.

Rather than working toward an explicit recognition of a right of humanitarian intervention, the participants gave some support for the view that ICISS's final report should reinforce the value of the nonintervention rule. This position criticizes the Secretary-General's attempt to counterpoise sovereignty and intervention, the argument being that it would be more productive to view humanitarian intervention as an extraordinary exception to the principle of nonintervention. It was suggested that there is merit in thinking of humanitarian intervention as a "tolerated practice," rather than explicitly recognizing a right under international law. Two examples cited by participants were the international response to India's intervention in East Pakistan and Tanzania's intervention in Uganda. In the case of the latter, it was argued that whatever President Nyerere's stated reasons had been, it was obvious that humanitarian considerations had motivated the action. It was pointed out by one participant that it is possible for the international community to simultaneously applaud and criticize an action.

There was agreement in the group that there is no chance of getting states to accept a general legal right of humanitarian intervention. Indeed, one participant argued that to think in terms of the language of a right is unhelpful. Discussion then turned to the question of what might be gained by shifting the language from one of rights to one of duties. In reflecting on whether there is a duty to act, it was agreed by some that there is advantage in limiting a duty to the requirement that actors give consideration to what ought to be done. However, a minority felt that a "duty to consider" does not leave enough substance and would create too many loopholes for states to slip through. Nevertheless, it was broadly agreed that there is no prospect of securing international agreement on a duty to intervene.

Instead of thinking in terms of a right or duty of intervention, it was suggested from the ICISS side that it might be helpful to think in terms of a "responsibility to protect." This is a more holistic concept than a right and has the merit of emphasizing that international intervention should encompass preventive aspects and the responsibility to participate in the mending of war-torn societies. There was some support for this idea, but one speaker felt that this reformulation still does not avoid the fundamental difficulties with the language of rights and duties.

## Motives and Political Will

A central question debated throughout the day concerns the place of humanitarian motives in judging the legitimacy of particular interventions. There was no support for the view, held by many international lawyers, that intervening states should be motivated by primarily humanitarian reasons. The majority viewpoint was that mixed motives would be an inevitable feature of interventions, and what matters is the character of these interests: the international community should not worry too much about the purity of motives if an armed intervention rescues the victims of oppression and does not threaten wider order. A number of participants cited Vietnam's intervention in Cambodia in December 1978 as a good example of this. How to judge the reasonableness of another state's professed interests and decide whether its humanitarian justifications are bona fide were questions raised but not discussed.

It was suggested that motives should not be focused on to the exclusion of questions of political will. The obstacle to intervention in Rwanda had not been doctrinal concerns about sovereignty, but a question of the lack of political will on the part of UN member states. This led to an exchange about the willingness of Western societies to accept casualties in defence of strangers. It was agreed that the claim that the US has a "body-bag" culture is probably overstated and certainly does not apply to the United Kingdom (UK) and France. However, it was also agreed that there is a clear limit to the casualties that political authorities would be willing to incur in wars other than those fought for national survival. A few participants suggested that NATO's reluctance to risk casualties in Kosovo undermined the humanitarian claims of NATO's action. But it was pointed out by others that flying at 15,000 ft is not necessarily any less accurate than flying low where there is greater risk to the safety of pilots. In discussing the casualties issue, one proposal that met with some approval was to rely on private military force. A suggestion viewed as a political nonstarter was to resurrect the idea of a UN rapid-reaction force.

## Hard versus Soft Codification

The idea of ICISS developing guidelines was raised, and this led to a lengthy discussion of the difference between hard and soft codification. The latter was defined by one participant as rules that serve as guidance devices – an "internal ethical checklist" – for policy makers. By contrast, hard codification involves drafting a convention or the highly controversial idea of amending the Charter to permit a right or duty of humanitarian intervention. There was general agreement that such a change of the Charter is not feasible in the foreseeable future and that any attempt to initiate such reform would meet with considerable opposition at the UN. Some participants were opposed to any form of codification – it is unwise to put too much weight on criteria, because every case would have to be treated on its political and legal merits, and, at best, criteria would only be one consideration. Against this, others argued that criteria are important in reducing the risk that states would employ humanitarian justifications as a pretext for the use of force. One speaker suggested that the political costs of codification could be overcome by conducting any debate over criteria through private diplomatic channels. However, another speaker considered that to raise this issue at all would be "poisonous" and "divisive."

Those who were opposed to any form of codification argued for reliance on what one participant called the "common-law" approach to developing a new norm. It was suggested that this approach of building up precedents might be accelerated by greater recourse to the International Court of Justice (ICJ), and reference was made to the case before the ICJ concerning the legality of "Operation Allied Force" in Kosovo. However, this position received little support in the general discussion.

## Southern Perspectives on Intervention

A key purpose of ICISS, stated several times during the day, is to create a new North–South consensus on intervention. It was noted that Southern states generally view the Northern agenda of humanitarian intervention with great suspicion, pointing to the selective character of Northern interventions. Consequently, they are mistrustful of the humanitarian claims made by the North, which they see as a smoke screen for the pursuit of selfish interests. The example of French intervention in Rwanda was cited in this context.

One participant pointed out that there is support among African states for a norm of collective intervention in cases where a democratically elected government has been overthrown. ECOWAS, for example, recognized that intervention was permissible to restore democratic government, an example being the favourable regional response that greeted Nigeria's intervention in Sierra Leone.

One participant argued that while the Security Council did not authorize the Nigerian intervention, it was possible to read into subsequent Council resolutions approval of this action. In legitimating future humanitarian interventions, the Security Council, it was suggested, might only authorize intervention with the consent of the relevant regional organization. This would address the concern among Southern states that intervention not take place without the consent of the affected parties. In discussing the prospects for regional intervention, one participant pointed to concerns about ulterior motives on the part of regional powers.

More broadly there was a consensus in the group that any progress on legitimating humanitarian intervention has to be located within the wider context of what one participant called a "duty of care" on the part of the North towards the South.

# MAPUTO

## REGIONAL ROUNDTABLE CONSULTATION WITH NONGOVERN-MENTAL AND OTHER INTERESTED ORGANIZATIONS

### MARCH 10, 2001

PARTICIPANTS

Richard J. Goldstone, Constitutional Court of South Africa (Chair)

Emmanuel Kwesi Aning, Institute of Economic Affairs, Ghana
Adonia Ayebare, Embassy of Uganda in Rwanda
Domitille Barancira, Collectif des associations et ONG féminines du Burundi
Mwesiga Baregu, Southern African Regional Institute for Policy Studies, Zimbabwe
Arcilia Barreto, UNHCR
Nelson Cosme, Economic Community of Central African States, Gabon
Emmanuel Dieckx de Casterle, UN Development Programme, Mozambique
Samuel Gbaydee Doe, West Africa Network for Peacebuilding, Ghana
Neuma Grobbelaar, Landmines and Demining Program, South African Institute for
    International Affairs, South Africa
Manuela Lucas, Ministry of Foreign Affairs, Mozambique
Mark Malan, Institute for Security Studies, South Africa
Mohammed Ibrahim Mansour, Institute for Future Studies, Egypt
Venantie Nabintu, Réseaux des femmes pour la défense des droits et la paix, Democratic
    Republic of the Congo
Paul Nantulya, African Centre for the Constructive Resolution of Disputes, South Africa
Laurie Nathan, Institute for Conflict Resolution, University of Cape Town, South Africa
Pauline Riak, Sudanese Women's Association, Kenya
Severine Rugumamu, OAU Secretariat, Ethiopia
Jeremy Rutledge, Quaker Peace Centre, South Africa
Leonardo Simão, Minister of Foreign Affairs, Mozambique
Elisabete Siqueira, Progresso, Mozambique
Elizabeth Siridopoulos, South African Institute of International Affairs, South Africa
Christiana Solomon, Campaign for Good Governance, Sierra Leone
John Stremlau, University of Witwatersrand, South Africa
Jamisse Taimo, Higher Institute for International Relations, Mozambique
Augustine Toure, Democracy Watch, Liberia
Yao Turkson, Africa Foundation for Democratic Institutions of Development, UK
Carlo von Flue, ICRC, Zimbabwe

## SUMMARY

### Definitions and Conditions

The first item to be discussed was the need for a coherent framework to capture the dynamics and complexity of intervention and state sovereignty. It was also suggested that a consensus was needed for some terminological reconceptualizations, such as a shift from a term like "humanitarian intervention." Many NGOs are sensitive to, and uncomfortable with, the association of "humanitarian" with military mandates. Furthermore, the application of the terminology restricts the debate on intervention in the sense that it creates the impression that if it is humanitarian, then it is automatically good. Similarly, a "right of intervention" conjures a diversity of images, especially since it does not reflect the views of the needy.

There was general consensus that discussions of intervention and sovereignty should also include the role of the Bretton Woods institutions. Participants considered the criteria to be applied to determine when intervention should take place. Reference was made to the OAU's conditions for intervention, which include 1) a breakdown of law and order; 2) circumstances where human suffering is intense; 3) preemptive involvement to control or contain complex political emergencies; 4) intervention to consolidate democracy and election monitoring; and 5) warlordism, or the criminalization of post-intervention states. In relation to point 5, participants seemed to agree on certain general factors that contribute to the rise of warlordism: mercenaries and the privatization of security, diverse agendas under the guise of humanitarianism, and the role of globalization and the undermining of state structures. All participants agreed that military interventions should only ever be made as a last resort.

Such guidelines, notwithstanding, participants discussed possible benchmarks for interventions. Some of the points agreed upon were 1) adequate and thorough discussions with involved parties; 2) interventions should have permanent and sustainable impact; 3) proactive prevention and early-warning and response mechanisms are needed; and 4) post facto interventions are normally not comprehensive, but usually a case of "too little, too late."

As a result, participants considered the applicability of, or the need for, a terminological shift, such as that being considered by ICISS from a "right to intervene" to a "responsibility to protect." The latter was seen to have broader implications. It implies a requirement to prevent crises a good deal in advance. It also implies notions of follow-through of issues dealing with reconciliation, rehabilitation, and post-conflict reconstruction of societies. Therefore, when one talks about the responsibility to protect, it does not imply only military entry and exit strategies but a consistent and sustainable responsibility. Furthermore, a responsibility to protect also connotes reciprocal responsibility between North and South. Questions were raised concerning whose responsibility it is to protect, since intervention by outsiders increasingly encompasses territorial, economic, and security interests of the intervenors.

## Interventions in the African Context

Participants believed Africa has been marginalized by the Security Council, as indicated by an unwillingness to provide adequate resources for intervention in the continent. A frequent example given was the contrast between the UN response in the Balkans, where the international community expended billions of dollars, while in Liberia it had not been possible to obtain pledges totalling $150 million to support subregional efforts.

Part of the discussion centred on the need to tackle the root causes of conflict in Africa, where there is a strong nexus between poverty and conflict. There was general consensus that the seeds of both current and future conflicts are deeply embedded and that all of them have the characteristics of humanitarian tragedies. Nevertheless, the nature and scope of international responses have been inconsistent, and sometimes totally absent. While welcoming recent international rhetoric about trade and not aid, participants complained about the increasing deterioration of the terms of trade and the sharp reduction in the disbursement of bilateral aid, estimated to be as high as 20 percent.

The best response by the international community was proactive prevention through appropriate strategies. While preventive strategies should not be excessively intrusive, the discussion dealt with the circumstances under which intrusiveness is justified. There is a consensus that intervention should be internally generated and externally assisted and supported.

The discussion also centred on the reality of sovereignty to African states. There was some consensus on the view that sovereignty has been elusive for most African states and that therefore one can talk of a crisis of legitimacy. This arises from the tensions and polarization between state and society, as well as being a result of globalization. As such, the concept of sovereignty that deals with state-building processes has become increasingly alien and has increasingly been replaced by a notion of sovereignty arising from an international regime external to, and minimizing of, state borders. As a result, the sovereignty of most African states has become superficial, and not deeply rooted in society. It was also recognized that sovereign states can and do mishandle their responsibilities as governing authorities and are therefore not immune from intervention.

There is also a need to redefine the concept to involve issues of citizen participation in decision making processes that affect their lives, human security, economic justice, and governance. Most African states that lack empirical sovereignty are characterized by one or more of the following: 1) classical political tensions; 2) robber barons; 3) gun runners; 4) drug barons; 5) weak states; 6) warlords seeking political power; and 7) "Lords of Poverty" profiting from the misery of their compatriots. Debate about sovereignty of the people must, as a result, be seen more as a paradigm shift. Two concluding points came out of this discussion. First, state and popular sovereignty are not mutually exclusive. Second, weak states and weak societies are mutually reinforcing.

While the above debate gave the impression of a dichotomy between the rhetoric and reality of the African state, participants were of the view that Africa must begin to define solutions to her problems. There was a strong feeling that in Africa people have been erceived as objects, and not actors. There has to be an awareness that people matter, and oreign actors could assist in this by facilitating issues defined by local actors. They should also practice what they preach – that is, good governance, transparency, and accountability – and should avoid imposing only their views on the management of conflicts.

Participants were also of the view that Africa should not always be seen as a problem to be solved. Rather, there is a need to understand some of the new dynamics arising in Africa, namely, the recent decision to transform the OAU into the "African Union," the Millennium African Recovery Programme, the presentation of the *Constitutive Act of the African Union* (Article 4), and the African Union Protocol's "Principle G," all of which permit the right of the Union to intervene under grave circumstances. Despite these potentially positive sea changes in African perceptions about intervention and sovereignty, participants were concerned that these new developments are not rooted within society.

## Modalities and Conditions for Intervention

Participants considered intervention to be a fact of life in the African context but sought to navigate between the politics surrounding the decision to intervene and its implementation. They also considered whether it should be undertaken at subregional or continental levels, or by a global body, that is, the UN. There was an awareness of, and consensus on, the nature of the international system that marginalizes African issues. There was also agreement that since the UN Charter permitted subregional organizations to intervene such institutions should be used as far as possible, but would need to be strengthened.

Participants then considered the post-intervention phase, which involves rehabilitation and reconstruction. There was concern that in cases where African states have shown a proactive willingness and initiative to resolve crises through a coalition of the willing, not of the weak, the responses from, and support of, the international community have been, at best, lukewarm. Citing the struggle between the the Economic Community of West African States' Cease-fire Monitoring Group (ECOMOG) and the international community, the participants generally agreed that while the UN Mission in Sierra Leone has been a dismal failure, there was nevertheless an unwillingness to support ECOMOG, because Africa should not succeed where the international community has failed. Concern was also voiced about the role and motives of agencies that provide assistance to victims of conflict, and particularly about the necessity to negotiate with warring factions and thus cross lines of confrontation. While this may be necessary at times, the consequences of such actions should be understood within the context of the incentives and disincentives thus created for war-profiteering.

Despite the implicit acceptance that intervention has become a fixture of international relations, there were differing views on the rationales for intervention and the reasons why nonmilitary options tend not to be pursued. It was suggested that a decision to intervene militarily signifies an unwillingness to understand the structural causes of conflicts. As an alternative to intervention, suggestions were made about measures to prevent the outbreak of conflicts and thereby avoid the intervention option. These included an examination of development processes as a mechanism for peace building; the establishment of early-warning mechanisms; capacity building of social institutions; the implementation of proactive measures, such as giving sovereignty to citizens, building societies, and creating a healthy relationship between states and societies; the need for restorative justice processes; and the need to draw on traditional practices.

While accepting the fact that post-conflict reconstruction and rehabilitation are important, participants were of the view that if structural disparities within states are not addressed, then the causes of conflict would continue. The structural deficiencies in the UN system, participants argued, may result from the inability of existing UN mechanisms to deal with newer sorts of conflict. However, the responsibility deficit that currently characterizes the UN also arose from factors such as complicity, policy paralysis, and illegality. Unwillingness to deal with symptoms of deeper crisis was seen as a possible manifestation of the power dynamics in the UN system. These can only be addressed by implementing proposals for the democratization of the decision making processes of the UN system by widening and revisiting the veto mechanism within the Security Council and reviving the General Assembly.

There followed a discussion of operational and practical matters related to intervention. Some of the more pertinent issues raised dealt with the clarification of mandates, access and security for intervenors, acceptance of the complementarity of roles among diverse actors during conflicts, a need for the establishment of peacekeeping academies, a code of conduct for combatants (necessary, since most combatants are not conversant with the rules of warfare) and for identifying and punishing misconduct by peacekeepers, and the recognition that private security armies would defend their own economic agendas.

In addition to the political costs of intervention, participants were of the view that Africans must begin to consider the social and economic costs. Among the social costs noted were an increase in prostitution and HIV–AIDS, a negative impact on the socioeconomic status of women and children, and a destruction of the family structure. A major economic impact noted was the weakening of local economies resulting from an influx of unregulated foreign currency with intervening troops.

# WASHINGTON, DC

## ROUNDTABLE CONSULTATION

### MAY 2, 2001

PARTICIPANTS

Harriet Hentges, US Institute of Peace (Co-Chair)
Richard Solomon, US Institute of Peace (Co-Chair)

Pamela Aall, US Institute of Peace
Daniel Augstburger, ICRC, Washington
Esther Brimmer, US Department of State
Chester Crocker, Georgetown University and US Institute of Peace Board of Directors
Donald Daniel, National Intelligence Council
Graham Day, US Institute of Peace
Alton Frye, Council on Foreign Relations
Paul Gaffney, National Defense University and US Institute of Peace Board of Directors
Toby Trister Gati, Akin, Gump, Strauss, Hauer and Feld, L.L.P.
Dan Guttman, Johns Hopkins University
Chuck Hagel, US Senate
Morton Halperin, Council on Foreign Relations
Inga Hawley, Stimson Center
Bruce Jentleson, Duke University
Zalmay Khalilzad, RAND Corporation and US Institute of Peace Board of Directors
Mary Locke, The Fund for Peace
Jane Holl Lute, UN Foundation
Dayton Maxwell, US Agency for International Development
Doris Meissner, Carnegie Endowment for International Peace
Charles Nelson, US Institute of Peace
Deepa Ollapally, US Institute of Peace
David Scheffer, US Institute of Peace
Eric Schwartz, Woodrow Wilson Center
Anita Sharma, Woodrow Wilson Center
Henryk Sokalski, US Institute of Peace
Donald Steinberg, US Department of State
Jane Stromseth, Georgetown University
Shibley Telhami, University of Maryland and US Institute of Peace Board of Directors
George Ward, US Institute of Peace
Theresa Whitfield, Ford Foundation
James Young, US Department of State

## SUMMARY

### The Role of the United States

A central assertion was made that the debate in the US is not so much over whether there is a responsibility to intervene, but whether there is an obligation to do so. It was suggested that the US, as the world's preeminent power, should not be indifferent to genocide or major human rights abuses: there is a role, in other words, for good international citizenship as a central national interest of the US. If it cannot develop or sustain a system to deal with major abuses, there is not much hope for the future. What is needed is more consistent application of values.

An opposite argument was made that for the US policy community, the rules of sovereignty are for others, not the US. In effect, the US reserves the right to do what it wants, including intervening in the affairs of others. That same community regards the mere discussion of this subject as dangerous because it can, on the one hand, serve to emphasis the central role of the Security Council and thus limit US action or, on the other hand, make others think that they too can reserve the right to intervene when they want.

It was argued that the US could not be expected to do everything, especially on the military front. It had been involved in multiple military operations internationally between 1990 and 1999, and there was a growing feeling internationally that US involvement is necessary to an intervention if it is to be successful. There was thus a growing feeling in official and defence circles in the US that the country should be much more selective about the interventions in which it becomes involved. More emphasis should now be put on nonmilitary prevention and as far as possible on supporting victims in ways that would have them defending themselves.

Another participant argued that the US should only become involved in interventions when its presence is needed, welcomed, or otherwise irresistible. However, the US should do more listening and less preaching and be more willing to share credit, so as to encourage other countries to join a coalition of the willing.

US public opinion was identified as a central factor in US decisions to intervene. However, it is also ambivalent about the value of interventions and can be easily swayed, positively or negatively, by the CNN effect. There is no ingrained or historical tendency for the US public to want to protect non-Americans. Sustaining public interest in any one situation for long is also difficult. However, while a decision to intervene is probably one of the most difficult a US President could make, once made it would be rare that it would not be supported by the public.

### Role of the Security Council

One participant queried the methodology used by the Security Council in authorizing interventions. Essentially, the Council has had an unfettered power to declare any situation a threat to international peace and security, and after that can do what it likes. The lack of accountability is unacceptable. Somalia was cited as an example of where an internal situation was probably not in fact a real threat to international peace and security, yet the Security Council nevertheless declared it to be so, and an inappropriate and ultimately disastrous intervention followed.

It was argued that interpretation of the UN Charter has evolved over time and that this has affected not only the rights of the Security Council but also those of states, particularly in situations where the Council has been unable or unwilling to act. One participant argued that in fact the Security Council is not the sole source of authority for interventions. The *Citizen's Guide to US Foreign Policy* (produced by the US State Department) noted – albeit controversially – that Council authorization is preferable but not always necessary. The trick was to get the Council to fulfill its functions better and not allow it to abdicate responsibility. Another participant suggested that the goal of ICISS should be to establish guidelines for Security Council action, but make it clear that if the Council fails to act, despite the guidelines being met, then any subsequent intervention by others would have increased legitimacy. It was also suggested that if authorization by the Council is blocked by one veto while all or most other members favour action, this too would confer a large degree of legitimacy on the intervention.

There is a place for double standards in all this. There are clearly places where the international community cannot and should not intervene, as the costs would be too high (for example, Chechnya). But this does not mean that interventions that could achieve positive results should not be undertaken elsewhere.

## Conditions for Intervention

While there was general agreement about interventions only being undertaken in response to the most serious abuses, it was noted that ICISS should not only be thinking in terms of such abuses being sudden and cataclysmic. In Indonesia, Sudan, and many other places the abuses are systematic and massive, but they are "slow burners."

Once a military intervention becomes necessary, however, then a certain number of basic conditions should be met: 1) the objective must be achievable and should not be transformed drastically (as occurred in Somalia); 2) the intervenors should prevail rapidly, using the level of force necessary to achieve this; 3) the US should preferably be part of a coalition; 4) there should be prior agreement on command structures, goals, criteria for withdrawal – more than a withdrawal date is needed, since otherwise parties to a conflict or abusers would only try to sit out the intervention; and 5) the armed forces should not be used for essentially police duties or other functions that they are not well equipped to perform. In the latter regard, more effort should be made to build up a capacity in the local population to take over those duties. However, to date this had been done badly.

It was also suggested that there should be timely sharing of intelligence among interested states to ensure that any action is based on common understandings. Another participant noted that a related problem is that in the hasty preparation that precedes most interventions, there is usually insufficient analysis of the situation. The result of this often is that greater importance is assigned to superficial problems, while the deeper seated causes are underestimated or ignored.

## Responsibility to Protect

Changing the terms of the debate to a "responsibility to protect," as suggested by ICISS, was greeted positively. It widens the scope of discussion, since local actors, including the government of the country that is the subject of possible intervention, also have a responsibility to protect. In some cases, moreover, these actors also have greater authority than international ones. Defining the success of an action or intervention is also easier if protection is the central focus.

One participant said that ICISS should stress the point about local actors having primary responsibility to protect. Otherwise, there is the risk that people would automatically start looking outside their own borders for others to protect them.

## Prevention

While there was agreement around the table that prevention is preferable to intervention, it was noted that prevention is not politically easy, because there is usually little happening on the ground that could grab international attention. Equally, from a political viewpoint, an intervention often only becomes practicable once a situation has deteriorated to the point that the chances of a successful intervention have become minimal (as occurred in Rwanda). The central question that people should thus be considering is how to generate positive public opinion well enough in advance of an atrocity to prevent it from occurring or worsening.

Another factor cited as undermining preventive strategies to an extent is the feeling in many Western capitals that more successful interventions are needed in order to build credibility and demonstrate a deterrent effect for future situations.

One participant argued that the material costs of intervention mean that countries would only intervene if there is strong public support for it. This, however, means that in effect there is a bias that favours interventions by countries with the strongest interest in the issues in dispute, thus undermining any notion of impartiality.

A note of caution was sounded about global interests – which is where the notion of protection fits – usually taking a back seat to national interests in any decision to act or not. This applies equally to prevention as to intervention.

# SANTIAGO

## REGIONAL ROUNDTABLE CONSULTATION WITH NONGOVERN- MENTAL AND OTHER INTERESTED ORGANIZATIONS

### MAY 4, 2001

PARTICIPANTS

Francisco Rojas Aravena, Faculdad Latinamericana de Ciencias Sociales, Chile (Chair)

María Soledad Alvear, Minister of Foreign Affairs, Chile
Rodrigo Atria, Advisory Committee to the Ministry of Defence, Chile
Carmen Avila, Ministry of Foreign Affairs, Panama
Mario José Avila Romero, Ministry of Foreign Affairs, El Salvador
Silvio Aviléz Gallo, Ministry of Foreign Affairs, Nicaragua
Enrique Bernales, Comisión Andina de Juristas
Luis Bitencourt, Latin America Program, Woodrow Wilson Center, US
Lara Blanco, Arias Foundation, Costa Rica
Arturo Cabrera, Ministry of Foreign Affairs, Ecuador
Roberto Cajina, Head of Project on Civil–Military Relations, Nicaragua
Policarpo Callejas Bonilla, Ministry of Foreign Affairs, Honduras
Fernando Cepeda, Universidad de los Andes, Colombia
Juan de Dios Parra, Associación Latinoamericana de Derechos Humanos, Ecuador
Paul Durand, Canadian Embassy in Chile
Juan Eduardo Eguiguren, Ministry of Foreign Affairs, Chile
Rodrigo Espinosa, Ministry of Foreign Affairs, Chile
Dra Berta Feder, Ministry of Foreign Affairs, Uruguay
Clemencia Forero Ucrós, Ministry of Foreign Affairs, Colombia
Andelfo García, Academic, Chile
Paulina García Donoso de Larrea, Ministry of Foreign Affairs, Ecuador
Jorge Luis Gómez, Ministry of Foreign Affairs, Argentina
Juan Manuel Gómez-Robledo Verduzco, Ministry of Foreign Affairs, Mexico
Antonio González, Ministry of Foreign Affairs, Colombia
Gerard Granado, Caribbean Conference of Churches, Barbados
Ivelaw Griffith, Florida International University, US
Jorge Heine, Fundación Chile XXI, Chile
Maria Teresa Infante, Ministry of Foreign Affairs, Chile

Jeannete Irigoin, Institute of International Studies, Chile
Gustavo Iruegas, Ministry of Foreign Affairs, Mexico
Javier Jiménez, Ministry of Foreign Affairs, Bolivia
Oscar Llanes Torres, Diplomatic Academy of Paraguay, Paraguay
Salomón Lerner Ghitis, Transparencia, Peru
Ernesto Lopez, University of Quilmes, Argentina
Delma Miralles, Ministry of Foreign Affairs, Venezuela
Wagner Obando, Ministry of Foreign Affairs, Costa Rica
Elda Paz, Ministry of Foreign Affairs, Mexico
Helí Peláez Castro, Ministry of Foreign Affairs, Peru
Bernardo Pericás, Ministry of Foreign Affairs, Brazil
Miguel Pichardo, Ministry of Foreign Affairs, Dominican Republic
Rodrigo Qintana, Ministry of Foreign Affairs, Chile
Juan José Quintana, Ministry of Foreign Affairs, Colombia
Augusto Saá Corriere, Ministry of Foreign Affairs, Ecuador
Guillermo Saenz de Tejada, Ministry of Foreign Affairs, Guatemala
Andrea Sanhueza, Corporation Participa, Chile
Elizabeth Spehar, Organization of American States Secretariat, US
Gabriel Szekèly, Citizens' Alliance, Mexico
Carlos Portales, Ministry of Foreign Affairs, Chile
Claudio Troncoso, Ministry of Foreign Affairs, Chile
Juan Gabriel Valdes, Permanent Mission of Chile to the UN
Alberto Van Klaveren, Ministry of Foreign Affairs, Chile
Augusto Varas, Ford Foundation, Chile
Edmundo Vargas, Ministry of Foreign Affairs, Chile
José Miguel Vivanco, Human Rights Watch, US
Luís Winter, Ministry of Foreign Affairs, Chile

## SUMMARY

In an opening address, Soledad Alvear, Chile's Minister of Foreign Affairs referred to intervention as a subject closely related "to life and death" and one that international organizations, despite all their technological progress, have been unable to address effectively. Indeed, massacres and other major aggressions against humankind continue to occur, to the dismay of the international community. All this urgently requires international organizations and UN state members to compromise on a common approach. On the other hand, the history of Latin American and the Caribbean countries gives them an important doctrinal framework that opposes unilateral interventions and favours respect for the sovereignty of states. When the issue is intervention, the region's policy makers trust the UN Charter. Yet, Security Council decisions can be blocked by the conflicting positions of its members, and it has sometimes been unable to respond quickly enough to situations demanding international intervention. The Minister concluded by suggesting that since saving lives should always be the superior interest, we should be able to find ways to create new and original mechanisms.

### Intervention, Sovereignty, and Security in Latin America and the Caribbean

An introductory paper proposed the idea of "cooperative multilateralism" as a basis for building consensus and decision making on the international system's key issues, including humanitarian intervention. Unlike the current approach, this system would be positive and practical and based on ideals such as peace and prosperity. In addition, it is necessary to adopt a more holistic approach to the concept of security.

Several participants endorsed this viewpoint. Since the end of the Cold War demands have frequently been made to revise the international-security concept that dominated Western strategic thinking in earlier decades. This desire has a direct connection with the intervention issues being discussed. Although there is consensus on the need for a new conceptual paradigm, no consensus exists on the concept itself. Two main possibilities have been considered. Because of a lack of comprehensive theoretical tools to explain the most recent phenomena within the international arena, new tag names, such as "environmental security," "citizen security," and "human security," have appeared. Others have preferred to broaden the traditional concept of international security to include new threats, actors, and power relationships.

Many suggested that globalization has made the concept of sovereignty obsolete. Others thought that current threats – new or old – have a transnational nature that ignores territorial borders. Consequently, transnational relations, including economic and cultural aspects, are increasingly taking place well beyond state control. Although some thought that sovereignty has become less important for nation-states, others thought that the opposite is true: because of lessened control over what happens inside their borders, governments have become more sensitive to, and interested in, preserving their sovereignty.

## When External Military Intervention Should Be Considered and Why: Intervention Priorities and Thresholds

A further discussion paper was presented on why and when military intervention is necessary and justifiable. This paper also covered the priorities and thresholds for a decision on intervention. It cited the case of violence in East Timor following the independence ballot. The Secretary-General could only have exerted the intense pressure he did on the Indonesian Government to end the violence or allow for international intervention because the international community had achieved a notable consensus on the need to intervene with military force to stop the violence. When such conditions are not present, a decision might still be taken if, for instance, it is a situation that would motivate global concern and criticism, such as a case of genocide. Even so, military intervention should still only be a last resort, and it should do more good than harm. A basic criterion should also be that the victims are non-fighting civilians. Other factors may militate against a decision to intervene, such as if the aggressor is a nuclear power or there is a risk of partiality in the use of force – which may arise particularly in cases of a decision of only one state to intervene. Similarly, hidden agendas, as opposed to altruistic or humanitarian concerns, should be a further reason not to intervene.

During the ensuing debate, consensus was reached on the basic conditions that legitimate the decision to intervene: the existence of multilateral support for the action, the use of intervention as a last resort, and the assurance that intervention would not worsen the problem. In addition, participants agreed that past situations that had been used to justify unilateral interventions in Latin America and the Caribbean no longer exist.

It became clear that intervention had a particular connotation in the Latin America and Caribbean region. An ever-present concern was the role of the US, either as an intervening state or as the most influential actor in multilateral organizations. Military interventions were thus seen as sharpening the contrast between the real power – but sometimes questionable legality – of an effective military power (the US), and the smaller power – but legitimacy of – multilateral organizations (the UN).

One participant noted the need to consider unarmed interventions. In addition, suggestions were made for changing the general attitude toward intervention. It should not be seen as a decision between the right to intervene or not, but as part of a duty or responsibility to protect. Finally, it was clear that issues requiring intervention are largely interdependent. It would also be helpful to increase the monitoring and early-warning capacity of the UN and to emphasize actions that could prevent situations from escalating. In this regard, three possible levels of intervention should be considered for adoption in a gradually escalating sequence: diplomatic measures, sanctions and incentives, and military force.

The UN nevertheless can only do what its member states decide and is thus dependent on the political interests of those states. However, it is not organized in ways that facilitate making quick decisions. It clearly needs a system to allow for global oversight. Therefore, in order to speed up decisions in situations where a regime is committing atrocities, suggestions were made for modification of the UN Security Council and creation of a tribunal or other body within the General Assembly to make pronouncements upon the gravity of human rights abuses and the related necessity or otherwise of an intervention. It was also suggested that the UN should sponsor analysis of case studies to assess both the effectiveness and the influence of interventions on the political climate of the states in which they take place.

## When Not to Intervene and Why: Alternatives to External Military Intervention

A further two papers were delivered and discussed together. The first related to when intervention is not advisable and alternatives to external military interventions. It noted that interventions involve many risks and perplexities. Because of the difficulty of distinguishing circumstances that require intervention and those that do not, the paper suggested the adoption of a new conceptual context, based on the "globalization" paradigm, rather than on the outdated one of the Cold War. It suggested that the protection of fundamental human rights should be the essential motivation for decisions to intervene. "Sustainability," the assurance that intervention will solve or at least stop the problem, was argued to be the essential operational factor. "If there is doubt about the sustainability of an intervention, it is better not to intervene," though "sovereignty cannot be a barrier when the protection of fundamental rights is at stake." The paper also suggested that fear of intervention may help to prevent abuses of human rights. However, there are two main circumstances when intervention should not take place: 1) when the state concerned is exercising full and complete sovereignty; and 2) when a fundamental value is not at stake. The problem is that situations that may suggest the need for intervention are usually complex. For example, civil war is often a situation that creates objective circumstances requiring intervention, but it is also a complex situation in which right and wrong cannot be easily distinguished.

## The Impact of External Military Intervention: Political, Economic, and Social

The second paper analyzed the political, economic, and social impacts of military intervention. The following variables are relevant: the situation of the country, the size of the intervention force, the necessity of rebuilding the country after intervention, and the level of economic deterioration following the intervention. To evaluate the local impact of military intervention within the context of the Americas, it is important to take into account the history and the role of the OAS, which is currently developing a wide range of instruments to cope with post-intervention situations and the necessity to use force. An example was Haiti. Although the intervention there had been successful in solving the immediate crisis, it was less successful afterward. Moreover, the situation was, at the time of the discussion, quickly deteriorating. From a purely economic standpoint, the intervention in Haiti is excessively expensive and not cost-effective. However, it is difficult to objectively assess the value of military intervention. Military interventions are designed to control a crisis, not address the roots of the problems. Preventive action is extremely important.

During the ensuing discussion, some of the most sensitive factors relating to the decision to intervene were identified as including the time when intervention is necessary and advisable, what is necessary to legitimize interventions, and who can make decisions to intervene. Participants agreed that the most accepted institution to take decisions on multilateral interventions is the UN Security Council. However, there was no consensus on what should happen when there is a widespread sentiment for intervention, but the Security Council chooses not to act.

*Wider Impacts* – Although participants agreed that decisions to intervene often give scant consideration to the intervention's impacts on a wider regional system, they agreed that this variable should be considered during a decision to intervene. Positions were divided between those who considered that sovereignty should not be an obstacle to intervention when human rights are at stake and those who were concerned about negative regional impacts. Examples discussed included the intervention in Nicaragua and the prospects for the Colombian crisis.

Concerned with post-intervention impacts on the population, one participant suggested the assessment of the psychological impacts of intervention, in addition to economic, political, social, and military impacts.

## Intervention "for Democracy"

A heated debate developed on this issue, with no real consensus emerging. There was a feeling that while international consensus might build rapidly in cases of intervention for humanitarian reasons, it does not do so when the intervention is politically motivated, as is the case with preservation of democracy. Although democracy has become a norm and almost a moral value in the region, the overthrow of democracy does not seem a valid motivation for military intervention. Nevertheless, agreement formed around the idea that measures short of military ones, such as diplomatic warnings and sanctions, would be useful tools for the protection of democracy. On the other hand, since democracy has become a cherished value, threats to democratic rule might be followed by major violations of humanitarian values and thus justify intervention. Nevertheless, it was clear that most of those present saw "intervention to protect or promote democracy" as a sensitive and potentially dangerous issue, since the concept of democracy itself is relative and subject to distinct interpretations. The region's direct experience with past US military interventions that claimed to have been aimed at protecting democracy was also relevant here. In this region, therefore, the initial reaction to military intervention would always be cautious.

One participant concerned with the idea of protecting democracy suggested the creation of a supranational institution to oversee and evaluate democracies and their shortcomings in the region. This idea, however, was also criticized on the basis of the relativity of the concept of democracy.

The conclusion was thus reached that in this region, any decision to intervene militarily could only be legitimate if based on severe abuse of fundamental human rights. However, even if the Security Council could not decide to intervene, despite the existence of objective grounds, it would be very difficult to classify as legitimate a "unilateral" military intervention (that is, one taking place without Security Council mandate.) Despite its shortcomings, the UN Charter should be kept as the key paradigm for the analysis of cases eventually requiring military intervention.

# CAIRO

## REGIONAL ROUNDTABLE CONSULTATION WITH NONGOVERN-MENTAL AND OTHER INTERESTED ORGANIZATIONS

### MAY 21, 2001

PARTICIPANTS

Nabil Elaraby, Egyptian Council for Foreign Affairs (Chair)

Livia Leu Agosti, Embassy of Switzerland, Egypt
Mohammed Sid Ahmad, Al-Ahram Centre for Diplomatic and Strategic Studies, Egypt
Salah Amer, Egyptian Association for International Law
Soliman Awad, Ministry of Foreign Affairs, Egypt
Marie-Andrée Beauchemin, Canadian Embassy in Egypt
Abdelaziz Bennani, Euro-Mediterranean Network for Human Rights, Morocco
Bishar El Kassawneh, international law and human rights expert, Jordan
Omran El Shafei, Egyptian Council for Foreign Affairs
Rana Husseini, *Jordan Times*, Jordan
Ahmed Tawfic Khalil, Egyptian Council for Foreign Affairs
Bassma Kodmani, Ford Foundation, Egypt
Sam Menassa, University of Balamand, Lebanon
Hassan Nafaa, Cairo University, Egypt
Atef Obidat, Regional Human Security Centre, Jordan
Bernard Pfefferlé, ICRC, Egypt
Mohammed Shaker, Egyptian Council for Foreign Affairs
Elsayed Amin Shalaby, Egyptian Council for Foreign Affairs
Nageeb Shamiry, Supreme Court and Supreme Judicial Council, Yemen
Massoud Younes, Law and Society Centre for Comparative Studies, Lebanon

## SUMMARY

During opening remarks and in other comments, a number of participants from all backgrounds expressed regret that no Palestinian participant was present, especially in light of the massive violations of human rights committed in the occupied territories and the passivity of the international community. It was stressed that the current situation in the occupied territories could not reasonably be divorced from the issues being discussed at the roundtable.

A discussion paper was presented that recalled past and contemporary experience of military intervention in the region and beyond, noting that it is a sensitive and complex issue. At the regional level, the sanctity of borders has been enshrined in the charters of both the Arab League and the OAU. All diplomatic means have to be exhausted before a military intervention could be contemplated; and, moreover, the intervention has to have a good chance of success. It should also be proportionate to the situation. The rules of international humanitarian law (IHL) should be respected.

Commissioners then referred to some of their current considerations, which included the need to develop working mechanisms for intervention; the responsibility to protect; the need for transparency; the need to avoid double standards; the need to strike a balance between action and inaction; the need for preventive strategies; and the responsibility to assist developing countries in order to tackle the root causes of humanitarian crises. They stressed that they were seeking innovative solutions.

Some participants argued that innovation should not be confined to the question of terminology. The post-war international order that produced the UN is suffering from increasing incoherence. In light of the ongoing changes in the international situation, conventional perceptions in the age of globalization can be viewed as obstacles. The UN does not any longer reflect the contemporary international situation. There is an urgent need to reform the UN system in order for it to be more responsive to the needs of the international community.

### When External Intervention Should Be Considered

A participant made a presentation on the question of when and why external military intervention should be considered, and on intervention priorities and thresholds. It was pointed out that the issue of humanitarian intervention includes a number of normative and moral factors, though the decision making and the undertaking of intervention are to be carried out by politicians. The Middle East has witnessed a number of humanitarian crises that are, or could be, subject to international intervention. The flagrant examples are Palestine and Iraq, but other possibilities are Libya and Sudan. Despite the fact that the intervention that took place in Iraq was justifiable, this intervention has become a source of ongoing humanitarian suffering for innocent Iraqi civilians. The case of Palestine represents the opposite extreme. It involves a number of severe factors (disproportionate use of force, severe abuses of human rights, denial of the right to self-determination), yet no international intervention is envisaged, despite appeals to the international community.

Objectively, there are a number of problematic thresholds to intervention, including the extent of atrocities, war crimes, crimes against humanity, genocide, and threats to fundamental human rights. The problem lies in the definition and identification of these abuses, as this can be a subjective and politicized process. There is a real need to develop an impartial political mechanism for this purpose. At the same time, independent states should be more amenable to the idea of devolution of sovereignty to a supranational body for crisis prevention, monitoring, and management.

The majority of participants agreed that there are thresholds and limitations on intervention that must always be observed. Furthermore, the mechanisms and procedures of the intervention process must be subject to objective international regulation. In this context, it is mentioned that the UN Charter contains apparently contradictory provisions concerning noninterference in internal affairs and the prohibition on the use of force, on one hand, and the provision for collective intervention, on the other. Two important reservations were mentioned in this regard. First, a decision by a state to become party to any international treaty (including the UN Charter) means that it is relinquishing part of its sovereignty to a supranational entity (ideally the UN). Second, the action taken by the Security Council in exercising its responsibility for peacekeeping or peace making is referred to in the UN Charter as legal enforcement measures and not "intervention."

Reservations were expressed about use of the term "humanitarian intervention." One point of view was that "humanitarian" should not be associated with war. Another point of view stressed that the concept of "humanitarian intervention" itself is regarded sceptically in most Third World countries. It has brought back bad memories from the colonial era, when Western colonialism was portrayed as a sort of humanitarian effort to help civilize and free the peoples of the South.

Reasons for intervention include genocide, crimes against humanity, war crimes, major atrocities, self-determination, mass violations of human rights – including, importantly in the Third World, economic, social, and cultural rights. One participant mentioned the concept of human security. Emphasis was put on the urgent need to narrow these concepts, since the more diffuse they are, the more problematic they could become.

On the question of when to intervene, the need to determine the extent of atrocities was noted. This is of particular relevance, since there are cases when intervention is more advisable earlier rather than later. On the other hand, some Western countries argue that having an ongoing, political (peace) process constitutes an impediment to intervention.

On the issue of procedures and how to intervene, reference was made to a wide variety of existing UN mechanisms and tools, ranging from treaty-based mechanisms and bodies, to special rapporteurs, to the Security Council. The majority of participants agreed that any form of use of force should be conducted strictly in conformity with the UN Charter. However, this raises problems, since giving the Security Council exclusive responsibility would simply mean leaving it in the hands of a "not really democratic organ" to decide when and how to intervene. Furthermore, Arab public opinion does not give full credence to the Security Council, because of its double-standard approach to the issues in this region.

The issue of "legality versus legitimacy" was also raised. In some cases, legal governments that lack legitimacy would object to humanitarian intervention on the grounds that it infringes on their sovereignty. In other cases, there might be a legitimate need for intervention, but the Security Council fails to provide the legal framework in which an intervention could take place.

Finally, participants agreed that while there is no substitute for the existing framework on the use of force (that is, mandated by the Security Council under Chapter VII), this must be coupled with the Council's reform, if the object is to secure an intervention that is objective, nonselective, and free from double standards.

### The Impact of Military Intervention and Alternatives

The second working session tackled the question of alternatives to external military intervention and the impacts of external military intervention: political, economic, and social. The paper presented on the first subject drew attention to the fact that in some cases authoritarian regimes in the South are fuelling civil wars in order to maintain their own power. Some Western powers back these regimes, though the regimes lack the support of their own people. In other cases, Western countries are sometimes invited to intervene in situations of internal chaos, but instead of helping ease tensions they add to them in pursuit of their own interests. This evoked the fear of many Third World countries that the West would misuse the concept of human rights to intervene in their internal affairs. A proposal was made for the creation of an international monitoring body to observe the situation in various areas of tension in the world in order to prevent the eruption of violence.

The presentation on the political, economic, and social impacts of external military intervention used Somalia as an example. The point was made that there existed three levels of problems in Somalia, namely the existence of various political entities, a deteriorating economic situation, and a social disaster consisting of a flood of refugees. International "humanitarian" intervention helped to solve none of them. Instead, one could say that as some of the problems worsened, international interest faded. In such circumstances, there is a graduated series of responses that should be considered concerning the phases of intervention. It should be initiated by neighbouring countries, then move up to regional organizations, then to the Security Council, and if the Council fails to take action, the General Assembly should act under the "Uniting for Peace" formula.

Reform of the UN was discussed at length. One participant claimed that what is needed is a totally new organization to reflect the ongoing changes in the international situation. Some participants responded that the lack of balanced representation of the international community in the UN does not necessarily mean abandoning the system. Instead, the Security Council should be reformed, or the "Uniting for Peace" mechanism should be revived.

The role and scope of power in the Security Council were also discussed. It was stated that while the responsibility and authority to maintain peace and security are vested in the Security Council, it is not clear to whom the Security Council is accountable. It was suggested that there is a need to have judicial supervision of the Council and that the ICJ is – theoretically – the best placed body to do so.

The majority of the participants expressed frustration over the current performance and legitimacy of the Security Council when it comes to the Middle East. The Palestinian problem, Iraq, Sudan, and the *Lockerbie* case were mentioned as flagrant examples of unfairness and double standards. Moreover, the credibility, as well as the legitimacy, of the Security Council is being eroded because of its ineffectiveness in certain cases. It is also unrepresentative and undemocratic. Some participants suggested that as a result of these defects, the world cannot depend on the Security Council as the only vehicle to maintain international peace and security. If the Security Council remains the starting point when it comes to international military intervention, it should not necessarily be the finishing point. There is a serious need for institutional change and reform, including revision of the veto power. Some participants suggested that true reform of the Council would be lacking as long as the veto power remains.

There was general agreement that prevention should always be preferable to intervention but that international protection through military intervention might be needed in cases of flagrant humanitarian violations. However, the right system for its implementation does not as yet exist. Unequivocal and agreed criteria and safeguards have to be established. Intervention should be the responsibility of a collective body that reflects the will of the majority of the international community.

One Commissioner pointed out that the enlargement of the Security Council would not by itself help improve the situation. The problem lies more in the Council's working methods, rather than its membership. Resorting to the General Assembly is no better and can even make the situation more chaotic. It was suggested that an international board of eminent persons be created to make recommendations to the president of the Security Council or to the Secretary-General as to when collective intervention might be required in specific cases. The recommendations, moreover, should be made public. Participants expressed reservations. They noted that for the majority of the Third World, the General Assembly, while flawed, is still the most democratic of the existing international bodies, and it is, at the very least, a better reflection of world public opinion. As for the proposed international board of eminent persons, it would inevitably become just one more bureaucratic body.

It was argued that regional organizations, authorized by the Security Council under Chapter VIII of the UN Charter, may well be in a better position to contribute to conflict resolution because of their proximity and their probably greater acceptability to parties in conflict in that region. Regional organizations could also monitor humanitarian crises, which could be particularly helpful for early warning and conflict prevention. A number of participants argued, to the contrary, that in some cases a regional organization could not play an effective role, because of sensitivities over the motives of major regional states.

The role of civil society and NGOs was raised. NGOs can play a very constructive role in forming international consensus as the basis for an intervention. This can be achieved through a coalition of the more important and influential human rights NGOs at the international level, as part of the global civil society initiative of the Secretary-General.

## Conclusions

The ICISS side said that at least four threads were evident in the discussion. The first was that ICISS needs to seriously consider Arab experience in relation to double standards and selectivity, with Palestine a good example. Secondly, there was a feeling that the existing structures of the UN Charter are no longer helpful in all situations and that new structures and processes (pursuant to the Geneva Conventions, the International Criminal Court (ICC), or other treaty-based mechanisms) should have a role, as well as the Security Council. Thirdly, there was a strong need felt for an objective process and concrete safeguards: it is important to ensure both that intervention happens in the right cases and that it does not happen in the wrong ones. The Security Council, as presently constituted, lacks some credibility in making the decision. Fourthly, there is a need to focus on prevention as very important and integral to the notion of the responsibility to protect.

In his concluding remarks, the Chair of the roundtable said that the international community needs to work out norms, criteria, rules, and guidelines to authorize and regulate interventions. At the same time, the existing legal framework enshrined in the UN must not be undermined. The Charter allows for a liberal and flexible interpretation of Article 2 (7) in order to cope with the evolution and expansion of issues that are increasingly considered to be of international concern. So, many forms of intervention short of the use of force are envisaged in the Charter. The use of force, however, is strictly regulated in Article 2 (4). Moreover, the prohibition of the use of force is universally considered as the greatest achievement of the contemporary international legal order in the 20th century. It is a cardinal rule from which no derogation is permitted. He concluded by stressing the importance of prevention and the need to always work by evolution and not revolution, making sure that striving to attain a lofty objective does not occur at the expense of undermining the existing international legal order.

# PARIS I

## ROUNDTABLE CONSULTATION WITH FRENCH GOVERNMENT OFFICIALS AND PARLIAMENTARIANS

### MAY 23, 2001

PARTICIPANTS

Jill Sinclair, Director-General, Global Issues Bureau, Department of Foreign Affairs and International Trade, Canada (Chair)

Ronny Abraham, Ministry of Foreign Affairs, France
François Alabrune, Ministry of Foreign Affairs, France
Raymond Chrétien, Canadian Embassy in France
Guillaume Etienne, Ministry of Defence, France
Pierre Lellouche, Member of Parliament, Defence Commission, France
Jean Félix Paganon, Ministry of Foreign Affairs, France
Marc Perrin de Brichambault, Ministry of Foreign Affairs, France
Béatrice Pouligny, Centre for the Study of International Relations, France
Térèse Pujolle, Ministry of Foreign Affairs, France
Harold Valentin, Ministry of Foreign Affairs, France
Hubert Védrine, Minister of Foreign Affairs, France
Denys Wibaux, Ministry of Foreign Affairs, France

# SUMMARY

This consultation was part of ICISS's efforts to engage the P-5. The session took place at the Canadian Cultural Centre in Paris on the morning of May 23 and was opened by Hubert Védrine, the French Minister for Foreign Affairs. Representatives from the French Department of Foreign Affairs, Department of Defence, think-tanks, and opposition parties in the National Assembly attended the session.

Minister Védrine detailed the French position on intervention and efforts to reform the UN Security Council. He said sovereignty is not an absolute. States, by actions such as negotiating treaties, recognize the inherent limits of their sovereignty, which have been further eroded by the increasing role of civil society. However, it is simply not possible, morally or politically, to establish a world order on a "right to interfere" (*droit d'ingérence*), regardless of how noble the goal might be.

In Kosovo, all political and diplomatic measures had failed; the Rambouillet conference had proved as much. Although he personally thought NATO's intervention had been justifiable juridically, others had argued it did not meet all the traditional legal requirements. The two preceding UN Security Council resolutions on the situation had, nevertheless, declared it to be a threat to international peace and security, even if they had not specifically authorized the use of force. In other words, there was three-quarters of a Chapter VII mandate, and the NATO action was at the very least legitimate.

However, interventions such as Kosovo must not become the norm or be considered the basis for a new system of international law, which would undoubtedly lead to rule by the strongest nations. It was an *exception* to the usual rules. The solution lies in a new system, which must answer the question: Who can intervene, where, and to do what? A new way of thinking must be brought about and that change must take place at the core of the UN Security Council.

Minister Védrine proposed a "Code of Conduct" for the use of the veto by the P-5. The hope was that this would allow the Security Council as a whole to react more quickly to crises, even when one of the P-5 is involved. This in turn would create greater reliability, predictability and credibility for the Security Council. The criteria need to be practical, rather than only "intellectual," and fairly specific, given the gravity and urgency of the situations necessitating action. He said that he did not think that more "radical" solutions are very realistic, especially since 120 or 130 of the UN's members still place overwhelming priority on their sovereignty.

Although participants could be said to have expressed a generally "Northern" view of these issues, more global concerns were voiced, such as the discrepancy between rhetoric and action and the usual lack of consideration for the sociopolitical repercussions of an intervention. Discussions generally centred on military intervention, with some references made to prevention and the importance of development issues.

## Sovereignty

A number of participants made the point that sovereignty is no longer an absolute rampart, behind which perpetrators of atrocities can hide; most states have in any case voluntarily reduced their sovereignty by becoming party to all sorts of treaties. In other words, the protection of human rights is, today, seen as some justification for the violation of state sovereignty. This leads to the misconception that state sovereignty and human rights are incompatible concepts. Although sovereignty might no longer be seen as the sole basis on which international society is organized, it is nonetheless a prerequisite for the development of democracy and human rights, without which the international order would be seriously compromised.

## Intervention

The debate on the means to intervene stemmed from the acknowledgement that not to act has become unacceptable. Situations of overwhelming humanitarian necessity challenge the traditional framework where the UN Security Council has to authorize the intervention.

Two participants noted that the French public traditionally supports intervention. This has led to France intervening more than 60 times since the end of the Cold War, a reorganization of its military forces toward peacekeeping–making operations, and the participation in development of a European rapid-reaction force. The ideas and values motivating these interventions were regarded as universal, and intervention was seen as contributing to the birth of an "international conscience." Nevertheless, participants recognized the potential for humanitarian fatigue and disinterest, as could be observed in the French public's relative lack of interest in the Algerian crisis.

## The Question of Legitimacy and Means

Three elements have substantially changed the debate on the issues of intervention and state sovereignty since the end of the Cold War:

❏   the increased number of intrastate armed conflicts have shifted the debate to the re-sponsibility of states for their own nationals;

❏   the end of the Cold War paralysis of the Security Council has seen an increased capacity and will to act; and

❏   the international community's inadequate, insufficient, or late action and its lack of consistency have directly affected the credibility of the UN and its Security Council.

These factors culminated in the Kosovo intervention, which shifted discourse to the protection of individuals and discussions about a new international political order, in which the notions of legitimacy of intervention and the means to intervene had to be reevaluated.

It was suggested by several participants that although the criteria for legality are clear, those for legitimacy are not, and the ICISS could make a mark in this regard. Opération Turquoise was an example cited. Although highly contested by the local population and the international community, it was regarded as a legitimate action by the French military and public opinion, since ultimately it saved lives. (Some participants were nevertheless critical of the operation.) One participant noted that even though an intervention may have been authorized by the Security Council (and its legality would thus not be in question), the intervention might itself still not take place, for example, because of lack of troop contributions, such as occurred in the Congo in 1996 despite severe crimes against humanity. In other words, we should also be taking account of interventions that do not occur, as well as those that do.

Some participants argued that a consensus on what is legitimate is impossible, since by nature each actor interprets the concept according to his or her own perspective. Similarly, legality alone does not make an intervention legitimate. This is especially true of a "rubber stamp" by the Security Council set in a climate of inconsistency and double standards. Law is nothing without the support and commitment of public opinion.

Another view put was that a true measure of the legitimacy of an intervention should lie in the perspective of the local population. An intervening force must be seen by the local population as a partner, especially in cases where reconstruction is needed. The principles guiding the mission must be explained and accepted by the population. In the case of a military intervention, great care must be taken as to the behaviour of the intervening soldiers. An intervention might be legitimate at first, but quickly become illegitimate if the rights and freedoms of the local population are disregarded, as had happened in Somalia.

Several official participants noted that the French government believed the answer to these dilemmas lies within the UN Charter. The Charter establishes a clear link between human rights and international peace and security, but it is necessary to put more focus on the relevant provisions. The Security Council also needs to be restored to a central position in the intervention equation, but to do this it also needs to be fully reformed. Since this would be some time off, we have to go on expecting interventions that might occur outside the authority of the Security Council. One senior official noted that the search for new mechanisms, such as greater use the UN General Assembly's "Uniting for Peace" procedures, is not part of French policy.

## Criteria for Military Intervention

The official criteria for French military intervention were stated to include

❏ the presence of a clear mandate pursuant to Chapter VII of the UN Charter;

❏ strong rules of engagement;

❏ a clear chain of command;

❏ a predefined exit strategy; and

❏ an acceptable risk of casualties (the French threshold being higher than that of other countries, such as the US).

Nevertheless, in practice, future interventions would likely take place in three situations that do not necessarily respect these criteria:

❏ cases where public opinion dictates intervention;

❏ easy interventions, where operations would not be dangerous or onerous (for ex-ample, the Ethiopia–Eritrea mission, where the states in question consented to the intervention); and

❏ regional interventions, usually in Africa, where ground troops are supplied by African countries.

Within the P-5, France, England, and the US accept the idea of intervention, in general, but are very restrictive about becoming involved in specific cases. In contrast, China prefers a case-by-case approach. In reality, however, there could never be an intervention if the P-5 are either too interested or not interested enough in a crisis as a result of the influence of their own national politics in the international decision making process. Moreover, the threat of the P-5 veto is usually apparent well before any formal vote is taken, and this has led to the high number of inconsistencies in the application of UN policy, even within an intervention itself.

This led some participants to suggest that the pertinence of elaborating a set of criteria for when to intervene could be highly questionable. Even if criteria are clearly set up, their interpretation would be different from state to state (for example, how to define an international crisis). In some cases, the existence of criteria might even lead to a calculated escalation of hostilities to bring about an international intervention (for example, arguably, East Timor). Similarly, some regimes would feel confident they might never be the subject of intervention, because of, for instance, their low strategic importance.

## Why Interventions Fail

The mentality guiding today's interventions is responsible for the dismal record of the UN in recent years. Proposed solutions, such as those contained in the Brahimi report, try to simplify a situation where "us and them" is a continuing, though evolving, concept. Not enough importance is given to the local impact of a foreign intervention, and this is exacerbated by the growing divide between those who decide on the intervention, those who pay for it, and those who provide the ground troops. This is particularly the case in Africa.

Efforts have been made to depoliticize peace building and make mandates technical. Trying to depoliticize an intervention is usually wrong and ineffective, because it inevitably results in the imposition of an outside political framework on the internal situation of a state. Intervening forces rarely have an clear idea about how to impose such new policies effectively, as has been illustrated in Haiti. Peace is a highly political endeavour; and peace, rule of law, and a stable environment are notions not only defined differently among states but within the intervened state itself. Rhetoric about the impartial nature of interventions is similarly deceptive and counterproductive. A military intervention can never be neutral and impartial, as it fundamentally affects and changes the sociopolitical structure of the country in which the intervention has taken place. The local population only relates in terms of "ally or enemy" and would interpret the actions of the intervening forces through that framework. The historical presence of certain wealthy countries, be it through arms sales, companies exploiting natural resources, or mercenaries in countries later intervened in similarly taints their actions.

The Brahimi report recommended that the mandate of an intervention should always be clear. This is unrealistic, as the mandate of a mission is the result of a political compromise that often includes contradicting positions. Long-term objectives end up contradicting short-term ones (for example, Kosovo, where the task now is to rebuild the infrastructure destroyed by the intervention). Interventions whose aim is to start a dynamic evolution of the society are usually organized to achieve their goal by stabilizing the situation or maintaining the status quo. Likewise, predefined exit strategies make it easy for local extremists to simply wait until the storm passes.

Although a political crisis cannot be solved by military means, there is an increased dependence on military personnel. The roles are becoming blurred, as politicians play at being generals, and soldiers are asked to play political roles or undertake tasks they are unsuited for. This in turn leads to fatigue by the military but also distrust of its political leaders. At the same time, the judiciary is seen as being highly ineffective and often as contributing to additional confusion and destabilization of the situation, as it never effectively attains its main goal, dissuasion. Its credibility is further diminished, as usually no provisions are made to engage the collective and individual responsibility of foreign intervenors, both military and NGO, for misdeeds.

## Prevention

Most participants agreed that prevention is a preferred alternative to intervention, but again there is inconsistency between rhetoric and action. As one participant noted, although governments officially endorse prevention, there has been a sharp reduction in development assistance in recent years. Similarly, states are rarely unaware of emerging crises. The decision to ignore early warnings is motivated by calculations of profit for armament industries, for instance, and the conviction that war is more profitable than peace. For one participant, the real challenge was to drive home to people that peace is really more valuable than war and costs far less.

More effective preventive mechanisms are needed. Suggestions included

❑ the revival of a proposal made in 1974 by President Valérie Giscard d'Estaing and later supported by President François Mitterand to establish a major new international prevention agency, which would include an early-warning mechanism;

❑ increase the role and competence of the ICC; and

❑ increase the regional capacity to respond to crises (for example, the European rapid-reaction force).

# PARIS II

## ROUNDTABLE CONSULTATION WITH NONGOVERNMENTAL AND OTHER INTERESTED ORGANIZATIONS

### MAY 23, 2001

PARTICIPANTS

Jill Sinclair, Department of Foreign Affairs and International Trade, Canada (Chair)
Jean-François Bayart, Centre for the Study of International Relations, France
Mario Bettati, Université de Paris II
Philippe Chabasse, Handicap International
Raymond Chrétien, Canadian Embassy in France
Loiscono Clouet, Handicap International
Emmanuel Decaux, Université de Paris II, member of the National Commission on Human Rights
Olivier De Frouville, Université de Paris X–Nanterre
Patrick de Louvain, Amnesty International
Ghislaine Doucet, ICRC
Carolle Dubrulle, Action internationale contre la faim
Pierre Hassner, Institute of Political Studies, Paris
Claude Lefort, philosopher
Béatrice Pouligny, Centre for the Study of International Relations, France
Robert Verdier, Human Rights League

## SUMMARY

### Defining Sovereignty

Sovereignty was defined by one participant as the power to govern territory, independence from other states, and respect for international law. It follows particularly from the latter that the exercise of sovereignty is not a tool to rule arbitrarily, for example by murdering one's own people. In absolute terms, sovereignty has always had strict limits.

Some participants rejected the notion that the proliferation of internal armed conflicts is associated with a new post-Cold War order that equates lessening of conflict with attacking state sovereignty. According to this view, conflicts have changed little throughout the last century; and although today's world is based on interdependence, Third World – and indeed some First World – countries are still very sensitive about their recently acquired independence. Internal conflicts are in a sense mechanisms to reinforce nationalism. Globalization is an important factor in state-building in modern times but could become negative when it clashes with sovereignty. War in such circumstances is a means used, for example, by some sub-Saharan states to reassert their sovereignty over international forces that they see as trying to diminish the importance of their national borders through financial restructuring and foreign-aid programmes.

### Defining Intervention and the Right of Interference

Intervention was defined as action by a state or an international organization in the affairs of another state. The intervention could, moreover, be civilian or military and could in general terms be aimed at saving or protecting human life.

Two types of interventions were identified:

❑ "interventions for humanity": unilateral, nonauthorized interventions motivated by the protection of national interests externally, such as rescue of nationals, self-defence; and

❑ multilateral, Chapter VII-authorized interventions aimed at protecting the citizens of another state.

The intervention in Bosnia was humanitarian, since its only aim was to separate the belligerents and protect the population impartially. The one in Kosovo was not. Its aim has been to protect human rights and therefore oblige intervening states to take sides against the perpetrators of the violations.

Countries such as the US do not distinguish between these two types. They, moreover, use the term "humanitarian" in a blanket way, which leads to confusion. Several participants opposed altogether the idea of using the term "humanitarian" for any type of intervention where force, military or otherwise, is used. They insisted the term should only apply to purely relief operations, since its use otherwise leads to a skewed perception by the local population of the true nature of an intervention.

Several French interventions in the past based their legitimacy on the doctrine of a "right to interfere" (*droit d'ingérence*). Confusion exists over this term. Some believe an intervention that respects international law is not interference, since all states have implicitly bound themselves to the precepts of the law. Similarly, "interventions" by bodies such as the ICC do not amount to judicial interference, as they apply the statutes agreed upon by states. The claimed legal basis for a "right to interfere" lies in international instruments, such as the Geneva Conventions (Article 3) and UN General Assembly resolutions. Even the strongest proponents of a right to intervene, such as Bernard Kouchner, have never argued that sovereignty should not be respected as far as possible. The Geneva Conventions also make it clear that nothing in them should challenge the basic rules of sovereignty.

### The Responsibility to Act

There was some agreement that the international community is less and less accepting of violations of humanitarian principles. These days, states are not only regarded as respon-sible for their own territory or the actions of their nationals abroad, but also being asked to remedy abuses committed by other states against their own populations and within their own territories. The framework provided by the UN was not seen as the only means to achieve this goal. There are other instruments, such as the Geneva Conventions, that provide such extraterritorial jurisdiction. The criteria elaborated by Antonio Cassese for state intervention without UN mandate were mentioned by one participant:

❑ massive and systematic violations of human rights;

❑ absence of political will by the state to stop such violations;

❑   paralysis of the UN Security Council pursuant to a veto;

❑   all peaceful means of settling the situation have failed;

❑   the intervention should best be conducted by a coalition of states; and

❑   force should be used only to end the abuses – there should be no hidden agenda.

A number of participants indicated that the problem does not lie with the law but with its implementation. Resources allocated for responding to crises have been steadily reduced. The influence of multinational companies, sometimes more powerful than some states, has negatively impacted on foreign policy making. Although states that oppose interventions are usually seen as having something to hide, military intervention is seldom the best way to deal with humanitarian crises. Similarly, states that usually recommend intervention are frequently the largest providers of arms fuelling the conflict.

Most participants agreed that states cannot intervene everywhere but criticized the apparently arbitrary selectivity of where interventions actually do take place, and blatant double standards. There was also criticism of the method of implementing interventions, which often leads to a perpetuation of the conflict (with ECOMOG in Liberia and the British intervention in Sierra Leone as claimed examples). Other points made were that states often commit to intervention half-heartedly and inconsistently, with little will to engage in long-term operations. Moreover, the political component is often lacking, and no long-term strategy is put in place to consider the political and economic repercussions of the intervention.

This led to the question of the responsibility of nonstate actors: armed rebel groups, mercenaries–private security companies, multinational companies, international organizations, NGOs, think-tanks, and, above all, individuals. The last three UN Secretaries-General insisted that the Charter provides for the protection of human rights and that interventions for that purpose, especially military, signify the emergence of the individual as a distinct subject of international law. New bodies, such as the ICC, in fact give the power to individuals to not only influence the policy of their governments but also intervene at a judicial level, on such issues as the starvation of the population (considered a war crime by the ICC).

It was suggested that even in military interventions, nonmilitary actors should also be brought in as soon as possible. Relief operations and assistance to the victims of war should be left to organizations such as the ICRC, and states should only intervene in the politico-military process. During the Kosovo intervention, NATO was the coordinating body for humanitarian affairs, which led to a confusion between military and humanitarian goals.

Some participants nevertheless expressed concern lest the shift in focus to non-state actors becomes an excuse for states not to assume the responsibility that is properly theirs. For example, in Angola the criminalization of the Union for the Total Independence of Angola might not have been wholly positive, as it ignored the role of neighbouring countries in rekindling the hostilities; similarly in Sierra Leone, the demonization of the Revolutionary United Front might have facilitated a political solution, but it did not address the original problems that led the group to rebel in the first place. This is particularly counterproductive, since other actors are usually only subject to nonbinding codes of conduct. Moreover, some nonstate actors simply do not have the capacity for effective political action.

## Prevention

The definition of peace has evolved from the old negative approach, namely, the absence of war, to a new positivistic view, viz. a permanent end to war attainable by affecting the root causes of conflict. A number of participants were pleased with ICISS's focus on a "responsibility to protect," as this emphasizes the victims and clearly encompasses prevention. Some other participants nevertheless warned that once you pass the wrapping, the essential questions remain the same and still have to be addressed.

Although participants diverged on the roles of the main actors during a crisis, all agreed on the importance of cooperation in elaborating effective, new preventive strategies through dialogue, fighting against racism and similar ideologies that lead to war, repressing international crimes, and instituting clear measures, such as the suspension of all international aid to countries taking part in a conflict. Most participants agreed that the use of military force should always be the last resort, but some considered that the targeted use of force early in a crisis could be construed as a preventive strategy, used to avoid the escalation of hostilities.

### Reforming the United Nations

Recent events, such as the intervention in Kosovo, have highlighted an apparent gap between legality and legitimacy. This discrepancy is further complicated within the UN, where structures are often ill-adapted to the objectives of the organization. A number of participants proposed reforms aimed at changing the composition of the Security Council to include new permanent members. Others noted that this is not a realistic goal in the short term. Moreover, although such reform might increase the Council's legitimacy, it would not necessarily improve its effectiveness. Similarly, reforms aimed at eliminating the veto tend to see the veto as a block to needed and legitimate interventions, rather than as a regulatory mechanism that, if ignored, could lead to greater crisis.

One solution suggested was to put human rights more firmly at the centre of policy making in the UN. Human rights are a universal criterion for legitimacy, recognized both in the UN Charter and in instruments of customary international law, such as the Universal Declaration of Human Rights. Concrete steps could include reinforcing human rights programmes and the Office of the UN High Commissioner for Human Rights to give them the means to implement policy effectively. Institutionalizing civil society within the UN system would also contribute, although a distinction must be made between NGOs with a global and wide-ranging agenda and those whose aim is to lobby for a specific, narrow goal.

This view based on the UN Charter was criticized by some participants. The Charter is not seen as all-unifying, but rather as a conglomerate of contradictory and antiquated principles, such as the concept of just war. The UN claims to be a democracy on a world scale, but does not recognize the diverse ideals of its members. Not all regimes have accepted or implemented the human rights principles contained in the Charter. The sheer diversity of the cultural values of its members makes a consensus on fundamental values and legitimacy difficult, if not impossible. This consensus cannot be imposed, since the organization itself is not really an effective supranational state with the means to enforce the application of those principles. The proponents of this perspective believed the answer lies in working toward a greater autonomy of action for states, individually or in unison, but not necessarily within the framework of the UN.

One participant warned, moreover, that it also has to be borne in mind that the people who were most interested in obtaining greater individual rights these days also tend to be those who are also interested in the creation of more states (though states that behave in a better way, both internally and internationally). In other words, such people are also strong supporters of sovereignty in the traditional sense.

# NEW DELHI

## REGIONAL ROUNDTABLE CONSULTATION WITH NONGOVERN-MENTAL AND OTHER INTERESTED ORGANIZATIONS

### JUNE 10, 2001

PARTICIPANTS

Satish Nambiar, United Services Institution, India (Chair)

Dipankar Banerjee, Regional Centre for Strategic Studies, Sri Lanka
Farhan Bokhari, correspondent, Pakistan
Chin Kin Wah, Singapore Institute of International Affairs, Singapore
Aiko Doden, NHK Bangkok Bureau, Thailand
I.K. Gujral, former Prime Minister of India
Colin James, Synapsis Ltd., New Zealand
Manoj Joshi, *The Times of India*
Sylvie Junod, ICRC, India
C.K. Lal, Himal Khabarpatrika, Nepal
William Maley, Refugee Council of Australia, Australia
Sriprapha Petcharamesree, Human Rights Studies Program, Mahidol University, Thailand
Melinda Quintos de Jesus, Centre for Media Freedom and Responsibility, the Philippines
Ok Serei Sopheak, Centre for Peace and Development, Cambodia
Peter Sutherland, Canadian High Commission in India
Jacob Tobing, Member of Parliamentary Assembly, Indonesia
Tran Ngoc Thach, Institute for International Relations, Vietnam
N.N. Vohra, India International Centre, India
Yuan Jian, China Institute of International Studies, China

## SUMMARY

The extent to which humanitarian intervention can become a legitimate practice in international society was the central issue of discussion. The concept of sovereignty, lessons learned from past interventions in various regions, the context and circumstances in which intervention can take place, the principles and criteria for intervention, the role of the media, and the limits and challenges of humanitarian intervention were all discussed.

Intervention and state sovereignty were stated to be incompatible concepts. However, with globalization, interdependence, and the new international order, the normative principle of state sovereignty has been undermined. While states no longer enjoy absolute sovereignty, the legitimacy of intervention remains a controversial issue.

Article 2 (4) of the UN Charter restricts the right to use force unilaterally, except in cases of self-defence. It has been widely accepted, especially during the Cold War, that military intervention to save the victims of even gross human rights abuses is a violation of the Charter. As strong adherents to this provision and the principle of nonintervention, countries in Asia – such as China, India, and many ASEAN members – are key opponents of intervention. Nevertheless, there is room to manoeuvre. Chapter VII of the UN Charter allows the use of force to maintain "international peace and security." The controversy lies in how international peace and security should be interpreted and how far this permits the Security Council to authorize interventions to stop intrastate humanitarian emergencies. Problems stemming from crises, such as the influx of refugees, must also be dealt with in the context of an intervention.

The gap between international commitments and the instruments for enforcing them allow some governments to abuse their citizens with impunity. Outside interventions to rescue these people provoke charges of interference in the internal affairs of another state. On the other hand, failing to act can lead to accusations of moral indifference and an abrogation of international responsibility.

### Lessons Learned

The Indian experiences of intervention in Bangladesh, Sri Lanka, and the Maldives, the NATO intervention in Kosovo, and UN interventions in Cambodia, East Timor, and other cases were raised for discussion. While these cases are diverse in nature (unilateral in the case of the Indian interventions, multilateral but outside the framework of the UN in the case of Kosovo, and multilateral, under the aegis of the UN, in the remaining cases), there are similarities among them, particularly in the ad hoc nature of those operations.

Nevertheless, participants generally agreed that the nature of each conflict differs markedly, according to varying political contexts and cultural settings, among other factors. Conflicts are rampant across the globe, but international law does not provide satisfactory principles or guidelines for intervention, and armed forces are not trained or intended for humanitarian operations. Faced with these difficulties, interventions have at times resulted in failure.

Very often, the morality and claimed legitimacy of interventions have in reality only been those of dominant nations or groups of nations. Although in some cases the effect of military intervention has been to rescue the victims of mass murder or grave violations of human rights, the use of force has been strongly condemned by the international community. Too often, intervention for humanitarian purposes has been criticized for inconsistency, selectivity, and hypocrisy.

Past experience suggests the following as the sorts of conditions that have to be met in carrying out an intervention:

❑ an intervention and its mandate have to flow from a global conscience;

❑ strategies and available resources have to be assessed carefully;

❑ operations must be well-planned, with clear and accepted, impartial, transparent polcies and must be implemented by trained (armed) forces;

❑ political and international-relations perspectives must be taken into consideration;

❑ territorial integrity must be respected;

❑ the objective must be to increase democratization, good governance, and economic development and strengthen the process of nation-building;

❑ discrimination in the ways or means of implementing an intervention must be avoided;

❑ safe areas and demilitarized zones must be redefined; and

❑ attempts must be made to predict and prevent undesirable consequences.

Participants noted that international society still lacks an international framework of laws and an authoritative, objective decision maker to adjudicate the applicability of intervention.

## Principles and Guidelines for Military Intervention

Participants discussed ways to mitigate the perverse effects of intervention by focusing on principles and guidelines for intervention that might be acceptable to the international community. Broad consensus was reached on the following criteria:

- ❏ Humanitarian intervention must be restricted to the most heinous crimes, such as genocide, imminent or ongoing gross human rights violations and mass murder.

- ❏ Military intervention must be seen as a last resort and must have a high likelihood of success. The use of force must be considered in conjunction with Chapter VI, Article 33 of the UN Charter.

- ❏ Intervention should be premised and based on existing internationally recognized and accepted norms. It should also be consistent with international laws and principles, including IHL.

- ❏ A multilateral intervention by the UN, or authorized by the UN, is preferable to a direct intervention by a regional organization, but the latter is preferable to one undertaken by a group of states or an individual state.

- ❏ Intervention must be implemented in a timely way and must be swift and decisive.

- ❏ The use of force must be proportionate to the desired ends and must be impartial.

- ❏ Policies for intervention must be developed by means of a democratic process, and decision making must be transparent.

- ❏ Intervening powers would have to withdraw as soon as the mandate has been achieved, and the sovereignty of the state must be immediately reinstated.

- ❏ Humanitarian intervention is justified not only on moral grounds, but also on grounds relating to the maintenance of peace and security, as well as economic development and the protection of cultural heritage.

- ❏ Intervention must address the root causes of violations and must be well intended, and not in the pursuit of state self-interest.

- ❏ The primary goal of intervention must be to remedy humanitarian crises and restore the rule of law, and not the pursuit of self-interest by intervening states.

- ❏ If at all possible, intervention should occur on the basis of the invitation of the government of the state in which the intervention is to occur.

Intervention must be considered on a case-by-case basis. It was agreed that the proposed criteria are incomplete and leave much open to interpretation, such as the definition of what constitutes gross violations of human rights, mass murder, etc. The question of who should decide to enforce standards and how and what the process of scrutiny should be were also discussed. Although in general participants tended to favour entrusting the authority to intervene to the Security Council, many called for a review of its structure and composition, citing problems of coherence, effectiveness, representation, democratic practice, and legitimacy. For many participants, the Security Council is in crisis, and there is uncertainty as to whether it could properly fulfill its mandate. One participant suggested that an international independent body be established outside the UN system in order to make sure that standards and conditions are met by intervenors.

## Impacts of External Military Intervention

It was argued that if military intervention is the only way to put an end to human crises and barbarism, it would be rather difficult to avoid their perverse effects. In this regard, one participant put forward a number of principles on the potential impacts of military intervention:

❏ Rather than addressing the deep-rooted problems of disrupted states, which requires a long-term strategy, intervention more readily and rapidly addresses the short-term symptoms of disorder.

❏ Intervention is likely to have significant impact on particular individuals or groups influenced by the access to, and distribution of, goods.

❏ Intervention brings a range of new actors to the local and international landscape.

❏ Intervention is merely the starting point in a complex process of political change. It is not designed to end conflict altogether but can at least be expected to "civilize" politcal conflict.

❏ Intervening forces will find it difficult to confront the problems of political culture, the elite structure, and institutional structure and design in the intervened country.

❏ Post-intervention peace processes might be hindered by the agendas of local authorities ("limited, greedy, or total spoilers"), whose principal targets are vulnerable populations;

❏ Intervention might have significant potential impacts on trust, social capital, and the character of a society (a lack of trust could spoil all good intentions);

❏ Intervention and (or) international assistance can produce negative effects on the reconstruction of a civilian economy if the presence of intervening powers causes distortions in local incentive structures, creates an unacceptably dependent state, or inadvertently provides space for criminal elements to flourish; and

❏ Any of the aforementioned issues can result in the fragmentation of a coalition of intervening powers.

## Role of the Media

It was noted that the legitimacy of intervention is based on public support. Without the media, military intervention would not win public support. The problem lies in the fact that

❏ in general, the need for instantaneous information precludes the transmission of confirmed information;

❏ the media's interest in comprehensive information can hinder operational, and, particularly, military strategies;

❏ the media is not adequately sensitized to the importance of political control over interventions; and

❏ information (and intelligence) is not adequately shared, but the media appears to be the main actor involved in gathering and disseminating information.

Participants concluded that it is important to win the support of the media in order to win public support over an intervention. From the perspective of the media, it is important that intervening parties understand international media norms; from the perspective of intervening parties, the media need to practice "preventive journalism."

## Conclusions

Seen from various dimensions, it was agreed that intervention is a complex question and needs to be addressed with caution. Cooperation is an essential element. International responsibility must be felt by all if intervention or cooperation is to succeed.

There are now too many conflicts crying out for an international response. The society of states has a duty to act. However, if principles and guidelines are necessary, there is also a need to consider the modalities for any particular action. Participants called for recharacterizing preventive responsibilities.

While military intervention might be the only means to enforce humanitarian norms, it should not be considered a right. Rather, it must be seen as a responsibility. As such, coercive intervention needs to be properly justified. While protective and preventive intervention is preferable to military intervention at all times, military intervention will, at times, be a "necessary evil," and though it should only ever be attempted "with a trembling hand," it should in some cases be attempted nonetheless.

# BEIJING

## ROUNDTABLE CONSULTATION WITH NONGOVERNMENTAL AND OTHER INTERESTED ORGANIZATIONS

### JUNE 14, 2001

PARTICIPANTS

Gareth Evans, ICISS (Co-Chair)
Mohamed Sahnoun, ICISS (Co-Chair)

Chen Luzhi, former Ambassador and senior UN official
Duanhong, China Institute of International Studies
Fan Guoxiang, UN Sub-Commission on Human Rights and China Society for Human Rights Studies
Su Ge, China Institute of International Studies
Wu Miaofa, China Institute of International Studies
Yan Guanqun, Former Deputy Permanent Representative of China to the UN Economic and Social Commission for Asia and the Pacific
Yuan Jian, China Institute of International Studies
Zhao Huaipu, Institute of International Relations at the Academy of Foreign Affairs, China
Zhou Qi, Institute of American Studies at the Chinese Academy of Social Sciences
Zhu Feng, School of International Studies, Peking University
Zhu Liqun, Institute of International Relations at the Academy of Foreign Affairs, China

## SUMMARY

At the request of the ICISS (which was established by Canadian Prime Minister Jean Chrétien's announcement at the Millennium Assembly of the UN, in September 2000), a meeting with the China Institute of International Studies and ICISS was held on June 14, 2001, in Beijing. The purpose of the meeting was to discuss the following three questions, put forward by ICISS: 1) when should external military intervention be considered and why: intervention priorities and thresholds; 2) when not to intervene and why; and 3) alternatives to external military intervention and the impact of external military intervention: political, economic, and social.

The participants realized that the day was significant and that it would be useful for both sides to move this discussion forward. No doubt such productive discussion and frank exchanges would improve our understanding and friendship. At the same time, we had to deepen the study of these issues that the international community is facing today.

The views from the Chinese side were summarized as follows:

❑ Theoretically, the conceptualization of humanitarian intervention is a total fallacy.

Practically, actions of humanitarian intervention posed grave problems for international laws and international relations.

The theorization of the doctrine of humanitarian intervention is flawed in several respects. First of all, it lacks a legal basis. Nowhere in the UN Charter can one find a clause that permits using force, except for national defence under Article 51 and for restoring international peace, as specified in Chapter VII. Using force for moral or conceptual reasons is questionable and dangerous, because such reasons are often controversial. In practice, legalization of humanitarian intervention is counterproductive to halting massive killings in targeted countries, for it can facilitate interventionists exploiting the legality for their own purposes and encourage warring parties inside a country to take an irresponsible stand in mediation processes.

Secondly, the assertion of "human rights transcending sovereignty" has serious fallacies in theory and lends no help to the legalization of humanitarian intervention. This assertion maintains that the rights of the people transcend the rights of states. It is allegedly based on Western human rights theory; however, it is misleading to see this claim as a logical derivative of Western values. Western human rights theory is based on the rights of individual persons who are born with some indefinite rights, and traditional Western philosophy tends to play down, if not deny, collective rights. Nonetheless, in the thesis of "human rights transcending sovereignty," rights of individuals are suddenly turned into rights of the people or collective rights. This deviation indicates that "human rights transcending sovereignty" is neither a coherent development of Western values nor a reflection of the views of most non-Western nations. It is highly politicized thinking with ulterior political motives.

Thirdly, the sporadic, unpredictable, and incoherent words and actions of the Western powers regarding humanitarian intervention suggest that they have not seriously pursued a policy of protecting human rights and safeguarding world peace. On the contrary, Western powers often approach international human rights issues with dual standards. Evidence of this can be found in the policy of the US toward racialist rule in South Africa and Southern Rhodesia, Washington's grudging attitude in carrying out a solution by the Security Council of the UN to stop civil war in Rwanda in 1994, NATO's military intervention in Kosovo, NATO's double standards in averting ethnic cleansing in the Balkans, and so on. It is clear that certain Western powers have played with noble principles to serve their own hegemonic interests.

❑ A clear distinction must be drawn between humanitarian assistance and humanitarian intervention.

Humanitarian intervention is a fallacious concept, tantamount to marrying evil to good. Humanitarianism is an admirable virtue, but interventionism is a red herring and widely condemned by the world; grafting humanitarian considerations onto intervention adds no lustre to the idea of meddling but will, contrarily, smear the lofty cause with dirt.

To appreciate and support efforts undertaken both within and outside the UN to provide humanitarian assistance, international society should draw a clear distinction between humanitarian assistance and humanitarian intervention. Humanitarian assistance is not an alternative means of politics, nor should it be an instrument for the pursuit of political and military goals of individual states. It must be free of ulterior political motives.

In practice, one can differentiate humanitarian actions from humanitarian intervention according to some key principles, the core one being respect for sovereignty. Sovereignty is enshrined in the UN and remains the most important pillar in today's international order; humanitarian actions must conform to this basic principle. Derived directly from the principle of respecting sovereignty are several other guiding norms that are concerned with the legitimacy of humanitarian actions. Consent of conflicting parties concerned to a third party's involvement is a precondition for taking humanitarian actions. This principle is a logical reflection of respecting sovereignty. The third principle is concerned with mandate. Humanitarian actions involving military personnel should have the authorization of the UN Security Council in accordance with the UN Charter. Without the authorization of the UN, military coercion by any single state or a group of states, even with the target of protecting human rights, constitutes a breach of the UN Charter and is not legitimate. Impartiality is also essential for the legitimacy of the third party's involvement in an internal conflict. And the principle of nonuse of force except for self-defence is the trademark of a peacekeeping operation whose central objective is to ensure a cessation of violence.

Though the complex reality of the causes and backgrounds of regional conflicts will sometimes make it difficult to conform to the above principles, without the guidance of these principles humanitarian actions would lose their innocence.

❑   Proposals for humanitarian assistance in regional conflicts.

Considering the misleading effects of humanitarian intervention and the complexity of protecting human rights, it is imperative to establish a framework for humanitarian assistance that reflects the interests of most countries in the world. Seven proposals are as follows:

First, international society should reaffirm Article 3 (4) of the UN Charter and the principles of nonencroachment upon state sovereignty and noninterference in internal affairs by any means specified in the Declaration of Principles of International Law and the Declaration of Non-Interference in Internal Affairs.

Secondly, if peace is threatened and undermined, the UN Security Council should take necessary air, sea, and land actions to maintain or restore peace and security. Before taking action, with the consent of relevant states, a fact-finding mission should be sent as quickly as possible to conduct an investigation. The investigation's report should be submitted immediately, and after the verification of the facts, the UN Security Council would send in a peacekeeping force according to Article 37 of the UN Charter.

Thirdly, if there is no agreement on the issue within the UN Security Council, the UN General Assembly should discuss it immediately according to Article 11 of Chapter IV of the UN Charter and put forward its proposals for peacekeeping actions.

Fourthly, in the course of conducting peacekeeping actions in a state, UN peacekeeping forces and personnel should remain strictly neutral. They should not support or oppose either side.

Fifthly, by the end of peacekeeping actions, personnel concerned should withdraw immediately. They should conduct no actions that may undermine the national sovereignty of the state concerned. They should submit an impartial and objective report on the peacekeeping actions.

Sixthly, peacekeeping actions can only be taken in the case of especially severe situations that endanger regional stability and world peace.

Finally, peacekeeping actions should always be authorized by the UN Security Council. Otherwise, the UN reserves the right to impose punishment according to Article 6 of Chapter 2 of the UN Charter.

# ST PETERSBURG

## ROUNDTABLE CONSULTATION WITH NONGOVERNMENTAL AND OTHER INTERESTED ORGANIZATIONS

## JULY 16, 2001

PARTICIPANTS

Vataniar Saidovich Yagya, St Petersburg Legislative Assembly and St Petersburg University (Chair)

Dmitri N. Barishnikov, Information and Documentation Centre on the Council of Europe, St Petersburg
Dimitri Danilov, Department for European Security Studies Institute of Europe, Moscow
Sylvia Gourova, International Relations Department, Kaliningrad
Barbara Hay, British Consulate, St Petersburg
Konstantin Khudoley, St Petersburg State University
Boris Kuznetsov, Center for Integration Research, St Petersburg
Mikhail Vladimirovitch Leontyev, Odnako, Moscow
Igor Leshukov, Centre for Integration Research and Programs, St Petersburg
Lev Yakovlich Lurie, Kariera-Kapital, St Petersburg
Aleksander Nikitin, Centre for Political and International Research, Moscow
Sergei Oznobishchev, Russian Academy of Sciences
Boris Pustintsev, Citizens' Watch, St Petersburg
Alexander Sergounin, University of Nizhni Novgorod
Viktor Sheinis, Institute of World Economy and International Relations, Moscow
Stanislav L. Tkachenko, St Petersburg State University
Bakhtiyar Raïssovitch Tuzmuhamedov, Diplomatic Academy, Moscow
Natalia A. Vasileva, St Petersburg University
Alexandr Ivanovich Yuriev, St Petersburg State University

## SUMMARY

### Russian Perspectives

A discussion paper was presented that gave an objective analysis of Russia's generally negative position on interventions of all kinds. This was for reasons of historical baggage, which came with interventions into Russia at the time of the 1917 Revolution and subsequently from the Cold War Soviet opposition to Western interventions within the Soviet sphere of influence. More recently, concern has arisen over Western unilateralism, which has characterized some interventions in the past decade and has seen the Security Council sidelined and double standards involved. Moreover, most of these interventions have been poorly conceived and have not achieved their objectives. Nevertheless, in the past few years, there have been signs that the Russian Government might be more prepared to reconsider the issues involved in the ultimate resort to force by the international community to resolve conflicts within states – a recent poll of 200 academic specialists in the subject showed that only 16 percent support the classical Russian position, with the rest taking a variety of more progressive views. There is also a slow realization that traditional rules of sovereignty are eroding and that increased intervention is inevitable. Moreover, Russia is coming to accept that the whole international community is responsible for conflict resolution. Globalization is important in this regard; and though its final effects are not yet clear, common human security is likely to emerge as a central theme.

One participant argued that the Russian public is not really interested in foreign conflicts, even those in neighbouring Slavic countries. The ethnocultural ties are too ephemeral, and people are too busy just surviving. It is thus meaningless to talk about public reaction to interventions as being an influence on governmental decision making in this regard.

## Russian Military Operations

Another discussion paper was presented that proceeded from the position that NATO and the Western European Union tend to concentrate more on military operations, whereas Russia is more inclined to the Organization for Security and Co-operation in Europe focus on conflict prevention. Traditionally, Russia has not voted for UN military or peacekeeping operations and has provided no troops or finance. This has now changed, and around 13,000 Russian troops were involved in UN operations in Bosnia, Kosovo, and Sierra Leone, as well as in conflicts within the old Soviet borders in Moldova, Abkhazia, Ossetia, and Tadjikistan. In Moldova, Russia was trying the innovative idea of involving troops from the opposing sides in peacekeeping deployments. The UN might usefully follow this example. In operations within the Commonwealth of Independent States (CIS), however, Russia has shown no preference for impartiality. In the Abkhazia operation, for example, Russia began by supporting one side; but as the situation evolved, it ended by the supporting the other. It also tends to work only with the six CIS members who signed the military cooperation protocol. On the other hand, Russia is now tending to apply UN peacekeeping operation standards, including using some enforcement methods in what they continue to describe in classic peacekeeping operation terms.

It was noted that Russian field commanders often complain about being given inappropriate functions, more suited to police forces, and also about having to assume political functions because the decision making process in Moscow is too slow. A Commissioner argued in reply that police forces need a functioning judicial system in which to operate, and this often does not exist in intervened countries. It is thus probably better to start an intervention off as a full military operation and then gradually bring in police as judicial structures are built or resurrected.

## Consent

One participant argued that Russian operations within the CIS could not be described as "humanitarian interventions" as the decision making process was quite different: there was no reference to the UN, or any international consensus as such. Moreover, CIS national parliaments were rarely if ever consulted. It was argued separately that Russia usually obtains a form of consent for an intervention from – often puppet – authorities in the territory concerned, whereas a "humanitarian intervention" is generally understood not to have such consent. East Timor was a similar case, where Indonesian consent for the International Force in East Timor had in effect been coerced. While some saw the subsequent military operation in East Timor as a model intervention, it could not properly be called a "humanitarian intervention" because consent existed, however coerced.

## Sovereignty

A further discussion paper was presented that canvassed sovereignty issues. The central point was that while understandings of sovereignty might have changed, the basic rules are still there and are still the organizing principle for international relations. Talk about new developments relating to democracy and human rights also has to be seen against the background that in reality they occur in fits and starts. A new international system could not be based on something so sporadic and uncertain.

It was noted, however, that the Russian Constitution seems to give priority to human rights over sovereignty, as it stipulates that international law should prevail when there is a conflict with national law.

In answer to a question why Luxembourg, say, should have the right to sovereign status, but not Chechnya or Kosovo, it was noted that Luxembourg independence has been the result of a historical process. Kosovo and Chechnya are not regarded as having similar rights, because their independence would challenge borders established in that same historical process.

## International Law

It was noted that attitudes toward intervention and sovereignty are conditioned according to the prevailing legal system in states: the common law tends to favour the rights of the individual, while the Napoleonic systems place more importance on the force of written law.

It was also argued that recent interventions are based largely on imaginative interpretations of vague and poorly defined provisions of the UN Charter. If new guidelines are being sought, attention should instead be paid to recent practice, regardless of whether specific cases are described at the time as not being precedents. Russia places too much importance on double standards, since these are inevitable, although in a sense the standards should at least be objective. A participant suggested that if a country or group of countries carrying out an intervention is clearly biased, then perhaps the intervention should be implemented by another, more objective group. Another participant suggested that double standards should not always be seen as black or white. The Soviet judge in the Nuremberg trials was notoriously biased, but the end result of those trials was to establish at least a more accountable form of international law.

A more legalistic view was presented that suggested that the rules of international law are binding and that the unilateral action of a group of countries outside its context risks undermining the whole international system. The Milosevic government probably would have collapsed of its own corruption without the NATO action in Kosovo, which actually strengthened internal support for Milosevic. Another participant argued that international law is really only the law of whoever the winners happen to be in specific circumstances.

## Kosovo

One interesting suggestion made was that the threatened Russian veto in the lead-up to the NATO action in Kosovo was not undertaken for capricious reasons. Russia genuinely believed that other measures falling short of military intervention had not been fully explored over a sufficient period and that conditions within Kosovo at that time were not of sufficient gravity in any case to warrant immediate military intervention. Another view, however, was that the threat of veto was only an indication of Russian irritation over insufficient involvement in Western decision making circles in the post-Cold War world generally.

## Guidelines

Apart from the thresholds identified by ICISS (massive loss of life, whether genocidal or not, or the threat thereof, and ethnic cleansing), one participant wondered whether intervention against major drug trafficking (as had happened in the case of Noriega) would be justifiable grounds.

The thresholds for involvement in conflicts within the CIS were identified as being 1) preventing the spread of conflict; 2) massive exodus of refugees; and 3) preventing major violations of human rights.

It was suggested that prudential considerations examined by ICISS should include "constructive abstentions," as practised by China, in lieu of imposing the veto. If more time and effort had been spent talking to Russia at the time, this might even have been the result over Kosovo.

If general guidelines were to be developed by ICISS, it was argued that it would be impossible to amend the UN Charter to incorporate them.

## When Not to Intervene

Situations where intervention should not occur were identified as 1) when intervention is opposed by the local population – treating the population of an intervened country as "defeated" would quickly alienate these people; 2) where there are large numbers of warring factions (as in Somalia); and 3) when the intervening powers base their decisions on factors that are not reflective of human rights values. One participant noted that it is strange that Western concepts of human rights could see the use of force as being necessary to maintain them. Another participant noted that early termination of an intervention often causes more harm than good, although overly long interventions are also to be avoided. If they do not address the root causes of the conflict, they should not take place.

Interventions were identified as promoting corruption among local elites, although the same participant acknowledged that when the basic issue is crimes against humanity, inaction would make the international community complicit in the crimes.

## Regional Bodies

It was noted that it has taken some time for the CIS to realize that it is a regional organization within the meaning of Chapter VIII of the Charter. In a sense, this explains why the CIS has never sought Security Council approval for any of its actions. One other view was that the actions carried out in the name of the CIS might not in fact be those of such a "regional organization," since only six members of the CIS are party to the CIS security arrangement. The operations are usually also carried out without status-of-forces agreements, although one participant asked rhetorically between whom such an agreement could be reached in those cases.

## Humanitarian Descriptor

There was some endorsement of ICISS's decision to drop the word "humanitarian" when talking about intervention. Some took the former Soviet position of characterizing all interventions as aggression and in no way humanitarian. Others took a more temperate position and argued that interventions are almost always against a certain class of states, hence they are discriminatory and thus cannot be called humanitarian. Yet others noted that regardless of the outcomes, most interventions are conducted in the national interests of the intervening states and thus cannot properly be called humanitarian. The current international system is not based on morality – this might be a "nice goal," but it does not reflect current realities.

### Responsibility to Protect

Despite promptings by Commissioners, there was no discussion of the "responsibility to protect" theme being considered by ICISS. One participant did, however, note that interventions have to empower the local population to rehabilitate itself. Otherwise, dependency would result, and the intervention would have to be judged a failure.

### Role of the Security Council

Similarly, there was no substantive discussion of the role of the Security Council, apart from those references noted above – and, again, despite urgings by Commissioners. One participant did, however, note that the "Uniting for Peace" procedure might not be liked by the P-5, including Russia, but that it would certainly be preferred by most of the remaining 184 members of the UN.

# INDEX